LAW AND SOCIETY

Printed and bound in the United States of America by
Edwards Brothers Malloy on sustainably sourced paper

Printed and bound in the United States of America by
Edwards Brothers Malloy on sustainably sourced paper

TENTH EDITION

LAW AND SOCIETY

Steven Vago

Professor Emeritus
Saint Louis University

Routledge
Taylor & Francis Group

LONDON AND NEW YORK

Printed and bound in the United States of America by
Edwards Brothers Malloy on sustainably sourced paper

Please visit the companion website at www.routledge.com/9780205820382

First published 2012 by Pearson Education, Inc.

Published 2016 by Routledge
2 Park Square, Milton Park, Abingdon, Oxon OX14 4RN
711 Third Avenue, New York, NY, 10017, USA

Routledge is an imprint of the Taylor & Francis Group, an informa business

ISBN: 9780205820382 (pbk)

Cover Designer: Suzanne Behnke

Library of Congress Cataloging-in-Publication Data

Vago, Steven.
    Law and society / Steven Vago. — 10th ed.
        p. cm.
    Includes bibliographical references and index.
    ISBN-13: 978-0-205-82038-2 (alk. paper)
    ISBN-10: 0-205-82038-7 (alk. paper)
    1. Sociological jurisprudence. I. Title.
    K370.V33 2012
    340'.115—dc22

                                                                      2010042387

Printed and bound in the United States of America by
Edwards Brothers Malloy on sustainably sourced paper

For Kathe

Printed and bound in the United States of America by
Edwards Brothers Malloy on sustainably sourced paper

Printed and bound in the United States of America by
Edwards Brothers Malloy on sustainably sourced paper

CONTENTS

Printed and bound in the United States of America by
Edwards Brothers Malloy on sustainably sourced paper

Printed and bound in the United States of America by
Edwards Brothers Malloy on sustainably sourced paper

Printed and bound in the United States of America by
Edwards Brothers Malloy on sustainably sourced paper

Printed and bound in the United States of America by
Edwards Brothers Malloy on sustainably sourced paper

PREFACE

For well over a quarter of a century, the preceding and progressively more comprehensive editions of this internationally acclaimed and successful book not only became popular with law and society scholars, but also over time were adopted as textbooks in more than 450 colleges and universities in the United States and abroad. Multiple printings for each edition along the way confirmed the usefulness of the text and the rapidly growing interest in the subject matter. This tenth edition is a result of the wide acceptance and demonstrated utility of the earlier versions. Upon the recommendations and satisfactions of those who used the earlier editions, I have retained the well-received and proven format, organizing framework and table of contents, themes, and features of the previous editions, and readers will also be pleased that now I have greatly enhanced, enlivened, and contemporized the relevant content. While still reflecting the intent, perspectives, and basic plan of preceding versions, this edition continues to enhance the message with extensive fresh input. The material is more focused, reorganized, and presented in a more integrated and relevant way for the benefit of students. The book remains in tune with ongoing national and global changes in legal systems resulting from the aftermath of the war on terror, climate change, and economic turbulence and extensively incorporates the most recent theoretical developments and the latest research results. Much of the book once again has been rewritten to further increase clarity and readability; to include new trends, concerns, and controversies; and to provide coherent, lively, and accessible accounts of the subject matter. The temptation to engage in merely cosmetic changes and verbiage alterations that are all too tempting in revisions has been successfully resisted. If a particular section was current, clear, relevant, and useful, I did not change it just for the sake of change. Throughout the various revisions, my purpose remained the same: to prepare a book that is pedagogically sound; intellectually stimulating; complete with ideas and insights; informative; provocative and enjoyable to read; comprehensive in its coverage; and clear, distinctive, and concise in its presentation of the subject. That mission, judging by the continuous positive feedback over the past three decades, has been accomplished.

The field of law is continuously evolving, and to capture the complexity and magnitude of recent developments, a substantial amount of new material has been included in this edition. The coverage now includes detailed and up-to-date discussions on the ongoing transformation of legal systems in Central and Eastern Europe and the former Soviet Union and some of the unintended consequences that promoted organized crime; new developments; critical feminist and race theories; community policing in Japan; trends in law enforcement and sentencing guidelines; changes in the legal landscape on drugs; lobbyists; current issues and controversies in the use and abuse of the death penalty; topical, social, and technological changes as causes of legal changes; a variety of new trends in alternative dispute resolution; emerging controversies in the education of future lawyers and the role of computer technology in their training; and billing practices and compensation of legal professionals. The many useful and insightful changes that have been suggested by students and reviewers have been considered and incorporated. All the chapters have been fully updated and expanded to reflect ongoing trends and current developments. There are now close to 850 new resources and references, a significantly expanded list of suggested further readings at the end of each chapter, and I have greatly increased the number of cross-cultural illustrations. As with earlier editions, I made a point once again of further emphasizing clarity of language at the expense of professional jargon.

The objective of this book is to serve as an undergraduate text in a one-term course. Although the book was written primarily for college students, anyone with an interest in law and society will find it useful, informative, and provocative. The classroom-tested and refined material over the past 30 years has been organized and presented in a logical fashion, and each chapter builds on the previous one. Should one prefer a different organization of the contents, it would not detract from the value of the book. For example, if one desires, Chapter 9, Researching Law in Society, can be read after Chapter 2, Theoretical Perspectives, rather than at the end of the book. For a quick chapter overview, some readers may want to look at the detailed summaries. The suggested further readings, emphasizing both classic and current material, are designed to provide a starting point for interested readers to pursue further a particular topic in depth and to reflect on alternative perspectives.

I wish to point out again, as I did in previous editions, that the study of the interplay between law and society is fundamentally eclectic. Knowledge about it has accumulated haphazardly. Intellectual developments in the field are influenced by a number of theoretical perspectives, resulting in a variety of strains of thought and research. In a sense, once again, more questions will be raised than answered. The profusion of unanswered questions and unexpected developments keeps the study of law and society fascinating, challenging, appealing, and intellectually stimulating.

Writing a book always requires the cooperation, support, and encouragement of many people. Throughout the evolution of this book to its present state, the various Prentice Hall reviewers over the years along with colleagues here and abroad made insightful and valuable suggestions. I would like to thank the following tenth edition reviewers for their helpful feedback: Becky da Cruz, Armstrong Atlantic State University; Robert Koulish, Philadelphia University; and Kenneth Mentor, University of North Carolina at Pembroke. Special thanks are due to Olga Zuber-Schmitt for her assiduous efforts to check and double check data and references and for her cogent literature and research reviews. In the unlikely event that something escaped Olga's scrutiny, the responsibility for the mistake(s) is mine. I also thank the many students (who over the years wittingly or unwittingly read and commented on and constructively criticized the numerous versions of the manuscript) for their no-nonsense feedback, demand for clarity, aversion to redundancy and verbosity, reluctance to take things for granted, insistence on proper and current documentation, and willingness to talk back to their professor. As with prior editions and other scholarly endeavors, this work could not have been realized without the unremitting generous financial, moral, and spiritual support of the Vago Foundation, which alone provided the necessary infrastructure, secretarial services, and library assistance and, despite the general economic decline and the prevalence of tight budgets or budget cuttings, once again generously covered all expenses incurred in the preparation of this book, including national and international travel over time for scientific work and cross-cultural contact.

Steven Vago
Bellingham, Washington, and Harrison Hot Springs,
British Columbia.

CHAPTER

1

Introduction

At the beginning of the second decade of the twenty-first century, law increasingly permeates all forms of social behavior. Its significance and pervasiveness resonate on all walks of life. In subtle and, at times, not so subtle ways, a complex and voluminous set of laws governs our entire existence and our every action. It determines registration at birth and the distribution of possessions at death. Laws regulate dating and mating behaviors, prenuptial agreements, marriage, divorce, pet ownership, hanging laundry outdoors to dry, and the conduct of professors in the classroom and at faculty parties. Laws demarcate the relationships between employers and employees, parents and children, and husbands and wives as opposed to girlfriends and boyfriends. Laws set the speed limit and the length of school attendance. Laws control what we eat and where; what we buy and when; how we use our computers; and what we can see in movie theaters or on television. Laws dictate what we wear and where. Laws protect ownership and define the boundaries of private and public property. Laws regulate business, raise revenue, provide for redress when agreements are broken, and uphold social institutions, such as the family. Laws protect the prevailing legal and political systems by defining power relationships, thus establishing who is superordinate and who is subordinate in any given situation. Laws maintain the *status quo* and provide the impetus for change. Finally, laws, in particular criminal laws, not only protect private and public interests but also preserve order. There is no end to the ways in which the law has a momentous effect upon our lives.

The principal mission of this book is to serve as a text in undergraduate courses on law and society. The large number of predominantly recent, diverse national and cross-cultural references cited also makes the text a valuable and indispensable source for graduate students engaging in research on the sociology of law, instructors who may be teaching this subject for the first time, and anyone else wanting to gain greater insight and understanding of the intricacies of law and society. Because the book has been written primarily for the undergraduate student, I opted for an eclectic approach to the often-controversial subject matter without embracing or advocating a particular position, ideology, or theoretical stance. To have done so would have been too limiting for a text, because important contributions would have been excluded or would have been considered out of context. Thus, the book does not propound a single thesis or position; instead, it exposes the reader to the dominant theoretical perspectives and sociological methods used to explain the interplay between law and society in the social-science literature. Should any reader care to follow up on a theoretical perspective or practical concern, or advocate or defend a certain position, the chapter topics, references, and the abundant and diversified suggested further readings will provide the necessary first step toward the further exploration of most law- and society-related issues.

OVERVIEW

All through history, in every human society there have been mechanisms for the declaration, alteration, administration, and enforcement of the rules and definitions of relationships by which people live (Glenn, 2010). Not all societies, however, utilize a formal legal system (courts, judges, lawyers, and law enforcement agencies) to the same degree (Grillo et al., 2009). For example, throughout the third world, the formal systems of property rights taken for granted in advanced nations simply do not exist. As the renowned economist Hernando de Soto (2001) presciently pointed out in his oft-quoted influential book, *The Mystery of Capital*, 80 percent of the poor people in the developing world cannot identify who owns what, addresses cannot be verified, and the rules that govern property vary from neighborhood to neighborhood or even from street to street. The notion of holding title to property is limited primarily to a handful of elites whose assets are "paperized" in the formal documents and legal structures common in the West.

Moreover, traditional societies rely almost exclusively on custom as the source of legal rules and resolve disputes through conciliation or mediation by village elders, or by some other moral or divine authority (see, for example, Pottage and Mundy, 2004). As for law, such societies need little of it. Traditional societies are more homogeneous than modern industrial ones. Social relations are more direct and intimate, interests are shared by virtually everyone, and there are fewer things to quarrel about. Because relations are more direct and intimate, nonlegal and often informal mechanisms of social control are generally more effective.

As societies become larger, more complex, and modern, homogeneity gives way to heterogeneity. Common interests decrease in relation to special interests. Face-to-face relations become progressively less important, as do kinship ties. Access to material goods becomes more indirect, with a greater likelihood of unequal allocation, and the struggle for available goods becomes intensified. As a result, the prospects for conflict and dispute within the society increase. The need for explicit regulatory and enforcement mechanisms becomes increasingly apparent. The development of trade and industry requires a system of formal and universal legal rules dealing with business organizations and commercial transactions, subjects that are not normally part of customary or religious law. Such commercial activity also requires guarantees, predictability, continuity, and a more effective method for settling disputes than that of trial by ordeal, trial by combat, or decision by a council of elders. As one commentator has noted: "The paradox . . . is that the more civilized man becomes, the greater is man's need for law, and the more law he creates. Law is but a response to social needs" (Hoebel, 1954:292).

In the powerful words of Oliver Wendell Holmes, Jr. (1963:5), "the law embodies the story of a nation's development through many centuries." Every legal system stands in close relationship to the ideas, aims, and purposes of society. Law reflects the intellectual, social, economic, and political climate of its time. Law is inseparable from the interests, goals, and understandings that deeply shape or compromise social and economic life

(Morales, 2003; Posner, 2001, 2007; Sarat and Kearns, 2000). It also reflects the particular ideas, ideals, and ideologies that are part of a distinct "legal culture" — those attributes of behavior and attitudes that make the law of one society different from that of another, that make, for example, the law of the Eskimos different from the law of the French (Friedman, 1998, 2002).

In the academic discipline of sociology, the study of law embraces a number of well-established areas of relevant inquiry (see, for example, Abadinsky, 2008; Cotterrell, 2006; Friedrichs, 2010). The discipline is concerned with values, interaction patterns, and ideologies that underlie the basic structural arrangements in a society, many of which are embodied in law as substantive rules. Both sociology and law are concerned with norms — rules that prescribe the appropriate behavior for people in a given situation. The study of conflict and conflict resolution are central in both disciplines. Both sociology and law are concerned with the nature of legitimate authority, the definition of relationships, mechanisms of social control, issues of human rights, power arrangements, the relationship between public and private spheres, and formal contractual commitments (Baumgartner, 1999; Griffin, 2009; McIntyre, 1994; Selznick, 1968:50). Both sociologists and lawyers are aware that the behavior of judges, jurors, criminals, litigants and other consumers of legal products is charged with emotion, distorted by cognitive glitches and failures of will, and constrained by altruism, etiquette, or a sense of duty.

Historically, the rapprochement of sociology (along with anthropology, economics, psychology, and other social sciences) (Canter and Zukauskiene, 2009; Donovan, 2008; Freeman and Goodenough, 2010; Kapardis, 2003; Parisi, 2008; Posner, 2001, 2007; Roesch et al., 1999; Zamir and Medina, 2010) and law is not novel. Early American sociologists, after the turn of the twentieth century, emphasized the various facets of the relationship between law and society. E. Adamson Ross (1922:106) considered law as "the most specialized and highly furnished engine of control employed by society." Lester F. Ward (1906:339), who believed in governmental control and social planning, predicted a day when legislation would endeavor to solve "questions of social improvement, the amelioration of the conditions of all the people, the removal of whatever privations may still remain, and the adoption of means to the positive increase of the social welfare, in short, the organization of human happiness."

The writings of these early sociologists have greatly influenced the development of the school of legal philosophy that became a principal force in American sociological jurisprudence. (Sociological jurisprudence is the study of law and legal philosophy, and the use of its ideas in law to regulate conduct [Lauderdale, 1997:132]. It is based on a comparative study of legal systems, legal doctrines, and legal institutions as social phenomena and considers law as it actually is — the "law in action" as distinguished from the law as it appears in books [see, for example, Wacks, 2009]). Roscoe Pound, the principal figure in sociological jurisprudence, relied heavily on the findings of early sociologists in asserting that law should be studied as a social institution. For Pound (1941:18), law was a specialized form of social control that exerts pressure on a person "in order to constrain him to do his part in upholding civilized society and to deter him from anti-social conduct, that is, conduct at variance with the postulates of social order."

Interest in law among sociologists grew rapidly after World War II, which ended in 1945. In the United States, some sociologists became interested in law almost by accident.

As they investigated certain problems, such as race relations, they found law to be relevant. Others became radicalized in the mid- and late-1960s, during the period of the Vietnam War, and their work began to emphasize social conflict and the functions of stratification in society. It became imperative for sociologists of the left to dwell on the gap between promise and performance in the legal system. By the same token, those sociologists defending the establishment were anxious to show that the law dealt with social conflict in a legitimate fashion. At the same time, sociological interest in law was further enhanced by the infusion of public funds into research evaluating a variety of law-based programs designed to address social problems in the United States (Ross, 1989:37). These developments provided the necessary impetus for the field of law and society, which got its start in the mid-1960s with the formation of the Law and Society Association and the inauguration of its official journal, the *Law & Society Review* (Abel, 1995:9; *Law & Society Review*, 1995:5), and the 2007 publication of the monumental three-volume set of the *Encyclopedia of Law and Society* (Clark, 2007). There is also a growing number of professional journals providing scholarly outlets for the mounting interest in law and society topics, such as *Law & Social Inquiry, Law and Anthropology Journal of Law and Society, Journal of Empirical Legal Studies, Indiana Journal of Global Legal Studies*, and *European Law Journal.*

These efforts are further sustained by the aftermath of the tragic events such as, for example, those following the World Trade Center and Pentagon terrorist attacks on September 11, 2001; the March 11, 2004 simultaneous bombing of several railroad stations in Madrid, Spain, resulting in almost 200 deaths and over 1,500 injuries; and the July 11, 2006 bombing of seven rail passenger cars during the rush hour in Mumbai (formerly known as Bombay), India, causing some 200 deaths and over 700 injuries followed by an attack on hotels and public facilities in 2008 resulting in dozens of deaths and injuries; and the recurrent threats of terrorism such as the 2009 Christmas Day attempt to blow up an American airliner using explosives hidden in the terrorist's underwear.

Nowadays, a number of universities offer undergraduate, graduate major, specialization, or joint degree programs in law and society, such as the School of Justice Studies at Arizona State University; the Jurisprudence and Social Policy at University of California, Berkeley; the Department of Law, Jurisprudence and Social Thought at Amherst College; University of Wisconsin; and University of Massachusetts, Amherst. Other law schools emphasize international relations, with pronounced social-science components, along with their programs in line with the trend toward further internalization of the social sciences (Kuhn and Weidemann, 2010). Some, such as Harvard, are offering joint degree programs with overseas universities (Gilgoff, 2004). There are also a number of major long-standing research institutes, such as the Center for Law & Society at Berkeley, the Institute for Law & Society at New York University, and the Institute for Legal Studies at the University of Wisconsin, that are well established and remain influential (Abel, 1995:10).

Of course, interest in law and society is not confined to the United States (Johns, 2010). Adam Podgorecki, a renowned Polish sociologist, has analyzed a number of distinct national styles in social-science work related to law. Scandinavian scholars have emphasized the social meaning of justice. In particular, they have investigated knowledge of the law and attitudes toward it. Italian social scientists have been concerned with empirical investigations of judges and the process of judging. With the end of the Soviet Union, the legitimacy of its law also died. Russian social scientists, encouraged and supported by the prominence of the often-controversial Prime Minister Vladimir Putin and President Dmitry Medvedev, are looking into the processes involved in the transformation of socialist legal systems into more Western, market-oriented ones with studies on privatization, joint ventures, leadership successions, and the reintroduction of juries in criminal cases. German sociologists are studying the socio-legal implications of reunification, changing demographic composition of the population due to immigration, the assimilation (and lately of the possible repatriation) of large numbers of guest workers, and the ways of coping with growing economic problems and unbalances and the rising and often-violent nationalism. Additionally, there is a flourishing interest in law and society in Japan, initiated by the many problems Japan experienced with the reception of European law and more recently by the growing anti-Japan sentiments brought about by perceptions of "unfair" trade practices and internal pressures to modernize the quasi-feudal criminal justice system (*Economist*, 2004; Oda, 2009; West, 2005). Both nationally and internationally, a number of organizations have been formed and centers established to study the multifaceted interaction between law and society (Rehbinder, 1975:13–48), and there is even a collection of essays by international authors devoted to the interplay between law and happiness (Posner and Sunstein, 2010). In 1988, the International Institute for the Sociology of Law (IISL) was founded jointly by the International Sociological Association (Research Committee on Sociology of Law) and the Basque government in Spain. The institute is located in the Old University of Onati (Spain). By mid-1990s, it had a full-fledged masters program (at a very reasonable tuition rate of €2,200 for the 2010–2011 academic year with scholarship opportunities) and an international doctorate in sociology of law program. By 2010, the success and reputation of the institute created a long list of applicants anxious to gain admission. IISL also has a sought-after program for a cadre of international visiting scholars including the members of the International Court of Justice and international law experts from the various UN (United Nations) organizations such as UNESCO (United Nations Educational, Scientific and Cultural Organization) (see, for example, Abass, 2011; Johns, 2010). There is, of course, awareness that the world's problems cannot be substantially reduced by simply creating more institutions, more facilities, and more international law, but they can perhaps be better understood and analyzed (Posner, 2009).

Undoubtedly, not many sociologists concerned with the study of law and society would question Eugen Ehrlich's oft-quoted dictum that the "center of gravity of legal development lies not in legislation, nor in juristic science, nor in judicial decision, but in society itself" (Ehrlich, 1975:Foreword). I share I. D. Willock's (1974:7) position that "in so far as jurisprudence seeks to give law a location in the whole span of human affairs it is from sociology that it stands to gain most." Sociological knowledge, perspectives, theories, and methods are not only useful but also axiomatic for the understanding and possible improvement of law and the legal system in society.

But the study of law by sociologists is somewhat hampered by difficulties of interaction between sociologists and lawyers. Both nationally and internationally, language-based approaches to issues are different in the two professions (Conley and O'Barr, 2005; Wagner and Cacciaguidi-Fahy, 2008). Edwin M. Schur correctly notes, "In a sense . . . lawyers and sociologists 'don't talk the same language,' and this lack of communication undoubtedly breeds uncertainty in both professions concerning any involvement in the other's domain, much less any cooperative interdisciplinary endeavors." He goes on to say "Sociologists and lawyers are engaged in quite different sorts of enterprises," and notes that "the lawyer's characteristic need to make decisions, here and now, may render him impatient with the sociologist's apparently unlimited willingness to suspend final judgment on the issue . . ." (Schur, 1968:8). The complexity of legal terminology further impedes interaction. There is a special rhetoric of law (Garner, 2001; Sarat and Kearns, 1994), and it has its own vocabulary; terms like *subrogation* and *replivin* and *respondeat superior* and *chattel lien* abound. Lawyers use a special arcane writing style, at times replete with multiple redundancies such as *made and entered into, cease and desist, null and void, in full force and effect*, and *give, devise and bequeath*, and they occasionally sue each other over the placement of a comma (Robertson and Grosariol, 2006). Not surprisingly, "Between specialized vocabulary and arcane style, the very language of the law defies lay understanding" (Chambliss and Seidman, 1982:119). There is a move under way to combat such legalese, and lawyers and law schools are beginning to learn that good English makes sense (Gest, 1995). The "linguistically challenged profession" (Glaberson, 2001) is further beset by difficulties involving the complexities of legal writing (and the need to translate it into plain English [Garner, 2001]) and the forms of irritating documentation called *sentence citations* (see, for example, *Bush v. Gore*, 531 U.S. 98, 121 S. Ct. 525, 148 L. Ed. 2d 388 [2000]), which tend to appear in mid-sentence. Not surprisingly, there is now a move under way to clean up legal documents by providing citations at the bottom of the page. Legal citations can include references to the date, volume, and page number of legal publications where precedents can be found.

Problems of interaction are also brought about and reinforced by the differences in professional cultures (Davis, 1962). Lawyers are advocates; they are concerned with the identification and resolution of the problems of their clients. Sociologists consider all evidence on a proposition and approach a problem with an open mind. Lawyers to a great extent are guided by precedents, and past decisions control current cases. In contrast, sociologists emphasize creativity, theoretical imagination, and research ingenuity. Law represents specific individuals and organizations within the legal system (Walker and Wrightsman, 1991:179). The pronouncements of law are predominantly prescriptive: They tell people how they should behave and what will happen to them if they do not. In sociology, the emphasis is on description, on understanding the reasons why certain groups of people act in certain ways in specific situations. The law *reacts* to problems most of the time; the issues and conflicts are brought to its attention by clients outside the legal system. In sociology, issues, concerns, and problems are generated within the discipline on the basis of what is considered intellectually challenging, timely, or of interest to the funding agencies.

These differences in professional cultures are, to a great extent, due to the different methods and concepts lawyers, sociologists, and other social scientists (see, for example, Mattei, 1997; Samuels, 2006) use in searching for "truth." Legal thinking, as Vilhelm

Aubert (1973:50–53) already explained in some detail decades ago, is different from scientific thinking for the following reasons:

1. Law seems to be more inclined toward the particular than toward the general (for example, what happened in a specific case).
2. Law, unlike the physical and social sciences, does not endeavor to establish dramatic connections between means and ends (for example, the impact the verdict has on the defendant's future conduct).
3. Truth for the law is normative and nonprobabilistic; either something has happened or it has not. A law is either valid or invalid (for example, did a person break a law or not).
4. Law is primarily past and present oriented and is rarely concerned with future events (for example, what happens to the criminal in prison).
5. Legal consequences may be valid even if they do not occur; that is, their formal validity does not inevitably depend on compliance (for example, the duty to fulfill a contract; if it is not fulfilled, it does not falsify the law in question).
6. A legal decision is an either-or, all-or-nothing process with little room for a compromise solution (for example, litigant either wins or loses a case).

These generalizations, of course, have their limitations. They simply highlight the fact that law is an authoritative and reactive problem-solving system that is geared to specific social needs. Because the emphasis in law is on certainty (or predictability or finality), its instrumentation often requires the adoption of simplified assumptions about the world. The lawyer generally sees the law as an instrument to be wielded, and he or she is more often preoccupied with the practice and pontification of the law than with its consideration as an object of scholarly inquiry.

Possibly the question most frequently asked of any sociologist interested in law is, "What are you doing studying law?" Unlike the lawyer, the sociologist needs to "justify" any research in the legal arena and often envies colleagues in law schools who can carry out such work without having to reiterate its relevance or their own competence. Yet, this need for justification is not an unmixed evil because it serves to remind the sociologist that he or she is not a lawyer but a professional with special interests. Like the lawyer, the sociologist may be concerned with the understanding, the prediction, and perhaps even the development of law. Obviously, the sociologist and the lawyer lack a shared experience—a common quest. At the same time, increasingly, sociologists and lawyers work together on problems of mutual interests (such as research on jury selection, capital punishment, conflict resolution, privacy, same sex marriage, immigration, undocumented workers, delinquency, crime, demographic concerns, consumer problems, and so on) and are beginning to see the reciprocal benefits of such endeavors. Sociologists also recognize that their research has to be adapted to the practical and pecuniary concerns of lawyers if it is to capture their interest. In view of the vocational and bar examination orientation of law schools and the preoccupation of lawyers with pragmatic legal doctrine (and billable events), it is unlikely that research aimed at theory building will attract or retain the attention of most law students and professors (Posner, 1996:327–330).

DEFINITIONS OF LAW

In ordinary parlance, the term *law* conjures up a variety of images (see, for example, Clark, 2007). For some, law may mean getting a speeding ticket, not being able to get a beer legally if under age, or complaining about the local "pooper-scooper" ordinance. For others, law is paying income tax, taking off shoes and going through a body scanner at the airport, signing a prenuptial agreement, being evicted, or going to prison for growing marijuana. For still others, law is concerned with what legislators enact or judges declare. Law means all the above and more. Even among scholars, there is no agreement on the term. Some of the classic and contemporary definitions of *law* are introduced here to illustrate the diverse ways of defining it.

The question "What is law?" still haunts legal thought at the onset of the second decade of 2010, and probably more scholarship has gone into defining and explaining the concept of law than into any other concept still in use in sociology and jurisprudence. Comprehensive reviews of the literature by Ronald L. Akers and Richard Hawkins (1975:5–15), Lisa J. McIntyre (1994:10–29), and Robert M. Rich (1977) indicate that there are almost as many definitions of law as there are theorists. E. Adamson Hoebel (1954:18) comments that "to seek a definition of the legal is like the quest for the Holy Grail." He cites Max Radin's warning: "Those of us who have learned humility have given over the attempt to define law." In spite of these warnings, law *can be* defined. In any definition of law, however, we must keep Julius Stone's (1964:177) admonition in mind that "'law' is necessarily an abstract term, and the definer is free to choose a level of abstraction; but by the same token, in these as in other choices, the choice must be such as to make sense and be significant in terms of the experience and present interest of those who are addressed."

In our illustrative review of the diverse definitions of law, let us first turn to two great American jurists, Benjamin Nathan Cardozo and Oliver Wendell Holmes, Jr. Cardozo (1924:52) defines law as "a principle or rule of conduct so established as to justify a prediction with reasonable certainty that it will be enforced by the courts if its authority is challenged." Holmes (1897:461) declares that "the prophecies of what the courts will do in fact, and nothing more pretentious, are what I mean by the law." For Holmes, judges make the law on the basis of past experience. In both of these definitions, the courts play an important role. These are pragmatic approaches to law as revealed by court-rendered decisions. Although implicit in these definitions is the notion of courts being backed by the authoritative force of a political state, these definitions of law seem to have a temporal character: What is the law at this time?

From a sociological perspective, one of the most influential and timeless definitions of law is that of Max Weber. Starting with the idea of an *order* characterized by legitimacy, he suggests: "An order will be called *law* if it is externally guaranteed by the probability that coercion (physical or psychological), to bring about conformity or avenge violation, will be applied by a *staff* of people holding themselves especially ready for that purpose" (Weber, 1954:5). Weber argues that law has three basic features that, taken together, distinguish it from other normative orders, such as custom or convention. First, pressures to comply with the law must come externally in the form of actions or threats of action by others regardless of whether a person wants to obey the law or does so out of habit. Second, these external actions or threats always involve coercion or force. Third, those who instrument the coercive threats are individuals whose official role is to enforce the law. Weber refers to "state" law when the persons who are charged to enforce the law are part of an agency of political authority.

Weber contends that customs and convention can be distinguished from law because they do not entail one or more of these features. Customs are rules of conduct in defined situations that are of relatively long duration and are generally observed without deliberation and "without thinking." Customary rules of conduct are called *usages*, and there is no sense of duty or obligation to follow them. Conventions, by contrast, are rules for conduct, and they involve a sense of duty and obligation. Pressures, which usually include expressions of disapproval, are exerted on individuals who do not conform to conventions. Weber (1954:27) points out that, unlike law, a conventional order "lacks specialized personnel for the instrumentation of coercive power."

Although a number of scholars accept the essentials of Weber's definition of law, they question two important points. First, some contend that Weber places too much emphasis on coercion and ignores other considerations that may induce individuals to obey the law. For example, Philip Selznick (1968, 1969:4–8) argues that the authoritative nature of legal rules brings about a special kind of obligation that is not dependent on the use or threat of coercion or force. Many laws are obeyed because people feel it is their duty to obey. The second point concerns Weber's use of a special staff. Some scholars claim that Weber's definition limits the use of the term *law* in cross-cultural and historical contexts. They argue that the word *staff* implies an organized administrative apparatus that may not exist in certain illiterate societies. E. Adamson Hoebel (1954:28), for instance, proposes a less-restrictive term by referring to individuals possessing "a socially recognized privilege," and Ronald L. Akers (1965:306) suggests a "socially authorized third party." Of course, in modern societies, law provides for a specific administrative apparatus. Still, these suggestions should be kept in mind while studying the historical developments of law or primitive societies (see, for example, Mundy, 2002; Pospisil, 1971, 1978; Pottage and Mundy, 2004).

From a different perspective, Donald Black (1976:2, 1989:121, 1998:1–26, 2002:118), a leading figure in law and society studies, contends that law is essentially governmental social control. In this sense, law is "the normative life of a state and its citizens, such as legislation, litigation, and adjudication" (Black, 1976:2). He maintains that several styles of law may be observed in a society, each corresponding to a style of social control. Four styles of social control are represented in law: penal, compensatory, therapeutic, and conciliatory. In the penal style, the deviant is viewed as a violator of a prohibition and an offender is to be subjected to condemnation and punishment (for example, a drug pusher). In the compensatory style, a person is considered to have a contractual obligation and, therefore, owes the victim restitution (for example, a debtor failing to pay the creditor). Both of these styles are accusatory where there is a complainant and a defendant—a winner and a loser. According to the therapeutic style, the deviant's conduct is defined as abnormal; the person needs help, such as treatment by a psychiatrist. In the conciliatory style, deviant behavior represents one side of a social conflict in need of resolution without consideration as to who is right or who is wrong (for example, marital disputes). These last two styles are remedial, designed to help people in trouble and ameliorate a bad social situation. Elements of two or more of these styles may appear in a particular instance; for example, when a drug addict is convicted of possession and is granted probation contingent upon his or her participation in some kind of therapy program.

The above-mentioned definitions illustrate some of the alternative ways of looking at law. It is the law's specificity in substance, its universality of applicability, and the formality of its enactment and enforcement that set it apart from other devices for social control. Implicit in these definitions of law is the notion that law can be analytically separated from other normative systems in societies with developed political institutions and specialized lawmaking and law-enforcement agencies. The paramount function of law is to regulate and constrain the behavior of individuals in their relationships with one another. Ideally, law is to be employed only when other formal and informal methods of social control fail to operate or are inadequate for the job. Finally, law can be distinguished from other forms of social control primarily in that it is a formal system embodying explicit rules of conduct, the planned use of sanctions to ensure compliance with the rules, and a group of authorized officials designated to interpret the rules and apply sanctions to violators (Davis, 1962:39–63). From a sociological perspective, the rules of law are simply a guide for action. Without interpretation and enforcement, law would remain meaningless (Benda-Beckman et al., 2009). As Henry M. Hart (1958:403) points out, law can be analyzed sociologically as a "method" of doing something. In this context, law can be studied as a social process, instrumented by individuals during social interaction. Sociologically, law consists of the behaviors, situations, and conditions for making, interpreting, and applying legal rules that are backed by the state's legitimate coercive apparatus for enforcement.

TYPES OF LAW

The content of law may be categorized as *substantive* or *procedural*. *Substantive* laws consist of rights, duties, and prohibitions administered by courts—which behaviors are to be allowed and which are prohibited (such as prohibition against murder or the sale of narcotics). *Procedural* laws are rules concerning just how substantive laws are to be administered, enforced, changed, and used by players in the legal system (such as filing charges, selecting a jury, presenting evidence in court, or drawing up a will).

At times, a distinction is made between *public* law and *private* law (Johnson, 1977:59–60). *Public* law is concerned with the structure of government, the duties and powers of officials, and the relationship between the individual and the state (Tomkins, 2003). "It includes such subjects as constitutional law, administrative law, regulation of public utilities, criminal law and procedure, and law relating to the proprietary powers of the state and its political subdivisions" (Davis, 1962:51). *Private* law is concerned with both substantive and procedural rules governing relationships between individuals (the law of torts or private injuries, contract, property, will, inheritance, marriage, divorce, adoption, and the like).

A more familiar distinction is between *civil* law and *criminal* law. As noted, *civil* law, as private law, consists of a body of rules and procedures intended to govern the conduct of individuals in their relationships with others. Violations of civil statutes, called *torts*, are private wrongs for which the injured individual may seek redress in the courts for the harm he or she experienced. In most cases, some form of payment is required from the offender to compensate for the injury he or she has caused. Similarly, one company may be required to pay another a sum of money for failing to fulfill the terms of a business contract. The complainant firm is thus "compensated" for the loss it may have suffered as a result of the other company's neglect or incompetence. *Criminal* law is concerned with the definition of crime and the prosecution and penal treatment of offenders. Although a criminal act may cause harm to some individual, crimes are regarded as offenses against the state or "the people." A crime is a "public," as opposed to an "individual" or "private," wrong. It is the state, not the harmed individual, that takes action against the offender. Furthermore, the action taken by the state differs from that taken by the plaintiff in a civil case. For example, if the case involves a tort, or civil injury, compensation equivalent to the harm caused is levied. In the case of crime, some form of punishment is administered. Henry M. Hart suggests that a crime ". . . is not simply antisocial conduct which public officers are given a responsibility to suppress. It is not simply any conduct to which a legislature chooses to attach a 'criminal' penalty. It is a conduct which, if duly shown to have taken place, will incur a formal and solemn pronouncement of the moral condemnation of the community" (1958:404). In Hart's view, both the condemnation and the consequences that follow may be regarded as constituting the punishment. Occasionally, a criminal action may be followed up by a civil suit, such as in a rape case where the victim may seek financial compensation in addition to criminal sanctions.

A distinction can also be made between *civil* law and *common* law. In this context, civil law refers to legal systems whose development was greatly influenced by Roman law, a collection of codes compiled in the Corpus Juris Civilis (Code Civil). Civil-law systems are codified systems, and the basic law is found in codes. These are statutes that are enacted by national parliaments. France is an example of a civil-law system. The civil code of France, which first appeared in 1804, is called the Code Napoleon and embodies the civil law of that country. By contrast, common law resisted codification. Law is not based on acts of parliament but on case law, which relies on precedents set by judges to decide a case (Friedman, 1998, 2002; see also Bennion, 2009). Thus, it is "judge-made" law as distinguished from legislation or "enacted law." In the United States, law may be further divided into the following branches: constitutional law, case law, statutory law, executive orders, and administrative law. Constitutional law is a branch of public law. It determines the political organization of the state and its powers while also setting certain substantive and procedural limitations on the exercise of governing power. Constitutional law consists of the application of fundamental principles of law based on that document, as interpreted by the U.S. Supreme Court. Case law is enacted by judges in cases that are decided in the appellate courts. Statutory law is legislated law—law made by legislatures. Executive orders are regulations issued by the executive branch of the government at the federal and state levels. Finally, administrative law is a body of law created by administrative agencies in the form of regulations, orders, and decisions. These various categories of laws will be discussed and illustrated later in the text.

MAJOR LEGAL SYSTEMS

In addition to the types of law, there is a large variety of legal systems (see, for example, Clark, 2007; Gillespie, 2009; Johansen, 1998; Kritzer, 2002; Oda, 2009; Richland and Deer, 2010 [the only available comprehensive introduction to tribal law]). The dominant legal systems that exist in various forms throughout the world are the Romano-Germanic (civil) law, common law, socialist law, and Islamic law (David and Brierley, 1985). The Romano-Germanic systems predominate in Europe, in most of the former colonies of France, Germany, Italy, Spain, Portugal, and Belgium, and in countries that have westernized their legal systems in the nineteenth and twentieth centuries. Common-law systems are predominant in English-speaking countries. Islamic systems are found in the Middle East and some other parts of the world to which Islamic religion has spread. Socialist legal systems prevail in the People's Republic of China, Vietnam, Cuba, and North Korea. Remnants of socialist systems are still found in the former Soviet Union and Eastern European countries.

Romano-Germanic System

The Romano-Germanic, or civil, law refers to legal science that has developed on the basis of Roman *ius civile* or civil law (Abel and Lewis, 1988, Vol. 2; Mousourakis, 2007; Plessis, 2010). The foundation of this system is the compilation of rules made in the sixth century A.D. under the Roman emperor Justinian. These rules are contained in the Code of Justinian and have evolved essentially as private law, as a means of regulating private relationships between individuals (see, for example, Mears, 2004). After the fall of the Roman Empire, the Code of Justinian competed with the customary law of the Germanic tribes that had invaded Europe. The code was reintroduced in law school curricula between A.D. 1100 and A.D. 1200 in northern Europe, then spread to other parts of the continent. Roman law thus coexisted with the local systems throughout Europe up to the seventeenth century. In the nineteenth century, the Napoleonic code, and, subsequently, the code of the new German Empire of 1900 and the Swiss code of 1907 are examples of the institutionalization of this legal system.

Codified systems are basic laws that are set out in *codes*. A *code* is simply a body of laws (see, for example, Kevelson, 1994; Mears, 2004). These statutes are enacted by national parliaments that arrange entire fields of law in an orderly, comprehensive, cumulative, and logical way. Today, most European countries have national codes based on a blend of customary and Roman law that makes the resulting systems members of the Romano-Germanic legal tradition.

Common-Law System

Common law is characteristic of the English system, which developed after the Norman Conquest in 1066 (Cownie, 2010). The law of England as well as those laws modeled on English law (such as the laws of the United States, Canada, Ireland, and India) resisted codification. Law is not based on acts of parliament but on case law, which relies on precedents set by judges in deciding a case (Friedman, 1998, 2002). Thus, it is "judge-made" law as distinguished from legislation or "enacted" (statutory) law. The doctrine of "precedent" is strictly a common law practice. The divisions of the common law; its concepts, substance, structure legal culture, and vocabulary; and the methods of the common-law lawyers and judges are very different, as will be demonstrated throughout the book, from those of the Romano-Germanic, or civil, law systems (see, for example, Abel and Lewis, 1988, Vol. 1).

Socialist Legal System

Discussions of the socialist legal system have always been fascinating for Western students due to the specialized and often emotionally laden coverage of it. Even though there are multiple versions of it, the origins of the socialist legal system can be traced back to the 1917 Bolshevik Revolution, which gave birth to the Union of Soviet Socialist Republics. The objectives of classical socialist law are threefold. First, law must provide for national security. Ideally, the power of the state must be consolidated and increased to prevent attacks on the socialist state and to assure peaceful coexistence among nations. Second, law has the economic task of developing production and distribution of goods on the basis of socialist principles so that everyone will be provided for "according to his needs." The third goal is that of education: to overcome selfish and antisocial tendencies that were brought about by a heritage of centuries of poor economic organization.

The source of socialist law is legislation, which is an expression of popular will as perceived and interpreted by the Communist party. The role of the court is simply to apply the law, not to create or interpret it. Even today, for example, judges in China are not required to have any legal training, and few do, and they are mostly in large urban areas. Most hold their positions because they have close connections with local governments, who are eager for quick convictions (Diamant et al., 2005; Muhlhahn, 2009; Oleinik, 2003; Smith, 2001).

Socialist law rejects the idea of separation of powers. The central notion of socialist law is the concept of ownership. Private ownership of goods has been renamed "personal ownership," which cannot be used as a means of producing income. It must be used only for the satisfaction of personal needs. Socialist law is unique with respect to "socialist" ownership, of which there are two versions: collective and state. A typical example of collective ownership is the *kolkhoz*, or collective farm, which is based on nationalized land. State ownership prevails in the industrial sector in the form of installations, equipment, buildings, raw materials, and products. In a socialist legal system, the real question of property is not who owns it, but by whom it is owned and how such property is exploited (David and Brierley, 1985). Versions of this type of legal system still exist in China, Cuba (Zatz, 1994), North Korea, and Vietnam (see, for example, Calvi and Coleman, 2008).

The collapse of communism in the Soviet Union and the former Eastern-bloc countries in 1989, the dissolution of the political and economic institutions that guaranteed the conservation of communist structures, the reintroduction of a multiparty system, and general democratization of political life had immediate implications for the socialist legal system (Hesli, 2007; Priban et al., 2003; Tismaneanu, 1992). These developments brought about by transitions require a reconceptualization of the basic notions of property, environmental protection (Agyeman and Ogneva-Himmelberg, 2009), authority, legitimacy, and power, and even of the very idea of law (see, for example, Elster, 1995).

As part of the unexpected and unforeseen dramatic transformations that are still taking place in Eastern Europe and the former Soviet Union (Collins, 1995), the newly established independent states are experimenting with workable alternatives to the socialist rule of law in their attempts to create a climate for a system of laws receptive to and facilitative of democratic forms of market economies and civil liberties (Alexander and Skapska, 1994; Bryant and Mokrzycki, 1994; Hesli, 2007; Milor, 1994; Priban et al.,

2003). Although the problems involved in the transition vary from country to country according to unique historical and political circumstances, all these states face common concerns, such as establishment of a new political ideology (Feuer, 2010), creation of new legal rights, the imposition of sanctions on former elites, and new forms of legitimization. Among the practical problems are the creation of new property rights; the attainment of consensus in lawmaking; the formulation and instrumentation of new laws on such matters as privatization; joint ventures; restitution for and rehabilitation of victims of the overturned regime; revision of criminal law; the rise of nationalistic, antiforeign, and anti-Semitic sentiments; and multiparty electoral behavior (Oleinik, 2003). There is also a whole slate of legal issues previously denied public attention by socialist law, such as prostitution, drug abuse, unemployment, and economic shortages. There are also significant structural changes taking place that are composed of newly democratic parliamentary lawmaking, conversion of the judicial system (see, for example, Piana, 2010), and the awakening of alternative political parties. There are, finally, concerns with the development of new law school curricula, selection of personnel, and replacement or resocialization of former members of the Communist party still occupying positions of power.

So far, the transition has been slow, uneven and its scope limited, especially in more remote rural areas. There has been no effort to remove judges who grew up under the old regime. The constitutions have yet to be fully revised, although there is much talk about them (Klingsberg, 1992). There is a shortage of defense attorneys (Erlanger, 1992). (The paucity of both new judges and defense attorneys can be accounted for, in part, by the relatively small number of law school graduates between 1989 and 2010, many of whom prefer the more lucrative civil law fields). As of November 1993, Russian law permits accused criminals to request a trial by jury (Stead, 1994). But the powers of prosecutors have remained largely unreformed since Stalin's day. They remain hugely influential, heavy-handed, unaccountable, and corrupt, and prosecutors can get almost anyone arrested under Russia's vague and contradictory laws, and usually convicted too (Oleinik, 2003; *Economist*, 2001).

Perhaps the biggest task facing the new lawmakers is the creation of a legal climate aimed at stimulating foreign investments. Westerners need to be assured about the safety of their investments, which requires the creation of a legal infrastructure based on democratic principles. New laws are still needed on repatriation of profits, property rights, privatization, and the movement of goods.

But the greatest challenge confronting the post-Communist regimes is crime management (see, for example, Friedman, 2000; Hesli, 2007; Oleinik, 2003; Perlez, 1995). In Russia and in its former satellites, the Soviet criminal code has not been significantly altered, and this resulted in some unexpected developments. It is better suited to catch political dissidents than to inspire respect for law and order. The laws were aimed at defending the totalitarian state, not the individual. Presidential decrees and legislative acts have expanded the boundaries of life—from the right to buy and sell property to the freedom to set up banks and private corporations—but the notoriously inefficient courts have no legal basis for interpreting these decrees, much less enforcing them. Consequently, the police cannot formally tackle organized criminal activity, because under present law, only individuals can be held criminally culpable. Not surprisingly, the number of organized criminal groups in Russia more than quadrupled during the last decade of the twentieth century. (Gaddy et al., 1995; Friedman, 2000; Oleinik, 2003; Priban et al., 2003; Ryan and Rush, 1997).

Criminal groups now operate in every region, and the *Mafiya* is ubiquitous internationally and nationally (Friedman, 2000; Handelman, 1995). For example, prostitution networks in Western Europe, involving several hundreds of thousands of women each year from former Soviet-bloc countries, are run mostly by Russians and Ukrainians, and generate huge profits (see, for example, Canter et al., 2009). They collect several thousand dollars per woman at each stage of her odyssey (passport, journey, placement, and so on) and "middlemen" average about $20,000 per person (Paringaux, 1998:18).

In cities all across the former Soviet-bloc countries, gangs operate with near impunity, practicing fraud and extortion, conducting illegal trade, bribing and corrupting officials, and viciously murdering anyone who gets in their way. One base of support for the Russian Army's invasion of Chechnya in late 1994 was competing crime syndicates elsewhere in Russia (Meier, 1995; Oleinik, 2003). In 1993, Russia saw 335,000 crimes officially designated as racketeering and nearly 30,000 premeditated murders. In Moscow, the slaughter included over 1,400 gangland assassinations, with probably thousands more that went unrecorded. By the end of the first quarter of 1994, the toll was running at 84 murders a day, giving Russia the dubious distinction of surpassing the United States' homicide rate—in fact more than doubling it. The bulk were contract killings due to conflicts in commercial and financial activities (Viviano, 1995). Although contract killings declined in the early years of this decade, by 2006, they seemed to have made a comeback with a series of high-profile cases (Buckley, 2006), and in 2010, a number of such incidents were reported in the media. In 2003, the murder rate in Moscow was about 18 per 100,000 residents (Wines, 2004) as compared to 5 per 100,000 in New York City. Almost a decade later, these figures have remained relatively constant.

Almost every small business across Russia pays protection money to some gang. Some authors even raise questions such as "Is Sicily the future of Russia?" (Varese, 2001). Vast fortunes in raw materials—from gold to petroleum—are smuggled out through the porous borders in the Baltics by organized groups who have bribed their way past government officials, and ministries and municipal governments peddle property and favors. Official corruption is rampant, and along with that, tax instability, licensing confusion, and disregard for intellectual property rights serve as disincentives to the kind of private Western investment Russia needs to create jobs and a functioning market economy (see, for example, Eicher, 2009; Erlanger, 1995).

In spite of attempts to establish a "dictatorship of law" in the new Russia (Buckley, 2006; Priban et al., 2003; Wines, 2001), the conditions remain chaotic, and the authors of an influential paper in the *Brookings Review* contend that many Russians still believe that organized crime is beneficial for the economy (Gaddy et al., 1995). Business people perceive organized crime as a necessary evil. Although it is hard to acknowledge, the Mafia confers certain benefits. The protection rackets offer security against other types of "disorganized" crime that might affect their clients. Dispute resolution is another Mafia service. But perhaps the biggest contribution of the Mafia to orderly market transactions is contract enforcement. In today's Russia, contracts have little force. Failure to adhere to a contract—to pay for goods or services ordered or delivered—exacts virtually no official sanctions. Close to half of the aggregate volume of accounts receivable in all

Russian industry are delinquent. Because the Russian state is unwilling or unable to provide public enforcement of private contracts, despite public claims by the current government, the interim alternative is to privatize enforcement. It is one of the private solutions business people use when they need protection for their transaction. It also makes a nice argument in support of functionalist theorizing in sociology.

Islamic Legal System

Islamic law, unlike the previously discussed systems, is not an independent branch of knowledge (Ende and Steinbach, 2010). Law is integral to Islamic religion, which defines the character of the social order of the faithful who create laws in the name of God (Ahmed, 2001; Al-Azmeh, 1988; An-Na'im and Baderin, 2010; Barzilai, 2007; Cooper et al., 2000; Ghanim, 2010; Hallaq, 2004, 2009; Lippman et al., 1988; Neusner and Sonn, 1999). *Islam* means "submission" or "surrender" and implies that individuals should submit to the will of God. Islamic religion states what Muslims must believe, and includes the *Shari'a* ("the way to follow"), which specifies the rules for believers based on divine command and revelation. Unlike other systems of law based on judicial decisions, precedents, and legislation, Islamic law is derived from four principal sources, and there is a traditional preference for eyewitness testimony (Shaham, 2010). The principal source of Islamic law is the *Koran*, the word of God as given to the Prophet. The second source is the *Sunna*, which are the sayings, acts, and allowances of the Prophet as recorded by reliable sources in the Tradition (*Hadith*). The third is *judicial consensus*; like precedent in common law, it is based on historical consensus of qualified legal scholars, and it limits the discretion of the individual judge. *Analogical reasoning* is the fourth primary source of Islamic law. It is used in circumstances not provided for in the Koran or in other sources. For example, some judges inflict the penalty of stoning for the crime of sodomy, contending that sodomy is similar to the crimes of adultery, out-of-wedlock sex, and drinking alcohol, and thus should be punished by the same penalty the Koran indicates for adultery (*Economist*, 2010:48). (In Saudi Arabia, sodomy remains punishable by death, and the kingdom maintains a long list of prohibitions—against smoking, drinking, going to discos, and socializing between men and women, which, interestingly, "has made it easier to be gay than straight in a society that forbids all sexual activity outside of marriage" [*Wall Street Journal*, 2007].) In the same vein, a female would get half the compensation a male would receive for being the victim of the same crime, because a male is entitled to an inheritance twice that of a female. In addition to these principal sources, various supplementary sources, such as custom, judge's preference, and the requirements of public interest, are generally followed (see, for example, Nielsen and Christoffersen, 2010).

Shari'a legal precepts can be categorized into five acts: commanded, recommended, reprobated, forbidden, and left legally indifferent. Islamic law mandates rules of behavior in the areas of social conduct, family relations, inheritance, and religious rituals, and defines punishments for heinous crimes including adultery, false accusation of adultery, intoxication, theft, and robbery. For example, in the case of adultery, the proof of the offense requires four witnesses or confession. [In some instances, such as Islamic decrees introduced in Pakistan in 1979, collectively known as the Hadood Ordinance, there is a controversial clause stating that to prove rape, a woman must have at least four male witnesses. If the woman fails to provide proof, she herself faces the charge of adultery, and in early 2006, there were close to 5,000 women in Pakistan awaiting trial for Hadood violations (Masood, 2006).] If a married person is found guilty, he or she is stoned to death. Stones are first thrown by witnesses, then by the judge, followed by the rest of the community. For a woman, a grave is dug to receive the body. The punishment for an unmarried person is 100 lashes (Lippman et al., 1988:42). Such punishments are still common in Islamic countries: for example, in late 2009, in Somalia, a young woman alleged to have committed adultery was stoned to death in front of a crowd, the second of such punishment within a short period of time (*Economist*, 2009:9).

For theft, the penalty of hand amputation is often used. From time to time, the classic retribution of the notion "eye for an eye" is invoked in a literary sense. For example, in December 2003, a judge in Bahawalpur, a city in the eastern Pakistani province of Punjab, has ruled that a man convicted of attacking and blinding his fiancée with acid be blinded with acid himself. "This is an Islamic way of doing justice," the judge wrote in his verdict and ordered that a doctor perform the punishment publicly at a sports stadium (*Seattle Times*, 2003:A8). This severe punishment may be an attempt at deterrence because violence against women, including acid attacks, is common in Pakistan, particularly in rural and deeply conservative tribal regions. In late 2009 in Malaysia, the pending sentence of caning given to a woman who was caught drinking beer has made the international headlines and provoked a series of protests against that country.

Even grooming can be a man's undoing. In Afghanistan, even in the early twenty first century, as the Taliban interprets the Koran, an adult male is obliged not only to grow a beard but also to leave the hairy underbrush unmolested by scissors. Patrols from the General Department for the Preservation of Virtue and Prevention of Vice, revived as the Vice and Virtues Ministry, were rather tough in the past on trimmed beards in Kabul and used to snatch violators from the bazaars and took them to a former maximum security prison for ten days of religious instruction (Bearak, 1998). Based on news reports in 2010, this practice is being selectively revived. So is in Iran where "decency crackdowns" are on the increase with new rules governing men's appearance with periodic police raids on barber shops and stores that sell neckties—seen as vestiges of the decadent West. The "correct fashion" on how women should look is also being enforced by hard-liners who try to revive the lost zeal of Iran's 1979 revolution. For example, in May, 2007, in a one-week period, some 16,000 women and about 500 men were "cautioned" about their appearance, and police were hunting streets and parks for immodestly dressed women and wildly coiffed men (Higgins, 2007).

Although such practices are susceptible to interpretations that can and do create conflicts between religious doctrine and human rights (see, for example, Mayer, 2007; Saeed, 2004), they must be examined within the philosophy of Islam and in the spirit of true theoretical inquiry for justification; Islamic justice is based on religious and philosophical principles that are quite alien to most western readers (Souryal and Potts, 1994). (For instance, in September 2005, a Danish newspaper published twelve cartoons of the prophet Muhammad. Shortly after, tens of thousands of Muslims took to the streets from Asia to Europe in protest, many violent, and inundated the newspaper with outpourings of anger and grief by phone, mail, and e-mail [Klausen, 2009].) Punishments and rules not defined by historical sources of Shari'a are left to decision by contemporary government regulations and Islamic judges. This practice permitted an evolution of Shari'a law to reflect changing social, political, and economic conditions.

It is important to remember that the sanctions attached to the violation of Islamic law are religious rather than civil. Commercial dealings, for example, between Muslims and Westerners are covered by governmental rules comparable to administrative law in the United States. The fundamental principle of Islam is that of an essentially theocratic society, and Islamic law can be understood only in the context of some minimum knowledge of Islamic religion and civilization. Thus, care should be exercised in discussing or analyzing components of Islamic law out of context and in isolation.

PRINCIPAL FUNCTIONS OF LAW

Why do we need law, and what does it do for society? More specifically, what functions does law perform? As with the definition of law, there is no agreement among scholars of law and society on the precise functions, nor is there consensus on their relative weight and importance. A variety of functions are highlighted in the literature (see, for example, Aubert, 1969:11; Bredemeier, 1962:74; Clark, 2007; Mermin, 1982:5–10; Nader and Todd, 1978:1; Pollack, 1979:669; Rawls, 2001; Sampford, 1989:116–120) depending on the conditions under which law operates at a particular time and place. The recurrent focal themes include social control, dispute settlement, and social change. I shall now consider them briefly. These functions of the law will be examined in detail in the chapters dealing with social control, conflict resolution, and social change.

Social Control

In a small, traditional, and homogeneous society, behavioral conformity is ensured by the fact that socializing experiences are very much the same for all members. Social norms tend to be consistent with each other, there is consensus about them, and they are strongly supported by tradition. Social control in such a society is primarily dependent upon self-sanctioning. Even on those occasions when external sanctions are required, they seldom involve formal punishment. Deviants are mostly subjected to informal mechanisms of social control, such as gossip, ridicule, or humiliation. Although they exist, banishment, or forms of corporal punishment are rare in modern societies (see, for example, Gram, 2006).

Even in a complex, heterogeneous society, such as the United States, social control rests largely on the internalization of shared norms. Most individuals behave in socially acceptable ways, and, as in simpler societies, fear of disapproval from family, friends, and neighbors is usually adequate to keep potential deviants in check (Matza, 2010). Nevertheless, the great diversity of the population; the lack of direct communication between various segments; the absence of similar values, attitudes, and standards of conduct; economic inequities, rising expectations; and the competitive struggles between groups with different interests have all led to an increasing need for formal mechanisms of social control. Formal social control is characterized by "(1) explicit rules of conduct, (2) planned use of sanctions to support the rules, and (3) designated officials to interpret and enforce the rules, and often to make them" (Davis, 1962:43).

In modern societies, there are many methods of social control, both formal and informal. Law is considered one of the forms of formal social control. In the inimitable words of Roscoe Pound (1941:249): "I think of law as in one sense a highly specialized form of social control in developed politically organized society—a social control through the systematic and orderly application of the force of such a society."

Lawrence M. Friedman calls attention to two ways in which law plays an important role in social control:

> In the first place, legal institutions are responsible for the making, care and preservation of those rules and norms which define deviant behavior; they announce (in a penal code, for example) which acts may be officially punished and how and which ones may not be punished at all. In the second place, the legal system carries out many rules of social control. Police arrest burglars, prosecutors prosecute them, juries convict them, judges sentence them, prison guards watch them, and parole boards release them. (1977:11)

Of course, as we shall see, law does not have a monopoly on formal mechanisms of social control. Other types of formal mechanisms (such as firing, promotion, demotion, relocation, compensation manipulation, and so forth) are found in industry, academe, government, business, and various private groups (Selznick, 1969).

Dispute Settlement

As Karl N. Llewellyn so elegantly put it close to half a century ago:

> What, then, is this law business about? It is about the fact that our society is honeycombed with disputes. Disputes actual and potential, disputes to be settled and disputes to be prevented; both appealing to law, both making up the business of law. . . . This doing of something about disputes, this doing of it reasonably, is the business of law. (1960:2)

By settling disputes through an authoritative allocation of legal rights and obligations, the law provides an alternative to other methods of dispute resolution. Increasingly, people in all walks of life let the courts settle matters that were once resolved by informal and nonlegal mechanisms, such as negotiation, mediation, or forcible self-help measures. It should be noted, however, that law deals only with disagreements that have been translated into legal disputes. A legal resolution of conflict does not necessarily result in a reduction of tension or antagonism between the aggrieved parties. For example, in a case of employment discrimination on the basis of race, the court may focus on one incident in what is a complex and often not very clear-cut series of problems. It results in a resolution of a specific legal dispute, but not in the amelioration of the broader issues that have produced that conflict.

Social Change

Many scholars contend that a principal function of law in modern society is social engineering. It refers to purposive, planned, and directed social change initiated, guided, and supported by the law. Roscoe Pound captures the essence of this function of law in stating:

> For the purpose of understanding the law of today, I am content to think of law as a social institution to satisfy social wants—the claims and demands involved in the existence of civilized society—by giving effect to as much as we need with the least sacrifice, so far as such wants may be satisfied or such claims given effect by an ordering of human conduct through politically organized society. For present purposes I am content to see in legal history the record of a continually wider recognizing and satisfying of human wants or claims or desires through social control; a more embracing and more effective securing of social interests; a continually more complete and effective elimination of waste and precluding of friction in human enjoyment of the goods of existence—in short, a continually more efficacious social engineering. (1959:98–99)

In many instances law is considered a "desirable and necessary, if not a highly efficient means of inducing change, and that, wherever possible, its institutions and procedures are preferable to others of which we are aware" (Grossman and Grossman, 1971:2). Although some sociologists disagree with this contention (for example, Quinney, 2002), law is often used as a method of social change, a way of bringing about planned social change by the government. Social change is a prominent feature of modern welfare states (Vago, 2004). For example, part of the taxes a government collects goes to the poor in the form of cash, food stamps, medical and legal benefits, and housing (Friedman, 1998, 2002). I shall return to this social change function of the law in the discussion of law and social change in Chapter 7.

DYSFUNCTIONS OF LAW

Although law is an indispensable and ubiquitous institution of social life, it possesses—like most institutions—certain dysfunctions that may evolve into serious operational difficulties if they are not seriously considered (see, for example, Clark, 2007). These dysfunctions stem in part from the law's conservative tendencies, the rigidity inherent in its formal structure, the restrictive aspects connected with its control functions, and the fact that certain kinds of discriminations are inherent in the law itself.

The eminent social scientist Hans Morgenthau (1993:418) suggests that "a given status quo is stabilized and perpetuated in a legal system" and that the courts, being the chief instruments of a legal system, "must act as agents of the status quo." Although this observation does not consider fully the complex interplay between stability and change in the context of law, it still contains an important ingredient of truth. By establishing a social policy of a particular time and place in constitutional and statutory precepts, or by making the precedents of the past binding, the law exhibits a tendency toward conservatism. Once a scheme of rights and duties has been created by a legal system, continuous revisions and disruptions of the system are generally avoided in the interests of predictability and continuity. Social changes often precede changes in the law. In times of crisis, the law can break down, providing an opportunity for discontinuous and sometimes cataclysmic adjustments. Illustrations of this include the various first-aid legal measures used during an energy crisis, such as the rationing of gasoline purchases.

Related to these conservative tendencies of the law is a type of rigidity inherent in its normative framework. Because legal rules are couched in general, abstract, and universal terms, they sometimes operate as straitjackets in particular situations. An illustration of this is the failure of law to consider certain extenuating circumstances for a particular illegal act; for example, stealing because one is hungry or stealing for profit.

A third dysfunction of the law stems from the restrictive aspects of normative control. Norms are shared convictions about the patterns of behavior that are appropriate or inappropriate for the members of a group. Norms serve to combat and forestall anomie (a state of normlessness) and social disorganization. Law can overstep its bounds, and regulation can turn into overregulation, in which situation control may become transformed into repression. For example, in nineteenth-century America, public administration was sometimes hampered by an overrestrictive use of the law, which tended to paralyze needed discretionary exercises in governmental power (Pound, 1914:12–13).

Donald Black's (1989) contention that certain kinds of discrimination are inherent in law itself can also be construed as a fourth dysfunction. Rules, in principle, may apply to everyone, but legal authority falls unevenly across social place. A quote from his oft-cited book, *Sociological Justice*, aptly illustrates this point: "The law in its majestic equality. . . forbids the rich as well as the poor from sleeping under bridges, begging in the streets, and stealing bread" (1989:72). He argues that social status (regardless of race), the degree of intimacy (for example, family members versus friends versus strangers), speech, organization, and a number of other factors all greatly influence the use and application of law. For example, when a black person is convicted of killing a white person in America, the risk of capital punishment far exceeds every other racial combination. In Ohio, the risk of capital punishment is approximately 15 times higher than when a black is convicted of killing another black; in Georgia, over 30 times higher; in Florida, nearly 40; and in Texas, nearly 90 times higher. Similarly, sentencing for negligent homicide with a car is by far the most severe when the victim's status is higher than that of the offender (1989:10).

Undoubtedly, the list of dysfunctions of law is incomplete. One may also include a variety of procedural inefficiencies, administrative delays, and archaic legal terminologies. At times, justice is denied and innocent people are convicted (Yant, 1991). There is the cost of justice to the middle class and its unavailability to the poor, to the consumer, and to minority-group members (Sen, 2009). Questions also can be raised regarding the narrowness of legal education, the failure of ethical indoctrination, and the polarization of faculty and students along economic, racial, and gender ways, which remain pronounced during the early years of the second decade of the twenty-first century. One can also talk about laws being out-of-date, inequitable criminal sentencing, lack of clarity of some laws resulting in loopholes and diverse interpretations, and the dominating use of law by one class against another (Rostow, 1971; Strick, 1977). Finally, critics of the law point to the current rage for procedure and to "government by judges" as being particularly dysfunctional in a world as complex as ours (Crozier, 1984:116–117).

PARADIGMS OF SOCIETY

Deliberations by sociologists on law in society, at the time of writing this book in 2010, continue to take place in the context of one of two ideal and classic conceptions of society: the *consensus* and the *conflict* perspectives. The former describes society as a functionally integrated, relatively stable system held together by a basic consensus of values. Social order is considered as more or less permanent, and individuals can best achieve their interests through cooperation. Social conflict is viewed as the needless struggle among individuals and groups who have not yet attained sufficient understanding of their common interests and basic interdependence. This perspective stresses the cohesion, solidarity, integration, cooperation, and stability of society, which is seen as united by a shared culture and by agreement on its fundamental norms and values.

The conflict perspective, in direct opposition, considers society as consisting of individuals and groups characterized by conflict and dissension and held together by coercion. Order is temporary and unstable because every individual and group strives to maximize its own interests in a world of limited resources and goods. Social conflict is considered as intrinsic to the interaction between individuals and groups. In this perspective, the maintenance of power requires inducement and coercion, and law is an instrument of repression, perpetuating the interests of the powerful at the cost of alternative interests, norms, and values.

But, as Ralf Dahrendorf aptly points out, it is impossible to choose empirically between these two sets of assumptions: "Stability and change, integration and conflict, function and 'dysfunction,' consensus and constraint are, it would seem, two equally valid aspects of every imaginable society" (1958:174–175). When law in society is viewed in one of these two perspectives, not surprisingly, quite disparate conceptions of its basic role emerge (see, for example, Dahrendorf, 1990). Let us examine in some detail the role of law in these two perspectives.

The Consensus Perspective

The consensus perspective considers law as a neutral framework for maintaining societal integration. One of the best-known and most influential legal scholars, Roscoe Pound (1943, 1959), views society as composed of diverse groups whose interests often conflict with one another but are in basic harmony. He considers certain interests as essential for the well-being of society and maintains that the reconciliation between the conflicting interests of the diverse groups in society is essential to secure and maintain social order. In his words, law

> is an attempt to satisfy, to reconcile, to harmonize, to adjust these overlapping and often conflicting claims and demands, either through securing them directly and immediately, or through securing certain individual interests, or through delimitations or compromises of individual interests, so as to give effect to the greatest total of interests or to the interests that weigh most in our civilization, with the least sacrifice of the scheme of the interests as a whole. (Pound, 1943:39)

In Pound's view, law in a heterogeneous and pluralistic society, such as the United States, is best understood as an effort at social compromise with an emphasis on social order and harmony. Pound argues that the historical development of law demonstrates a growing recognition and satisfaction of human wants, claims, and desires through law. Over time, law has concerned itself with an ever-wider spectrum of human interests. Law has more and more come to provide for the common good and the satisfaction of social wants (Pound, 1959:47). He considers law a form of "social change" directed toward achieving social harmony. Pound argues that the purpose of law is to maintain and to en-sure those values and needs essential to social order, not by imposing one group's will on others, but by controlling, reconciling, and mediating the diverse and conflicting interests of individuals and groups within society. In brief, the purpose of law is to control interests and to maintain harmony and social integration.

Talcott Parsons (1962:58), a most influential sociologist of the twentieth century, concurs with this view by suggesting that "the primary function of a legal system is in-tegrity. It serves to mitigate potential elements of conflict and to oil the machinery of so-cial intercourse." Other sociologists, such as Harry C. Bredemeier (1962), accept this perspective and believe that it is necessary for society to supplement informal with for-mal mechanisms for generating and sustaining interpersonal cooperation. Proponents of the consensus perspective further maintain that law exists to maintain order and stability. Law is a body of rules enacted by representatives of the people in the interests of the people. Law is essentially a neutral agent, dispensing rewards and punishments without bias. A fundamental assumption of this perspective is that the political system is pluralis-tic; that is, society is composed of a number of interest groups of more or less equal power. The laws reflect compromise and consensus among these various interest groups and the values that are fundamental to the social order (Chambliss, 1976:4). This perspec-tive is alluded to in various sections of this book.

The Conflict Perspective

In marked contrast to the consensus perspective, the conflict view considers law as a "weapon in social conflict" (Turk, 1978) and an instrument of oppression "employed by the ruling classes for their own benefit" (Chambliss and Seidman, 1982:36). From this perspective, the transformation of society from a small, relatively homogeneous social group to a network of specialized groups is brought about by the evolution of both dis-tinct sets of interests and differences in real power between groups. When diverse groups come into conflict, they compete to have their interests protected and perpetuated through the formalization of their interests into law. On the basis of this idea, Richard Quinney argues that rather than being a device to control interests, law is an expression of interests, an outgrowth of the inherent conflict of interests characteristic of society. According to Quinney:

> Society is characterized by diversity, conflict, coercion, and change, rather than by consensus and stability. Second, law is a *result* of the operation of interests, rather than an instrument that functions outside of particular interests. Though law may control interests, it is in the first place *created* by interests of specific

persons and groups; it is seldom the product of the whole society. Law is made by men, representing special interests, who have the power to translate their interests into public policy. Unlike the pluralistic conception of politics, law does not represent a compromise of the diverse interests in society, but supports some interests at the expense of others. (1970:35)

Proponents of the conflict perspective believe that law is a tool by which the ruling class exercises its control. Law both protects the property of those in power and serves to repress political threats to the position of the elite. Quinney (1975:285) writes that whereas the state, contrary to conventional wisdom, is the instrument of the ruling class, "law is the state's coercive weapon, which maintains the social and economic order," and supports some interests at the expense of others, even when those interests are that of the majority.

But advocates of this position overstate their case. Not all laws are created and operated for the benefit of the powerful ruling groups in society. Laws prohibiting murder, robbery, arson, incest, and assault benefit all members of society, regardless of their economic position. It is too broad an assumption that powerful groups dictate the content of law and its enforcement for the protection of their own interests. As we shall see in Chapter 4, all kinds of groups are involved in lawmaking, although the powerful groups do have a substantial voice in the lawmaking process.

These two perspectives of society—consensus and conflict—are ideal types (that is, abstract concepts used to describe essential features of a phenomenon). Considering the operation of legal systems in society, there may be an element of truth in both. Sociologists who are influenced by Karl Marx, Georg Simmel, Lewis Coser, and Ralf Dahrendorf generally tend to embrace the conflict perspective of law in society (Goldstein, 2005). One of their justifications for taking this theoretical stance is that this approach emphasizes the role of special-interest groups in society. For example, the power of economic and commercial interests to influence legislation is illustrated by William J. Chambliss in his study of vagrancy statutes. He notes that the development of vagrancy laws paralleled the need of landowners for cheap labor during the period in England when the system of serfdom was collapsing. The first of these statutes, which came into existence in 1349, threatened criminal punishment for those who were able-bodied and yet unemployed—a condition that existed when peasants were in the process of moving from the land into the cities. The vagrancy law served "to force laborers (whether personally free or unfree) to accept employment at a low wage in order to insure the landowner an adequate supply of labor at a price he could afford to pay" (Chambliss, 1964:69). Subsequently, vagrancy statutes were modified to protect the commercial and industrial interests and to ensure safe commercial transportation. In the late nineteenth and early twentieth centuries in the United States, vagrancy laws were used again to serve the interests of the wealthy. Agricultural states during harvest time enforced vagrancy laws to push the poor into farm work. In periods of economic depression, similar laws were used to keep the unemployed from entering the state (Chambliss and Seidman, 1982:182). This is just one illustration to show how law came to reflect the particular interests of those who have power and influence in society. I shall return to the role of interest groups dealing with decision-making processes in the context of lawmaking in Chapter 4.

OPTIONS FOR SOCIOLOGISTS

As with the approaches to the study of law and society, divergences of opinion also characterize the question of what role sociologists should play in such endeavors. This question, to a substantial degree, polarized the discipline (see, for example, Mertz, 2008). Some sociologists consider their role primarily to synthesize material, to provide instructional packages, and to design software programs with interactive components for students and interested laymen (see, for example, Calavita, 2010; Friedrichs, 2010; Sutton, 2001). Others consider their role as describing and explaining social phenomena objectively (see, for example, Sherwin, 2006). They are concerned with the understanding of social life and social processes, and they go about their research in an alleged value-neutral and empirical fashion. They accept as scientific only those theoretical statements whose truth can be proven empirically. They are guided by Max Weber's notion of sociology as "a science which seeks to understand social action interpretively, and thereby to explain it causally in its course and its effects" (Weber, 1968:3). They believe that the discovery of causal laws is the ultimate goal of sociology, but the understanding of people's motives is central.

Others, however, go beyond the notion of *verstehen* (understanding). Sociologists who claim to be dialectical and critical in their orientation do not seek merely to describe and explain social events. They, as scientists, assert their right to criticize. The standards of evaluation upon which their criticism is based, and which these sociologists deduce from the nature of human beings and from considerations about social development, cannot always be empirically tested. To them, empirical research is necessary insofar as it provides and explains the data, but it is, so to speak, only a first step toward the essential criticism. They believe that the task of sociology is to account for human suffering. They aim at demystifying the world; to show people what constrains them and what their routes to freedom are. Their criticisms are prompted by their belief that the human condition and the social order have become unbearable. These critics believe that they have a responsibility not only to identify the factors that have precipitated a deleterious condition but also to provide, through theoretical and empirical efforts, ways to rectifying or redressing it. In the context of law and society studies, illustrations of such attempts over the past three decades are (many with self-explanatory titles) Jerold S. Auerbach's *Unequal Justice* (1976); Maureen Cain and Christine B. Harrington's *Lawyers in a Postmodern World: Translation and Transgression* (1994); Paul Campos's *Jurismania: The Madness of American Law* (1998); Alan M. Dershowitz's *The Abuse Excuse: And Other Cop-outs, Sob Stories, and Evasions of Responsibility* (1994); Leonard Downie's *Justice Denied* (1972); Daniel A. Farber and Suzanna Sherry's *Beyond All Reason: The Radical Assault on Truth in American Law* (1997); Macklin Fleming's *Lawyers, Money, and Success: The Consequences of Dollar Obsessions* (1997); Owen Fiss's *The Law As It Could Be* (2004); Mary Ann Glendon's *A Nation Under Lawyers: How the Crisis in the Legal Profession Is Transforming American Society* (1994); Paul G. Haskell's *Why Lawyers Behave As They Do* (1998); Philip K. Howard's four critical volumes (arguing over and over that the legal system has substantially disabled the judgment of the people with responsibility): *The Death of Common Sense: How Law Is Suffocating America* (1994), *The Lost Art of Drawing the Line: How Fairness Went Too Far* (2001), *The Collapse of the Common Good: How*

America's Lawsuit Culture Undermines Our Freedom (2003), and *Life Without Lawyers: Restoring Responsibility in America* (2010); David Nelken's *Beyond Law in Context: Developing a Sociological Understanding of Law* (2009); Charles J. Ogletree, Jr. and Austin Sarat's compelling collection of essays, *When Law Fails: Making Sense of Miscarriages of Justice* (2009); Richard Quinney's *Critique of Legal Order* (2002); Geoffrey Rivlin's *Understanding the Law* (2009); Gerry Spence's *With Justice for None* (1989); Cameron Stracher's *Double Billing: A Young Lawyer's Tale of Greed, Sex, Lies, and the Pursuit of a Swivel Chair* (1998); Ann Strick's *Injustice for All* (1977); and Martin Yant's *Presumed Guilty: When Innocent People Are Wrongly Convicted* (1991).

Finally, for some sociologists, criticism is interconnected with practice. They endorse the role of being simultaneously a student and an agent of social action. They are guided by *praxis*, or the wedding of theory and action. Because of their knowledge of social conditions, they are obligated to take action (see, for example, McLaren and Kincheloe, 2007; Schram, 2002). This position is associated with a Marxist tradition. It is based on the notion that knowledge generated from an analysis of a specific historical situation may be used as an argument for intervention, and politically engaged scholarship can contribute to the struggle for social justice. Sociologists in such situations try to demystify, clarify, and show individuals the source of their misery and the means of overcoming it. In a Marxian context, praxis means what people do, as contrasted with what they think. "Praxis is a revolutionary form of social practice (that is, it contributes to the humanization of people by transforming reality from alienation to hopefully better future). The concept is both a means of consciously shaping historical conditions and a standard for evaluating what occurs in any historical order. Marx maintains that a dialectical relationship exists between theory and praxis" (Reasons and Rich, 1978:431). Thus, sociologists of this perspective actively advocate changes in law and legal institutions wherever needed and work for the reformation of both the criminal system and the criminal law when warranted (Krisberg, 1978).

These controversies beset the "proper" role of sociologists in the discipline of law. Based on one's values, ideologies, and conception of sociology, and a plethora of other considerations, one may prefer to be a detached observer of social life, a critic of the social order, or an active agent of change. These roles, fortunately, are not mutually exclusive. Depending on the nature of the issue under consideration, the degree of commitment to and involvement in that issue, one may freely select among these alternatives. As an intellectual enterprise, sociology is flexible enough to accommodate these diverse positions. In a sense, they contribute to a greater understanding of the complicated interplay between law and society.

SUMMARY

The study of law in the field of sociology touches a variety of well-established areas of inquiry. It incorporates values, ideologies, social institutions, norms, power relations, and social processes. Since World War II, there has been a growing interest in law among sociologists both in the United States and abroad. Some of the examples of the study of law and society include the effectiveness of law, the impact of law on society, methods of dispute resolution, and research on judicial, legislative, and administrative processes. There are still some obstacles to interaction between sociologists and lawyers, however, as a consequence of differences in terminology, perception of the role of law in society, methodology, and professional culture. Yet, in spite of these difficulties, collaboration is on the increase between members of the two professions.

Academic debate over a proper definition of law has long preoccupied scholars in jurisprudence and in the social sciences. In our illustrative definitions, it was noted that law is a form of social control with explicit sanctions for noncompliance, and it consists of the behaviors, situations, and conditions for creating, interpreting, and applying legal rules.

The content of law may be considered as substantive or procedural. A distinction is made between public law and private law, as well as between civil law and criminal law. Common law generally refers to "judge-made" law or "case" law, as differentiated from statutory or enacted law. The principal legal systems in the world today are the Romano-Germanic (civil) law, common law, socialist law with its current ramifications and problems of transition, and Islamic law.

Law performs a multitude of functions in society. It is difficult to arrive at a satisfactory and meaningful list of functions. Still, there seems to be a great deal of emphasis in the literature on the recurrent social control, dispute settlement, and social change functions of law. But law, like other social institutions, possesses certain dysfunctions as a result of its conservative tendencies, the rigidity inherent in its formal structure, the restrictive aspects connected with its social control functions, and the fact that certain kinds of discriminations are inherent in the law itself.

Sociological analyses of law and society are generally based on two ideal views of society—consensus and conflict perspectives. The former considers society as a functionally integrated, relatively stable system held together by basic consensus of values. The latter conceives of society as consisting of groups characterized by conflict and dissension on values and held together by some members who coerce others. These dialectic models of society are ideal types. Taken toward the operation of the lawmaking organizations, there may be an element of truth in both. In this context, perhaps an eclectic approach is best.

In addition to divergences in the way of studying law in society, controversies also beset the "proper" role sociologists should play in the study of law and society. Some sociologists maintain that their role is to try to understand, describe, and empirically analyze social phenomena in a more or less value-free context. Others argue that it is the responsibility of social scientists to criticize malfunctioning components of, and processes in, a social system. Still others are guided by the notion of praxis; they seek to combine theory with practice, and their objective is to try to redress deleterious social conditions by means of legal action. Of course, these divergent positions are not mutually exclusive, and an awareness of these perspectives on the role of sociologists can contribute to a greater understanding of the intricate interplay between law and society.

SUGGESTED FURTHER READINGS

Richard L. Abel (ed.), *The Law & Society Reader*. New York: New York University Press, 1995. A series of often-cited groundbreaking articles that have all appeared in the *Law & Society Review*.

Mary P. Baumgartner (ed.), *The Social Organization of Law*. 2nd ed. San Diego, CA: Academic Press, 1999. A set of empirical studies on how social factors affect legal behavior. See also Sarat's compendium of the same title below that covers additional areas on the topic.

Franz von Benda-Beckman, Keebet von Benda-Beckman, and Julie Eckert (eds.), *Rules of Law and Laws of Ruling*. Burlington, VT: Ashgate, 2009. A compendium from the perspective of anthropology of law on the changing relationship between law and governance and how law is used both as a constitutive legitimation of governance and as a medium through which governance processes take place.

Kitty Calavita, *Invitation to Law and Society: An Introduction to the Study of Real Law*. Chicago, IL: University of Chicago Press, 2010. A brief introduction to the basics of the field and a starting point for additional readings.

James V. Calvi and Susan Coleman, *American Law and Legal Systems*. 6th ed. Upper Saddle River, NJ: Prentice-Hall, 2008. An informative up-to-date discussion of law and the various legal systems.

David S. Clark (ed.), *Encyclopedia of Law and Society*. Three volumes. Thousand Oaks, CA: Sage Publications, 2007. It is the largest, most current, comprehensive and international treatment of the law and society field with more than 700 biographical, historical, comparative, topical, thematic and methodological entries.

John M. Conley and William M. O'Barr, *Just Words: Law, Language, and Power*. 2nd ed. Chicago, IL: University of Chicago Press, 2005. An attempt to show how the microdynamics of the legal process and the major questions of justice can be explored through the field of socio-linguistics.

John Cooper, Ronald L. Nettler, and Mohamed Mahmoud (eds.), *Islam and Modernity*. New York: I. B. Tauris Publishers, 2000. A compendium of articles that provides a background for the interplay between law and Islamic religion.

Roger Cotterrell, *Law, Culture and Society: Legal Ideas in the Mirror of Social Theory*. Burlington, VT: Ashgate, 2006. Through a range of specific studies, the author seeks to integrate the sociology of law with other kinds of legal analysis and discusses current justice debates in legal theory and comparative law.

Neil J. Diamant, Stanley B. Lubman, and Kevin J. O'Brien (eds.), *Engaging the Law in China: State, Society, and Possibilities for Justice*. Stanford, CA: Stanford University Press, 2005. A collection of interdisciplinary articles on the various facets of law and legal system in contemporary China.

James E. Duke, *Conflict and Power in Social Life*. Provo, Utah: Brigham Young University Press, 1976. A primer on influential and important conflict theories in sociology. It provides several ramifications of the conflict model of society.

Werner Ende and Udo Steinbach (eds.), *Islam in the World Today: A Handbook of Politics, Religion, Culture, and Society*. Ithaca, NY: Cornell University Press, 2010. A single-volume authorative reference work on Islam providing background information on religious, cultural, social and political life essential for understanding Islamic law.

Lawrence M. Friedman, *Total Justice*. New York: Russell Sage Foundation, 1985. A short, influential, and highly readable book on law and the legal system in the United States.

Robert I. Friedman, *Red Mafiya: How the Russian Mob Has Invaded America*. Boston, MA: Little, Brown and Company, 2000. An interesting account of Russian organized crime. It is bloodier than Corleone's *Godfather*, and reads almost as well.

Bryan A. Garner, *Legal Writing in Plain English: A Text with Exercises*. Chicago, IL:

University of Chicago Press, 2001. Just to show that it can be done.

Patrick Glenn, *Legal Traditions of the World: Sustainable Diversity in Law*. 4th ed. New York: Oxford University Press, 2010. An overview of the legal traditions that serve the foundation of the world's major societies.

Wael B. Hallaq (ed.), *The Formation of Islamic Law*. Burlington, VT: Ashgate, 2004. A collection of fourteen essays on the rise of Islamic law.

Wael B Hallaq, *An Introduction to Islamic Law*. Cambridge, UK: Cambridge University Press, 2009. Another illuminating publication by Hallaq on Islamic law in its premodern habitat, how the law was transformed during the colonial period, and how the law emerged as primarily textual entity focusing on fixed punishments and ritual requirements.

E. Adamson Hoebel, *The Law of Primitive Man: A Study in Comparative Legal Dynamics*. Cambridge, MA: Harvard University Press, 1954. A classic and highly influential treatise on the cross-cultural study of the dynamics of law. A must for students interested in law from an anthropological perspective.

Herbert Jacob, *Law and Politics in the United States*. 2nd ed. Fort Washington, PA: Harper-Collins College Publishers, 1995. An informative and clear overview of the components and processes of the American legal system.

Herbert M. Kritzer (ed.), *Legal Systems of the World: A Political, Social, and Cultural Encyclopedia*. Santa Barbara, CA: ABC-CLIO, 2002. A comprehensive review of legal systems and an excellent source of background information on the topic,

Richard Lempert and Joseph Sanders, *An Invitation to Law and Social Science: Desert, Disputes, and Distribution*. New York: Longman, 1986. A timeless and influential interdisciplinary analysis of law and the legal system written by two law professors for students in both law and the social sciences.

Lisa J. McIntyre, *Law in the Sociological Enterprise: A Reconstruction*. Boulder, CO: Westview Press, 1994. A sophisticated discussion of how law permeates the relationships of modern society.

Peter McLaren and Joe L. Kincheloe (eds.), *Critical Pedagogy: Where Are We Now?* New York: Peter Lang, 2007. An interesting collection reconsidering Marx in post-Marxist times with a review of the educational left after September 11 and critical pedagogy as revolutionary praxis.

John Monahan and Laurens Walker, *Social Science in Law: Cases and Materials*. 7th ed. New York: Thomson Reuters/ Foundation Press, 2010. See especially the material on the jurisprudential origins of social science in law.

Alfonso Morales (ed.), *Renascent Pragmatism: Studies in Law and Social Sciences*. Burlington, VT: Ashgate, 2003. A series of essays on theory, method, public policy, and empirical scholarship by well-known contributors in social sciences, law, and philosophy.

George Mousourakis, *A Legal History of Rome*. New York: Routledge, 2007. The book traces the historical development of Roman law from the earliest period of Roman history up to and including Justinian's codification in the sixth century A.D. and its implications on modern law.

David Nelken, *Beyond Law in Context: Developing a Sociological Understanding of Law*. Burlington, VT: Ashgate, 2009. This volume examines from a fresh perspective the relationship between law, society and social theory with an emphasis on the ideal fit between law and its social context.

Anton N. Oleinik, *Organized Crime, Prison and Post-Soviet Societies*. Burlington VT: Ashgate, 2003. A fascinating exploration of the social roots of organized crime and the concept of Mafia in the former Soviet Union. Should be read along with *Red Mafiya: How the Russian Mob Has Invaded America*, cited earlier.

Alain Pottage and Martha Mundy (eds.), *Law, Anthropology, and the Constitution of the Social: Making Persons and Things*. New York: Cambridge University Press, 2004. An assortment of cross-cultural articles on the various facets of the relationship between law and anthropology.

Justin B. Richland and Sarah Deer, *Introduction to Tribal Legal Studies.* 2nd ed. Lanham, MD: AltaMira Press, 2010. This is the only comprehensive introduction (to my knowledge) to tribal law covering the intricate relationship between tribal, federal, and state laws.

Ronald Roesch, Steven D. Dart, and James R. P. Ogloff (eds.), *Psychology and the Law: The State of the Discipline.* New York: Plenum Publishing Corporation, 1999. A good overview of major issues and contributions of psychology to the understanding of law, legal systems, and processes. A useful supplement to the law and society literature.

Norbert Rouland, *Legal Anthropology.* Translated by Philippe G. Planel. Stanford, CA: Stanford University Press, 1994. An excellent discussion of a number of law and legal systems throughout the world from an anthropological perspective.

Patrick J. Ryan and George E. Rush (eds.), *Understanding Organized Crime in a Global Perspective.* Thousand Oaks, CA: Sage Publications, Inc., 1997. See in particular the articles on organized crime in Russia and Eastern Europe and the interesting predictions for the twenty-first century — some of which are way off target but worth glancing at.

Austin Sarat (ed.), *Social Organization of Law.* Los Angeles, CA: Roxbury Publishing Company, 2004. A collection of articles by noted scholars on the various aspects of the social organization of law in society. See also Baumgartner's book mentioned above that covers additional areas on the topic.

Austin Sarat and Thomas R. Kearns (eds.), *Law in the Domains of Culture.* Ann Arbor, MI: University of Michigan Press, 2000. A collection of essays on law's relations to culture and on the role of cultural analysis of law.

A. W. B. Simpson, *Invitation to Law.* Oxford, UK: Basil Blackwell, 1988. A provocative and mordant examination of law and the emergence of the British legal system.

June Starr and Jane F. Collier (eds.), *History and Power in the Study of Law: New Directions in Legal Anthropology.* Ithaca, NY: Cornell University Press, 1989. A compendium of 14 articles by leading anthropologists, sociologists, and law professors from North America and Europe on the various facets of the interplay between law and society.

Marjorie S. Zatz, *Producing Legality: Law and Socialism in Cuba.* New York: Rutledge, 1994. A fascinating exploration of the various facets of Cuba's legal system that are still in place today and a good resource for anyone interested in the comparative study of legal systems.

REFERENCES

Abadinsky, Howard. 2008. *Law and Justice: An Introduction to the American Legal System*, 6th ed. Upper Saddle River, NJ: Prentice-Hall.

Abass, Ademola. 2011. *Complete International Law.* New York: Oxford University Press.

Abel, Richard L. 1995. "What We Talk About When We Talk About Law." Pp. 1–10 in Richard L. Abel (ed.), *The Law & Society Reader.* New York: New York University Press.

Abel, Richard L., and Philip S. C. Lewis (eds.). 1988. *Lawyers in Society: The Common Law World.* Vol. 1. Berkeley and Los Angeles, CA: University of California Press. 1988. *Lawyers in Society: The Civil Law World.* Vol. 2. Berkeley and Los Angeles, CA: University of California Press.

Agyeman, Julian, and Yelena Ogneva-Himmelberg. 2009. *Environmental Justice and Sustainability in the Former Soviet Union.* Cambridge, MA: The MIT Press.

Ahmed, Ali. 2001. *Cosmopolitan Orientation of the Process of International Environmental Lawmaking: An Islamic Law Genre.* Lanham, MD: University Press of America.

Akers, Ronald L. 1965. "Toward a Comparative Definition of Law," *Journal of*

Criminal Law, Criminology, and Police Science, 56 (September): 301–306.

Akers, Ronald L., and Richard Hawkins (eds.). 1975. *Law and Control in Society*. Englewood Cliffs, NJ: Prentice-Hall.

Alexander, Gregory S., and Grazyna Skapska (eds.). 1994. *A Fourth Way? Privatization, Property, and the Emergence of New Market Economies*. New York: Routledge.

Al-Azmeh, Aziz (ed.). 1988. *Islamic Law: Social and Historical Contexts*. London: Routledge.

An-Na'im, Abdullahi, and Mashood Baderin. 2010. *Islam and Human Rights*. Burlington, VT: Ashgate.

Aubert, Vilhelm (ed.). 1969. *Sociology of Law*. "Introduction." Pp. 9–14. Harmondsworth, UK: Penguin. 1973. "Researches in the Sociology of Law." Pp. 48–62 in Michael Barkun (ed.), *Law and the Social System*. New York: Lieber-Atherton.

Auerbach, Jerold S. 1976. *Unequal Justice*. New York: Oxford University Press.

Barzilai, Gad (ed.). 2007. *Law and Religion*. Burlington, VT: Ashgate.

Baumgartner, Mary P. (ed.) 1999. *The Social Organization of Law*. 2nd ed. San Diego, CA: Academic Press.

Bearak, Barry. 1998. "Afghan Beard Code: Like Castro Si, Pavarotti No," *New York Times* (October 13): A4.

Benda-Beckman, Franz von, Keebet von Benda-Beckman, and Julie Eckert (eds.). 2009. *Rules of Law and Laws of Ruling*. Burlington, VT: Ashgate.

Bennion, F.A.R. 2009. *Understanding Common Law Legislation*. New York: Oxford University Press.

Black, Donald. 1976. *The Behavior of Law*. New York: Academic Press. 1989. *Sociological Justice*. New York: Oxford University Press. 1998. *The Social Structure of Right and Wrong*. Revised ed. San Diego, CA: Academic Press. 2002. "The Geometry of Law: An Interview with Donald Black," *International Journal of the Sociology of Law*, 30 (2): 101–129

Bredemeier, Harry C. 1962. "Law as an Integrative Mechanism." Pp. 73–90 in

William J. Evan (ed.), *Law and Sociology: Exploratory Essays*. New York: Free Press.

Buckley, Neil. 2006. "Contract Killers Return to Russia." *Financial Times* (October 15): 3.

Bryant, Christopher, and Edmund Mokrzycki (eds.). 1994. *The Great Transformation? Change and Continuity in East-Central Europe*. New York: Routledge.

Cain, Maureen, and Christine B. Harrington (eds.). 1994. *Lawyers in a Postmodern World: Translation and Transgression*. New York: New York University Press.

Calavita, Kitty. 2010. *Invitation to Law and Society: An Introduction to the Study of Real Law*. Chicago, IL: University of Chicago Press.

Calvi, James V., and Susan Coleman. 2008. *American Law and Legal Systems*. 6th ed. Upper Saddle River, NJ: Prentice-Hall.

Campos, Paul F. 1998. *Jurismania: The Madness of American Law*. New York: Oxford University Press.

Canter, David, Maria Ioannou, and Donna Youngs (eds.). 2009. *Safer Sex in the City: The Experience and Management of Street Prostitution*. Burlington, VT: Ashgate.

Canter, David, and Rita Zukauskiene. 2009. *Psychology and Law: Bridging the Gap*. Burlington, VT: Ashgate.

Cardozo, Benjamin Nathan. 1924. *The Growth of the Law*. New Haven, CT: Yale University Press.

Chambliss, William J. 1964. "A Sociological Analysis of the Law of Vagrancy," *Social Problems*, 12 (1) (Summer):67–77. 1976. "Functional and Conflict Theories of Crime: The Heritage of Emile Durkheim and Karl Marx." Pp. 1–28 in William J. Chambliss and Milton Mankoff (eds.), *Whose Law? What Order? A Conflict Approach to Criminology*. New York: John Wiley.

Chambliss, William, and Robert Seidman. 1982. *Law, Order, and Power*. 2nd ed. Reading, MA: Addison-Wesley.

Clark, David S. (ed.) 2007. *Encyclopedia of Law and Society*. Three volumes. Thousand Oaks, CA: Sage Publications.

Collins, Randall. 1995. "Prediction in Macrosociology: The Case of the Soviet Collapse,"

American Journal of Sociology, 100 (6) (May): 1552–1593.

Conley, John M., and William M. O'Barr. 2005. *Just Words: Law, Language, and Power.* 2nd ed. Chicago, IL: University of Chicago Press.

Cooper, John, Ronald L. Nettler, and Mohamed Mahmoud (eds.). 2000. *Islam and Modernity.* New York: I. B. Tauris Publishers.

Cotterrell, Roger. 2006. *Law, Culture, and Society: Legal Ideas in the Mirror of Social Theory.* Burlington, VA: Ashgate.

Cownie, Fiona. 2010. *English Legal System in Context.* 4th ed. New York: Oxford University Press.

Crozier, Michel. 1984. *The Trouble with America.* Trans. Peter Heinegg. Berkeley and Los Angeles, CA: University of California Press.

Dahrendorf, Ralf. 1958. "Toward a Theory of Social Conflict," *Journal of Conflict Resolution,* (2) (June): 170–183. 1990. *The Modern Social Conflict: An Essay on the Politics of Liberty.* Berkeley, CA: University of California Press,

David, Rene, and John E. Brierley. 1985. *Major Legal Systems in the World Today.* 3rd ed. London: Stevens & Sons.

Davis, F. James. 1962. "Law as a Type of Social Control." Pp. 39–63 in F. James Davis et al. (eds.), *Society and the Law: New Meanings for an Old Profession.* New York: Free Press.

de Soto, Hernando. 2001. *The Mystery of Capital: Why Capitalism Triumphs in the West and Fails Everywhere Else.* New York: Basic Books.

Dershowitz, Alan M. 1994. *The Abuse Excuse: And Other Cop-Outs, Sob Stories, and Evasions of Responsibility.* Boston, MA: Little, Brown and Company.

Diamant, Neil J., Stanley B. Lubman, and Kevin J. O'Brien (eds.). 2005. *Engaging the Law in China: State, Society, and Possibilities for Justice.* Stanford, CA: Stanford University Press.

Donovan, James M. 2008. *Legal Anthropology: An Introduction.* Lanham, MD: AltaMira Press.

Downie, Leonard. 1972. *Justice Denied.* Baltimore, MD: Penguin.

Economist. 2001. "A Survey of Russia: Putin's Choice," (July 21): 1–16. 2004. "The People Come to Court" (March 6): 35–36. 2009. "The World This Week," (November 21): 9. 2010. "Justice in the United Arab Emirates: What a Muddle." (January 16): 48.

Ehrlich, Eugen. 1975. *Fundamental Principles of the Sociology of Law,* Foreword. Trans. Walter L. Mall. New York: Arno Press. Originally published by Harvard University Press, 1936.

Eicher, Sharon (ed.). 2009. *Corruption in International Business: The Challenge of Cultural and Legal Diversity.* Burlington, VT: Ashgate.

Elster, Jon. 1995. *Archives Europeenes de Sociologie.* 36 (1) (Sommaire): 105–134.

Ende, Werner, and Udo Steinbach (eds.). 2010. *Islam in the World Today: A Handbook of Politics, Religion, Culture, and Society.* Ithaca, NY: Cornell University Press.

Erlanger, Steven. 1992. "Two Novelties in Russian Courts: Defense Lawyers and Jury Trial," *New York Times* (May 11): A1, A4. 1995. "A Corrupt Tide in Russia from State-Business Ties," *New York Times* (July 3): A1, A5.

Farber, Daniel A., and Suzanna Sherry. 1997. *Beyond All Reason: The Radical Assault on Truth in American Law.* New York: Oxford University Press.

Feuer, Lewis S. 2010. *Ideology and the Ideologists.* With a new introduction by Irving Louis Horowitz. Piscataway, NJ: Transaction Publishers.

Fiss, Owen. 2004. *The Law As It Could Be.* New York: New York University Press.

Fleming, Macklin. 1997. *Lawyers, Money, and Success: The Consequences of Dollar Obsessions.* Westport, CN: Quorum.

Foster, Nigel, and Satish Sule. 2010. *German Legal System and Laws.* New York: Oxford University Press.

Freeman, Michael, and Oliver G. Goodenough (eds.). 2010. *Law, Mind and Brain.* Burlington, VT: Ashgate.

Friedman, Lawrence M. 1975. *The Legal System: A Social Science Perspective.* New York: Russell Sage Foundation. 1977. *Law and Society: An Introduction.* Englewood Cliffs, NJ: Prentice-Hall. 1998. *American Law: An Introduction.* 2nd ed. New York: W.W. Norton & Co., Inc. 2002. *American Law in the Twentieth Century.* New Haven, CT: Yale University Press.

Friedman, Robert I. 2000. *Red Mafiya: How the Russian Mob Has Invaded America.* Boston, MA: Little, Brown and Company.

Friedrichs, David O. 2010. *Law in Our Lives: An Introduction.* 2nd ed. Los Angeles, CA: Roxbury Publishing Co.

Gaddy, Clifford, Jim Leitzel, and Michael Alexeev. 1995. "Mafiosi and Matrioshki: Organized Crime and Russian Reform," *Brookings Review* 13 (1) (Winter): 26–30.

Garner, Bryan A. 2001. *Legal Writing in Plain English: A Text with Exercises.* Chicago, IL: University of Chicago Press.

Ghanim, David. 2010. *Gender and Violence in the Middle East.* Santa Barbara, CA: Prager.

Gest, Ted. 1995. "Combating Legalese: Law Schools are Finally Learning That Good English Makes Sense," *U.S. News & World Report* (March 20): 78–81.

Gilgoff, Dan. 2004. "Law Schools Go International," *U.S. News & World Report* (April 12): 58–62.

Gillespie, Alisdair. 2009. *The English Legal System.* New York: Oxford University Press.

Glaberson, William. 2001. "Legal Citations on Trial in Innovation v. Tradition," *New York Times* (July 8): A1.

Glendon, Mary Ann. 1994. *A Nation Under Lawyers: How the Crisis in the Legal Profession Is Transforming American Society.* New York: Farrar, Straus, and Giroux.

Glenn, Patrick. 2010. *Legal Traditions of the World. Sustainable Diversity in Law.* 4th ed. New York: Oxford University Press.

Goldstein, Philip. 2005. *Post-Marxist Theory.* Albany, NY: State University of New York Press.

Gram, David. 2006. "As Part of Sentence, Man Told He Can't Go Home Again." *Seattle Times* (July 5): A4.

Griffin, James. 2009. *On Human Rights.* New York: Oxford University Press.

Grillo, Ralph, Roger Ballard, Allesandro Ferrari, Andre Hoekema, Marcel Maussen, and Prakash Shah (eds.). 2009. *Legal Practice and Cultural Diversity.* Burlington, VT: Ashgate.

Grossman, Joel B., and Mary H. Grossman (eds.). 1971. "Introduction." Pp. 1–10 in *Law and Change in Modern America.* Pacific Palisades, CA: Goodyear.

Hallaq, Wael B. (ed.) 2004. *The Formation of Islamic Law.* Burlington, VT: Ashgate.

Hallaq, Wael B. 2009. *An Introduction to Islamic Law.* Cambridge, UK: Cambridge University Press.

Handelman, Stephen. 1995. *Comrade Criminal: Russia's New Mafiya.* New Haven, CT: Yale University Press.

Hart, Henry M., Jr. 1958. "The Aims of the Criminal Law," *Law and Contemporary Problems* (23) (Summer): 401–441.

Haskell, Paul G. 1998. *Why Lawyers Behave As They Do.* Boulder, CO: Westview Press.

Hesli, Vicki L. 2007. *Governments and Politics in Russia and the Post-Soviet Region.* Boston, MA: Houghton Mifflin.

Higgins, Andrew. 2007. "A Word to the Wise in Iran: Don't Ever Wear a Tie to Work. Men, Too, Now Must Worry about the Fashion Police; Barber Shop Dos & Don'ts," *Wall Street Journal* (May 12–13): A1, A5.

Hoebel, E. Adamson. 1954. *The Law of Primitive Man: A Study of Comparative Legal Dynamics.* Cambridge, MA: Harvard University Press.

Holmes, Oliver Wendell. 1897. "The Path of the Law," *Harvard Law Review* (10) (March): 457–461. 1963. *The Common Law.* Cambridge, MA: Harvard University Press. Mark D. Howe (ed.). Originally published in 1881.

Howard, Philip K. 1994. *The Death of Common Sense: How Law Is Suffocating America.* New York: Random House. 2001. *The Lost Art of Drawing the Line: How Fairness Went Too Far.* New York: Random House. 2003. *The Collapse of the Common Good: How America's Lawsuit Culture Undermines Our Freedom.* New York: Random House. 2010. *Life Without Lawyers: Restoring Responsibility in America.* New York: W. W. Norton.

Johansen, Bruce Elliott (ed.). 1998. *The Encyclopedia of Native American Legal Tradition.* Westport, CT: Greenwood Publishing Group.

Johns, Fleur (ed.). 2010. *International Legal Personality.* Burlington, VT: Ashgate.

Johnson, Alan V. 1977. "A Definition of the Concept of Law," *Mid-American Review of Sociology* 2 (1) (Spring): 47–71.

Kapardis, Andreas. 2003. *Psychology and Law: A Critical Introduction.* 2nd ed. New York: Cambridge University Press.

Kevelson, Roberta (ed.). 1994. *Codes and Customs: Millennial Perspectives.* New York: Peter Lang.

Klausen, Jytte. 2009. *The Cartoons That Shook the World.* New Haven, CT: Yale University Press.

Klingsberg, Ethan. 1992. "Judicial Review and Hungary's Transition from Communism to Democracy: The Constitutional Court, the Continuity of Law, and the Redefinition of Property Rights," *Brigham Young University Law Review 1992* (1): 41–144.

Krisberg, Barry. 1978. "The Sociological Imagination Revisited." Pp. 455–470 in Charles E. Reasons and Robert M. Rich (eds.), *The Sociology of Law: A Conflict Perspective.* Toronto, Canada: Butterworths.

Kritzer, Herbert M. (ed.) 2002. *Legal Systems of the World: A Political, Social, and Cultural Encyclopedia.* Santa Barbara, CA: ABC-CLIO.

Kuhn, Michael, and Doris Weidemann (eds.). 2010. *Internalization of the Social Sciences. Asia – Latin America – Middle East – Africa – Eurasia.* Piscataway, NJ: Transaction Publishers.

Law & Society Review. 1995. "From the Editor," 29 (1): 5–9.

Lauderdale, Pat. 1997. "Indigenous North American Jurisprudence," *International Journal of Comparative Sociology* 38 (1–2) (June): 131–149.

Lippman, Matthew, Sean McConville, and Mordechai Yerushalmi. 1988. *Islamic Criminal Law and Procedure.* New York: Praeger.

Llewellyn, Karl N. 1960. *The Bramble Bush.* Dobbs Ferry, NY: Oceana Publications, Inc. Originally published in 1930.

Masood, Salman. 2006. "Pakistani Rape Victims Jailed for Adultery." *Seattle Times* (July 9): A17.

Mattei, Ugo. 1997. *Comparative Law and Economics.* Ann Arbor, MI: University of Michigan Press.

Matza, David. 2010. *Becoming Delinquent.* Piscataway, NJ: Transaction Publishers.

Mayer, Ann Elizabeth. 2007. *Islam and Human Rights: Tradition and Politics.* 4th ed. Boulder, CO: Westview Press.

McIntyre, Lisa J. 1994. *Law in the Sociological Enterprise: A Reconstruction.* Boulder, CO: Westview Press.

McLaren, Peter, and Joe L. Kincheloe (eds.). 2007. *Critical Pedagogy: Where Are We Now?* New York: Peter Lang.

Mears, T. Lambert. 2004. *The Institutes of Gaius and Justinian: The Twelve Tables, and the CXVIIth and CXXVIIth Novels, with Introduction and Translation.* Clark, NJ: Lawbook Exchange.

Meier, Andrew. 1995. "The Chechen Mafia: The Real Reason Yeltsin Invaded," *New Republic* 212 (17) (April 24): 16–18.

Mermin, Samuel. 1982. *Law and the Legal System: An Introduction.* 2nd ed. Boston, MA: Little, Brown and Company.

Mertz, Elizabeth (ed.). 2008. *The Role of Social Science in Law.* Burlington, VT: Ashgate.

Milor, Vedat (ed.). 1994. *Changing Political Economies: Privatization in Post-Communist and Reforming Communist States.* Boulder, CO: Lynne Rienner Publishers.

Morales, Alfonso (ed.). 2003. *Renascent Pragmatism: Studies in Law and Social Sciences.* Burlington, VT: Ashgate.

Morgenthau, Hans. 1993. *Politics among Nations.* New York: McGraw-Hill. Revised by Kenneth W. Thompson.

Mousourakis, George. 2007. *A Legal History of Rome.* New York: Routledge.

Muhlhahn, Klaus. 2009. *Criminal Justice in China: A History.* Cambridge, MA: Harvard University Press.

Mundy, Martha (ed.). 2002. *Law and Anthropology.* Aldershot, Hants, UK; Burlington, VT: Ashgate/Dartmouth.

Nader, Laura, and Harry F. Todd, Jr. (eds.) 1978. "Introduction." Pp. 1–40 in *The Disputing Process—Law in Ten Societies.* New York: Columbia University Press.

Nelken, David. 2009. *Beyond Law in Context: Developing a Sociological Understanding of Law.* Burlington, VT: Ashgate.

Neusner, Jacob, and Tamara Sonn. 1999. *Comparing Religions Through Law: Judaism and Islam.* New York: Routledge.

Nielsen, Jorgen S., and Lisbet Christoffersen (eds.). 2010. *Shari'a as Discourse: Legal Traditions and the Encounter with Europe.* Burlington, VT: Ashgate.

Oda, Hiroshi. 2009. *Japanese Law.* 3rd ed. New York: Oxford University Press.

Ogletree, Charles J. Jr., and Austin Sarat (eds.). 2009. *When Law Fails: Making Sense of Miscarriages of Justice.*

Oleinik, Anton N. 2003. *Organized Crime, Prison and Post-Soviet Societies.* Burlington, VT: Ashgate.

Paringaux, Roland-Pierre. 1998. "Prostitution Takes a Turn for the West," *Guardian Weekly* 158 (21) (May 24): 18.

Parisi, Francesco. 2008. *The Economics of Lawmaking.* New York: Oxford University Press.

Parsons, Talcott. 1962. "The Law and Social Control." Pp. 56–72 in William M. Evan (ed.), *Law and Sociology: Exploratory Essays.* New York: Free Press.

Perlez, Jane. 1995. "Poles Dismayed at Unchecked Crime," *New York Times* (June 19): A5.

Piana, Daniela. 2010. *Judicial Accountabilities in New Europe: From Rules of Law to Quality of Justice.* Burlington, VT: Ashgate.

Plessis, Paul du. 2010. *Borkowski's Textbook on Roman Law.* 4th ed. New York: Oxford University Press.

Pollack, Ervin H. 1979. *Jurisprudence: Principles and Applications.* Columbus, OH: Ohio State University Press.

Posner, Eric A. 2009. *The Perils of Global Legalism.* Chicago, IL: University of Chicago Press.

Posner, Eric A., and Cass R. Sunstein (eds.). 2010. *Law and Happiness.* Chicago, IL: University of Chicago Press.

Posner, Richard A. 1996. *The Federal Courts: Challenge and Reform.* Cambridge, MA: Harvard University Press. 2001. *Frontiers of Legal Theory.* Cambridge, MA: Harvard University Press. 2007. *Economic Analysis of Law.* 7th ed. New York: Aspen Publishers.

Pospisil, Leopold J. 1971. *Anthropology of Law: A Comparative Theory.* New York: Harper & Row, Publishers. 1978. *The Ethnology of Law.* 2nd ed. Menlo Park, CA: Cummings Publishing Company.

Pottage, Alain, and Martha Mundy (eds.). 2004. *Law, Anthropology, and the Constitution of the Social: Making Persons and Things.* New York: Cambridge University Press.

Pound, Roscoe. 1914. "Justice According to Law," *Columbia Law Review* 14 (1): 1–26. 1941. *In My Philosophy of Law.* Saint Paul, MN: West Publishing Company. 1943. "A Survey of Social Interests," *Harvard Law Review* (57) (October): 1–39. 1959. *An Introduction to the Philosophy of Law.* New Haven, CT: Yale University Press.

Priban, Jiri, Pauline Roberts, and James Young (eds.). 2003. *Systems of Justice in Transition: Central European Experiences since 1989.* Burlington, VT: Ashgate.

Quinney, Richard. 1970. *The Social Reality of Crime.* Boston, MA: Little, Brown and Company. 1975. *Criminology: Analysis and Critique of Crime in America.* Boston, MA: Little, Brown and Company. 2002. *Critique of Legal Order: Crime Control in Capitalist Society.* New Brunswick, NJ: Transaction Books.

Rawls, John. 2001. *Justice as Fairness: A Restatement.* Ed. Erin Kelly. Cambridge, MA: Belknap Press/Harvard University Press.

Reasons, Charles E., and Robert M. Rich (eds.). 1978. *The Sociology of Law: A Conflict Perspective.* Toronto, Canada: Butterworths.

Rehbinder, Manfreid. 1975. *Sociology of Law: A Trend Report and Bibliography.* The Hague, Netherlands: Mouton.

Rich, Robert M. 1977. *The Sociology of Law: An Introduction to Its Theorists and Theories.* Washington, DC: University Press of America.

Richland, Justin B., and Sarah Deer. 2010. *Introduction to Tribal Legal Studies.* 2nd ed. Lanham, MD: AltaMira Press.

Rivlin, Geoffrey. 2009 *Understanding the Law.* New York: Oxford University Press.

Robertson, Grant, and Beppi Grosariol. 2006. "Litigation. Grammarians Take Heed of Telecomma Dispute: Legal and Business Scholars Are Riveted by Rogers, Aliant Punctuation Debate," *Globe and Mail* (December 29): B4.

Roesch, Ronald, Steven D. Dart, and James R. P. Ogloff (eds.). 1999. *Psychology and the Law: The State of the Discipline.* New York: Plenum Publishing Corporation.

Ross, E. Adamson. 1922. *Social Control.* New York: MacMillan. Originally published in 1901.

Ross, Laurence H. 1989. "Sociology and Legal Sanctions," Pp. 36–49 in Martin Lawrence Friedland (ed.), *Sanctions and Rewards in the Legal System: A Multidisciplinary Approach.* Toronto, Canada: University of Toronto Press.

Rostow, Eugene V. (ed.) 1971. *Is Law Dead?* New York: Simon & Schuster.

Ryan, Patrick J., and George E. Rush (eds.). 1997. *Understanding Organized Crime in a Global Perspective.* Thousand Oaks, CA: Sage Publications, Inc.

Saeed, Abdullah. 2004. *Freedom of Religion, Apostasy and Islam.* Burlington, VT: Ashgate.

Sampford, Charles. 1989. *The Disorder of Law: A Critique of Legal Theory.* Oxford, UK: Basil Blackwell.

Samuels, Suzanne. 2006. *Law, Politics, and Society: An Introduction to American Law.* Boston, MA: Houghton Mifflin.

Sarat, Austin, and Thomas R. Kearns (eds.). 1994. *The Rhetoric of Law.* Ann Arbor, MI: University of Michigan Press. 2000. *Law in the Domains of Culture.* Ann Arbor, MI: University of Michigan Press.

Schram, Sanford F. 2002. *Praxis for the Poor: Piven and Cloward and the Future of Social Science in Social Welfare.* New York: New York University Press.

Schur, Edwin M. 1968. *Law and Society: A Sociological View.* New York: Random House.

Selznick, Philip. 1968. "Law: The Sociology of Law," *International Encyclopedia of the Social Science* (9): 50–59. 1969. *Law, Society, and Industrial Justice.* New York: Russell Sage Foundation.

Sen, Amartya. 2009. *The Idea of Justice.* Cambridge, MA: Harvard University Press.

Shaham, Ron. 2010. *The Expert Witness in Islamic Courts: Medicine and Crafts in the Service of Law.* Chicago, IL: University of Chicago Press.

Sherwin, Richard K. (ed.) 2006. *Popular Culture and Law.* Burlington, VT: Ashgate.

Smith, Craig S. 2001. "Torture Hurries New Wave of Executions in China," *New York Times* (September 9): A1, A8.

Souryal, Sam S., and Dennis W. Potts. 1994. "The Penalty of Hand Amputation for Theft in Islamic Justice," *Journal of Criminal Justice* 22 (3) (May–June): 249–265.

Spence, Gerry. 1989. *With Justice for None.* New York: Times Books.

Stone, Julius. 1964. *Legal System and Lawyer's Reasonings.* Stanford, CA: Stanford University Press.

Stracher, Cameron. 1998. *Double Billing: A Young Lawyer's Tale of Greed, Sex, Lies, and the Pursuit of a Swivel Chair.* New York: William Morrow and Company.

Strick, Anne. 1977. *Injustice for All.* New York: Penguin.

Stead, Deborah. 1994. "Crime and Punishment—And Now Trial by Jury," *Business Week* (January 17): 20–22.

Sutton, John R. 2001. *Law/Society: Origins, Interactions, and Change.* Thousand Oaks, CA: Pine Forge Press.

Seattle Times. 2003. "Judge Orders Acid Attacker Be Blinded," (December 13): A8.

Tismaneanu, Vladimir. 1992. *Reinventing Politics: Eastern Europe from Stalin to Havel.* New York: Free Press.

Tomkins, Adam. 2003. *Public Law.* New York: Oxford University Press.

Turk, Austin T. 1978. "Law as a Weapon in Social Conflict." Pp. 213–232 in Charles E. Reasons and Robert M. Rich (eds.), *The Sociology of Law: A Conflict Perspective.* Toronto, Canada: Butterworths.

Vago, Steven. 2004. *Social Change.* 5th ed. Upper Saddle River, NJ: Prentice-Hall.

Varese, Federico. 2001. "Is Sicily the Future of Russia? Private Protection and the Rise of the Russian Mafia," *Archives Europeennes de Sociologie* 42 (1): 186–221.

Viviano, Frank. 1995. "The New Mafia Order: Organized Crime in Russia, Mexico, and Elsewhere," *Mother Jones* 20 (3) (May–June): 44–55.

Wacks, Raymond. 2009. *Understanding Jurisprudence: An Introduction to Legal Theory.* 2nd ed. New York: Oxford University Press.

Wagner, Anne, and Sophie Cacciaguidi-Fahy (eds.). 2008. *Obscurity and Clarity in the Law: Prospects and Challenges.* Burlington, VT: Ashgate.

Walker, Nancy Perry, and Lawrence S. Wrightsman. 1991. *The Child Witness: Legal Issues and Dilemmas.* Newbury Park, CA: Sage Publications.

Wall Street Journal.2007. "Saudi Arabia: Gay Life Thrives Despite Strict Islamic Law," (April 4): B11.

Ward, Lester F. 1906. *Applied Sociology.* Boston, MA: Ginn & Company.

Weber, Max. 1954. *Law in Economy and Society.* Ed. Max Rheinstein and trans. Edward Shils and Max Rheinstein. Cambridge, MA: Harvard University Press. 1968. *Economy and Society.* Trans. Guenther Roth and Claus Wittich. New York: Bedminster Press.

West, Mark D. 2005. *Law in Everyday Japan: Sex, Sumo, Suicide, and Statutes.* Chicago, IL: University of Chicago Press.

Willock, I. D. 1974. "Getting on with Sociologists," *British Journal of Law and Society* 1 (1): 3–12.

Wines, Michael. 2001. "Russian's Latest Dictator Goes by the Name of Law," *New York Times* (January 21): WK3. 2004. "Crime Reports Defy Russian Claims of Greater Calm in Chechnya" *New York Times* (April 13): A2.

Yant, Martin. 1991. *Presumed Guilty: When Innocent People Are Wrongly Convicted.* Buffalo, NY: Prometheus Books.

Zamir, Eyal, and Barak Medina. 2010. *Law, Economics, and Morality.* New York: Oxford University Press.

Zatz, Marjorie S. 1994. *Producing Legality: Law and Socialism in Cuba.* New York: Rutledge.

CHAPTER

2

Theoretical Perspectives

The objective of this chapter is to examine the evolution of legal systems and review some of the principal classical and contemporary theories of law and society. At the outset, it should be recognized that there is no single, widely and commonly accepted, comprehensive theory of law and society (or, as a matter of fact, of anything else in the social sciences). The field is enormously complex and polemical, and individual explanations have thus far failed to capture fully this complexity and diversity. This is, of course, not due to lack of effort. On the contrary, sociological, sociolegal (and other social science) theories of law abound (see, for example, Abadinsky, 2008; Arrigo and Milovanovic, 2010; Banakar, 2003; Banakar and Travers, 2002; Barnett, 2010; Cotterrell, 2006; Henry and Lukas, 2009; Nelken, 2009; Patterson, 2010; Rich, 1978; Ransome, 2010; Rokumoto, 1994; Seron, 2006; Trevino, 2007, 2008). Of the vast amount of law and society literature, this chapter deals briefly with only a few of the important classical and contemporary theories of law and society. This approach serves certain purposes. It provides the reader with some conception of the development and content of these different theories and how they relate to one another. Although the discussion of these theories clearly shows the complex and multifaceted nature of the relationship between law and society, it also serves as a means of differentiating, organizing, and understanding a great mass of material. Thus, although the concern is to suggest the magnitude and diversity of the field, an attempt is also made to lend order to that magnitude and diversity.

A cautionary note is in order with regard to the procedures followed in this chapter for grouping various theories. It will become clear that many theories of law and society tend to overlap. For example, the reader may find that a theory placed under the heading of "The European Pioneers" will contain similar elements to those embodied in "Classical Sociological Theorists." Any such effort at classification of theories should be viewed as essentially a heuristic device to facilitate discussion rather than to reflect the final status of the theories considered.

Just like with general sociological theories (see, for example, Adams and Sydie, 2002; Shoemaker et al., 2004; Turner et al., 2007), there are many ways of (more or less arbitrarily) categorizing the more specific law and society theories. They may be considered from the disciplinary perspectives of jurisprudence, philosophy of law, sociology of law, and anthropology of law. They can also be listed under the headings of sociology of civil law, sociology of criminal law, sociological jurisprudence, and anthropology of law (Pottage and Mundy, 2004; Rich, 1978); grouped by various theoretical trends, such as natural law, historical and analytical jurisprudence, utilitarianism, positivism, and legal realism (Bodenheimer, 1974; Pollack, 1979; Seron, 2006); listed under emerging trends such as global law (Capaldo, 2009; Kirton and Madunic, 2010); or classified under various perspectives such as Marxian, Weberian, and Durkheimian (Trevino, 2007, 2008). Any attempt to categorize theories under particular labels is obviously open to question. The present effort should not be an exception. The categories used are in some ways subjective, because they can be increased or decreased depending on one's objectives. These categorizations simply provide some semblance of order for the principal theoretical approaches to law and society. In the schema employed, the diverse theories are presented in a chronological order, with an emphasis on influential classical and contemporary theories. Finally, due to the tyranny of space, and the already widespread and continuously growing interest in the topic, there are more theorists and theories omitted than included. Those who wish to gain further knowledge about classical or modern theoretical concerns, the suggested further readings section will provide a useful initial point of departure.

EVOLUTION OF LEGAL SYSTEMS

Formal codified law emerges when the social structure of a given society becomes so complex that regulatory mechanisms and methods of dispute settlement can no longer be dependent on informal customs and social, religious, or moral sanctions (see, for example, Zifcak, 2005). Formal and institutionalized regulatory mechanisms come into being when other control devices are no longer effective. Changes in the organization of a society from kinship and tribe to a territorially based political organization inevitably result in changes in the legal system. The basic content of the law and legal system concomitantly will become more complex, specialized, and statutory as the economy grows more complex and diversified, industrialization increases, and social institutions become more stratified and specialized.

Historically, legal development and industrialization, urbanization, and modernization, and lately globalization, are closely intertwined (see, for example, Grossi, 2010). In a small, isolated and homogeneous society with little division of labor and a high degree of solidarity, informal sanctions are sufficient to keep most behavior in line with the norms. An ideal example is the community on Tristan da Cunha, an isolated island in the middle of the South Atlantic Ocean. A few hundred people live there, growing potatoes and catching fish. When social scientists visited the island in the 1930s, they were amazed to see how *law abiding* these people were, even though they had nothing resembling law as we know it. There was no serious crime on the island that anyone could recall, no police, courts, jails, or judges. There was no need for such controls. People in the community relied on informal mechanisms of social control such as shaming and open disapproval, which can be effective and severe in their own way. Such forms of control work in small, homogeneous, face-to-face communities (Friedman, 1998, 2002).

But, in a modern, heterogeneous, and complex society with a high division of labor, formal norms and sanctions are necessary to control behavior so that society can continue to function in an orderly and predictable fashion. The presence of some kind of law and a legal system is essential to the maintenance of social order (see, for example, Kritzer, 2002).

The reciprocal relationships between society and the legal system during their parallel development are perplexing issues that have been conceptualized vaguely in the sociological literature. Jonathan H. Turner points out that

> linkages between law and society are often left implicit; change in the relative importance of these linkages is frequently not discussed; and there is a tendency to place too heavy an emphasis on single variables and thereby ignore the multiplicity of institutional influences on legal development. (1974:3)

Turner (1972:242), whose perspectives are widely recognized in the law and society literature, views legal development as a form of institutional adjustment to the ubiquitous problems of control and coordination facing modernizing society. He reasons that modernization inevitably generates conflict, tension, strains, and disjunctures, which force the development of law in society. It should be noted, however, that although there is some overall pattern of legal development, the specifics vary from society to society as a result of unique conditions, such as geographical location, historical events, conquest, and prevailing political and social forces. As a result, it is impossible to trace legal development from a primitive to a modern profile for one society because changes in geographical boundaries, wars, and other events would obscure unilinear development. For instance, a highly developed system of Roman law was imposed upon primitive legal systems during the expansion of the Roman Empire, "with the result that a developmental jump occurred in these primitive legal systems" (Turner, 1972:242).

Developmental models, although controversial, have been used and are being used in almost every field of social science. Their use is justified by the attempt to make sense of history, which requires an appreciation of directionality, growth, and decay (Nonet and Selznick, 2001:19). The early sociologists all believed in the progressive development of social patterns over long periods of time (Vago, 2004:51–58). Similar beliefs are also present in psychology. Take, for example, the stages of growth to psychological maturity in Freudian theory, or the development of personality in the theories of Piaget (1965). Similarly, in economics, Walt W. Rostow (1961) talks about the stages of economic growth from preconditions for takeoff to the age of high mass consumption. In the same vein, students of modern organization talk rather freely of three stages—prebureaucratic, bureaucratic, and postbureaucratic (Bennis, 1966:3–15). Developmental models can deal with transformations at various levels in society, such as individual, group, community, organization, and social institution, or they may deal with the transformation of entire societies. The underlying theme in developmental models is the identification of forces that, having been set in motion at one stage, produce a characteristic outcome in another stage.

Thus, it is not surprising that Pound (1959:366), among others, finds it "convenient to think of . . . stages of legal development in systems which have come to maturity." The law and society literature suggests that the more complex the society, the more differentiated the legal system (Schwartz and Miller, 1975). Underlying this proposition is the notion that legal development is conditioned by a series of integrative demands stemming from society's economic, political, educational, and religious institutions. Based on the complexity and magnitude of the interplay among these institutions and between these institutions and the law, several types of legal systems may be identified in the course of societal development. There is practically no limit to the variability of legal systems, and many scholars have developed typologies to capture this diversity (Diamond, 1971; Mundy, 2002; Pospisil, 1971:97–126; Pottage and Mundy, 2004; Wormser, 1962). These typologies seldom correspond fully to the real world, but they are essential in an analytical discussion dealing with the types of legal systems. From a developmental perspective, some general types can be isolated, and following Turner's illustrative and timeless and often-cited categories (1972:216–230), the primitive, transitional, and modern legal systems will be examined. Before proceeding, it should be noted that the terms *primitive* and *traditional* law and legal systems are often used interchangeably in the literature (see, for example, Rouland, 1994), and one should fight the temptation to construe the word *primitive* as *politically incorrect* in the present context.

Primitive Legal Systems

Primitive legal systems are typically found in hunting and gathering and simple agrarian societies. The laws are not written or codified; they are permeated by customs, tradition, religious dogmas, and values. Primitive laws often coexist with ancient norms, and are also comparatively undifferentiated. There is, however, some distinction between *substantive* and *procedural* laws. *Substantive* laws consist of rights, duties, and prohibitions concerning what is right, wrong, permissible, and impermissible. *Procedural* laws are rules regarding just how substantive law is to be administered, enforced, changed, and used in the mediation of disputes. Subsequent differentiation of types at later stages of legal evolution can be encompassed under these two general types of law.

The functions of law in primitive societies are essentially the same as those in more advanced societies (Rouland, 1994: 153–299). Laws preserve important cultural elements; they coordinate interaction, settle disputes, check deviance, and regularize exchanges. Laws also legitimize existing inequalities. In addition, "By codifying, preserving, and enforcing certain key kinship rules (usually descent and authority), religious rituals and dogmas, and the chief's right to enact laws, differences in power and privilege are preserved and made to seem appropriate" (Turner, 1972:220).

In primitive societies, there are no well-developed political subsystems, and the polity is composed of kin leaders, councils of elders or chiefs, and various religious leaders. Legislators are political bodies and, as such, do not formally exist in primitive societies. In such societies, judges and political leaders (elders and the like) are one and the same. The emphasis is on court-enacted law (common law) rather than on legislative law enacted by political bodies (statutory law). Although the distinction between the two in primitive societies does not exist (because courts are political and their decisions constitute legislation), chiefs or elders can enact both substantive and procedural laws. Because there are no written laws, the chief legislator can strike, rescind, or change old laws more easily than the modern legislator; and if such action appears reasonable, little resistance is offered. Obviously, getting old laws off the books in modern societies is rarely that easy.

Courts, like the police force, are temporarily assembled and then dispersed as disputes arise and are settled. Although they are provisional, the courts comprise at least two clearly differentiated roles: that of the judges, who hear evidence and make decisions in accordance with laws, and that of litigants, who have to abide by the judges' decision. Occasionally, a third role can be identified in such courts, that of a representative *lawyer* who pleads the case for a litigant. As the legal system develops, these roles become more clearly differentiated. In primitive societies, however, these three procedures are sufficient to maintain a high degree of societal integration and coordination.

Transitional Legal Systems

Transitional legal systems are characteristic of advanced agrarian and early industrial societies where the economic, educational, and political subsystems are increasingly differentiated from kinship relationships. As a result of increases in integrative problems, the legal subsystem becomes more complex and extensive, as evidenced by a clear-cut differentiation in basic legal elements—laws, courts, enforcement agencies, and legislative structures. In the transitional stage, most of the features of the modern legal system are present, but not to the same degree. Law becomes more differentiated from tradition, customs, and religious dogma. There is a distinction between *public* and *private* law. The former is concerned with the structure of government, the duties and powers of officials, and the relationships between the individual and the state, and the latter regulates relations among nonpolitical units. *Criminal* law also becomes distinguishable from *torts*. *Criminal* law denotes wrongs against the state, the community, and the public. Torts are laws pertaining to private wrongs of parties against each other rather than against the state or the public. There is, similarly, a clearer differentiation between procedural and substantive laws, and as the types of laws increase, laws become systems of rules (Friedman, 1975:291–309).

The increased differentiation of laws is reflected in the increased complexity of the courts. Accompanying this differentiation is the emergence of at least five distinct types of statuses: judge, representative or lawyer, litigant, court officials and administrators, and jurors. The roles of judges and lawyers become institutionalized, requiring specialized training. In transitional legal systems, written records of court proceedings become more common, contributing to the emergence of a variety of administrative roles, which, in turn, leads to the initial bureaucratization of the court.

With the development of clearly differentiated, stable, and autonomous courts, legal development accelerates for the following reasons:

> (1) Laws enacted by the growing legislative body of the polity can be applied systematically to specific circumstances by professionals and experts. This means that laws enacted by the centralizing polity have institutional channels of application. (2) Where political legislation of laws is absent, an established court can enact laws by handing down Common-Law precedents. Such common laws tend to fit nicely the structural conditions in a society, since they emerge out of attempts to reconcile actual and concrete conflicts. (Turner, 1972:222)

Initially, courts are localized and characterized by common-law decisions. In time, their conflicting and overlapping rules provide an impetus for the unification of a legal system, eventually leading to a more codified system of laws.

There is also the emergence of explicit, relatively stable, and somewhat autonomous police roles in transitional legal systems. Concomitant with the development of police roles is the emergence of legislative structures. This results in a clear differentiation of legislative statuses from judicial (courts) and enforcement (police) statuses. Legislating new laws or abolishing old ones is no longer a matter of a simple decree. In transitional legal systems, a small cluster of statuses, whether organized in a forum, a senate, or a royal council, can enact laws. Initially, these laws were dominated by political elite and were responsive to its demands. Later on, legislative changes became more comprehensive, involving a group of laws pertaining to general problem areas. With the enactment of more comprehensive statutes and codes, a system of civil law began to emerge to supplement common law. The development of civil codes is stimulated by an established court system and police force, a pool of educated lawyers and judges, a background of common law, and a degree of political and national unity. The functions of law in transitional legal institutions are essentially similar to those in primitive systems, perhaps a bit more complex, but less successful in resolving integrative problems. Structural differentiation becomes more complex. Political development increases, bringing with it inequities in power and wealth. In such situations, civil law tends to legitimize these inequalities.

Modern Legal Systems

In modern legal systems, we find all the structural features of transitional systems present, but in greater and more elaborate arrangements. Turner notes, "Laws in modern legal systems are extensive networks of local and national statutes, private and public codes, crimes and torts, common and civil laws, and procedural and substantive rules" (1972:225). A distinctive feature of modern legal systems is the proliferation of public and procedural laws, referred to as *administrative* law. Another aspect is the increasing proportion of statutory law over common law. Legislation, as a result of political development, becomes a more acceptable method of adjusting law to social conditions. There are also clear hierarchies of laws, ranging from constitutional codes to regional and local codes.

Courts, in modern legal systems, have an important role in mediating and mitigating conflict, disputes, deviance, and other sources of malintegration. The roles of lawyers and judges become highly professionalized, with licensing requirements and formal sanctions. The various administrative statuses—clerks, bailiffs, and public prosecutors—specialize, proliferate, and become heavily bureaucratized. The jurisdictions of courts are specified with clearly delineated appeal procedures. Cases unresolved in lower courts can be argued in higher courts that have the power to reverse lower court decisions (see, for example, Dixon et al., 2007).

In modern legal systems, laws are enforced and court decisions are carried out by clearly differentiated and organized police forces, which are organized at the local, state, and federal levels. Each force possesses its own internal organization, which becomes increasingly bureaucratized at the higher levels. In addition to police forces, regulatory agencies (such as the U.S. Food and Drug Administration, the Federal Trade Commission, or the Federal Aviation Administration) regularly enforce and oversee compliance with laws. Administrative agencies, as will be discussed in Chapters 4 and 5, also make and interpret laws in the context of their own mandates.

Legislative bodies at various levels proliferate. There is a greater emphasis on integrative problems and on enacting comprehensive laws. Accompanying the emergence of a stable legislature, a well-planned and comprehensive law enactment can become an effective mechanism of social change (Zifcak, 2005).

Inherent in modern legal systems is the notion of *modern* law. Marc Galanter (1977) in a classic and influential article, "The Modernization of Law," sets forth a comprehensive conceptualization of contemporary law that remains among the most widely cited even today. His model, not a description, includes 11 salient features that characterize the legal systems of the industrial societies of the last century, and many of them can be found in modern societies as well. He argues that "modern law consists of rules that are uniform and unvarying in their application" (1977:1047). The same rules and regulations are applicable to everyone. Modern law is also *transactional*. Rights and duties stem from *transactions*. They are not *aggregated in unchanging clusters* prescribed to an individual by ascribed status. Galanter insists that modern legal norms are *universalistic*; that is, their application is predictable, uniform, and impersonal. Further, the system, to be uniform and predictable, operates on the basis of written rules and has a regular chain of command. The system is *rational* in the Weberian sense, and "rules are valued for their instrumental utility in producing consciously chosen ends, rather than for their formal qualities" (1977:1048). Such a system is run by full-time professionals whose "qualifications come from mastery of the techniques of the legal system itself, not from possession of special gifts or talents or from eminence in some other area of life" (1977:1048). Professionals run the law; lawyers replace "mere general agents" as the legal system grows more complex. The system is "amenable." It can be changed and it does not have "sacred fixity." Says Galanter, "Legislation replaces the slow reworking of customary law" (1977:1048). It is also "political"—that is, tied to the state, which has a monopoly on law. Finally, legislative, judicial, and executive functions are "separate and distinct" in modern law.

Thus far, we have identified some of the preconditions necessary for the development of modern legal systems. Let us now consider some of the theories accounting for those developments.

THEORIES OF LAW AND SOCIETY

The preceding section dealt with some general types of legal systems as they correspond to various stages of modernization and social development. The present section addresses two questions emerging from the previous discussion: Why did changes in the legal system take place? And what factors contributed to legal development from a historical perspective? In attempting to answer these questions, we can distinguish two general issues. The first is the issue of legal development in any society. The second concerns forces that produce or prevent change in the legal system.

Theorists of law and society have long been preoccupied with efforts to describe the broad historical course of legal development and to analyze the factors that influence legal systems. The literature is extensive, going back several centuries. The investigation of legal development has traditionally been the concern of scholars in a variety of fields. In view of the limits set for this study, no attempt is made here to provide a comprehensive and systematic review of principal theories and schools. Certain prominent theorists will, however, be considered.

Among the theorists to be presented, there is more or less general agreement that societal and legal complexities are interrelated. Beyond that, there is little consensus. The particular theorists differ as to detail and interpretation of the general relationship between legal change and social change. It is hoped that the following sample of theorists from various disciplines, historical periods, and countries will provide a better understanding of the diverse issues involved in the investigation of the multifaceted relations between law and other major institutions of society.

The European Pioneers

For centuries, in Europe, law has been considered as an absolute and autonomous entity, unrelated to the structure and function of the society in which it existed (see, for example, Feinberg and Coleman, 2008). The idea of natural law constitutes the basis for this exposition of law (see, for example, Donnelly, 2007; George, 2003). The origins of natural law can be traced back to ancient Greece. Aristotle maintains that natural law has a universal validity and is based on reason that is free from all passion (see, for example, Brooks and Murphy, 2003; Daston and Stolleis, 2010). St. Thomas Aquinas argues that natural law is part of human nature, and through natural law, human beings participate as rational beings in the eternal laws of God.

The idea of natural law is based on the assumption that the nature of human beings can be known through reason, and that this knowledge can provide the basis for the social and legal ordering of human existence (see, for example, Belliotti, 1992:17–44). Natural law is considered superior to enacted law. It is "the chief tenet of natural law that arbitrary will is not legally final" (Selznick, 1961:100). An appeal to higher principles of justice is always permissible from the decrees of a lawmaker. When enacted law does not coincide with the principles of natural law, it is considered unjust. For example, pro-life proponents argue that laws providing for abortion on demand are contrary to the tenets of natural law.

Under the influence of natural law, many European scholars believed that law in any given society was a reflection of a universally valid set of legal principles based on the idea that through reason, the nature of man can be ascertained (see, for example, Daston and Stolleis, 2010). This knowledge could then become the basis for the social and legal order of human existence. From the middle of the nineteenth century, however, the idea of natural law was largely displaced by historical and evolutionary interpretations of law and by legal positivism, which considered the legal and the moral to constitute two quite separate realms. These two views of the law sought to explain the law causally in terms of ethnological factors, or by reference to certain evolutionary forces that pushed the law forward along a predetermined path. Many theorists sought to discourage philosophical speculation about the nature and purposes of law and concentrated on the development and analysis of positive law laid down and enforced by the state. The most notable among these scholars include Baron de Montesquieu in France, Herbert Spencer, and Sir Henry Sumner Maine in England. I shall now consider their theories in some detail.

Baron de Montesquieu (1689–1755) Charles-Louis de Secondat, Baron de Montesquieu was born near Bordeaux, France, to a wealthy family. He inherited a seat in the parliament of Bordeaux and was active in politics most of his life. Well educated by his family, he was a most influential writer against the absolutism of the French monarchy (see, for example, Carrithers, 2010).

Montesquieu challenges the underlying assumptions of natural law by presenting a radically different conceptualization of law and society. He considers law integral to a particular people's culture. The central thesis of his *Spirit of Laws* (1886) is that laws are the result of a number of factors in society, such as customs, physical environment, and antecedents, and that laws can be understood only in the context of particular societies. He further posits that laws are relative and that there are no *good* or *bad* laws in the abstract. This proposition ran contrary to the opinions of the day. Each law, Montesquieu maintains, must be considered in relation to its background, its antecedents, and its surroundings. If a law fits well into this framework, it is a good law; if it does not, it is bad.

But Montesquieu's fame rests above all on his political theory of the separation of powers. According to this theory, a constitution is composed of three different types of legal powers—legislative, executive, and judicial—each vested in a different body or person. The role of the legislature is to enact new laws; of the executive, to enforce and administer the laws as well as to determine policy within the framework of those laws; and of the judiciary, simply to interpret the laws established by the legislative power. This neat classification had considerable influence on the form of constitution subsequently adopted by the newly created United States of America after the Declaration of Independence (Bodenheimer, 1974:49) and would greatly affect constitutional thinkers in other countries as well throughout the late eighteenth and nineteenth centuries.

Leopold Pospisil (1971:138), in his analysis of Montesquieu's contributions, aptly remarks, "With his ideas of the relativity of law in space as well as in time, and with his emphasis on specificity and empiricism, he can be regarded as the founder of the modern sociology of law in general and of the field of legal dynamics in particular."

Herbert Spencer (1820–1903)   This British philosopher and sociologist was a major figure in the intellectual life of the Victorian era. He was born in Derby, England, and was a product of an undisciplined and largely informal education, strongly influenced by his family's antiestablishment and anticlerical views, which are reflected in his writings.

Contrary to the doctrines of natural law, in nineteenth-century England, Herbert Spencer provides the philosophical underpinnings for the theory of unregulated competition in the economic sphere. Strongly influenced by Charles Darwin, Spencer draws a picture of the evolution of civilization and law in which natural selection and the survival of the fittest are the primary determining factors. Evolution for Spencer consists of growing differentiation, individuation, and increasing division of labor. Civilization is the progress of social life from primitive homogeneity to ultimate heterogeneity. He identifies two main stages in the development of civilizations: a primitive or military form of society, with war, compulsion, and status as regulatory mechanisms, and a higher or industrial form of society, with peace, freedom, and a contract as the controlling devices.

Spencer is convinced that in the second stage, human progress will be marked by a continual increase in individual liberty and a corresponding decrease in governmental activities. Government, he believes, would gradually confine its field of action to the enforcement of contracts and the protection of personal safety. He strongly opposes public education, public hospitals, public communications, and any governmental programs designed to alleviate the plight of the economically weaker groups in society. He was convinced that social legislation of this type is an unwarranted interference with the laws of natural selection (Spencer, 1899).

Spencer's ideas on law influenced a number of early sociologists in the United States (McCann, 2004). For example, William Graham Sumner advocates a position essentially similar to that of Spencer. He, too, sees the function of the state limited to that of an overseer who guards the safety of private property and sees to it that the peace is not breached. He favors a regime of contract in which social relations are regulated primarily by mutual agreements, not by government-imposed legal norms. He argues that society does not need any supervision. Maximum freedom of individual action should be promoted by law. He considers attempts to achieve a greater social and economic equality among men ill-advised and unnatural.

> Let it be understood that we cannot go outside of this alternative: liberty, inequality, survival of the fittest; not liberty, equality, survival of the unfittest. The former carries society forward and favors all its best members; the latter carries society downward and favors all its worst members. (Sumner, 1940:25)

To a great extent, the *laissez-faire* doctrines of courts and legislatures in the United States, perhaps consciously or unconsciously, reflected the economic and social philosophy of Spencer and Sumner. Up until fairly recently, for example, legislative policies designed to equalize the bargaining power of management and labor, to protect the health and subsistence of marginal groups, or to interfere with that freedom of contract that was considered the true birthmark of an advancing civilization did not appear to be widespread. In part, these are still discernible in the current conservative attitudes that place the rights of wealthier groups above those of the disfavored members of society.

Sir Henry Sumner Maine (1822–1888)   The founder and principal proponent of the English historical school of law, Maine was born in Scotland and died in Cannes, France. He was educated at Cambridge, and after various teaching positions in England and administrative appointments in India, he returned to Cambridge where he was elected master of Trinity Hall and ended his career as professor of international law. He was among the first theorists to argue that law and legal institutions must be studied historically if they are to be understood.

Maine contends that the legal history of people shows patterns of evolution, which recur in different societies and in similar historical circumstances. He argues that there do not exist infinite possibilities for building and managing human societies; certain political, social, and legal forms reappear in seemingly different garb, and if they reappear, they manifest themselves in certain typical ways. For example, Roman feudalism produced legal rules and legal institutions strikingly similar to English feudalism, although differences can also be demonstrated.

One of Maine's general laws of legal evolution is set forth in his classical treatise, *Ancient Law*:

> The movement of the progressive societies has been uniform in one respect. Through all its course it has been distinguished by the gradual dissolution of

family dependency and the growth of individual obligation in its place. The Individual is steadily substituted for the Family, as the unit of which civil laws take account. The advance has been accomplished at varying rates of celerity, and there are societies not absolutely stationary in which the collapse of the ancient organization can only be perceived by careful study of the phenomena they present. But, whatever its pace, the change has not been subject to reaction or recoil, and apparent retardations will be found to have been occasioned through the absorption of archaic ideas and customs from some entirely foreign source. Nor is it difficult to see what is the tie between man and man which replaces by degrees those forms of reciprocity in rights and duties which have their origin in the Family. It is Contract. Starting, as from one terminus of history, from a condition of society in which all the relations of Persons are summed up in the relations of Family, we seem to have steadily moved towards a phase of social order in which all these relations arise from the free agreement of Individuals. (1861:170)

Thus, Maine arrives at his often-quoted dictum that "the movement of the progressive societies has hitherto been a movement from Status to Contract" (1861:170). Status is a fixed condition in which an individual is without will and without opportunity. Ascribed status prevails, and legal relations depend on birth or caste. It is indicative of a social order in which the group, not the individual, is the primary unit of social life. Every individual is enmeshed in a network of family and group ties. With the progress of civilization, this condition gradually gives way to a social system based on contract. Maine argues that a progressive civilization is manifested by the emergence of the independent, free, and self-determining individual, based on achieved status, as the primary unit of social life. He suggests that the emphasis on individual achievement and voluntary contractual relations set the conditions for a more mature legal system that uses legislation to bring society and law into harmony. In essence, his argument is that, in modern societies, legal relations are not conditioned by one's birth but depend on voluntary agreements.

Classical Sociological Theorists

Early sociologists have recognized the essential interrelation between legal institutions and the social order. In this section, the influential theoretical explanations of law and society of Karl Marx, Max Weber, and Émile Durkheim are explored.

Karl Marx (1818–1883) Karl Heinrich Marx was born into a comfortable middle-class family in Trier, Germany. He studied law and literature at the universities of Bonn and Berlin before moving to Paris and subsequently to England where he did most of his writing, much of it in collaboration with his financial mentor, Friedrich Engels. He died on March 14, 1883, in London.

Of all the social theorists, few are as important, brilliant, or original as Karl Marx. Part philosopher, part economist, part sociologist, and part historian, Marx combines political partisanship with deep scholarship. Marx, and the subsequent ideology of Marxism, may have caused more social change than any other force in the modern world, in both developed and developing societies (Barber, 1971:260; see also King and Szelényi, 2004).

base= superstructure

Marx postulates that every society, whatever its stage of historical development, rests on an economic foundation. He calls this "mode of production" of commodities, which has two elements. The first is the physical or technological arrangement of economic activity. The second is "the social relations of production," or the indispensable human attachments that people must form with one another when engaged in economic activity. In his words:

> The sum total of these relations of production constitutes the economic structure of society—the real foundation, on which rise legal and political superstructures and to which correspond definite forms of social consciousness. (Marx, 1959:43)

For Marx, the determinant variable is the mode of production. Changes in this produce changes in the way in which groups are attached to production technology. This economic determinism is reflected in Marx's theory of law.

Marx's theory of law, which has greatly influenced social and jurisprudential thinking throughout the world, may be summarized in three principal assumptions: (1) Law is a product of evolving economic forces; (2) law is a tool used by a ruling class to maintain its power over the lower classes; and (3) in the communist society of the future, law as an instrument of social control will "wither away" and finally disappear.

The idea that law is a reflection of economic conditions is integral to the doctrine of *dialectical materialism.* According to this doctrine, the political, social, religious, and cultural order of any given epoch is determined by the existing system of production and forms a "superstructure" on top of this economic basis. Law, for Marx, is part of this superstructure whose forms, content, and conceptual apparatus constitute responses to economic developments. This view maintains that law is nothing more than a function of the economy but without any independent existence (see, for example, Easton, 2009).

In societies with pronounced class distinctions, the means of production are owned and controlled by the ruling class. Marx's theory of law characterizes law as a form of class rule and dominance (Collins, 1996). While addressing the bourgeoisie of his day in his *Communist Manifesto*, Marx (1955:47) writes, "Your jurisprudence is but the will of your class made into a law for all, a will whose essential character and direction are determined by the economic conditions of existence of your class." Marx further argues that law, as a form of class rule, is sanctioned by public authority, which has the power of enforcement through the use of armed bodies.

Finally, Marx suggests that after the revolution, when class conflict is resolved and the institution of private property is replaced by a communist regime, law and the state, hitherto the main engines of despotism and oppression, will "wither away." There will be no need for coercion, because everyone's needs will be fulfilled and universal harmony will prevail. According to this view, there will be no need for law in the future—a future that will be the final stage of humanity's evolution because stateless and lawless communism shall exist forever.

Max Weber (1864–1920)   Max Weber holds a central position among the law and society theorists. He was born near Erfurt in Central Germany into a middle-class professional family and studied at Heidelberg and Berlin, earned a Ph.D., and became a

F + R = D
(fact) (rule) (decision)

professor of economics. He traveled to the United States, and among other cities, visited St. Louis during the 1904 World's Fair. After his return to Germany, he devoted his life to writing and teaching. Max Weber played a crucial role in the development of sociology. His significance is not merely historical; he remains an ever-present force in contemporary sociology. Today, he occupies a central position among law and society theorists and remains among the most influential social thinkers of our time (see, for example, Camic et al., 2005; Chalcraft et al., 2010; Lassman, 2006; Ringer, 2004).

Weber's typology of legal systems is based on two fundamental distinctions (1954:63). First, legal procedures are rational or irrational. *Rational* procedures involve the use of logic and scientific methods to attain specific objectives (see also Berg and Meadwell, 2004). *Irrational* procedures rely on ethical or mystical considerations, such as magic or faith in the supernatural. Second, legal procedures can proceed, rationally or irrationally, with respect to formal or substantive law. *Formal* law refers to making decisions on the basis of established rules, regardless of the notion of fairness. *Substantive* law takes the circumstances of individual cases into consideration along with the prevailing notion of justice. These two distinctions create four ideal types, which are seldom, if ever, attained in their pure form in specific societies.

SI **1.** *Substantive irrationality.* This exists when a case is decided on some unique religious, ethical, emotional, or political basis instead of by general rules. An example of this would be when a religious judge makes a decision without any recourse to explicit rules or legal principles. (unpredictable)

FI **2.** *Formal irrationality.* This involves rules based on supernatural forces. It is irrational because no one tries to understand or clarify why it works and formal because strict adherence is required to the procedures. The Ten Commandments, for example, were enacted in a formally irrational way: Moses, claiming direct revelation, presented the tablets and announced, "This is the Law." Other examples include the use of ordeals and oaths. (unpredictable)

SR **3.** *Substantive rationality.* This is based on the application of rules from nonlegal sources such as religion, ideology, and science. It is rational because rules are derived from specific and accepted sources and substantive because there is a concern for justness of outcomes in individual cases. The efforts of Ayatollah Khomeini in Iran to make decisions on the basis of the Koran would be an example of substantive rationality. (predictable)

FR **4.** *Formal rationality.* This involves the use of consistent, logical rules independent of moral, religious, or other normative criteria that are applied equally to all cases. An example of this is modern American or Western law. (predictable)

While referring to both formal and substantive rationality, Weber identifies three types of administration of justice: (1)*Kahdi* justice, (2) empirical justice, and (3) rational justice. *Kahdi* justice is dispensed by the judge of the Islamic *Shari'a* Court. (See Chapter 1 for a detailed discussion of Islamic law; also see Huff and Schlucter, 1999.) It is based on religious precepts and is so lacking in procedural rules as to seem almost completely arbitrary. The *Koran* contains the revealed word of God, and this bible forms the heart of the Islamic legal system in such countries as Iran and Pakistan. Empirical justice, the deciding of cases by referring to analogies and by relying on and interpreting precedents, is

external →

internal →

external →

internal →

more rational than *Kahdi* justice, but notably short of complete rationality. Weber argues that modern law is rational, whereas traditional and primitive laws were irrational or, at least, less rational. Rational justice is based on bureaucratic principles. The rational legal system is basically universalistic; the irrational system is particularistic. The rational legal system looks toward contract, not toward status (Parsons, 1964:339). Rationality can be further based on adherence to "eternal characteristics" (observable concrete features) of the facts of the case. However, Weber perceives that Western law, with its specialized professional roles of judges and lawyers, is unique in that it is also reliant on the "logical analysis of meaning" of abstract legal concepts and rules.

Modern society differs from its past in many ways, which Max Weber sums up in a single concept: the *rational*. Modern society is in pursuit of the rational. Weber contends that the modern law of the West has become increasingly institutionalized through the bureaucratization of the state. He points out that the acceptance of the law as a rational science is based on certain fundamental and semilogical postulates, such as that the law is a "gapless" system of legal principles and that every concrete judicial decision involves the application of an abstract legal proposition to a concrete situation. There is little doubt that Weber captures, in his idea of rationality, a crucial feature of modern legal systems. It is rather ironic that soon after Max Weber's death in 1920, rational law in Germany was in part replaced by a faith in the intuition of a charismatic leader—Adolph Hitler.

Émile Durkheim (1858–1917)   Émile Durkheim was born in Epinal, France, and following several generations of rabbis, he was destined for the rabbinate. Part of his early education was spent in a rabbinical school. But soon after his arrival in Paris, he broke with Judaism. He attended the prestigious *École Normale Supérieure*, and taught at the Faculty of Letters at Bordeaux and was subsequently appointed professor and chair of sociology and education at the Sorbonne. He was the founder of L'*Année sociologique,* the first social science journal in France, and the author of several very important treaties in sociology (see, for example, Cotterrell, 2010; Schmaus, 2004).

Émile Durkheim outlines his thesis on law in society in his influential work, *The Division of Labor in Society* (1964). While tracing the development of social order through social and economic institutions, Durkheim sets forth a theory of legal development by elucidating the idea that law is a measure of the type of solidarity in a society. Durkheim maintains that there are two types of solidarity: mechanical and organic. *Mechanical* solidarity prevails in relatively simple and homogeneous societies where unity is ensured by close interpersonal ties and similarity of habits, ideas, and attitudes. *Organic* solidarity is characteristic of modern societies that are heterogeneous and differentiated by a complex division of labor. The grounds for solidarity are the interdependence of widely different persons and groups performing a variety of functions.

Corresponding to these two forms of solidarity are two types of law: repressive and restitutive. Mechanical solidarity is associated with repressive and penal law. In a homogeneous, undifferentiated society, a criminal act offends the collective conscience, and punishment is meant to protect and preserve social solidarity. Punishment is a mechanical reaction. The wrongdoer is punished as an example to the community that deviance will not be tolerated. There is no concern with the rehabilitation of the offender.

[margin annotations: "restorative → non-suffer → organic solidarity"; "mechanical solidarity"; "make people suffer →"; "criminal law → mechanical solidarity"]

In contemporary heterogeneous societies, repressive law tends to give way to restitutive law with an emphasis on compensation (see, for example, Strickland, 2004). Punishment deals with restitution and reparations for harm done to the victim—which basically provides the philosophical underpinning of the contemporary restorative justice approach in criminal justice (Alexander, 2006; Eriksson, 2009; Hayden and Gough, 2010; Ptacek, 2009; Zernova, 2008). Crimes are considered acts that offend others and not the collective conscience of the community. Punishment is evaluated in terms of what is beneficial for the offender and is used for rehabilitation.

Stated concisely, Durkheim's position is that penal law reflects mechanical solidarity. Modern society is bound together by organic solidarity—interdependence and division of labor flowing out of voluntary acts. Society is complex; its parts are highly specialized. Through contracts, which are the main concern of modern law, people arrange their innumerable, complex relationships. Contracts and contract laws are central to modern society and influence the course of societal development through the regulation of relationships.

Although Durkheim's concern is not with the elaboration of a general framework or methodology for the sociological analysis of law, his interest in law "resulted in the school that formed around him developing a considerable interest in the study of law as a social process" (Hunt, 1978:65). His ideas on law also provided an important background to subsequent discussions concerning the nature of primitive law and the nature of crime. Although it may be questionable that "he made a serious contribution to the development of systematic legal sociology" (Gurvitch, 1942:106), he certainly made an important contribution to our understanding of the relationship between law and social solidarity and legal evolution (McIntyre, 1994:77–78).

Sociolegal Theorists

The theorists considered in this section argue that law cannot be understood without regard for the realities of social life. Since the beginning of the twentieth century, scholars of jurisprudence and of related disciplines on both sides of the Atlantic have reflected the influence of the social sciences in their analyses of legal development. The more prominent ones who are included in our synoptic analysis are Albert Venn Dicey, Justice Oliver Wendell Holmes, Jr., and Edward Adamson Hoebel.

Albert Venn Dicey (1835–1922)   Dicey, an English legal scholar, was born in Lutterworth, Northhamptonshire. For several generations, his family owned and edited a newspaper, and over time, they became prosperous. Dicey was educated at Oxford, assisted in the founding of law schools in Manchester where he was elected the prestigious Vinerian Chair, then he accepted a professorship and returned to Oxford where he would spend the rest of his life (see, for example, Collins, 2000).

He offers what has become a classic theory on the influence of public opinion on social change in his lectures given at Harvard Law School in 1898. He traces the growth of statutory lawmaking and the legal system in the context of the increasing articulateness and power of public opinion. He notes that the process begins with a new idea that "presents itself to some one man of originality or genius." He has in mind such individuals as Adam Smith and Charles Darwin. Next, the idea is adopted by supporters who "preach" it to others. As time passes, "the preachers of truth make an impression, either directly upon the general public or upon some person of eminence, say a leading states-man, who stands in a position to impress ordinary people and thus to win the support of the nation" (Dicey, 1905:23). As Dicey points out, however, something must happen so that people will listen to a truly new idea and change their values. He talks of "accidental conditions" that enable popular leaders to seize the opportunity. As an example he gives the Irish famine, which enabled Cobden and Bright to gain acceptance of Adam Smith's doctrine of free trade.

Public opinion for Dicey is "the majority of those citizens who have at a given mo-ment taken an effective part in public life" (1905:10). Dicey talks of the "gradual, or slow, and continuous" (1905:27) developments of tides of public opinion in England. Gener-ally, he maintains, there are few abrupt changes. Ideally, legislators should reflect and act upon public opinion, but judges (even more than legislators) lag behind public opinion. Dicey concedes that although judges are "guided to a considerable extent by the domi-nant current of public opinion" (1905:363), "they are also guided by professional opin-ions and ways of thinking which are, to a certain extent, independent of and possibly opposed to the general tone of public opinion" (1905:364). He then concludes, "they are men advanced in life. They are for the most part persons of a conservative disposition" (1905:364).

Dicey is also known for his famous doctrine of "the rule of law." The doctrine has three aspects: First, no one is punishable except for a distinct breach of law, and there-fore, the rule of law is not consistent with arbitrary or even wide discretionary authority on the part of the government. Second, the rule of law means total subjection of all classes to the law of the land, as administered by the law courts. Third, individual rights derive from court precedents rather than from constitutional codes.

From a sociological perspective, Dicey's most crucial contribution to law and soci-ety is the recognition of the importance of public opinion in legal development. As Lord Tangley (1965:48) observes, "We are indebted to Professor Dicey for many things—he es-tablished for all time the relationship between public opinion and law reform and traced its course through the nineteenth century."

Oliver Wendell Holmes, Jr. (1841–1935)   Holmes was born in Boston, Massachusetts, and was named after his famous father, the writer and physician. After his service in the American Civil War, he entered Harvard Law School and subsequently became a profes-sor there. He was appointed to the U.S. Supreme Court in 1902 where he remained for three decades.

The distinguished American judge and legal philosopher Oliver Wendell Holmes, Jr., is considered one of the founders of the "legal realism" school (Novick, 1989; White, 2006). This school is based on the conception of the judicial process whereby judges are responsible for formulating law, rather than merely finding it in law books. The judge al-ways has to exercise choice when making a decision. He decides which principle will pre-vail and which party will win. According to the legal realists' position, judges make decisions on the basis of their conceptions of justness before resorting to formal legal precedents. Such precedents can be found or developed to support almost any outcome. The real decisions are based on the judge's notion of justness, conditioned, in part, by values, personal background, predilections, and so forth. They are then rationalized in the written opinion (Holmes, 2004).

Holmes stresses the limits that are set to the use of deductive logic in the solution of legal problems. He postulates that the life of law has been experience and not logic and maintains that only a judge or a lawyer who is acquainted with the historical, social, and economic aspects of the law will be in a position to fulfill his or her functions properly.

Holmes assigns a large role to historical and social forces in the life of law, while de-emphasizing the ethical and ideal elements. He considers law largely as a body of edicts representing the will of dominant interests in society, backed by force. Although he admits that moral principles are influential in the initial formulation of the rules of law, he is inclined to identify morality with the taste and value preferences of shifting power groups in society. Schwartz notes, "Holmes was part of the generation that had sat at the feet of Darwin and Spencer and he could never shed his Darwinist outlook" (1974:151). Holmes's basic philosophy is that life is essentially a Darwinian struggle for existence and that the goal of social effort was to "build a race" rather than to strive for the attainment of humanitarian ethical objectives.

In his often-quoted essay "The Path of the Law," Holmes (1897:458) outlines some of his basic propositions and states that "a legal duty so called is nothing but a prediction that if a man does or omits certain things he will be made to suffer in this or that way by judgment of a court." A pragmatic approach to law, he declares, must view the law from the point of view of the "bad man." Such a person does not care about the general moral pronouncements and abstract legal doctrines. What is important is simply what the courts are in fact likely to do.

He argues that any sense of absolute certainty about the law was bound to be illusory.

> Behind the logical forms lies a judgment as to the relative worth and importance of competing legislative grounds, often an inarticulate and unconscious judgment, it is true, and yet the very root and nerve of the whole proceeding. You can give any conclusion a logical form. (Holmes, 1897:465–466)

Lawyers and judges should be aware of this and should "consider the ends which the several rules seek to accomplish, the reasons why those ends are desired, what is given up to gain them, and whether they are worth the price" (Holmes, 1897:476).

Edward Adamson Hoebel (1906–1993) Edward Adamson Hoebel was born in Madison, Wisconsin. He received his A.B. from the University of Wisconsin, M.A. from New York University, and a Ph.D. in anthropology from Columbia University. He was president of the American Ethnological Society and the American Anthropological Association and was Regents' Professor of Anthropology at University of Minnesota for 18 years until his retirement in 1972.

A leading and highly respected and influential American scholar in the field of anthropology of law, Hoebel was much influenced by Karl N. Llewellyn, a brilliant lawyer with social-science skills and interests. The two men collaborated on an analysis of the "law ways" in traditional Cheyenne society. The emphasis on the "law-jobs" having both a "pure survival" or "bare bones" aspect for the society and a "questing" or "betterment" value (Llewellyn and Hoebel, 1941: Ch. 3) contributed significantly to the development of a modern functional approach to the legal system. I shall return to this point in the discussion on the functionalist approach later in this chapter.

Hoebel's (1954:288–333) views on the development of legal systems are presented in the concluding chapter, entitled "The Trend of the Law," in his book *The Law of Primitive Man.* Hoebel (1954:288) notes that "there has been no straight line of development in the growth of law." His description of trends in legal development is based on the assumption that cultures of contemporary primitive societies exhibit characteristics that are similar "to those that presumably prevailed in the early cultures of the infancy of mankind" (1954:290). He considers law and the legal system as a property of a specific community or subgroup of a society, and states, "Without the sense of community there can be no law. Without law there cannot be for long a community" (1954:332). Consequently, law exists to some extent even in the simplest societies.

Hoebel begins his description of the trend of law with a discussion of the "lower primitive societies"—the hunters and gatherers, such as the Shoshone Indians and the Andaman Islanders. Almost all relations in such a society are face-to-face and intimate. The demands imposed by culture are relatively few. Ridicule is a potent mechanism of social control. Taboo and the fear of supernatural sanctions control a large area of behavior. Special interests are few, for there is little accumulated wealth. Conflict arises mostly in interpersonal relations. Repetitive abuse of the customs and codes of social relations constitutes a crime, and the offender may be beaten or even killed by the members of the community. Hoebel writes, "Here we have law in the full connotation of the word—the application, in threat or in fact, of physical coercion by a party having the socially recognized privilege-right of so acting. First the threat—and then, if need be, the act" (1954:300).

Among the more organized hunters, the pastoralists, and the rooter-gardening peoples, such as the Cheyenne, Comanche, Kiowa, and Indians of the northwest coast of North America, the size of the group and the increased complexity of the culture make possible a greater divergence of interests among the members of society. Conflicts of interest grow, and the need arises for legal mechanisms for settlement and control of the internal clash of interests. Private law emerges and spreads, although much of the internal social control problems are handled on other than a legal basis.

In the tribes, a more formalized chieftainship develops, with a tendency toward hereditary succession (Hoebel, 1954:309–310). Although homicide and adultery still represent major difficulties, the development of criminal law remains weak.

"The real elaboration of law begins with the expansion of the gardening-based tribes," such as the Samoans and the Ashanti (Hoebel, 1954:316). The gardening activity provides an economic foundation for the support of larger populations that can no longer maintain face-to-face relationships. With the formation of more communities, "The pressures to maintain peaceful equilibrium between the numerous closely interacting communities become intensified. The further growth of law and a more effective law is demanded" (1954:316). The attempt to establish the interest of the society as superior to the interests of kinship groups is the prime mover of law in this type of society. Allocation of rights, duties, privileges, powers, and immunities with regard to land becomes important, and "the law of things begins to rival the law of persons" (1954:316). "Clear-cut crimes" (1954:319) are established in the legal systems of these societies, and action for damages becomes even more frequent than on the preceding level.

For Hoebel, the "trend of law" is one of increasing growth and complexity in which the tendency is to shift the privilege right of prosecution and imposition of legal sanctions from the individual and the kinship group to clearly defined public officials representing the society as such. Hoebel notes, "Damages have generally replaced death as penalties in civil suits" (1954:329). Hoebel maintains that this is how law developed in human societies through the ages, but the laws of particular societies have not followed a single line of development through fixed, predetermined, and universal stages. The development of legal systems in particular societies is characterized by a trend that only in general exhibits the features described here.

Contemporary Law and Society Theorists

A brief explanation is necessary for the inclusion of the particular contemporary theorists. Comprehensive macrolevel theoretical works on law and society are few. My intention in this section is to describe influential (and possibly controversial) theoretical developments that have taken place since the 1970s. The rationale for this preference is to illustrate some of the relatively recent advances in sociolegal theorizing on law and society. There are, of course, a number of other theorists (who will be alluded to in specific contexts) who could have been discussed. They are Raymond A. Belliotti (1992), *Justifying Law*; Calvi and Coleman (2008), *American Law and Legal Systems*; William Chambliss and Robert Seidman (1982), *Law, Order, and Power*; William M. Evan (1990), *Social Structure and Law: Theoretical and Empirical Perspectives*; Hyman Gross (1979), *A Theory of Criminal Justice*; Alan Hunt (1993), *Explorations in Law and Society: Toward a Constitutive Theory of Law*; Philippe Nonet and Philip Selznick (2001), *Law and Society in Transition: Toward Responsive Law*; Harold E. Pepinsky (1976), *Crime and Conflict: A Study of Law and Society*; Charles E. Reasons (1974), *The Criminologist: Crime and the Criminal*; and Charles Sampford (1989), *The Disorder of Law: A Critique of Legal Theory*. As illustrations of contemporary theorists, these and similar works tend to be limited in scope. By contrast, the ones chosen for examination attempt to account for law and society in their treatises from different but, at the same time, complementary perspectives. Their alternative viewpoints are also broad enough to include both the older theoretical perspectives and the more contemporary, specialized advancements.

Donald Black   Black received his doctorate in sociology in 1968 at the University of Michigan. He held dual appointments in the Department of Sociology and the Law School at Yale and Harvard universities. He joined University of Virginia in 1985 where he is presently university professor of social sciences.

In three influential volumes, *The Behavior of Law*; *Sociological Justice;* and *The Social Structure of Right and Wrong*, Donald Black (1976, 1989, 1998) sets forth a theory of law that he contends explains variations in law from a cross-national perspective, as well as among individuals within societies. As noted in Chapter 1, he considers law as governmental social control, which makes use of legislation, litigation, and adjudication. He distinguishes between behavior that is controlled by these means and behavior that is subject to other forms of social control, such as etiquette, custom, and bureaucracy.

Black contends that law is a quantitative variable that can be measured by the frequency by which, in a given social setting, statutes are enacted, regulations are issued, complaints are made, offenses are prosecuted, damages are awarded, and punishment is meted out. Consequently, the quantity of law varies from society to society and from one historical period to another in a given society. Different organizations in a society may have more or less law both for themselves and in regard to other groups and organizations.

The direction of law (that is, the differential frequency and success of its application by persons in different social settings) also varies. So is the style of law that, as I mentioned earlier, may be accusatory (with penal or compensatory consequences) or remedial (with therapeutic or conciliatory consequences).

Next, Black develops a number of propositions that explain the quantity, direction, and style of law in regard to five measurable variables of social life: stratification, morphology, culture, organization, and social control. *Stratification* (inequality of wealth) can be measured in such ways as differences in wealth and rates of social mobility. *Morphology* refers to those aspects of social life that can be measured by social differentiation or the degree of interdependence (for example, the extent of division of labor). *Culture* can be measured by the volume, complexity, and diversity of ideas, and by the degree of conformity to the mainstream of culture. *Organization* can be measured by the degree to which the administration of collective action in political and economic spheres is centralized. Finally, the amount of nonlegal *social control* to which people are subjected is a measure of their respectability, and differences between people indicate normative distance from each other.

On the basis of sociological, historical, and ethnographic data, Black arrives at a number of conclusions. He points out that the quantity of law varies directly with stratification rank, integration, culture, organization, and respectability, and inversely with other forms of social control. Thus, stratified societies have more law than simple ones, wealthy people have more law among themselves than poor people, and the amount of law increases with the growth of governmental centralization.

The relationships between the quantity of law and the variables of differentiation, relational distance, and cultural distance are curvilinear. Law is minimal at either extreme of these variables and accumulates in their middle ranges. For example, law relating to contractual economic transaction is limited in simple societies where everyone engages in the same productive activity, and in the business world where manufacturers operate in a symbiotic exchange network.

The style of law varies with its direction: In relation to stratification, law has a penal style in its downward direction, a compensatory or a therapeutic style in its upward direction, and a conciliatory style among people of equal rank. In regard to morphology, law tends to be accusatory among strangers and therapeutic or conciliatory among intimates. Less organized people are more vulnerable to penal law, and more organized people can count on compensatory law.

These patterns of stylistic variation explain, for example, why an offense is more likely to be punished if the rank of the victim is higher than that of the offender, but is more likely to be dealt with by compensation if their ranks are reversed, why accusatory law replaces remedial law in societies undergoing modernization, why members of subcultures are more vulnerable to law enforcement than conventional citizens, and why organizations usually escape punishment for illegal practices against individuals.

Over the years, Black's theory of law has generated considerable critical debate and analysis (see, for example, Wong, 1998). It has been referred to as a "crashing classic" (Nader, cited by Gottfredson and Hindelang, 1979:3) and as "the most important contribution ever made to the sociology of law. It is that and more" (Sherman, 1978:11). It should be noted, however, that Black's thesis has been subjected only to limited empirical investigation, mostly at the microsociological level. Consequently, it is criticized for being "circular" (Michaels, 1978:11) and because some of the propositions derived from the theory do not stand up well to the rigors of empirical testing at the macrosociological level (Doyle and Luckenbill, 1991; Gottfredson and Hindelang, 1979:3–18; Lessan and Sheley, 1992). Regardless of these and other criticisms, Black's theory of law will continue to provide the impetus for a great deal of empirical work in coming years (see, for example, Cooney, 1997, on the decline of lethal conflict among social elites). His propositions are likely to be subjected to further testing, criticism, revision, reformulation, and possible rejection, especially his recently compiled ideas on the "geometry of law" (Black, 2002). But, as Sherman presciently noted shortly after the publication of *The Behavior of Law*, "whatever the substance or method, social research on law cannot ignore Black" (1978:15).

Roberto Mangabeira Unger   The internationally prominent and prolific Unger is currently a professor of law at Harvard University. Unger has long been active in Brazilian politics (demonstrating that theoretical knowledge can be translated into practical applications and real life situations), as a candidate, as a political activist, and as an advisor to world leaders. From 2007 to 2009, he took leave from his position at Harvard to serve in the Brazilian government as minister of strategic affairs.

In *Law in Modern Society*, Unger (1976) revives the sweeping scope of Max Weber's theorizing on law and places the development of rational legal systems within a broad historical and comparative framework. Unger locates the study of law within the major questions of social theory in general: the conflicts between individual and social interests, between legitimacy and coercion, and between the state and society. His main thesis is that the development of the rule of law, law that is committed to general and autonomous legal norms, could take place only when competing groups struggle for control of the legal system and when there are universal standards that can justify the law of the state.

Unger's analysis emphasizes the historical perspective. His goal is an understanding of modern law and society. He examines the nature of society and compares rival systems (for example, the Chinese) with the Western tradition with the range of special types of law—customary or interactional law, regulatory law, and autonomous legal order. Customary or interactional law is "simply any recurring mode of interaction among individuals and groups, together with the more or less explicit acknowledgment by these groups and individuals that such patterns of interaction produce reciprocal expectations of conduct that ought to be satisfied" (1976:49). Bureaucratic or regulatory law for Unger "consists of explicit rules established and enforced by an identifiable government" (1976:50). This type of law is not a universal characteristic of social life. "It is limited to situations in which the division between state and society has been established and some standards of conduct have assumed the form of explicit prescriptions, prohibitions, or permissions, addressed to more or less general categories of persons and acts" (1976:51). Unger calls the third type of law the legal order or legal system, which is both general and autonomous, as well as public and positive (1976:52). From an evolutionary perspective, these different types of law turn out to be stages, for they build upon one another—regulatory law upon customary law and the autonomous legal order upon regulatory law.

For Unger, law is indicative of the normative structure of social life. He contends that there are two competing forms of normative integration: consensual and instrumental. "Consensual law expresses the shared values of a group or community and manifests the stable structure in recurring interactions. Regulatory law is instrumental social control by political institutions through positive and public rules" (Eder, 1977:142). Unger considers autonomous law as both instrumental and consensual.

Unger accounts for these different types of law in an evolutionary context. The change of customary law into bureaucratic law is characterized by an extension of instrumental rules that have normative quality (state law and governmental sanctions). This extension of the instrumental rule is dependent upon the recognition of the consensual basis of law. Unger argues that sacred and natural law can provide the cultural context within which instrumental norms can be legitimized. The development of an autonomous legal order brings about a further extension of instrumental rules to everybody. Everyone can pursue his or her personal objectives as long as they do not infringe upon those of others. Laws set these limits. He notes, however, that this situation requires a further legitimization of the principles of law, and consensus must be generated by social contract and by agreement upon the criteria of substantive justice.

Unger (1998, 2004, 2009; Unger and West, 1998) is a prolific writer, and provides a fresh and unified, albeit somewhat controversial, solution to a number of problems in social theory—the problem of social scientific method, the problem of social order, and the problem of modernity (Sampford, 1989:145). His theory of law is useful for the analysis of changes in law, and he has generated a number of testable propositions that enable sociologists to study law at the synchronic and diachronic levels (Eder, 1977:143). His works are becoming increasingly recognized and appreciated in sociological circles.

CURRENT INTELLECTUAL MOVEMENTS IN LAW

As discussed in Chapter 1, sociological deliberations of the role of law in society generally take place in the context of two ideal conceptions of society: the consensus and conflict perspectives. The consensus perspective is grounded in the functionalist approach and the conflict perspective, in the conflict and Marxist approaches to the study of law in society. These are the two prevailing approaches in the sociological literature. Most sociologists opt for either a version of the functionalist or the conflict and Marxist approach to law and the legal system.

Functional analysis examines social phenomena with respect to their consequences for the broader society. Proponents of this approach ask specific questions such as: What does a kinship system do for society? What does law do for society? What are the "functions" of government, of social classes, or of any social phenomenon? (Turner, 2003: 11–87). In the context of the analysis of law, functionalists are concerned with the identification of the characteristics of legal phenomena, as well as indicating how legal institutions fit into the workings of the overall structure. Theorists embracing conflict and Marxist approaches emphasize the structuring of economic relations that provide, for them, the foundation for various specific studies of legal trends. I shall now consider these two approaches in some detail.

The Functionalist Approach

"Functionalism is," writes Robert A. Nisbet (1969:228), "without any doubt, the single most significant body of theory in the social sciences in the present century. It is often thought to be essentially a theory of order, of stability, of how society is possible." Historically, functionalism was brought into sociology by borrowing directly, and developing analogies for, concepts in the biological sciences. Biology, since the middle of the nineteenth century, frequently referred to the "structure" of an organism, meaning a relatively stable arrangement of relationships between the different cells, and to the "function" of the organism that considered the consequences of the activity of the various organs in the life process. The principal consideration of this organic analogy was how each part of the organism contributed to the survival and maintenance of the whole.

Sociologists distinguish between the manifest and the latent functions (Merton, 1957:19–84). Manifest functions are those that are built into a social system by design. They are well understood by group members. Latent functions are, by contrast, unintentional and often unrecognized. They are unanticipated consequences of a system that has been set up to achieve other ends. For example, the minimum wage law was enacted to provide unskilled laborers with an income slightly above poverty level. Unintentionally, however, this law contributed to the increase in teenage unemployment, particularly among black youths (Herbers, 1979), and reduced job prospects of low-wage earners. When the minimum wage increased, employers tended to hire more part-time than full-time workers, and the overall level of hiring was lower.

The basic tenets of functionalism are summarized in the following key assumptions (Van den Berghe, 1967:294–295):

1. Societies must be analyzed "holistically as systems of interrelated parts."
2. Cause-and-effect relations are "multiple and reciprocal."
3. Social systems are in a state of "dynamic equilibrium," such that adjustment to forces affecting the system is made with minimal change within the system.
4. Perfect integration is never attained so that every social system has strains and deviations, but the latter tend to be neutralized through institutionalization.
5. Change is fundamentally a slow adaptive process, rather than a revolutionary shift.
6. Change is the consequence of the adjustment of changes outside the system, growth by differentiation, and internal innovations.
7. The system is integrated through shared values.

In sociology, functional analysis is as old as the discipline. Comte, Spencer, Durkheim, Malinowski, Radcliffe-Brown, Merton, and Parsons, to name a few, have engaged in the functional analysis of the social world (Turner and Maryanski, 1979:XI). The early theorists viewed the world in systematic terms (Turner and Maryanski, 1995:49–55).

For them, such systems were considered to have needs and prerequisites that had to be met to ensure survival. They viewed such systems as having normal and pathological states, thus suggesting a system of equilibrium and homeostasis. The social world was seen as composed of mutually interrelated parts, and the analysis of these connected and interdependent parts focused on how they fulfilled the requisites of the systems as a whole and how, thus, system equilibrium was maintained.

Ever since the classical sociological theorist Émile Durkheim postulated the notion that deviance could serve certain social functions in a society, sociologists have looked for evidence to support this contention. Durkheim had in mind the idea that a society needed deviance to continually reaffirm its boundaries of propriety. Functional arguments for the importance of deviance are intriguing. They provide a novel way of showing how certain institutions in a society, if not the society itself, continue to operate. Durkheim points out, for example, that without the existence of sinners, a church could not exist. Their very existence provides the opportunity for believers to reaffirm the faith that has been offended by the sinner. Thus, the worst thing that could happen to a church is to completely eliminate sin from the world and completely propagate the faith to society.

Functionalism is also present in legal anthropology. For example, in *The Cheyenne Way*, Karl N. Llewellyn and E. Adamson Hoebel (1941) outline their law-job theory about society as a whole. For societies to survive, there are certain basic needs that must be met. It is within this context that the wants and desires of individuals, their "divisive urges," assert themselves. The conflicts produced are unavoidable but, at the same time, essential to group survival. "The law-jobs entail such arrangement and adjustment of people's behaviour that the society (or the group) remains a society (or a group) and gets enough energy unleashed and coordinated to keep on functioning as a society (or as a group)" (1941:291). They consider the law-jobs as universal, applicable, and necessary to all groups and to all societies.

Functionalism is also evident in other writers. For example, in Jerome Frank's (1930) *Law and the Modern Mind,* the entire discussion of the "basic legal myth" and the associated "legal magic" is grounded in an examination of their functional consequences for the legal system. Similarly, Thurman Arnold's (1935) concern with the role of symbolism within legal institutions is consciously functionalist. Felix Cohen (1959) also resorts to functional analysis in his elaboration of "functional jurisprudence." Also, the writing of Lon Fuller (1969) on law morality, Julius Stone's (1966) *Law and the Social Sciences*, Philippe Nonet's (1976) ideas on jurisprudential sociology, and Andras Sajo's (2003) study of the nature and politically determined functions of governmental corruption in postcommunist transition and how political structure itself creates corrupt practices that become a structural feature of transition societies are illustrative of the functionalist approach to the study of law and society (see also Nuijten and Anders, 2009).

Almost from the beginning, however, the functionalist approach was attacked both for alleged theoretical shortcomings and on ideological grounds. Criticisms included complaints that the whole notion of function is oversimplified. Questions such as "Functional for whom?" were raised, and not without grounds, for the interests and needs of different groups in a society are often in conflict. What may be functional for one group may be dysfunctional for another. Others argue that functional analysis is a static, antihistorical mode of analysis with a bias toward conservatism. Some sociologists even suggest that there is an implicit teleology in functional analysis, in that this mode of analysis inappropriately attributes purposes to social institutions as if they were conscious beings. As expected, a sizable amount of literature in the field has been devoted to both formulating and refuting these charges (see, for example, Turner and Maryanski, 1979, 1995). In spite of these criticisms, as Rich correctly points out, "It can be concluded that most sociology of law theorists are adherents to structural-functionalist theory" (1978:153).

Conflict and Marxist Approaches

Conflict and Marxist approaches are based on the assumption that social behavior can best be understood in terms of tension and conflict between groups and individuals (see, for example, Goldstein, 2005). Proponents of these approaches suggest that society is an arena in which struggles over scarce commodities take place. Closely intertwined with the idea of conflict in society is the Marxian notion of *economic determinism.* Economic organization, especially the ownership of property, determines the organization of the rest of society. The class structure and institutional arrangements, as well as cultural values, beliefs, and religious dogmas, are, ultimately, a reflection of the economic organization of a society.

According to Marx, law and the legal system are designed to regulate and preserve capitalist relations. For the Marxists, law is a method of domination and social control used by the ruling classes. Law protects the interests of those in power and serves to maintain distinctions between the dominated and the domineering classes. Consequently, law is seen as a set of rules that arise as a result of the struggle between the ruling class and those who are ruled. The state, which is the organized reflection of the interests of the ruling class, passes laws that serve the interests of this domineering class.

This breakdown of society into two classes—a ruling class that owns the means of production and a subservient class that works for wages—*inevitably* leads to conflict. Once conflict becomes manifest in the form of riots or rebellions, the state, acting in the interest of the ruling class, will develop laws aimed at controlling acts that threaten the interests of the status quo. As capitalism develops and conflict between social classes becomes more frequent, more acts will be defined as criminal.

It is not surprising; therefore, that many sociologists interested in law, particularly criminal law, have espoused this perspective. The conflict view of criminal law is most noticeable in the now controversial writings of Marxist criminologists. Quinney (1974), for example, argues that law in capitalist society gives political recognition to powerful social and economic interests. The legal system provides the mechanism for the forceful control of the majority in society. The state and the legal system reflect and serve the needs of the ruling class. In *The Critique of Legal Order,* Quinney (2002:16) argues that as capitalist society is further threatened, criminal law is increasingly used in the attempt to maintain domestic order. The underclass will continue to be the object of criminal law as the dominant class seeks to perpetuate itself. To remove the oppression, and to eliminate the need for further reward, would necessarily mean the end of that class and its capitalist economy.

Similarly, William Chambliss and Robert Seidman take a conflict approach in their analysis of law. While emphasizing conflicting interests in society, they argue that "the state becomes a weapon of a particular class. Law emanates from the state. Law in a society of classes must therefore represent and advance the interests of one class or the other" (1982:72–73). For them, law is an instrument sought after and employed by powerful interest groups in society. Chambliss (1978:149) further reinforces the notion of law as an instrument of the powerful in society by specifically pointing out that "acts are defined as criminal because it is in the interests of the ruling class to so define them." Austin Turk (1978) also sees law as "a weapon in social conflict," an instrument of social order that serves those who are in power. The control of legal order represents the ability to use the state's coercive authority to protect one's interests. The control of the legal process further means the control of the organization of governmental decisions and the workings of the law, which diverts attention from more deeply rooted problems of power distribution and interest maintenance. Reasons (1974:103–104) considers crime as a phenomenon created by special interests who, with their definition of rectitude, create the laws of society.

Conflict theorists point out that most of the American criminal law comes directly from English common law. C. Ray Jeffery (1957) contends that acts such as murder, theft, trespassing, and robbery, problems that were once resolved in the kinship group, became crimes against the state when Henry II, King of England, centralized political power and declared them wrongs against the crown. Jerome Hall (1952) traces the growth of property and theft laws to the emergence of commerce and industrialization. With the advent of commerce and trade, a new economic class of traders and industrialists emerged, and the need to protect their business interests grew. As a result, new laws were established to protect the interests and economic well-being of the emergent class. These laws included the creation of embezzlement laws and laws governing stolen property and obtaining goods under false pretense. According to conflict theorists, notions of crime have their origins less in general ideas about right or wrong than in perceived threats to groups with the power to protect their interests through law.

Critics have not been kind to this type of argumentation, holding that it involves enormous simplification, reification, and absence of sensitivity to the complexity of social interaction (Manning, 1975:12). There are many who concede the validity of conflict and interest-group arguments but who, at the same time, contend that bold assertions about the "ruling class" conceal more than they reveal. Surely, lawmaking phenomena are more complex than implied in these statements that hint at a monolithic ruling class that determines legislative behavior and the creation of rules. In spite of these and other criticisms, Marxism exists in contemporary sociological theorizing and "must exist—because alienation exists. Alienation refers to the way in which human beings under capitalism do not control their work, but instead are dominated by their work and by the requirements of the profit-system" (Agger, 1979:1). Elements of the Marxist approach enter into a number of sociological studies on law and society and are influential on epistemological, methodological, and theoretical approaches, as evidenced, for example, in the works of Charles E. Reasons and Robert M. Rich (1978), who present the major paradigms in the sociology of law, with a particular emphasis on conflict and Marxist approaches. The collapse of the Soviet planned economy ended the most extensive attempt to implement Marxism ever, and it is unlikely that another attempt will ever be made to create an economy of any scale that rejects private property, markets, money, financial instruments, prices, money wages, profits, and interest. Thus, the Marxist conception of an economy that would be the negation of capitalism is a dead letter today. This is not to say that the

Marxist ideas have no continuing (albeit nowadays limited) appeal; they can be expected to retain some of their allure for approaching the study of law in society.

Critical Legal Studies Movement

Critical legal studies (CLS but also referred to as CRITS in more popular parlance) is a vibrant, refreshing, controversial, and enduring addition to the ongoing jurisprudential debate on law, legal education, and the role of lawyers in society (Belliotti, 1992:162–189; Kennedy, 2007; Kramer, 1995; Neacsu, 2000; Sampford, 1989:143–146; Tushnet, 2008; Unger, 1983, 1986, 2004). It is widely considered, by critics and followers alike, to comprise some of the most exciting sociolegal scholarship around, and one sociologist of law described it as being "where the action is" (Trubek, 1984). The movement began with a group of junior faculty members and law students at Yale in the late 1960s who have since moved to other places. In 1977, the group organized itself into the Conference on Critical Legal Studies, which now has over 400 members and holds an annual conference that draws more than 1,000 participants.

The movement has been greatly influenced by Marxist-inspired European theorists, and its roots can be traced back to American legal realism (Tomasic, 1985:18). Legal realists in the 1920s and 1930s argued against the nineteenth-century belief that the rule of law was supreme. They contended, because a good lawyer could argue convincingly either side of a given case, there was actually nothing about the law that made any judicial decision inevitable. Rather, they pointed out, the outcome of a case depended largely, if not entirely, on the predilections of the judge who happened to be deciding it. Thus, far from being a science, the realists argued, law was virtually inseparable from politics, economics, and culture. They rejected the idea that law is above politics and economics.

Proponents of the movement reject the idea that there is anything distinctly legal about legal reasoning. As with any other kind of analysis, legal reasoning, they maintain, cannot operate independently of the personal biases of lawyers or judges, or of the social context in which they are acting (see, for example, Bankowski and MacLean, 2007). Furthermore, law is so contradictory that it allows the context of a case to determine the outcome. That attribute of law—its inability to cover all situations—is called *indeterminacy* (Trubek, 1984:578). Because law consists of a variety of contradictions and inconsistencies, judicial decisions cannot be the self-contained models of reasoning as they claim to be. Decisions rest on grounds outside of formal legal doctrine, which are inevitably political.

Critical scholars also reject law as being value-free and above political, economic, and social considerations. Laws only *seem* neutral and independent, even those that reflect the dominant values in society. Moreover, laws legitimize those values that predominate in society. Therefore, laws legitimate the status quo. They maintain that law is actually part of the system of power in society rather than a protection against it.

Although proponents of the movement insist that their ideas are still tentative and evolving, their attacks on law and legal training have created a good deal of criticism. The movement has been called Marxist, utopian, hostile to rules, and incoherent. Critical legal scholars have been accused of favoring violence over bargaining, of advocating the inculcation of leftist values in legal education, and of being preoccupied with "illegitimate hierarchies" such as the bar (Schwartz, 1984); their approach to law is "nihilistic," and they teach cynicism to their students, which may result in "the learning of the skills of corruption." Nihilist law teachers with a proclivity for revolution are likely to train criminals and, they have, therefore "an ethical duty to depart from law school" (Carrington, 1984:227). It is unlikely that the controversy between proponents and opponents of the movement will be settled in the foreseeable future (Trubek and Esser, 1989). Further, although the movement has been fairly successful in questioning the validity of the Western legal system, it has failed, as the following sections will demonstrate, its major objective of developing and gaining broader support for new legal doctrines that are more representative of class, gender, and race differences. So far, the most useful function of the movement is indicating the extent to which politics influences the legal system (Goodrich, 1993).

Feminist Legal Theory

Feminist legal theory is another intellectual movement of considerable influence, significance, and impact. It is concerned with issues that are central to a broader intellectual and political feminist movement: sex-based equality at the work place, reproductive rights, domestic violence, sexual harassment, sexual preferences, and rape, just to mention a few (see, for example, Barclay et al., 2009; Fineman et al., 2009; Ford, 2006; Horvath and Brown, 2009; Kolmar and Bartkowski, 2010; Lloyd et al., 2010; Paxton and Hughes, 2007; Rhode and Sanger, 2005). It draws from the experiences of women and from critical perspectives developed in other disciplines in analyzing the relationship between law and gender (Frazier and Hunt, 1998; Frug, 1992a; Greenberg et al., 2008; Heinzelman, 2010; Sullivan, 2004; Williams, 2004). Unlike critical legal studies, which started in elite law schools and were inspired predominantly by notions of what may be considered contemporary Marxism, feminist legal theories emerged against the backdrop of mass political movements (Rhode, 1991:334). These political backlashes for feminists included the defeat of the Equal Rights Amendment, setbacks in abortion rights, same-sex marriage obstacles, continued sexual subordination and exploitation in the profession of law, and the general prevalence of sexism in most walks of life. The "tough on crime" policies are also thought to have had a series of negative consequences on women: cuts from social services to pay for crime control can disproportionately affect women; women incur increased responsibility for family while men serve longer sentences, and women are often victimized as third parties by government when women are associated with criminals (Chesney-Lind and Pasko, 2004a, 2004b; Miller, 1998).

A dominant tendency in feminist legal theories is to regard men as the source of women's problems (Lorber, 2009; Naffine, 1990:20, Wing, 2003). There is a strong conviction that male-dominated jurisprudence perpetuates women as objects (Abrams, 1995; Eskridge and Hunter, 1997). Society is viewed as basically patriarchal, organized and dominated by men, and, as a result, not very hospitable to women. Not surprisingly, proponents of the theory consider it one of the most crucial challenges to contemporary law and legal institutions (Bartlett and Kennedy, 1991:1).

There are at least three predominant, although by no means mutually exclusive, themes in feminist legal literature (see, for example, Delamont, 2003; Moran, 2006). The first deals with women's struggle for equality in a male-dominated legal profession and in the broader society. Feminists challenge legal claims of fairness and the impartiality of law in dealing with women (Grana, 2009). The argument is that men directly or indirectly have endeavored to maintain their own power and to keep women in their place. There are many structural constraints to perpetuate inequality. One is law's respect for precedent. But for feminists, the emphasis on precedents raises two concerns. First, existing precedents tend to support and reinforce a status quo that may be more favorable to male than to female interests. Second, reasoning not based on precedent or accepted doctrine is often viewed as extreme and is less likely to be successful than arguments based on precedents. Examples of these two concerns are male-only combat rules, job security for pregnant women, and maternal child-custody preferences.

In the second broad theme of feminist legal scholarship, the argument of male bias is extended to include practically every feature of law. The law, according to this theme, is a reflection of a typical male culture, a masculine way of doing things. Law, therefore, is corrupted for women by its inherent masculinity. The task feminists face is to come up with a completely new law for women. Such law should be devoid of norms and characteristics that reinforce male prerogatives and female powerlessness about gender roles and private intentions. For example, the male legal culture dismisses or trivializes many problems that women face, such as sexual harassment and date-rape (Horvath and Brown, 2009; Stein, 1999). They capture different subjective experiences of shared social realities: For the man, an office pass is sex (and pleasurable); for the woman, it is harassment (and painful). For the man, the dinner and its aftermath is a date (with certain expectations); for the woman, it is rape and frightening. Many gender-specific injuries are still dismissed as trivial (sexual harassment on the street); consensual (sexual harassment on the job); humorous (nonviolent marital rape); deserved or private (domestic violence); nonexistent (pornography); legally predetermined (marital rape, in states where legislatures have yet to outlaw it) (Frug, 1992b:808); or the use of battered women syndrome defense as an excuse for a variety of crimes, ranging from homicide to fraud (Coughlin, 1994).

The third dominant theme challenges the very concepts law invokes to support its contention that it is a just and fair institution. Contrary to professed notions, law is not value-neutral, objective, rational, dispassionate, and consistent. This is because law defines those concepts in a typically masculine way, ignoring or devaluing the qualities associated with the experience of women. Essentially, the problem is that law claims to be neutral in relation to the sexes (and other social categories); yet, the very way it argues for its neutrality is gender-biased. The particular style of maleness can best be illustrated by the concept of "rational person," a mythical legal subject who is coherent, rational, acts on *his* free will, and in ordinary circumstances can be held fully accountable for *his* actions (Naffine, 1990:1–23).

Feminists are pragmatists (Chafetz, 1997; Heinzelman, 2010; Radin, 1991) and rely on feminist legal methods (Bartlett, 1991; Jarviluoma et al., 2003; Kleinman, 2007; Ramazanoglu and Holland, 2002) to advance their cause. Feminists contend that without understanding feminist methods, law will not be perceived as legitimate or "correct." These methods, although not unique to feminists, seek to reveal features of a legal concern that more traditional approaches tend to ignore or suppress. There are three such basic methods (Bartlett, 1991:370–403).

One method asks the *woman question*, which is designed to probe into the gender implications of a social practice or rule. Asking the woman question compensates for law's failure to take into account experiences and values that are more typical of women than of men. Nowadays, feminists ask the woman question in many areas of the law. In the case of rape, they ask why the defense of consent deals with the perspective of the defendant and what he "reasonably" thought the woman wanted rather than the point of view of the woman and what she "reasonably" thought she conveyed to the defendant. The woman question asks why pregnancy is virtually the only medical condition excluded from state employee disability plans; why women cannot be prison guards on the same terms as men; and why conflict between family and work responsibilities is considered a private matter for women to resolve rather than a public concern involving the restructuring of the workplace. Essentially, the woman question shows how the predicament of women reflects the organization of society rather than the inherent characteristics of women.

Another method, *feminist practical reasoning*, deals with features not usually reflected in legal doctrine. The underlying assumption is that women approach the reasoning process differently from men, that women are more sensitive to situation and context, and that they tend to resist universal generalizations and principles. An example is minors' access to abortion. The notion of family autonomy seems to justify the legal requirement that a minor obtain parental consent before abortion. The young woman is immature, and parents are best suited to help her to decide whether or not to terminate her pregnancy. However, the often tragic and wrenching circumstances under which a minor may want to avoid notifying a parent about an abortion demonstrate the practical difficulties of the matter. Often, minors are traumatized by their parents' knowledge of their pregnancy. Women may be compelled to continue their pregnancy and subsequently give up the child for adoption, which is contrary to their intentions. Or they may be subjected to various forms of parental rejection or manipulation. Feminist practical reasoning challenges the legitimacy of the norms of those who claim to speak on behalf of the community, and they seek to identify perspectives not represented in the dominant monolithic male culture.

A third method, *consciousness-raising,* provides an opportunity to test the validity of legal principles through personal experiences of those who have been affected by those principles. The idea is to explore common experiences and patterns that come about from shared recollection of life events. It enables feminists to draw insights from their own experiences and those of other women and to use these newly formed insights to challenge dominant versions of social reality. In consciousness-raising sessions, women share their experiences publicly as victims of marital rape, pornography, sexual harassment on the job, or other forms of oppression or exclusion based on sexual orientation (Lloyd et al., 2010; Robson, 1994; Williams, 2004), in an attempt to alter public perception of the meaning to women of practices that the dominant male culture considers harmless or flattering.

Of course, feminist legal theory and its methods are not without their detractors. In part as a reaction to feminist legal scholarship, there is a nascent intellectual movement of critical studies of masculinity (see, for example, Collier, 1995; Hearn, 1992). The contention is that men are oppressed within patriarchy in a fashion comparable to women's oppression. It is not yet an institutionalized attempt at "men's liberation," albeit there are already efforts to legitimize the endeavors of politically powerful individuals and organizations to "improve" the legal rights of men (Collier, 1995:26). There is also a call for the development of a lesbian legal theory, "a theory about law that is relentlessly and intelligently lesbian," as a component of contemporary legal scholarship (Robson, 1992:37; see also Fineman et al., 2009; Richardson and Seidman, 2002).

The assumption of a dominant androcentric homogenous legal culture is an exaggeration. It is more of a rhetorical than a factual contention. The classical Marxist polarization of the sexes into a dominant and a subordinate class, with the concomitant proletarianization of gender, represents a forceful argument but one of limited intellectual substance and appeal. In an attempt to depict the benefits that accrue to men in what is considered an essentially sexist institution, many feminists have overlooked the fact that not all men benefit equally from legal sexism. Indirectly and perhaps unintentionally, allusions are made only to successful white middle-class males, with their unique form of white middle-class masculinity while minority and gay males are excluded (Cante, 2010; Keen and Goldberg, 1998). A close examination of the principles and methods of law also reveals that there are many people who are omitted or maltreated on the basis of class, race, and ethnic background, in addition to gender. Thus, to assume that we are dealing with a clear-cut issue of "us versus them" gender-based exploitation is an oversimplification.

There are also some perplexing dilemmas confronting feminists. For example, there is no consensus in the literature about various options. In the context of male-only draft, statutory rape laws, and pregnancy, feminists have two choices: Either they claim equality for women on the basis of similarities between the sexes or they demand special treatment for women on the grounds of basic sexual differences. This difference-versus-similarity argument carries over into a variety of other areas. It is an either/or proposition, and critics maintain that feminists cannot have it both ways (Williams, 1991). Feminist legal theory also fails to address issues of democracy and citizenship (Higgins, 1997) and age (should a 4-year-old pre-kindergarten boy be suspended for "inappropriately hugging" a teacher's aide or a 5-year-old for "sexually harassing" a girl in his class by pinching her bottom? [Hunter, 2006]), and neglects the formulation of a positive theory of female sexuality (Franke, 2001). It should also be noted that a century or so ago, in 1913, Toronto already launched an experiment in feminist ideals: a woman's police court. This particular court offered a separate venue to hear cases that involved criminalized women (prostitutes, vagrants, thieves, alcoholics, and so on) gathered and struggled with the meaning of justice (Glasbeek, 2010).

The cult of victimhood has also become widespread; women are viewed as defenseless and oppressed, social and sexual violence are treated as the same, and men are guilty and are to be held accountable. But by conflicting real and false victims, feminism runs the risk of losing credibility with the younger generation. Preoccupied by putting men on trial, the movement of recent years has reactivated old stereotypes and ignored the issues that were the reasons for its existence and thus coming to a dead end (Badinter, 2006). Still, in spite of these criticisms, feminist legal theory and its methods represent an important intellectual movement challenging traditional legal doctrine both in the United States (Bartlett and Kennedy, 1991; Bartlett et al., 2009; Ford, 2006; Frug, 1992; Greer, 2000; Naffine, 1990) and in Europe (Bernstein 1994).

Critical Race Theory

Critical race theory (CRT) is an eclectic, dynamic, and growing movement in law with close to 900 leading law review articles and dozens books directly or indirectly devoted to it (see, for example, Ayres, 2003; Delgado, 2004; Delgado and Stefancic, 2000; López, 2006, 2007; Valdes et al., 2002).

Like feminist legal theory, CRT is concerned with questions of discrimination, oppression, difference, equality, and the lack of diversity in the legal profession (Johnson, 1997). Although its intellectual origins go back much farther, the inception and formal organization of the movement can be traced back to a 1989 workshop on CRT in Madison, Wisconsin (Delgado, 1994, 2004; Delgado and Stefancic, 2000; Harris, 1994; Hayman, 1995; Scheppele, 1994). Many of the proponents have been previously involved with critical legal studies or feminist jurisprudence, and the 1989 conference effectively ratified CRT as an important component of legal theory. The CRT movement, along with the Latino-focused critical legal scholarship or LatCrit (Bender, 2004; Valdes, 1997; Valdes et al., 2002), attempts to rectify the wrongs of racism while acknowledging that racism is an inherent part of modern society. Racism is embedded in the system, and proponents recognize that its elimination is impossible; but at the same time, they insist that an ongoing struggle to countervail racism must be carried out.

In a way, the word *critical* reflects a continuity between critical legal studies and critical race studies. Both seek to explore the ways in which law and legal education and the practices of legal institutions work to support and maintain a system of oppressive and inegalitarian relations. But CRITS do not generally look outside of the law to identify the forces that actually determine the content of legal rules while CRT prompts a recognition of the urgency of racial problems and an uncompromising search for real solutions rather than temporary and comforting stopgap measures (Chang, 1993; Culp, 1994; Farber, 1994). The basic premise is that persons of color in the United States are oppressed and being oppressed creates fundamental disadvantages for those who are so treated. CRT focuses on the experiences and situations of oppressed people of color, and provides an outlet for the concrete experiences of subordinates. Because of oppression, people of color perceive the word differently than those who have not had such experience. CRT scholars can thus bring to legal analyses perspectives that were previously excluded. Through narratives and "story telling," some scholars share their experiences or the experiences of other people of color to make their presence felt in legal scholarship.

Critical race theorists extend traditional civil rights scholarship to locate problems beyond the surface of doctrine to the deep structure of American law and culture (see, for example, Fleury-Steiner and Nielsen, 2006). Racism is viewed not only as a matter of individual prejudice and everyday practice, but also as a phenomenon that is deeply embedded in language and perception. Racism is in a ubiquitous and inescapable feature of modern society, and despite official rhetoric to the contrary, race is always present even in the most neutral and innocent terms. Concepts such as *justice*, *truth*, and *reason* are open to questions that reveal their complicity with power. This extraordinary pervasiveness of unconscious racism is often ignored by the legal system.

Proponents of CRT have a commitment to a vision of liberation from racism through reason and efforts to separate legal reasoning and institutions from their alleged racist roots. Justice is still possible, and it is the property of both whites and nonwhites. CRT seems confident that coming up with the correct theory of race and racism will lead to enlightenment, empowerment, and, eventually, to emancipation.

As all other intellectual developments, CRT has also come in for criticism (see, for example, Ayres, 2003). As a matter of formal law, blacks and other people of color are no longer barred from professional jobs. Evolving laws and social norms have opened the door, particularly for *qualified people of color*. How widely this door has opened is the subject of debate. But for present purposes, it is enough to observe that, over the past thirty years, changes in our laws and norms have increased the representation of people of color in professional workplaces. The diversification of the professional workplace renders these workplaces important *social contexts* for thinking about racial formation—that is to say, the social construction of race.

Another concern is that CRT articulates its conception of race as a social construction at the macro level, focusing primarily on legal and sociopolitical processes. It has not paid attention to the interpersonal ways in which race is produced. That is, CRT often ignores the racial productivity of the *choices* people of color make about how to present themselves as racialized persons. As a general matter, CRT's race-as-a-social-construction thesis does not include an analysis of the race-producing practices reflected in the daily negotiations people of color perform in an attempt to shape how people (especially white) interpret their nonwhite identities. For example, a Latina may decide not to speak Spanish at work, she may decide to *hold her tongue*, or she may refrain from socializing with other Latina workers. These are all race-constructing choices: How a Latina exercises them will inform how her employer and fellow employees experience her as a Latina.

There also seems to be a contradiction between its commitment to radical criticism and its emphasis on racial emancipation. If the very language used to describe justice is infected by racism and gradations of power, what is the objective of critique? Another criticism is that it lacks a standard methodology and a set of common tenets. Further, it is also seen as a reformist project, not really new and distinguishable from traditional civil rights scholarship (which is different from the current controversies surrounding civil rights and counterterrorism policies [see, for example, Dyzenhaus, 2009]), which was set to eliminate discrimination but failed to achieve fully its stated objective. In the final analysis, CRT is a young intellectual movement that has the potential to have a profound effect on legal scholarship in the coming years.

SUMMARY

This chapter has traced the development of legal systems and has examined the principal theories of law and society. In a historical context, legal development, industrialization, urbanization, and modernization are closely intertwined. Legal development is conditioned by a series of integrative demands, stemming from society's economic, political, educational, and religious institutions. From a developmental perspective, the primitive, transitional, and modern legal systems were discussed. These three types are still present in the world's societies. Although one should be careful not to emphasize unilinear evolution, it can be inferred from the discussion that, to the extent legal change takes place in a society, it will follow more or less the pattern outlined. What distinguishes these legal systems from each other is the comparative degree of differentiation between basic legal elements. In the process of development, the once-blurred elements of law, courts, legislation, and enforcement become increasingly separated from one another. Accompanying the emergence of laws, court systems, police force, and legislation is a trend toward increasing size, complexity, differentiation, and bureaucratization.

Among the theorists discussed, there seems to be more or less a general consensus that societal and legal complexities have gone hand in hand. Beyond that, there is little agreement. Many of the European pioneers discussed reacted in various ways to the influence of natural law and attempted to account for it from an evolutionary perspective. The classical sociological theorists covered have recognized the essential role of legal institutions in the social order and have made important explorations of the interplay between law and society. The sociolegal theorists were guided by social science principles in the development of their diverse perspectives on law and society. Making sense of the idea of law remains an ongoing enterprise, as evidenced by the efforts of the contemporary theorists discussed.

These efforts at explaining the interplay between law and society should be seen in the context of intellectual, political, and social climates of the particular theorists. In each historical epoch, every interpretation of social reality posits certain questions and provides certain answers. According to S. N. Eisenstadt (1972), tension is inherent in intellectual life because of the tendency to challenge the intellectual construction of social reality. If a theory of law and society is developed by one group of intellectuals, this will provide an incentive for others to view the matter in another way. Eisenstadt's insights account, in part, for the diverse explanations of the relationship between law and society and the nature, province, and function of law in society.

Currently, there are two widely accepted approaches to the study of law and society. Sociologists embracing the functionalist approach attempt, in various ways, to account for law in society within the overall framework of the theory that society consists of interrelated parts that work together for the purpose of maintaining internal balance. Sociologists advocating conflict and Marxist approaches to the study of law in society consider conflict inevitable and ubiquitous in societies, as a result of inescapable competition for scarce resources. They are preoccupied with debunking myths about society and advocating changes in what they regard as harmful social relations, structures, and processes that exist in today's social order. Proponents of the CLS movement argue that there is nothing inherently rational, scientific, or neutral about the law—nothing that would dictate the outcome of a particular case. They maintain that law is riddled with contradiction and prejudice and that it is heavily in favor of the wealthy and powerful. Another movement of considerable influence is that of the feminist legal theory. Proponents challenge the impartiality of law in dealing with women and argue that law is a reflection of a typical male culture. Feminists rely on feminist methods that seek to reveal aspects of law that more traditional methods tend to ignore or suppress. Finally, proponents of CRT argue that the root causes of racial inequality still persist in American society, embedded in law, language, perception and structural conditions, and there must be an uncompromising search for real solutions rather than convenient stopgaps.

SUGGESTED FURTHER READINGS

Bruce A. Arrigo and Dragan Milovanovic (eds.), *Postmodernist and Post-Structuralist Theories of Crime.* Burlington, VT: Ashgate, 2010. A collection of critical approaches by well-known contemporary theorists to law, crime, and the criminal justice system.

Reza Banakar and Max Travers (eds.), *An Introduction to Law and Social Theory.* Portland, OR: Hart Publishing, 2002. This compilation of essays outlines six major sociological views and perspectives that have been developed to study law and society: classical sociology of law, systems theory, critical approaches, interpretive approaches, postmodernism, and pluralism and globalization.

Katharine T. Bartlett and Rosanne Kennedy (eds.), *Feminist Legal Theory: Readings in Law and Gender.* Boulder, CO: Westview Press, 1991. A balanced and provocative anthology of early articles on feminist legal theory and methods.

Katharine T. Bartlett, Angela P. Harris, and Deborah L. Rhode, *Gender and Law: Theory, Doctrine, Commentary.* 5th ed. New York: Aspen Law and Business, 2009. A comprehensive resource on feminist jurisprudence.

Raymond A. Belliotti, *Justifying Law: The Debate over Foundations, Goals, and Methods.* Philadelphia, PA: Temple University Press, 1992. A clear and concise review of historical and contemporary trends in jurisprudential thought.

Steven W. Bender, *Greasers and Gringos: Latinos, Law, and the American Imagination.* New York: New York University Press, 2004. An insightful examination of Latino negative stereotypes, their evolution and possible rectification.

Edgar Bodenheimer, *Jurisprudence: The Philosophy and Method of the Law* (rev. ed.). Cambridge, MA: Harvard University Press, 1974. A classic review of the historical materials dealing with the development of jurisprudential thought with an emphasis on philosophical, sociological, historical, and analytical components of legal theory.

David Chalcraft, Fanon Howell, Marisol Lopez Menendez, and Hector Vera (eds.), *Max Weber Matters: Interweaving Past and Present.* Burlington, VT: Ashgate, 2010. This insightful compendium illustrates the multidisciplinary relevance of Weber's work and will be of interest to scholars of law and society.

William J. Chambliss and Milton Mankoff (eds.), *Whose Law, What Order? A Conflict Approach to Criminology.* New York: John Wiley, 1976. A good early illustration of the fundamental perspectives of conflict criminologists.

Richard Collier, *Masculinity, Law and the Family.* New York: Routledge, 1995. A controversial and thought-provoking book on the legal ramifications of critical studies of masculinity as a reaction in part to race and feminist legal scholarship.

Hugh Collins, *Marxism and Law.* New York: Oxford University Press, 1996. A clear and thorough treatment of the relationship between Marxian theory and law.

Roger Cotterrell (ed.), *Émile Durkheim. Justice, Morality and Politics.* Burlington, VT: Ashgate, 2010. This volume dwells on three interrelated aspects of Durkheim's work: his sociology of justice, his sociology of morality, and his political sociology. These ideas are considered most relevant and practical in view of the fundamental problems of contemporary society and provide important insight of his social theory.

Richard Delgado. *Justice at War: Civil Liberties and Civil Rights During Times of Crisis.* New York: New York University Press, 2004. Delgado, one of the founding figures of the CRT movement, expands on his earlier works dealing with topical social issues. A judicious supplement to his compendium on race theory cited in text.

Richard Delgado and Jean Stefancic (eds.), *Critical Race Theory: The Cutting Edge.* Philadelphia, PA: Temple University Press, 2000. A collection of the best writings of a new generation of civil rights scholars in the fast growing legal genre of CRT.

William M. Evan (ed.), *The Sociology of Law: A Social-Structural Perspective.* New York: Free Press, 1980. *Social Structure and Law: Theoretical and Empirical Perspectives.* New York: Macmillan, 1990. Handy references for alternative theoretical approaches to the study of law in society.

Martha Albertson Fineman, Jack E. Jackson, and Adam P. Romero (eds.), *Feminist and Queer Legal Theory: Intimate Encounters and Uncomfortable Conversations.* Burlington, VT: Ashgate, 2009. This compendium brings together positions in feminist and queer theory to create interdisciplinary dialogues and to explore further the legal, cultural, and social implications of the various theoretical approaches.

Lawrence M. Friedman, *American Law: An Introduction.* 2nd ed. New York: W.W. Norton, 1998. A seminal work on the history and development of American law and legal system. *American Law in the Twentieth Century,* New Haven, CT: Yale University Press, 2002. An excellent overview of law in the United States during the last century.

Robert P. George (ed.), *Natural Law.* Burlington, VT: Ashgate, 2003. A gathering of essays by leading contemporary natural law theorists and their critics.

Philip Goldstein, *Post-Marxist Theory.* Albany, NY: State University of New York Press, 2005. An overview of topical trends in Marxist theorizing.

Judith G. Greenberg, Martha L. Minow, and Dorothy E. Roberts, *Women and the Law.* 4th ed. New York: Foundation Press, 2008. A detailed overview of concrete legal problems of particular and current concern to women. The problems are grouped into three categories: women and work, women and family, and women and their bodies.

Alan Hunt, *The Sociological Movement in Law.* Philadelphia, PA: Temple University Press, 1978. A comprehensive examination of the intellectual precursors of modern sociology of law, with an emphasis on Roscoe Pound, American legal realism, Émile Durkheim, and Max Weber.

Law and Human Behavior. "Special Issue: Gender and the Law," 22 (1) (February), 1998. The entire issue is devoted to the examination of gender and law concerns. A good source for research and applications.

Lawrence Peter King and Iván Szelényi, *Theories of the New Class: Intellectuals and Power.* Minneapolis, MN: University of Minnesota Press, 2004. Addressing the intellectual history of Marxism and socialism, theories of the increasing role of the state and technocratic elites in capitalism, and theories of contemporary social change, the book provides useful background information for theorizing about law and legal systems.

Ian Haney López (ed.), *Race, Law, and Society.* Aldershot, Hants, UK/Burlington, VT: Ashgate, 2007. An edited volume of important articles on race and race-related topics in American and a variety of cross-cultural contexts.

Susan L. Miller (ed.), *Crime Control and Women: Feminist Implications of Criminal Justice Policy.* Thousand Oaks, CA: Sage Publications, Inc., 1998. Using a feminist perspective, the collection of articles explores the adverse affects and unintended consequences of the U.S. crackdown on crime.

David Nelken (ed.), *Beyond Law in Context: Developing a Sociological Understanding of Law.* Burlington, VT: Ashgate, 2009. An international collection of essays on the relationship between law, society, and social theory and on the ideal fit between law and its social context.

Ervin H. Pollack, *Jurisprudence: Principles and Applications.* Columbus, OH: Ohio State University Press, 1979. A lengthy examination of diverse legal theories and their applications. A very useful book for prelaw students and essential for law students.

Charles E. Reasons and Robert M. Rich (eds.), *The Sociology of Law: A Conflict Perspective.* Toronto, Canada: Butterworths, 1978. A compendium designed to present the major paradigms in the sociology of law, with particular emphasis on conflict and Marxist approaches.

Robert M. Rich, *The Sociology of Law: An Introduction to Its Theorists and Theories.* Washington, DC: University Press of America, 1978. A pioneering review of principal theorists under the headings of sociology of law, sociology of criminal law, sociological jurisprudence, and anthropology of law.

Kahei Rokumoto (ed.), *Sociological Theories of Law.* New York: New York University Press, 1994. A handy collection of classic, contemporary, and cross-cultural articles on theoretical perspectives.

Charles Sampford, *The Disorder of Law: A Critique of Legal Theory.* Oxford, UK: Basil Blackwell, 1989. A useful source for additional discussion of a large number of important contemporary theorists from a critical perspective.

Kim Lane Scheppele, "Legal Theory and Social Theory," *Annual Review of Sociology, Annual 1994,* 20: 383–407, 1994. A concise and comprehensive review of trends in legal theory.

Pamela J. Shoemaker, James William Tankard, Jr., and Dominic L. Lasorsa. *How to Build Social Science Theories.* Thousand Oaks, CA: Sage, 2004. A discussion of the various ways of theory construction.

Roman Tomasic, *The Sociology of Law.* London, UK: Sage Publications, 1985. A compact overview of the various theoretical approaches to law and society, with a bibliography of close to a thousand references.

A. Javier Trevino, *The Sociology of Law: A Biography of Theoretical Literature.* 3rd ed. Lewiston, NY: Mellen Press, 2003. A useful list of over a thousand different references, culled from journal articles and books, which deal directly with the field of legal sociology.

A. Javier Trevino (ed), *The Classic Writings in Law and Society: Contemporary Comments and Criticisms.* New Brunswick, NJ: Transaction Books, 2007. A valuable and critical supplement on current perspectives regarding many of the influential classical theories.

A. Javier Trevino, *The Sociology of Law: Classical and Contemporary Perspectives.* New Brunswick, NJ: Transaction Publishers, 2008. A review of classical and contemporary perspectives incorporating some original writings by theorists.

Francisco Valdes, Jerome McCristal Culp, and Angela P. Harris (eds.), *Crossroads, Directions, and a New Critical Race Theory.* Philadelphia, PA: Temple University Press, 2002. The majority of the essays in this volume were delivered at the last major CRT conference, which was held at Yale in 1997. The essays represent the past, present, and future of CRT. The book is a must-read for those who are interested in the genesis of CRT, in how CRT positions itself against other legal discourses, and in the current debates within the CRT literature.

Max Weber, *Law in Economy and Society.* Ed. Max Rheinstein, and trans. Edward Shils and Max Rheinstein. Cambridge, UK: Harvard University Press, 1954. Weber's most important writings on law, rich in historical material and major theoretical formulations. The articles in David Chalcraft et al., collection mentioned earlier should be read along with this work.

G. Edward White, *Oliver Wendell Holmes: Sage of the Supreme Court.* New York: Oxford University Press, 2006. An insightful and informative biography of Holmes along with a review of some of his most important ideas and contributions.

Adrien Katherine Wing (ed.), *Critical Race Feminism: A Reader.* 2nd ed., New York: New York University Press, 2003. Both a forceful statement and a platform for change, the anthology addresses an ambitious range of subjects, from life in the workplace and motherhood to sexual harassment, domestic violence, and other criminal justice issues. Extending beyond national borders, the volume tackles global issues such as the rights of Muslim women, immigration, multiculturalism, and global capitalism.

REFERENCES

Abadinsky, Howard. 2008. *Law and Justice: An Introduction to the American Legal System,* 6th ed. Upper Saddle River, NJ: Prentice Hall.

Abrams, Kathryn. 1995. "Sex War Redux: Agency and Coercion in Feminist Legal Theory," *Columbia Law Review,* 95 (2) (March): 304–376.

Adams, Bert N., and R. A. Sydie. 2002. *Contemporary Sociological Theory.* Thousand Oaks, CA: Pine Forge Press.

Agger, Ben. 1979. *Western Marxism: An Introduction.* Santa Monica, CA: Goodyear.

Alexander, Rudolph, Jr. 2006. "Restorative Justice: Misunderstood and Misapplied," *Journal of Policy Practice,* 5 (1): 67–81.

Antalffy, Gyorgy. 1974. *Basic Problems of State and Society.* Budapest, Hungary: Akademiai Kiado.

Arnold, Thurman. 1935. *The Symbols of Government.* New Haven, CT: Yale University Press.

Arrigo, Bruce A., and Dragan Milovanovic (ed.). 2010. *Postmodernist and Post-Structuralist Theories of Crime.* Burlington, VT: Ashgate.

Ayres, Ian. 2003. BOOK REVIEW SYMPOSIUM: Prevention Perspectives on "Different" Kinds of Discrimination: From Attacking Different "Isms" to Promoting Acceptance in Critical Race Theory, Law and Economics, and Empirical Research: Pervasive Prejudice? Unconventional Evidence of Race and Gender Discrimination. *Stanford Law Review,* 55 (June): 2293–2364.

Badinter, Elisabeth. 2006. *Dead End Feminism.* Malden, MA: Blackwell Publishing.

Banakar, Reza. 2003. *Merging Law and Sociology: Beyond the Dichotomies in Socio-Legal Research.* Glienicke, Berlin/Madison, WI: Wilch Verlag/Galda.

Banakar, Reza, and Max Travers (eds.). 2002. *An Introduction to Law and Social Theory.* Portland, OR: Hart Publishing.

Bankowski, Zenon, and James MacLean (eds.). 2007. *The Universal and the Particular in Legal Reasoning.* Burlington, VT: Ashgate.

Barber, Bernard. 1971. "Function, Variability, and Change in Ideological Systems." Pp. 244–262 in Bernard Barber and Alex Inkeles (eds.), *Stability and Social Change.* Boston, MA: Little, Brown.

Barclay, Scott, Mary Bernstein, and Anna-Maria Marshall. 2009. *Queer Mobilizations. LGBT Activists Confront the Law.* New York: New York University Press.

Barnett, Larry D. 2010. *Legal Construct, Social Concept: A Macrosociological Perspective on Law.* Piscataway, NJ: Transaction Publishers.

Bartlett, Katharine T. 1991. "Feminist Legal Methods." Pp. 370–403 in Katharine T. Bartlett and Rosanne Kennedy (eds.), *Feminist Legal Theory: Readings in Law and Gender.* Boulder, CO.: Westview Press.

Bartlett, Katharine T., and Rosanne Kennedy (eds.). 1991. *Feminist Legal Theory: Readings in Law and Gender.* Boulder, CO.: Westview Press.

Bartlett, Katharine T., Angela P. Harris, and Deborah L. Rhode. 2009. *Gender and Law: Theory, Doctrine, Commentary.* 5th ed. New York: Aspen Law and Business.

Belliotti, Raymond A. 1992. *Justifying Law: The Debate over Foundations, Goals, and Methods.* Philadelphia, PA: Temple University Press.

Bennis, Warren G. 1966. *Changing Organizations.* New York: McGraw-Hill.

Bernstein, Anita. 1994. "Law, Culture, and Harassment: Law and Workplace Harassment in the US and Europe," *University of Pennsylvania Law Review,* 142 (4): 1227–1311.

Bender, Steven W. 2004. *Greasers and Gringos: Latinos, Law, and the American Imagination.* New York: New York University Press.

Berg, Axel van den, and Hudson Meadwell (eds.). 2004. *The Social Sciences and Rationality: Promise, Limits, and Problems.* New Brunswick, NJ: Transaction Publishers.

Black, Donald. 1976. *The Behavior of Law.* New York: Academic Press. 1989. *Sociological Justice.* New York: Oxford University Press. 1998. *The Social Structure of Right and Wrong.* Revised ed. San Diego, CA: Academic Press. 2002. "The Geometry of Law: An Interview with Donald Black," *International Journal of the Sociology of Law,* 30 (2): 101–129.

Bodenheimer, Edgar. 1974. *Jurisprudence: The Philosophy and Method of the Law.* Rev. ed. Cambridge, MA: Harvard University Press.

Brooks, Richard O., and James Bernard Murphy (eds.). 2003. *Aristotle and Modern Law.* Burlington, VT: Ashgate.

Calvi, James V., and Susan Coleman. 2008. *American Law and Legal Systems.* 6th ed. Upper Saddle River, NJ: Prentice-Hall.

Camic, Charles, Philip S. Gorski, and David M. Trubek (eds). 2005. *Max Weber's Economy and Society: A Critical Companion.* Stanford, CA: Stanford University Press.

Cante, Richard C. 2010. *Gay Men and the Forms of Contemporary US Culture.* Burlington, VT: Ashgate.

Capaldo, Giuliana Ziccardi. 2009. *The Pillars of Global Law.* Burlington, VT: Ashgate.

Carrington, Paul D. 1984. "Of Law and the River," *Journal of Legal Education,* 34 (2) (June): 222–236.

Carrithers, David (ed.). 2010. *Charles-Louis de Secondat, Baron de Montesquieu.* Burlington, VT: Ashgate.

Chafetz, Janet Saltzman. 1997. "Feminist Theory and Sociology: Underutilized Contributions for Mainstream Theory," *Annual Review of Sociology,* 23: 97–121.

Chalcraft, David, Fanon Howell, Marisol Lopez Menendez, and Hector Vera (eds.). 2010. *Max Weber Matters: Interweaving Past and Present.* Burlington, VT; Ashgate.

Cooney, Mark. 1997. "The Decline of Elite Homicide," *Criminology,* 35 (3) (August): 381–401.

Coughlin, Anne M. 1994. "Excusing Women," *California Law Review,* 82 (1) (January): 1–93.

Chambliss, William J. 1978. "Toward a Political Economy of Crime." Pp. 191–211 in Charles

E. Reasons and Robert M. Rich (eds.), *The Sociology of Law: A Conflict Perspective.* Toronto, Canada: Butterworths.

Chambliss, William, and Robert Seidman. 1982. *Law, Order, and Power.* 2nd ed. Reading, MA: Addison-Wesley.

Chang, Robert S. 1993. "Toward an Asian American Legal Scholarship: Critical Race Theory, Post-Structuralism, and Narrative Space." *California Law Review,* 81 (5) (October): 1241–1323.

Chesney-Lind, Meda, and Lisa Pasko. 2004a. *The Female Offender: Girls, Women, and Crime.* 2nd ed. Thousand Oaks, CA: Sage Publications.

Chesney-Lind, Meda and Lisa Pasko (eds.). 2004b. *Girls, Women, and Crime: Selected Readings.* Thousand Oaks, CA: Sage Publications.

Cohen, Felix. 1959. *Ethical Systems and Legal Ideals.* New York: Cornell University Press.

Collier, Richard. 1995. *Masculinity, Law, and the Family.* New York: Routledge.

Collins, Hugh. 1996. *Marxism and Law.* New York: Oxford University Press.

Collins, Lawrence (ed.). 2000. *Dicey and Morris on the Conflict of Laws.* 13th ed. London, UK: Sweet & Maxwell.

Cotterrell, Roger (ed). 2006. *Law in Social Theory.* Burlington, VA: Ashgate. 2010. *Émile Durkheim. Justice, Morality and Politics.* Burlington, VT: Ashgate.

Culp, Jerome McCristal, Jr. 1994. "Colorblind Remedies and the Intersectionality of Oppression: Policy Arguments Masquerading as Moral Claims," *New York Law Review,* 69 (1) (April): 162–196.

Daston, Lorraine, and Michael Stolleis (eds.). 2010. *Natural Law and Laws of Nature in Early Modern Europe: Jurisprudence, Theology, Moral and Natural Philosophy.* Burlington, VT: Ashgate.

Delamont, Sara, 2003. *Feminist Sociology.* London, UK: Sage.

Delgado, Richard. 1994. "Rodrigo's Ninth Chronicle: Race, Legal Instrumentalism, and the Rule of Law," *University of Pennsylvania Law Review,* 143 (2) (December): 379–416. 2004. *Justice at War: Civil Liberties and Civil*

Rights During Times of Crisis. New York: New York University Press.

Delgado, Richard, and Jean Stefancic (eds.). 2000. *Critical Race Theory: The Cutting Edge.* Philadelphia, PA: Temple University Press.

Diamond, Arthur S. 1971. *Primitive Law: Past and Present.* London, UK: Methuen and Company, Ltd.

Dicey, Albert Venn. 1905. *Lectures on the Relation between the Law and Public Opinion in England During During the Nineteenth Century.* London, UK: MacMillan.

Dixon, Jo, Aaron Kupchik, and Joachim Savelsberg (eds.). 2007. *Criminal Courts.* Burlington, VA: Ashgate.

Donnelly, Bebhinn. 2007. *A Natural Law Approach to Normativity.* Burlington, VT: Ashgate.

Doyle, Daniel P., and David F. Luckenbill. 1991. "Mobilizing Law in Response to Collective Problems: A Test of Black's Theory of Law," *Law & Society Review,* 25 (1): 103–116.

Durkheim, Émile. 1964. *The Division of Labor in Society.* Trans. George Simpson. New York: Free Press. Originally published in 1893.

Dyzenhaus, David (ed.). 2009. *Civil Rights and Security.* Burlington, VT: Ashgate.

Easton, Susan (ed.). 2009. *Marx and Law.* Burlington, VT: Ashgate.

Eder, Klaus. 1977. "Rationalist and Normative Approaches to the Sociological Study of Law," *Law & Society Review,* 12 (1) (Fall): 133–144.

Eisenstadt, S. N. 1972. "Intellectuals and Tradition," *Daedelus,* 101 (2): 1–19.

Eriksson, Anna. 2009. *Justice in Transition: Community Restorative Justice in Northern Ireland.* Devon, UK: Willan Publishing.

Eskridge, William N. Jr., and Nan D. Hunter. 1997. *Sexuality, Gender, and the Law.* Westburry, NY: The Foundation Press, Inc.

Evan, William M. 1990. *Social Structure and Law: Theoretical and Empirical Perspectives.* Newbury Park, CA: Sage Publications.

Farber, Daniel A. 1994. "The Outmoded Debate Over Affirmative Action," *California Law Review,* 82 (4) (July): 893–934.

Feinberg, Joel, and Jules Coleman (eds.). 2008. *Philosophy of Law.* 8th ed. Belmont, CA: Wadsworth Publishing Company.

Fineman, Martha Albertson, Jack E. Jackson, and Adam P. Romero (eds.). 2009. *Feminist and Queer Legal Theory: Intimate Encounters and Uncomfortable Conversations.* Burlington, VT: Ashgate.

Fleury-Steiner, Benjamin, and Laura Beth Nielsen (eds). 2006. *The New Civil Rights Research: A Constitutive Approach.* Aldershot, Hants, UK/Burlington, VT: Ashgate.

Ford, Lynn E. 2006. *Women and Politics: The Pursuit of Equality.* 2nd ed. Boston, MA: Houghton Mifflin.

Frank, Jerome. 1930. *Law and the Modern Mind.* New York: Coward-McCann.

Franke, Katherine M. 2001. "Theorizing Yes: An Essay on Feminism, Law, and Desire," *Columbia Law Review* (January): 101–181.

Frazier, Patricia A., and Jennifer S. Hunt. 1998. "Research on Gender and the Law: Where Are We Going, Where Have We Been," *Law and Human Behavior,* 22 (1) (February): 1–16.

Friedman, Lawrence M. 1975. *The Legal System: A Social Science Perspective.* New York: Russell Sage Foundation. 1998. *American Law: An Introduction.* 2nd ed. New York: W.W. Norton & Co., Inc. 2002. *American Law in the Twentieth Century,* New Haven, CT: Yale University Press.

Frug, Mary Joe. 1992a. *Postmodern Legal Feminism.* New York: Routledge. 1992b. *Women and the Law.* Westbury, NY: The Foundation Press, Inc.

Fuller, Lon. 1969. *The Morality of Law.* Rev. ed. New Haven, CT: Yale University Press.

Galanter, Marc. 1977. "The Modernization of Law." Pp. 1046–1060 in Lawrence M. Friedman and Stewart Macaulay (eds.), *Law and the Behavioral Sciences.* 2nd ed. Indianapolis: Bobbs-Merrill.

George, Robert P. (ed.). 2003. *Natural Law.* Burlington, VT: Ashgate.

Glasbeek, Amanda. 2010. *Feminized Justice. The Toronto Women's Court, 1913–34.* Vancouver, BC: UBC Press.

Goldstein, Philip. 2005. *Post-Marxist Theory.* Albany, NY: State University of New York Press.

Goodrich, Peter. 1993. "Sleeping with the Enemy: An Essay on the Politics of Critical

Legal Studies in America," *New York University Law Review,* 68 (2) (May): 389–425.

Gottfredson, Michael R., and Michael J. Hindelang. 1979. "A Study of *The Behavior of Law,*" *American Sociological Review* 44 (1) (February): 3–18.

Grana, Sheryl. 2009. *Women and Justice.* 2nd ed. Lanham, MD: Rowman & Littlefield.

Greenberg, Judith G., Martha L. Minow, and Dorothy E. Roberts. 2008. *Women and the Law.* 4th ed. New York: Foundation Press.

Greer, Edward. 2000. "Awaiting Cassandra: The Trojan Mare of Legal Dominance Feminism (Part I)," *Women's Rights Law Reporter,* 21 (2) (Spring): 95–116.

Gross, Hyman. 1979. *A Theory of Criminal Justice.* New York: Oxford University Press.

Grossi, Paolo. 2010. *A History of European Law.* New York: Wiley-Blackwell.

Gurvitch, Georges. 1942. *Sociology of Law.* New York: Philosophical Library.

Hall, Jerome. 1952. *Theft, Law and Society.* 2nd ed. Indianapolis, IN: Bobbs-Merrill.

Harris, Angel P. 1994. "Forward: The Jurisprudence of Reconstruction. Symposium: Critical Race Theory," *California Law Review,* 82 (4) (July): 741–785.

Hayden, Carol, and Dennis Gough. 2010. *Implementing Restorative Justice in Children's Residential Care.* Bristol, UK: The Foundation Press.

Hayman, Robert L., Jr. 1995. "The Color of Tradition: Critical Race Theory and Postmodern Constitutional Traditionalism," *Harvard Civil Rights-Civil Liberties Law Review,* 30 (1) (Winter): 57–108.

Hearn, Jeff. 1992. *Men in the Public Eye.* London, UK: Routledge.

Heinzelman, Susan Sage. 2010. *Riding the Black Ram: Law, Literature, and Gender.* Palo Alto, CA: Stanford University Press.

Henry, Stuart, and Scott A. Lukas (eds.). 2009. *Recent Developments in Criminological Theories.* Burlington, VT: Ashgate.

Herbers, John. 1979. "Changes in Society Holding Back Youth in Jobless Web," *New York Times* (March 11): A1, A44.

Higgins, Tracy E. 1997. "Democracy and Feminism," *Harvard Law Review,* 110 (8) (June): 1657–1703.

Hoebel, E. Adamson. 1954. *The Law of Primitive Man: A Study in Comparative Legal Dynamics.* Cambridge, MA: Harvard University Press.

Holmes, Oliver Wendell. 1897. "The Path of Law," *Harvard Law Review,* (10) (March): 457–478. 2004. *The Common Law.* With a new introduction by Tim Griffin. New Brunswick, NJ: Transaction Publishers.

Horvath, Miranda, and Jennifer Brown (eds.). 2009. *Rape: Challenging Contemporary Thinking.* Devon, UK; Willan Publishing.

Huff, Toby E., and Wolfgang Schlucter (eds.). 1999. *Max Weber & Islam.* New Brunswick, NJ: Transaction Publishers.

Hunt, Alan. 1978. *The Sociological Movement in Law.* Philadelphia, PA: Temple University Press. 1993. *Explorations in Law and Society: Toward a Constitutive Theory of Law.* New York: Routledge.

Hunter, Ian. 2006. "What Next? Anti-Harassment Training in the Crib?" *The Globe and Mail* (December 29): A15.

Jarviluoma, Helmi, Pirkko Moisala, and Anni Vilkko. 2003. *Gender and Qualitative Methods.* Thousand Oaks, CA: Sage Publications.

Jeffery, C. Ray. 1957. "The Development of Crime in Early English Society," *Journal of Criminal Law, Criminology and Police Science,* 47:647–666.

Johnson, Alex M., Jr. 1997. "The Underrepresentation of Minorities in the Legal Profession: A Critical Race Theorist's Perspective," *Michigan Law Review,* 95 (4) (February): 1005–1062.

Keen, Lisa, and Suzanne B. Goldberg. 1998. *Strangers to the Law: Gay People on Trial.* Ann Arbor, MI: The University of Michigan Press.

Kennedy, Duncan. 2007. *Legal Education and the Reproduction of Hierarchy: A Polemic Against the System. A Critical Edition.* New York: New York University Press.

King, Lawrence Peter, and Iván Szelényi. 2004. *Theories of the New Class: Intellectuals and*

Power. Minneapolis, MN: University of Minnesota Press.

Kirton, John J., and Jelena Madunic (eds.). 2010. *Global Law.* Burlington, VT: Ashgate.

Kleinman, Sherryl. 2007. *Feminist Fieldwork Analysis.* Thousand Oaks, CA: Sage Publications.

Kolmar, Wendy K., and Frances Bartkowski (eds.). 2010. *Feminist Theory: A Reader.* 3rd ed. Boston, MA: McGraw-Hill Higher Education.

Kramer, Matthew H. 1995. *Critical Legal Theory and the Challenge of Feminism: A Philosophical Reconception.* Lanham, MD: Rowman & Littlefield Publishers, Inc.

Kritzer, Herbert M. (ed.). 2002. *Legal Systems of the World: A Political, Social, and Cultural Encyclopedia.* Santa Barbara, CA: ABC-CLIO.

Lassman, Peter (ed.). 2006. *Max Weber.* Burlington, VT: Ashgate.

Lessan, Gloria T., and Joseph F. Sheley. 1992. "Does Law Behave? A Macrolevel Test of Black's Propositions on Change in Law," *Social Forces,* 70 (3) (March): 655–678.

Llewellyn, Karl N., and E. Adamson Hoebel. 1941. *The Cheyenne Way: Conflict and Case Law in Primitive Jurisprudence.* Norman, OK: University of Oklahoma Press.

Lloyd, Sally A., April L. Few, and Katherine R. Allen. 2010. *Handbook of Family Studies.* Thousand Oaks, CA: Sage.

López, Ian Haney. 2006. *White by Law: The Legal Construction of Race.* New York: New York University Press.

López, Ian Haney (ed.). 2007. *Race, Law, and Society.* Aldershot, Hants, UK/Burlington, VT: Ashgate.

Lorber, Judith. 2009. *Gender Inequality: Feminist Theories and Politics.* 4th ed. New York: Oxford University Press.

Maine, Sir Henry Sumner. 1861. *Ancient Law.* London, UK: J. Murray. 2003. *Ancient Law,* 5th ed. *Its Connection with the Early History of Society, and its Relation to Modern Ideas.* Holmes Beach, FL: Gaunt.

Manning, Peter K. 1975. "Deviance and Dogma," *British Journal of Criminology,* 15 (1) (January): 1–20.

Marx, Karl. 1959. "A Contribution to the Critique of Political Economy.".Pp. 42–46 in L. S. Feuer (ed.), *Marx and Engles: Basic Writing on Politics and Philosophy.* Garden City, NY: Doubleday.

Marx, Karl, and Friedrich Engels. 1955. *The Communist Manifesto.* New York: Appleton-Century-Crofts. Originally published in 1848.

McCann, Charles R. 2004. *Individualism and the Social Order: The Social Element in Liberal Thought.* New York: Routledge.

McIntyre, Lisa J. 1994. *Law in the Sociological Enterprise: A Reconstruction.* Boulder, CO: Westview Press.

Merton, Robert K. 1957. *Social Theory and Social Structure.* New York: Free Press.

Michaels, Priscilla. 1978. "Review of Black's *The Behavior of Law,*" *Contemporary Sociology,* 7 (1) (January): 10–11.

Miller, Susan L. (ed.). 1998. *Crime Control and Women: Feminist Implications of Criminal Justice Policy,* Thousand Oaks, CA: Sage Publications, Inc.

Moran, Leslie J. (ed.). 2006. *Sexuality and Identity.* Burlington, VA: Ashgate.

Montesquieu, Baron De. 1886. *The Spirit of Laws.* Trans. Thomas Nugent. Cincinnati, OH: Robert Clarke and Co. Originally published 1748.

Mundy, Martha (ed.). 2002. *Law and Anthropology.* Aldershot, Hants, UK/Burlington, VT: Dartmouth/Ashgate.

Naffine, Ngaire. 1990. *Law and the Sexes: Explorations in Feminist Jurisprudence.* Sydney, Australia: Allen & Unwin.

Neacsu, E. Dana. 2000. "CLS Stands for Critical Legal Studies, If Anyone Remembers," *Journal of Law and Policy,* 8:415.

Nelken, David (ed.). 2009. *Beyond Law in Contex:. Developing a Sociological Understanding of Law.* Burlington, VT: Ashgate.

Nisbet, Robert A. 1969. *Social Change and History.* New York: Oxford University Press.

Nonet, Philippe. 1976. "For Jurisprudential Sociology," *Law & Society Review,* 10 (4) (Summer): 525–545.

Nonet, Philippe, and Philip Selznick. 2001. *Law and Society in Transition: Toward Responsive*

Law. New Brunswick, NJ: Transaction Publishers.

Novick, Sheldon M. 1989. *Honorable Justice: The Life of Oliver Wendell Holmes, Jr.* Boston, MA: Little Brown.

Nuijten, Monique, and Gerhard Anders (eds.). 2009. *Corruption and the Secret of Law: A Legal Anthropological Perspective.* Burlington, VT: Ashgate.

Parsons, Talcott. 1964. "Evolutionary Universals in Society," *American Sociological Review,* 29 (3) (June): 339–357.

Patterson, Dennis (ed.). 2010. *A Companion to Philosophy of Law and Legal Theory.* 2nd ed. Hoboken, NJ: Wiley-Blackwell.

Paxton, Pamela, and Melanie M. Hughes. 2007. *Women, Politics, and Power: A Global Perspective.* Thousand Oaks, CA: Pine Forge Press.

Pepinsky, Harold E. 1976. *Crime and Conflict: A Study of Law and Society.* New York: Academic Press.

Piaget, Jean. 1965. *The Moral Judgment of the Child.* New York: Free Press. Originally published in 1932.

Podgorecki, Adam. 1974. *Law and Society.* London, UK: Routledge & Kegan Paul. 1985. "Social Systems and Legal Systems—Criteria for Classification." Pp. 1–24 in Adam Podgorecki, Christopher J. Whelan, and Dinesh Khosla (eds.), *Legal Systems & Social Systems.* London, UK: Croom Helm.

Pollack, Ervin H. 1979. *Jurisprudence: Principles and Applications.* Columbus, OH: Ohio State University Press.

Pospisil, Leopold. 1971. *Anthropology of Law: A Comparative Theory.* New York: Harper & Row Publishers.

Pottage, Alain, and Martha Mundy (eds.). 2004. *Law, Anthropology, and the Constitution of the Social: Making Persons and Things.* New York: Cambridge University Press.

Pound, Roscoe. 1959. *Jurisprudence.* St. Paul, MN: West Publishing Company, Vols. 1 and 2.

Ptacek, James (ed.). 2009. *Restorative Justice and Violence Against Women.* New York: Oxford University Press.

Quinney, Richard. 1974. *Criminal Justice in America.* Boston, MA: Little Brown. 2002.

The Critique of Legal Order: Crime Control in Capitalist Society. New Brunswick: NJ: Transaction Books.

Radin, Margaret Jane. 1991. The Pragmatist and the Feminist." Pp. 127–153 in Michael Brint and William Weaver (eds.), *Pragmatism in Law and Society.* Boulder, CO: Westview Press.

Ramazanoglu, Caroline, and Janet Holland. 2002. *Feminist Methodology: Challenges and Choices.* Thousand Oaks, CA: Sage Publications.

Ransome, Paul. 2010. *Social Theory for Beginners.* Bristol, UK: The Policy Press.

Reasons, Charles E. 1974. *The Criminologist: Crime and the Criminal.* Pacific Palisades, CA: Goodyear.

Reasons, Charles E., and Robert M. Rich (eds.). 1978. *The Sociology of Law: A Conflict Perspective.* Toronto, Canada: Butterworths.

Rhode, Deborah L. 1991. "Feminist Critical Theories." Pp. 333–350 in Katharine T. Bartlett and Rosanne Kennedy (eds.), *Feminist Legal Theory: Readings in Law and Gender.* Boulder, CO: Westview Press.

Rhode, Deborah L., and Carol Sanger (eds.). 2005. *Gender Rights.* Burlington, VT: Ashgate.

Rich, Robert M. 1978. *The Sociology of Law: An Introduction to Theorists and Theories.* Washington, DC: University Press of America.

Richardson, Diane, and Steven Seidman (eds.). 2002. *Handbook of Lesbian and Gay Studies.* Thousand Oaks, CA: Sage Publications.

Ringer, Fritz. 2004. *Max Weber—An Intellectual Biography.* Chicago, IL: University of Chicago Press.

Robson, Ruthann. 1992. "Embodiment(s): The Possibilities of Lesbian Legal Theory in Bodies Problematized by Postmodernisms and Feminisms," *Law & Sexuality: A Review of Lesbian and Gay Legal Issues,* 2 (Summer): 37–80. 1994. "Resisting the Family: Repositioning Lesbians in Legal Theory," *Signs,* 19 (4) (Summer): 975–997.

Rokumoto, Kahei (ed.). 1994. *Sociological Theories of Law.* New York: New York University Press.

Rostow, Walt W. 1961. *The Stages of Economic Growth: A Non-Communist Manifesto.* New York: Cambridge.

Rouland, Norbert. 1994. *Legal Anthropology.* Trans. Philippe G. Planel. Stanford, CA: Stanford University Press.

Sajo, Andras. 2003. From Corruption to Extortion: Conceptualization of Post-communist Corruption. *Crime, Law, and Social Change,* 40 (2–3) (October): 171–195.

Sampford, Charles. 1989. *The Disorder of Law: A Critique of Legal Theory.* Oxford, UK: Basil Blackwell.

Scheppele, Kim Lane. 1994. "Legal Theory and Social Theory," *Annual Review of Sociology, Annual 1994,* 20: 383–407.

Schmaus, Warren. 2004. *Rethinking Durkheim and His Tradition.* New York: Cambridge University Press.

Schwartz, Bernard. 1974. *The Law in America: A History.* New York: McGraw-Hill.

Schwartz, Louis B. 1984. "With Gun and Camera through Darkest CRITS-Land," *Stanford Law Review,* 36 (1 & 2) (January): 413–464.

Schwartz, Richard D., and James C. Miller. 1975. "Legal Evolution and Societal Complexity." Pp. 52–62 in Ronald L. Akers and Richard Hawkins (eds.), *Law and Control in Society.* Englewood Cliffs, NJ: Prentice-Hall.

Selznick, Philip. 1961. "Sociology and Natural Law," *Natural Law Forum* 6:84–108.

Seron, Carroll (ed.). 2006. *Law and Society Cannon.* Burlington, VA: Ashgate.

Sherman, Lawrence W. 1978. "Review of *The Behavior of Law*," *Contemporary Sociology* 7 (1) (January): 10–15.

Shoemaker, Pamela J., James William Tankard, Jr., and Dominic L. Lasorsa. 2004. *How to Build Social Science Theories.* Thousand Oaks, CA: Sage.

Spencer, Herbert. 1899. *The Principles of Sociology. Vol.* II. New York: D. Appleton and Company.

Stein, Laura. 1999. *Sexual Harassment in America: A Documentary History.* Westport, CT: Greenwood Publishing Group, Inc.

Strickland, Ruth Ann. 2004. *Restorative Justice.* New York, NY: Peter Lang Publisher.

Sullivan, Nikki. 2004. *A Critical Introduction to Queer Theory.* New York: New York University Press.

Sumner, William Graham. 1940. "The Challenge of Facts." Pp. 67–93 in Maurice R. Davie (ed.), *Sumner Today.* New Haven, CT: Yale University Press. Originally published in 1886.

Tangley, Lord. 1965. *New Law for a New World.* London, UK: Stephens and Sons.

Tomasic, Roman. 1985. *The Sociology of Law.* London, UK: Sage Publications.

Trevino, A. Javier. 2008. *The Sociology of Law: Classical and Contemporary Perspectives.* New Brunswick, NJ: Transaction Publishers.

Treviño, A. Javier (ed). 2007 *The Classic Writings in Law and Society: Contemporary Comments and Criticisms.* New Brunswick, NJ: Transaction Books

Trubek, David M. 1984. "Where the Action Is: CRITS and Empiricism," *Stanford Law Review* 36 (1 & 2) (January): 575–622.

Trubek, David M., and John Esser. 1989. "Critical Empiricism in American Legal Studies: Paradox, Program, or Pandora's Box?" *Law & Social Inquiry,* 14 (1): 3–52.

Turk, Austin T. 1978. "Law as a Weapon in Social Conflict." Pp. 213–232 in Charles E. Reasons and Robert M. Rich (eds.), *The Sociology of Law: A Conflict Perspective.* Toronto, Canada: Butterworths.

Turner, Jonathan H. 1972. *Patterns of Social Organization: A Survey of Social Institutions.* New York: McGraw-Hill, 1974. "A Cybernetic Model of Legal Development," *Western Sociological Review,* (5): 3–16. 2003. *The Structure of Sociological Theory.* 7th ed. Belmont, CA: Wadsworth Publishing Company.

Turner, Jonathan H., and Alexandra R. Maryanski. 1979. *Functionalism.* Menlo Park, CA: Benjamin/Cummings. 1995. "Is 'Neofunctionalism' Really Functional?" Pp. 49–62 in Donald McQuarie (ed.), *Readings in Contemporary Sociological Theory: From Modernity to Post-Modernity.* NJ: Prentice Hall.

Turner, Jonathan H., Leonard Beeghley, and Charles H. Powers. 2007. *The Emergence of*

Sociological Theory. 6th ed. Belmont, CA: Thomson Higher Education.

Tushnet, Mark (ed.). 2008. *Legal Scholarship and Education.* Burlington, VT: Ashgate.

Unger, Roberto Mangabeira. 1976. *Law in Modern Society: Toward a Criticism of Social Theory.* New York: Free Press. 1983. "The Critical Legal Studies Movement," *Harvard Law Review,* 96 (3) (January): 561–675. 1986. *The Critical Legal Studies Movement.* Cambridge, MA: Harvard University Press. 1998. *Democracy Realized: The Progressive Alternative.* New York: Verso. 2004. *Politics: A Work in Constructive Social Theory.* New York: Verso. 2009. *The Left Alternative.* New York: Verso.

Unger, Roberto Mangabeira, and Cornel West. 1998. *The Future of American Progressivism: An Initiative for Political and Economic Reform.* Boston, MA: Beacon Press.

Vago, Steven. 2004. *Social Change.* 5th ed. Upper Saddle River, NJ: Prentice-Hall.

Valdes, Francisco. 1997. "Under Construction: LatCrit Consciousness, Community, and Theory," *California Law Review,* 85 (5) (October): 1087–1142.

Valdes, Francisco, Jerome McCristal Culp, and Angela P. Harris (eds.). 2002. *Crossroads, Directions, and a New Critical Race Theory.* Philadelphia, PA: Temple University Press

Van den Berghe, Pierre L. 1967. "Dialectic and Functionalism: Toward a Synthesis." Pp. 294–310 in N. Demerath and R. A. Peterson (eds.), *System Change and Conflict: A Reader on Contemporary Sociological Theory and the Debate over Functionalism.* New York: Free Press.

Weber, Max. 1954. *Law in Economy and Society.* Ed. Max Rheinstein and trans. Edward Shils and Max Rheinstein. Cambridge, MA: Harvard University Press. 1968. *Economy and Society.* Trans. Guenther Roth, and Claus Wittich. New York: Bedminster Press.

White, G. Edward. 2006. *Oliver Wendell Holmes: Sage of the Supreme Court.* New York: Oxford University Press,

Williams, Susan H. 2004. *Truth, Autonomy, and Speech: Feminist Theory and the First Amendment.* New York: New York University Press.

Williams, Wendy W. 1991. "The Equality Crisis: Some Reflections on Culture, Courts, and Feminism." Pp. 15–34 in Katharine T. Bartlett and Rosanne Kennedy (eds.), *Feminist Legal Theory: Readings in Law and Gender.* Boulder, CO: Westview Press.

Wing, Adrien Katherine (ed.). 2003. *Critical Race Feminism, A Reader,* 2nd ed. New York: New York University Press.

Wong, K. C. 1998. "Black's Theory on the Behavior of Law Revisited II: A Restatement of Black's Concept of Law," *International Journal of Sociology,* 26 (1) (March): 75–120.

Wormser, Rene. 1962. *The Story of Law.* Rev. ed. New York: Simon & Schuster.

Zernova, Margarita. 2008. *Restorative Justice. Ideals and Realities.* Burlington, VT: Ashgate.

Zifcak, Spencer (ed.). 2005. *Globalisation and the Rule of Law.* New York: Routledge.

CHAPTER

3

The Organization of Law

Nowadays, one way or another, more than ever before, law touches all of us. The contact may be pleasant or unpleasant, tangible or intangible, direct or indirect, but law is nonetheless a constant force and presence in our lives. For a sociological understanding of law in society, we need to know about the social organization of law, the types of social arrangements and relations involved in the legal process, and the social characteristics of people who interpret and administer the law (see, for example, Abadinsky, 2008; Higgins and Mackinem, 2010; Sarat, 2004, 2011). The intention of this chapter is to look at the social organization of legal systems in the framework of the judicial, legislative, administrative, and enforcement agencies that carry out the official (and, at times, the unofficial) business of law.

COURTS

Of the various functions of courts, unquestionably the most important is to process disputes (see, for example, Mays and Gregware, 2009). By definition, a dispute is a conflict of claims or rights—an assertion of right, claim, or demand on one side, met by contrary claims on the other. When courts hear disputes, they attempt to decide (adjudicate) between or among those who have some disagreement, misunderstanding, or competing claims. Such disputes may arise between individuals, between organizations (private or governmental), or between an individual and an organization. Jones may sue Smith to recover damages caused by a traffic accident; acting under the provisions of a civil rights statute, the federal government may sue the state of Mississippi to force its officials to stop discriminating against blacks in the electoral process; and the state of Washington may charge Doe with burglary and bring him to court to answer the charge. When a judge renders the official judgment of the trial court in a civil or a criminal case as to the defendant's guilt or innocence, the process is called *adjudication*.

Unlike legislative and administrative bodies, courts do not place issues on their own agendas (see, for example, Abadinsky, 2008; Abraham, 1998; Dixon, 2007). Judges generally do not decide to make rulings about voting rights, racial discrimination, or abortion, and then announce their "decisions." Rather, courts are passive; they must wait until matters are brought to them for resolution. The passivity of courts places the burden on citizens or organizations to recognize and define their own needs and problems and to determine which require legal judgments. As Donald Black (1973:138) notes, this method of acquiring cases "assumes that each individual will voluntarily and rationally pursue his own interests." The courts are indifferent to those issues or disputes that individuals or organizations fail to notice or wish to ignore. This reactive nature of courts ensures that they consider disputes only after the injuries have taken place or after the problems have developed.

In theory, courts differ from other kinds of dispute-regulation methods in that they are available to all members of society. In principle, everyone who has a dispute for which there is legal redress ought to be able to use the courts regardless of ethnic, racial, cultural, or other differences (Connolly, 2010). Unlike dispute-settlement methods that are available only to specific groups in society (for example, college grievance committees or religious tribunals), courts are truly public. Judicial resolution of disputes entails both the application of legal knowledge and the interpretation of events. The role of courts is to interpret and to apply law. Such judicial interpretation of law is expected to be impartial. Judges are expected to be governed by legal principles, not by personal preferences or by political pragmatism. In other countries, such as China, courts also have a propaganda function in adjudication and sentencing, which carry images and messages about the state, order, legitimacy, and the consequences of punishment, and are part of a wider program of social control and socialization (Peerenboom, 2009; Trevaskes, 2004).

Dispute Categories

The dispute-processing function of American courts, which will be discussed in detail in Chapter 6, is on the increase (see, for example, Palmer and Roberts, 1998, for the onset of precipitating factors). To understand what courts do, it is necessary to examine the kinds of disputes they process. Sheldon Goldman and Austin Sarat (1989:4–6) suggest that three important categories of disputes provide the bulk of work of American courts.

The first is called the *private* dispute. This kind of dispute is characterized by the absence of any initial participation by public authorities. For example, when a husband and wife quarrel, when two businesspersons debate the terms of a contract, and when two automobiles collide, these events are likely to give rise to private disputes. Although they may occur in public places and may involve competing interpretations of law, they remain private as long as the government is not a party. Because these disputes arise more or less spontaneously in the course of normal social life, they are usually processed and managed without the intervention of government. Many of these private disputes can be dealt with in the general context of ongoing relationships or through some kind of bargaining and negotiation. For example, the husband and wife may seek marriage counseling, the businessperson may arrive at a compromise through negotiation, and a settlement may be reached for the car accident through an insurance company. At times, however, nonlegal intervention is insufficient for the disputing parties. The courts may be asked to settle disputes in a large variety of civil cases where a party seeks legal redress in a private interest, such as for a breach of contract or for the use of a copyrighted story without permission.

The second category of disputes is called the *public-initiated* dispute. It occurs when the government seeks to enforce norms of conduct or to punish individuals who breach such norms. These kinds of public disputes emerge when society attempts to control and channel social behavior through the promulgation of binding legal norms. An illustration of the public-initiated dispute is the ordinary criminal case in which the state, or some official acting on its behalf, seeks to use the courts to determine whether a particular breach of law has occurred and whether sanctions should be applied. Public-initiated dispute is unique because it always involves and is governed by the law of the entire community. In the case of criminal law violation, dispute processing must occur in a public forum, for no society could allow the development of private mechanisms for the enforcement of breaches of public norms, since that could easily lead to anarchy. It should be noted, however, that not all public-initiated disputes are resolved or processed by means of judicial action. A variety of informal mechanisms, ranging from the warnings that a police officer may give to a traffic violator, to the prosecutor's choice not to go ahead with a criminal case, to the practice of plea bargaining, may be used to deal with breaches of public norms (Eisenstein and Jacob, 1977; Fisher, 2003; Forester, 2009). Furthermore, disputes involving the breach of public norms are, at times, not called to the attention of public authorities. For instance, the husband who beats his wife may have committed a violation of public norms, but until a complaint is lodged with or an arrest made by law enforcement agencies, their dispute remains private.

The third kind of dispute is the ***public defendant*** dispute. In this type, the government participates as a defendant. Such disputes involve challenges to the authority of some government agency or questions about the propriety of some government action that may be initiated by an individual or by an organization. In such cases, the courts are called upon to review the action of other branches of government. These disputes involve claims that the government has not abided by its own rules or followed procedures that it has prescribed. For instance, parents of children in racially segregated public schools might claim that school officials violated the U.S. Constitution's guarantee of equal protection of the laws. In general, such disputes come to court only after the aggrieved party has failed to remedy his or her grievance either through the political process or through procedures provided by the offending government agency.

These three types of disputes—private, public-initiated, and public defendant—represent, for the most part, the workload of American courts. It should be noted that, contrary to widespread beliefs, courts, in general, process rather than solve disputes. A court decision is seldom the last word in a dispute. For example, after a divorce decree, the aggrieving parties may continue to argue, not about settlements, but about visiting rights or proper supervision of children (see, for example, Sarat and Felstiner, 1995). Similarly, in many cities, court-ordered desegregation and busing did not resolve the issue of where children should go to school, not to mention the more enduring and underlying racial issues. Thus, it should be remembered that whether the disputes involve only two individuals who bring the case to court or whether cases have broader ramifications, court decisions are seldom the final word in a dispute. Let us now consider the structure of courts where decisions are rendered.

The Organization of Courts

The American court system is characterized by dual hierarchies. There are both state and federal courts, and their operation is sketched out in the American Courts System (see Figure 3-1). The structure is decentralized. Throughout American history, courts have been considered the third branch of government. Because they do not have an independent constitutional or political base, courts depend on the same political processes that sustain legislative and executive institutions. Each of the 50 states of the United States

FIGURE 3-1 American Court Systems Flowchart

Top Level Courts of Last Resort on Appeal

U.S. Supreme Court

The U.S. Supreme Court is free to accept or reject the cases it will hear. It must, however, hear certain rare mandatory appeals and cases within its original jurisdiction as specified by the U.S. Constitution.

State Supreme Courts of Appeal

Called the *State Supreme Court* in almost all states, it's the final court of appeal for all but a small number of state cases. If a case involves a right protected by the U.S. Constitution, the concerned party may appeal to the U.S. Circuit Court of Appeals.

U.S. Circuit Courts of Appeal

There are 12 of these courts based on state boundaries. Each state and U.S. District Court is in one of the 12 circuits. Each circuit court reviews cases from the U.S. district courts in its circuit. Appeals go to the U.S. Supreme Court.

U.S. Court of Appeals for the Federal Circuit (CAFC)

This court reviews civil appeals dealing with minor claims against the U.S. government, appeals in patent-right cases, and cases involving international trade disputes.

State Intermediate Courts of Appeal (ICAs)

Forty states have ICAs. These courts are the first court of appeals for most state cases. In 10 states, the state supreme court is the only court of appeals.

U.S. District Courts

There are 94 federal district courts, which handle criminal and civil cases involving:
– federal statutes
– U.S. Constitution
– citizens from different states and the amount of money at stake is more than $75,000. (This is the most common type of case in the U.S. district court.)

Most appeals from here go to the U.S. circuit courts of appeals; some go to the U.S. Court of Appeals for the Federal Circuit.

U.S. Court of International Trade

This court specializes in cases that involve international trade. Appeals go to the CAFC

U.S. Claims Court

This court deals with federal cases involving amounts over $10,000, conflicts from Indian Claims Commission, and cases involving some government contractors. Appeals go to the CAFC.

State Trial Courts

Almost all cases involving state civil and criminal laws are initially filed in state or local trial courts. They are typically called *municipal, county, district, circuit, or superior courts*. In the state of Washington, they are called *district courts*.

Appeals from the state trial court usually go to the state intermediate court of appeals.

About 95% of all court cases in the United States come through the state trial courts.

has its own court system, and, in addition, there is the federal court system. No two state court systems are alike; indeed, the differences both in the functions and in the labels given to American courts are many and bewildering, and no generalization is absolutely reliable for all states. Court systems have rarely been the product of long-range planning. Nearly all represent a series of patchwork accommodations to changing needs (see, for example Spohn and Hemmens, 2009, on court complexities).

Although the organization and the structure of state court systems vary widely, in most states there are (1) trial courts (commonly called district courts), where most civil and criminal cases are originally heard, often before a jury; (2) intermediate courts of appeals, which primarily review cases decided at the trial court level; and (3) a court of last resort (commonly called a state supreme court), whose primary function is to review cases decided by the lower appeals courts. In 2010, total justice expenditures comprised approximately 8 percent of all state and local public expenditures.

Federal and state court systems are separate from each other (Hughes, 1995). Most of the nation's legal business is settled in state courts under the provision of state law. However, state court decisions that involve a "federal question"—that is, decisions that present a question involving the Constitution (such as free speech) or federal laws (such as racial or sexual discrimination)—may be appealed to the U.S. Supreme Court (Pfander, 2009).

The federal district courts carry most of the workload of the federal courts. At least one court of this type exists in every state, although some of the larger states are subdivided into several districts. There are 94 district courts and 649 district court judges. The number of judges and case filings ranges from 2 judges and a caseload of 589 in Vermont to 28 judges and 11,169 filings in Manhattan, New York (Yackle, 2010). A single judge usually presides over trials in the district courts for various cultural and sociological dimensions of trials (see, for example, Umphrey, 2009). Juries are used in about half of the more than one million criminal and civil cases decided each year by these courts.

In the hierarchy of the federal judiciary, the several courts of appeals are immediately above the district courts. The nation is divided into 12 geographically defined jurisdictions, called "circuits," and 1 nationwide specialized jurisdiction. There is a court of appeals with a panel of three judges in each circuit. The chief function of these courts is to review decisions made by the district courts within their jurisdictions. They are also empowered to review the decisions of federal regulatory agencies, such as the Federal Trade Commission.

Thus, the typical court case begins in a trial court in the state or federal court system. Most cases go no further than the trial court. For example, the criminal defendant is convicted (by a trial or by a guilty plea) and sentenced by the trial court, and his or her case ends. The personal injury suit ends in a judgment by a trial court (or an out-of-court settlement by the parties while the court suit is pending), and the disputants leave the court system. Some litigants, however, who are not fully satisfied with the decision of a trial court may, by right, file an appeal. An appeal may take one of two forms: a trial *de novo* (a new trial) or a more limited review of specific aspects of a trial proceeding. For example, a criminal defendant who believes that his or her conviction was based on errors by the trial judge (such as the admission of evidence that should have been excluded) may seek a new trial. In other instances, a litigant may seek a review of certain aspects of the trial based on procedural grounds. Most states have only one appellate court, usually known as the state supreme court. This court hears appeals from all trial court decisions, criminal and civil, except those of minor courts. State supreme courts render the final decision for all cases involving state law. The U.S. Supreme Court renders the final verdict on all matters involving federal law or the federal Constitution (see, for example, Baum, 2010; McCloskey, 2010; Pfander, 2009).

In the lower court, the burden of appealing falls on the losing party. In a criminal case, the prosecutor is prohibited from appealing an acquittal. The sole function of appellate courts is to correct errors committed in law by the trial courts. As disputes move from the trial to the appellate level, they are typically transformed. They become almost exclusively disputes about law or about procedures; issues of law or questions concerning the way the trial was conducted are argued in appellate courts. Usually, the facts produced by the trial proceedings are not disputed at the appellate level. Time allotted for oral arguments before appellate courts is limited. Disputes are conducted primarily through briefs, motions, and memoranda. In a sense, disputes in appellate courts are a "lawyers' game." In trial courts, decisions are rendered by a single judge or shared by a judge and jury. In appellate courts, the decision-making process involves only judges. Some appellate courts have only a single judge, although most have several judges. Disputing in appellate courts is far removed in time and substance from the events that gave rise to the original disagreement. The original parties, their dispute, and its specific resolution become less important than the legal context into which they are placed.

Participants in Court Processes

In the United States, courts, as dispute-processing institutions, are composed of four distinct groups of participants—litigants, lawyers, judges, and juries. (In other countries, such as the Netherlands, there is also lay participation in court processes, which theoretically could constitute a fifth group [see, for example, Malsch, 2010].) These participants, in turn, bring to the judicial process diverse interests, values, and perspectives that influence the ways in which disputes are processed. I shall discuss these different types of participants separately.

Litigants Because the principal function of courts is to process disputes, the most obvious participants are the disputants. This group includes individuals, organizations, and government officials who are trying to settle disagreements and to regulate their own behavior and the behavior of others. Clearly, not all individuals, groups, or organizations can resort or are willing to resort to courts in their attempts to settle disputes. Questions of cost, efficiency, availability, the fulfillment of the legal requirements of a suit, and the nature of the dispute affect the potential users of courts differently. Consequently, two distinct types of litigants emerge.

In an often-cited classic study, Marc Galanter (1974) designates the two types of litigants as "one-shotters" and "repeat players" who have not changed over the years. The litigants are distinguished by the relative frequency with which they resort to court services. As will be shown in Chapter 6, those who use the courts only occasionally are called one-shotters. Illustrations of one-shotters include an author suing his publisher for breach of contract and a female professor filing charges against her university for alleged sexual discrimination in promotion. Repeat players are those who engage in many similar litigations over a period of time. Whereas one-shotters are usually individuals, repeat players are organizations, such as finance companies, moving companies, the Internal Revenue Service (IRS), or insurance companies. Their investment and interest in a particular case are moderately small. Because of their high frequency of participation in litigation, repeat players are more concerned with the ways a decision may affect the disposition of similar cases in the future than with the outcome of a single case (Ross, 1980). Repeat players can also invest greater resources in litigation than one-shotters, and their frequent appearances in court enable them to develop expertise. Such expertise is reflected in the way in which they select cases for litigation and in the manner in which they carry on disputes that have been transformed into lawsuits.

By contrast, participants who have only a one-time interest in litigation are generally more concerned with the substantive result of their case than the way in which the outcome may in the future affect the disposition of other cases. For example, the author in the preceding illustration is more concerned with winning his case against the publisher than with setting a precedent for similar cases. The IRS, on the other hand, is more interested in maintaining specific rules (such as those governing charitable deductions or computers) than with winning one particular case. Organizations, in general, participate in litigation as plaintiffs, and individuals participate as defendants. Both governmental and nongovernmental organizations have greater access to resources, and they are the most frequent initiators of court cases to process disputes between themselves and private individuals with whom they are dealing.

Lawyers   Law is a technical game, and the players have to be highly trained in its complex rules and elusive categories. Without the assistance of attorneys, most individuals would be unable to activate the courts on their own behalf. The operation of courts is based on special standards and rules established by law. The process of identifying and applying rules requires special training and expertise, which is provided by members of the legal profession. Lawyers occupy an intermediary position between disputants and courts and transform litigants' complaints into legal disputes. Disputants generally need to retain the services of lawyers to receive advice about legal rules and how those rules apply to specific issues in dispute. By being familiar with both court operations and legal rules, lawyers are instrumental in determining whether a particular dispute warrants judicial intervention. Lawyers in effect play the role of gatekeepers for the judiciary (Hughes, 1995:109).

Lawyers are repeat players in the adjudication process. Only a small proportion of lawyers are involved in actual litigation. Most are concerned with specific nontrial activities, such as writing wills or carrying out routine transactions. As will be discussed in Chapter 8, some of the trial attorneys specialize in particular areas of the law (such as divorce law or criminal law), and others represent only particular kinds of clients (such as corporations or universities) or limit themselves to particular clients within specified areas of law (such as taxes). Jonathan Casper (1972), in an often-cited study, distinguishes among types of trial lawyers by the manner in which they perceive their clientele. He argues that a small number of attorneys view themselves principally as representatives of public interests. These attorneys are concerned, for example, with consumer interests or with the protection of the environment. For them, individual cases are simply vehicles for achieving broad public objectives that generally necessitate major changes in the law. They prefer to take only cases they believe involve significant issues. The second type of lawyer represents particular interests or organizations. For example, some companies have their in-house lawyers whose principal role is to represent members of the organization.

The third type of lawyer, typically criminal defense lawyers, is most often involved in actual court work and, therefore, is considered in greater detail in this chapter. These lawyers are legal specialists who most closely approximate the public's preconception of lawyers. They handle a broad range of felonies and misdemeanors, with only a rare petty offense, traffic, or personal injury case (Wice, 1978:29–30). Although the role of defense lawyers is most often couched in the general term of "defending a client," defense lawyers perform a number of specific roles. These include the roles of advocate, intermediary, and counselor (Cohn, 1976:261). In the primary role of *advocate*, defense lawyers take all possible steps within legal and ethical bounds to achieve a victory for the client, while protecting the rights of the client at each step of the criminal justice process. Often, this can best be accomplished by acting as an *intermediary* between the client and the law, working through negotiation and compromise to secure the best possible benefits from the system. The third role is that of *counselor*. It is the responsibility of defense to give advice to the client as to what to expect and what appears to be in the client's best interest. Although most people would agree that defense attorneys should perform the foregoing functions, it is often suggested that they fail to do so. For example, Abraham S. Blumberg echoes some of the still prevailing criticisms of defense lawyers. He argues:

> The real key to understanding the role of defense counsel in a criminal case is the fixing and collection of his fee. It is a problem which influences to a significant degree the criminal court process itself, not just the relationship of the lawyer and his client. In essence, a lawyer–client "confidence game" is played. (Blumberg, 1979:242)

Blumberg charges that defense lawyers make sure that the clients know that there is an important connection between fee payment and the zealous exercise of professional expertise, secret knowledge, and organizational "connections" in their behalf. He contends that defense lawyers manipulate their clients and stage-manage cases to offer at least the appearance of services. He calls the criminal lawyer a "double agent" because the main concern of a criminal lawyer is to maintain good relations with members of the court organization. The defense lawyer may give the impression of being an impartial professional who will do everything possible for the client; however, he or she is, in reality, dependent on the goodwill of the prosecutor and the court.

The fourth type of trial lawyer perceives a lawyer's role primarily as serving individuals who retain him or her as opposed to government-appointed attorneys. These lawyers are often referred to as "hired guns" (Blumberg, 1979:238). They are interested only in the case in which they are involved, and they will do everything within legal and ethical limits to ensure favorable outcomes for their clients. In their view, they serve a case, not a cause. These different types of lawyers behave differently in advising clients whether to litigate and in preparing strategies of litigation.

Judges Although a variety of officials work around courtrooms, none has the prestige of the judge, who is responsible for the administration of the court and its reputation for honesty and impartiality and the occasional controversial decisions (Posner, 2009). The courtroom is designed so that attention is focused on the judge, who sits on a pedestal above the other participants. Any visitor to a courtroom will notice that the visitors' gallery never rises above the judge and that those who work in the courtroom are not allowed to sit or stand at the judge's level. The judge is the only official in the courtroom who wears special attire—a robe. When the judge enters the courtroom, everyone rises, and all attention is directed at him or her. The judge is addressed as "Your Honor," regardless of individual predilections (Jacob, 1984:10). The judge alone interprets the rules that govern the proceedings, although this power may be shared with a jury of laypersons, and the judges see themselves as autonomous decision makers whom nobody bosses around (Jacob, 1997:3; see also Spohn, 2009, for the broader picture).

In addition to the basic adjudication functions and the control of the flow of litigation in the courtroom, the judge is also responsible for administering his or her own court. This entails a variety of "housekeeping" tasks, such as appointing clerical assistants, drawing up a budget, and making certain that the physical facilities are adequate for the court's operation. The judge is also instrumental in pretrial conferences and, by law, has a great deal of discretionary power (such as jury instruction on admission of evidence), which has important implications on the consideration and outcome of cases (Philips, 1998; Pinkele and Louthan, 1985). Because of this prestigious role, the judge also performs a variety of nonjudicial functions, such as appointing officials to public agencies (for example, to the board of education, as district attorneys in some states, and, at times, to lucrative patronage positions).

Judges come from the middle or upper classes and have a history of party identification, nomination, and appointment (see, for example, the stacking of the judiciary during the second term of the presidency of George W. Bush), if not activism (Carp et al., 2010; Schmidhauser, 1979:49–55). Federal court judges are nominated by the president and confirmed by a majority vote in the U.S. Senate. These federal judges hold office for life, subject to removal only by impeachment or by conviction of a major crime. State and local judges are chosen by a variety of methods: Some are elected, some are appointed, and some are chosen by a method that combines election and appointment. In the combined election and appointment system, judges are appointed by an executive (such as a governor), and after completing a term in office, they must secure voter support to serve further terms. This type of system also has a selection procedure in which the executive's choice for a judgeship is screened through a commission or limited to nominees made by a commission. When elected, a majority of judges at the state level serve for a limited period, such as a six-year term (Volcansek and Lafon, 1988). Nowadays, running for judgeship can be an expensive proposition; judicial campaigns in many states now include large war chests, consultants, and attack advertising (Streb, 2009). Some candidates for state supreme courts spend more than $1 million for campaigns. To combat interest-group pressures, increased campaign fund-raising for judicial races, and the resulting cynicism about the courts, public financing of judicial campaigns is an idea whose time has come (Glaberson, 2001). Table 3-1 reviews the selection processes and retention terms for judges by states as of June 1, 2010.

TABLE 3-1   Judicial Selection and Retention by States as of June 1, 2010

ALABAMA

Supreme Court
Elective System: Partisan election
Initial Term of Office: 6 years
Method of Retention: Reelection (6-year term)

Court of Civil Appeals
Elective System: Partisan election
Initial Term of Office: 6 years
Method of Retention: Reelection (6-year term)

Court of Criminal Appeals
Elective System: Partisan election
Initial Term of Office: 6 years
Method of Retention: Reelection (6-year term)

Circuit Court
Elective System: Partisan election
Initial Term of Office: 6 years
Method of Retention: Retention election (6-year term)

ALASKA

Supreme Court
Appointive System: Merit selection through nominating commission
Initial Term of Office: 3 years
Method of Retention: Retention election (10-year term)

Court of Appeals
Appointive System: Merit selection through nominating commission
Initial Term of Office: 3 years
Method of Retention: Retention election (8-year term)

Superior Court
Appointive System: Merit selection through nominating commission
Initial Term of Office: 3 years
Method of Retention: Retention election (6-year term)

ARIZONA

Supreme Court
Appointive System: Merit selection through nominating commission
Initial Term of Office: 2 years
Method of Retention: Retention election (6-year term)

Court of Appeals
Appointive System: Merit selection through nominating commission
Initial Term of Office: 2 years
Method of Retention: Retention election (6-year term)

ARKANSAS

Supreme Court
Elective System: Nonpartisan election
Initial Term of Office: 8 years
Method of Retention: Reelection for additional 8-year terms

Court of Appeals
Elective System: Nonpartisan election
Initial Term of Office: 8 years
Method of Retention: Reelection for additional 8-year terms

Circuit Court
Elective System: Nonpartisan election
Initial Term of Office: 4 years
Method of Retention: Reelection for additional 4-year terms

Chancery Court and Probate Court
Elective System: Nonpartisan election
Initial Term of Office: 6 years
Method of Retention: Reelection for additional 6-year terms

CALIFORNIA

Supreme Court
Appointive System: Gubernatorial appointment without nominating commission
Initial Term of Office: 12 years
Method of Retention: Retention election (12-year term)

Courts of Appeal
Appointive System: Gubernatorial appointment without nominating commission
Initial Term of Office: 12 years
Method of Retention: Retention election (12-year term)

Superior Court
Elective System: Nonpartisan election
Initial Term of Office: 6 years
Method of Retention: Nonpartisan election (6-year term)

COLORADO

Supreme Court
Appointive System: Merit selection through nominating commission
Initial Term of Office: 2 years
Method of Retention: Retention election (10-year term)

Court of Appeals
Appointive System: Merit selection through nominating commission
Initial Term of Office: 2 years
Method of Retention: Retention election (8-year term)

District Court
Appointive System: Merit selection through nominating commission
Initial Term of Office: 2 years
Method of Retention: Retention election (6-year term)

CONNECTICUT

Supreme Court
Appointive System: Merit selection through nominating commission
Initial Term of Office: 8 years
Method of Retention: Commission reviews incumbent's performance on noncompetitive basis;
governor renominates and legislature confirms

(Continued)

TABLE 3-1 (Continued)

Appellate Court
Appointive System: Merit selection through nominating commission
Initial Term of Office: 8 years
Method of Retention: Commission reviews incumbent's performance on noncompetitive basis; governor renominates and legislature confirms

Superior Court
Appointive System: Merit selection through nominating commission
Initial Term of Office: 8 years
Method of Retention: Commission reviews incumbent's performance on noncompetitive basis; governor renominates and legislature confirms

DELAWARE

Supreme Court
Appointive System: Merit selection through nominating commission
Initial Term of Office: 12 years
Method of Retention: Reappointment

Court of Chancery
Appointive System: Merit selection through nominating commission
Initial Term of Office: 12 years
Method of Retention: Reappointment

Superior Court
Appointive System: Merit selection through nominating commission
Initial Term of Office: 12 years
Method of Retention: Reappointment

DISTRICT OF COLUMBIA

Court of Appeals
Appointive System: Merit selection through nominating commission
Initial Term of Office: 15 years
Method of Retention: Reappointment by judicial tenure commission

Superior Court
Appointive System: Merit selection through nominating commission
Initial Term of Office: 15 years
Method of Retention: Reappointment by judicial tenure commission

FLORIDA

Supreme Court
Appointive System: Merit selection through nominating commission
Initial Term of Office: 1 year
Method of Retention: Retention election (6-year term)

District Court of Appeal
Appointive System: Merit selection through nominating commission
Initial Term of Office: 1 year
Method of Retention: Retention election (6-year term)

Circuit Court
Elective System: Nonpartisan election
Initial Term of Office: 6 years
Method of Retention: Reelection for additional 6-year terms

GEORGIA

Supreme Court
Elective System: Nonpartisan election
Initial Term of Office: 6 years
Method of Retention: Reelection for additional 6-year terms

Court of Appeals
Elective System: Nonpartisan election
Initial Term of Office: 6 years
Method of Retention: Reelection for additional 6-year terms

Superior Court
Elective System: Nonpartisan election
Initial Term of Office: 4 years
Method of Retention: Reelection for additional 4-year terms

HAWAII

Supreme Court
Appointive System: Merit selection through nominating commission
Initial Term of Office: 10 years
Method of Retention: Reappointed to subsequent term by the judicial selection commission
(10-year term)

Intermediate Court of Appeals
Appointive System: Merit selection through nominating commission
Initial Term of Office: 10 years
Method of Retention: Reappointed to subsequent term by the judicial selection commission
(10-year term)

Circuit Court and Family Court
Appointive System: Merit selection through nominating commission
Initial Term of Office: 10 years
Method of Retention: Reappointed to subsequent term by the judicial selection commission
(10-year term)

IDAHO

Supreme Court
Elective System: Nonpartisan election
Initial Term of Office: 6 years
Method of Retention: Reelection for additional 6-year terms

Court of Appeals
Elective System: Nonpartisan election
Initial Term of Office: 6 years
Method of Retention: Reelection for additional 6-year terms

District Court
Elective System: Nonpartisan election
Initial Term of Office: 4 years
Method of Retention: Reelection for additional 4-year terms

ILLINOIS

Supreme Court
Elective System: Partisan election
Initial Term of Office: 10 years
Method of Retention: Retention election (10-year term)

(Continued)

TABLE 3-1   (Continued)

Appellate Court
Elective System: Partisan election
Initial Term of Office: 10 years
Method of Retention: Retention election (10-year term)

Circuit Court
Elective System: Partisan election
Initial Term of Office: 6 years
Method of Retention: Retention election (6-year term)

INDIANA

Supreme Court
Appointive System: Merit selection through nominating commission
Initial Term of Office: 2 years
Method of Retention: Retention election (10-year term)

Court of Appeals
Appointive System: Merit selection through nominating commission
Initial Term of Office: 2 years
Method of Retention: Retention election (10-year term)

IOWA

Supreme Court
Appointive System: Merit selection through nominating commission
Initial Term of Office: 1 year
Method of Retention: Retention election (8-year term)

Court of Appeals
Appointive System: Merit selection through nominating commission
Initial Term of Office: 1 year
Method of Retention: Retention election (6-year term)

District Court
Appointive System: Merit selection through nominating commission
Initial Term of Office: 1 year
Method of Retention: Retention election (6-year term)

KANSAS

Supreme Court
Appointive System: Merit selection through nominating commission
Initial Term of Office: 1 year
Method of Retention: Retention election (6-year term)

Court of Appeals
Appointive System: Merit selection through nominating commission
Initial Term of Office: 1 year
Method of Retention: Retention election (4-year term)

District Court (17 districts)
Appointive System: Merit selection through nominating commission
Initial Term of Office: 1 year
Method of Retention: Retention election (4-year term)

District Court (14 districts)
Elective System: Partisan election
Initial Term of Office: 4 years
Method of Retention: Reelection for additional 4-year terms

KENTUCKY

Supreme Court
Elective System: Nonpartisan election
Initial Term of Office: 8 years
Method of Retention: Reelection for additional 8-year terms

Court of Appeals
Elective System: Nonpartisan election
Initial Term of Office: 8 years
Method of Retention: Reelection for additional 8-year terms

Circuit Court
Elective System: Nonpartisan election
Initial Term of Office: 8 years
Method of Retention: Reelection for additional 8-year terms

LOUISIANA

Supreme Court
Elective System: Partisan election
Initial Term of Office: 10 years
Method of Retention: Reelection for additional 10-year terms

Court of Appeals
Elective System: Partisan election
Initial Term of Office: 10 years
Method of Retention: Reelection for additional 10-year terms

District Court
Elective System: Partisan election
Initial Term of Office: 6 years
Method of Retention: Reelection for additional 10-year terms

MAINE

Supreme Judicial Court
Appointive System: Gubernatorial appointment without nominating commission
Initial Term of Office: 7 years
Method of Retention: Reappointment by governor, subject to legislative confirmation

Superior Court
Appointive System: Gubernatorial appointment without nominating commission
Initial Term of Office: 7 years
Method of Retention: Reappointment by governor, subject to legislative confirmation

MARYLAND

Court of Appeals
Appointive System: Merit selection through nominating commission
Initial Term of Office: 15 years
Method of Retention: Retention election (10-year term)

(Continued)

TABLE 3-1 (Continued)

Court of Special Appeals
Appointive System: Merit selection through nominating commission
Initial Term of Office: 10 years
Method of Retention: Retention election (10-year term)

Circuit Court
Appointive System: Merit selection through nominating commission
Initial Term of Office: 15 years
Method of Retention: Nonpartisan election (15-year term)

MASSACHUSETTS

Supreme Judicial Court
Appointive System: Merit selection through nominating commission
Initial Term of Office: Until age 70
Method of Retention: NA

Appeals Court
Appointive System: Merit selection through nominating commission
Initial Term of Office: Until age 70
Method of Retention: NA

Trial Court of Massachusetts
Appointive System: Merit selection through nominating commission
Initial Term of Office: Until age 70
Method of Retention: NA

MICHIGAN

Supreme Court
Elective System: Partisan election
Initial Term of Office: 8 years
Method of Retention: Reelection for additional 8-year terms

Court of Appeals
Elective System: Partisan election
Initial Term of Office: 6 years
Method of Retention: Reelection for additional 6-year terms

Circuit Court
Elective System: Partisan election
Initial Term of Office: 6 years
Method of Retention: Reelection for additional 6-year terms

MINNESOTA

Supreme Court
Elective System: Nonpartisan election
Initial Term of Office: 6 years
Method of Retention: Reelection for additional 6-year terms

Court of Appeals
Elective System: Nonpartisan election
Initial Term of Office: 6 years
Method of Retention: Reelection for additional 6-year terms

District Court
Elective System: Nonpartisan election
Initial Term of Office: 6 years
Method of Retention: Reelection for additional 6-year terms

MISSISSIPPI

Supreme Court
Elective System: Nonpartisan election
Initial Term of Office: 8 years
Method of Retention: Reelection for additional 8-year terms

Court of Appeals
Elective System: Nonpartisan election
Initial Term of Office: 8 years
Method of Retention: Reelection for additional 8-year terms

Chancery Court
Elective System: Nonpartisan election
Initial Term of Office: 4 years
Method of Retention: Reelection for additional 4-year terms

Circuit Court
Elective System: Nonpartisan election
Initial Term of Office: 4 years
Method of Retention: Reelection for additional 4-year terms

MISSOURI

Supreme Court
Appointive System: Merit selection through nominating commission
Initial Term of Office: 1 year
Method of Retention: Retention election (12-year term)

Court of Appeals
Appointive System: Merit selection through nominating commission
Initial Term of Office: 1 year
Method of Retention: Retention election (12-year term)

Circuit Court (excluding Jackson, Clay, Platte, and Saint Louis counties)
Elective System: Partisan election
Initial Term of Office: 6 years
Method of Retention: Reelection for additional 6-year terms

Circuit Court (Jackson, Clay, Platte, and Saint Louis counties only)
Appointive System: Merit selection through nominating commission
Initial Term of Office: 1 year
Method of Retention: Retention election (6-year term)

MONTANA

Supreme Court
Elective System: Nonpartisan election
Initial Term of Office: 8 years
Method of Retention: Reelection; unopposed judges run for retention

(Continued)

TABLE 3-1 (Continued)

District Court
Elective System: Nonpartisan election
Initial Term of Office: 6 years
Method of Retention: Reelection; unopposed judges run for retention

NEBRASKA

Supreme Court
Appointive System: Merit selection through nominating commission
Initial Term of Office: 3 years
Method of Retention: Retention election (6-year term)

Court of Appeals
Appointive System: Merit selection through nominating commission
Initial Term of Office: 3 years
Method of Retention: Retention election (6-year term)

District Court
Appointive System: Merit selection through nominating commission
Initial Term of Office: 3 years
Method of Retention: Retention election (6-year term)

NEVADA

Supreme Court
Elective System: Nonpartisan election
Initial Term of Office: 6 years
Method of Retention: Reelection for additional 6-year terms

District Court
Elective System: Nonpartisan election
Initial Term of Office: 6 years
Method of Retention: Reelection for additional 6-year terms

NEW HAMPSHIRE

Supreme Court
Appointive System: Merit selection through nominating commission
Initial Term of Office: Until age 70
Method of Retention: NA

Superior Court
Appointive System: Merit selection through nominating commission
Initial Term of Office: Until age 70
Method of Retention: NA

NEW JERSEY

Supreme Court
Appointive System: Gubernatorial appointment without nominating commission
Initial Term of Office: 7 years
Method of Retention: Reappointment by governor (until age 70) with advice and consent of the U.S. Senate

Appellate Division of Superior Court
Appointive System: Gubernatorial appointment without nominating commission
Initial Term of Office: 7 years
Method of Retention: Reappointment by governor (until age 70) with advice and consent of the U.S. Senate

Superior Court
Appointive System: Gubernatorial appointment without nominating commission
Initial Term of Office: 7 years
Method of Retention: Reappointment by governor (until age 70) with advice and consent of the U.S. Senate

NEW MEXICO

Supreme Court
Appointive System: Merit selection through nominating commission
Initial Term of Office: Until next general election
Method of Retention: Retention election

Court of Appeals
Appointive System: Merit selection through nominating commission
Initial Term of Office: Until next general election
Method of Retention: Retention election

District Court
Appointive System: Merit selection through nominating commission
Initial Term of Office: Until next general election
Method of Retention: Retention election

NEW YORK

Court of Appeals
Appointive System: Merit selection through nominating commission
Initial Term of Office: 14 years
Method of Retention: Gubernatorial appointment from nominating commission with Senate consent

Appellate Division of the Supreme Court
Appointive System: Merit selection through nominating commission
Initial Term of Office: 5 years
Method of Retention: Commission reviews and recommends for or against reappointment by governor

Supreme Court
Elective System: Partisan election
Initial Term of Office: 14 years
Method of Retention: Reelection for additional 14-year terms

County Court
Elective System: Partisan election
Initial Term of Office: 10 years
Method of Retention: Reelection for additional 10-year terms

NORTH CAROLINA

Supreme Court
Elective System: Nonpartisan election
Initial Term of Office: 8 years
Method of Retention: Reelection for additional 8-year terms

Court of Appeals
Elective System: Nonpartisan election
Initial Term of Office: 8 years
Method of Retention: Reelection for additional 8-year terms

(Continued)

TABLE 3-1 (Continued)

Superior Court
Elective System: Nonpartisan election
Initial Term of Office: 8 years
Method of Retention: Reelection for additional 8-year terms

NORTH DAKOTA

Supreme Court
Elective System: Nonpartisan election
Initial Term of Office: 10 years
Method of Retention: Reelection for additional 10-year terms

District Court
Elective System: Nonpartisan election
Initial Term of Office: 6 years
Method of Retention: Reelection for additional 6-year terms

OHIO

Supreme Court
Elective System: Partisan election
Initial Term of Office: 6 years
Method of Retention: Reelection for additional 6-year terms

Court of Appeals
Elective System: Partisan election
Initial Term of Office: 6 years
Method of Retention: Reelection for additional 6-year terms

District Court
Elective System: Partisan election
Initial Term of Office: 6 years
Method of Retention: Reelection for additional 6-year terms

OKLAHOMA

Supreme Court
Appointive System: Merit selection through nominating commission
Initial Term of Office: 1 year
Method of Retention: Retention election (6-year term)

Court of Criminal Appeals
Appointive System: Merit selection through nominating commission
Initial Term of Office: 1 year
Method of Retention: Retention election (6-year term)
Court of Appeals
Appointive System: Merit selection through nominating commission
Initial Term of Office: 1 year
Method of Retention: Retention election (6-year term)

District Court
Elective System: Nonpartisan election
Initial Term of Office: 4 years
Method of Retention: Reelection for additional 4-year terms

OREGON

Supreme Court
Elective System: Nonpartisan election
Initial Term of Office: 6 years
Method of Retention: Reelection for additional 6-year terms

Court of Appeals
Elective System: Nonpartisan election
Initial Term of Office: 6 years
Method of Retention: Reelection for additional 6-year terms

Circuit Court
Elective System: Nonpartisan election
Initial Term of Office: 6 years
Method of Retention: Reelection for additional 6-year terms

Tax Court
Elective System: Nonpartisan election
Initial Term of Office: 6 years
Method of Retention: Reelection for additional 6-year terms

PENNSYLVANIA

Supreme Court
Elective System: Partisan election
Initial Term of Office: 10 years
Method of Retention: Retention election (10-year term)

Superior Court
Elective System: Partisan election
Initial Term of Office: 10 years
Method of Retention: Retention election (10-year term)

Commonwealth Court
Elective System: Partisan election
Initial Term of Office: 10 years
Method of Retention: Retention election (10-year term)

Court of Common Pleas
Elective System: Partisan election
Initial Term of Office: 10 years
Method of Retention: Retention election (10-year term)

RHODE ISLAND

Supreme Court
Appointive System: Merit selection through nominating commission
Initial Term of Office: Life
Method of Retention: NA

Superior Court
Appointive System: Merit selection through nominating commission
Initial Term of Office: Life
Method of Retention: NA

(Continued)

TABLE 3-1 (Continued)

Workers' Compensation Court
Appointive System: Merit selection through nominating commission
Initial Term of Office: Life
Method of Retention: NA

SOUTH CAROLINA

Supreme Court
Appointive System: Legislative appointment
Initial Term of Office: 10 years
Method of Retention: Reappointment by legislature

Court of Appeals
Appointive System: Legislative appointment
Initial Term of Office: 6 years
Method of Retention: Reappointment by legislature

Circuit Court
Appointive System: Legislative appointment
Initial Term of Office: 6 years
Method of Retention: Reappointment by legislature

SOUTH DAKOTA

Supreme Court
Appointive System: Merit selection through nominating commission
Initial Term of Office: 3 years
Method of Retention: Retention election (8-year term)

Circuit Court
Elective System: Partisan election
Initial Term of Office: 8 years
Method of Retention: Reelection for additional 8-year terms

TENNESSEE

Supreme Court
Appointive System: Merit selection through nominating commission
Initial Term of Office: Until next biennial general election
Method of Retention: Retention election (8-year term)

Court of Appeals
Appointive System: Merit selection through nominating commission
Initial Term of Office: Until next biennial general election
Method of Retention: Retention election (8-year term)

Court of Criminal Appeals
Appointive System: Merit selection through nominating commission
Initial Term of Office: Until next biennial general election
Method of Retention: Retention election (8-year term)

Chancery Court
Elective System: Partisan election
Initial Term of Office: 8 years
Method of Retention: Reelection for additional 8-year terms

Criminal Court
Elective System: Partisan election
Initial Term of Office: 8 years
Method of Retention: Reelection for additional 8-year terms

Circuit Court
Elective System: Partisan election
Initial Term of Office: 8 years
Method of Retention: Reelection for additional 8-year terms

TEXAS

Supreme Court
Elective System: Partisan election
Initial Term of Office: 6 years
Method of Retention: Reelection for additional 6-year terms

Court of Criminal Appeals
Elective System: Partisan election
Initial Term of Office: 6 years
Method of Retention: Reelection for additional 6-year terms

Court of Appeals
Elective System: Partisan election
Initial Term of Office: 6 years
Method of Retention: Reelection for additional 6-year terms

District Court
Elective System: Partisan election
Initial Term of Office: 4 years
Method of Retention: Reelection for additional 4-year terms

UTAH

Supreme Court
Appointive System: Merit selection through nominating commission
Initial Term of Office: 3 years after appointment
Method of Retention: Retention election (10-year term)

Court of Appeals
Appointive System: Merit selection through nominating commission
Initial Term of Office: First general election > 3 years after appointment
Method of Retention: Retention election (6-year term)

District Court
Appointive System: Merit selection through nominating commission
Initial Term of Office: 3 years after appointment
Method of Retention: Retention election (6-year term)

Juvenile Court
Appointive System: Merit selection through nominating commission
Initial Term of Office: First general election > 3 years after appointment
Method of Retention: Retention election (6-year term)

(Continued)

TABLE 3-1 (Continued)

VERMONT

Supreme Court
Appointive System: Merit selection through nominating commission
Initial Term of Office: 6 years
Method of Retention: Retained by vote of the state general assembly (6-year term)

Superior Court
Appointive System: Merit selection through nominating commission
Initial Term of Office: 6 years
Method of Retention: Retained by vote of the state general assembly (6-year term)

District Court
Appointive System: Merit selection through nominating commission
Initial Term of Office: 6 years
Method of Retention: Retained by vote of the state general assembly (6-year term)

VIRGINIA

Supreme Court
Appointive System: Legislative appointment without nominating commission
Initial Term of Office: 12 years
Method of Retention: Reappointment by legislature

Court of Appeals
Appointive System: Legislative appointment without nominating commission
Initial Term of Office: 8 years
Method of Retention: Reappointment by legislature

Circuit Court
Appointive System: Legislative appointment without nominating commission
Initial Term of Office: 8 years
Method of Retention: Reappointment by legislature

WASHINGTON

Supreme Court
Elective System: Nonpartisan election
Initial Term of Office: 6 years
Method of Retention: Reelection for additional 6-year terms

Court of Appeals
Elective System: Nonpartisan election
Initial Term of Office: 6 years
Method of Retention: Reelection for additional 6-year terms

Superior Court
Elective System: Nonpartisan election
Initial Term of Office: 4 years
Method of Retention: Reelection for additional 4-year terms

WEST VIRGINIA

Supreme Court
Elective System: Partisan election
Initial Term of Office: 12 years
Method of Retention: Reelection for additional 12-year terms

Circuit Court
Elective System: Partisan election
Initial Term of Office: 8 years
Method of Retention: Reelection for additional 8-year terms

WISCONSIN

Supreme Court
Elective System: Nonpartisan election
Initial Term of Office: 10 years
Method of Retention: Reelection for additional 10-year terms

Court of Appeals
Elective System: Nonpartisan election
Initial Term of Office: 6 years
Method of Retention: Reelection for additional 6-year terms

Circuit Court
Elective System: Nonpartisan election
Initial Term of Office: 6 years
Method of Retention: Reelection for additional 6-year terms

WYOMING

Supreme Court
Appointive System: Merit selection through nominating commission
Initial Term of Office: 1 year
Method of Retention: Retention election (8-year term)

District Court
Appointive System: Merit selection through nominating commission
Initial Term of Office: 1 year
Method of Retention: Retention election (6-year term)

Almost all judges are lawyers in the United States, but only a small fraction of lawyers ever become judges (Badinter and Breyer, 2004; Friedman, 1998, 2002). By contrast, in civil law countries, such as France and Italy, judges are civil servants and have different training and experience from practicing lawyers. Those who aspire to become a judge take a competitive examination after law school. The ones who pass will become judges with a career of their own. Previous practice of law is not required. It is also unlikely that they will ever practice law. Their roles and functions are also different from their American counterparts of the adversarial system. Unlike in common law countries, judges rely on the inquisitorial method, which has its roots in ecclesiastical courts (see, for example, Parisi, 2004). The French criminal trial is a good example of this method. The main figures at the trial are the investigating magistrate and the presiding judge. The magistrate is responsible for the investigation. He sends the material to the trial, where the judge dominates the proceedings and interrogates the defendant and the witnesses, who are the same for both the defense and the prosecution. Obviously, there is no "coaching" of witnesses. The interrogation of the judge resembles more of a conversation than a cross-examination (Loh, 1984:497–498). The judges in civil law countries are much more active than in the United States: They play a greater role in building and deciding a case, they put the evidence together, and they go far beyond the "refereeing" role characteristic of common law judges. France's 600 or so investigating judges can put suspects under formal investigation, order wiretaps, raid and search premises, summon witnesses, and confiscate documents. The investigating judges also weigh the evidence and decide whether to send a suspect for trial. In recent years, there have been attempts to curtail the wide-ranging judicial powers of investigating judges, and the debate remains a central issue among French politicians (*Economist*, 2009:57).

Juries   An ancient Welsh king, Morgan of GlaMorgan, established trial by jury in A.D. 725, and the origins of the American jury system can be traced back to civil and criminal inquiries conducted under old Anglo-Saxon law in England (Adler, 1995; Abramson, 2000; Brooks, 2009; Jonakait, 2003; Kleining and Levine, 2005; Ramirez, 1994; Vidmar, 2000; Vidmar and Hans, 2007; Wolf and Sarat, 1997). The original concept of the jury was most likely imported into England after the Norman Conquest. The Normans started the practice of placing a group of local people under oath (hence the term "juror") to tell the truth. Early jurors acted as sources of information on local affairs, and they gradually came to be used as adjudicators in both civil and criminal cases.

Before the twelfth century, criminal and civil disputes were resolved by ordeal. It took many forms. There was ordeal by water. The accused person was bound by rope and dropped into a body of water. If the person floated, it was a sign of guilt; if he or she sank, it was a sign of innocence. There was also ordeal by fire—carrying heated stones or iron, and if the subsequent burn did not get infected in three days, the accused was declared innocent—and ordeal of the morsel that did or did not choke the accused. Civil disputes were often resolved by oaths on the assumption that a false oath would expose someone to the judgment of God.

The jury system came to American shores with the British settlers in 1607 (Simon, 1980:5). One of the important symbols during the struggle for independence, the jury system is prominently referred to in three of the first ten amendments to the Constitution. As noted earlier, juries are used in about half of the criminal and civil cases in federal district courts. Although the Constitution provides the right to a jury trial for both criminal and civil cases involving more than $20, in the state trial courts, juries render verdicts in fewer than 10 percent of all cases. One-quarter to one-half of all the cases that go before a jury are settled out of court. Many of them involve liability claims in which the impaneling of a jury may be another strategy in the insurance companies' bargaining process. Of the three million or so people called to jury duty annually, for an average of 10 days each, only 60 percent will serve on a jury (*Time*, 1981:45). Lately, more and more Americans are evading jury duty, and the widespread failure to respond to jury-service summons is delaying trials and inconveniencing judges, lawyers, and court administrators (Gerlin, 1995:B1). In a recently started pilot program, several counties in Washington State are experimenting with better pay to lure more jurors to report for service; they have increased the daily compensation from $10 to $60. They also want to find out if higher pay affects the diversity of jury pools (*Seattle Times*, 2007). The findings, once available, should shed some light on the relationship between jury pay and showing up for service.

At the state and federal levels, generally, "only criminal trials make extensive use of juries" (Jacob, 1984:165). In some jurisdictions, the prosecutor also has the right to have a case tried by a jury. In such jurisdictions, the jury may be used even if the defendant prefers to have the case tried by a judge, although how the proceedings are carried out is determined by the trial judge. A prosecutor may seek a jury trial because of the belief that a jury is more likely to convict than a particular judge, that a jury is more likely to impose the desired sentence, or that a jury trial will attract more public attention to a defendant's heinous crime (Dalrymple, 2005). Though the right to a jury trial is often waived, juries are essential to the operation of American courts. The jury is used in all death penalty cases, and a fundamental law in the United States is that no person may be convicted of a capital crime except by the unanimous verdict of a 12-member jury. That is the law in all of the 38 states that have the death penalty, as well as in federal cases. There is, however, one exception. A jury of five is all that is required to sentence a member of the armed services to death in a court-martial (Bonner, 2001).

Though they invented the jury system, the British have been steadily dismantling it for decades. There are no juries in British civil cases, except those involving libel or police misconduct (Beggs and Davies, 2009). Around 93 percent of the criminal cases are heard before panels of three lay magistrates. Unlike in the United States, there is no voir dire and cross-examination of juries, and criminal cases do not require unanimous verdicts.

Juries are used predominantly in common law countries (Friedman, 1998, 2002; Hans, 2006), although Russian law now permits accused criminals to request a trial by jury as of November 1993. The old tribunal method in Russia, which only involved a judge and two assistants, was unfairly biased against the defendants, who now are entitled to a fair trial (Stead, 1994). It is estimated that 80 percent of all jury trials worldwide take place in the United States (Hans and Vidmar, 1986:31). A prominent federal judge, Richard A. Posner (1995), comments that this unique fidelity to the jury system is to a great extent due to the legacy of American distrust of officials, which has its roots in colonial times, and to a lesser extent to the political power of trial lawyers. Although this distrust is present in federal courts in both civil and criminal cases, it is much more pronounced in the state courts where it is reinforced by the low professional quality and rampant politicization of many of the state judiciaries. The distrust toward the judiciary retards government funding at all levels that would help to obtain better officials, and the resulting poor performance of the officials further reinforces the distrust.

Juries are used exclusively in trial courts. Dispute processing in trial courts involves two basic types of issues—issues of law and issues of fact. Issues of law emerge as participants in the dispute seek to identify and interpret norms that will legitimize their behavior. In a sense, a trial is a contest of interpretation and legal reasoning (see, for example, Bankowski and MacLean, 2007). The judge has the authority to determine which interpretations of law are proper and acceptable, but a trial is more than a question of legal reasoning. It also provides the opportunity for a reconstruction, description, and interpretation of events (that is, issues of fact). The purpose of a trial is to answer the question of who did what to whom and whether such conduct is legal. The function of the jury is to listen to and decide among competing and conflicting interpretations of events. The jury acts as a referee in an adversary contest dealing with the presentation of differing versions of the same event. By a crude division of labor, the jury is the authority on facts; the judge is the authority on law. But judges also control the jury, and the common law provides several mechanisms by which judges can and often intervene to prevent juries from going overboard, including the discretion to exclude prejudicial evidence, the power to split trials into separate phases so that liability can be decided before jurors hear of the terrible pain suffered by the plaintiffs, the prerogative to instruct the jury in the law, the use of special verdicts to ensure that factual determinations are rational, the power to reduce jury awards, and the ability to order new trials when a jury reaches an absurd result (See, for example, Bogus, 2001; Kleining and Levine, 2005; Umphrey, 2009).

One of the most important (if not the most important function as many attorneys claim) functions of a trial lawyer is jury selection (Donner and Gabriel, 2000; Kassin and Wrightsman, 1988:22–27). Some attorneys contend that by the time the jury has been chosen, and there has been a trend in recent years toward abbreviating jury selection (Davies and Emshwiller, 2006), the case has been decided. During the process of voir dire (literally, "to see, to tell"), prospective jurors are questioned first by the judge, then by the attorneys representing defense and prosecution. The purpose of the voir dire is threefold. First, it is used to obtain information to assist in the selection of jurors and to ferret out any juror bias (Jonakait, 2003; Lilley, 1994). Second, it enables the attorneys to develop rapport with potential jury members. Finally, there is an attempt by both sides to try to change the attitudes, values, and perspectives of jurors (Klein, 1984:154). If a juror admits to a racial, a religious, a political, or some other bias that would influence his or her decision, the lawyers whose client would be harmed can ask the judge to excuse the juror for cause.

But lawyers know and many studies have indicated, in criminal psychology in particular (Pakes and Pakes, 2009), that when people are questioned before an authority figure (the judge) and a number of strangers in crowded seating conditions, they are under stress and they tend to give socially acceptable answers and to conceal or deny their prejudices about litigants (Andrews, 1982:68). For example, national polls have shown that one-third or more of Americans consider a criminal defendant probably guilty ("The person wouldn't be on trial if there wasn't something to it"), but few would admit that in the courtroom (Hunt, 1982:82).

The hypothesis that the composition of the jury is the most important determinant of the trial's outcome is implicit in the practice of law (Saks and Hastie, 1978:48). Lawyers rely on their private judgments about how jurors are likely to be biased, and by using their peremptory challenges, they eliminate those who worry them most. Decisions to exclude or include a juror are based on a variety of considerations—gut reactions to the juror's looks and manner, advice passed down by other lawyers, and various maxims or rules of thumb (Hoffman, 2004). Examples of this legal folklore are admonitions that clergymen, schoolteachers, and wives of lawyers do not make desirable jurors because they are often sought out for advice and tend to be opinionated. Or, cabinetmakers should be avoided because they want everything to fit neatly together, and Germans or Scandinavians should be shunned because they are too exacting (Saks and Hastie, 1978:49). Body language also influences the selection process (Dimitrius and Mazzarella, 1998). For example, sweating; shaking; sincere, furrowed-brow look; running tongue over teeth; inappropriate familiarity (backslapping, touching, or invading personal space) are considered signs of dishonesty. Arms, legs, or ankles crossed; short or rapid breath; stiff, rigid posture; and pointing fingers are viewed as signs of anger and volatility. Even television-viewing habits enter into the selection equation. For example, as a result of the influence of crime-oriented television programs (such as the popular 2009–2010 season "CSI: Crime Scene Investigation" and "Law and Order" shows) where viewers are exposed to indisputable forensic evidence, would-be jurors in criminal cases are closely questioned about their television-watching activities because of the possible impact it can have on cases without forensic data (Deutsch, 2006). In a recent study, David W. Durnal (2010) further demonstrated that exposure to television drama series that focus on forensic science has altered the legal system in America in complex and far reaching ways. For example, jurors seem to think that they have a complete understanding of science presented on television, when in fact they do not, and they have unrealistic expectations of forensic science. As a result, it has to be ensured during the jury selection process that prospective jurors are not judging scientific evidence by television standards.

Many lawyers assume that Catholics will favor a Catholic litigant and Jews a Jewish one; that union members will be anticorporation; and that women, especially mothers of daughters, will be quicker to convict an alleged rapist than men. Some jurors are avoided because they are wearing a loud sport jacket, white socks, or a hairpiece. In damage suits, some people are eliminated because they are fat, on the assumption that fat persons tend to dish out overly generous portions. In criminal cases, legal cookbooks on jury selection would recommend men, Republicans, upper-income groups, bankers, engineers, and certified public accountants for the prosecution, and women, Democrats, middle- and lower-income groups, social scientists, and members of racial and ethnic groups such as Latinos or Jews for the defense (Simon, 1980:35).

For centuries, folklore, intuition, and unsystematic past experience provided the basis for jury selection (see, for example, Jonakait, 2003). Scientific jury selection enabled this process to move to a more sophisticated and predictable level (Hans, 1992:61–63). Since the early 1970s, lawyers have made increasing use of social sciences and social scientists in jury selection (see, for example, Lieberman and Krauss, 2010a, 2010b). Scientific jury selection was first used in the winter of 1971–1972 in the conspiracy trial of the Berrigan brothers and other antiwar activists in Harrisburg, Pennsylvania (Saks and Hastie, 1978:55). They were accused of plotting to blow up the heating pipes of the Pentagon and kidnap the secretary of state. Scientific jury selection has been used in the Angela Davis trial, in the conspiracy trial of John Mitchell and Maurice Stans for allegedly impeding a U.S. Securities and Exchange Commission (SEC) investigation of a fugitive financier, and in a score of other cases (Hunt, 1982).

In essence, scientific jury selection consists of three steps. First, a random sample is drawn from the population, and the demographic profile of this sample is compared with that of the prospective jurors (Pope, 1989). If the jurors were randomly selected, the profile should match. If there is substantial over- or underrepresentation of particular characteristics (ethnic groups, age, occupation, and so forth), the jury pool can be challenged. Second, after it is established that the prospective jurors represent the population at large, a random sample is drawn from the jury pool to determine the demographic, personal, and attitudinal characteristics considered to be favorable to one's own side. Third, after establishing the psychological and demographic profile of a "favorable" juror, the social scientist can make recommendations for selection of individual jurors (Loh, 1984:400). This basic procedure is often supplemented with additional information. For example, in the Angela Davis trial, investigators for the defense questioned prospective jurors' neighbors and friends to learn about the prospective jurors' attitudes. In another case, a research firm representing a corporate defendant called all potential jurors and questioned them, pretending to be conducting a random telephone survey.

An expansion of the technique is the use of a shadow jury. A number of social scientists feel that because the opposing attorneys present conflicting views of the facts, jurors tend to make decisions based more on empathy than on evidence. Thus, techniques of effective communication and persuasion need to be called to the attention of lawyers. To this end, simulated or "shadow" juries are used to gain feedback for lawyers on how to try their cases. The pioneering work with shadow juries took place during the antitrust case brought by California Computer Products of Anaheim against IBM. The IBM attorneys hired Litigation Sciences, a consulting firm, to help in IBM's defense. The researchers recruited six people with backgrounds and attitudes similar to the real jury. The six shadow jurors sat in the courtroom each day during the course of the trial, and each evening, they telephoned the researchers to report on their impressions of the day's proceedings. Because the plaintiffs presented their case first, the researchers learned how shadow jurors reacted to the arguments and what issues they considered important. Although the judge ruled in favor of IBM after the plaintiff presented its side, IBM attorneys would have used the knowledge gained from the shadow jury in presenting their side of the case (Hans and Vidmar, 1986:89). In 1989, Litigation Sciences (which has grown to more than 100 sociologists, psychologists, marketers, graphic artists, and technicians) has helped Pennzoil Company win a $10.5 billion jury verdict against Texaco Inc. Litigation Sciences' annual revenue is in excess of $25 million (Adler, 1989).

In addition to using shadow juries, some attorneys practice their arguments in front of simulated juries, with social scientists making suggestions about their persuasiveness (see, for example, Decaro and Matheo, 2004). In an often-cited case, the law firm representing MCI Communications in an antitrust suit against AT&T hired consultants to develop a profile of potentially favorable jurors. The consultants arranged mock juries made up of such people, in front of whom the MCI attorneys practiced their arguments. The researchers also videotaped MCI's witnesses and then advised them on how their testimony could be presented more succinctly and persuasively. MCI won the case and was awarded $600 million. Of course, with amounts like this at stake, the fees paid to social-science consultants—ranging from $50,000 to $500,000—may be a bargain (even in 1980 dollars) if they actually help (Hunt, 1982:72).

Such mock trials are the most useful early in a case. They can help a lawyer pinpoint the main issue of a case and assemble pertinent evidence around it, and also show jurors' probable reactions to arguments, which might contradict their basic beliefs. Most mock trials are conducted by jury consulting or market research firms and contain abbreviated versions of all parts of a regular trial (Clifford, 1995; Fuente et al., 2004).

There are serious reservations about the appropriateness of the use of scientific jury selection. Lawyers, when they are being candid, admit that their goal is not fairness but the selection of biases that benefit them. In the words of an attorney, "I don't want an impartial jury. I want one that's going to find in my client's favor" (Hunt, 1982:85). But, critics of the method contend that it tends to undermine the American adversarial system of justice. The techniques for surveying the community and assessing juror values during the voir dire are clearly designed to achieve juror partiality. It leads to an imbalance in the composition of the jury (see, for example, Lieberman and Krauss, 2010a, 2010b). Thus, it is an advantage only to rich defendants in criminal cases and the richer side in civil suits. One with greater resources will have more lawyers, better lawyers, and a larger staff. Jury research is one more such advantage. The ability of the adversary system to guarantee a fair and impartial jury and trial is obviously tested when the adversaries possess unequal resources (Hans and Vidmar, 1986:94).

There is also the danger that prosecutors may start relying on scientific jury selection if they lose too many cases because of the defendants' use of experts (which is a lucrative growth industry in the legal landscape that has transformed business litigation and where experts charge $850 an hour or more for their "insights" [Anders, 2007]). In such cases, as Amitai Etzioni decades ago pointed out, "Could any but the most affluent Americans compete with the state, once it began to apply these procedures to the prosecution?" (quoted in Andrews, 1982:73). Finally, there is the question of the public perception of the trial. There is a possibility that the legitimacy of the trial and subsequent verdict are undermined by the use of scientific methods in jury selection. The entire system of peremptory challenges may come under attack if these issues are not confronted by those who carry out jury research and by those who benefit from the results. If the judges release the list of prospective jurors to lawyers only one day before the trial, and not several days before, which is the current practice, many of the dangers and ethical problems inherent in scientific jury selection could be minimized. This would drastically reduce the time available for experts to conduct thorough background investigations of prospective jurors and the subsequent advantages for one party in the litigation.

In addition to problems of jury selection, there are other important issues concerning the involvement of jurors in dispute processing in courts (Brooks, 2009; Duff and Findlay, 1997; Prentice and Koehler, 2003). The first is whether juries are effective checks on judicial power. There is really no way of determining whether juries ensure that judges will be more restrained in using their power than they would be otherwise. In a study by Harry Kalven and Hans Zeisel (1966), an attempt was made to determine the effectiveness of the jury in checking the judge's power by examining the percentage of cases in which the judges and juries involved in the same case agreed as to the appropriate verdict. The researchers found a high degree of agreement between judge and jury—approximately 75 percent. They also noted that in almost all criminal cases in which judge and jury disagreed, the jury tended to be more lenient. Whether the leniency of the jury can be construed as limiting the exercise of judicial power is open to question. It does, however, show that the participation of laypersons in the decision-making process does make a difference in the outcomes of court decisions.

Another issue deals with the question of representativeness of the jury. Three steps are involved in the selection of jurors: (1) the placement of names on a master list of prospective jurors, (2) the selection of names from this list and the summoning of these persons to the court to constitute a jury panel, and (3) the selection from the panel of persons to serve on juries. Ideally, a jury that is representative of the community it serves is one that provides judgment by peers. Studies show, however, that American juries, as well as juries in other countries, are not always representative, mainly because the sources from which potential jurors are drawn—typically voter registration lists—are not representative of the various ethnic, social, and economic groups in the community (Alker et al.,

1976; Forman, 2004; Israel, 1998). Defense lawyers often complain that the urban poor, many of them minorities, are more mobile than the middle class and thus less easy for jury commissioners to find. Therefore, fewer are located and called for jury service. Yet, having even a few members of a minority group on a jury panel can help enormously, because racist discussions are less likely to occur in a mixed-race setting (Kennedy, 1998).

This is why states such as New York and Arizona are initiating changes in the jury selection procedures to enlarge the jury pool to include people receiving unemployment or welfare benefits (Barge, 1995). Also, even a small number of jurors can hold together to block a verdict they consider unjust (Pollock and Adler, 1992:4). Obviously, the representativeness of juries is important, not only because of the need to ensure legitimacy of the jury, but also because different kinds of people bring different attitudes and values to the jury. This is particularly true in racially sensitive cases, as best illustrated in the 1992 trial and acquittal of four white Los Angeles policemen in a police-brutality case involving the videotaped beating of a black motorist. Jury representativeness in racially charged cases has become more difficult in the wake of the rioting that followed the acquittals. Notorious, controversial, and racially charged trials also raise the possibility that jurors will lean toward a verdict that is likely to keep the peace. There is no way of determining to what extent, if any, jurors will be influenced by the possibility of mob violence in highly controversial cases (Geyelin and Brannigan, 1992; *U.S. News & World Report,* 1992).

The representativeness of the jury is further jeopardized by the courts' generally lenient policy toward "no-shows," excuses, and deferments. For the nation as a whole, one author estimates the "no-show" rate around 55 percent (Adler, 1995). Although anyone can theoretically get a temporary postponement for "undue hardship or extreme inconvenience," certain groups may be excused permanently, if they wish. In most jurisdictions, for example, these include people who are over 70 years of age; active ministers and members of religious orders; men and women with the daily care of a child under 12 years of age; and active lawyers, law students, physicians, dentists, and registered nurses. Also excused are people who are engaged in teaching, supervisory, and administrative positions in schools and colleges, and those who are sole proprietors of a business. Elected public officials and members of the armed forces and fire and police departments are also exempted, as are those who can convincingly demonstrate that their presence is required in a particular business or occupation. In New York State, more than 20 occupations are exempted from jury duty including optometrists, podiatrists, embalmers, and people who fit artificial limbs (*New York Times,* 1995:A18) despite recent attempts to reduce the number of exemptions for professions (Rohde, 1998). There is also a trend to reduce the size of the jury in the wake of a 1970 Supreme Court ruling that the Constitution does not require that the jury be made up of 12 people. For other than capital offenses, Arizona allows an eight-member jury and Florida allows six, and other states are considering similar reductions (Hoffman, 1995).

As a result, jury panels are more likely to be composed of people who have the time or can (or want to) take time off from their places of employment. In many occupations and professions, the prospect of being absent for a prolonged period (average jury duty is 10 days) is not welcomed. Thus, it is not surprising that juries draw disproportionately from the lower-middle and middle classes. At the same time, in a disproportionate number of cases, upper- and middle-class persons are chosen as jury forepersons over lower-class persons (Deosaran, 1993). The makeup of a jury, a dozen persons randomly pulled together, is vividly described by a college professor who served as the jury foreman in a Manhattan murder trial, as 12 idiosyncratic individuals thrown together in tight quarters for hours and days of sequestered deliberations—pushing civics into realms normally reserved for extreme sports (Burnett, 2002).

As a final point, there are serious concerns about the ability of jurors to comprehend the judge's instructions, which can be particularly important in capital trials (Luginbuhl, 1992) where juries making decisions must properly understand legal instructions if they are to perform their duties properly (Cho, 1994) so that they do not make up their mind about the sentence before the evidence is presented as many do (Coyle, 1995), and about their bias against business and their competence in civil cases. Studies show that jurors tend not to be biased against business, are generally skeptical of plaintiff tort claims against businesses, question more the motivations and actions of plaintiffs than the responsibilities of business, and tend to be conservative, in most cases, in awarding damages (Hans, 2006; Hans and Lofquist, 1992). Regarding competence, some observers argue that many disputes are so complex that an average person is incapable of understanding either the nature of the dispute or the complicated issues involved. For example, to decide whether IBM had monopolized various markets claimed in Memorex's $900 million antitrust suit, jurors needed a detailed understanding of things like "reverse engineering," "cross elasticity of supply," and "subordinated debentures." (And just try to imagine the complexity of cyber jargon in the recently settled Microsoft antitrust case that lasted three years, from 2001 to 2004 [for other cases, see, for example, Bissonette, 2009]. Incidentally, lawyers who persuaded Microsoft to settle their class-action lawsuit accusing the company of price-fixing are asking for $258 million in legal fees, the largest amount so far in an antitrust case. It amounts to about $3,000 per hour for one lawyer, more than $2,000 an hour each for 34 other attorneys, and $1,000 an hour for administrative work [Kravets, 2004].) The trial lasted 96 days. The jury heard 87 witnesses and examined some 3,000 exhibits. As a result of the inability to comprehend such a multitude of complex issues, some jurors may become susceptible to appeals to their emotions, or increased levels of stress may influence their disposition toward the case (Hafemeister and Ventis, 1994; Whittemore and Ogloff, 1995). Some commentators would limit the role of jurors and even eliminate juries in civil cases such as litigations involving the 2004 egregious market-timing activities of some mutual fund companies that adversely impacted shareholders. Others assert that, to the contrary, juries generally do grasp the facts (Corboy, 1975:186–187), and data from hundreds of jury trials and jury simulations show that actual incompetence is a rare phenomenon (Hans and Vidmar, 1986:129). Further, in a report by the *New York Times* (2001) on a comprehensive study of nearly 9,000 trials across the country, it was noted that judges award punitive damages as often as juries and generally in about the same proportion, suggesting that juries may be far less arbitrary, irresponsible, and incompetent than is widely believed. This study is expected to be controversial not only because it concludes that jurors may be more rational than they were believed to be, but also because it contradicts other research. It should be noted, however, that past studies on civil juries have been hampered by lack of data on verdicts spanning a sufficiently long time period. Average jury awards tend to be highly variable from year to year, making it difficult to distinguish trends over relatively short periods of time (Seabury et al., 2004).

By way of constructive measures to increase the still-debated jury competence, some researchers encourage note taking by jurors, allowing them to ask questions during the proceedings (Dilworth, 1995; Jonakait, 2003; Penrod and Heuer, 1997) and structuring cases around specific themes with strong jury appeal such as family or work, which are presented with a minimum of legal language (Baum, 1994).

THE FLOW OF LITIGATION

Several characteristics of the flow of litigation are significant. The processes by which cases are decided differ widely according to the type of dispute, the participants involved, and the stage of the judicial process at which the dispute is settled. In many instances, civil and criminal cases are quite different, and I shall review them separately.

Criminal Cases   A high degree of discretion is characteristic of every phase of criminal prosecution (see, for example, Johnstone and Ward, 2010; Stolzenberg, and D'Alessio, 2002). The process begins with an alleged crime and the arrest of the suspect. At this point, the police may or may not exercise the option of arresting the lawbreaker, as, for example, in cases of a traffic violation, prostitution, public drunkenness, or gambling. Once an arrest is made, however, the next step is to file charges against the prisoner and to set the amount of bail. Most defendants do not plead guilty at the time of arrest. Bail is simply a method to assure the court that the defendant will appear for later proceedings. Again, at this stage, judges can exercise a great deal of discretion in setting the amount of bail, which frequently results in many defendants having to wait in prison for trial. Individuals who are unable to pay their bail suffer consequences, such as being treated like convicted prisoners, spending a long time in jail before the case is decided where some 21 percent of the prisoners report at least one episode of forced sexual contact and 7 percent claim that they have been raped since being incarcerated (Lewin, 2001a:14), and losing their jobs while in prison, thus forfeiting their chances for probation—all of which make it difficult for them to prepare a defense. The poor are very much at a disadvantage in this respect. In New York City, for example, a study showed that 25 percent of those arrested could not come up with the $25 that would have enabled them to be set free on bail before trial (President's Commission on Law Enforcement and Administration of Justice, 1967:131). Further, a 1996 law barring the federal Legal Services Corporation from financing legal-aid organizations that represent prisoners reduced the number of lawyers available to litigate on behalf of the inmates (Lewin, 2001a:1).

Following bail, the next step depends on the prosecutor, the defendant, and, at times, the judge. Although a date is set for a trial during the arraignment or preliminary hearing, only 10 percent of the cases nationwide go to trial. This is due, in part, to the inability of law enforcement agents to establish accurately the identity of the perpetrator on the basis of eyewitness testimony (Levi, 1998; Webber, 2010; Worrall and Hemmens, 2005). The use of eyewitness identification is most prevalent in robberies. In other property crimes, such as burglaries and auto theft, the proof of identity is seldom by eyewitness. Personal crimes such as rapes and assaults usually involve parties who know each other (Loh, 1984:551).

There are four basic types of police identification practices. The first is a showup, which involves a confrontation between a suspect and a witness. It may take place either at the crime scene if the police are available or at the police station. The second is the lineup at the police station, which is basically a "multiple choice recognition test" where a witness is presented with several suspects (Tredoux, 1998). The third is a photographic identification, which may take place in either showup or lineup form. Finally, there is informal identification in the field, which may involve riding around in an unmarked police car in search of the suspect or an "accidental" encounter with him or her at the time of a bail hearing.

Following the initial identification of a suspect, the question of the accuracy of eyewitness evidence and testimony also comes up on the witness stand during a trial (Inbau et al., 1997:639–692; Kassin and Wrightsman, 1988:79–86; Williams et al., 1992; Worrall and Hemmens, 2005). The unreliability of eyewitness identification and the fallibility of testimony on the witness stand are brought about by three general problems of human memory (Woocher, 1977). To start, the perception of an event is not merely a passive recording. People can perceive only a limited number of events at the same time, and the number remembered is even smaller. Even trained observers find it difficult to describe accurately such basic physical characteristics as height, weight, and age. Humans also find it difficult to judge time, and because of the amount and variety of activities that occur during an action-packed event such as a crime, there is a tendency to overestimate the length of time. Often, crimes take place under poor observation conditions, making subsequent recall difficult. The presence of stress and anxiety decreases perceptual abilities. As a result, witnesses often compensate for perceptual selectivity by reconstructing what has occurred from what they assume must have occurred. In essence, they state what they think should have taken place rather than what actually transpired. Finally, eyewitness accuracy is further reduced in situations of cross-racial identifications. People are poorer at identifying members of another race than of their own. For example, whites have greater difficulties recognizing black or oriental faces than they do recognizing white faces.

The second problem is that memory decays over time. People forget quickly and easily. When it comes to recall at the police station or at the witness stand, people have a tendency to fill gaps in memory by adding extraneous details so that "things make sense." For example, a witness may recall an individual accurately but is completely wrong in remembering the circumstances under which he or she encountered that person. A salesperson may identify the defendant as having been in the store with the murder victim when, in reality, the defendant had been in that store on a few earlier occasions but was out of town at the time of the crime.

Finally, the way in which information is recalled from memory invariably reduces the accuracy of eyewitness testimony. The recall of witnesses is influenced by the subtle suggestions they receive under questioning by a police officer or a lawyer (Wasby and Brody, 1997). Many people also feel compelled to answer questions completely despite incomplete knowledge in an attempt to please their interrogators. So they rely on their imagination to supplement factual information. Lawyers are cognizant of these concerns, and try to use voir dire as a safeguard to identify and excuse prospective jurors who are unable or unwilling to critically evaluate eyewitness testimony (Narby and Cutler, 1994).

Even after positive identification of defendants, the majority of cases are settled by negotiations between the prosecutor and the defendant's lawyer. In these cases, the prosecutor is placed in a bargaining situation and may "trade" with the defendant for an admission of a lesser crime. The process is called *plea bargaining*. It can be traced back to earliest days of common law (Nasheri, 1998). There is evidence that plea bargaining was used prior to the American Civil War (Alschuler, 1995:144)

Today, in many cases involving plea bargaining, the prosecutor acts as a de facto judge and makes most of the decisions regarding the disposition of a case (see, for example, Scheck et al., 2003). If the defendant, on the advice of his or her lawyer, does not plead guilty, the person goes to trial. Contrary to popular belief, the ones who plead guilty do not, on the average, receive a lighter sentence than those who do not. It is really the criminal justice system that benefits by saving time and the expense of conducting a trial (Klein, 1984:77). Studies show that there is a growing reliance on plea bargaining, especially by federal prosecutors—in 1980, 18 percent of criminal cases handled by federal prosecutors were decided at trial; by 1987, only 9 percent ended in trials (Glaberson, 1989). Nowadays, it is estimated that roughly 90–95 percent of all criminal convictions are arrived at through plea bargaining (Palermo et al., 1998:112).

In felony convictions, for example, 91 percent of the defendants plead guilty. When a felony case does not result in a dismissal or a guilty plea and goes to trial, the chances are five in six that the defendant will be convicted. The growth in recent years in plea bargaining is considered to be a sign of the increasing professionalization of the judicial system. Criminal convictions are usually upheld on appeal (Hanson and Ostrom, 1993).

Plea bargaining is not limited to criminal cases. A version of it can be found even in traffic courts (Cunningham, 2009). For example, an investigation in the metropolitan St. Louis area discovered that accused speeders retain attorneys (who specialize in traffic cases) to get the charges "adjusted" to nonmoving offenses such as having a loud muffler or a burned-out headlight—offenses that do not result in point penalties for driving records (Osborne, 1992). Missouri drivers are allowed eight points in any 12-month period or twelve points in 18 months. A speeding conviction, depending on its severity, can cost the driver two or three points. Three speeding tickets can result in the loss of the driver's license. The city deals with about 300 traffic tickets per judge per hour. Prosecutors, who want to clear the docket, prefer plea bargaining, lawyers make money by charging about $250 to negotiate a city ticket, and the accused speeders are not faced with the loss of their driving privileges. There is a silent understanding among the plea bargain participants that if an offender paid the lawyer, "that's punishment enough." Poor people and those who insist on pleading not guilty on their own are the ones who are likely to have their licenses suspended.

Plea bargaining, as a form of negotiated justice, is a baffling and controversial topic in the sociological literature (see, for example, Feeley, 1979; Lynch and Evans, 2004; Mulcahy, 1994; Palermo et al., 1998). There are many objections to plea bargaining, the most common being that criminals are allowed to obtain "cheap" convictions (that is, ones in which they do not pay for the real crimes they committed), that it is moving criminal justice into an administrative process rather than an adversarial one, and that it is generating cynicism about criminal justice among the accused, the system's participants, and the public at large.

In explaining the widespread use of plea bargaining, Arthur Rosett and Donald R. Cressey (1976:85–97) assert that court personnel, including prosecutors, "develop a group sense of justice," which differs from attitudes generally held in the community, and which is generally more humane and pragmatic than that of the public. They maintain that prosecutors use caseloads as their public excuse for plea bargaining (there is evidence that plea bargaining affects positively the courts' ability to move the felony docket efficiently [Holmes et al., 1992]) but rarely consider caseloads in deciding whether to deal with specific cases before them (such as whether to prosecute on the basis of initial charges or to negotiate). The real reasons for plea bargaining, they argue, are the weaknesses in cases that could result in acquittals; the desire to adjust the charges to more reasonable levels, depending on the facts and the character of the defendant; and the desire to comply with the courthouse consensus on concepts of fairness and justice. For a typical defendant, it is often his or her own defense lawyer who initiates negotiations and urges a settlement by plea bargaining. In one study, for example, Abraham S. Blumberg (1979:223) found that over half of the 724 defendants entering guilty pleas indicated that their defense counsel first suggested the guilty plea, usually during the first or second meeting between lawyer and client. The situation is similar in other countries; in England, for example, attorneys often justify the use of plea bargaining based on their desire to avoid going to trial, their belief that most defendants are guilty, and their desire to control crime (Mulcahy, 1994; Passas, 2003).

Another form of "negotiated justice" aimed at reducing a sentence is "cooperation with the Government" (Hoffman, 1992). It is becoming quite common for prosecutors, particularly in organized crime cases and extensive white-collar cases, to ask the defendant to testify against a former colleague or associate in return for a reduced sentence or, occasionally, freedom. People who profit most from informing are usually the worst offenders, and testifying has little to do with justice but a great deal to do with giving a reward for the conviction of one's associate. Often, the defendants have to gamble that prosecutors will fulfill their end of the bargain for a reduced sentence. Recent and highly publicized examples of defendant-witnesses are Michael R. Milken, who testified against his former Wall Street colleagues, and Sammy Gravano, who informed against his former friend and employer, John Gotti, the convicted head of the Gambino crime family. In addition to legal questions (for example, should the judge or the prosecutor have the power to grant a "reward" for cooperation?), this practice raises some moral dilemmas, for it goes against a highly cherished American value—loyalty.

The final step in most criminal proceedings is sentencing the defendants who have been found guilty. Although sentencing decisions are made within a specific legal framework (see, for example, Savelsberg, 1992; Tonry, 1996), most jurisdictions permit the exercise of considerable discretion. The extent of judicial discretion allowed by legislation varies from state to state. As a result, the decisions handed down by judges vary within and across jurisdictions. This is the case, in particular, with white-collar crimes (Wheeler et al., 1988). Similarly, in some states, virtually no sentencing discretion is allowed in felony cases, whereas in others, judges may effectively determine not only the nature of punishment (probation, fine, or imprisonment) but also the extent of punishment (the length of a prison term).

There are five common structures for prison sentences, each illustrating a different combination of legislative provisions and judicial discretion:

(1) Both maximum and minimum terms of imprisonment are set by the judge at any point within legislative outer limits; (2) maximum terms are fixed by statute,

but the judge may set a minimum at any point up to the maximum; (3) maximum and minimum terms are set by the judge, but the minimum cannot exceed some fraction, usually one-third, of the maximum; (4) the maximum term is set by the judge, but the minimum is fixed by statute; and (5) both maximum and minimum terms are fixed by statutory law allowing the judge no discretion. (Anderson and Newman, 1998)

Thus, judges do have some choice between different sentencing options for most crimes, and they tend to exercise it. Generally, the judge's decision is influenced by the recommendations of the prosecutor and probation officers. Other factors that might influence a judge's decision include the race, sex, age, and socioeconomic and criminal background of the defendant and the type of lawyer involved (for example, privately retained or court appointed). The decision to plea bargain is also a factor. Although legal norms set the framework for the process, they do not control whether violators will be actually subjected to these legal norms. Instead of the judge or the defense attorney, the prosecutor plays the key role in administering criminal justice. Negotiation, bargaining, and compromise play an important part in the litigation process. Consequently, in many instances, offenders consider trials dangerous because they incite the judge and the prosecutor to "throw the book" at the defendant (see, for example Hemmens et al., 2010, on activities in criminal courts).

Throughout the world in recent years, there have been several developments in sentencing (see, for example, Tonry and Hatlestad, 1997). Most recently in Brazil, there are efforts under way to reform the judiciary, which, according to the *Economist* (2004a), is "dysfunctional"—agonizingly slow, beset with frivolous cases designed to evade justice, and enmeshed in useless procedure. The 16,900 judges seem old-fashioned, out of touch, and unaccountable to the citizens they serve. A police operation called "Anaconda" in 2003 caught judges selling favorable sentences to criminals. Of the 49,000 murders committed annually in Brazil (almost three times as many as in the United States with much less than half of its population) just 7.8 percent every year are "prosecuted with success." Currently, the defendants have endless rights of appeal, not merely against a verdict but against minor decisions along the way. Because one court's rulings are not binding on another, a single legal question can be tried separately several times.

In the United States, the trends in sentencing include the use of mandatory minimums, various forms of popular determinate sentencing such as "three strikes and you are out" (see, for example, Barker, 2009), truth-in-sentencing, and guidelines-based sentencing. These measures are aimed at ensuring that some time will be served for violent offenses, limiting judicial discretion in sentence variation for the same offenses, and increasing the predictability of penalties (see, for example, Stolzenberg and D'Alessio, 1997).

As a response to the growing preoccupation with violent crime, a number of states have adopted mandatory sentencing laws to fight high crime rates. These laws require a minimum amount of incarceration upon conviction and were designed for specific offenses such as rape, murder, drug trafficking, and dangerous weapons violations. Studies show that mandatory minimums have dramatically increased the number of offenders in prison, and the prison terms are longer. But other than keeping offenders off the streets for a longer time—specific deterrence, which will be discussed in Chapter 5—mandatory sentencing provisions did not act as general deterrence and had no measurable impact on crime rates (O'Connell, 1995).

Other law and order initiatives such as the three-strikes and two-strikes (and you are out) sentencing measures mandating life without parole for repeaters of certain violent or drug-related crimes, first passed in Washington State in 1993 then in California in 1994, did not fare much better (Cox, 1994; Garland, 2001; Rodriguez, 2003; Stolzenberg and D'Alessio, 1997). They too fail to combat crime and recidivism and ignore questions of rehabilitation and reform. For example, a 2001 study by the Sentencing Project, a nonprofit research group, showed that, in California, these laws had no significant effect on the state's decline in crime. In California, with three-strikes and two-strikes laws, crimes dropped by 41 percent from 1993 to 1999; New York, with no such laws, showed the same decline for the same period (Lewin, 2001b). Such measures also waste precious jail space on minor offenders (the majority of convictions, at least in California, are for property, drug, and other nonviolent offenses), strain resources, contribute to the aging of the prison population, denigrate the independence of the judiciary, and rob judges of the discretion needed to tailor sentences to offenders and their life situations (Broderick, 1994; Franklin, 1994). In recognition of these concerns, some smaller states, such as Louisiana, Connecticut, Indiana, and North Dakota, in 2001 have quietly started to roll back some of their most stringent anticrime measures, including those imposing mandatory minimum sentences and forbidding early parole (Butterfield, 2001).

Truth-in-sentencing measures reflect continued attention to discretion and to the association between sentences and time served (Wood and Dunaway, 2003). Truth-in-sentencing is intended to reduce the discrepancy between the sentence imposed upon those who are sent to prison and the actual time they serve. Data indicate that violent offenders released from state prisons in 1992 served 48 percent of the sentence they had received—an average of 43 months on an average sentence of 89 months (U.S. Department of Justice, 1995).

In federal courts, the amount of discretion judges may exercise is limited by the controversial Sentencing Reform Act, which took effect on November 1, 1987 (Margolick, 1992; see also Lax, 2004). One of the primary objectives of the act was to eliminate the problem of unwarranted disparity—that is, two similarly situated offenders could go into two different courtrooms, even in the same courthouse at the same time, and come out with two vastly different sentences. Under the guidelines, all crimes are ranked on a scale from 1 to 43; the greater the heinousness and severity, the higher the number. For example, murder is assigned a score of 43; hijacking, 38; and blackmail, 9. The base score is affected by a variety of aggravating and mitigating circumstances, such as acknowledgment of guilt and cooperation with the government. Since the instrumentation of the guidelines, the range of sentences has been noticeably reduced. Critics complain, however, that it is difficult to master the complex guidelines (with amendments, the manual is three inches thick), and at times it can be tricky. For instance, robbery has a base score of 20. But if a post office or a bank is robbed, the score goes up to 22. If a weapon was fired, it rises 7 more; if a gun was merely "used," it goes up by 6, and if the gun was "brandished, displayed or possessed," by 5. Despite these and other criticisms, the act is working by reducing and checking the power of judges and effectively eliminating what was sardonically referred to as a "system of roulette" in sentencing. It also filters out variations based on the philosophies of particular judges and probation officers, docket pressures in some courts, and other criteria, such as race, sex, and socioeconomic background of the defendant, that have been considered decisive in the literature (see, for example, Albonetti, 1992). Not surprisingly, there is widespread dissatisfaction among federal judges with the sentencing guidelines, and they loath to have much of their discretion in sentencing taken away (Reske, 1994).

Civil Proceedings

In civil cases, a dispute reaches the court when it is filed by the plaintiff's attorney. The attorney generally has the option to choose a court based on a number of considerations, such as the quality and known biases of judges, the delay that may be expected in hearing a case, and the relative convenience of the court for the litigant (Jacob, 1984:213–215). Generally, the litigant has little voice in the selection of courts. It is left to the attorney who handles the case.

Just as in the case of criminal proceedings, bargaining governs negotiating settlements in civil courts. For example, in personal injury cases, plaintiffs who are represented by lawyers usually win a greater settlement than those who attempt to handle their own negotiations (Ross, 1980). Courts are often instrumental in expediting the settlement of cases through pretrial conferences. At times, the judge may even suggest a particular amount that seems reasonable, based on his or her experience with similar cases.

If a satisfactory settlement cannot be reached, the case goes to trial. Only a small proportion of cases that are filed end up in trial. In some types of cases, such as automobile accidents, the plaintiffs generally prefer a jury trial in anticipation of a larger settlement.

At times, disputes are settled before civil cases go to trial, and, in such instances, the trial is used to legitimize the outcome. This is particularly true in divorce suits. In such cases, a separation agreement has been reached by husband and wife, and then the wife generally takes action in court to formalize and legitimize the agreement.

LEGISLATURES

To commence the study of the organization of legislatures, we first need to look at what legislatures do. A legislature is defined as a collection of individuals who are elected as members of the formal parliamentary bodies prescribed by national and state constitutions. The functions of the legislature, at both the federal and the state levels, are numerous (see, for example, Grossback and Peterson, 2004). Of course, the hallmark of legislative bodies is their lawmaking function, and part of Chapter 4 will be concerned with how this function is carried out. Yet, lawmaking takes up only a portion of the legislature's time. Legislative bodies are also engaged in conflict management and integrative functions.

Conflict Management Functions   Even though conflict management is part of both the administrative and the judicial subsystems, the legislature may be distinguished by the extent to which compromise, as a mode of conflict management, is institutionalized in the system. The emphasis is on conflict management rather than on conflict resolution for, in a sense, few political decisions are final (Boulding, 1956:103).

The conflict management functions of legislative bodies can be seen in the context of their deliberative, decisional, and adjudicative activities (Jewell and Patterson, 1986:5–10). Frequently, legislative bodies deliberate without arriving at a decision or taking action. However, the deliberation process itself and the rules under which it takes place contribute to the reconciliation of divergent interests. In addition to formal debates, deliberation is carried on in the hearing rooms, in the offices of legislators, or in the lobbies or cloakrooms surrounding the chambers. At times, these informal deliberations are more important for they provide an opportunity to incorporate a variety of viewpoints and interests.

Some adjudicative activities are routinely undertaken by legislative bodies, and the principles of dispute resolution currently being applied in the judicial system also benefit the legislators (Melling, 1994). For example, the work of some legislative committees has been adjudicative, as when hearings before investigating committees have been, in effect, trials during the course of which sanctions have been applied. A most celebrated and classic illustration of the application of sanctions by the Senate for the violation of its norms is that of the late Senator Joseph McCarthy. As chairperson of the Permanent Subcommittee on Investigations of the Committee on Government Operations, McCarthy engaged in a communist witchhunt during 1953 and 1954, which focused mainly on the U.S. Department of State and the U.S. Army. In December 1954, the Senate voted to censure McCarthy for his conduct—not for indiscriminately accusing people of being communists and abusing the investigatory powers of Congress, but for attacking the integrity of the Senate itself.

Integrative Functions   Legislative bodies contribute to the integration of the polity by providing support for the judicial and executive and administrative systems. They provide this support through authorization, legitimization, and representation (Jewell and Patterson, 1986:10). A characteristic of any constitution is the specific, and often mandated, delegation of authority to different components of government. In the United States, the legislative branch is given various kinds of authority over the executive branch. The legislative branch is also the source of power in most instances of administrative agencies. Perhaps the most important of these is the budgetary process through which legislative bodies authorize a particular agency or body to collect taxes and disburse funds. Legislative bodies also authorize the courts to establish jurisdiction, to create their organizational machinery, and to qualify their members. Moreover, legislatures oversee bureaucratic activities and attempt to balance them against prevailing special interests in a community.

The integrative functions are also promoted through legitimization of activities. Legislative actions are considered by most people as legitimate. For example, when Congress gives the IRS permission to collect more taxes, its exercise of authority is legitimized in the process, and the IRS has the right (meaning legitimate authority) as well as the power to collect more taxes.

The Organization of Legislatures

Because of the similarities in organizational patterns, I shall consider the federal and state legislative bodies together. Congress consists of two separate bodies—the Senate and the

House of Representatives. These two bodies differ in several respects and are eager to protect their privileges and power. The House members are apportioned among the states on the basis of population. After each census, the apportionment of representatives among the states normally changes: States with the fastest-growing populations gain representation, and those with little or no population growth or with declining populations lose representation (but usually not without a fight). U.S. senators are not affected by apportionment or districting. Each state is entitled to two senators. Unlike the situation in the House, where members come up for election at the same time, Senate terms are staggered, so that only one-third of the Senate is up for election every two years, which ensures a greater continuity of both formal and informal organizational arrangements.

Herbert Asher (1973) points out that behavior in both the Senate and the House is influenced by a set of informal rules and norms: (1) Newcomers to the legislative body serve a period of apprenticeship in which they accept their assignments, do their homework, and stay in the background while learning their jobs; (2) members become specialists in the work of the committees to which they are assigned; (3) members avoid personal attacks on each other; (4) members are willing to reciprocate by compromising and trading votes (supporting each other's proposals) when possible; and (5) legislators do nothing that will reflect adversely upon the integrity of the legislative body and Congress as a whole. The same informal norms and rules operate in state legislatures.

Avoidance of personal disputes, restriction of full participation in the legislative process to senior members, and the norm of reciprocity all function to minimize conflict within legislative bodies. The emphasis on specialization provides Congress with the opportunity to deal with the increasingly complex issues it must consider, though specialization may also create some organizational problems. In general, House members are more likely than senators to specialize in the work of the committees on which they serve. Senators, on the other hand, are more apt to draw the attention of the media and have presidential ambitions. This is due, in part, to the length of time they are elected to serve. The norm of protecting the integrity of the legislative body may, and often has, led to controversy between the Senate and the House, and between Congress as a whole and the president.

Participants in the Legislative Process

The legislative process encompasses a variety of participants (Hall, 2004). In this section, I have chosen to give attention to three sets of participants who are particularly relevant to legislative activity—legislators, executives, and lobbyists. These three sets of participants in the legislative process are examined separately.

Legislators Who are the legislators who make laws? Are legislatures composed of men and women who represent a cross-section of the population? What groups are "overrepresented" and what groups are "underrepresented" in the legislature? Social scientists have carried out a number of investigations on the social origins and occupational backgrounds of political decision makers. A few of these studies have focused on legislators. Despite substantial gaps in factual knowledge about legislative personnel, certain generalizations about the individuals who serve as legislators can be made.

Most legislators come from a middle-class or an upper-class background. A survey on the characteristics of legislators of the 1990s, for example, based on 900 state lawmakers in

16 states, reveal that lawmakers have an average age of 50 years, are married (83 percent as contrasted to 42 percent of the general population), have 2.4 children, are well educated, and are successful with a much higher than average income. They are predominantly males (70 percent) and white (89 percent). The average legislator was reared in a comfortable, stable family that provided a strong work ethic and values (Woo, 1994). These characteristics remain the same in the early years of the twenty-first century.

Contrary to popular beliefs, legislators are not representative of the population at large, and obviously not all citizens have an equal chance to be elected to legislative office. As a group, legislators have a much higher educational attainment than the general population. In part, this high educational level can be accounted for by their relatively high social origins. Protestant Anglo-Saxon males are substantially overrepresented among legislators. (And the situation was similar in 2001 in the national legislatures of European Union nations [Daley, 2001].) Women, blacks, and foreign-born Americans are conspicuously underrepresented. The religious composition of most state legislatures and both houses of Congress is predominantly Protestant (Ornstein et al., 1990:32–36).

The recruitment of legislators is very selective by occupational status. By and large, those in the professional and business occupations dominate the legislative halls in the United States at both the state and the national levels. The most obvious fact about the occupations of legislators is that lawyers are predominant (Ornstein et al., 1990:20–31). Well over one-half of the members of Congress are lawyers, and overrepresentation is also found at the state level, where they account for 20 percent of legislators. Although lawyers remain the largest occupational group among legislators, the profession's "share" of state legislative seats decreased by 6 percent since 1966. The president of the American Bar Association considers this decline a "bad sign"; in his words, "I don't think it's good for the country, and I don't think it's good for the profession" (Slonim, 1980:30). Those who echo this highly debatable view believe that the absence of a large number of lawyers "bodes ill for the quality of legislation," because lawmaking by laypeople lends itself to ambiguity.

In addition to lawyers, it is common to find state legislatures in which over one-third of the members are businesspeople. Those engaged in the insurance business, real estate, and banking and investment are particularly numerous. In the less urbanized states of the Midwest and the South, legislators engaged in farming are likely to be about as numerous as those engaged in either business or law. Farmers, however, are not often elected to Congress. Educators account for a small fraction of state legislators, and women are significantly underrepresented at both the federal and the state levels.

From the preceding discussion, it is evident that no legislature comes close to representing a cross-section of the population it serves. The political system inevitably has built-in biases and numerous devices for the containment of minority-group aspirations for office and for the advancement of dominant segments of the population. Some groups win often; others lose often.

The Executive   There are three main functions for the president and the governors in the legislative process. First, they serve as a source of ideas for the programs that legislative bodies consider; second, they function as catalytic agents; and third, they instrument the law.

Although the extent of executives initiating ideas for legislative programs varies among the states, and certainly between the state and national levels, in most instances executive recommendations are the principal items on the legislators' agenda. Legislative recommendations emerge from individual cabinet departments or from agencies and are sent to the president far in advance of presentation to Congress. The presidential initiative is a permanent and ubiquitous feature of the legislative process (see, for example, Jones, 2005, 2009).

The president and the governors also function as catalytic agents in the legislative process. They not only offer programs but also strive to structure support, both directly within legislative bodies and indirectly through interest groups, party leaders, and other political activists. They are also greatly concerned with the manipulation of public opinion (see, for example, Brooker and Schaefer, 2006.)

The instrumentation of law constitutes a third executive contribution to the legislative process. The legislative process seldom ends when the executive has signed a bill into law. In many instances, the enactment of a law is not the most important step in making public policy. Much legislation is phrased in general terms to apply to a diversity of concrete situations. Law is interpreted and given new dimensions as it is applied under the direction of the executive. An awareness of the relationships between law instrumentation and lawmaking is reflected in legislative eagerness to oversee administrative behavior.

Lobbyists   Organizations and groups that attempt to influence political decisions that might have an impact on their members or their goals are called *interest groups* (Baumgartner et al., 2009). Whom do interest groups represent? At the most general level, the interest-group system in the United States has a distinct bias favoring and promoting upper-class and predominantly business interests (see, for example, Johnston, 2004). Interest groups are usually regarded as self-serving—with some justification (Rozell et al., 2006). The very word "interest" suggests that the ends sought will primarily benefit only a segment of society such as, for example, prison management companies pushing for tougher sentencing—to fill beds in private prisons (see, for example, *Economist,* 2007). Still, not all the groups, such as large corporations or industry associations that attempt to influence legislative bodies, profit directly. Quite a number of groups claim to represent the public, such as the Sierra Club and the League of Women Voters, or advocate for progressive causes, such as consumer rights, homelessness, children's rights, gay rights, animal rights, and so on (Seligman, 1995). (Note that the word "advocate" sounds much better than "lobbyist."). Other groups represent foreign governments, small or medium-sized political groups, public and private universities, and various charitable organizations (Hopkins, 1992).

The legislative bodies are the natural habitat of political interest groups. These interest groups enter the legislative process through their lobbying activities. Lobbyists are individuals who are paid to try to influence the passage or defeat of a legislation. Lobbying is considered a professional undertaking, and full-time experienced lobbyists are considered essential by most interest groups (Hrebenar and Morgan, 2010). It is estimated that in Washington alone, as many as 4,500 groups are represented by lobbyists covering a wide range of activities such as labor, education, business, health, welfare, banking, and farming. There are some 35,000 registered lobbyists in Washington (*Economist,* 2006a), including many former members of Congress (Abramson, 1998:A22). They collectively spend over $2 billion a year in an effort to influence lawmakers although this figure is likely to decrease due to a recent Senate rule (based on voluntary compliance) forbidding senators, their aides, and other Senate officers to accept privately paid travel to "recreational" events, gifts, or meals in excess of $50, or more than $100 worth of gifts and meals from any person in a year (Clymer, 1995). This is in addition to the 4,618 political action committees (PACs)—groups that are not affiliated directly with a candidate or a political party—whose annual expenditures are well in excess of half a billion dollars (Salant and Cloud, 1995). If these figures sound a bit excessive, recall that the average amount spent by a winning candidate for a seat in the House of Representatives is around $556,000 and the average cost of a seat in the U.S. Senate is over $4 million (Coleman, 2006; see also Gerber, 2004). And once again, the Senate resurrected a bill to overhaul the nation's campaign finance laws, which was buried in a series procedural vote for about a year. Still there are no signs that it will pass.

The lobbyist plays a variety of roles in the legislative process. As a contact person, the lobbyist devotes his or her time and energies to walking the legislative halls, visiting legislators, establishing relationships with administrative assistants and others of the legislator's staff, cultivating key legislators on a friendship basis, and developing contacts on the staffs of critical legislative committees. As a campaign organizer, the lobbyist gathers popular support for his or her organization's legislative program. As an informant, the lobbyist conveys information to legislators without necessarily advocating a particular position. Finally, as a watchdog, the lobbyist scrutinizes the legislative calendars and watches legislative activities carefully. This way, the lobbyist can be alert to developments in the legislative bodies that might affect his or her client groups (Jewell and Patterson, 1986; Levine, 2009).

Large-scale lobbying efforts directed toward the enactment or defeat of certain legislations, such as school finance reforms (Paris, 2010), are omnipresent features at both the state and the federal levels (Abramson, 1998; Godwin, 1988:73–100; Mahood, 2000). In all probability, a professional lobbyist will be an ex-congressperson, an ex-senator, an ex-governor, or a former government employee who once occupied a high position in the administration and, ideally, still living up to the "highest standards of probity" (to borrow a term from the British Parliament) to maintain credibility. Some, such as former longtime congressman and presidential candidate Dick Gephardt of Missouri, become "consultant" or "advisor" to large corporations to help them with their ability to serve clients in the areas of government, public policy, and international affairs (Kardos, 2007). Lobbying groups are willing to pay dearly for the services of an experienced ex-senator or House member, particularly a former chairman or senior member of a top committee. And there is no shortage of them. Twenty-two percent of senators and representatives who left Congress in the 1990s are listed in the 1998 edition of *Washington Representatives,* a directory of lobbyists. Overall, 12 percent of those who left Congress since 1970 are listed (Abramson, 1998:A22). Many top officials of the Clinton administration are still in Washington, trying to influence the actions of their successors in government (Salant, 2003).

What these groups are buying, by and large, are prestige and access to the inner sanctum of government. In Washington especially, an ex-lawmaker has privileges that set him or her apart from other lobbyists—including access to the House and Senate chambers and members' private dining rooms, gymnasiums, and swimming pools. But there are some restrictions. A former senator who is a registered lobbyist must wait a year before visiting the Senate for the purpose of influencing his former colleagues. The House has no such rule but forbids a former member to enter the chamber if he or she has an interest in an issue that is being debated. Still, there is really not much to prevent a lawmaker-turned-lobbyist from making his or her pitch elsewhere (Baker, 2008:159–185). Former members can always call themselves "consultants," as they started to do so in the 2010s, and essentially carry out the same activities as registered lobbyists.

Supplementing his or her personal efforts, the lobbyist often turns to public relations firms to stir up grassroots sentiment. As a result, a stream of phone calls, letters, and cables will deluge the offices of legislators. The efforts of the National Rifle Association (NRA) (see, for example, Brown and Abel, 2003; Spitzer, 2008), American Association of Retired Persons (AARP), American Association of University Professors (AAUP), or the tobacco industry (Abramson, 1998), among many other organizations, are illustrative of these practices. Contributions in conjunction with these efforts can also be discreetly used among certain legislators to muster support when needed.

At times, however, a "discreet contribution" may turn out to be outright bribery in an attempt to buy political favors in the form of special bills, the right vote on a particular piece of legislation, or assistance in winning government contracts because individual lawmakers have immense power to take money out of the public purse for the narrowest of purposes or to oppose or support a particular project. But bribery can lead to criminal prosecution of political figures, and 42 percent of the criminal indictments against congressional office holders since 1940 involved some sort of bribery charges. A most notorious example of this was the Federal Bureau of Investigation's (FBI) sting operation known as ABSCAM. FBI agents posed as representatives of an alleged Arab sheik who wanted some Washington favors. Eight officials were persuaded to sponsor special bills or use their influence in the government in return for cash or other rewards. One senator was given stock certificates in a bogus titanium mine for his assistance in obtaining government contracts. Another representative was videotaped stuffing $20,000 in his pocket. Those involved in ABSCAM were convicted of various crimes and given fines and prison terms (Coleman, 2006). Another notorious incident involved Jack Abramoff who pleaded guilty to fraud early 2006 and was sentenced to six years of imprisonment. His clients gave money to at least 195 Republicans and 88 Democrats, and one congressman tearfully admitted that he accepted brides from defense contractors (*Economist,* 2006a). Fortunately, most lobbyists do not resort to such extreme and illegal measures as outright bribery, nor do they wish to test the limits of politicians' resistance to temptation. But lobbyists often give small personal presents, free samples of company products such as perfume, and free meals at expensive restaurants to create a receptive climate for their efforts.

There are several types of lobbying efforts and techniques that are deployed with varying degrees of efficiency, depending on the cause. First, there are activities directed at influencing legislation during the electoral process by supporting the election of a person to the legislative body whose program one favors. Second, there are activities directed at influencing legislation by "educational work." If one happens to oppose a particular legislative action, one can substitute the phrase "educational work" for "propaganda work." The educational propaganda may be specifically directed toward a particular bill, or it may be directed only at the establishment of a political or an economic philosophy that will condition subsequent legislation (Ripley, 1988:272–273).

ADMINISTRATIVE AGENCIES

Reminiscent of the study of legislation, the investigation of regulatory and administrative agencies has been neglected by legal sociologists, who tend to focus their attention primarily upon courts and litigations. As a result, there is a paucity of research and theorizing on administrative and regulatory bodies in the sociological literature (Tomasic, 1985:111). These agencies deal with an important sociological process, *social control,* which is a leading concern in the study of law and society. This section will describe the context within which that control is exercised. In the U.S. government in the twentieth century, the most striking development has been the growth and multiplication of administrative agencies and the extension of their power and activities (Box, 2009; Calvi and Coleman, 2008; Cann, 2006). Today, numerous local, state, and federal administrative agencies have a tremendous impact on American lives. They are often called "the fourth branch of government." On the federal level, there are some 50 agencies in Washington alone (Hill and Hill, 2004). The average state probably has more than 100 administrative agencies with powers of adjudication or rulemaking or both (Davis, 1975a:8). Individuals are much more directly and much more frequently affected by the administrative process than by the judicial process. The pervasiveness of the effects of just the federal administrative process and the ubiquitousness of the government can quickly be appreciated by considering the following hypothetical scenario (see, for example, Seib, 1995).

A typical couple is awakened by the buzz of an electric clock or perhaps by a clock radio. This marks the beginning of a highly regulated existence. The clock or radio that wakes them up is run by electricity provided by a utility company, regulated by the Federal Energy Regulatory Commission and by state utility agencies. The couple listen to the weather report, generated by the National Weather Service, part of the United States Department of Commerce. When they go into the bathroom, they use products, such as mouthwash and toothpaste, made by companies regulated by the U.S. Food and Drug Administration (FDA). The husband might lose his temper trying to open a bottle of aspirin that has the child-proof cap required by the U.S. Consumer Product Safety Commission (CPSC). In the kitchen, his wife reaches for a box of cereal containing food processed by a firm subject to the regulations of the United States Department of Agriculture (USDA) and required to label its products under regulations of the Federal Trade Commission (FTC). The husband, who is conscious of his weight, uses an artificial sweetener in his coffee. Since the banning of cyclamates by the FDA, he has switched to saccharine, but he is worried because that, too, is on the FDA's proposed ban list. Obviously, it does not help his ulcer.

As they get in their car to go to work, the couple are reminded by a buzzer to fasten the seat belts, compliments of the National Highway Traffic Safety Administration. They paid slightly more for the car than they wanted to, because it contains a catalytic converter and other devices stipulated by the United States Environmental Protection Agency (EPA). They also pay more for gas, because the car can use only unleaded gasoline, another government requirement. On the way to work, they drive at speeds regulated by state and municipal ordinances and subject to the federally mandated 65 miles per hour speed limit. They listen to the car radio, which is regulated by the Federal Communications Commission (FCC), as is the telephone that they use at home or at their place of work. Our typical wife works in an office, and during the course of the day, she provides information about the financial activities of her company to the SEC, and she is also likely to fill out a variety of statistical forms for the U.S. Census Bureau. She finds out in the office that she has lost her retirement benefits; the small company where she worked recently terminated its pension plan because of the onerous requirements imposed by the IRS and the United States Department of Labor under the Employee Retirement Income Security Act (ERISA).

In the meantime, the husband begins his work in the factory under conditions negotiated by his union, which was chosen after a lengthy strike in an election supervised by the National Labor Relations Board (NLRB). The equipment he uses in his job and in the lavatory must meet the requirements of the Occupational Safety & Health Administration (OSHA). The material he uses at work was shipped to his company under the guidelines of the Interstate Commerce Commission (ICC) for rail and truck, the Civil Aeronautics Board (CAB) for air, and the Federal Maritime Commission for sea. One of his company's outside contractors is late for a meeting because the Federal Aviation Administration (FAA) prohibits airplanes to take off without an ashtray in the lavatory—even on nonsmoking flights. The search for a replacement ashtray delayed the flight by the now defunct TWA by 90 minutes (*St. Louis Post-Dispatch,* 2001).

They take off time from work to negotiate a mortgage on the house they are buying with financing from a savings and loan association regulated by a Federal Home Loan Bank (FHLB) with a guarantee by the Federal Housing Administration of the U.S. Department of Housing and Urban Development (HUD). They also plan to go to a commercial bank (regulated by the Federal Reserve System) to get a loan for the furniture they will need. On the way home, they stop for a hamburger, which is the subject of 41,000 federal and state regulations, many of those stemming from 200 laws and 111,000 precedent-setting court cases (*U.S. News & World Report,* 1980:64).

At home, they decide to watch commercial television, the programming and advertising of which are regulated by the FCC. They light up a cigarette with a package label mandated by the Office of the Surgeon General in the U.S. Department of Health & Human Services. But they have to cut their television watching short because of a letter they have received from the IRS questioning their tax return for the previous year. After a while, the husband decides to clean his shotgun, regulated by the Bureau of Alcohol, Tobacco, Firearms and Explosives of the United States Department of Justice. He has yet to find out that these regulations cost every consumer thousands of dollars a year.

The Organization of Administrative Agencies

Administrative agencies are authorities of the government other than the executive, legislative, and judicial branches, created for the purpose of administering particular legislation. They are sometimes called commissions, bureaus, boards, authorities, offices, departments, administrations, and divisions (Box, 2005). They may be created by legislative acts, by executive orders authorized by statutes, or by constitutional provisions. The powers and functions of an agency are generally contained in the legislation that created it (Breyer and Stewart, 2006:9–15).

At the federal level, all the agencies derive their power from Congress, which created them under its constitutional authority to regulate interstate commerce. Congress long ago began delegating this authority when it became clear that the job was too complex and technical to be handled entirely by legislation in the amount of time available and with the limited expertise of the lawmakers. As economic activity became more complex, legislative bodies were unable or unwilling to prescribe detailed guidelines for regulation. Traditional agencies of government could no longer regulate big businesses (Friedman, 2005). Agencies were established and given considerable discretion in determining the applicability of often vaguely written legislation to specific situations such as mass transport and communication. These agencies were expected to provide certain advantages over the courts in the instrumentation of public policy. These advantages included speed, informality, flexibility, expertise in technical areas, and continuous surveillance of an industry or an economic problem.

In general, administrative agencies were created to deal with a crisis or with emerging problems, requiring supervision and flexible treatment. For example, when Congress decided in the nineteenth century not to permit railroads to operate without close public control, it established, in 1887, the Interstate Commerce Commission—the first federal independent regulatory agency. ICC's assignment was to supervise the railroads to guarantee cheap, safe service and rates that would be fair to small towns all across the country. The phenomenal development of radio, with its concomitant crowding of airwaves, brought about the creation of the Federal Radio Commission—the forerunner of today's FCC. This agency was charged with allocating licenses to stations to be operated "in the public interest." More recently, when environmental issues became a serious national concern, two agencies—the Council on Environmental Quality, and the EPA—were established.

There is substantial variation in the responsibilities, functions, and operations of the various agencies. Some, such as the EPA and the FTC, are concerned with only a few activities of a large number of firms (Harris and Milkis, 1996), and others, such as the ICC, oversee a great many matters involving a relatively small number of firms (in this case, transportation). Many agencies in the first category have the official mission of protecting the interests of the general public in regard to health, safety, and activities in the marketplace. Most of the agencies in the second category are expected not only to perform public protection functions but also to safeguard and promote the health of specific occupations, industries, or segments of the economy subject to their jurisdiction.

Administrative agencies are just as subject to pressures of interest groups as are all other policymakers (Rozell et al., 2006). Although many of the agencies were originally established in response to protests by various consumer groups against dangerous practices by various industries, their orientation has changed over the years. The agencies gradually shifted their orientation and became the "captive" of the groups they were supposed to regulate. Often appointees were (and still are) selected from the very industries that the agencies were created to regulate. Agency heads frequently take high-level jobs in such industries after finishing their governmental service. There have also been frequent revelations of agency heads fraternizing with representatives of regulated industries and of their willingness to accept favors, such as industry-paid vacations. For these reasons, critics have often pointed out that some high-level agency members seem more interested in protecting the interests of airlines, drug companies, trucking firms, stockbrokers, and other industries that they are supposed to regulate than in protecting the interests of the public (Schwartz, 1959).

The activities of the ICC illustrate this tendency. Originally, it was set up to protect consumers against predatory practices by the railroad monopolies. By 1920, the agency was almost solely responsive to the railroads, against the interests of consumers, and against other forms of interstate transportation. In case after case, the ICC's rulings benefited the railroads. Nowadays, the ICC is trying to strike a balance between the interests of railroads and trucking companies, but the interests of consumers are still virtually ignored. Witness, for example, the progressive discontinuation of passenger-train services.

Administrative agencies have also been criticized by conservatives as being uncontrollable monsters that threaten the civil liberties of businesspeople and the proper functioning of the economic system (Weidenbaum, 1979). In a somewhat contradictory fashion, conservatives have also depicted regulatory agencies as inefficient, bungling bureaucracies that do little more than waste the taxpayers' money. Liberals have often been able to muster enthusiasm over the creation of new agencies but have become disappointed with their performance. Agencies are often seen by liberals as becoming the captive of the regulated, and thus unwilling to pursue their public-interest obligations. At this juncture, it is interesting to note the differences in attitudes toward regulatory agencies in the United States and Japan. Public trust of agencies is high in Japanese society (see, for example, Oda, 2009). Citizens believe that social order can be maintained and progress facilitated by administrative agencies and that public administrators are honest, are free from corruption, serve the public, and are loyal and competent in carrying out their technical responsibilities. In the United States, by contrast, there is endemic distrust of regulatory agencies reinforced by the impression that administrators have failed to solve a phalanx of complex social, economic, and environmental problems (Box, 2005; Jun and Muto, 1995).

On an ideological level, governmental regulation has also been controversial because it raises questions regarding the proper role of government in the economy. The conservative of the "free enterprise" position has generally called for a hands-off policy by government in regulating economic activity. According to this view, the same protections against regulation are to be given to corporations. The pursuit of business profits, moreover, is seen by economic conservatives as being in the best interests of the general public. We are all familiar with the cliché, "What is good for General Motors is good for the country." Liberals, by contrast, are more likely to seek restrictions on the rights of businesspeople or corporations to protect what they consider to be the important rights of workers, consumers, and the general public. Perhaps a case could be made that the public is not so much interested in *less* regulation in the abstract as they are in having *effective* regulation, and having it confined to areas where there is consensus on the need for it (Foreman, 1991:13).

The Administrative Process

Administrative agencies affect the rights of individuals and businesses by exercising powers of investigation, rulemaking, enforcement, and adjudication. This combination of functions does not conflict with the doctrine of the separation of powers; the constitutional principle that the legislative, executive, and judicial functions of government should not exist in the same person or groups of persons. Notes Freedman (1978:17), "Administrative agencies were deliberately created as instruments of blended powers. In many instances they were expressly created to combine legislative, executive, and judicial powers." Although a wide range of powers are delegated to an agency by the enabling act, there are checks on its activities (see, for example, Box, 2005; Mashaw, 1994). The creator of an agency, which is generally the legislature, retains the power to destroy it or alter the rules governing it. The judiciary retains the power of final review of the determinations of administrative agencies, but this right is, as a practical matter, rather limited. The principal administrative processes are investigation, rulemaking, and adjudication. I shall consider these separately.

Investigation   The authority to investigate is given to practically all administrative agencies. Without information, administrative agencies would not be in the position to regulate industry, protect the environment, prosecute fraud, collect taxes, and attempt to reduce the consequences of identity theft or issue grants. Most administrative actions in both formal and informal proceedings are conditioned by the information obtained through the agency's prior investigation. As regulation has expanded and intensified, the agency's quest for facts has gained momentum. Some agencies are created primarily to perform the fact-finding or investigative function. The authority to investigate is one of the functions that distinguishes agencies from courts. This authority is usually exercised to perform properly another primary function, that of rulemaking.

Statutes usually grant an agency the authority to use several methods to carry out its information-gathering function. Requiring reports from regulated businesses and conducting inspections are methods of accomplishing this information-gathering task. Necessary information is often available from the staff, from the agencies' accumulated records, and from private sources. If these resources prove inadequate, the agency may seek further information by calling in witnesses or documents for examination, or by conducting searches. The authority of an agency to investigate is intertwined with the objectives of administrative investigation. The purposes of investigations vary, ranging over the entire spectrum of agency activity. For example, if an agency is responsible for enforcing a statute, its investigations may set the groundwork for detecting violations and punishing wrongdoers. To illustrate, the U.S. Department of Labor may seek to inspect employers' payroll records when checking for compliance with minimum wage laws.

Congress has traditionally conferred broad investigative powers upon the agencies. Important and typical are the provisions of the Federal Trade Commission Act of 1914, empowering the commission to (1) instruct corporations to file annual or special reports and answer specific questions in writing (this may account, in part, for the fact that the federal government is using 4,987 different kinds of information-gathering forms [*Time*, 1978:26]), (2) obtain access to corporate files for examination and reproduction of their contents, and (3) subpoena the attendance of witnesses and the production of documentary evidence (Gellhorn and Levin, 1997). It would be difficult to devise a broader authorization for fact gathering.

Rulemaking   Rulemaking is the single-most important function performed by government agencies (Kerwin, 2003:xi). It defines the mission of the agency and essentially involves the formulation of a policy or an interpretation that the agency will apply in the future to all persons engaged in the regulated activity. As quasi-legislative bodies, administrative agencies issue three types of rules—procedural, interpretive, and legislative.

Procedural rules identify an agency's organization, describe its methods of operation, and list the requirements of its practice for rulemaking and adjudicative hearings. Interpretive rules are issued by an agency to guide both its staff and regulated parties as to how the agency will interpret its statutory mandate. These rules range from informally developed policy statements announced through press releases to authoritative rulings binding upon the agency and are issued usually after a notice and hearing. Legislative rules are, in effect, administrative statutes. In issuing a legislative rule, the agency exercises lawmaking power delegated to it by the legislature.

Kenneth Culp Davis considers rulemaking one of the greatest inventions of modern government and argues that the United States is entering the age of rulemaking (Davis, 1977:241). Rulemaking is an agency process for formulating, amending, or repealing a rule, and most rulemaking falls into the "notice and comment" category. The Administrative Procedure Act of 1946 requires simply that the proposed rule be announced in advance and that interested parties should be afforded an opportunity to present their views. Rulemaking generally involves policy issues (value judgments), which depend upon the agency's knowledge about current practices, the impact of the proposed rule, the need for public protection against inadequate safeguards, and the possible burden (cost) of government regulation on private or public interests.

The rulemaking process, more often than not, is lengthy and complicated. Usually a lawyer's expertise is needed to master the procedural maze and technical requirements imposed by administrative agencies. Even so, an average person may initiate and participate in the process. Unlike legislatures and courts, access to administrative agencies is often direct. No middlemen stand between agencies and their clients (Jacob, 1995).

Adjudication Administrative agencies, of all kinds and at all levels, must settle disputes or mediate among conflicting claims. Adjudication is the administrative equivalent of a judicial trial. It applies policy to a set of past actions and results in an order against (or in favor of) the named party.

Much of this adjudication is handled informally through the voluntary settlement of cases at lower levels in an agency. At these levels, agencies dispose of disputes relatively quickly and inexpensively, and they take an immense burden off the courts. Moreover, they are handled by individuals who are experts in technical areas. But this practice is not without criticism. Many individuals—in particular, lawyers pleading cases before the agencies—have expressed concern over the extent of judicial power vested in agencies. They complain that administrators violate due process of law by holding private and informal sessions, by failing to give interested parties an adequate hearing, and by basing their decisions on insufficient evidence.

These complaints stem, in part, from the institutional differences between agency and court trials. Agency hearings, unlike court hearings, tend to produce evidence of general conditions, as distinguished from the facts relating specifically to the respondent. This distinction is due to one of the original justifications for administrative agencies—the development of policy. Another difference is that, in an administrative hearing, a case is tried by a trial examiner and never by a jury. As a result, the rules of evidence applied in jury trials, presided over by a judge, are frequently inapplicable in an administrative trial. The trial examiner decides both the facts and the law to be applied. Finally, the courts accept whatever cases the disputants present. As a result, their familiarity with the subject matter is accidental. By contrast, agencies usually select and prosecute their cases. Trial examiners and agency chiefs either are experts or at least have a substantial familiarity with the subject matter, because their jurisdictions tend to be restricted.

Partly in response to these complaints and differences, the Administrative Procedure Act of 1946 was passed, providing for broader judicial review of administrative decisions. The courts have always had the power to overturn the agencies' judgments on points of law, as in cases where an agency has exceeded its authority or misinterpreted the law, or simply been unfair. Under the 1946 act, however, the courts acquired more authority to examine questions of *fact*—that is, to go over the mass of technical evidence examined by the agencies. Though this tendency has not gone far, it sheds light on the problem of maintaining the balance between judicial control and administrative expertise. Judicial review of agency activities also deals with procedural safeguards, such as more formalized hearings and proper notice of action (Box, 2005; Edley, 1990). But the role of the courts is essentially limited to procedural matters—advising agencies, sometimes repeatedly; to go about their business in a fairer manner and to pay serious attention to all affected interests. In technical, complex disputes, courts cannot decide major issues. They will not set tariffs, allocate airline routes, or control the development of satellite communications (Breyer and Stewart, 2006).

LAW ENFORCEMENT AGENCIES

Most people, even the law abiding, have ambiguous feelings toward the police. Police are a salvation when it comes to protecting life, limb, and property, but their efforts are possibly less welcome when one's foot happens to slip momentarily on the gas pedal. Few would argue, however, that human societies could completely dispense with their activities. Even in primitive societies with a reliance on informal methods of social control to discourage criminal acts, there is some form of reassuring police presence. Interestingly, the practice of policing is not uniquely human; it is also present in simian society (*Economist*, 2006b; Flack, 2006).

The word *police* comes from the Greek world, *polis*, meaning "city." The word also includes the idea of the city's "government," and by more modern extension that of the state. The principal functions of the police are law enforcement, maintenance of order, and community service (see, for example, Bell, 2006; Choudhary, 2010; Dempsey and Forst, 2010; Dunham and Alpert, 2005; John et al., 2009; Langworthy and Travis, 2008; Lemieux, 2010; Thurman and Zhao, 2004). Like other components of the American legal system, the origins of the American police can be traced to early English history (Novak, 1989). In the ninth century, Alfred the Great started paying private citizens for arresting offenders. The population was broken down into units of ten families or "tithings," and each person was responsible for watching over the others. Subsequently, the unit was expanded tenfold to the "hundred," and one person, designated as the constable, was in charge of maintaining order. In time, the hundred was increased to include the countrywide "shire," under the control of an appointed "shire-reeve," who later on became known as the "sheriff." The first citywide police force was created by Sir Robert Peel in

London in 1829; and in 2004, one in every 115 employed Londoners was a police officer (*Economist,* 2004b; Smith and Henry, 2007). Police officers were uniformed, organized along military lines, and called "Bobbies" after their founder. The American colonists adopted the English system of law enforcement, and the first metropolitan police force was created in Philadelphia in 1833 (Loh, 1984:276).

In September 2004, the latest year for which data are available, some 18,000 publicly funded state and local law enforcement agencies were operating in the United States (U.S. Department of Justice, 2007). The state and local law enforcement agencies had about 1 million full-time personnel (but still fewer than the 1.1 million lawyers or the 1.3 million or so real estate agents [Hagerty, 2006]), with an operating budget of around $57 billion.

The local police departments had about 581,000 full-time employees, including about 452,000 sworn personnel. There were about 11,000 more sworn and 4,000 more nonsworn employees than in 2000. Racial and ethnic minorities comprised 23.6 percent of full-time sworn personnel in 2004, up from 22.6 percent in 2000 and 14.6 percent in 1987. Women comprised 11.3 percent of officers in 2004, up from 10.6 percent in 2000 and 7.6 percent in 1987. From 2000 to 2004, the number of black or African American local police officers increased by 1,500, or 3 percent; Hispanic or Latino officers by 4,700, or 13 percent; officers from other minority groups by 850, or 7 percent, and female officers by 4,400, or 9 percent. Sixty-one percent of departments had officer separations during the 12-month period ending June 30, 2004. Overall, about 32,100 officers separated, including 16,100 resignations, 9,400 retirements, and 2,600 dismissals. Sixty percent of departments hired new officers during the 12-month period ending June 30, 2004. Overall, about 34,500 officers were hired, including 28,800 entry-level hires and 5,300 lateral transfers/hires. During the 12-month period ending June 30, 2004, 21 percent of local police departments had full-time sworn personnel called up as full-time military reservists. Overall, about 7,500 officers were called up. Departments had total operating budgets of $43.3 billion during fiscal year 2004–2005, 10 percent more than in 2000 after adjusting for inflation. Operating expenditures in 2004 averaged $93,300 per sworn officer and $200 per resident. In 2004, starting salaries for local police officers ranged from an average of about $23,400 in the smallest jurisdictions to about $37,700 in the largest.

The new local police recruits were required to complete an average of about 1,600 hours of academy and field training in departments serving 100,000 or more residents, compared to about 800 hours in those serving a population of less than 2,500. New deputy recruits in sheriffs' offices serving 100,000 or more residents were required to complete an average of 1,400 hours of training compared to about 780 hours in those serving a population of less than 10,000 (U.S. Department of Justice, 2002, 2006, 2007).

The largest police department is in New York City; it has over 46,000 full-time employees. Three in four departments nationwide serve a population less than 10,000. Most local police departments are in small towns; most local police officers are not. About half of all officers work in jurisdictions with a population of 100,000 or more, and one in five officers works for a department that serves one million or more residents. In 2004, local police departments cost about $80,600 per sworn officer and $179 per resident to operate for the year. Sheriffs' offices cost about $107,900 per officer and $65 per resident for the year. On the average, local police departments cost some $59,000 per officer to operate per year. In cities over 250,000 residents, that figure is around $69,000 (U.S. Department of Justice, 2002, 2006, 2007).

The level of police service is determined to a great extent by personnel policy and by recruiting standards (Hess et al., 2011; Kerley, 2005; Leonard and More, 2000:379). Only a small percentage (about 7 percent) of local police departments require new recruits to have at least some college education. About 18 percent of state police departments have such a requirement. It is interesting to note that local police departments serving fewer than 2,500 residents require an average of 400 hours of training for new officers in contrast to 1,000 hours in state and large city police departments (U.S. Department of Justice, 2002, 2006, 2007). In most smaller city departments, personnel are provided little guidance regarding professional development and personal growth, and the concept of career development is typically viewed in terms of promotion to the next higher rank (Gibbons, 1995).

In the United States, there is no unified system of law enforcement. As Thomas F. Adams observes:

> A police system—if one were to exist in the United States—would be a rank ordering of all the local police agencies in sequence, according to their relative importance; then higher up the scale would be placed the many state agencies, and finally a rank ordering up through all of the federal agencies to a single head or committee. Such a system does not exist in the United States. (2007:69)

In a classic and often-cited work, Bruce Smith (1960) identified five types of public law enforcement systems in the United States, conforming roughly to the major levels of government: (1) the police agencies of the federal government; (2) the state police forces and criminal investigation agencies of the 50 states; (3) the sheriffs in more than 3,000 counties, plus a few county police forces that either duplicate the sheriff's police jurisdiction or displace it; (4) the police of 1,000 cities and more than 20,000 townships or New England towns, to which must be added an unknown number of magisterial districts and county districts in the South and the West; and (5) the police of 15,000 villages, boroughs, and incorporated towns, together with a small number of special-purpose forces serving quasi-public corporations and ad hoc districts. If we add to these the law enforcement activities of private police agencies, we end up with a large number of systems of law enforcement, related in their functions and at times overlapping in their jurisdictions.

In addition, within these systems are specific police agencies. Some federal agencies have law enforcement powers, such as the FBI, United States Secret Service, Drug Enforcement Administration, United States Postal Inspection Service, IRS, U.S. Customs and Border Protection, U.S. Immigration and Customs Enforcement, and Alcohol and Tobacco Tax and Trade Bureau of the U.S. Department of Treasury (Adams, 2007). The federal government also maintains the U.S. Marshals Service as a law enforcement agency; marshals are appointed by the president to a four-year term, whose duties are to preserve order in the courtrooms, handle subpoenas and summonses, seize goods, transport prisoners, and serve as a disbursing officer (Souryal, 1995).

Law enforcement at the state level was established, for the most part, at the beginning of the twentieth century. Although their jurisdictions vary from state to state, police agencies perform a myriad of varied functions, such as enforcing traffic laws, investigating fires, combating occult and cult crime (Hicks, 1991), enforcing liquor laws, arresting juvenile offenders, and inspecting property. State police agencies also assist local police agencies by providing technical expertise in criminal identification and laboratory and community services.

No review of law enforcement agencies is complete without mention of the private police (Button, 2007; Davis et al., 1991; Nemeth, 2010; Shearing and Stenning, 1987; Simonsen, 1998; Steden, 2008) (and its international version of the some $100 billion worth of privatized military industry where private companies, so-called "corporate warriors," take on military support roles including combat [Singer, 2003]). Special needs of private sectors of the community require the services of private police patrols and investigation agencies. Businesses, industries, residential complexes, and others use private agencies, such as Pinkerton's Incorporated, to guard property, apprehend thieves, investigate offenses, and detect fraud and embezzlement. There are approximately 8,500 such firms in the United States, the largest 10 employing more than 30,000 employees. In the early 1990s, annual spending for private security was already over $64.5 billion (*U.S. News & World Report*, 1994:13), and private security agencies employed more than 1.5 million people, almost twice as many as in public law enforcement (Munk, 1994). By the year 2010, public expenditures for law enforcement exceeded $70 billion; they were dwarfed by private security expenditures, which reached $180 billion. (All told, the United States spent in 2010 close to $240 billion for police protection, corrections, and judicial and legal activities [see, for example, Clear et al., 2011].) The average annual rate of growth in private security is 8 percent; double that of public law enforcement. Policy expenditures represent a substantial part of the municipal budget (see, for example, Leonard and More, 2000:380–381), and many budget-conscious communities are exploring the privatization of police as a way to contain costs, and it may be a trend to watch in the years to come (O'Leary, 1994) along with developments to privatize death row and correctional institutions (Steinhauer, 2009). While on the subject of money, the annual cost of crime in the United States was already in excess of $700 billion in the mid-1990s (*U.S. News & World Report*, 1994:13) and is expected to be much higher in 2010 although there are no current estimates available (Nemeth, 2010).

Finally, many large corporations have their own private police. As an example, General Motors over two decades ago already had more than 4,200 plant guards, a police force larger than the police departments in all but the five biggest cities in the country (Friedman, 1998, 2002). As a matter of interest, it is not unusual for urban universities to have a campus police department of several hundred officers, a police force larger than that of many medium-sized towns in Western Europe. The rest of this section will be devoted to the structural features of municipal police departments.

The Organization of Law Enforcement Agencies

Municipal and other police organizations have evolved in response to changes in technology, social organization, and political governance at all levels of society (Carter, 2002; Reiss, 1992; Thurman and Jamieson, 2005). They are structured along the lines of complex bureaucratic organizations (see Figure 3-2). A variety of specific organizational tables or patterns describe how the police divide up tasks. In every case, a formal and highly complex

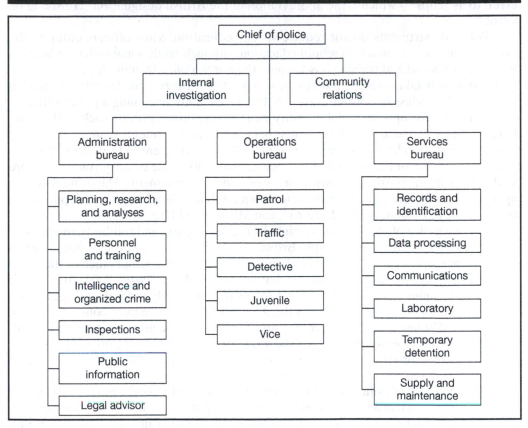

FIGURE 3-2   One Form of a Well-Organized Municipal Police Department

division of labor characterizes these systems (see, for example, Wilson and McLaren, 1972). In addition to their bureaucratic characteristics, law enforcement agencies are structured like quasi-military institutions, which gives these agencies their special character. Bittner (1970:53) notes, "Both institutions are instruments of force and for both institutions the occasions for using force are unpredictably distributed. Thus, the personnel in each must be kept in a highly disciplined state of alert preparedness. The formalism that characterizes military organization, the insistence on rules and regulations, on spit and polish, on obedience to superiors, and so on, constitute a permanent rehearsal for 'the real thing.'"

The municipal police system of law enforcement is built on a subordinating chain of command (Bordua and Reiss, 1966; Loveday, 1998). Although all units of a particular department may be related to a central command, the overall chain of command is divided into units so that different precincts or squads are immediately responsible to a localized authority. The functional divisions of police departments follow the kinds of activities they handle, such as traffic patrol, investigative work, undercover work (for example, in vice and narcotics), crowd control, and uniformed patrol, whose officers are popularly referred to as "cops"—which is the abbreviation of the British designation "constable on patrol."

Police departments do not require special education. Most officers entering the force have no more than a high school education, although lately some college education without any specialized training has become the norm. Police training is pragmatic and brief and usually takes place in a police academy. Most officers come from lower-middle-class or working-class backgrounds (Jacob, 1995). For many, becoming a police officer is an opportunity for upward social mobility, and in some ethnic groups, such as the Irish, there is a high proportion of family members in law enforcement. Women are slowly making inroads into law enforcement, and in 2007, they represented 15 percent of sworn police officers. Out of the some 18,000 police departments in the country, roughly 200 are headed by women, mostly small town forces or campus departments. The trend is changing, though, and more and more women are appointed to head large city departments such as those in Boston, Portland, Detroit, and Milwaukee (Tyre, 2004).

Among police officers, there is a high degree of cohesion and solidarity, much more so than in other occupational groups (Brown, 1988). They are by virtue of occupational expectations suspicious, and tend to be skeptical toward outsiders, and much of their outlook and conduct have an authoritarian character (Bartol and Bartol, 2004, 2011). Their subculture includes a code of silence, and fellow officers rarely incriminate each other. They socialize and make friends within the department, and some even conceal their police identity (Skolnick, 1994). In recent years, there has been a growing incidence of suicides among police personnel. Studies show that police suicides are caused by a variety of factors such as job stress, frustration, easy access to firearms, alcohol abuse, and fear of separation from the police subculture (Violanti, 1995).

The activities of police both in the United States and in other parts of the world consist of routine patrol and maintaining order—such duties as attending to domestic disturbances, handling drunks, assisting motorists, controlling traffic, escorting dignitaries, and processing juveniles (Bayley, 1992: 523–527; Lyman, 2010; Skolnick and Bayley, 1988; Smith and Henry, 2007; Thurman and Jamieson, 2005). Contrary to popular image, police officers, with the exception of detectives, spend only about 20 percent of their time in criminal investigations (Brown, 1988:322).

The effectiveness of law enforcement agencies (as determined usually by arrest and clearance rates) depends on the size of the department and the way it is organized (Kerley, 2005). Small departments often lack the training or equipment for proper handling of serious crimes. The experience of officers may be limited predominantly to traffic control and routine patrol, and in complex cases, the diversity in expertise is sorely absent (Glaberson, 1992). Whether or not departments are organized along professional criteria also has a bearing on their effectiveness. For example, in a study of a nonprofessionalized police department in a West Coast city, James Q. Wilson (1968a) found that the nonprofessionalized department's members had no strong sense of urgency about police work and produced low rates of official actions on offenders. In the professionalized department, however, violations of the law were more likely to be detected, and offenders were more likely to be arrested, producing a higher crime rate.

In another well-known and influential study, James Q. Wilson (1968b) identified three styles of police work—the watchman style, the legalistic style, and the service style. Although elements of all three can be found in any law enforcement agency, different agencies tend to emphasize one style more than the others and, as a result, practice different law enforcement policies.

The *watchman* style emphasizes the responsibility for maintaining public order, as contrasted with traditional law enforcement (see, for example, Crank, 1994). The police officer in such an agency is viewed as a peace officer, ignoring or handling informally many violations of the law and paying much greater attention to local variations in the demand for law enforcement and maintenance of order. The role of peace officer is characterized by a great amount of discretion, because peacekeeping is poorly structured by law or by agency regulation. Underenforcement, corruption, and low arrest rates characterize watchman-style departments.

The *legalistic* style is just the opposite of the watchman style. Agencies characterized by this style tend to treat all situations, even commonplace problems of maintaining order, as if they were serious infractions of the law. Members of such agencies issue a high rate of traffic tickets, arrest a high proportion of juvenile offenders, and crack down on illicit enterprises. The police typically act as if there were a single standard of conduct rather than different standards for different groups. As a result, some groups, especially juveniles, blacks, and migrants, are more likely to be affected by law enforcement than others considered "respectable" by the police. Although this style of law enforcement is characterized by technical efficiency and high arrest rates, it also results in inequality in law enforcement, with complaints of harassment and police brutality by groups who are most often subjected to police scrutiny.

The *service* style combines law enforcement and maintenance of order. An emphasis is placed on community relations, the police on patrol work out of specialized units, and command is decentralized. The pace of work is more leisurely, and more promotional opportunities are available. This style differs from the watchman style in that the police respond to all groups and apply informal sanctions in the case of minor offenses. It differs from the legalistic style in that fewer arrests are made for minor infractions, and the police are more responsive to public sentiments and desires. In this sense, the service style is less arbitrary than the watchman style and more attuned to the practical considerations of public service than the legalistic style. There is little corruption, and complaints against police in service-style departments tend to be low. Such departments are also characterized by community-oriented policing. The emphasis is on problem-solving policing where attention is focused on the problems that lie behind incidents, rather than on the incidents only (Moore, 1992; Zhao and Thurman, 1997). This style aims at reducing alienation and distrust between police and minorities and between police and the poor—potentially explosive situations that can escalate a simple traffic stop into a riot. Community-oriented policing tries to improve neighborhood quality of life, involves citizens in crime fighting (in particular, against drugs), and undertakes more concerted effort at crime prevention (Peak and Glensor, 2008; Thurman et al., 2001). Although it is more expensive and labor intensive, more than 400 cities have already adopted community-oriented policing (Boyce, 1992). But the approach is not without criticisms and enthusiasm for it is being tempered by training needs, costs, and overall effectiveness (Joseph, 1994). Community-oriented policing, as a recent study contends, also colonizes community life and increases the capacity of police departments to shield themselves from criticism (Lyons, 1999).

Community-oriented policing is not limited to the United States. It is widely practiced in many European countries (see, for example, *Economist*, 2004b), and it was more or less "invented" in Japan (Kristof, 1995). In Japan, the police are highly respected and considered almost incorruptible. In every Japanese city, each neighborhood has its own *koban*, or police box. It is a one- or two-room office, staffed around the clock by police officers called "Honorable Walkabouts" for they spend much of their time strolling or bicycling around the neighborhood. They advise homeowners how to avoid burglaries, make teenagers rip up and throw away their cigarettes—"but in the trash can, not just on the ground"—issue a newsletter for the area, and visit homes at least once a year. The police have broad powers; they can stop people who look suspicious, and they can ask them to come to the *koban* for a "discussion," to empty their pockets, or to avoid the neighborhood. The police also have the right to detain people for up to 23 days for questioning often without the presence of an attorney before being charged, the interviews with suspects are not taped, deprive them of sleep, and do their best to make them feel guilty and to confess. In fact, the police bring charges to the court only when they have a cast-iron case, almost always based on confession (and the courts almost invariably convict) (*Economist,* 2004c). But despite appearances, Japanese police are much less powerful than their American counterparts; they are usually not allowed to infiltrate subversive organizations, to pay informers, to tap telephones or to plea bargain with defendants. Even though the crime rate is much lower, Japan spends a greater proportion of its GNP on the police than the United States does. New York City police, for example, have to answer more than twice as many emergency calls than the police in *all* of Japan. Adopting the Japanese style policing in the United States would increase costs substantially. Placing police in *kobans* tends to cost more than keeping them in station houses. But Japan does have the lowest crime rate in the industrialized world, and its high efficient model of policing deserves further scrutiny.

Police Discretion

A significant feature of law enforcement—indeed of the entire judicial process and the criminal justice system—is the discretionary power officials can exercise in specific situations (Gilbert, 1997; Miller, 2006; Schulenberg, 2003). The exercise of discretion is integral to the daily routine of police officers in a large variety of activities ranging from routine traffic stops to responding to domestic violence calls (Campbell, 1999; Guyot, 1991:36–61; Kane, 1999; Williams, 1984). Is highly institutionalized in the American system of criminal justice (Reiss, 1992:74) and questions about police discretion increasingly appear in lawsuits against the police (Worrall, 1998). Albert J. Reiss and David J. Bordua (1967) point out that police discretion and disparity stem in large part from the general organization of modern police work. As a largely reactive force, primarily dependent on citizen mobilization, the police officer functions in criminal law much like a private attorney functions in civil law—determining when the victim's complaint warrants formal action and encouraging private settlement of disputes whenever possible. Among such private arrangements protected by the police are those of their own relationships with various categories of citizens, so the degree to which formal legality is extended by police to different categories of individuals varies substantially. In view of the highly decentralized police operation, with minimal direct supervision, it is difficult to control such disparate treatment. Many of the decisions of police officers on the beat do not lend themselves to either command or review. As a result, police exercise a considerable amount of discretionary power, as reflected in disparities in the volume of arrests, parking tickets, and pedestrian stops. For example, James Q. Wilson's (1968a:95) investigation of eight police agencies showed that, among other things, the arrest rates for moving traffic violations ranged from 11.4 to 247.7 per 1,000 population in the cities he studied, about the same as in around 2010.

Because of their discretionary power, "the police are among our most important policymaking administrative agencies. One may wonder whether any other agencies—federal, state, or local—make so much policy that so directly and vitally affects so many people" (Davis, 1975a:263). The police need to make policy with regard to nearly all their activities, such as deciding what types of private disputes to mediate and how to do it, breaking up sidewalk gatherings, helping drunks, deciding what to do with runaways, breaking up fights and matrimonial disputes, entering and searching premises, controlling juveniles, and managing race relations. The police exercise discretion in both reactive and proactive policing.

Reactive police work is a response to citizen mobilization. But even before a citizen can reach a police officer, discretionary power is exercised by police dispatchers at the communication center. A member of the dispatch crew answers the telephone call made to the police emergency number, interviews the caller to identify the nature and location of the reported problem, and decides whether to dispatch a patrol car. In a study of telephone calls to three departments, T. E. Bercal (1970) found that 20 to 40 percent of the calls are handled without dispatching a car. If the dispatcher decides to send a patrol car, then the nature of the assignment (for example, burglary or robbery) and which car to assign must be determined. When a car is dispatched, the officer may informally turn down the assignment, or may procrastinate on the way, or even lie about having investigated the call (Rubinstein, 1973:87–123). If the officer follows up on the call, he or she often has to decide whether a crime has been committed. Albert J. Reiss (1971:73) found that, in Chicago, whereas citizens considered 58 percent of their complaints as criminal matters, officers responding to those dispatches officially processed only 17 percent as criminal matters. One study found in domestic violence cases that over half of the offenders were gone upon police arrival (Kane, 1999:68). Harold E. Pepinsky (1976:21–22) suggests that police officers' decisions are determined mainly by the dispatcher's characterization of the incident and officers' experience with similar cases in their jurisdiction.

A great deal of police work is undertaken on the initiative of the police themselves without citizen mobilization (Reiss, 1971:88–114). The activities of traffic and tactical divisions are primarily proactive policing, as are the various nondispatched activities of detectives and vice divisions. In proactive policing, discretionary power is exercised in the context of whether or not to stop a suspicious pedestrian or automobile for investigation or to engage in various types of crime preventing measures such as hot-spot policing (Braga and Weisburd, 2010).

In both reactive and proactive policing, the use of discretion can take a number of forms—investigation, confrontation, disposition, and decisions about the use of force.

Police officials have the option (although limited) of investigating some acts and not others. The police, for example, may elect to ignore or to actively pursue a citizen's complaint. In some cases, the police arrest a suspect, and in others—even though the act and circumstances may be similar—the individual is released. And some people are "roughed up" by the police, whereas others are handled with respect. All along the line, decisions are made by the police.

Kenneth Culp Davis (1975a:264) notes that the power of the police not to enforce the law in any particular circumstances is enormous. It can even be turned into an affirmative weapon. Jerome H. Skolnick, in *Justice without Trial* (1994), discusses an Oakland ordinance that permits holding every woman arrested for prostitution for eight days for a venereal check. The ordinance conferred no discretionary power on the police, but officers assumed a discretionary power not to enforce the ordinance against women who cooperated: They detained for testing only 38 percent of the women who were arrested. As one officer explained: "If a girl gives us a hard time . . .we'll put a hold on her. I guess we're actually supposed to put a hold on everybody, so there's nothing wrong in putting a hold on her . . . but you know how it is, you get to know some of the girls, and you don't want to give them extra trouble" (Skolnick, 1994:108). In this context, Davis (1975a:264) contends that because the ordinance requires holding every woman arrested, assumption of discretion not to enforce against 62 percent of those arrested was contrary to the terms of the ordinance. Here, discretion not to enforce was converted into an affirmative weapon: "If a girl gives us a hard time . . . we'll put a hold on her." This policy of enforcement discriminates against the innocent woman, because she is more likely to resist, and the experienced woman is more likely to cooperate. The discrimination appears clearly unjust.

There is, indeed, a thin line between discretion and discrimination in discretionary law enforcement. If the likelihood that an individual will be considered a criminal is dependent on the discretionary power of the police to respond to or to ignore a citizen's complaint, to arrest or to release a suspect, and the like, then the probability that any one person will be labeled a criminal increases or decreases depending on that person's correspondence to police conceptions of the criminal. Some individuals are more likely than others to have their behavior treated as a crime by the police and, consequently, are more likely to be labeled as criminal. For example, Nathan Goldman (1963:35–47) found that 65 percent of the black offenders arrested by the police were referred to the juvenile court, as contrasted with 34 percent of the white youths apprehended (see also Bernard and Kurlychek, 2010). Similarly, Donald J. Black and Albert J. Reiss (1970:68) found that 21 percent of black teenagers, but only 8 percent of the white youths, encountered by the police were arrested. Although evidence is sketchy, there is reason to assume that young adults, poor citizens, minority members, migrants, and individuals who look disreputable by police standards are more likely to experience one or another form of police brutality and to be arrested than are more "respectable" citizens. They also tend to be less deferential toward officers, and in general, the police are likely to sanction suspects who fail to defer to police authority, whether legal grounds exist or not (Black, 1980:77).

Police discretion not to enforce the law is attributed to a number of conditions. These include the police belief that (1) the legislative body does not desire enforcement, (2) the community wants nonenforcement or lax enforcement, (3) other immediate duties are more urgent, (4) the offenders promise not to commit the act again, (5) there is a lack of adequate police manpower, (6) there is sympathy with the violator, (7) a particular criminal act is common within a subculture, (8) the victim is likely to get restitution without arrest, (9) nonenforcement can be traded for information, (10) the probable penalty is likely to be too severe, and (11) the arrest would unduly harm the offender's status (Davis, 1975a:264–265; see also Beggs and Davies, 2009).

But as Kenneth Culp Davis (1975b:140) emphatically argues, "Police discretion is absolutely essential. It cannot be eliminated. Any effort to eliminate it would be ridiculous. Discretion is the essence of police work, both in law enforcement and in service activities. Police work without discretion would be something like a human torso without legs, arms, or head." Selective enforcement represents low-visibility interaction between individual officers and various citizens. The exercise of discretion is not guided by clear policy directives, nor is it subject to administrative scrutiny. For such reasons, selective enforcement can easily deteriorate into police abuse and discriminatory conduct. Although it cannot be eliminated, Joseph Goldstein (1960) proposes that an impartial civilian body should scrutinize the decisions as to which laws should be enforced. In that way, discretionary conduct would become more visible and might result in selective law enforcement that would then become a subject for open public dialogue. Discretionary law enforcement can also become an area in police-community relations (Clark, 1979:213–218; Miller, 2006; Skinns, 2010; Thurman et al., 2001).

SUMMARY

This chapter has been concerned with the organization of law in society in the context of judicial, legislative, administrative, and enforcement agencies.

Court cases generally begin with a dispute. Private-initiated, public-initiated, and public defendant disputes constitute, for the most part, the workload of American courts. There are 51 court systems in the United States—one federal court and 50 state court organizations. This dual hierarchy operates side by side. When disputes move from the trial to the appellate level, they are typically transformed and become almost exclusively disputes about law or about procedures.

Courts, as dispute-processing institutions, are composed of four distinct groups of participants—litigants, lawyers, judges, and juries. Litigants can be distinguished by the relative frequency with which they resort to court services. There are two types—the "one-shotters" and the "repeat players." The most important distinction that can be made among types of litigating lawyers is the manner in which they perceive their clientele. These types are public-interest lawyers, private-interest lawyers, criminal defense lawyers, and client-oriented attorneys. The judges are the most prestigious participants in court processes. In addition to basic adjudication functions and the control of the flow of litigation in the courtrooms, judges are responsible for administering their courts. Judges' personal backgrounds and values affect their decisions, which in turn are bases for their recruitment to the higher bench. Juries are used exclusively in trial courts. The principal issues surrounding the participation of jurors in the processing of disputes are their effectiveness on checking the power of judges; the use of the scientific method in jury selection, the degree of their representativeness of the community; and their competence. Although the flow of litigation is different in criminal and civil cases, a high degree of discretion at every level is characteristic of both.

Although the principal function of legislative bodies is lawmaking, they also engage in conflict management and integrative functions. At the federal level and in most states, legislatures comprise two separate bodies—the House and the Senate—which differ in several respects. Differences exist between the House and the Senate in organization, procedure, and the regular activities of their members. The House operates under more formal rules than does the Senate. Behavior in both houses is influenced by a set of informal rules and norms. Much of the important work is done by standing committees and subcommittees.

The participants in the legislative process are legislators, executives, and lobbyists. The majority of legislators come from a middle-class or an upper-class background. The recruitment of legislators is selective by education, religion, and occupational status. Protestant Anglo-Saxon males are substantially overrepresented among legislators. Executives perform three main functions in the legislative process: They serve as a source of ideas; they function as catalytic agents; and they instrument the law. The lobbyist plays a variety of key roles in the legislative process, such as contact person, campaign organizer, and watchdog.

Administrative agencies, often called the fourth branch of government, reach into virtually every corner of American life. Administrative rules affect the food we eat, the cars we drive, the fuel we use, the clothes we wear, the houses we live in, the investments we make, the water we drink, and even the air we breathe. These agencies are authorities of the government other than the executive, legislative, and judicial branches, created for the purpose of administering particular legislations. Administrative agencies are just as subject to pressures of interest groups as are all other lawmakers. Administrative agencies have powers of investigation, rulemaking, and adjudication. Information is essential for administrative agencies to carry out their functions. Rulemaking is administrative lawmaking, and it consists of the power to make or alter rules and regulations. Adjudication is the administrative agency's equivalent of a judicial trial. Much of it is handled informally through the voluntary settlement of cases at lower levels in an agency. In case of disagreement, administrative decisions can be subjected to judicial review, and the courts have the power to overturn an agency's judgment, both on points of law and on questions of fact.

The police are expected and empowered to enforce the law. In the United States, there is no unified system of law enforcement. An important characteristic of law enforcement is the strongly bureaucratic and militaristic organization of the police. The effectiveness of law enforcement agencies depends on the way in which departments are organized. In professionalized departments, there is a greater tendency to detect violators and a higher arrest rate than in nonprofessionalized departments. Law enforcement is characterized by a high amount of discretion. Both in reactive and in proactive policing, the use of police discretion can take a number of forms—investigation, confrontation, disposition, and the decision to use force. There is a thin line between discretion and discrimination in a discretionary law enforcement.

SUGGESTED FURTHER READINGS

Don J. Lofgren, *Dangerous Premises: An Insider's View of OSHA Enforcement*. Ithaca, NY: Cornell University, 1989. A discerning and revealing narrative of the author's experience as an OSHA investigator, written in nontechnical language.

Larry W. Yackle, *Regulatory Rights: Supreme Court Activism, the Public Interest, and the Making of Constitutional Law*. Chicago, IL: University of Chicago Press, 2007.

Michael Tonry (ed.), *Why Punish? How Much? A Reader on Punishment*. New York: Oxford University Press, 2010. A compendium on some time and provocative aspects of punishment.

Michael Tonry and Norval Morris (eds.), *Modern Policing*. Chicago, IL: University of Chicago Press, 1992. An outstanding classic collection of essays on the various facets of policing based on a good historical analysis.

REFERENCES

Abadinsky, Howard. 2008. *Law and Justice: An Introduction to the American Legal System*. 6th ed. Upper Saddle River, NJ: Prentice Hall.

Abraham, Henry J. 1998. *The Judicial Process: An Introductory Analysis of the Courts of the United States, England, and France*. 7th ed. New York: Oxford University Press.

Abramson, Jeffrey. 2000. *We, the Jury: The Jury System and the Ideal of Democracy*. Cambridge, MA: Harvard University Press.

Abramson, Jill. 1998. "The Business of Persuasion Thrives in Nation's Capital," *New York Times* (September 29): A1, A22–23.

Adams, Thomas F. 2007. Police Field Operations. 7th ed. Upper Saddle River, NJ: Prentice Hall.

Adler, Stephen J. 1989. "Consultants Dope Out the Mysteries of Jurors for Clients Being Sued," *Wall Street Journal* (October 24): A1, A10. 1995. *The Jury: Trial and Error in the American Courtroom*. New York: Times Books.

Albonetti, Celesta A. 1992. "An Integration of Theories to Explain Judicial Discretion," *Social Problems* 38 (2) (May): 247–266.

Alker, Hayward R. Jr., Carl Hosticka, and Michael Mitchell. 1976. "Jury Selection as a Biased Social Process," *Law & Society Review* 11 (1) (Fall): 9–41.

Alschuler, Albert W. 1995. "Plea Bargaining and Its History." Pp. 138– 160 in Richard L. Abel (ed.), *The Law & Society Reader*. New York: New York University Press.

Anders, George. 2007. "Economist an Expert at Being Called to Testify." *Seattle Times* (March 25): F1, F7.

Anderson, Patrick R., and Donald J Newman. 1998. *Introduction to Criminal Justice*. 6th ed. Boston, MA: McGraw-Hill.

Andrews, Lori B. 1982. "Mind Control in the Courtroom," *Psychology Today* (March): 66–73.

Asher, Herbert. 1973. "The Learning of Legislative Norms," *American Political Science Review* 67 (June): 499–513.

Badinter, Robert, and Stephen Breyer (eds.). 2004. *Judges in Contemporary Democracy: An International Conversation*. New York: New York University Press.

Baker, Ross K. 2008. *House and Senate*. 4th ed. New York: W.W. Norton & Co., Inc.

Bankowski, Zenon, and James MacLean (eds.). 2007. *The Universal and the Particular in Legal Reasoning*. Burlington, VT: Ashgate.

Barge, Jeff. 1995. "Reformers Target Jury Lists; Seeking Diversity, Jurisdictions May Call Benefit Recipients," *ABA Journal*, 81 (January): 26–28.

Barker, Vanessa. 2009. The Politics of Imprisonment. How the Democratic Process

Shapes the Way America Punishes Offenders. New York: Oxford University Press.

Bartol, Curt R., and Anne M. Bartol. 2004. *Psychology and Law: Theory, Research, and Application.* 3rd ed. Belmont, CA: Thomson/Wadsworth. 2011. *Criminal Behavior: A Psychological Approach.* 9th ed. Boston, MA: Prentice Hall.

Baum, David B. 1994. "Creating a Theme," *Trial,* 30 (3) (March): 66–70.

Baum, Lawrence. 2010. *The Supreme Court.* 10th ed. Washington, DC: QC Press.

Baumgartner, Frank R., Jeffrey M. Berry, Marie Hojnacki, David C. Kimball, and Beth L. Leech. 2009. *Lobbying and Policy Change. Who Wins, Who Loses, and Why.* Chicago, IL: University of Chicago Press.

Bayley, David H. 1992. "Comparative Organization of the Police in English-speaking Countries." Pp. 509–545 in Michael Tonry and Norval Morris (eds.), *Modern Policing.* Chicago, IL: University of Chicago Press.

Beggs, John, and Hugh Davies. 2009. *Police Misconduct, Complaints, and Public Regulation.* New York: Oxford University Press.

Bell, Jeannine (ed.). 2006. *Police and Policing Law.* Burlington, VA: Ashgate.

Bercal, T. E. 1970. "Calls for Police Assistance: Consumer Demands for Governmental Service," *American Behavioral Scientist,* 13 (5–6) (May–August): 681–691.

Bernard, Thomas J., and Megan C. Kurlychek. 2010. *The Cycle of Juvenile Justice.* 2nd ed. New York: Oxford University Press.

Bissonette, Aimee M. 2009. *Cyber Law.* Thousand Oaks, CA: Corwin.

Bittner, Egon. 1970. *The Functions of the Police in Modern Society.* Chevy Chase, MD: National Institute of Mental Health.

Black, Donald. 1973. "The Mobilization of Law," *Journal of Legal Studies,* 2 (1) (January): 125–149. 1980. *The Manners and Customs of the Police.* New York: Academic Press.

Black, Donald J., and Albert J. Reiss, Jr. 1970. "Police Control of Juveniles," *American Sociological Review,* 35 (1) (February): 63–77.

Blumberg, Abraham S. 1979. *Criminal Justice: Issues & Ironies.* 2nd ed. New York: New Viewpoints.

Bogus, Carl T. 2001. *Why Lawsuits Are Good for America: Disciplined Democracy, Big Business, and the Common Law.* New York: New York University Press.

Bonner, Raymond. 2001. "Push Is On for Larger Jury in Military Capital Cases," *New York Times* (September 4): A1, A9.

Bordua, David J., and Albert J. Reiss, Jr. 1966. "Command, Control, and Charisma: Reflections on Police Bureaucracy," *American Journal of Sociology,* 72 (1) (July): 68–76.

Boulding, Kenneth E. 1956. *The Image.* Ann Arbor, MI: University of Michigan Press.

Box, Richard C. 2005. Dialogue and Administrative Theory & Praxis: Twenty-Five Years of Public Administrative Theory. *Administrative Theory & Praxis,* 27 (3) (September): 438–466. 2009. *Public Administration and Society: Critical Issues in American Governance.* 2nd ed. Armonk, NY: M.E. Sharpe.

Boyce, Joseph N. 1992. "Community Style Policing Takes Hold in Cities Like Takoma Park, Md.," *Wall Street Journal* (August 5): A1, A6.

Braga, Anthony A., and David L. Weisburd. 2010. *Policing Problem Places: Crime Hot Spots and Effective Prevention.* New York: Oxford University Press.

Breyer, Stephen G., and Richard B. Stewart. 2006. *Administrative Law and Regulatory Policy.* 6th ed. New York: Aspen Law & Business.

Broderick, Vincent L. 1994. "The Delusion of Mandatory Sentencing: The Wrong Approach to Fighting Crime," *Trial,* 30 (8) (August): 62–67.

Brooker, Russell, and Todd Schaefer. 2006. *Public Opinion in the 21st Century: Let the People Speak?* Boston, MA: Houghton Mifflin.

Brooks, Thom (ed.). 2009. *The Rights to a Fair Trial.* Burlington, VT: Ashgate.

Brown, Michael K. 1988. *Working the Street: Police Discretion and the Dilemmas of Reform.* New York: Russell Sage Foundation.

Brown, Peter Harry, and Daniel G. Abel. 2003. *Outgunned: Up against the NRA: The First Complete Insider Account of the Battle over Gun Control*. New York, NY: Free Press.

Burnett, Graham D. 2002. *A Trial by Jury*. New York: Alfred B. Knopf

Butterfield, Fox. 2001. "States Easing Stringent Laws on Prison Time," *New York Times* (September 2): A1, A5.

Button, Mark. 2007. *Security Officers and Policing: Powers, Culture, and Control in the Governance of Private Space*. Burlington, VT: Ashgate.

Campbell, Elaine. 1999. "Toward a Sociological Theory of Discretion,*" International Journal of the Sociology of Law*, 27:79–101.

Calvi, James V., and Susan Coleman. 2008. *American Law and Legal Systems*. 6th ed. Upper Saddle River, NJ: Prentice Hall.

Cann, Steven J. 2006. *Administrative Law*. 4th ed. Thousand Oaks, CA: Sage Publications, Inc.

Carp, Robert A., Ronald Stidham, and Kenneth L. Manning. 2010. *Judicial Process in America*. 8th ed. Washington, DC: CQ Press.

Carter, David L. 2002. *The Police and the Community*. 7th ed. Upper Saddle River: NJ: Prentice Hall.

Casper, Jonathan. 1972. *Lawyers before the Warren Court*. Urbana, IL: University of Illinois Press.

Cho, Susie. 1994. "Capital Confusion: The Effect of Jury Instructions on the Decision to Impose Death," *Journal of Criminal Law and Criminology*, 85 (2) (Fall): 532–561.

Choudhary, Rohit. 2010. *Policing: Reinventing Strategies in a Marketing Framework*. Thousand Oaks, CA: Sage.

Clark, Robert S. 1979. *Police and the Community: An Analytic Perspective*. New York: New Viewpoints.

Clear, Todd R., George F. Cole, and Michael D Reisig. 2011. *American Corrections*, 9th ed. Belmont, CA: Wadsworth.

Clifford, Robert A. 1995. "Mock Trials Offer Virtual Reality: Simulated Juries Can Be Used Most Effectively Early in the Litigation Process to Develop the Theory of the Case,"

National Law Journal, 17 (26) (February 27): 88.

Clymer, Adam. 1995. "Senate Votes 98-0 for Strict Limits on Lobbyist Gifts – Compliance Voluntary," *New York Times* (July 29): A1, A9.

Cohn, Alvin W. 1976. *Crime and Justice Administration*. Philadelphia, PA: Lippincott.

Coleman, James W. 2006. *The Criminal Elite: Understanding White Collar Crime*. 6th ed. New York: Worth Publishers.

Connolly, Anthony J. 2010. *Cultural Difference on Trial: The Nature and Limits of Judicial Understanding*. Burlington, VT: Ashgate.

Cox, Gail Diane. 1994. "Voters Tough on Criminals: Law and Order Initiatives Sweep the Polls, While Tort Reform and Others Lose," *National Law Journal*, 17 (12) (November 21): A6.

Corboy, Philip H. 1975. "From the Bar." Pp. 179–195 in Rita James Simon (ed.), *The Jury System in America: A Critical Overview*. Beverly Hills, CA: Sage Publications.

Coyle, Marcia. 1995. "Death Juries Get It Wrong – Study: Survey Reports They Mishear Judges' Instructions," *National Law Journal*, 17 (28) (March): 6.

Crank, John P. 1994. "Watchman and Community: Myth and Institutionalization in Policing," *Law and Society Review*, 28 (2) (May): 325–351.

Cunningham, Sally. 2009. *Driving Offences: Law, Policy, and Practice*. Burlington, VT: Ashgate.

Daley, Suzanne. 2001. "France's Most Courted: Women to Join the Ticket," *New York Times* (February 8): 1, 8.

Dalrymple, T. 2005. "Trial by Human Begins," *National Review*, 57 (7) (April 25): 30–31.

Davis, Kenneth Culp. 1975a. *Administrative Law and Government*. 2nd ed. St. Paul, MN: West Publishing Company. 1975b. *Police Discretion*. St. Paul, MN: West Publishing Company. 1977. A*dministrative Law: Cases—Text—Problems*. 6th ed. St. Paul, MN: West Publishing Company.

Davis, Melissa G., Richard J. Lundman, and Ramiro Martinez, Jr. 1991. "Private Corporate Justice: Store Police, Shoplifters, and Civil Recovery," *Social Problems,* 38 (3) (August): 395–411.

Davies, Paul, and John Emshwiller. 2006. "Split Verdict on Selecting Juries Quickly," *Wall Street Journal* (February 1): B1–B2.

Decaro, Lisa L., and Leonard Matheo. 2004. *The Lawyer's Winning Edge: Exceptional Courtroom Performance.* Denver, CO: Bradford Publishing Co.

Dempsey, John S., and Linda S. Forst. 2010. *An Introduction to Policing.* 5th ed. Belmont, CA: Wadsworth.

Deosaran, Ramesh. 1993. "The Social Psychology of Selecting Jury Forepersons," *British Journal of Criminology,* 33 (1) (Winter): 70–80.

Deutsch, Linda. 2006. "TV Distorting Jurors' Expectations?" *Seattle Times* (January 15): A9.

Dilworth, Donald C. 1995 "Arizona Commission Proposes Far-Reaching Changes in Jury Procedures," *Trial,* 31 (2) (February): 17–20.

Dimitrius, Jo-Ellan, and Mark Mazzarella. 1998. *Reading People: How to Understand People and Predict Their Behavior, Anytime, Anyplace.* New York: Random House.

Dixon, Jo, Aaron Kupchik, and Joachim Savelsberg. (eds.). 2007. *Criminal Courts.* Burlington, VA: Ashgate.

Donner, Ted A., and Richard K. Gabriel. 2000. *Jury selection: Strategy and Science.* 3rd ed. St. Paul, MN: West Group.

Dunham, Roger G., and Geoffrey P. Alpert (eds.). 2005. *Critical Issues in Policing, Contemporary Readings.* 5th ed. Prospect Heights, IL: Waveland Press, Inc.

Duff, P., and M. Findlay. 1997. "Jury Reform: Of Myths and Moral Panics," *International Journal of the Sociology of Law,* 25 (4) (December): 363–384.

Durnal, David W. 2010. "Crime Scene Investigation (As Seen on TV)." *Forensic Science International* (March 15): 2–17.

Economist. 2004a. "How to Reform Brazil's Justice System" (March 25): 66–67. 2004b. "London's Cops Look to New York" (February 21): 53–54. 2004c. "Justice in Japan: The People Come to Court" (March 6): 35–36. 2006a. "Pork and Scandals: Hobbling the Lobbyists" (January 28): 29–30. 2006b. "The Police Are a Bunch of Monkeys" (January 28): 77. 2007. "Private Jails: Locking in the Best Price" (January 27): 60–61. 2009. "A Delicate Judgment: Nicolas Sarkozy Wants to Reform Napoleon's Investigating Judges" (September 12): 57.

Edley, Christopher R. 1990. *Administrative Law: Rethinking Judicial Control of Bureaucracy.* New Haven, CT: Yale University Press.

Eisenstein, James, and Herbert Jacob. 1977. *Felony Justice.* Boston, MA: Little, Brown.

Feeley, Malcolm M. 1979. "Perspectives on Plea Bargaining." *Law & Society Review* (Special Issue on Plea Bargaining), 13 (2) (Winter): 199–209.

Fisher, George. 2003. *Plea Bargaining's Triumph: A History of Plea Bargaining in America.* Stanford, CA: Stanford University Press.

Flack, Jessica C. 2006. "Policing Stabilizes Social Niche Construction in Primates," *Nature,* 439: 426–429.

Forman, James Jr. 2004. "Juries and Race in the Nineteenth Century," *Yale Law Journal,* 113 (4) (January): 895–939.

Foreman, Tucker C. (ed.). 1991. *Regulating for the Future: The Creative Balance.* Washington, DC: Center for National Policy Press.

Forester, John. 2009. *Dealing with Differences: The Drama of Mediating Public Disputes.* New York: Oxford University Press.

Franklin, Daniel. 1994. "The Right Three Strikes," *Washington Monthly,* 26 (9) (September): 25–30.

Freedman, James O. 1978. *Crisis and Legitimacy: The Administrative Process and American Government.* Cambridge, UK: Cambridge University Press.

Friedman, Lawrence M. 1998. *American Law: An Introduction.* 2nd ed. New York: W. W. Norton & Co., Inc. 2002. *American Law in the Twentieth Century.* New Haven, CT: Yale University Press. 2005. *A History of American Law.* 3rd ed. New York: Simon & Schuster/Touchstone Book.

Fuente, Leticia de la, E. Inmaculada de la Fuente, and Juan García. 2004. "Effects of

Pretrial Juror Bias, Strength of Evidence and Deliberation Process on Juror Decisions: New Validity Evidence of the Juror Bias Scale Scores". *Psychology, Crime, and Law*, 9 (2): 197–209.

Galanter, Marc. 1974. "Why the 'Haves' Come Out Ahead: Speculations on the Limits of Legal Change," *Law & Society Review*, 9 (1) (Fall): 95–160.

Garland, David. 2001. *The Culture of Control: Crime and Social Order in Contemporary Society*. Chicago, IL: University of Chicago Press.

Gerber, A. S. 2004. "Does Campaign Spending Work?: Field Experiments Provide Evidence and Suggest New Theory," *American Behavioral Scientist*, 47 (5) (January): 541–575.

Gellhorn, Ernest, and Ronald M. Levin. 1997. *Administrative Law and Process in a Nutshell*. 4th ed. St. Paul, MN: West Publishing Company.

Gerlin, Andrea. 1995. "Jury-Duty Scofflaws Try Patience of Courts," *Wall Street Journal* (August 9): B1, B6.

Geyelin, Milo, and Martha Brannigan. 1992. "Jury Selection in Racially Charged Cases Becomes More Difficult after Rioting," *Wall Street Journal* (May 5): B1, B10.

Gibbons, Gary F. 1995. "Career Development in Smaller Departments," *FBI Law Enforcement Bulletin*, 64 (2) (February): 16–19.

Gilbert, Michael J. 1997. "The Illusion of Structure: A Critique of the Classical Model of Organization and the Discretionary Power of Correctional Officers," *Criminal Justice Review*, 22 (1) (Spring): 49–64.

Glaberson, William. 1989. "Study Sees More US Plea Bargains," *New York Times* (October 29): Y19. 1992. "With Au Pair Acquitted in Murder, the Focus Turns to the Police," *New York Times* (July 12): 20. 2001. "Lawyers' Study Says States Should Pay for Court Races," *New York Times* (July 23): 1.

Godwin, R. Kenneth. 1988. *One Billion Dollars of Influence: The Direct Marketing of Politics*. Chatham, NJ: Chatham House Publishers, Inc.

Goldman, Nathan. 1963. *The Differential Selection of Juvenile Offenders for Court Appearance*. New York: National Council on Crime and Delinquency.

Goldman, Sheldon, and Austin Sarat (eds.). 1989. *American Court Systems: Readings in Judicial Process and Behavior*. 2nd ed. New York: Longman.

Goldstein, Joseph. 1960. "Police Discretion Not to Invoke the Criminal Process: Low Visibility Decisions in the Administration of Criminal Justice," *Yale Law Journal*, 69 (March): 543–594.

Grossback, Lawrence J., and David A. M. Peterson. 2004. "Understanding Institutional Change: Legislative Staff Development and the State Policymaking Environment," *American Politics Research*, 32 (1): 26–51

Guyot, Dorothy. 1991. *Policing as though People Matter*. Philadelphia, PA: Temple University Press.

Hafemeister, Thomas L., and W. Larry Ventis. 1994. "Juror Stress: Sources and Implications," *Trial*, 30 (10) (October): 68–73.

Hagerty, James R. 2006. "Broker Commissions Are the Real Component to the Real-Estate Bubble," *Wall Street Journal* (February 6): A2.

Hall, Thad. 2004. *Authorizing Policy*. Columbus, OH: Ohio State University Press.

Hans, Valerie P. (ed.). 2006. *The Jury System: Contemporary Scholarship*. Burlington, VA: Ashgate.

Hans, Valerie P. 1992. "Jury Decision Making." Pp. 56–76 in Dorothy K. Kagehiro and William S. Laufer (eds.), *Handbook of Psychology and Law*. New York: Springer-Verlag.

Hans, Valerie P., and William S. Lofquist. 1992. "Jurors' Judgments of Business Liability in Tort Cases: Implications for the Litigation Explosion Debate," *Law & Society Review*, 26 (1): 85–115.

Hans, Valerie P., and Veil Vidmar. 1986. *Judging the Jury*. New York: Plenum.

Hanson, Roger A., and Brian J. Ostrom. 1993. "Litigation and the Courts: Myths and Misconceptions, *Trial*, 29 (4) (April): 40–45.

Harris, Richard A., and Sidney M. Milkis. 1996. *The Politics of Regulatory Change: A Tale of Two Agencies*. 2nd ed. New York: Oxford University Press.

Hemmens, Craig, David C. Brody, and Cassia C. Spohn. 2010. *Criminal Courts: A Contemporary Perspective.* Thousand Oaks, CA: Sage.

Hess, Karen M., Christine H. Orthmann, and Henry Lim Cho. 2011. *Police Operations: Theory and Practice.* 5th ed. Belmont, CA: Wadsworth.

Hicks, Robert D. 1991. *In Pursuit of Satan: The Police and the Occult.* Buffalo, NY: Prometheus Books.

Higgins, Paul, and Mitchell B. Mackinem (eds.). 2010. P*roblem-Solving Courts. Justice for the Twenty-First Century?* Santa Barbara, CA: Praeger.

Hill, Kathleen Thompson, and Gerald N. Hill. 2004. *Encyclopedia of Federal Agencies and Commissions.* New York: Facts on File.

Hoffman, Jan. 1992. "In Courtrooms, the Stoolie Is Pushed to Squeal Louder," *New York Times* (August 2): E18. 1995. "Why a Jury Can Be 12, Even 6, but Not 5," *New York Times* (June 11): E6. 2004. "Finding the Ideal Jury, Keeping Fingers Crossed," *New York Times* (March 11): B2.

Holmes, Malcolm D., Howard C. Daudistel, and William A. Taggart. 1992. "Plea Bargaining Policy and State District Court Caseloads: An Interrupted Time Series Analysis," *Law & Society Review,* 26 (1): 139–159.

Hopkins, Bruce R. 1992. *Charity, Advocacy, and the Law.* New York: John Wiley.

Hrebenar, Ronald J., and Bryson B. Morgan. 2010. *Lobbying in America: A Reference Handbook.* Santa Barbara, CA: ABC-CLIO.

Hughes, John C. 1995. *The Federal Courts, Politics, and the Rule of Law.* New York: HarperCollins College Publishers.

Hunt, Morton. 1982. "Putting Juries on the Couch," *New York Times Magazine* (November 28):70–87.

Inbau, Fred E., James R. Thompson, James B. Zagel, and James P. Manak. 1997. *Criminal Law and Its Administration.* 6th ed. Westbury, NY: The Foundation Press, Inc.

Israel, Mark. 1998. "Ethnic Bias in Jury Selection in Australia and New Zealand," *International Journal of the Sociology of Law,* 26: 35–54.

Jacob, Herbert. 1984. *Justice in America: Courts, Lawyers, and the Judicial Process.* 4th ed. Boston, MA: Little, Brown. 1995. *Law and Politics in the United States.* 2nd. ed. Fort Washington, PA: HarperCollins College Publishers. 1997. "The Governance of Trial Judges," *Law & Society Review,* 32 (1): 3–30.

John, Tim, Rhobert Lewis, and Colin Rogers. 2009. *Police Work: Principles and Practice.* Devon, UK: Willan Publishing.

Johnston, David Cay. 2004. *Perfectly Legal: The Covert Campaign to Rig Our Tax System to Benefit the Super Rich – and Cheat Everybody Else.* New York: Portfolio/Penguin Group.

Johnstone, Gerry, and Tony Ward. 2010. *Law and Crime.* Thousand Oaks, CA: Sage.

Jonakait, Randolph N. 2003. *The American Jury System.* New Haven, CT: Yale University Press.

Jones, Charles O. 2005. *The Presidency in a Separated System.* 2nd ed. Washington, DC: The Brookings Institution. 2009. *The American Presidency.* New York: Sterling Publishing Company.

Joseph, Thomas M. 1994. "Walking the Minefields of Community-Oriented Policing," *FBI Law Enforcement Bulletin,* 63 (9) (September): 8–13.

Jun, Jond S., and Hiromi Muto. 1995. "The Hidden Dimensions of Japanese Administration: Culture and Its Impact," *Public Administration Review,* 55 (2) (March–April): 125–134.

Jewell, Malcolm E., and Samuel C. Patterson. 1986. *The Legislative Process in the United States.* 4th ed. New York: Random House.

Kalven, Harry, Jr., and Hans Zeisel. 1966. *The American Jury.* Boston, MA: Little, Brown.

Kane, Robert J. 1999. "Patterns of Arrest in Domestic Violence Encounters: Identifying a Police Decision-Making Model," *Journal of Criminal Justice,* 27 (1): 65–79.

Kardos, Donna. 2007. "Dick Gephardt to Join FTI Consulting as an Advisor," *Wall Street Journal* (January 18): B7.

Kassin, Saul M., and Lawrence S. Wrightsman. 1988. *The American Jury on Trial.* New York: Hemisphere Publishing Corporation.

Kennedy, Randall. 1998. *Race, Crime, and the Law*. New York: Random House/Vintage.

Kerley, Kent R. (ed.). 2005. *Policing and Program Evaluation*. Upper Saddle River, NJ: Prentice Hall.

Kerwin, Cornelius M. 2003. *Rulemaking: How Government Agencies Write Law and Make Policies*. 3rd ed. Washington, DC: CQ Press.

Klein, Mitchell S. G. 1984. *Law, Courts, and Policy*. Englewood Cliffs, NJ: Prentice Hall.

Kleining, John, and James P. Levine. 2005. *Jury Ethics: Jury Conduct and Jury Dynamics*. Boulder, CO: Paradigm Publishers.

Kravets, David. 2004. "Lawyers Seek Record Pay in Microsoft Case." *Seattle Times* (May 13): E1–2.

Kristof, Nicholas D. 1995. "A Neighborly Style of Police State," *New York Times* (June 4): E5.

Langworthy, Robert H., and Lawrence F. Travis. 2008. *Policing in America: A Balance of Forces*. 4th ed. Upper Saddle River, NJ: Prentice Hall.

Lax, Jeffrey R. 2004. "Certiorari and Compliance in the Judicial Hierarchy: Discretion, Reputation, and the Rule of Four," *Journal of Theoretical Politics*, 15 (1): 61–79.

Lemieux, Frederic (ed.). 2010. *International Police Cooperation: Emerging Issues, Theory, and Practice*. Devon, UK: Willan Publishing.

Leonard, V. A., and Harry W. More. 2000. *Police Organization and Management*. 9th ed. New York: Foundation Press.

Levi, Avraham M. 1998. "Are Defendants Guilty If They Were Chosen in a Lineup?" *Law and Human Behavior*, 22 (4) (August): 389–408.

Levine, Bertram J. 2009. *The Art of Lobbying: Building Trust and Selling Policy*. Washington, DC: CQ Press.

Lewin, Tamar. 2001a. "Little Sympathy or Remedy for Inmates Who Are Raped," *New York Times* (April 15): 1, 14. 2001b. "3-Strikes Law Is Overrated in California, Study Finds," *New York Times* (August 23): 1, 8.

Lieberman, Joel D., and Daniel A. Krauss (eds.). 2010a. *Jury Psychology: Social Aspects of Trial Process: Psychology in the Courtroom*. Vol. 1. Burlington, VT: Ashgate.

2010b. *Psychological Expertise in Court: Psychology in the Courtroom*. Vol. 2. Burlington, VT: Ashgate.

Lilley, Lin S. 1994. "Techniques for Targeting Juror Bias," *Trial*, 30 (11) (November): 74–80.

Loh, Wallace D. 1984. *Social Research in the Judicial Process: Cases, Readings, and Text*. New York: Russell Sage Foundation.

Loveday, Barry. 1998. "Improving the Status of Police Patrol," *International Journal of the Sociology of Law*, 26: 161–196

Luginbuhl, James. 1992. "Comprehension of Judges' Instructions in the Penalty Phase of a Capital Trial," *Law and Human Behavior*, 16 (2) (April): 203–218.

Lyman, Michael D. 2010. *The Police: An Introduction*. 4th ed. Upper Saddle River, NJ: Prentice Hall.

Lynch, D.R., and T.D. Evans. 2004. "Attributes of highly effective criminal defense negotiators," *Journal of Criminal Justice*, 30 (5): 387–396.

Lyons, William T., Jr. 1999. *The Politics of Community Policing: Rearranging the Power to Punish*. Ann Arbor, MI: University of Michigan Press.

Mahood, H. R. 2000. *Interest Groups in American National Politics: An Overview*. Upper Saddle River, NJ: Prentice Hall.

Malsch, Marijke. 2010. *Democracy in the Courts: Lay Participation in European Criminal Justice Systems*. Burlington, VT: Ashgate.

Margolick, David. 1992. "Chorus of Judicial Critics Assail Sentencing Guides," *New York Times* (April 12): A1, A20.

Mashaw, Jerry L. 1994. "Improving the Environment of Agency Rulemaking: An Essay on Management, Games, and Accountability," *Law and Contemporary Problems*, 57 (2) (Spring): 185–257.

Mays, Larry G., and Peter R. Gregware (eds.). 2009. *Courts and Justice: A Reader*. 4th ed. Prospect Heights, IL: Waveland Press, Inc.

McCloskey, R. G. 2010. *The American Supreme Court*. 5th ed. Chicago, IL: University Chicago Press.

Melling, Tom. 1994. "Dispute Resolution within Legislative Institutions," *Stanford Law Review*, 46 (6) (July): 1677–1715.

Miller, Seumas (ed.). 2006. *Police Ethics*. Burlington, VT: Ashgate.

Moore, Mark Harrison. 1992. "Problem-Solving and Community Policing." Pp. 99–158 in Michael Tonry and Norval Morris (eds.), *Modern Policing*. Chicago, IL: University of Chicago Press.

Mulcahy, Aogan. 1994. "The Justification of 'Justice': Legal Practitioners' Accounts of Negotiated Case Settlements in Magistrates' Courts (United Kingdom)," *British Journal of Criminology*, 34 (4) (Autumn): 411–430.

Munk, Nina. 1994. "Rent-a-Cops," *Forbes*, 154 (8) (October 10): 104–106.

Narby, Douglas J., and Brian L. Cutler. 1994 "Effectiveness of Voir Dire as a Safeguard in Eyewitness Cases," *Journal of Applied Psychology*, 79 (5) (October): 724–730.

Nasheri, Hedie. 1998. *Betrayal of Due Process: A Comparative Assessment of Plea Bargaining in the United States and Canada*. Lanham, MD: University Press of America, Inc.

Nemeth, Charles. 2010. *Private Security and the Investigative Process*. 3rd ed. Boca Raton, FL: Taylor and Francis.

New York Times. 1995. "Toward Democratic Jury Service" (June 14): A18. 2001. "A Study's Verdict: Jury Awards Are Not Out of Control" (August 6): A1.

Novak, William J. 1989. "Intellectual Origins of the State Police Power: The Common Law Vision of a Well-Regulated Society," Working Papers Series 3. Legal History Program. Institute for Legal Studies. Madison, WI: University of Wisconsin. 3 (2) (June): 1–112.

O'Connell, John P., Jr. 1995. "Throwing Away the Key (and State Money): Study Reveals Ineffectiveness of Mandatory Sentencing Policies," *Spectrum: The Journal of State Government*, 68 (1) (Winter): 28–32.

Oda, Hiroshi. 2009. *Japanese Law*. 3rd ed. New York Oxford University Press.

O'Leary, Dennis. 1994. "Reflection on Police Privatization," *FBI Law Enforcement Bulletin*, 63 (9) (September): 21–26.

Ornstein, Norman J., Thomas E. Mann, and Michael J. Malbin. 1990. *Vital Statistics on Congress, 1989–1990*. Washington, DC: Congressional Quarterly Inc.

Osborne, Randal. 1992. "The Fixers," *Riverfront Times* (St. Louis), (June 17–23): 1, 14–15.

Pakes, Francis, and Suzanne Pakes. 2009. *Criminal Psychology*. Devon, UK: Willan Publishing.

Palermo, George B., Maxine Aldridge White, Lew A. Wasserman, and William Hanrahan. 1998. "Plea Bargaining: Injustice for All?" *International Journal of Offender Therapy and Comparative Criminology*, 42 (2) (June): 111–123.

Palmer, Michael, and Simon Roberts. 1998. *Dispute Processes: ADR and the Primary Forms of Decision Making*. London, UK: Butterworths.

Paris, Michael. 2010. *Framing Equal Opportunity: Law and the Politics of School Finance Reform*. Palo Alto, CA: Stanford University Press.

Parisi, F. 2004. "Rent-Seeking through Litigation: Adversarial and Inquisitorial Systems Compared," *International Review of Law and Economics*, 22 (2): 193–216.

Passas, Nikos (ed.). 2003. *International Crimes*. Aldershot, UK/Burlington, VT: Ashgate.

Peak, Kenneth J., and Ronald W. Glensor. 2008. *Community Policing and Problem Solving: Strategies and Practices*. 5th. ed. Upper Saddle River, NJ: Prentice Hall.

Peerenboom, Randall (ed.). 2009. *Judicial Independence in China: Lessons for Global Rule of Law Promotion*. Cambridge, UK: Cambridge University Press.

Penrod, Steven D., and Larry Heuer. 1997. "Tweaking Commonsense: Assessing Aids to Jury Decision Making," *Psychology, Public Policy, and Law*, 3 (2/3) (June/September): 259–284.

Pepinsky, Harold E. 1976. *Crime and Conflict: A Study of Law and Society*. New York: Academic Press.

Pfander, James E. 2009. *One Supreme Court: Supremacy, Inferiority, and the Judicial Department of the United States*. New York: Oxford University Press.

Philips, Susan U. 1998. *Ideology in the Language of Judges: How Judges Practice Law, Politics, and Courtroom Control*. New York: Oxford University Press.

Pinkele, Carl F., and William C. Louthan (eds.). 1985. *Discretion, Justice, and Democracy: A Public Policy Perspective*. Ames, IA: Iowa State University.

Pollock, Ellen Joan, and Stephen J. Adler. 1992. "Justice for All? Legal System Struggles to Reflect Diversity, but Progress Is Slow," *Wall Street Journal* (May 8): 1, 4.

Pope, Maurice. 1989. "Upon the Country—Juries and the Principle of Random Selection," *Social Science Information,* 28 (2): 265–289.

Posner, Richard A. 1995. "Juries on Trial," *Commentary*, 99 (3) (March): 49–53. 2009. *How Judges Think*. Cambridge, MA: Harvard University Press.

Prentice, Robert A., and Jonathan J. Koehler. 2003. "A Normality Bias in Legal Decision Making," *Cornell Law Review*, 88 (3) (March): 583–651.

President's Commission on Law Enforcement and Administration of Justice. 1967. *The Challenge of Crime in a Free Society*. Washington, DC: U.S. Government Printing Office.

Ramirez, Deborah A. 1994. "A Brief Historical Overview of the Use of Mixed Jury," *American Criminal Law Review*, 31 (3) (Summer): 1213–1224.

Reiss, Albert J., Jr. 1971. *The Police and the Public*. New Haven, CT: Yale University Press. 1992. "Police Organization in the Twentieth Century." Pp. 51–97 in Michael Tonry and Norval Morris (eds.), *Modern Policing*. Chicago, IL: University of Chicago Press.

Reiss, Albert J., Jr., and David J. Bordua. 1967. "Environment and Organization: A Perspective on the Police." Pp. 25–55 in David J. Bordua (ed.), *The Police: Six Sociological Essays*. New York: John Wiley.

Reske, Henry J. 1994. "Judges Irked by Tough-on-Crime Laws," *ABA Journal*, 80 (October): 18–18.

Ripley, Randall B. 1988. *Congress: Process and Policy*. 4th ed. New York: W. W. Norton & Co., Inc.

Rodriguez, Nancy. 2003. The Impact of "Strikes" in Sentencing Decisions: Punishment for Only Some Habitual Offenders," *Criminal Justice Policy Review*, 14 (1):106–127.

Rohde, David. 1998. "Jury Duty in Manhattan Lightens a Bit After Changes," *New York Times* (August 27): A21.

Rosett, Arthur, and Donald R. Cressey. 1976. *Justice by Consent: Plea Bargains in the American Courthouse*. Philadelphia, PA: Lippincott.

Ross, H. Laurence. 1980. *Settled Out of Court*. 2nd ed. Chicago, IL: Aldine.

Rozell, Mark J., Clyde Wilcox, and David Madland. 2006. *Interest Groups in American Campaigns*. 2nd ed. Washington, DC: CQ Press.

Rubinstein, Jonathan. 1973. *City Police*. New York: Farrar, Straus & Giroux.

Saks, Michael J., and Reid Hastie. 1978. *Social Psychology in Court*. New York: Van Nostrand Reinhold.

Sarat, Austin (ed.). 2004. *Social Organization of Law*. Los Angeles, CA: Roxbury Publishing Company. 2011. *Sovereignty, Emergency, Legality*. New York: Cambridge University Press.

Sarat, Austin, and William L. F. Felstiner. 1995. *Divorce Lawyers and Their Clients: Power and Meaning in the Legal Process*. New York: Oxford University Press.

Salant, Jonathan D. 2003. "Clinton-Era Officials Follow Tradition, Take Lobbying Jobs," *Seattle Times* (March 31): A10.

Salant, Jonathan D., and David S. Cloud. 1995. *Congressional Quarterly Weekly Report*, 53 (15) (April 15): 1055–1060.

Savelsberg, Joachim J. 1992. "Law That Does Not Fit Society: Sentencing Guidelines as a Neoclassical Reaction to the Dilemmas of Substantivized Law," *American Journal of Sociology,* 97 (5) (March): 1346–1381.

Scheck, Barry, Peter Neufeld, and Jim Dwyer. 2003. *Actual Innocence: When Justice Goes Wrong and How to Make it Right*. New ed. New York: New American Library.

Schmidhauser, John R. 1979. *Judges and Justices*. Boston, MA: Little, Brown.

Schulenberg, Jennifer L. 2003. "The Social Context of Police Discretion with Young Offenders: An Ecological Analysis," *Canadian Journal of Criminology and Criminal Justice*, 45 (2) (April): 127–158.

Schwartz, Bernard. 1959. *The Professor and the Commissions*. New York: Knopf.

Seabury, Seth A., Nicholas M. Pace, and Robert T. Reville. 2004. "Forty Years of Civil Jury Verdicts," *Journal of Empirical Legal Studies*, 1 (1): 1–25.

Seattle Times. 2007. "State Continues Testing Higher Pay for Jurors" (May 20): B6.

Seib, Gerald F. 1995. "You Can Get Away From Washington—But Not Government," *Wall Street Journal* (June 21): A1, A5.

Seligman, Daniel. 1995. "Advocates Unlimited," *Fortune,* 131 (4) (March 6): 217.

Shearing, Clifford D., and Philip C. Stenning (eds.). 1987. *Private Policing*. Beverly Hills, CA: Sage Publications.

Simon, Rita J. 1980. *The Jury: Its Role in American Society*. Lexington, MA: Lexington Books, DC Heath.

Simonsen, Clifford E. 1998. *Private Security in America: An Introduction*. Upper Saddle River, NJ: Prentice Hall.

Singer, Peter. 2003. *Corporate Warriors: The Rise of the Privatized Military Industry*. Ithaca, NY: Cornel University Press.

Skinns, Layla. 2010. *Police Custody*. Devon, UK: Willan Publishing.

Skolnick, Jerome H. 1994. *Justice without Trial: Law Enforcement in Democratic Society*. 3rd ed. New York: MacMillan.

Skolnick, Jerome H., and David H. Bayley. 1988. *Community Policing: Issues and Practices around the World*. Washington, DC: National Institute of Justice.

Slonim, Scott. 1980. "Survey Finds Fewer Lawyer-Legislators," *American Bar Association Journal,* 66 (January): 30.

Smith, Bruce. 1960. *Police Systems in the United States*. 2nd ed. New York: Harper & Row Publishing.

Smith, David J., and Alistair Henry (eds.). 2007. *Transformations of Policing*. Burlington, VT: Ashgate.

Souryal, Sam S. 1995. *Police Organization and Administration*. 2nd ed. Cincinnati, OH: Anderson Publishing Company.

Spitzer, Robert J. 2008 *The Politics of Gun Control*. 4th ed. Washington, DC: CQ Press.

Spohn, Cassia. 2009. *How Do Judges Decide? The Search for Fairness and Justice in Punishment*. 2nd ed. Thousand Oaks, CA: Sage.

Spohn, Cassia, and Craig Hemmens (eds.). 2009. *Courts: A Text/Reader*. Thousand Oaks, CA: Sage.

Stead, Deborah. 1994. "Crime and Punishment—And Now Trial by Jury," *Business Week* (January 17): 20–22.

Steden, van Ronald. 2008. *Privatizing Policing: Describing and Explaining the Growth of Private Security*. Devon, UK: Willan Publishing.

Steinhauer, Jennifer. 2009. "Death Row May Go Private in Arizona. Bids Sought. States Broke, Overburdened with Prisoners." *Seattle Times* (October 24): A2.

St. Louis Post-Dispatch, 2001. "Smoking Away" (April 15): A2.

Stolzenberg, Lisa, and Stewart J. D'Alessio. 1997. "'Three Strikes and You're Out': The Impact of California's New Mandatory Law on Serious Crime Rates," *Crime & Delinquency*, 43 (4) (October): 457–469.

Stolzenberg, Lisa, and Stewart J. D'Alessio (eds.). 2002. *Criminal Courts for the 21st Century*. Upper Saddle River, NJ: Prentice Hall.

Streb, Matthew J. (ed.). 2009. *Running for Judge: The Rising Political, Financial, and Legal Stakes of Judicial Elections*. New York: New York University Press.

Thurman, Quint C., and J. D. Jamieson. 2005. *Police Problem Solving*. Florence, KY: LexisNexis – Anderson Publishing.

Thurman, Quint C., and Jihong Zhao. 2004. *Contemporary Policing: Controversies, Challenges, and Solutions: An Anthology*. Los Angeles, CA: Roxbury Publishing Company.

Thurman, Quint C., Jihong Zhao, and Andrew Giacomazzi. 2001. *Community Policing in a Community Area: An Introduction and Exploration*. Los Angeles, CA: Roxbury Publishing Company.

Time. 1978. "Paper Chase: The Battle Against Red Tape" (July 10): 26. 1981. "We, the Jury, Find the . . . " (September 28): 44–56.

Tomasic, Roman. 1985. *The Sociology of Law*. London, UK: Sage Publications.

Tonry, Michael. 1996. *Sentencing Matters*. New York: Oxford University Press.

Tonry, Michael, and Kathleen Hatlestad (eds.). 1997 *Sentencing Reform in Overcrowded Times: A Comparative Perspective*. New York: Oxford University Press.

Tredoux, Colin G. 1998. "Statistical Inference on Measures of Lineup Fairness," *Law and Human Behavior*, 22 (2) (April): 217–238.

Trevaskes, S. 2004. China Propaganda Work in Chinese Courts: Public Trials and Sentencing Rallies as Sites of Expressive Punishment and Public Education in the Peoples Republic of China," *Punishment & Society*, 6 (1) (January 1): 5–22.

Tyre, Peg. 2004. "Ms. Top Cop," *Newsweek* (April 12): 48–49.

Umphrey, Marta Merrill (ed.). 2009. *Trial*. Burlington, VT: Ashgate.

U.S. Department of Justice. 1995. "Prison Sentences and Time Served for Violence," Bureau of Justice Statistics, Selected Findings. 4 (April). 2002. "Census of State and Local Law Enforcement Agencies, 2000," Bureau of Justice Statistics Bulletin (October). 2006. "Local Police Departments, 2003," Bureau of Justice Statistics (May). 2007. "Census of State and Local Law Enforcement Agencies, 2004" (June).

U.S. News & World Report. 1980. "Your Hamburger: 41,000 Regulations" (February 1): 64. 1992. "The Justice System: Getting a Fair Trial" (May 25): 36–38. 1994. "Outlook" (May 9): 13.

Vidmar, Neil (ed.). 2000. *World Jury Systems*. New York: Oxford University Press.

Vidmar, Neil, and Valerie P. Hans. 2007. *American Juries: The Verdict*. Amherst, NY: Prometheus Books.

Violanti, John M. 1995. "The Mystery Within: Understanding Police Suicide," *FBI Law Enforcement Bulletin*, 64 (2) (February): 19–24.

Volcansek, Mary L., and Jacqueline Lucienne Lafon. 1988. *Judicial Selection: The Cross-Evolution of French and American Practices*. New York: Greenwood Press.

Wasby, Stephen L., and David C. Brody. 1997. "Studies of Repressed Memory and the Issue of Legal Validity," *Law and Human Behavior*, 21 (6) (December): 687–692.

Webber, Craig. 2010. *Psychology and Crime*. Thousand Oaks, CA: Sage.

Weidenbaum, Murray L. 1979. *The Future of Business Regulation: Private Action and Public Demand*. New York: AMACOM, A division of American Management Associations.

Wheeler, Stanton, Kenneth Mann, and Austin Sarat. 1988. *Sitting in Judgment: The Sentencing of White-Collar Criminals*. New Haven, CT/London, UK: Yale University Press.

Whittemore, Karen E., and James R. P. Ogloff. 1995. "Factors that Influence Jury Decision Making: Disposition Instructions and Mental State at the Time of the Trial," *Law and Human Behavior*, 19 (3) (June): 283–304.

Wice, Paul B. 1978. *Criminal Lawyers: An Endangered Species*. Beverly Hills, CA: Sage Publications.

Williams, Gregory Howard. 1984. *The Law and Politics of Police Discretion*. Westport, CT: Greenwood Press.

Williams, Kipling D., Elizabeth F. Loftus, and Kenneth A. Deffenbacher. 1992. "Eyewitness Evidence and Testimony." Pp. 141–166 in Dorothy K. Kagehiro and William S. Laufer (eds.), *Handbook of Psychology and Law*. New York: Springer-Verlag.

Wilson, James Q. 1968a. "The Police and the Delinquent in Two Cities." Pp. 9–30 in Stanton Wheeler (ed.), *Controlling Delinquents*. New York: John Wiley. 1968b. *Varieties of Police Behavior*. Cambridge, MA: Harvard University Press.

Wilson, O. W., and Roy C. McLaren. 1972. *Police Administration*. 2nd ed. New York: McGraw-Hill.

Wolf, Robert V., and Austin Sarat. 1997. *The Jury System*. Philadelphia, PA: Chelsa House Publishers.

Woo, Lillian C. 1994. "Today's Legislators: Who They Are and Why They Run?" *State Legislatures*, 20 (4) (April): 28–32.

Woocher, Frederic D. 1977. "Did Your Eyes Deceive You? Expert Psychological Testimony on the Unreliability of Eyewitness Identification," *Stanford Law Review,* 29: 969–1030.

Wood, Peter B., and R. G. Dunaway. 2003. "Consequences of Truth-in-Sentencing: The Mississippi Case," *Punishment & Society*, 5 (2): 139–154.

Worrall, John L. 1998. "Administrative Determinants of Civil Liability Lawsuits against Municipal Police Departments: An Exploratory Analysis," *Crime & Delinquency*, 44 (2) (April): 295–313.

Worrall, John L., and Craig Hemmens. 2005. *Criminal Evidence: An Introduction.* Los Angeles, CA: Roxbury Publishing Company.

Yackle, Larry W. 2010. *Federal Courts: Habeas Corpus.* 2nd ed. New York: Foundation Press: Thomson/West.

Zhao, Jihong, and Quint C. Thurman. 1997. "Community Policing: Where Are We Now?" *Crime & Delinquency*, 43 (3) (July): 345–357.

CHAPTER

4

Lawmaking

Routinely and ostensibly mechanically, at the local, state, and federal levels, legislative, administrative, and judicial bodies grind out annually tens of thousands of new laws. But, despite the piecemeal appearance, each law is unique. Each has its own distinct set of precipitating factors, special history, and *raison d'être*. Still, some generalizations are possible about how laws are formed, the sociological factors that play a role in lawmaking, and the social forces that provide an impetus for making or altering laws. This chapter focuses on the more important sociological theories of lawmaking; the ways in which legislatures, administrative agencies, and courts make laws; the roles of vested interests, public opinion, and social science in the decision-making process; and the sources of impetus for laws.

PERSPECTIVES ON LAWMAKING

The creation and instrumentation of laws are routine and ongoing processes (Ball, 2004; Cheney, 1998), and theoretical perspectives dealing with the many facets of lawmaking abound in the sociological and sociolegal literature (see, for example, Chambliss, 1984:16–17; Chambliss and Zats, 1993; Hagan, 1980; Lange, 2009; Monahan and Walker, 2010; Parisi, 2008; Tomasic, 1985:101–106; Zander, 2005). Students of lawmaking have used a number of them in attempts to explain how laws are created or defeated. I will consider briefly four such theories to illustrate the diversity of perspectives—the rationalistic model, the functional view, conflict theory, and a "moral entrepreneur" thesis.

The *rationalistic* model proposes that laws (in particular, criminal laws) are created as rational means of protecting the members of society from social harm. In this perspective, crimes are considered socially injurious. This is not only the most widely accepted and popular but also the most unsophisticated theory of lawmaking (Goode, 2011). One of the principal difficulties with this perspective is that it is the lawmakers and powerful interest groups who define what activities may be harmful to the public welfare. Value judgments, preferences, and other considerations obviously enter into the process of definition (for example, why are certain types of behaviors, like prostitution or gambling—which will be discussed in Chapter 5—labeled as criminal?).

The *functionalist* view of lawmaking, as formulated by Paul Bohannan (1973), is concerned mainly with how laws emerge. Bohannan argues that laws are a special kind of "reinstitutionalized custom." Customs are norms or rules about the ways in which people must behave if social institutions are to perform their functions and society is to endure. Lawmaking is the restatement of some customs (for example, those dealing with economic transactions and contractual relations, property rights in marriage, or deviant behavior) so that they can be enforced by legal institutions.

This functionalist view suggests that failure in other institutional norms encourages the reinstitutionalization of the norms by the legal institution. As noted earlier, this perspective implies a consensual model of lawmaking in a society. From the functionalist perspective, laws are passed because they represent the voice of the people. Laws are essentially a crystallization of custom, of the existing normative order. Although there are conflicts in society, they are relatively marginal, and they do not involve basic values. In this view, conflict and competition between groups in a society actually serve to contribute to its cohesion and solidarity.

The *conflict* perspective cites value dissensus, unequal access to economic goods and the resulting structural cleavages of a society as the basic determinant of laws. Specifically, the origin of law is traced to the emergence of an elite class. These elites, it is suggested, use social-control mechanisms such as laws to perpetuate their own advantageous positions in society. In the event of conflict over the prescription of a norm, conflict theorists would argue that the interest group(s) more closely tied to the interests of the elite group would probably win the conflict. To define who the elites or the powerful groups of the society are, conflict theorists often employ structural indices of power. For example, William J. Chambliss (1964), as shown in Chapter 1, claims that the groups in England having the most power to create the vagrancy laws were those representing the dominant economic interests at the time. A more recent example would be how international organizations and national governments crafted legal responses, through corporate legal responses, to the turbulences of financial markets in 2009 (Halliday and Carruthers, 2009).

The *"moral entrepreneur"* theory attributes the precipitation of key events to the "presence of an enterprising individual or group. Their activities can properly be called *moral enterprise*, for what they are enterprising about is the creation of a new fragment of the moral constitution of society, its code of right and wrong" (Becker, 1963:146). The role of moral entrepreneurs in lawmaking is splendidly illustrated by Howard S. Becker's study (1963:121–146) of the development of criminal law designed to repress the use of marijuana. He notes that the Marijuana Tax Act of 1937 had its forerunners in earlier criminal statutes such as the Volstead Act (alcohol) and the Harrison Narcotics Tax Act (opium and derivatives). The Narcotics Bureau of the Treasury Department (now the U.S. Drug Enforcement Administration of the U.S. Department of Justice) was unconcerned with marijuana in its earlier years. It argued, instead, that the regulation of opiates was the real problem. However, shortly before 1937, the Narcotics Bureau redefined marijuana use as a serious problem. As a consequence, this agency acted in the role of moral entrepreneur, in that it attempted to create a new definition of marijuana use as a social danger. For example, the bureau provided information to the mass media on the dangers of marijuana, including "atrocity stories" that detailed gruesome features of marijuana smoking. Finally, in 1937, the Marijuana Tax Act was passed, ostensibly as a taxation measure but with the real purpose of preventing persons from smoking marijuana. But it had another little-known component to it. The campaign against marijuana was also colored by the fact that Harry Anslinger, the first drug czar, was appointed by Andrew Mellon, his wife's uncle. Mellon, the Treasury secretary, was banker to DuPont, and the sales of hemp threatened that firm's efforts to build a market for synthetic fibers.

Spreading scare stories about cannabis was a way to give hemp a bad name. Obviously, moral outrage is always more effective when backed by vested interests (*Economist,* 2001:4).

Another good example of the role of moral entrepreneurs in lawmaking is in the context of birth control. In a fascinating book, *Devices and Desires: A History of Contraceptives in America,* Andrea Tone (2001) points out that it was not until the mid-1800s that contraceptive technology jumped beyond methods in use for centuries, such as making condoms out of animal intestines. After Charles Goodyear invented the vulcanization of rubber in 1839, rubber manufacturers began supplying not just condoms but douching syringes and "womb veils" (or diaphragms and cervical caps), and what amounted to IUDs (intrauterine devices). By the 1870s, pharmacies were graphically advertising and selling chemical suppositories, vaginal sponges, and medicated tampons. The easy availability of birth control devices alarmed Anthony Comstock, a onetime salesman in New York City who believed that they assisted vice trade by divorcing sex from marriage and childbearing. In 1873, joined by like-minded allies, he successfully lobbied for Congressional passage of a bill that branded contraception obscene and prohibited its distribution across state lines or through the mails. Subsequently, versions of the Comstock law were enacted in 24 states.

Further, it should be noted that the passing of a law may also symbolize the supremacy of the groups that support it. The creation of a law is a statement that the illegal behavior is disreputable. Where groups differ significantly in prestige and status, or where two groups are competing for status, each sees the law as a stamp of legitimacy. They will seek to use it to affirm the respectability of their own way of life. According to Gusfield:

> The fact of affirmation through acts of law and government, expresses the public worth of one set of norms, or one subculture vis-à-vis those of others. It demonstrates which cultures have legitimacy and public domination, and which do not. Accordingly it enhances the social status of groups carrying the affirmed culture and degrades groups carrying that which is condemned as deviant. (1967:178)

These are the currently prominent theories on lawmaking in the law and society literature. None of these theories can account for the creation of all laws. On the basis of research evidence, however, some models come closer to providing a general explanation than do others. But how much closer they come depends on one's theoretical perspective. Some would argue that "the paradigm that is most compatible with the facts is one that recognizes the critical role played by social conflict in the generation of . . . law" (Chambliss, 1976:67). Others, in a similar vein, would argue for the explanatory power of *their* respective theoretical stances. Because a large number of laws are made by the legislative, administrative, and judicial bodies each day, it is always possible to select a few examples that illustrate almost any conceivable theoretical position. At best, the theories I have discussed explain in part how laws are made. Probably all these theories are at least partially correct, but it is doubtful that any single theory fully explains the creation of law, although one or another may account for the formation of any particular law or kind of law. With these considerations in mind, let us now turn to an examination of the processes of legislative, administrative, and judicial lawmaking.

LEGISLATION

The most important and most obvious legal task of legislative bodies is to make law (Loewenberg et al., 2002). The term "legislation" describes the deliberate creation of legal precepts by a body of government that gives articulate expression to such legal precepts in a formalized legal document. Legislation, as such, must be distinguished from normative pronouncements made by the courts. The verbal expression of a legal rule or principle by a judge does not have the same degree of finality as the authoritative formulation of a legal proposition by a legislative body. Furthermore, although both adjudication and legislation involve the deliberate creation of laws by a body of government, it should be remembered that the judiciary is not a body set up primarily for the purpose of lawmaking. As pointed out earlier, its main function is to decide disputes under a pre-existing law, and the law-creating function of the judges should be considered incidental to their primary function of adjudication.

There are several other differences that should be kept in mind between legislative and judicial lawmaking. Judge-made law stems from the decision of actual controversies. It provides no rules in advance for the decision of cases but waits for disputes to be brought before the court for decision. Legislators, by contrast, formulate rules in anticipation of cases. A judicial decision is based on a justification for applying a particular rule, whereas a statute usually does not contain an argumentative or justificatory statement; it simply states that this is forbidden, this is required, and this is authorized. An opinion supporting a court decision is normally signed by the judge who wrote it. By contrast, a statute carries no signature (Fuller, 1968:89–93). In general, legislators have much more freedom to make significant changes and innovations in the law than do the courts. The accumulation of precedents and the growth of an evermore complex body of principles have inevitably narrowed the scope of most judicial innovations. Legislators are also more responsive to public and private pressures than judges. Whereas judges deal with particular cases, legislators consider general problem areas with whole classes of related situations. At times, the attention of legislative bodies is drawn to a problem by a particular incident, but the law it eventually passes is designed for general applicability. For example, when Congress passed the Federal Kidnapping Act of 1932, the kidnapping and death of the Lindbergh baby were fresh in the legislators' minds, but the law that was enacted was designed to deal with a whole class of such possible occurrences. Thus, it may be concluded that legislators are solely responsible for formulating broad new rules and for creating and revising the institutions necessary to put those laws into effect.

Legislative lawmaking, at times, represents a response to some kind of problem, one acute enough to intrude on the well-being of a large number of individuals and their organizations or on the well-being of the government itself or conspicuous enough to attract the attention of at least some legislators. But, legislation can also be generated, among other ways, by apprehension, social unrest, conflict, environmental deterioration (Lazarus, 2004), and technological innovation.

Federal pure food and drug laws resulted from an exposure of the practices of food and drug manufacturers and processors (Friedman and Macaulay, 1977:610–613). More recent examples are internal security laws were the outgrowth of apprehension over the activities of American communists; manpower retraining and area redevelopment legislation to provide for more rigorous control over the testing of drugs was passed in the wake of disclosures of the effects of thalidomide, a drug that caused numerous babies to be born malformed; and legislation to establish a system of communication satellites was passed shortly after the successful experiment with Telstar. The list of legislation passed in response to the emergence of new problems or to the successful dramatization of old ones could be extended infinitely.

But neither legislators' recognition of a social problem nor their recognition of a group's particular claims for action is certain to lead to legislation. The probability of some form of legislative response increases when (1) powerful interest groups mobilize their members to seek legislative action; (2) the unorganized public becomes intensely concerned with an issue, as in the controversy over thalidomide, or conversely, is indifferent to the particular measures advocated by an interest group; and (3) there is no pressure to maintain the status quo or opposition to the proposed legislation.

Typically, the introduction of a legislative plan is preceded by a series of prelawmaking "stages" of activity. The first stage is the *instigation and publicizing* of a particular problem (such as nuclear waste disposal). Typical instigators are the mass media (such as special TV programs like *60 Minutes* or a series of articles or editorials in major newspapers or news magazines), a representative who highlights an issue through investigative hearings, or an author (as we shall see later in this chapter) who documents and dramatizes a social problem. The second stage is *information gathering*. It entails collecting data on the nature, magnitude, and consequences of a problem; the alternative schemes for solving the problem and their costs, benefits, and inherent difficulties; the likely political impact of each scheme; and the feasibility of various compromises. The third stage is *formulation,* or devising and advocating a specific legislative remedy for the problem. The fourth stage is *interests-aggregation,* or obtaining support for the proposed measure from other lawmakers through trade-offs and compromises (that is, if you support my proposal, I will support yours); the championing of one interest group over others; or mediating among conflicting groups. The fifth stage is *mobilization,* the exertion of pressures, persuasion, or control on behalf of a measure by one who is able, often by virtue of his or her institutional position, to take effective and relatively direct action to secure enactment. Whether an issue goes beyond the first three stages usually depends on the support it receives from individuals, groups, or governmental units that possess authority and legitimacy in the policy area, and on the support that the proponents of a proposal are able to muster from key figures in the legislature. The last stage is *modification*, the marginal alteration of a proposal, sometimes strengthening it and sometimes granting certain concessions to its opponents to facilitate its introduction (Price, 1972:4–5).

These six stages, although they show a certain sequential character and complementarity, do not simply represent the components the legislative process must "necessarily" include. They also illustrate the norms that govern the legislative process (for example, the airing of an issue and the attempt to accommodate diverse interests). They further illustrate the thoroughly political character of the legislative lawmaking process.

ADMINISTRATIVE LAWMAKING

Administrative agencies engage in lawmaking through rulemaking and through the adjudication of cases and controversies arising under their jurisdiction. They pursue both civil remedies and criminal sanctions to promote compliance with regulatory and administrative laws (Beermann, 2006; Harrington and Carter, 2009; Kerrigan et al., 1993; Warren, 2010). Administrative lawmaking plays an increasingly important role in modern society (Evan, 1990:89–96), and its consequences are felt in all walks of life. The intent of this section is to examine the fundamental processes involved in that kind of lawmaking in the context of administrative rulemaking and adjudication.

Administrative Rulemaking

Administrative rulemaking is the single most important function carried out by a government agency. While the president and Congress provide a general framework for the government's tasks, rulemaking provides the specifics that define the law and delineate how administrative agencies implement their responsibilities. Administrative rulemaking refers to the establishment of prospective rules (Beermann, 2006; Bryner, 1987; Kerwin and Furlong, 2010; Pierce, 1995; Warren, 2010; West, 1985). *A rule is a law made by an administrative agency.* Through rulemaking, a particular administrative agency legislates a policy. Under the requirements of the Federal Administrative Procedure Act, general notice of proposed rulemaking must be published in the *Federal Register* (the daily compendium of new, revised, and proposed rules). The fact that the register grew from 20,000 pages in 1968 to well over 53,000 in 1988 (Ornstein et al., 1990:160) and in excess of 160,000 pages in 2010 is indicative of the considerable increase in administrative rulemaking. The notice must specify the location of the proceedings, the legal authority under which the rules are being proposed, and the substance of the proposed rules. After such a notice is given, interested parties are to be provided with the opportunity to participate in the rule-making proceedings through the presentation of written data. At the discretion of the agency, oral presentation may be made. Unless notice or a hearing is required by the statutes governing the agency's operation, notice of rulemaking can be withheld if the agency considers it to be impractical, unnecessary, or contrary to the public interest. This provision potentially excludes a number of administrative rule-making proceedings from any possibility of public participation (Davis, 1977:241–269).

The flexibility of agencies in rule-making procedures is much greater than in administrative adjudication. Formal hearings are not held unless required by statute. Administrators are free to consult informally with interested parties and are not bound by the more rigid requirements of adjudicative hearings. The number of parties that may participate is also potentially far greater than in adjudicative proceedings, where only those directly affected by an administrative order have standing (that is, are directly involved in litigation).

Much of the immense code of federal regulations is composed of the substantive rules of administrative agencies. The Internal Revenue Code, for example, is part of this compendium of regulations, which consists of a seemingly endless number of rules interpreting statutes that have been passed by Congress. At this point, it should be noted that administrative agencies issue a variety of pronouncements less formal and binding than their "legislative" regulations, which are designed to clarify the laws they are administering (see, for example, Beermann, 2006; Schwartz, 1995). Some of these are described as "interpretative regulations" (for example, the Internal Revenue Service [IRS] regularly issues interpretations of the Internal Revenue Code, such as under what circumstances a college professor may deduct his or her office at home as a business expense). Moreover, in response to inquiries, agencies sometimes issue "advisory rulings," which interpret the law with reference to particular types of situations such as the disposal of certain types of potentially hazardous wastes. In addition, some agencies also publish instructions, guides, explanatory pamphlets, and so forth.

Regulatory agencies state many of their regulatory policies through rulemaking. For example, the U.S. Food and Drug Administration determines policies governing the labeling, availability, shelf life, and safety of drugs by rulemaking (Parisian, 2001). Rate-setting proceedings (for example, the limits on fees that brokerage houses may charge for certain class of services) of regulatory bodies are also considered to be rulemaking. The United States Department of Transportation, among others, is concerned with airline passengers' rights and monitors and issues rules on what airlines should do about schedule changes, flight cancellation, long delays, compensation for missed flights, lost luggage, being bumped from flights, keeping passengers on a plane while it is one the tarmac, and so on (McCartney, 2010). Outside of the regulatory realm, departments such as the U.S. Department of Commerce and the U.S. Department of Defense are constantly stating their general policies through the issuance of rules ranging from banking practices to dress codes in the military.

Administrative Adjudication

The second way in which agencies create rules is through their adjudicative powers, given to them by congressional grants of authority. *Administrative adjudication is the process by which an administrative agency issues an order.* Adjudication is the administrative equivalent of a judicial trial. As I pointed out in Chapter 3, adjudication differs from rulemaking in that it applies only to a specific, limited number of parties involved in an individual case before the agency. Administrative orders have retroactive effect, as contrasted with the prospective effect of rulemaking. In rulemaking, the agency is apprising in advance those under its jurisdiction of what the law is. When an agency opens proceedings with the intention of issuing an order, it must eventually interpret existing policy or define new policy to apply to the case at hand. The parties involved do not know how the policy is going to be applied until after the order is issued, giving the agency decision retroactive effect. Adjudicative lawmaking tends to produce inconsistencies because cases are decided on an individual basis. The rule of *stare decisis* (requiring precedent to be followed, which will be discussed in the context of judicial lawmaking) need not prevail (West, 1985:53–55), and the high turnover of top-level administrators often results in a lack of continuity.

Because many agencies have both the power to issue regulations and the power to adjudicate cases, they can choose between the two methods of lawmaking. When an agency believes that the time has come to formulate a policy decision in an official text, it can draft and issue a regulation (for example, when the U.S. Securities and Exchange Commission (SEC) formulates law by writing rules that describe what disclosures must be made in a prospectus). But when an agency prefers to wait until the contours of a problem become clearer, it can continue to deal with the problem on a case-by-case basis, formulating a series of decisional rules couched in terms that ensure continuing flexibility (for example, individual workers' compensation claims). Furthermore, an agency, unlike a court, does not have to wait passively for cases to be brought before it. Its enforcement officials can go out looking for cases that will raise the issues its adjudicating officials want to rule on. And because the agency can decide for itself what enforcement proceedings to initiate, it can choose cases that present the issues in such a way that the court will be likely to uphold the agency's ruling if an appeal is taken.

JUDICIAL LAWMAKING

Over the years, there has been a steady increase in judicial lawmaking in the United States (Canon and Johnson, 1999; Glazer, 1975; Glendon, 1994; McCloskey, 2010; Rabkin, 1989). In many instances, legislators and administrators are willing to let judges take the heat for controversial actions, such as allowing or disallowing abortion or ordering busing to desegregate schools. Similarly, it is often politically expedient to allow courts to handle such sensitive jobs as reapportioning legislatures, regulating employment practices, supervising land use and development or urban planning, and managing school systems (Stone, 1979:76). In addition, "an increasing number of judges hold the belief that law and the courts are the most appropriate and effective means of redressing the perceived ills of our society" (Rusthoven, 1976:1340). As a result, the judiciary in recent years has assumed a powerful role in our society. As Henry J. Abraham (1996:21) aptly remarks: "It is simply a fact of life that in the United States all social and political issues sooner or later seem to become judicial!"

Although traditional cases still occupy most of the court's time, the scope of judicial business has broadened. Courts have tended "to move from the byways onto the highways of policy making" (Horowitz, 1977:9). In fact, Nathan Glazer argues that we have developed an "Imperial Judiciary"—that is, the courts now have so much power and play such a great role in lawmaking that they pose a threat to the vitality of the political system—a rather controversial position in academic circles, which is not without criticism (see, for example Kozlowski, 2003). Glazer (1975:110) contends that too much power has moved from the elected, representative branches of government to the largely nonelective judiciary, and the courts "are now seen as forces of nature, difficult to predict and impossible to control." Judicial activity is now extended, for example, to welfare, prison, and mental-hospital administration, to education and employment policy, to road and bridge building, to automotive safety standards, and to management of natural resources. Some activist judges are called by May Ann Glendon (1994) as "romantic judges" who follow their passions of "do-gooding" and use due process and equal protection to justify making law rather than interpreting it. These judges are bold, creative, compassionate, and result oriented, who do not let tradition, precedent, or nonromantic readings of the Constitution get in the way.

In recent years, courts altered laws requiring a period of instate residence as a condition of eligibility for welfare; laid down elaborate standards for food handling, hospital operations, inmate employment, and education; and ordered some prisons closed. Courts have established comprehensive programs of care and treatment for the mentally ill who are confined in hospitals. They have ordered the equalization of school expenditures on teachers' salaries, decided that bilingual education must be provided for Mexican-American children, ruled for and ruled against same-sex marriage, and eliminated the requirement of a high-school diploma for a firefighter's job. Courts have enjoined the construction of roads and bridges on environmental grounds and suspended and then reinstituted performance requirements for automobile tires and air bags.

In some now classic, broad-ranging and often-cited examples such as *Brown v. Board of Education* (347 U.S. 483 [1954]), the judiciary set a precedent in establishing new policies in interracial relations with its decisions forbidding official segregation in public schools with dramatic long-ranging consequences (see, for example, Gold, 2005; *U.S. News & World Report,* 2004). The judiciary also established a new set of laws for processing criminal cases, requiring that indigents be given attorneys at public expense in all but minor cases (*Gideon v. Wainwright,* 372 U.S. 355 [1963]); defendants must be warned that whatever they say to the police may be used against them and that they will be permitted attorneys during police interrogation if they request them (*Miranda v. Arizona*, 384 U.S. 436 [1966]); and juveniles must be given some of the same rights as adult offenders in hearings that may lead to their imprisonment (*In re Gault,* 387 U.S. 1 [1967]). Reapportionment of national, state, and local legislative bodies has followed the decisions in *Baker v. Carr* (369 U.S. 186 [1962]) and *Reynolds v. Sims* (377 U.S. 533 [1964]), which required that all legislative districts be approximately the same size. The courts have been, "to put it mildly, very busy, laboring in unfamiliar territory" (Horowitz, 1977:5).

Judicial activism is not without criticism (Bryden, 1993; Dow, 2009; Leo and Thomas, 1998; Lindquist and Cross, 2009). There are questions about the policy-making role of judges in the American system of governments. The role of judges is to apply the law, and the policy-making activities carried out by the U.S. Supreme Court in interpreting the Constitution in view of social changes are considered an impermissible expansion of the powers granted to the judicial branch. The increase in judicial activism, it is argued, created a legislative body that is not accountable to the American people (Graglia, 1994). Judicial activism is not limited to the United States, and the will of legislators is often altered by the courts in other countries such as Canada (Markin, 2004).

Prior to discussing when and how judges make law, it is important to review the salient features of the adjudicative process. Adjudication is focused. The typical question before the judge is simply: Does one party have a right? Does another party have a duty? This should be contrasted with the question before legislators and administrators: What are the alternatives? Adjudication is also piecemeal, and the lawsuit is a good illustration of incremental decision making. Furthermore, courts must act when litigants present their cases before them. In the end, a judgment cannot be escaped. Moreover, fact-finding in adjudication is poorly adapted to the ascertainment of social facts. The unrepresentative character of the litigants makes it difficult to generalize from their situation to a wider context. Finally, adjudication makes no provision for policy review. Judges base their decisions on behavior that antedates the litigation. Consequential facts—those that relate to the impact of a decision on behavior—are equally important but much neglected. This results in an emphasis on rights and duties rather than on alternatives (Horowitz, 1977:33–56).

All these statements suggest that judicial lawmaking is different from legislative or administrative lawmaking. There are three types of judicial lawmaking: by precedents, by interpretation of statutes, and by interpretation of constitutions. I shall examine these three types separately.

Lawmaking by Precedents

Judicial formulation of rules is based frequently on the principle that judges should build on the precedents established by past decisions, known as the *doctrine of stare decisis* ("stand by what has been decided"), which is both expeditious and a deeply rooted common law tradition (Carp and Stidham, 1996:295–296). By contrast, civil law countries, such as France and Germany, have a codified legal system where the basic law is stated in *codes*. These are statutes enacted by the national parliament, which arranges whole fields of law (family law, housing law, and so forth) in an orderly, logical, and comprehensive way. The judges follow the basic principles of law found in acts of parliament. In common law countries, such as England and the United States, judges base their decisions on *case law*, a body of opinion developed by judges over time in the course of deciding particular cases. The doctrine of precedent, the notion that the judge is bound by what has already been decided, is a strictly common law doctrine (Friedman, 1998, 2002).

In the common law system, following precedents is often much easier and less time-consuming than working out all over again solutions to problems that have already been faced. It enables the judge to take advantage of the accumulated wisdom of preceding generations. It minimizes arbitrariness and compensates for weakness and inexperience. It conforms to the belief that "like wrongs deserve like remedies" and to the desire for "equal justice under the law." More important, the practice of following precedents enables individuals (with the assistance of attorneys) to plan their conduct in the expectation that past decisions will be honored in the future. Although certainty, predictability, and continuity are not the only objectives of law, they are certainly important ones. Many disputes are avoided, and others are settled without litigation simply because individuals are familiar with how the courts will likely respond to certain types of behavior (see, for example, Geel, 2009).

But judicial formulations of rules are frequently revised and restated by the courts in cases presenting the same or similar problems. A judge may also be confronted with a case for which there is simply no precedent. For example, consider a problem that judges first had to face during the 1920s when farmers began to complain that airplanes were disturbing the peace and frightening their livestock. Obviously, there were no precedents dealing with the rights and duties of landowners and of individuals who flew aircraft over their land. To make a decision, judges searched through property-law cases for any analogies that seemed applicable. Through the selection of appropriate and desirable analogies (which is, indeed, a value judgment), judges make law in instances when they are not guided by precedents. In general, in view of the way courts deal with legal rules laid down in earlier decisions (by rephrasing, qualifying, broadening, narrowing, or changing such rules, or by analogies), a precedent must be considered as a weaker and less authoritative source of law than a statute.

Lawmaking by Interpretation of Statutes

In interpreting statutes, judges determine the effects of legislative decisions. For many, a legislative decree is not a law until enforced and interpreted by the courts (Jacob, 1984:37). In the vast majority of cases involving the application of statutes, the courts have no trouble determining how to apply the statute. Most cases fall squarely inside or outside the law's provisions.

In some cases, however, the intent of a legislature is ambiguous. Some statutes contain unintentional errors and ambiguities because of bad drafting of the law. Other statutes are unclear because those who pushed them through the legislature sought to avoid opposition by being vague or silent on potentially controversial matters. An important reason for the lack of clarity in many instances is that the proponents have not been able to foresee and provide for all possible future situations. This provides the courts with an opportunity to engage in lawmaking. For example, antitrust statutes permit much judicial lawmaking, for Congress has set up only the most general guidelines. Exactly what constitute a restraint of trade or monopolization are questions that the court determines. In doing so, courts not only make law but also set explicit policy to guide other businesses and government agencies.

On rare occasions, judges find that all their efforts to discover the legislative intent of a statute are in vain. It is simply not clear how the statute applies to the case before them. In those cases, the judges must do just what they do when faced with a case for which there are no precedents. They must perform a creative act of lawmaking. In all probability, this is exactly what the legislature, unwilling to prescribe details for an unknown future, counted on them to do. It is the duty of judges to infer a purpose that is applicable to a particular case from what they know of the legislature's broader purposes and of the shared purposes and aims of the community.

The Interpretation of Constitutions

In addition to the U.S. Congress playing a major role in constitutional interpretation (Bloom, 2009; Davidson, 1993), the courts are regularly called upon to interpret the Constitution (Baum, 2010; McCann and Housemann, 1989; Wellington, 1991). Every controversial statute and a variety of controversial executive actions are challenged in the courts on grounds of unconstitutionality (Jacob, 1984:38). For example, in an attempt to avert a threatened strike, the president orders federal officials to seize and operate the nation's steel mills. The steel companies challenge his power to do so under Article II of the Constitution, which deals with the powers and duties of the president. Or an overzealous sheriff in a small town breaks into the offices of a business firm and searches for evidence of illegal sales without a search warrant. When the firm's owners are brought to trial for unlawful operations, they challenge the admission of the evidence offered against them on the grounds that it has been illegally obtained and that admitting it would violate the "due process" clause of the Fourteenth Amendment, which is supposed to protect individuals against irregular official procedures.

The opportunities to interpret constitutional provisions arise more often in federal than in state courts, because the national Constitution is considered more ambiguous in many of its key provisions (McCloskey, 2010). State constitutions, by contrast, are much more detailed documents and leave much less room for judicial interpretations. Usually both state and federal courts ratify the decision of the governmental officials by finding the challenged legislation or executive action constitutional. At times, however, they declare the law or action unconstitutional. When deciding on the constitutionality of a government action, the courts have to decide what meaning they wish to give to the Constitution and which social objectives to pursue. For example, the Supreme Court "has given quite different interpretations to the 'due process of law' clauses of the Fifth and Fourteenth Amendments, ranging from a guarantee of property against governmental intervention to a guarantee of civil rights against official abuse" (Jacob, 1984:38).

Judicial lawmaking is usually directed at other government agencies rather than at private individuals. Courts interpret statutes and constitutional provisions, and in so doing, they permit or prohibit the action of other government agencies. For example, courts have prohibited racial discrimination by government agencies in schools, parks, and elections, but they have not prohibited racial discrimination (on constitutional grounds) by private individuals (for example, obtaining professional services such as dental, medical, or legal). Most judicial lawmaking efforts are concerned with the regulatory activities of agencies (Shapiro, 1968). There are, however, some issues that are rarely decided in courts. Foreign affairs (because they are considered political and not judicial issues) are generally beyond the scope of court action. For example, when the American participation in the Vietnam conflict was challenged, the Supreme Court, by a six to three vote, refused to rule on its constitutionality. Moreover, courts are seldom involved in matters such as the appropriation of funds or the levying of taxes.

INFLUENCES ON THE LAWMAKING PROCESSES

Lawmaking is a complex and continuous process, and it exists as a response to a number of social influences that operate in society. The forces that influence lawmaking cannot always be precisely determined, measured, or evaluated. At times, a multitude of forces are in operation simultaneously. Although a variety of forces of diverse intensity can exert influence on the lawmaking process (for example, male legislators who have daughters vote more liberally on women's issues [Washington, 2006]), in this section, I shall consider only the roles of vested interests, public opinion, and the social sciences—the ones most prominently discussed in the law and society literature.

Interest Groups

The interest-group thesis contends that laws are created because of the special interests of certain groups in the population (Mahood, 2000). The image of society reflected by this view stresses cultural differences, value clashes, inequities, and social conflict (Hajnal and Clark, 1998). Examples of interest-group influence in lawmaking and policy making abound (see, for example, Gioacchino et al., 2004; Rozell et al., 2006). Laws governing the use of alcohol, regulations concerning sexual conduct, abortion bills, pure food and drug legislation, antitrust laws, automobile safety standards, and the like are all documented instances of interest-group activity (Quinney, 1970:49–94). Even alterations in existing statutes are not immune from influence by those who see some threat or advantage in the proposed changes. For example, Pamela A. Roby (1969) demonstrated, in a study of the New York State Penal Code regarding prostitution, that the changes originally proposed in this law were drastically altered by the time the new statute took effect. Throughout the legislative process, various groups (for example, the police, the Hotel Association of New York City, the American Civil Liberties Union, and the mayor's office) were all involved in shaping the legislation to fit their interests or views. Often, interest groups also act as a communication network for social movements, facilitating the dissemination of their ideas in a manner that helps to legitimize movements, exert public pressure for legal change, attract some politicians to the movements' objectives, and effect policy change (Yarnold, 1992:115).

The nature of the interaction between interest groups and lawmakers varies to an extent based on the branch of the government. Judges, although they are not immune to interest-group pressures, are generally not lobbied in the same way as legislators or administrators. To reach the courts, a lawyer must be hired, formal proceedings must be followed, and grievances must be expressed in legal terminology. Minorities and the poor find the courts attractive because they are more readily available. To influence legislators, a group must be economically powerful or able to mobilize a large number of voters (Jacob, 1984:150). No such prerequisites are needed in the courts. If a group has enough money to hire an attorney, it can seek court action to further its interests. Further, interest groups may also turn to courts because they assume that the judicial branch may be more sympathetic to their objectives than the other two branches (Carp et al., 2010). As a result, minority groups are often among the most active lobbies in courts. The National Association for the Advancement of Colored People (NAACP), for example, has instituted and won numerous cases in its efforts to improve the legal protection of blacks. The technique is not new, of course, but in recent decades, urban interests, feeling underrepresented in state and national legislatures, have turned increasingly to the lawsuit.

The techniques used by interest groups to influence courts are different from those used to influence legislative or administrative bodies. Notes Jacob (1984:151), "The principal techniques are: to bring conflicts to a court's attention by initiating test cases, to bring added information to the courts through *amicus curiae* (friend of the court) briefs, and to communicate with judges indirectly by placing information favorable to the group's cause in legal and general periodicals." By instituting test cases, interest groups provide judges with opportunities to make policies by which they overcome the otherwise passive nature of the judicial process. Often, such briefs communicate relevant social science research findings to a particular case (Roesch et al., 1991). By providing information through *amicus curiae* briefs, interest groups expand the confines of the judicial process and build coalitions with other groups (McGuire, 1994). For example, the American Civil Liberties Union with other interest groups that share similar goals files many such briefs with the Supreme Court in cases that raise questions of constitutional liberty. The final technique is to publish decisions in legal periodicals. Judges generally read these journals to keep abreast of legal scholarship and sometimes even cite them as authority for their ruling. Publication in these journals gets one's views before the courts and before the attentive public.

Interactions between interest groups and legislative and administrative lawmakers are more overtly political in nature. Many interest groups maintain Washington and state capital offices staffed with people who keep track of developments in the legislative and administrative branches and attempt to influence their activities. Some groups pay for the services of law firms in dealing with legislators or administrators. These firms provide expertise in such areas as antitrust and tax regulations and use their personal contacts with important lawmakers on behalf of their clients.

A number of specific conditions can be identified that enhance the potential influence of interest groups on lawmakers (Ripley, 1988). In many instances, there may not be two competing groups on an issue. When only one point of view is presented, the group is likely to get much of what it wants. For example, when banking and other money-lending interests (Monchuk, 2006), such as pawnshops, push for a higher ceiling for usury laws in a state, they are more likely to succeed if there is no organized opposition. Similarly, if the groups on one side of a controversy are unified and coordinated on the principal issues they want to push (or if they can minimize their disagreements), they will enhance their chances of success. For instance, the walnut growers are represented by a single highly organized group and are thus likely to get what they want. By contrast, chicken farmers are dispersed and have no effective single group to speak for them. Consequently, they have difficulty in achieving their legislative ends. If certain key members of legislative bodies (such as a subcommittee chairperson) believe in the interest group's position, the probability of success is greatly enhanced. The visibility of an issue is another consideration in influencing lawmakers. When the issue is not too visible or when interest groups seek single distinct amendments to bills (such as to alter soybean export quotas in addition to others proposed by farming interests), as contrasted with large legislative packages, the chances for success increase. Conversely, as the visibility of issues increases and public attention grows (such as draft registration or wage and price controls), the influence of interest groups tends to diminish. Interest groups are likely to have greater influence on issues that coincide with the interests of the groups they purport to represent. For example, the AFL-CIO may be very influential in matters concerning working conditions, but it is likely to receive less attention from lawmakers when it advocates higher tariffs for imported goods or when it makes attempts to guide foreign policy. Finally, interest groups are likely to have greater influence on amendments than on entire pieces of legislation. This is because amendments are generally technical and less understood by the public.

In general, the effectiveness of interest groups in influencing lawmakers is related to such considerations as their financial and information resources, their offensive or defensive positions, and the status of the group in the eyes of lawmakers. Financial resources determine the ability of an interest group to support court suits, lobbying, public relations, and other activities (Abramson, 1998). Interest groups that support the status quo have an advantage over groups trying to bring change, because whereas the latter must overcome several obstacles in the lawmaking process, the former may frustrate change at any of several points in the process. But the influence of an interest group depends mainly on its status as perceived by lawmakers. An interest group is particularly influential in situations where a lawmaker shares the same group affiliation (for example, when farm groups talk to legislators who are farmers), where the group is considered important to the legislator's constituency, and where the group is recognized as a legitimate and reliable source of information. In addition, a group's competence to influence lawmaking is enhanced by its ability to bring about social or economic disruptions. Threats of disorder, disruption, and mass violence have been, at times, effective bargaining weapons of relatively powerless groups (see, for example, Shaw et al., 2010). Similarly, the threat of a decline in the supply of such necessities as food, medical services, and energy has been used to influence lawmakers. For example, energy-supply problems have been employed to justify the removal of price controls on oil and natural gas. There is little doubt that the ability of an interest group to create a crisis, whether a social disorder, an economic slowdown, or the reduction of supply of a needed product or service, gives it considerable clout in the lawmaking process.

Public Opinion

When the relationship between law and popular will was refined in the nineteenth century, theorists of law and society were concerned with the origins of law and the development of legal institutions (see Chapter 2; Althaus, 2003). Legal development was viewed as a sequence of events. First, practices and sentiments occur in a group of people, without their awareness that they are the "right" ones or the "only" ones. Eventually, particularly on occasions of deviance from prior practice, *a* way of acting or believing becomes *the* way of acting or believing. Custom becomes law.

It is easier to substantiate the association between popular sentiments and law in so-called *primitive societies* (Llewellyn and Hoebel, 1941:10–15). As a society becomes larger, more complex, and heterogeneous, there is a less direct correspondence between public opinion and the law. In a primitive society, one comes to know intimately the law of one's tribe. It is highly unlikely that today one can know, let alone tinker with, much of the law that could affect one's life. As a result of such limited awareness, there is a fair amount of selectivity involved in the expression of opinions toward the law. Some questions, therefore, arise in the discussion of the influence of public opinion on lawmaking. One concerns the timing of the relationship between public opinion and lawmaking. At what point does the accumulation of practice and belief make the reflection of those practices and beliefs in law inevitability? For example, how many marijuana violations cause the law relating to marijuana to be changed?

A related question concerns the identification of those individuals whose opinion is expressed in lawmaking and the means of translating those opinions into legal outcomes. The *people* may mean a numerical majority, an influential elite, blacks, women, the poor, the middle class, the young, the aged, migrant workers, students, college professors, and so forth. Popular views may be similar throughout all segments of the population, but on many important issues, opinions will differ (Norrander and Wilcox, 2009).

A more meaningful way of looking at the influence of public opinion on lawmaking would be to consider the diverse opinions of many "publics" (that is, segments of society) bearing on specific concerns such as sentencing offenders for particular crimes (Walker and Hough, 1988). These opinions are expressed through a multitude of channels, such as the media, political parties, and the various types of interest groups. Care should be exercised, however, not to overestimate the catalytic part played by public opinion in lawmaking, which is conditioned by economic forces. As Friedman states:

> The "public opinion" that affects the law is like the economic power which makes the market. This is so in two essential regards: Some people, but only some, take enough interest in any particular commodity to make their weight felt; second, there are some people who have more power and wealth than others. At one end of the spectrum stand such figures as the president of the United States and General Motors; at the other, migrant laborers, babies, and prisoners at San Quentin. (1975:163)

The differential influence of public opinion on lawmaking processes is a well-known phenomenon and is recognized by lawmakers. Lawmakers are aware that some people are more equal than others because of money, talent, or choice. Notes Friedman:

> They know that 100 wealthy, powerful constituents passionately opposed to socialized medicine, outweigh thousands of poor, weak constituents, mildly in favor of it. Most people do not shout, threaten, or write letters. They remain quiet and obscure, unless a head count reveals they are there. This is the "silent majority"; paradoxically, this group matters only when it breaks its silence—when it mobilizes or is mobilized by others. (1975:164)

Lawmakers also know that most people have no clear opinions on most issues with which judicial, administrative, and legislative bodies must deal. This means that they have a wide latitude within which to operate. Thus, for example, when a legislator claims to be representing the opinion of his or her district, he or she is, on most issues, representing the opinion of only a minority of the constituents (for example, developers versus residents of a community) because most do not know or care about the issue at hand and do not communicate their views on it.

Despite these considerations, public opinion does exert an influence on the lawmaking process (Carp et al., 2010). Dennis S. Ippolito and his associates (1976) identify three types of influences that press lawmakers into formulating certain decisions. These three types are direct, group, and indirect influences.

Direct influences refer to constituent pressures that offer rewards or sanctions to lawmakers. Rewards for compliance and sanctions for noncompliance may be votes in an election or reelection campaign, financial assistance, and other forms of pressure that could possibly range from the representative's standing in lawmaking bodies to prestige in his or her own particular community. But this kind of influence is not confined to legislators. Members of the judiciary are also pressured by partisan publications to make certain decisions consistent with opinions and interests that run throughout the jurisdiction of a particular court.

The second type of influence is distinctly that of organized interest groups representing a special constituency. Political parties, interest groups, and citizen action groups are continually influencing the lawmaking process. In the area of administrative law, for example, special-interest groups press regulatory agencies for rules and regulations that are in keeping with their own immediate interests. Public opinion in these and other areas is represented by organization leaders. The motivation behind joining such groups is the perceived need for expressing a point of view in a manner that will influence lawmakers. In this context, public opinion becomes organized around a specific issue or an immediate objective (for example, pros and cons of gun control or abortion). Through the process of organizing, interests are made specific, and public-opinion backing is sought in the attempt to gain an advantage in pressing for change or redress through the legal machinery.

The third type of public-opinion model is that which influences the lawmaking process indirectly. Here a lawmaker acts in the capacity of an "instructed delegate." The decisions made are on behalf of the desires of a particular constituency; for example, residents living around an airport who oppose expansion of facilities. Ippolito and his colleagues (1976:3) state that indirect influence occurs when legislators act in accordance with constituent preferences because they either share such preferences or believe such preferences should prevail over their own judgment. This type of influence is indicative of the importance attached to public-opinion polls.

Public-opinion polls seek to determine the aggregate view people hold in a community on current important issues. Polling, in the late 2000s, is flourishing in the United States. Today, there are numerous well-established commercial firms that take public-opinion polls. Among the most respected are the Gallup, Harris, Yankelovich, and Sindlinger, Opinion Research Corporation, Roper, and Cambridge Reports polls. They often work jointly with major TV networks such as CBS, CNN, and NBC or newspapers and magazines such as *the New York Times, U.S. News & World Report, Time,* and *Newsweek.* In addition, there are a variety of smaller, specialized public and private and university polling organizations. Scores of surveys have been commissioned by federal agencies and by various state bodies. A typical sample size for national polls is around 1,500 respondents. Pollsters claim that with a sample of that size, there is a 95-percent probability that the results obtained are no more than three percentage points off the figure that would be obtained if every adult in the country were interviewed.

It has been demonstrated that opinion polls clearly influence what lawmakers do (Lipset, 1976). On a variety of domestic issues, for example, public opinion led or prompted lawmakers toward passage of a program that might have otherwise been delayed for months or years. Legislation concerning minimum wages, social security, and medical programs are examples of issues on which public opinion has preceded and prompted legislative action. However, in other instances, such as civil liberties and civil rights, public opinion has either lagged behind government policy or tended to support measures that are repressive of constitutional rights. For example, since the mid-1950s, the Supreme Court has played a leading role in interpreting and formulating policies on civil rights that were more progressive than the views reflected in public-opinion polls (Simon, 1974). It should be noted, however, that whether the U.S. Supreme Court does—or should—reflect majority public opinion has been a recurring controversy in American legal thought (see, for example, Baum, 2010; Marshall, 1989).

Generally, the use of polls in lawmaking is encouraged. For example, Irving Crespi suggests that lawmakers could be more effective if they learned to draw upon the full fruits of survey research. Direct evidence—unfiltered by the interpretations of special interests or lobby groups—of the wants, needs, aspirations, and concerns of the general public needs to be accounted for in lawmaking activities. In lawmaking processes, Crespi argues that first there should be an attempt to determine the views of both the general public and that segment of the public that would be directly affected by a particular law. Then that public opinion should be made part of the formative stages of the lawmaking process, and not simply a force to be coped with after the fact. Says Crespi (1979:18), "The difference between treating public attitudes and opinions as a relatively minor variable instead of an influence that should be authoritative is ultimately the difference between technocratic and democratic government."

Lawmaking and Social Science

Lawmakers have long been aware of the contribution that social scientists can make to the lawmaking process. For example, the Brandeis Brief of 1908, defending the constitutionality of limited working hours for women, is considered an early landmark for the use of social science in lawmaking (Zeisel, 1962:142). The ideas of the economist John R. Commons (1934) influenced the way most states in the United States deal with compensation for industrial accidents and unemployment. In the major U.S. Supreme Court decision of *Brown v. Board of Education of Topeka* (347 U.S. 483 [1954]), the court drew upon a spectrum of the social sciences—ranging from discrete psychological experiments to broad-ranging economic and social inquiry—in reversing an earlier ruling that had established the separate-but-equal standards in racial matters. The Court ruled that racial segregation in elementary schools is psychologically harmful. In a footnote—the famous footnote 11—the Court also cited a number of social science studies summarizing evidence showing that segregation retards black children's educational development.

In an era increasingly dominated by scientific and technical specialists, it is not surprising that lawmakers reflect the quest for specialization and expertise (see, for example, Costanzo et al., 2007). Experts abound in a variety of fields (Smith, 1992), and there is a growing reliance on social scientists and the research data they generate in diverse areas ranging from school desegregation studies (Wolf, 1976) to consumer surveys in trademark suits. With the aid of social scientists, ad hoc committees of legislative bodies have, at times, also produced important studies on matters such as insurance, investment banking, and public utilities (Zeisel, 1962).

Efforts to bring social science to bear on lawmaking processes involve the use of quantitative social science data and the reliance on the social scientist as an expert witness in specific legal cases. Social science data may be collected and analyzed for academic purposes and later utilized by one or more sides of a dispute as it was, for example, in *Brown v. Board of Education* (Gold, 2005). Social science research may also be reactive in the sense that it is initially requested by parties in a dispute. In such instances, the materials may address facts in the case (for example, research on sex discrimination in the jury selection for the Attica trial) or initiate an intervention in a lawmaking process (for example, the disparate effects of wage garnishment on blacks). Social science research may also be undertaken in a proactive fashion. In such a situation, a social scientist may undertake an investigation (such as the social impact of mandatory day care for companies with more than 500 employees) with the anticipation of subsequent use of the results by lawmakers (Berk and Oppenheim, 1979:125).

Social scientists can also participate in the lawmaking process as expert witnesses who testify typically for one of the litigants or appear before a legislative body. The demand for such service is evidenced by the various directories of expert witnesses and a growing body of literature on the intricacies of testifying in court or in front of legislative bodies (Brodsky, 2004). At times, social scientists are asked to directly assist either the court or the legislator in the preparation of background documents pertinent to a particular issue or to serve on presidential commissions intended for policy recommendations.

Although social science influences what lawmakers do, there are controversies surrounding the role of social scientists in lawmaking. Consider, for example, the controversy that broke out in the late 1960s over reinterpretations of the Equal Educational Opportunity Report, commonly known as the Coleman Report after its principal author, James S. Coleman (1966, 1967). In the late 1960s, Coleman's data on pupil achievement were the basis for a number of important court decisions calling for school busing. With the use of extensive busing to achieve "racial balance" in public schools, social science findings about the effects of integration on black children have been hotly debated (Howard, 1979:104). In reviewing the studies on busing, David J. Armor (1972) has questioned the assumption that school integration enhances blacks' educational achievement, aspirations, self-esteem, and opportunities for higher education. He contends that it is possible that desegregation actually retards race relations. Other scholars, such as Thomas F. Pettigrew and Robert L. Green (1976), have accused Armor of presenting a distorted and incomplete review of a politically charged topic. Incidentally, the entire controversy could have been avoided, for Coleman had not found any race effect as such in his analysis of student-body characteristics and educational achievement. Instead, he had found a social class effect. At the time of his testimony, this fact was not made clear to the court.

The late Daniel Patrick Moynihan (an eminent sociologist, a prolific writer, and a ranking member of the U.S. Senate from New York State from 1977 to 2001) proposed two general reasons why social scientists have been criticized for their involvement in lawmaking processes. First, he points out that social science is basically concerned with the prediction of future events, whereas the purpose of the law is to order them. Notes Moynihan (1979:16), "But where social science seeks to establish a fixity of *relationships* such that the consequences of behavior can be known in advance—or, rather, narrowed to a manageable range of possibilities—law seeks to dictate future performance on the basis of past *agreements.*" For example, it is the function of the law to order alimony payments; it is the function of social science to attempt to estimate the likelihood of their being paid and of their effect on work behavior and remarriage in male and female parties, or similar probabilities. The second reason he suggests is that "social science is rarely dispassionate, and social scientists are frequently caught up in the politics which their work necessarily involves" (1979:19). Social scientists are, to a great extent, involved with problem solving, and the identification of a "problem" usually entails a political statement that implies a solution. Moynihan (1979:19) states, "Social scientists are never more revealing of themselves than when challenging the objectivity of one another's work. In some fields almost *any* study is assumed to have a more-or-less-discoverable political purpose." Furthermore, there is a distinct social and political bias among social scientists. As a result, social sciences attract many people who are more interested in shaping the future than in preserving the past. Moynihan feels that this orientation coupled with "liberal" tendencies and the limited explanatory power of social sciences results in a weakening of influence on lawmakers. He points out, for example, that after examining a number of recent studies concerning the effects of rehabilitation programs on criminals, no consistent effects could be shown one way or the other. Moynihan (1979:20) notes, "Seemingly, all that could be established for certain about the future behavior of criminals is that when they are in jail they do not commit street crimes." Similarly, there are still controversies concerning the deterrent effects of the death penalty (see for example, Wolfgang, 1998). Obviously, when social science data yield uncertain results, the root causes of major problems remain elusive. When well-intentioned social scientists dispute about alternatives, it is not surprising that lawmakers are, at times, skeptical about social science and social scientists.

SOURCES OF IMPETUS FOR LAW

An impetus is a fundamental prerequisite for setting the mechanism of lawmaking in motion. Demands for new laws or changes in existing ones come from a variety of sources. In the following pages, several of the more widely analyzed and prominent sources of impetus for law creation are considered. These sources, which are not mutually exclusive, are detached scholarly diagnosis, a voice from the wilderness, protest activities, social movements, public-interest groups, and the mass media.

Detached Scholarly Diagnosis

The impetus for law may come from a detached scholarly undertaking. From time to time, academicians may consider a given practice or condition as detrimental in the context of existing values and norms. They may communicate their diagnoses to their colleagues or to the general public through either scholarly or popular forums. In some cases, they may even carry the perceived injustice to the legislature in search of legal redress. Perhaps the best way to illustrate how an impetus for law can be provided by a member of an academic community is to refer to my study on wage garnishment (a legal process that enables a creditor upon a debtor's default to seize his or her wages from the employer before the debtor is paid), carried out some years ago (Vago, 1968).

I investigated the impact of wage garnishment on low-income families. The findings indicated that existing wage garnishment laws at that time in Missouri were more counterproductive than functional as a collection device. Approximately 20 percent of the debtors were dismissed by their employers upon the receipt of the first garnishment suit. Such an action was detrimental not only to the debtor, but also to his or her family, creditor, and employer, and to society at large.

As a result of the deleterious and unintended consequences of garnishment (for example, broken homes or engaging in illegal behavior), I proposed a simple procedure in the study to provide the debtor whose wages were subject to garnishment with legal safeguards so that he or she will not be dismissed from a job or be forced into bankruptcy. At the same time, a provision was made also to enable creditors to maintain an effective collection method.

On the basis of my data and recommendations, House Bill 279 was designed and introduced in the 75th General Assembly of the State of Missouri. Under the proposed bill, the service of the writ would be made upon the defendant only, and the employer of the defendant would not be involved in the litigation process. Upon entry of the judgment, the court may order the debtor to make payments to the clerk of the court, which would be disbursed in turn by the clerk. In settling the amount of these payments, the court would take into consideration the circumstances of the defendant, including his or her income and other obligations or considerations bearing on the issue. If the debtor fails to obey the order of the court, *then, and only then,* the creditor may summon the employer as a garnishee. The primary intention of the bill was to prohibit employers from discharging employees upon the receipt of the first garnishment suit, thus saving thousands of jobs for low-income individuals annually in Missouri. It was estimated that, on the national level, approximately 500,000 individuals are fired each year as a direct result of the practice of wage garnishment. The societal implications of the proposed changes were obvious (Vago, 1968:7–20). Today, wage garnishment is regulated nationally (Bryant, 2004). This is the result of the Consumer Credit Protection Act (PL 90-32), passed in 1968. The act protects consumers from being driven into bankruptcy by excessive garnishment of wages by limiting the amount of wages subject to garnishment to 25 percent of the employee's weekly disposable income although it still played a role in the some 1.6 million personal bankruptcies filed annually during the past decade (Gordon, 2003; Murray, 2009; Murray and Daugherty, 2010). It also forbids the firing of an employee because of wage garnishment.

There have been a number of attempts by university professors in a variety of disciplines to provide an impetus for lawmaking as an outgrowth of their investigations. For example, publications by David Caplovitz, such as *The Poor Pay More* (1963) and *Consumers in Trouble: A Study of Debtors in Default* (1974), resulted in proposals for much-needed reform of the consumer credit laws. In *Genetic Fix* (1973), Amitai Etzioni examines the implications of "human engineering" and suggests that the Mondale bill (the establishment of a scientific review committee in the form of a health-ethics commission) should be used as a model for safeguarding such activities. Marc F. Plattner's influential article "Campaign Financing: The Dilemmas of Reform" (1974) stimulated further reexamination of existing procedures in this domain. Martin S. Feldstein (1975a, 1975b) is concerned with changes in unemployment insurance and social security laws, as the titles of his articles indicate: "Unemployment Insurance: Time for Reform" and "Toward a Reform of Social Security." Anthony Downs, in *Urban Problems and Prospects* (1976), calls a series of specific solutions on housing, community schools, and transportation dilemmas to the attention of lawmakers. The list could go on ad infinitum. But the point has been argued and illustrated that detached scholarly diagnoses can, indeed, stimulate lawmaking. The source of impetus, however, is not limited to ivory towers. It can have other origins, as the following sections will demonstrate.

A Voice from the Wilderness

Through their writings, many people outside of academe succeed, or even excel, in calling public attention to a particular problem or social condition. There is a long list of those whose literary efforts stimulated changes in the law. For our purposes, it will suffice to call attention to a few better-known such ventures.

Around the turn of the twentieth century, there was a fair amount of concern in the United States about the quality of food products. In particular, numerous scandals had arisen over the quality of meat products. It was alleged that during the Spanish-American War, American soldiers were forced to eat cans of "embalmed beef." A number of horrible practices of manufacturers were revealed in the mass media, but a federal food and drug law had still not passed when, in 1906, Upton Sinclair published *The Jungle,* a novel about life in Chicago, centering on the stockyards.

The first half of the book deals with a vivid description of conditions in the Chicago meatpacking plants. To illustrate:

> Tubercular pork was sold for human consumption. Old sausage, rejected in Europe and shipped back "mouldy and white," would be "dosed with borax and glycerin, and dumped into the hoppers, and made over again for home consumption." Meat was stored in rooms where "water from leaky roofs would drip over it, and thousands of rats would race about on it." The packers would put out poisoned bread to kill the rats; then the rats would die, and "rats, bread and meat would go into the hoppers together." Most horrifying of all was the description of the men in the "cooking rooms." They "worked in tankrooms full of steam," in some of which there were "open vats near the level of the floor." Sometimes they fell into the vats "and when they were fished out, there was never enough of them left to be worth exhibiting—sometimes they would be overlooked for days, till all but the bones of them had gone out to the world as Durham's Pure Leaf Lard." (Quoted by Friedman and Macaulay, 1977:611–612)

When it was published, the book created a furor. A copy was sent to President Roosevelt, who, in turn, appointed two investigators whose report confirmed Sinclair's findings. It is hard to say to what extent Sinclair's book provided an impetus for the passage of the Pure Food and Drug Act and the Meat Inspection Act in 1906, but it is indisputable that it played an important role in it.

In the domain of environmental protection laws, it would be difficult not to consider the book *Silent Spring* by Rachel Carson (1962). It was the first time that the environmental threat posed by pesticides was announced to a wide audience. Others in the same vein were Richard Falk's *This Endangered Planet* (1971), Fairfield Osborn's *Our Plundered Planet* (1948), and *Moment in the Sun* by R. Reinow and L. T. Reinow (1967).

Even a short list of influential authors would be incomplete without a reference to Ralph Nader. He was an unknown young lawyer at the time he published his book, *Unsafe at Any Speed* (1965), which alerted the public to the automobile industry's unconcern for safety in the design and construction of American cars. This book is a model of the kind of muckraking journalism that, at times, initiates the rise of public concern over a given issue. As a result of his book, and General Motors' reaction to it, Nader became front-page news, and his charges took on new weight. More than anyone else, he has contributed to and provided the impetus for the passing of a substantial number of auto safety provisions. Since 1966, Nader "has been responsible almost entirely through his efforts for the passage of seven major consumer-related laws—the National Traffic and

Motor Vehicle Safety Act (1966), Natural Gas Pipeline Safety Act (1968), Wholesale Meat Act (1967), Radiation Control Act (1968), Wholesale Poultry Products Act (1967), Coal Mine Health and Safety Act (1969), and the Occupational Health and Safety Act (1970)" (Buckhorn, 1972:226).

There are other ways of transforming "private troubles into public issues" (Spector and Kitsuse, 1973:148). For example, we are all familiar with Rosa Parks, a black seamstress who, on December 1, 1955, sat down in the back of a city bus in Montgomery, Alabama, then refused to relinquish her seat to a white man when the "noncolored" section became overcrowded. Her action launched the famous black boycott of the buses that created a new era in the civil rights struggle and provided considerable impetus for civil rights legislation. And let's not forget Carrie Nation's efforts to demonstrate the advantages of Prohibition by chopping up saloons with her celebrated hatchet.

Protest Activities

Protest activities involve demonstrations, sit-ins, strikes, boycotts, and more recently various forms of electronic civil disobedience or "hacktivism" both in the United States and abroad (Harmon, 1998; Jordan and Taylor, 2004; Whyte, 2011) that dramatically emphasize, often with the help of the media, a group's grievances or objectives (Rooy, 2004). (For example, the Spring 2010 activities . . . as illustrations of demonstrations in support and against President Obama's government policies.) Often, such strategies, along with rioting or other use of mass violence, have been considered tools of those who are unable or unwilling to engage in the more conventional lawmaking or who regard it useless (Gamson, 1990; see also Shaw et al., 2010). It should be noted at the outset that "the relationship among law, protest, and social change is neither unidirectional nor symmetrical—nor always predictable. One major function of protest may be to secure changes in the law as a means of inducing change in social conditions. Another may be to bring about change directly without the intervention of the law. Still a third may be to bring about legal change which ratifies or legitimizes social change accomplished by other means. These functions are not mutually exclusive" (Grossman and Grossman, 1971:357). But the impact of protest activities on law creation is clearly evident, for "the law in general, and the Court in particular, lacks a self-starter or capacity for initiating change on its own" (Grossman and Grossman, 1971:358).

Racial minorities, poverty organizations, antiwar groups, and opponents of nuclear power have been among those who have employed protest techniques in recent years in attempts to create laws in favor of their objectives (see, for example, Lipschutz, 2006). Much of this activity is designed to generate favorable media coverage and, through this, the support of organizations and persons important in the eyes of lawmakers. But the young, the poor, and minority groups have not been the only ones to use protest techniques such as strikes and boycotts. Strike action has long been a central tactic of organized labor, including the unions of public employers in pursuing political and economic goals. In the mid-1970s, physicians used the strike weapon as a method of seeking governmental relief from medical malpractice insurance costs. Boycotts have been used by consumers protesting high prices. The national meat boycott of 1973 is an important example of such consumer action. It helped to generate enough pressure to force President Nixon to place a ceiling on meat prices. The controls, however, caused a meat shortage as farmers cut back on their supply.

To what extent protest activities provide an impetus for lawmaking is difficult to say. But, "few major social movements or great changes have occurred without the unrest and disorder which, if one approves is called protest or civil disobedience, and if one disapproves, it is called breaking the law, violence, or worse. Violence in particular is as much a part of enforcing the law as it is of seeking changes in the law" (Grossman and Grossman, 1971:358).

Social Movements

Over the years, there have been many examples of social movements that have culminated in proposals for or the actual creation of new laws and social policies (Almeida and Stearns, 1998; Johnston, 2010; Lipschutz, 2006; McCann, 2006; Santoro and McGuire, 1997; Snow et al., 2004; Tarrow, 1998; Tilly and Tarrow, 2007; Yarnold, 1992:109–128). By definition, a social movement is a type of collective behavior whereby a group of individuals organize to promote certain changes or alterations in certain types of behavior or procedures. Invariably, the movement has specified stated objectives, a hierarchical organizational structure, and a well-conceptualized and precise change-oriented ideology. The movement consciously and purposefully articulates the changes it desires through political, educational, or legal channels (see, for example, McAdam and Snow, 2010).

A classic example is the movement to legalize abortion (see, for example, Bennett, 2004). People had for some time regarded illegal abortion as dangerous, but efforts to prevent it (and thus end the death or serious injury of women) were unsuccessful. Then, a combination of women's rights and medical groups began to demand the legalization of abortion. Medical spokespersons argued that abortion is rightfully a medical decision to be made by a physician and his or her patient. Women's leaders argued that a woman has an unassailable right over her own body and ought to be able to choose whether or not to terminate the pregnancy. At the same time, no significant groups in society had a stake either in a high birthrate or in providing expensive illegal abortions. On the contrary, the general consensus was that the economic interests of the nation were concerned with the issues of overpopulation. Furthermore, with modern medical techniques, a legal abortion is classified as minor surgery, both cheap and safe.

With relative speed, in the 1960s, several states began to repeal or greatly liberalize laws against abortion. Within this climate of opinion, the Supreme Court completed the process in 1973 by declaring state laws against abortion unconstitutional except in the case of the last three months of pregnancy, and in regulating the physicians who perform the operation. The landmark 1973 decision that established a woman's right to abortion is still the law of the land, although it was narrowed in 1989 by a Supreme Court decision that sharply restricts the availability of public funds for abortion and requires physicians to test for the viability of a fetus at 20 weeks (*Newsweek*, 1989:14). Still, it remains a classic and routinely cited example of a social movement. Of course, there are many others, including ecology, antiglobalization, antiwar, civil rights, animal rights, victim rights, feminism, "crime without victims," "law and order movements," movements to combat sexual exploitation of women (Limoncelli, 2010), and ad infinitum. It should be pointed out that not all social movements are successful in bringing about changes through laws. As a matter of fact, at any given moment, hundreds of groups with hundreds of messages are trying to get public attention. Most fail as evidenced by the various "deviance liberation" movements, such those of prostitutes rights movements, both in the United States and in Europe (Poel, 1995). In the United States, winning public attention, thus public support, is becoming a highly professional activity requiring significant resources. Groups that can afford to hire or that can recruit public relations and advertising experts have a considerable advantage over other groups in getting a public hearing for their grievances. It is interesting to note that, regardless of the expertise available to them, all groups share the problem of developing an effective strategy to attract attention in a way that will not at the same time provoke outrage and opposition.

Public-Interest Groups

Lawmakers are fully cognizant of the fact that private interests are much better represented than public interests (see, for example, Maloney et al., 1994). There are literally hundreds of organizations and individuals in Washington and in state capitals who represent one or more private interests on a full- or part-time basis (Godwin, 1988; Mahood, 2000). They range from extremely well-financed organizations, such as the American Petroleum Institute, involved in worldwide affairs and supported by thousands of engineers, lawyers, and public relations experts, to small, single-issue groups, such as the Sportsman's Paradise Homeowners Association. Some, such as oil companies, regulate refinery output to maintain prices, and they lobby government representatives for favorable tax policies. Others, such as the Shipbuilders Union and the National Maritime Union, win direct and indirect subsidies from Congress in the guise of national defense requirements. Power utilities are legal monopolies whose rate structures are decided by utility commissions that are, in turn, the focus of tremendous pressures to allow expansion and higher rates for the benefit of managers and investors. There are over 23,000 entries of U.S. national associations, 19,000 international associations, and 159,000 U.S. regional, state, and local associations in the *2010 Encyclopedia of Associations*. Most of them represent specific, private interests.

By contrast, the number of groups that claim to represent public interests is quite small. The most notable among these are John Gardner's Common Cause, the Sierra Club, public interest research groups (PIRGs), and the various centers for law in the public interest focusing on public safety and other local problems (Reske, 1994). These groups have been instrumental in the initiation of a series of changes in the law designed to benefit and protect the public.

The Common Cause organization, founded in 1970, had an annual budget of over $6 million and around 300,000 dues-paying members in the mid-2000s and remains viable despite a reduction in both membership and budget since the early 1980s. It "has fought pitched battles on issues of the deepest concern to the American people—the Vietnam war, environmental pollution, racial injustice, poverty, unemployment, and women's rights" (Gardner, 1973:18). The organization is dedicated to "opening up the system" through the reform of campaign financing, open meeting laws, and disclosure laws. For example, in 1973, it initiated proposals for legislations that included making highway trust funds available for mass transit use, an unequivocal press-shield law, and "tax equity" (Wieck, 1973:21).

Spurred by the belief that the world faces an ultimate ecocatastrophe unless immediate and successful efforts are made to halt the abuse and deterioration of the environment, Sierra Club members "are no longer the outdoor recreationists of yesterday, but rather today's environmental politicos, in the vanguard of society's newest social movement" (Faich and Gale, 1971:282). The Sierra Club and similar organizations have been active in recent years in providing the impetus for a series of laws dealing with the protection of the environment. Some of these are the Air Quality Act of 1967, the Clean Air Act of 1970, and the Clean Water Act of 1972, in addition to the formation of a number of new federal agencies both to monitor compliance with the numerous existing pollution and environmental protection laws and to help establish new policies.

Modeled after Ralph Nader's Center for Study of Responsive Law, but independent of it, are the various PIRGs that now, after only a few years of organizing, include close to 400,000 student members at over 150 schools in 24 states. These groups are both funded and directed by students and are composed of a small professional staff of lawyers, scientists, and organizers, aided by hundreds of volunteer student researchers. For example, during the years from the late-1990s to late-2000s, the Missouri Public Interest Research Group (MoPIRG), among other things, drafted a new consumer code to protect poor people in St. Louis and have distributed a handbook on tenants' rights in Missouri. MoPIRG also participated in a study of the Educational Testing Service and is working with St. Louis unions to secure better enforcement of the occupational safety and health laws. Just recently, they have been instrumental in reforming health care in Missouri. In other states as well, the PIRGs are active in pointing out deficiencies in the system and proposing legal solutions for their improvement through research, public information, and law reform.

Impetus for law may also come from the various quasi-public specialized interest groups. They may represent certain economic interests, such as consumer groups, organized labor, or the National Welfare Rights organization. Or they may represent certain occupational interests, such as the American Medical Association, which not only exercises considerable control over the practice of medicine in this country, but also actively takes stands, raises money, and lobbies in favor of specific positions on such issues as abortion, euthanasia, drugs, and alcohol. The same can be said for the American Association of University Professors (though not on the same issues). Still others include groups representing what may be called moral interests, such as temperance, various types of antidrug concerns, various forms of "child saving" (for example, delinquency control), sexual deviance, the "work ethic," same-sex marriage, and antipornography. The important point to remember is that all these organizations can agitate for changes in the law and can provide the needed impetus for it.

For a group to effectively promote its interests and to provide an impetus for lawmaking, it naturally must have access to lawmakers. But access to lawmakers depends, at least in part, on the socioeconomic status of the group. Groups with the most financial resources, the most prestigious membership, and the best organization are likely to have the greatest access to legislators. It takes a substantial amount of money to maintain lobbyists in Washington and throughout the state capitals. Moreover, lawmakers, on the local as well as the higher levels, may be more sympathetic to groups that represent interests of the middle and upper classes than to groups representing poor people, welfare recipients, and the like. Generally, groups with "mainstream" views, seeking only small changes in the status quo, may be given more sympathetic hearing than those advocating large-scale radical changes.

The Mass Media

The mass media (newspapers, magazines, and radio and television stations) function in part as an interest group. Each component of the mass media is a business, and like other businesses, it has a direct interest in various areas of public policy. For example, the media have had a general objective of securing legislation, such as freedom of information (see, for example, Klosek, 2010) and open meeting laws that facilitate their access to the news and legislation or court decisions that allow them to protect the confidentiality of news sources. Associations like the National Association of Broadcasters are regularly concerned with the activities of the Federal Communications Commission, which controls their licensing of television and radio stations (Graber, 2009).

The mass media also function as conduits, although not altogether impartial ones, for others who would shape policy. Wealthier groups, for example, purchase media time or space in an effort to align public opinion behind their causes. Through the media, these groups may reach the ear of legislators and administrators by publicly exposing problems and proposals about which they might not otherwise hear or, in some instances, about which they might not want to hear.

The mass media, especially the news media, are able to generate widespread awareness and concern about events and conditions — to bring matters before the public so that they become problematic issues. For example, the well-known (late) columnist Jack Anderson, the irreverent muckraker, repeatedly sniffed out malodorous secrets that vested interests — oil companies, the Pentagon, the various juntas in Latin American countries, the distributors of chemical defoliants — do not want aired.

The Watergate case is a classic demonstration of the number of ways in which the mass media influence current events. Without dogged investigations by the mass media, the scandal probably would have remained buried. Without the blitz of mass-media coverage, the issues probably would not have achieved as rapid, widespread, or deep an impact on the public. Many of the most scandalous incidents of the Watergate affair have involved the improper solicitation and employment of campaign funds. Outraged segments of public opinion demanded the prevention of future "Watergates." The legislative response to this outcry was the passage of a bill in April 1974 that would drastically alter the way in which presidential and congressional campaigns are funded. This is illustrative of situations in which, as a result of investigative reporting, the mass media provide a direct impetus for legislation. Another example of the role of mass media in influencing current events is seen in the context of the Iran–Contra scandal. Special congressional committees have been impaneled to look into the precipitating events leading to the scandal, and the attorney general has opened a criminal investigation into the possibility that millions of dollars raised through secret U.S. arms sales to Iran had been diverted to the Contras to supply weapons in an attempt to topple Nicaragua's government, which was controlled by the leftist Sandinista Party (*St. Louis Post-Dispatch,* 1987:1B). Congress reacted by enacting the Intelligence Authorization Act of 1989, which President

Reagan signed into law, prohibiting any U.S. agency from providing assistance to the Nicaraguan paramilitary operations (Barron and Lederman, 2008).

Because public opinion is an important precursor of change, the mass media can set the stage by making undesirable conditions visible to a sizable segment of the public with unparalleled rapidity. Through the exposure of perceived injustices, the mass media play a crucial role in the formation of public opinion. Ralph Turner and Lewis M. Killian (1987) discuss six processes considered essential in understanding how the mass media can influence public opinion. First, the mass media *authenticate* the factual nature of events, which is decisive in the formation of public opinion. Second, the mass media *validate* opinions, sentiments, and preferences. It is reassuring to hear one's views confirmed by a well-known commentator. It also enables a person to express his or her views more effectively by borrowing the commentator's words. A third effect of the mass media is to *legitimize* certain behaviors and viewpoints considered to be taboo. Issues that were discussed only in private can now be expressed publicly, because they have already been discussed on television (for example, legal rights of homosexuals, gender violence, and family dysfunctions [Rapping, 2004]). Fourth, the mass media often *symbolize* the diffuse anxieties, preferences, discontents, and prejudices that individuals experience. By giving an acceptable identification for these perplexing feelings, the mass media often aid their translation into specific opinions and actions. By providing symbols—the "me" generation, Yuppies, law and order, war on terror, the new morality—the mass media create a number of objects toward which specific sentiments can be directed. Fifth, the mass media *focus* the preferences, discontents, and prejudices into lines of action. Finally, the mass media *classify into hierarchies* persons, objects, activities, and issues. As a result of the amount of consideration, preferential programming, and placement of items, they indicate relative importance and prestige.

The generalization that the views of individuals whose prestige and influence are established carry more weight than the views of others applies to public opinion. As a result, the "influences stemming from the mass media first reach 'opinion leaders,' who in turn, pass on what they read or hear to those of their everyday associates for whom they are influential" (Katz, 1957:61). Opinion leaders are usually leaders in only one sphere of activity. They tend to be different from the rest of the public in that they are more highly educated and are engaged in more prestigious occupations. They are also more powerful, active, and influential in specific community, interest group, or political affairs. Consequently, their opinions are considered much more influential and, therefore, are targeted by much of the media efforts.

In addition to investigative reporting and the shaping of public opinion, the mass media can pressure or challenge lawmakers into taking action on an issue or into changing their stand on a question. Influential newspapers such as the *New York Times* and the *Washington Post* can make or break legislators by the use of editorial pages. Endorsement by a major newspaper can greatly facilitate a candidate's chances for being elected. Conversely, opposition to a candidate on the editorial page can influence the outcome of an election. Legislators are quite aware of the power of the press, and as a result, editorial recommendations are given serious consideration. Similarly, articles in various influential weekly or monthly publications, such as *Commentary, Daedalus, Foreign Affairs, Monthly Review, Economist, Nation, New Leader, New Republic,* the now defunct *Public*

Interest, Progressive, and *Social Policy,* and the diverse specialized professional and legal journals can agitate for change.

Finally, an indirect way by which the mass media can furnish an impetus for lawmaking is through the provision of a forum for citizens' concerns. For example, the "letters to the editor" page in newspapers is a traditional outlet for publicizing undesirable conditions. Such letters can accomplish several objectives. First, the letter can alert the community that an issue is before a lawmaking body; second, it can persuade the reader to take a position; third, it can make clear that there are responsible and articulate people in the community who are concerned with the issue; and fourth, it can enlist the active support of others. Similarly, many radio and television stations have local talk shows and public-affairs programs that can be used to air grievances and to seek redress.

SUMMARY

This chapter has been concerned with the complex and continuous process of lawmaking in society. A number of theoretical perspectives to account for lawmaking have been reviewed. They are the rationalistic model, the functional view, conflict theory, and the "moral entrepreneur" thesis. None of these theories can account for the creation of all laws. At best, they explain in part how laws are made.

Three general types of lawmaking processes—legislative, administrative, and judicial—were analyzed. Legislators are solely responsible for formulating broad new roles and for creating and revising the institutions necessary to put them into effect. Legislative lawmaking basically consists of finding major and minor compromises to ideas advanced for legislation by the executive, administrative agencies, interest groups, and various party agencies and spokespersons. Administrative lawmaking consists of rulemaking and adjudication. Rulemaking is essentially legislation by administrative agencies. Adjudication differs from rulemaking in that it applies only to a specific, limited number of parties involved in an individual case and controversy before the agency. Judicial lawmaking is an accelerating trend in the United States. Three types of judicial lawmaking were examined—by precedent, by interpretation of statutes, and by interpretation of the Constitution. Judicial lawmaking is generally directed at other government agencies rather than at private individuals.

Interest groups, public opinion, and social science all exert an influence on the lawmaking process. Interest groups influence judicial lawmaking by initiating test cases, by providing additional information to the courts through *amicus curiae* briefs, and by communicating indirectly with judges by placing information in legal and general periodicals. Interactions between interest groups and legislative and administrative lawmakers are more overtly political in nature. The notion that laws reflect public opinion can be misleading. Some groups are more influential than others, and the differential influence of public opinion on lawmaking processes is a well-known phenomenon. Still, public opinion does exert an influence on lawmakers through rewards and sanctions (for example, voting for or against a particular legislator); through interest groups; and through the use of public opinion polls. Lawmakers are aware of the contributions social scientists can make to the lawmaking process. These contributions are based on social science research and expressed to lawmakers either directly in the form of expert testimony or indirectly through the use of research findings as they bear upon a particular piece of legislation or judicial and administrative decision. But, the participation of social scientists in the law-making process is not without controversies. There are questions about the use of research results, their validity and reliability, and the political bias of social scientists. Despite the controversies, it was noted that social science evidence cannot be kept out of the lawmaking process.

Demands for lawmaking come from a multitude of sources. Ideas for change are born in the minds of a few people who are ready and willing to articulate their dissatisfaction. They represent diverse interests and causes and channel their discontent through different means. Once in a while, a scholarly investigation generates concern over a social condition or practice and points to a legal solution. At times, a novel can detect or warn about a deleterious situation that affects the public. The impetus for lawmaking can also come from institutionalized forces, such as lobbying activities and public-interest groups. Occasionally, the creation of laws has been stimulated by organized protest activities or social movements. Finally, the mass media can set the stage for lawmaking by calling attention to an issue.

SUGGESTED FURTHER READINGS

William Dudley, *Mass Media.* San Diego, CA: Greenhaven Press, 2005.

Richard A. Harris and Sidney M. Milkis, *The Politics of Regulatory Change: A Tale of Two Agencies.* New York: Oxford University Press, 1989. A fascinating and timeless account of how regulatory policies are made and unmade.

Kamala Kempadoo and Jo Doezema, *Global Sex Workers: Rights, Resistance, and Redefinition.* New York: Routledge, 1998.

Roman A. Tomasic (ed.), *Legislation and Society in Australia.* Sydney, Australia: George Allen and Unwin, 1980. A series of case studies and theoretical articles on the making and instrumentation of law in Australia.

REFERENCES

Abraham, Henry J. 1996. *The Judiciary: The Supreme Court in the Governmental Process.* 10th ed. New York: New York University Press.

Abramson, Jill. 1998. "The Business of Persuasion Thrives in Nation's Capital," *New York Times (*September 29): A1, A22–23.

Almeida, Paul, and Linda Brewster Stearns. 1998. "Political Opportunities and Local Grassroots Environmental Movements: The Case of Minamata," *Social Problems,* 45 (1) (February): 37–57.

Althaus, Scott L. 2003. *Collective Preferences in Democratic Politics: Opinion Surveys and the Will of the People.* Cambridge, UK/New York: Cambridge University Press.

Armor, David J. 1972. "The Evidence on Busing," *Public Interest,* 25 (Summer): 90–126.

Ball, Howard. 2004. *The Supreme Court in the Intimate Lives of Americans: Birth, Sex, Marriage, Childbearing, and Death.* New York: New York University Press.

Barron, David J. and Martin S. Lederman. 2008. The Commander in Chief at the Lowest Ebb: A Constitutional History. *Harvard Law Review*, 121 (4) (February): 941–1111.

Baum, Lawrence. 2010. *The Supreme Court.* 10th ed., Washington, DC: QC Press.

Becker, Howard S. 1963. *Outsiders.* New York: Free Press.

Beermann, Jack M. 2006. *Administrative Law.* 2nd ed. New York: Aspen Publishers.

Bennett, Belinda (ed.). 2004. *Abortion.* Burlington, VT: Ashgate.

Berk, Richard A., and Jerrold Oppenheim. 1979. "Doing Good Well: The Use of Quantitative Social Science Data in Adversary Proceedings," *Law and Policy Quarterly,* 1 (2) (April): 123–146.

Bloom, Lackland H. 2009. *Methods of Interpretation: How the Supreme Court Reads the Constitution.* New York: Oxford University Press.

Bohannan, Paul. 1973. "The Differing Realms of the Law." Pp. 306–317 in Donald Black and Maureen Mileski (eds.), *The Social Organization of the Law.* New York: Seminar Press.

Brodsky, Stanley L. 2004. *Coping with Cross-examination and other Pathways to Effective Testimony.* Washington, DC: American Psychological Association.

Bryden, David P. 1993. "A Conservative Case for Judicial Activism," *Public Interest,* 111 (Spring): 72–87.

Bryant, Amorette Nelson. 2004. *Complete Guide to Federal and State Garnishment.* 3rd ed. New York: Aspen Publishers.

Bryner, Gary C. 1987. *Bureaucratic Discretion: Law and Policy in Federal Regulatory Agencies.* New York: Pergamon Press.

Buckhorn, Robert F. 1972. *Nader: The People's Lawyer.* Englewood Cliffs, NJ: Prentice Hall.

Canon, Bradley C., and Charles A. Johnson. 1999. *Judicial Policies: Instrumentation and Impact.* 2nd ed. Washington, DC: CQ Press.

Caplovitz, David. 1963. *The Poor Pay More.* New York: Free Press. 1974. *Consumers in Trouble: A Study of Debtors in Default.* New York: Free Press.

Carp, Robert A. and Ronald Stidham. 1996. *Judicial Process in America.* 3rd ed. Washington, DC: CQ Press.

Carp, Robert A., Ronald Stidham, and Kenneth L. Manning. 2010. *Judicial Process in America.* 8th ed. Washington, DC: CQ Press.

Carson, Rachel L. 1962. *Silent Spring.* Boston, MA: Houghton-Mifflin.

Chambliss, William J. 1964. "A Sociological Analysis of the Law of Vagrancy," *Social Problems,* 12 (1) (Summer): 67–77. 1976. "The State and Criminal Law." Pp. 66–106 in William J. Chambliss and Milton Mankoff (eds.), *Whose Law, What Order? A Conflict Approach to Criminology.* New York: John Wiley. 1984. *Criminal Law in Action.* 2nd ed. New York: John Wiley.

Chambliss, William J., and Marjorie S. Zatz (eds.). 1993. *Making Law: The State, the Law, and Structural Contradictions.* Bloomington, IN: Indiana University Press.

Cheney, Timothy D. 1998. *Who Makes the Law: The Supreme Court, Congress, the States, and Society.* Upper Saddle River, NJ: Prentice Hall.

Coleman, James S. 1966. "Equality Schools or Equal Students," *Public Interest,* 7 (Summer): 70–75. 1967. "Toward Open Schools," *Public Interest,* 9 (Fall): 20–27.

Commons, John R. 1934. *Institutional Economics.* New York: MacMillan.

Costanzo, Mark, Daniel Krauss, and Kathy Pezdek (eds.). 2007. *Expert Psychological Testimony for the Courts.* Mahwah, NJ: Lawrence Erlbaum Associates.

Crespi, Irving. 1979. "Modern Marketing Techniques: They Could Work in Washington, Too," *Public Opinion,* 2 (3) (June–July): 16–19, 58–59.

Davidson, Roger H. 1993. "The Lawmaking Congress," *Law and Contemporary Problems,* 56 (4) (Autumn): 99–119.

Davis, Kenneth Culp. 1977. *Administrative Law: Cases-Text-Problems.* 6th ed. St. Paul, MN: West Publishing Company.

Dow, David R. 2009. *America's Prophets. How Judicial Activism Makes America Great.* Santa Barbara, CA: Praeger/ABC-CLIO.

Downs, Anthony. 1976. *Urban Problems and Prospects.* 2nd ed. Chicago, IL: Markham Publishing Company.

Economist. 2001. "High Time: A Survey of Illegal Drugs" (July 28): 1–16.

Etzioni, Amitai. 1973. *The Genetic Fix.* New York: MacMillan.

Evan, William M. 1990. *Social Structure and Law: Theoretical and Empirical Perspectives.* Newbury Park, CA: Sage Publications.

Faich, Ronald G., and Richard P. Gale. 1971. "The Environmental Movement from Recreation to Politics," *Pacific Sociological Review,* 14 (July): 270–287.

Falk, Richard. 1971. *This Endangered Planet.* New York: Random House.

Feldstein, Martin S. 1975a. "Toward a Reform of Social Security," *Public Interest,* 40 (Summer): 75–95. 1975b. "Unemployment Insurance: Time for Reform," *Harvard Business Review,* 53 (March–April): 51–61.

Friedman, Lawrence M. 1975. *The Legal System: A Social Science Perspective.* New York: Russell Sage Foundation. 1998. *American Law: An Introduction.* 2nd ed. New York: W. W. Norton & Co., Inc. 2002. *American Law in the Twentieth Century.* New Haven, CT: Yale University Press.

Friedman, Lawrence M., and Stewart Macaulay. 1977. *Law and the Behavioral Sciences.* 2nd ed. Indianapolis, IN: Bobbs-Merrill.

Fuller, Lon. 1968. *Anatomy of the Law.* New York: Praeger.

Gamson, William. 1990. *The Strategy of Social Protest.* 2nd ed. Belmont, CA: Wadsworth.

Gardner, John W. 1973. *In Common Cause.* Revised ed. New York: W. W. Norton & Co., Inc.

Geel, Tyll R. van. 2009. *Understanding Supreme Court Opinions.* 4th ed. New York: Pearson Longman.

Gioacchino, Debora Di, Sergio Ginebri, and Laura Sabani (eds.). 2004. *The Role of Organized Interest Groups in Policy Making.* New York: Palgrave Macmillan.

Glazer, Nathan. 1975. "Towards an Imperial Judiciary?" *Public Interest,* 41 (Fall): 104–123.

Glendon, Mary Ann. 1994. *A Nation under Lawyers: How the Crisis in the Legal Profession is Transforming American Society.* New York: Farrar, Straus, and Giroux.

Godwin, R. Kenneth. 1988. *One Billion Dollars of Influence: The Direct Marketing of Politics.* Chatham, NJ: Chatham House Publishers, Inc.

Gold, Susan Dudley. 2005. *Brown v. Board of Education: Separate but Equal?* New York: Benchmark Books.

Goode, Erich. 2011. *Deviant Behavior.* 9th ed. Upper Saddle River, NJ: Pearson Prentice Hall.

Gordon, Marcy. 2003. "1.6 million file for bankruptcy; Debt Lingers from Free-Spending '90s." *Seattle Times* (November 15): A7.

Graber, Doris A. 2009. *Mass Media and American Politics.* 8th ed. Washington, DC: CQ Press.

Graglia, Lino A. 1994. "Do Judges Have a Policy-making Role in the American System of Government?" *Harvard Journal of Law & Public Policy,* 17 (1) (Winter): 119–130.

Grossman, Joel B., and Mary H. Grossman (eds.). 1971. *Law and Social Change in Modern America.* Pacific Palisades, CA: Goodyear.

Gusfield, Joseph R. 1967. "Moral Passage: The Symbolic Process in Public Designations of Deviance," *Social Problems,* 15 (2) (Fall): 175–188.

Hagan, John. 1980. "The Legislation of Crime and Delinquency: A Review of Theory, Method, and Research," *Law & Society Review,* 14 (3) (Spring): 603–628.

Hajnal, Zoltan L., and Terry Nichols Clark. 1998. "The Local Interest-Group System: Who Governs and Why?" *Social Science Quarterly,* 79 (1) (March): 227–242.

Halliday, Terrence C., and Bruce G. Carruthers. 2009. *Bankrupt: Global Lawmaking and Systemic Financial Crisis.* Palo Alto, CA: Stanford University Press.

Harmon, Amy. 1998. "'Hacktivists' of All Persuasions Take Their Struggle to the Web," *New York Times* (October 31): A1, A5.

Harrington, Christine B., and Lief H. Carter. 2009. *Administrative Law and Politics: Cases and Comments.* 4th ed. Washington, DC: Press.

Horowitz, Donald L. 1977. *The Courts and Social Policy.* Washington, DC: Brookings Institution.

Howard, A. E. Dick. 1979. "The Road from 'Brown,'" *Wilson Quarterly,* 3 (2) (Spring): 96–107.

Ippolito, Dennis S., Thomas G. Walker, and Kenneth L. Kolson. 1976. *Public Opinion and Responsible Democracy.* Englewood Cliffs, NJ: Prentice Hall.

Jacob, Herbert. 1984. *Justice in America: Courts, Lawyers, and the Judicial Process.* 4th ed. Boston, MA: Little, Brown and Company.

Johnston, Hank (ed.). 2010. *Culture, Social Movements, and Protest.* Burlington, VT: Ashgate.

Jordan, Tim, and Paul A. Taylor. 2004. *Hacktivism and Cyberwars: Rebels with a Cause?* New York: Routledge.

Katz, Elihu. 1957. "The Two-Step Flow of Communication: An Up-to-Date Report on an Hypothesis," *Public Opinion Quarterly,* 21 (1) (Spring): 61–78.

Kerrigan, Laura J., et al., 1993. "Project: The Decriminalization of Administrative Law Penalties: Civil Remedies, Alternatives, Policy, and Constitutional Implications," *Administrative Law Review,* 45 (4) (Fall): 367–434.

Kerwin, Cornelius M., and Scott R. Furlong. 2010. *Rulemaking: How Government Agencies Write Law and Make Policy.* 4th ed. Washington, DC: CQ Press.

Klosek, Jacqueline. 2010. *The Right to Know: Your Guide to Using and Defending Freedom of Information Law in the United States.* Santa Barbara, CA: Praeger.

Kozlowski, Mark. 2003. *The Myth of the Imperial Judiciary: Why the Right is Wrong about the Courts.* New York: New York University Press.

Lange, Marc. 2009. *Laws and Law Makers: Science, Metaphysics, and the Laws of Nature.* New York: Oxford University Press.

Lazarus, Richard J. 2004. *The Making of Environmental Law.* Chicago, IL: University of Chicago Press.

Leo, Richard A., and George C. Thomas III (eds.). 1998. *The Miranda Debate: Law, Justice, and Policing.* Boston, MA: Northeastern University Press.

Limoncelli, Stephanie A. 2010. *The Politics of Trafficking. The First International Movement to Combat the Sexual Exploitation of Women.* Palo Alto, CA: Stanford University Press.

Lipschutz, Ronnie D. (ed.). 2006. *Civil Societies and Social Movements.* Burlington, VT: Ashgate.

Lipset, Seymour Martin. 1976. "The Wavering Polls," *Public Interest,* 43 (Spring): 70–89.

Lindquist, Stefanie, and Frank Cross. 2009. *Measuring Judicial Activism.* New York: Oxford University Press.

Llewellyn, Karl N., and E. Adamson Hoebel. 1941. *The Cheyenne Way: Conflict and Case Law in Primitive Jurisprudence.* Norman, OK: University of Oklahoma Press.

Loewenberg, Gerhard, Peverill Squire, and D. Roderick Kiewiet (eds.). 2002. *Legislatures: Comparative Perspectives on Representative Assemblies.* Ann Arbor, MI: University of Michigan Press.

Mahood, H. R. 2000. *Interest Groups in American National Politics: An Overview.* Upper Saddle River, NJ: Prentice Hall.

Maloney, William A., Grant Jordan, and Andrew M. McLaughlin. 1994. "Interest Groups and Public Policy: The Insider/Outsider Model Revisited," *Journal of Public Policy,* 14 (1) (January–March): 17–39.

Markin, Kirk. 2004. "Critics of Supreme Court off Base, Study Says: Analysis by Academic Debunks Charges that Judicial Activism is on the Increase," *Globe and Mail* (February 2): A4.

Marshall, Thomas R. 1989. *Public Opinion and the Supreme Court.* Boston, MA: Unwin Hyman.

McAdam, Doug, and David A. Snow (eds.). 2010. *Readings on Social Movements: Origins, Dynamics, Outcomes.* 2nd ed. New York: Oxford University Press

McCann, Michael (ed.). 2006. *Law and Social Movements.* Burlington, VA: Ashgate.

McCann, Michael W., and Gerald L. Houseman (eds.). 1989. *Judging the Constitution: Critical Essays on Judicial Lawmaking.* Glenview, IL: Scott, Foresman/Little, Brown and Company.

McCartney, Scott. 2010. "Forcing Airlines to Play Nice with Fliers." *Wall Street Journal* (March 4): D1, D2.

McCloskey, Robert G. 2010. *The American Supreme Court.* 5th ed. Chicago, IL: University of Chicago Press.

McGuire, Kevin T. 1994. "Amici Curiae and Strategies for Gaining Access to the Supreme Court," *Political Research Quarterly*, 47 (4) (December): 821–838.

Monahan, John, and Laurens Walker. 2010. *Social Science in Law: Cases and Materials.* 7th ed. New York: Thomson Reuters/Foundation Press, Inc.

Monchuk, Judy. 2006. "Calgary Pawn-Shop Operator Convicted of Criminal Usury; Charged 207,891% Interest," *Globe and Mail* (December 29): A8.

Moynihan, Daniel Patrick. 1979. "Social Science and the Courts," *Public Interest,* 54 (Winter): 12–31.

Murray, Sara. 2009. "Personal Bankruptcy Filings Have Exceeded One Million." *Wall Street Journal (*October 3–4): A4.

Murray, Sara, and Conor Daugherty. 2010. "Personal Bankruptcy Filings Rising Fast." *Wall Street Journal* (January 5): A3.

Nader, Ralph. 1965. *Unsafe at Any Speed: The Designed-in Dangers of the American Automobile.* New York: Grossman.

Newsweek. 1989. "The Future of Abortion: The Court Drills a Crack in the Foundation of *Roe*" (July 17): 14–27.

Norrander, Barbara, and Clyde Wilcox (eds.). 2009. *Understanding Public Opinion.* 3rd ed. Washington, DC: CQ Press.

Ornstein, Norman J., Thomas E. Mann, and Michael Malbin. 1990. *Vital Statistics on Congress, 1989–1990.* Washington, DC: Congressional Quarterly Inc.

Osborn, Fairfield. 1948. *Our Plundered Planet.* Boston, MA: Little, Brown and Company.

Parisi, Francesco. 2008. *The Economics of Law Making.* New York: Oxford University Press.

Parisian, Suzanne. 2001. *FDA: Inside & Out.* Front Royal, VA: Fast Horse Press.

Pettigrew, Thomas F., and Robert L. Green. 1976. "School Desegregation in Large Cities," *Harvard Educational Review,* 46 (February): 1–53.

Pierce, Richard J., Jr. 1995. "Seven Ways to Deossify Agency Rule Making," *Administrative Law Review,* 47 (1) (Winter): 59–95.

Plattner, Marc F. 1974. "Campaign Financing: The Dilemmas of Reform," *Public Interest,* 37 (Fall): 112–130.

Poel, Sari Van Der. 1995. "Solidarity as Boomerang: The Fiasco of the Prostitutes' Rights Movement in the Netherlands," *Crime, Law & Social Change,* 23:41–65.

Price, David E. 1972. *Who Makes the Law? Creativity and Power in Senate Committees.* Cambridge, MA: Schenkman.

Quinney, Richard. 1970. *The Social Reality of Crime.* Boston, MA: Little, Brown and Company.

Rabkin, Jeremy. 1989. *Judicial Compulsions.* New York: Basic Books.

Rapping, Elayne. 2004. *Law and Justice as Seen on TV.* New York: New York University Press.

Reinow, R., and L.T. Reinow. 1967. *Moment in the Sun.* New York: Dial Press.

Reske, Henry J. 1994. "Ralph Nader's New Project: Law Centers to Help the Small Group Instead of the Little Guy," *ABA Journal,* 80 (May): 32–33.

Ripley, Randall B. 1988. *Congress: Process and Policy.* 4th ed. New York: W. W. Norton & Co., Inc.

Roby, Pamela. 1969. "Politics and Criminal Law: Revision of the New York State Penal Law on Prostitution," *Social Problems,* 17 (1) (Summer): 83–109.

Roesch, Ronald, Stephen L. Golding, Valerie P. Hans, and N. Dickon Reppucci. 1991. "Social Science and the Courts: The Role of Amicus Curiae Briefs," *Law and Human Behavior,* 15 (1) (February): 1–11.

Rooy, Alison Van. 2004. *The Global Legitimacy Game: Civil Society, Globalization, and Protest.* New York: Palgrave Macmillan.

Rozell, Mark J., Clyde Wilcox, and David Madland. 2006. *Interest Groups in American Campaigns.* 2nd ed. Washington, DC: CQ Press.

Rusthoven, Peter J. 1976. "The Courts as Sociologists," *National Review* (December 10): 1339–1341.

Santoro, Wayne A., and Gail M. McGuire. 1997. "Social Movement Insiders: The Impact of Institutional Activists on Affirmative Action and Comparable Worth Policies," *Social Problems,* 44 (4) (November): 503–519.

Schwartz, Bernard. 1995. "'Shooting the Piano Player'? Justice Scalia and Administrative Law," *Administrative Law Review*, 47 (1) (Winter): 1–57.

St. Louis Post-Dispatch. 1987. "Warning on Contras" (January 26): 1B.

Shapiro, Martin. 1968. *The Supreme Court and Administrative Agencies.* New York: Free Press.

Shaw, Rosalind, Lars Waldorf, and Pierre Hazan (eds.). 2010. *Localizing Transnational Justice: Interventions and Priorities after Mass Violence.* Palo Alto, CA: Stanford University Press.

Simon, Rita James. 1974. *Public Opinion in America: 1936–1970.* Skokie, IL: Rand McNally.

Smith, Anne Kates. 1992. "Opinions with a Price: More-Complex Court Cases Mean Jobs for Expert Witnesses," *U.S. News & World Report* (July 20): 64–66.

Snow, David A., Sarah A. Soule, and Hanspeter Kriesi (eds.). 2004. *The Blackwell Companion to Social Movements.* Malden, MA: Blackwell Publishers.

Spector, Malcolm, and John I. Kitsuse. 1973. "Social Problems: A Reformulation," *Social Problems,* 21 (2) (Fall): 145–159.

Stone, Marvin. 1979. "Should Judges Make Law?," *U.S. News & World Report* (June 4): 76.

Tarrow, Sidney. 1998. *Power in Movement: Social Movements and Contentious Politics.* 2nd ed. Cambridge, UK: Cambridge University Press.

Tilly, Charles, and Sidney Tarrow. 2007. *Contentious Politics.* Boulder, CO: Paradigm Publishers.

Tomasic, Roman. 1985. *The Sociology of Law:* London, UK: Sage Publications.

Tone, Andrea. 2001. *Devices and Desires: A History of Contraceptives in America.* New York: Hill & Wang.

Turner, Ralph, and Lewis M. Killian. 1987. *Collective Behavior.* 3rd ed. Englewood Cliffs, NJ: Prentice Hall.

U.S. News & World Report, 2004. "Special Report: 50 Years after Brown" (March 22–29): 65–96.

Vago, Steven. 1968. "Wage Garnishment: An Exercise in Futility under Present Law," *Journal of Consumer Affairs,* 2 (1) (Summer): 7–20.

Walker, Nigel, and Mike Hough (eds.). 1988. *Public Attitudes to Sentencing: Surveys from Five Countries.* Aldershot, UK: Gower.

Warren, Kenneth F. 2010. *Administrative Law in the Political System.* 5th ed. Boulder, CO: Westview Press.

Washington, Ebonya. 2006. "How Daughters Affect Their Legislator Fathers' Voting on Women's Issues" (January) Working Paper # 11924. Cambridge, MA: National Bureau of Economic Research.

Whyte, Martin King. 2011. *Myth of the Social Volcano. Perceptions of Inequality and Distributive Injustice in Contemporary China.* Stanford, CA: Stanford University Press.

Wellington, Harry H. 1991. *Interpreting the Constitution: The Supreme Court and the Process of Adjudication.* New Haven, CT: Yale University Press.

West, William F. 1985. *Administrative Rulemaking: Politics and Processes.* Westport, CT: Greenwood Press.

Wieck, Paul R. 1973. "The John Gardner Brigade," *New Republic,* 168: 21–22.

Wolf, Eleanor P. 1976. "Social Science and the Courts: The Detroit Schools Case," *Public Interest,* 42 (Winter): 102–120.

Wolfgang, Marvin E. 1998. "We Do Not Deserve to Kill," *Crime & Delinquency,* 44 (1) (January): 19–31.

Yarnold, Barbara M. 1992. *Politics and the Courts: Toward a General Theory of Public Law.* New York: Praeger.

Zander, Michael. 2005. *The Law-Making Process.* 6th ed. Cambridge, UK/New York: Cambridge University Press.

Zeisel, Hans. 1962. "Social Research on the Law: The Ideal and the Practical." Pp. 124–143 in William M. Evan (ed.), *Law and Sociology: Exploratory Essays.* New York: Free Press.

CHAPTER

Law and Social Control

Since the beginning of the discipline of sociology in the nineteenth century, a great deal has been written on various facets of social control, and the topic continues to occupy a central position in the sociological and law and society literature (see, for example, Hil and Tait, 2004; Norris and Wilson, 2007; Vold et al., 2009). Social control refers to the methods used by members of a society to maintain order and to promote predictability of behavior. There are many different forms of social control, and law is only one of them. The emphasis in this chapter is on social control through laws that are activated when other forms of control mechanisms are ineffective or unavailable. This chapter examines the processes of informal and formal social control, the use of criminal sanctions, the effectiveness of the death penalty, and civil commitment to regulate behavior. Part of this chapter is concerned with crimes without victims (drug addiction, prostitution, and gambling), white-collar crime, and the control of dissent. The chapter concludes with a consideration of administrative law as an instrument of control in the context of licensing, inspection, and the threat of publicity.

There are two basic processes of social control—the internalization of group norms and control through external pressures (Clinard and Meier, 2010). In the first instance, social control is the consequence of socialization, the process of learning the rules of behavior for a given social group. Individuals develop self-control by being taught early what is appropriate, expected, or desirable in specific situations. People acquire a motivation to conform to the norms, regardless of external pressures. Most students do not cheat because of the fear of being caught, and most people pay their taxes, most of the time. There is conformity to norms because individuals have been socialized to believe that they should conform, regardless of and independent of any anticipated reactions of other persons.

Mechanisms of social control through external pressures include both negative and positive sanctions. Negative sanctions are penalties imposed on those who violate norms. Positive sanctions, such as a promotion, a bonus, and encouragement, are intended to reward conformity. These positive and negative sanctions are forms of social control. Some types of social control are formal or official, and others are informal or unofficial in character. Typical reactions to deviance and rule breaking may generate both informal and formal sanctions. Although there is a considerable amount of overlapping between informal and formal mechanisms of social control, for analytical purposes they will be discussed separately.

INFORMAL SOCIAL CONTROLS

Methods of informal social controls are best exemplified by folkways (established norms of common practices such as those that specify modes of dress, etiquette, and language use) and mores (societal norms associated with intense feelings of right or wrong and definite rules of conduct that are simply not to be violated—for example, incest). These informal controls consist of techniques whereby individuals who know each other on a personal basis accord praise to those who comply with their expectations and show displeasure to those who do not (Shibutani, 1961:426). These techniques may be observed in expressions of opinion and specific behaviors, such as ridicule, gossip, praise, reprimands, criticisms, ostracism, and verbal rationalizations. Gossip, or the fear of gossip, is one of the more effective devices employed by members of a society to bring individuals into conformity with norms. Unlike formal social controls, these informal controls are not exercised through official group mechanisms, and there are no specially designated persons in charge of enforcement.

Informal mechanisms of social control tend to be more effective in groups and societies where relations are face to face and intimate and where the division of labor is relatively simple. For example, Emile Durkheim argues that in simple societies, such as tribal villages or small towns, legal norms more closely accord with social norms than in larger and more complex societies. Moral disapproval of deviance is nearly unanimous in such communities (Shilling and Mellor, 1998); and as Daniel Glaser (1971:32) notes, "Tolerance of behavioral diversity varies directly with the division of labor in a society." In simple societies, laws are often unwritten, necessitating the direct teaching of social norms to children. Socialization in such simple societies does not present children with contradictory norms that create confusion or inner conflict. Intense face-to-face interaction in such societies produces a moral consensus that is well known to all members; it also brings deviant acts to everyone's attention quickly.

There is substantial evidence in the sociological literature to support the contention that informal social control is stronger in smaller, traditional, more homogeneous communities than in larger, more modern, heterogeneous communities (Hanawalt, 1998). In a classic and influential study of deviance in the seventeenth-century Massachusetts Bay Colony, Kai T. Erikson found that the small size and the cultural homogeneity of the community helped control behavior, because everyone in the community pressured potential deviants to conform to dominant norms. There was a substantial amount of surveillance by neighbors in the community watching for acts of deviance. Moral censure immediately followed any observed act of deviance (Erikson, 1966:169–170). Even today, reaction to certain crimes (for example, rape or murder) in a small, homogeneous, and close-knit community may be so intense and immediate that justice for a defendant in a criminal case may be difficult, because public pressure on the legal system to exact harsh and immediate punishment may make the provision of due process rights doubtful. In such instances, it may be necessary to change the location of the trial to minimize public pressure. Such a change of venue order is more likely to take place in small communities than in larger ones where the court would not assume that the defendant cannot receive a fair trial because of prejudice (Friendly and Goldfarb, 1967:96–101; see also Brooks, 2009).

Undoubtedly, informal social controls operate more effectively in smaller communities where people know each other and regularly interact. In such communities, law enforcement agents can probably expect better cooperation. As a perceptive and innovative President's Commission on Law Enforcement and Administration of Justice (1967a:6) points out: "A man who lives in the country or in a small town is likely to be conspicuous, under surveillance by his community so to speak, and therefore under its control. A city man is often almost invisible, socially isolated from his neighborhood and therefore incapable of being controlled by it. He has more opportunities for crime."

The greater effectiveness of informal social-control mechanisms in small communities is demonstrated by Sarah L. Boggs's well-known study of formal and informal social controls in central cities, suburbs, and small towns in Missouri. Boggs found that residents of large cities were more apt than suburban or small-town residents to feel that crime was likely to occur in their community. City residents were also more likely to think that their neighbors would not report a burglary that they observed, and more urban residents knew of a crime or a suspicious incident in their community within the previous year. Most people in all areas felt that their own neighborhood was safe, but fewer felt that way in the cities. When they were asked *what* it was that made their neighborhood safe, 83 percent of those in rural areas and small towns said that it was informal controls; 70 percent in suburbs and 68 percent of those in the cities attributed safety to informal controls. When they said that their neighborhood was kept safe by informal social controls, the people meant that they felt secure because of the character of the community and its residents—"good, decent, law-abiding, middle-class citizens" (Boggs, 1971:323). Safety in a neighborhood was also attributed to the social network in the community that might lead to bystander intervention in a crime. Respondents who lived in suburbs and large cities were more likely than those who lived in rural areas and small towns to attribute safety to such formal control agents as the police (Boggs, 1971:234). Boggs concluded that people in cities were most inclined to expect crime but least likely to feel that they could rely on their neighbors rather than the police to protect their community. As a result, they were more likely to take precautions, such as purchasing weapons or a watchdog, than their counterparts who lived in suburbs, small towns, and rural areas.

Similar conclusions about the role of informal social-control mechanisms can be drawn from studies dealing with developing nations. For example, in comparing a low-crime-rate community and a high-crime-rate community in Kampala, Uganda, Marshall B. Clinard and Daniel J. Abbott found that the areas with less crime showed greater social solidarity, more social interaction among neighbors, more participation in local organizations, less geographical mobility, and more stability in family relationships. There was also greater cultural homogeneity and more emphasis on tribal and kinship ties in the low-crime community, helping to counteract the anonymity of recent migrants to the city. The stronger primary group ties among residents of the low-crime area made it more difficult for strangers in the community to escape public notice. To prevent theft, residents of an area must feel that it is wrong, share some responsibility for protecting their neighbors' property, be able to identify strangers in the area, and be willing to take action if they observe a theft (Clinard and Abbott, 1973:149).

These and other studies (see, for example, Garofalo and McLeod, 1989) show that if there is intense social interaction on an intimate face-to-face basis, the normative consensus, and the surveillance of the behavior of members of the community, informal social control will be strong to the extent that legal or formal controls may be unnecessary. This contention is reinforced by Roberto Mangabeira Unger's (1976) argument, which was discussed in Chapter 2. To reiterate, Unger contends that bureaucratic law emerges when state and society become differentiated and there is a felt need for an institution standing above conflicting groups. This occurs when the community disintegrates, that is, when individuals may no longer be counted on to act in set ways without overt guidance. Such disintegration comes about as the division of labor creates new opportunities for power and wealth, which, in turn, undercut old hierarchies determined by birth. This process is accompanied by an increased reliance on formal social controls.

Finally, the role of neighborhood committees (for example, little old ladies employed by the state to monitor their neighbors), such as those found in China, should be considered. The Chinese call them "KGB with little feet" (Ignatius, 1989). The "old lady" network, established in the 1950s as a bridge between the party and the people, still remains China's most effective means of grassroots social control (Diamant et al., 2005). In the mid-2000s, there were an estimated one million neighborhood committees in cities and villages around the country, employing 6.4 million retirees, virtually all women. In Beijing, there is, on the average, one old lady keeping watch on every 20 families. Their primary task is to seek out and resolve squabbles among neighbors. They report everything they see to higher-ups, investigate disturbances, routinely stop strangers, and pry into couples' plans for having children. In the summer of 1989, they were active in circulating photos of fugitive prodemocracy activists and helped to mobilize residents to attend mass rallies and public executions. This technique of community-based surveillance is modeled after the one introduced in the former Soviet Union in the 1920s, which was based on the principle of denouncement. People were encouraged, and rewarded, to report on friends and relatives who were suspected of engaging in activities contrary to the interests of the government. Various versions of this technique were subsequently used in Nazi Germany and other totalitarian regimes. Some of them are being revitalized in the post 9/11 war on terror endeavors by the police backing antiterrorism community watch programs to educate the public about behaviors that are truly suspicious and should be reported to the police. An example of this would be the Los Angeles iWATCH program designed to provide the public with concrete advice on how to follow the oft-repeated post-9/11 recommendation: "If you see something, say something" (Sullivan, 2009).

FORMAL SOCIAL CONTROLS

Although there is no clear-cut dividing line, formal social controls are usually characteristic of more complex societies with a greater division of labor, heterogeneity of population, and subgroups with competing values and different sets of mores and ideologies. Formal controls arise when informal controls alone are insufficient to maintain conformity to certain norms. Formal controls are characterized by systems of specialized agencies, standard techniques, and the general predictability of universal sanctions. The two main types are those instituted by the state and authorized to use force and those imposed by agencies other than the state, such as the church, business and labor groups, universities, and clubs.

[handwritten margin note: societal norms associated with intense feelings of right or wrong]

Formal social controls are incorporated in the institutions in society and are characterized by the explicit establishment of procedures and the delegation of specific bodies to enforce them (laws, decrees, regulations, and codes). Because they are incorporated in the institutions of society, they are administered by individuals who occupy positions in those institutions. Generally, anyone who attempts to manipulate the behavior of others through the use of formal sanctions may be considered an agent of social control (Clinard and Meier, 2010).

Social institutions are organized for securing conformity to established modes of behavior and consist of established procedures for satisfying human needs. These procedures carry a certain degree of compulsion and involve mechanisms of imposing conformity. Nonpolitical institutions may resort to a variety of penalties and rewards to ensure compliance (Vaughan, 1998). For example, an organization may fire an employee; a church may withhold religious services at a wedding or a burial, or even excommunicate a member; and a league owner may fine or suspend a professional athlete for infractions of rules. These same organizations may also use formal rewards to ensure conformity. To illustrate, through bonuses and promotion, an organization often rewards those who make an outstanding contribution. Dedicated church members may be commended for exemplary service, and professional athletes are often enticed by financial rewards.

It should be noted at the outset that control through law is seldom exercised by the use of positive sanctions or rewards. A person who, throughout his or her life, obeys the law and meets its requirements seldom receives rewards or commendations. State control is exercised primarily, but not exclusively, through the use or threat of punishment to regulate the behavior of citizens. The next two sections focus on the use of criminal sanctions, with particular emphasis on the death penalty debate and civil commitment to control certain types of behavior.

Criminal Sanctions

The social control of criminal and delinquent behavior exemplifies the most highly structured formal system (the criminal justice system) used by society (see, for example, Bosworth, 2010; Clinard and Meier, 2010; Husak, 2010; McBarnet, 2004; Simon, 2009). In 2010, the number of Americans under the control of the criminal justice system exceeded 6.7 million, 3.3 percent of adults in the United States, including some 2.2 million inmates in federal and state prisons and local jails—three times as many as in 1980—and another 4.5 million convicted criminals on probation and parole (Butterfield, 2004; Clinard and Meier, 2010; Currie, 1998; McDonald, 2006; *New York Times,* 2001a; U.S. Department of Justice, 2007, 2009). One person in 142 is behind bars, up from one in 218 a decade ago, with some 4.5 million on probation (Hallinan, 2001). Federal prisons are operating at more than 130 percent of capacity, and two dozen state prison systems are operating at 100 percent capacity or higher (McDonald, 2006; U.S. Department of Justice, 2009). More and more, state and federal governments are turning to private prison operators such as Corrections Corporation of America to cope with overcrowding. In the United States, around 7 percent of the inmates are held in private facilities, as compared to 17 percent in Australia and 10 percent in Britain (*Economist,* 2007a).

Some counties in the United States now have more than 30 percent of their residents behind bars (U.S. Department of Justice, 2007, 2009). Almost 10 percent of all inmates in state and federal prisons are serving life sentences, an increase of 83 percent from 1992. The jump in the number of inmates serving life sentences imposes large costs on states, about $1 million for each inmate who serves out his full sentence behind bars. The number of federal and state prisons grew from 592 in 1974 to over 1,200 in 2005. In 1923, the United States had 61 prisons. Spending on jails and prisons rose to $57 billion in 2005, the latest year for which data are available, from $9.6 billion in 1982. Spending on police protection and the courts also grew, though more slowly, with money for the police reaching $82 billion in 2005 and spending on the courts reaching $58 billion. Court spending includes the costs of judges, prosecutors, clerks, and public defenders. In total, the criminal justice system accounted for 7 percent of all state and local government spending in 2005, roughly equal to the amount spent on health and hospitals, the report found. The criminal justice system employed 2.3 million people in 2001, 747,000 of them as jail or prison guards (Butterfield, 2004; U.S. Department of Justice, 2007).

America not only has more people in prison than anywhere else, but also has a higher incarceration rate. This country imprisons people at fourteen times the rate of Japan, eight times the rate of France, and six times the rate of Canada. (The American prison system disgorges 600,000 angry, unskilled people each year—more than the city populations of Boston, Milwaukee, or Washington. In 2004, some 13 million people have been convicted of a felony and spent some time locked up [Butterfield, 2004]. That's almost 7 percent of the adult residents of the United States, larger than the population of many countries, including Sweden, Bolivia, Senegal, Greece, Hungary, or Somalia.)

To put this in some kind of perspective, there are some 8 million students enrolled full-time in four-year colleges and universities nationwide, and if current trends continue, the number of Americans behind bars and on probation will very soon match, and then possibly exceed, this number. While comparing prisons and higher education, it is worth noting that states collectively spend more to construct prisons than universities, and they spend $57 billion a year, well over $20,000 per prisoner, on keeping offenders behind bars. In this context, America's schools are losing the budget battle to prisons by a factor of more than two to one.

The laws enacted by legislators and modified by court decisions define criminal and delinquent behavior and specify the sanctions imposed for violations (see, for example, Beckett and Sasson, 2004; Husak, 2010). Over time, there has been an increasing reliance on law to regulate the activities and, thus, the lives of people. As the law has proliferated to incorporate more types of behavior, many changes in penalties for certain crimes have also occurred. These increases inevitably result in more social control and in further changes in the control methods. As more behaviors are defined as criminal, more acts become the interest of the police, the courts, and the prison system.

The term *legalization* is used to describe the process by which norms are moved from the social to the legal level. Not all social norms become laws; in fact, only certain norms are translated into legal norms. Why is it that the violation of certain norms, but not others, is chosen to be incorporated into the criminal code? Austin T. Turk (1972) suggests that there are certain social forces involved in the legalization and creation of legal norms: moral indignation, a high value on order, response to threat, and political tactics.

As discussed in Chapter 4, laws may be created by the actions of "moral entrepreneurs" who become outraged over some practice they regard as reprehensible; for example, smoking marijuana. Others prefer order and insist on provisions to regulate life and to make society as orderly as possible. They promulgate laws to ensure order and uniformity, as in the case of traffic regulation. Some people react to real or imaginary threats and advocate legal-control measures. For instance, some people may assume that the availability of pornographic material not only is morally wrong but also directly contributes to the increase of sex crimes (although rape and child molestation undoubtedly predate erotic books and pornographic magazines and videocassettes). In this instance, it would appear certain that these people would attempt to legally prohibit the sale of pornographic material (Irving, 1992). The final source of legalization of norms is political, where criminal laws are created in the interest of powerful groups in society. This source is identified with the conflict perspective that I have considered in the preceding chapters.

The process of legalization of social norms also entails the incorporation of specific punishments for specific kinds of criminal law violators. Rusche and Kirchheimer (2003:5) note, "Every system of production tends to discover punishments which correspond to its productive relationships." Michel Foucault (1977) tells us that before the industrial revolution, life was considered cheap and individuals had neither the utility nor the commercial value that is conferred on them in an industrial economy. Under those circumstances, punishment was severe and often unrelated to the nature of the crime (for example, death for stealing a chicken). When more and more factories appeared, the value of individual lives, even criminal ones, began to be stressed. Beginning in the last years of the eighteenth century and the early years of the nineteenth century, efforts were made to connect the nature of a given punishment to the nature of the crime.

Fitting the punishment to the crime is a difficult and at times controversial and politically sensitive task (see, for example, Brooks, 2010; Brudner, 2009; Cusac, 2009; Tonry, 2010). The definition of crime and the penalty for it and the components of the culture of control (Cusac, 2009; Garland, 2001) vary over time and from one society to another. For example, in rural areas in People's Republic of China, it is not uncommon to burn down the houses or to confiscate the property of those who violate birth control laws. In the words of a villager, "If you have more than one child, they will come and rip the engine out of your boat or destroy your house on the land" (Tyler, 1995:6). By contrast, in a democracy, the power to define crime and punishment rests with the citizenry. This power is largely delegated to elected representatives. Their statutes are often broad and subject to various interpretations. As Chapter 3 demonstrated, legislative enactments allow judges, prosecutors, and juries considerable flexibility and discretion in assessing guilt and imposing punishment.

But what does it mean to punish an individual who violates a criminal law? Edwin H. Sutherland and Donald R. Cressey (1974:298) provide the following definition of the ingredients of punishment as a form of social control: "Two essential ideas are contained in the concept of punishment as an instrument of public justice. (a) It is inflicted by the group in its corporate capacity upon one who is regarded as a member of the same group. . . . (b) Punishment involves pain or suffering produced by design and justified by some value that the suffering is assumed to have."

Punishment of lawbreakers has several purposes. Paul W. Tappan (1960:241–261) offers the now-established objectives of punishment. He suggests that punishment is designed to achieve the goal of *retribution* or *social retaliation* against the offender (see also

Zaibert, 2006). This means punishment of the offender for the crime that has been committed and, to an extent, punishment that (in principle) matches the impact of the crime upon its victim (for instance, a person or an organization). The state is expected to be the agent of vengeance on behalf of the victim. Punishment also involves *incapacitation* (for example, a prison term), which prevents a violator from misbehaving during the time he or she is being punished. Increasingly, judicially created public humiliations are also being introduced in courtrooms as alternatives to incarceration and to satisfy a "retributive impulse" (Karp, 1998:277). They are considered as "shaming penalties"—after punishments like the stocks favored by seventeenth-century Puritans—and they take a mea culpa message to the community. For example, the names of men who solicit prostitutes are identified in local papers or radio shows; Kansas City, Missouri, in late 1990s started the now popular "John TV," in which the names, mug shots, birth dates, and hometowns of men arrested for trying to buy sex, and women arrested trying to sell it, are broadcast on the municipal cable channel; drunken drivers carry signs on their cars announcing their problem and urging other drivers to report their erratic driving to the police; convicted shoplifters must take out advertisements in local papers running their photographs and stating their crimes; and the courts ordered people convicted of assault or child molestation to put signs in their yards announcing their transgression (Belluck, 1998; *Economist*, 2006a; Hoffman, 1997). In Peoria, Illinois, police park an unmanned former Brink's truck, nicknamed "Armadillo," bristling with video cameras in front of the homes of drug dealers and other offenders (Porter, 2009). Shaming and embarrassment are potent forces in social control, and various techniques are being more and more widely used nowadays and they are a good way to express communal values (Allyn, 2004).

Furthermore, punishment is supposed to have a *deterrent* effect, both on the law-breaker and on potential deviants. *Individual* or *specific deterrence* may be achieved by intimidation of the person, frightening him or her against further deviance, or it may be affected through reformation, in that the lawbreaker changes his or her deviant behavior. *General deterrence* results from the warning offered to potential criminals by the example of punishment directed at a specific wrongdoer. It aims to discourage others from criminal behavior by making an example of the offender being punished.

The theory of deterrence is predicated on the assumption that individuals weigh the costs and rewards associated with alternative actions, and select behaviors that maximize gains and minimize cost. Thus, crime takes place when law breaking is perceived as either more profitable (rewarding) or less costly (painful) than conventional activities. In this context, the purpose of punishment is to prevent crime (Bailey and Peterson, 1994). The concept of deterrence is often used to designate punishment in the form of threats directed at offenders or potential offenders so as to frighten them into law-abiding conduct. The effectiveness of these threats is conditioned by the operation of three variables: (1) the severity of the punishment for an offense (2) the certainty that it would be applied, and (3) the speed with which it would be applied (Friedland, 1989). Research generally supports the view that certainty of punishment is more important than severity for achieving deterrence, but there is little research data as yet on the swiftness of punishment. For example, in a study of a series of criminal offenses, Charles R. Tittle (1969) found strong and consistent negative relationships between certainty of punishment and crime rates for different states, as measured by the ratio between felony admissions to state prisons and the total crimes known to the police in different states. Those states with the lowest crime rates had a proportionately larger number of incarcerated persons. On the other hand, severity of punishment bore no marked relationship to crime rates. Tittle's findings led him to conclude that measures to improve the efficiency of police work probably would have significant effects on crime rates but that increasing the severity of punishment would be of limited effectiveness.

However, sociologists have long recognized that punishment may deter only some crimes and some offenders. For example, William J. Chambliss (1975) makes a distinction between crimes that are instrumental acts and those that are expressive. *Instrumental* offenses include burglary, tax evasion, embezzlement (American businesses lose $660 billion each year to embezzling [Ortiz, 2006]), motor vehicle theft (note that 15 percent of all auto thefts reported are fraudulent and made by the owner to collect on his or her insurance [Cook, 1989:68]), identity theft (Finch and Fafinski, 2010) that became very popular in the early part of the twenty-first century (annually in late 2000, for example, an estimated 3.6 million U.S. households—or about three out of every 1000—reported being victims of identity theft, including Ben Bernanke, chairman of the Federal Reserve Board [Hilsenrath and Kendall, 2009], resulting in a loss of $3.2 billion [Jelinek, 2006; U.S. Department of Justice, 2006, 2007]), and other illegal activities directed toward some material end. Examples of *expressive* acts are murder, assault, and sex offenses, where the behavior is an end in itself. Chambliss hypothesizes that the deterrent impact of severe and certain punishment may be greater on instrumental crimes because they generally involve some planning and weighing of risks. Expressive crimes, by contrast, are often impulsive and emotional acts. Perpetrators of such crimes are unlikely to be concerned with the future consequences of their actions.

Chambliss further contends that an important distinction can be made between individuals who have a relatively high commitment to crime as a way of life and those with a relatively low commitment. The former would include individuals who engage in crime on a professional or regular basis. They often receive group support for their activities, and crime for them is an important aspect of their way of life (such as prostitutes or participants in organized crime). For them, the likelihood of punishment is a constant feature of their life, something they have learned to live with, and the threat of punishment may be offset by the supportive role played by their peers. On the other hand, a tax evader, an embezzler, or an occasional shoplifter does not view this behavior as criminal and receives little, if any, group support for these acts. Fear of punishment may well be a deterrent for such low-commitment persons, particularly if they have already experienced punishment (for example, a tax evader who has been audited and then subjected to legal sanctions).

On the basis of these two types of distinctions—instrumental and expressive acts, and high- and low-commitment offenders—Chambliss contends that the greatest deterrent effect of punishment will be in situations that involve low-commitment individuals who engage in instrumental crimes. Deterrence is least likely in cases involving high-commitment persons who engage in expressive crimes. The role of deterrence remains questionable in situations that involve low-commitment individuals who commit expressive crimes (such as murder), which can be illustrated by the arguments used for or against the death penalty.

Discord over the Death Penalty

Throughout the world, as the most severe form of punishment, the death penalty is the most obvious, controversial, and emotional issue in the concept of deterrence (see for example, Bedau and Cassell, 2004; Christianson, 2004, 2010; *Economist*, 2007b, 2010; Johnson and Zimring, 2009; Sarat, 2001; Turow, 2004; Williams, 2003; Yorke, 2009). Historically, property offenses rather than violent crimes (Ferguson, 2010) accounted for the majority of executions. In the eighteenth century, the death penalty was imposed in England for more than 200 offenses, including poaching and smuggling. Executions were performed in public. They were a popular spectacle. The public applauded a skillful execution of a criminal much as aficionados today cheer the matador who skillfully slays a bull (Foucault, 1977). The standard methods of execution were hanging, beheading, disemboweling, and quartering. The increased severity and frequency of executions during this period were associated with the growth of urbanization and wealth. Notes Loh (1984:194), "Capital statutes 'served the interests of private property and commerce' against those who might seek to undermine them." Although the colonies inherited many of the capital punishments from England, by the middle of the nineteenth century, most of the colonies repealed capital punishments, and the death sentence was imposed primarily for murder and, to a lesser extent, rape.

In the 1972 decision *Furman v. Georgia*, capital punishment was declared unconstitutional by the U.S. Supreme Court. The Court held that the discretionary application of the death penalty to only a small fraction of those eligible to be executed was capricious and arbitrary and hence unconstitutional. However, a number of states since responded to the Court ruling by legislating modifications in state laws that make the death penalty mandatory for certain offenses, such as multiple killings; killing in connection with a robbery, rape, kidnapping, or hostage situation; murder for hire; killing a police officer or prison guard; and treason. Some of these revised statutes were held to be constitutional by the Supreme Court in 1976 when it voted 7-2 in *Gregg v. Georgia* to reinstate the death penalty. Over the past three decades or so, as Table 5-1 captures, several states passed capital punishment laws, and several other states are considering similar statutes as well. In 2006, the United States ranked sixth in the world per capita for the number executions (*Economist*, 2007b:70). By contrast, 47 percent of the world's countries had abolished capital punishment in law or practice by the end of 1993 (Worsnop, 1995), and South Africa was added to this list in mid-1995 (*U.S. News & World Report*, 1995:14). By 2007, 89 countries have abolished the death penalty for all crimes, another 10 for exceptional crimes, and an additional 30 are abolitionist in practice, having executed nobody for at least 20 years (*Economist*, 2007b:69). For the first time in Europe's recorded history, there was not a single execution in 2009 (*Economist*, 2010:50) although Amnesty International notes that 714 people were executed in other countries, led by Iran, Iraq, and Saudi Arabia where methods of execution included beheading, stoning, electrocution, hanging, firing squads, and lethal injection (McDonald, 2010). In China, however, death penalty is still widely practiced with more court-ordered executions than all other nations combined. During a fairly recent wave of death sentences, as many as 191 people were executed in a single day. In 2005, for example, an estimated 5,000 to 10,000 have been subjected to the death penalty for crimes ranging from murder to such nonviolent offenses

TABLE 5-1 Death Penalty Policy by States — 2010		
States with the Death Penalty		
Alabama	Louisiana	Pennsylvania
Arizona	Maryland	South Carolina
Arkansas	Mississippi	South Dakota
California	Missouri	Tennessee
Colorado	Montana	Texas
Connecticut	Nebraska	Utah
Delaware	Nevada	Virginia
Florida	New Hampshire	Washington
Georgia	North Carolina	Wyoming
Idaho	Ohio	
Indiana	Oklahoma	**ALSO**
Illinois	Oregon	- U.S. Government
Kansas	Louisiana	- U.S. Military
Kentucky	Maryland	Pennsylvania

States without the Death Penalty (*Year Abolished in Parentheses*)		
Alaska (1957)	Minnesota (1911)	Vermont (1964)
Hawaii (1948)	North Dakota (1973)	West Virginia (1965)
Iowa (1965)	New Jersey (2007)	Wisconsin (1853)
Maine (1887)	New Mexico (2009)	
Massachusetts (1984)	New York (2007)	**ALSO**
Michigan (1846)	Rhode Island (1984)	- District of Columbia (1981)

as tax evasion. In 2008, the number of executions seemed to have stabilized around 5,000, a rate per capita population dozens of times higher than in the United States (*Economist*, 2010:50; McDonald, 2010). The *Economist* (2007b:70) even noted that China had deployed a fleet of "death vans," vehicles equipped with the needed paraphernalia for lethal jabs—to make it easier for rural communities to dispose of criminals. In 2006, following criticisms that lower courts have arbitrarily imposed death sentences resulting in the execution of wrongly convicted people, the capital-punishment law was amended to require approval from the country's highest court before putting anyone to death (Ang, 2006). By 2010, an official policy of "kill less, kill carefully" is taking root (*Economist*, 2010:50). (Interestingly, an unanticipated consequence of tighter oversight of death penalty cases will be a further shortage of human organs for transplants because many organs used in transplants now are taken from executed prisoners—and many recipients are foreigners who pay hefty sums to avoid a long wait [Magnier and Zarembo, 2006].) Table 5-2 summarizes the various crimes punishable by the death penalty in states that have it.

In the United States, there is even a 54-page Execution Protocol, prepared by the Federal Bureau of Prisons. Work on the protocol began in 1993, when federal rules for executions were finalized, and it was released in April 2001 (*St. Louis Post-Dispatch*, 2001). It is a detailed, comprehensive, almost macabre document that spells out with exquisite, minute-by-minute precision every detail of an execution ranging from the

TABLE 5-2   Crimes Punishable by the Death Penalty by States — 2009

Alabama   Intentional murder with 18 aggravating factors (Ala. Stat. Ann. 13A-5-40(a)(1)–(18)).

Arizona   First-degree murder accompanied by at least 1 of 14 aggravating factors (A.R.S. § 13-703(F)).

Arkansas   Capital murder (Ark. Code Ann. 5-10-101) with a finding of at least 1 of 10 aggravating circumstances; treason.

California   First-degree murder with special circumstances; sabotage; train wrecking causing death; treason; perjury causing execution of an innocent person; fatal assault by a prisoner serving a life sentence.

Colorado   First-degree murder with at least 1 of 17 aggravating factors; first-degree kidnapping resulting in death; treason.

Connecticut   Capital felony with eight forms of aggravated homicide (C.G.S. § 53a-54b).

Delaware   First-degree murder with at least one statutory aggravating circumstance (11 Del. C. § 4209).

Florida   First-degree murder; felony murder; capital drug trafficking; capital sexual battery.

Georgia   Murder; aggravated kidnapping; rape; armed robbery; aircraft hijacking; treason.

Idaho   First-degree murder with aggravating factors; first-degree kidnapping; perjury resulting in death.

Illinois   First-degree murder with 1 of 21 aggravating circumstances (720 Ill. Comp. Stat. 5/9-1).

Indiana   Murder with 16 aggravating circumstances (IC 35-50-2-9).

Kansas   Capital murder with eight aggravating circumstances (KSA 21-3439, KSA 21-4625, KSA 21-4636).

Kentucky   Murder with aggravating factors; kidnapping with aggravating factors (KRS 32.025).

Louisiana   First-degree murder; treason (La. R.S. 14:30 and 14:113).

Maryland   First-degree murder, either premeditated or during the commission of a felony, provided that certain death eligibility requirements are satisfied.

Mississippi   Capital murder (Miss. Code Ann. § 97-3-19(2)); aircraft piracy (Miss. Code Ann. § 97-25-55(1)).

Missouri   First-degree murder (565.020 RSMO 2000).

Montana   Capital murder with one of nine aggravating circumstances (Mont. Code Ann. § 46-18-303); aggravated sexual intercourse without consent (Mont. Code Ann. § 45-5-503).

Nebraska   First-degree murder with a finding of at least one statutorily defined aggravating circumstance.

Nevada   First-degree murder with at least 1 of 15 aggravating circumstances (NRS 200.030, 200.033, 200.035).

New Hampshire   Murder committed in the course of rape, kidnapping, or drug crimes; killing of a law enforcement officer; murder for hire; murder by an inmate while serving a sentence of life without parole (RSA 630:1, RSA 630:5).

(Continued)

TABLE 5-2 (Continued)

New Mexico First-degree murder with at least one of seven statutorily-defined aggravating circumstances (Section 30-2-1 A, NMSA).

New York First-degree murder with 1 of 13 aggravating factors (NY Penal Law §125.27).

North Carolina First-degree murder (NCGS §14-17).

Ohio Aggravated murder with at least 1 of 10 aggravating circumstances (O.R.C. Secs. 2903.01, 2929.02, and 2929.04).

Oklahoma First-degree murder in conjunction with a finding of at least one of eight statutorily defined aggravating circumstances; sex crimes against a child under 14 years of age.

Oregon Aggravated murder (ORS 163.095).

Pennsylvania First-degree murder with 18 aggravating circumstances.

South Carolina Murder with 1 of 12 aggravating circumstances (§ 16-3-20(C)(a)); criminal sexual conduct with a minor with one of nine aggravators (§ 16-3-655).

South Dakota First-degree murder with 1 of 10 aggravating circumstances.

Tennessee First-degree murder with 1 of 15 aggravating circumstances (Tenn. Code Ann. § 39-13-204).

Texas Criminal homicide with one of nine aggravating circumstances (Tex. Penal Code § 19.03).

Utah Aggravated murder (76-5-202, Utah Code Annotated).

Virginia First-degree murder with 1 of 15 aggravating circumstances (VA Code § 18.2-31).

Washington Aggravated first-degree murder.

Wyoming First-degree murder; murder during the commission of sexual assault; sexual abuse of a minor; arson, robbery, escape from prison, resisting arrest, kidnapping, or abuse of a minor under 16.

---

length of the last meal to the surrender of the body to the coroner. It also deals with detailed contingency plans for handling disturbances that might be caused by protesters and sympathizers both with and outside of the facility.

Between 1976 and 2009, 7,713 executions were carried out in the United States, as depicted in Table 5-3. For illustrative purposes, Table 5-4 shows the number of inmates awaiting execution in 2009. Georgia joined other states in banning the electric chair, and its highest court struck down the use of the electric chair, saying the ghastly injuries inflicted and the risk of "excruciating pain" violate the state constitution's ban on cruel and unusual punishment; this leaves Alabama and Nebraska as the only states with the electric chair as the sole method of execution. There is also a mounting national debate over whether lethal injection is a cruel and unusual punishment because of recent medical information showing a risk of great pain if poorly trained personnel mishandle the anesthetic that is supposed to render inmates unconscious (Henderson, 2006). At the same time, medical groups warn physicians on aiding executions and the mandate from the American Board of Anesthesiology that "we are healers, not executioners" could result in the loss of certification of those who participate in lethal injection (Stein, 2010). Studies show that other things being equal, killers of white people are more likely to receive

TABLE 5-3 Death Sentences by Year in the United States: 1977–2009	
Year	*Sentences*
1976	233
1977	137
1978	185
1979	151
1980	173
1981	223
1982	267
1983	252
1984	284
1985	262
1986	300
1987	287
1988	291
1989	258
1990	251
1991	268
1992	287
1993	295
1994	328
1995	326
1996	323
1997	281
1998	306
1999	284
2000	235
2001	167
2002	169
2003	154
2004	140
2005	138
2006	122
2007	119
2008	111
2009	106
TOTAL	7,713

death sentences than killers of blacks. (For racial differences in sentencing, see Culver, 1992; Eckholm, 1995; Gross and Mauro, 1989; Lewin, 1995; Miethe and Moore, 1986; Radelet and Pierce, 1985.) Table 5-5 shows executions by race since 1976 and prisoners executed in 2006 spent an average of 7 years and 11 months awaiting execution (but it has taken 11 years, on the average, to establish reversible error in capital cases).

TABLE 5-4   Current Death Row Inmates by State as of July 1, 2009

Total Number of Death Row Inmates as of July 1, 2009: 3,279

State	Number of Inmates	State	Number of Inmates	State	Number of Inmates
California	690	S. Carolina	63	Connecticut	10
Florida	403	Mississippi	60	Kansas	10
Texas	342	U.S. Government	58	Utah	10
Penn.	225	Missouri	52	Washington	9
Alabama	200	Arkansas	43	U.S. Military	8
Ohio	176	Kentucky	36	Maryland	5
N. Carolina	169	Oregon	33	South Dakota	3
Arizona	129	Delaware	19	Colorado	3
Georgia	108	Idaho	18	Montana	2
Tennessee	92	Indiana	17	New Mexico	2
Oklahoma	86	Virginia	16	Wyoming	1
Louisiana	84	Illinois	15	New Hampshire	1
Nevada	78	Nebraska	11		

TABLE 5-5   Size of Death Row from 1968 to 2009

Year	Size	Year	Size	Year	Size
1968	517	1982	1,050	1996	3,219
1969	575	1983	1,209	1997	3,335
1970	631	1984	1,405	1998	3,452
1971	642	1985	1,591	1999	3,527
1972	334	1986	1,781	2000	3,593
1973	134	1987	1,984	2001	3,581
1974	244	1988	2,124	2002	3,557
1975	488	1989	2,250	2003	3,374
1976	420	1990	2,356	2004	3,315
1977	423	1991	2,482	2005	3,254
1978	482	1992	2,575	2006	3,228
1979	539	1993	2,716	2007	3,215
1980	691	1994	2,890	2008	3,207
1981	856	1995	3,054	2009	3,279

The dilemma of whether to kill the killers comes up only in a small fraction of homicides (see, for example, Roth, 2009; Smith and Zahn, 1998). The criteria for capital murder vary from state to state and from case to case. In general, there must be aggravating circumstances. These can be as specific as the murder of a police officer or a prison guard; as common as homicide committed along with a lesser felony such as burglary; or as vague as Florida's law citing "especially heinous, atrocious or cruel" killing. Some 10 percent of homicides qualify, representing about 2,000 murders in 2010. Those particularly heinous killings are the ones the threat of capital punishment is meant to prevent.

What are the preventive effects of capital punishment? The arguments for the death penalty are mostly anecdotal but, at times, can become visceral (see, for example, Peppers and Anderson, 2009). Proponents of the death penalty contend that it is a deterrent to others and that it protects society. It constitutes retribution for society and the victim's family and serves to protect police officers and prison guards. It also removes the possibility that the offenders will repeat the act. There is not much empirical evidence in support of the death penalty as a deterrent. Were it not for the work of Isaac Ehrlich, the deterrence debate would be very much one-sided. Using econometric modeling techniques to construct a "supply-and-demand" theory of murder, Ehrlich (1975), in a now-classic and frequently cited article subtitled "A Question of Life and Death," argued that the death penalty prevents more murders than do prison sentences. He speculates that because of the 3,411 executions carried out from 1933 to 1967, enough murderers were discouraged so that some 27,000 victims' lives were saved. As might be expected, his conclusions drew immediate criticisms.

An assortment of concerns were raised. Among others, Ehrlich did not compare the effectiveness of capital punishment with that of particular prison terms. When data from 1965 to 1969 are omitted, the relationship between murder rates and executions is not statistically significant (Loh, 1984:258). While considering the increases in homicides in the 1960s, he failed to account for the possible influences of rising racial tensions, the Vietnam War, and increased ownership of handguns. Moreover, for deterrence to be effective, murderers need to take into consideration the probable costs of their action. Emotions and passions at play can make a cost-benefit analysis unlikely. Most murderers, in Chambliss's words, are low-commitment individuals, often under the influence of drugs or alcohol, who are unlikely to assess rationally the consequences of their action. For them, the death penalty remains a highly questionable deterrent.

Aside from ethical and moral considerations, there are many arguments against the death penalty. For serial killers and particularly for female serial killers, capital punishment is not a deterrent (Fisher, 1997; Kelleher and Kelleher, 1998). Almost every study of capital punishment has shown that there is no material difference in the rate of homicides in states that have capital punishment and states that do not (Sellin, 1959:28). The homicide rate per 100,000 in Michigan, which did not have the death penalty in the 1950s, was 3.49. In Indiana, which did have the death penalty, the homicide rate for the same period was 3.50. Similarly, Minnesota and Rhode Island, states with no death penalty, had proportionately as many killings as their respective neighbors that had capital punishment, Iowa and Massachusetts. A study of different types of police killings for 1976–1989 involving 1,204 officers found no evidence that police are afforded an added measure of protection against death by capital punishment (Bailey and Peterson, 1994). Studies in Canada, England, and other countries also found nothing to suggest that the death penalty is a more effective deterrent than long prison sentences. Although a cause-and-effect relationship cannot be inferred between capital punishment and murder rates, Lawrence M. Friedman (1998:214) speculates that capital punishment may work efficiently in some societies "which use it quickly, mercilessly, and frequently. It cannot work well in the United States, where it is bound to be rare, slow, and controversial."

Opponents of the death penalty argue that prison terms without parole would deter as many potential murderers as capital punishment. Data indicate that the certainty of being punished is negated by the fact that the death penalty is seldom imposed and that juries are less willing to convict when the penalty is death. Trials of capital cases are also more costly and time-consuming than trials for other cases, and maintenance costs for inmates in death row are higher than for inmates in the rest of the prison. An exhaustive system of judicial review is required in capital cases. Today, no death-row inmate will be executed until his or her case has been brought to the attention of the state's highest court, a federal district court of appeals, and the U.S. Supreme Court. There are 20 federally founded centers for death-row appeals at an annual cost of around $30 million, and it would not be surprising if their numbers declined in the foreseeable future because of budget considerations. Already almost two decades ago, the total costs for trials and appeals were estimated to range between $3 million (Malcolm, 1989) and $5 million (*Economist*, 1990). By one study, each execution in North Carolina cost $2.16 million more than life imprisonment. California spent over $1 billion between 1977 and 1996 on its death penalty, but executed only five men during this period (Costanzo, 1997:61). A *New York Times* (1995a:F2) article mordantly remarks that it is because "quite simply, lawyers earn more than guards and it's lawyers who fly into action after a death sentence—with appeals, appeals and more appeals." The following is another way of illustrating the cost of death penalty: The 1995 reinstatement of capital punishment in New York State was correctly projected to cost over a five-year period the same as hiring 250 police officers and building prisons for 6,000 inmates. (On June 24, 2004, the New York Court of Appeals in *People v. LaValle* held part of the death penalty statute unconstitutional. Specifically, the court found that the statute's so-called deadlock provision—a sentencing instruction that trial courts were obligated to give the deliberating juries— was unduly coercive. Concluding that only the legislature could repair the statute, the court directed that, in the meantime, first-degree murder cases could proceed noncapitally. The legislature has not acted to repair the statute.)

Imprisoning one inmate for 50 years in most states would require less than $1 million or about $20,000 annually. This negates the argument that prison is too costly and there are good fiscal reasons for executing murderers. There is also the possibility that an innocent person will be executed. One study shows that some 139 innocent people were sentenced to death between 1900 and 1985 in the United States. Of those, 29 were actually executed (Haines, 1992:130). Other studies show that one innocent person has been convicted for every 20 executions carried out since the turn of the century (*St. Louis Post-Dispatch*, 1985:6B). In their 1992 book, *In Spite of Innocence*, the authors (Radelet et al., 1992) review more than 400 cases in which innocent people were convicted of capital crimes in the United States. In the past decade, eight men have been sentenced to die for murder in Illinois only to be later found innocent and released (Tuft, 1998). The greatest fear of opponents and supporters of death penalty—the execution of the innocent—was the topic of the three-day National Conference on Wrongful Convictions and the Death Penalty, held at Northwestern University in November 1998, and attended by more than 1,000 lawyers, law students, and professors. The conference documented that 28 of the 73 men and 2 women have been released from death rows across the country since 1972. Each was wrongfully convicted of murder and sentenced to death. It was also documented at the conference that for every seven executions in the United States since 1976, one condemned inmate has been freed (or one innocent is almost killed) after serving years on death row (Terry, 1998). Furthermore, federal judges have found constitutional errors in about 40 percent of the cases they have reviewed since 1976 (Smolowe, 1992:42).

The death penalty is also more likely to affect the poor and minority-group members than more affluent whites (Berlow, 2001; Ogletree and Sarat, 2006). This has to do in part with the quality of legal help available to murder defendants. Those with court-appointed lawyers are more likely to be sentenced to death than those represented by private attorneys. Court-appointed lawyers in most states are not required to stay on a homicide case after a conviction. Issues for appeal are likely to be raised by different court-appointed attorneys, if at all, for the poor. Defendants with more money get better legal defense. In a study carried out in Texas in 2000, it was found that people represented by court-appointed lawyers were 28 percent more likely to be convicted than those who hired their own lawyers. If convicted, they were 44 percent more likely to be sentenced to death (*New York Times*, 2001b). Between 1973 and 2002, 102 inmates on death row have been exonerated and freed. The most common reasons for wrongful convictions are mistaken eyewitness testimony, the false testimony of informants and "incentivized witnesses," incompetent lawyers, defective or fraudulent scientific evidence, prosecutorial and police misconduct, and false confessions. In recent years, DNA played a role in overturning 12 of these wrongful death row convictions.

Nevertheless, the debate on the penological effectiveness of capital punishment continues despite the paucity of empirical evidence in support of its alleged deterrent effect. Aside from the moral need for eliminating the death penalty, the evidence shows that capital punishment does not deter murder (Roth, 2009). Some even argue that it actually encourages homicide in certain circumstances. The threat of death penalty raises the stakes of getting caught, and anyone who is subject to death penalty has little to lose by killing again and again, which may be the case with serial killers (see, for example, Holmes and Holmes, 2010, on serial murder). Criminals who already face death for a previous crime are more likely to kill in order to avoid being captured or to silence possible witnesses. The death penalty is viewed by police as "the enemy of law enforcement" and is ranked last as a way of reducing violent crime (Morgenthau, 1995).

Yet, there is a growing advocacy of the death penalty in the United States. Public-opinion surveys show that those who are in favor of capital punishment for persons convicted of murder increased from 38 percent in 1972 to a high of 77 percent in 1996, then dropped to 64 percent in 2000 (Maguire and Pastore, 2001:538), and then in the late 2000s, it was again a high 79 percent, but opinion polls keep fluctuating (*Economist*, 2007b).

An influential study shows that even inmates, especially the most violent ones, favor capital punishment for some crimes—when applied to others' but not to their own criminal activity (Stevens, 1992). At this point, it should be noted that the majority of murders are committed by family members or acquaintances of the victim, and in more than half of all homicides, handguns are used. In many parts of the country, there is a dramatic increase in gun-related violence (Bruce and Wilcox, 1998; Hickey, 2003; Spitzer, 2008), and a former attorney general of the United States correlated homicide rates with the prevalence of guns and reported the highest rate of homicide in states where gun controls are lax and gun ownership is common (Clark, 1971:82–84). Seventy percent of the 24,526 homicides in 1993 were committed by guns (*New York Times*, 1995b:A6). Some startling figures to support this conclusion: In 1984, "handguns killed 48 people in Japan, 8 in Great Britain, 34 in Switzerland, 52 in Canada, 58 in Israel, 21 in Sweden, 42 in West Germany, 10,728 in the United States" (*Forbes*, 1985:28). In 2007, the figures were close to 11,000, and the homicide rate in the United States is 5.9 per 100,000, as compared to 1.5 per 100,000 in Britain, 1.1 in Japan, and 2.5 in Turkey (*Newsweek*, 2007:56). (For the sake of balance, there are many other ways of committing murder. For example, in China, rat poison is a lethal weapon of choice for those with a grudge [Hoo, 2003] and a particularly potent form has already been outlawed in the late 1990s.)

In the United States, noted for the world's highest rate of gun ownership— 90 weapons per 100 civilians (followed by Yemen at 61 weapons per 100 civilians, Finland at 56, and Iraq at 39), with at least one town (Kennesaw, Georgia) requiring its citizens to own a firearm and ammunition—controlling handguns might be a more effective but far less popular method of reducing homicide rates than capital punishment. The fact is that in mid-2000, some 36 states permitted adults to carry a concealed handgun (Henderson, 2005), and by 2010, 40 states adapted right-to-carry laws requiring that concealed-carry weapon licenses be issued to every qualified applicant (Patrick, 2010); 3 states require no background check and have no laws concerning concealed or open carry; and in 43 states, open carry is legal (that is, gun owners can carry holstered handguns in public places such as coffee shops or local parks [O'Connell and Jargon, 2010]). But current sentiments seem to be in favor of the right to carry and concealed-weapons laws (even after the April 16, 2007, Virginia Tech massacre of 32 students [Timiraos, 2007]); there were close to 15 million background checks during the first three months of 2010 for gun buyers (O'Connell, 2010). A University of Chicago economist, John R. Lott (2003, 2006, 2010), in three highly controversial and much-debated books, *The Bias against Guns: Why Almost Everything You've Heard about Gun Control Is Wrong; Straight Shooting: Guns, Economics, and Public Policy; and More Guns, Less Crime: Understanding Crime and Gun Control Laws*, claims that if more law-abiding citizens were allowed to carry guns, murder rates and crime would go down. The books claim to be the most comprehensive look ever at the effects of gun control laws on crime. In his first title, now in its third edition, using data from all 3,054 counties in the United States from 1977 to present, he has found that, for each year that a concealed-handgun law is in effect, the local murder rate declines by 3 percent, robberies by over 2 percent, and rape by 2 percent. Two groups most vulnerable to violent crime—women and blacks—benefit most from concealed-weapon laws. He also incorporated recent changes in the law and responded to a range of criticism of the second edition. Lotts's second book reinforces these conclusions and shows how the various proposed regulations, bans, and registration procedures are counterproductive, and in the third, he presents a collection of representative and well-documented pro-gun articles. The books touched off furious protests from gun-control lobbyists and criminologists (among many others) who question the methodologies used and suspect the conclusions. Gun availability continues to be a topic of contentious debate among social scientists and policy makers (see, for example, Burbick, 2006; Cukier and Sidel, 2006; *Focus on Law Studies*, 2003; Harcourt, 2003; Henderson, 2005; Melzer, 2009; Stolzenberg and D'Alessio, 2000; Wyatt, 2003).

An alternative to the death sentence may be life without parole. Thirty-one states have adopted a life prison term with no chance of parole for certain offenses (Malcolm, 1989).

Life without parole can also short-circuit lengthy and expensive appeals over a death sentence, some of which can go on for a decade or longer. Florida's Supreme Court now devotes one-third of its time to capital cases. Yet, 40 percent of death sentences are overturned on appeal anyway. Life without parole, by contrast, has been consistently upheld on appeal. And, contrary to popular impressions, convicts ineligible for parole have not posed special problems of discipline or control. Capital punishment appears to be more popular than ever, possibly a result of the public perception of an increase in violent crime, but as a deterrent, it remains ineffective and expensive (*Economist*, 1995:19–21). As Franklin Zimring concludes, "no one on either side can defend the current system, which is hypocritical and unprincipled" (Zimring, quoted by Kaplan, 1995:29).

Civil Commitment

The formal control of deviant behavior is not limited to criminal sanctions (see, for example, Arrigo, 2002; Diesfeld and Freckelton, 2003). There is another form of social control through laws that operate extensively, but not exclusively (Duff, 1997), in the United States—the civil commitment (Forst, 1978:1) through medicalization of deviance (Conrad, 1996:69). Medicalization refers to the process of defining behavior as a medical problem or illness and mandating the medical profession to provide treatment for it. Examples of this are drug abuse, alcoholism, and viewing violence as a genetic or psychological disorder.

Statutes governing civil commitment exist in every country and every state in America, although with some variations in the criteria for involuntary hospitalization (see, for example, Appelbaum, 1992; Boyd-Caine, 2009). Civil commitment is a noncriminal process that commits disabled or otherwise dependent individuals, without their consent, to an institution for care, treatment, or custody, rather than for punishment. It is based on two legal principles: (1) the right and responsibility of the state to assume guardianship over individuals suffering from some disability and (2) police power within constitutional limitations to take the necessary steps to protect society. Procedurally, the civil commitment is different from criminal commitment. In civil commitment, certain procedural safeguards are not available, such as a right to a trial by jury, which involves confronting witnesses against the defendant, and to avoid testifying against oneself. Moreover, the formal moral condemnation of the community is not an issue in civil commitment. Forst (1978:3) notes, "This situation may arise if the behavior is intentional but not morally blameworthy, as in a civil suit for damages, or if the behavior would have been morally blameworthy, but because of mental impairment, criminal culpability is either mitigated or negated. In the latter instance, the civil issue is not the person's *behavior* but his *status*." In this view, a heroin addict, a mental defective, or a sex offender is not held morally responsible for these actions. The general consensus is that the individual deserves treatment, not punishment, even though the treatment may entail the deprivation of his or her liberty in a mental institution without due process.

In the United States, about 1 in 12 people will spend some part of his or her life in a mental institution. On any given day of the year, nearly half a million Americans are in confinement in mental wards; in fact, nearly half of all hospital beds in the United States are occupied by people suffering from mental disorders. But civil commitment for mental illness (see, for example, McLeod and Wright, 2009) and incompetence is only one of the many types of civil commitments used to control deviant behavior (see, for example, Levine, 2009). Other types are the incarceration of juveniles in training schools or detention homes; the commitment of chronic alcoholics and alcohol-related offenders; the commitment of drug addicts; and the institutionalization, through the civil law, of sex offenders (variously known as sexual psychopaths, sexually dangerous persons, or mentally disordered sex offenders) and those who are considered "dangerous" to either themselves or the community as initially perceived by family members or the authorities (Dallaire et al., 2000). Martin L. Forst (1978:7) contends that the various types of civil commitments "constitute one of the primary forms of social control through law in American society." He further notes that this form of social control is more extensive than the social control exercised by the traditional criminal commitment.

The use of civil commitment as a form of social control is not limited to adults. Difficult, disruptive, disobedient adolescents—the ones who may have been sent to military schools or juvenile detention centers—are now being placed in mental hospitals. Commitment of children under 18 years of age has increased from 82,000 in 1980 to more than 112,000 in 1986, the last year for which data are available (due to the lack of funding) (Darnton, 1989:66). Most of the increase in admissions was to private hospitals; roughly 43,000 adolescents were admitted to free-standing private psychiatric hospitals in 1986, compared with 17,000 in 1980 and 6,452 in 1970. About 80 percent of these children are from white, middle- and upper-class families. Some are seriously disturbed, but others are simply rebellious teenagers fighting with their parents over anything—from the music they listen to to the boyfriend or girlfriend they choose. Regardless of the reason, they are often held behind locked doors, virtually without civil rights. In the name of therapy, they are subjected to a strict regimen of rewards and punishments.

Problem adolescents are being shifted from a legal to a medical forum. Because of the movement to treat teenage deviance with medicine, private psychiatric beds for young adults is the fastest-growing segment of the hospital industry. These teenagers are often diagnosed with common behavioral problems, such as "conduct disorder," "oppositional defiant disorder," and the popular "adolescent adjustment reaction." These terms sound impressive, but they cover a variety of teenage activities: running away, aggression, persistent opposition to parental values and rules, and engaging in "excessive" sexual activity (usually as defined by the parent). Not surprisingly, many adolescents are committed to mental hospitals not because they are troubled but because they are troubling to someone else (Darnton, 1989:67–68).

In the legal arena, the causes of criminal behavior and the responsibility for such behavior lie within the individual. But in a legal system that posits individual causation, complications arise in attempts to control individuals who are threatening yet have broken no law (see, for example, Peay, 2005). One way to control such individuals is to define their conduct as a mental disorder. Greenaway and Brickey (1978:139) state, "This definition has the combined effect of imputing irrationality to the behavior and providing for the control of the individual through ostensibly benign, but coercive psychiatric intervention." Thus, it is not surprising to find that many state mental hospitals include people who have committed trivial misdemeanors or who have not been convicted of any crime at all, but have been sent there for "observation." The police and courts may refer individuals whose behavior appears odd for psychiatric examination, and if they are found to be "insane," they can be confined in a mental hospital against their will for long periods, in some cases for life (Levine, 2009).

There are diverse explanations for the increased use of civil commitment as a mechanism of social control. Forst states:

> There are those (the positive criminologists) who view the increase as a beneficial shift from the traditional emphasis on punishing people to rehabilitating them. Another explanation for the increased use of civil commitments (the divestment of the criminal law) is that the civil commitment serves as a substitute for, or a supplement to, the criminal law in order to socially control undesirable forms of behavior. (1978:9–10)

The use of civil commitment is not without criticisms. Some critics advocate the abolition of all civil commitment laws because the constitutional rights of the individuals subjected to them are violated, despite the number of laws designed to protect the rights of the mentally ill. Others oppose it because it allows people to avoid the punishment they deserve. Although the issue remains controversial, the use of civil commitment as a form of social control is on the increase.

CRIMES WITHOUT VICTIMS

The United States invests enormous resources in controlling victimless crimes where harm occurs primarily to the participating individuals themselves (Schur, 1965:170). In 2009, there were around 14 million arrests recorded in the latest Federal Bureau of Investigation (FBI) *Uniform Crime Report*. Many of these arrests involved crimes without victims. For example, roughly 100,000 arrests were made for prostitution; 1.5 million for drunkenness and violation of liquor laws (driving under the influence of alcohol is excluded); well over 1 million for drug abuse violations; and around 17,000 for gambling (Federal Bureau of Investigation, 2010).

The criminalization of some acts that have no victims stems from the fact that society regards those acts as morally repugnant and wishes to restrain individuals from engaging in them. Many of those arrested for victimless crimes are never prosecuted: Arrest and overnight lockup are used simply as a means of exerting social control over the drunk or the prostitute without going through the bothersome lengths of creating a convincing prosecution case. For example, habitual drunks may build up formidable "criminal" records by being repeatedly arrested, even though they may never have harmed anyone except, possibly, themselves (La Fave, 1965:439). One study found that two-thirds of repeatedly arrested alcoholics have been charged with nothing more than public intoxication and related offenses, such as vagrancy, throughout their long "criminal" careers (Pittman, quoted by Landsman, 1973:288).

There is an extensive victimless crime literature dealing with drug addiction, prostitution, gambling, abortion, homosexuality, suicide, alcoholism, heterosexual deviance, pornography, and such obscene and lewd "offenses" as women going topless on public beaches (Winerip, 1992) or breast-feeding in public (Lewin, 2001). These are crimes *mala prohibita* (that is, behaviors made criminal by statute, but there is no consensus as to whether these acts are criminal of themselves). They are acts against public interest or morality and appear in criminal codes as crimes against public decency, order, or justice. Crimes like rape or murder are *mala in se* (that is, evils in themselves with public agreement on the dangers they pose) (Rich, 1978:27).

Victimless crimes are also differentiated from other crimes by the element of consensual transaction or exchange. These crimes are also differentiated from other kinds of crimes by the lack of apparent harm to others and by the difficulty in enforcing the laws against them as a result of low visibility and the absence of complainants. In other words, they are plaintiffless crimes—that is, those involved are willing participants who, as a rule, do not complain to the police that a crime has been committed. Although many people do not consider these activities "criminal," the police and the courts continue to apply laws against such groups as drug users, prostitutes, gamblers, homosexuals, and pornography distributors—laws that large sections of the community do not recognize as legitimate and simply refuse to obey. This situation is further compounded (and muddied) by technological breakthroughs such the use of computers to create pornographic images. Is there a line between "fake" pornography, where digital simulations are used to create images and "real" pornography with "live" subjects? The two are virtually indistinguishable from each other, and the criminalization of foul figments of cyber technology that does not involve human subjects raises some interesting First Amendment questions (Liptak, 2001).

The formal controls exerted on these types of behavior are expensive and generally ineffective. Still, they serve certain functions. Robert M. Rich (1978:28) notes that persons who are labeled as criminals serve as an example to community members. When the laws are enforced against lower-class and minority-group members, it allows the ones in power (middle- and upper-class people) to feel that the law is serving a useful purpose because it preserves and reinforces the myth that low-status individuals account for most of the deviance in society. Finally, the control of victimless crimes, in the forms of arrests and convictions, strengthens the notion in the community that the police and the criminal justice system are doing a good job in protecting community moral standards. Let us now consider law as a means of social control for certain victimless crimes such as drug addiction, prostitution, and gambling.

Drug Addiction

Although there have been several major periods of antidrug sentiments, crusades, and drug scares, the nonmedical use of drugs, such as opium and heroin, only relatively recently became a criminal act in the United States and in other countries (Bull, 2009; Liska, 2008; Natarajan, 2010a; Reinerman, 1996). Before 1914, there had been only sporadic attempts to regulate the use of drugs. Although some states attempted to control drug use by passing laws to provide for civil commitment to institutions for drug addicts and outlawing the use of particular narcotic substances, it was not until 1914 that any systematic attempt was made to regulate drug use in the United States (Szasz, 2003) and other substances that people may put in their bodies for which they were not legally intended (Smith and Deazley, 2010). In 1914, the *Harrison Narcotics Tax Act* was passed. It was the first attempt to deal comprehensively with the narcotics and dangerous drugs known at that time. It was essentially a tax measure or, more aptly, a series of prohibitive taxes. Drug use was restricted to medical purposes and research by licensed individuals and facilities. But in the act's interpretation, in court rulings in specific cases, and in supplementary laws, criminal sanctions were provided for the unauthorized possession, sale, or transfer of drugs. The states, too, have enacted a variety of antinarcotic laws. In the United States, penalties for violating drug laws have become more severe in recent years with increased and mandatory jail sentences for the sale and possession of many controlled substances, such as heroin, cocaine, and crack (Benjamin and Miller, 1992; Inciardi and McElrath, 2008; Liska, 2008; Natarajan, 2010b; Treaster, 1992). With increasing frequency, drug testing has become the norm in many workplaces, and potential employees are required to undergo drug testing (Tunnell, 2004).

The nation's prisons, which in 1980 housed fewer than 30,000 drug offenders, harbored nearly 300,000 less than two decades later (Massing, 1998a:48), and in 2006, more than 1.5 million people were arrested for drug offenses (Federal Bureau of Investigation, 2010). Drug offenders comprised a third of all persons convicted of a felony in state courts, and the average prison sentence for persons convicted of drug trafficking was 6 years and 2 months, of which they served 1 year and 11 months (U.S. Department of Justice, 1995:19–20).

In 2010, the United States had the highest substance abuse rate in any industrialized nation although the drug problem is ubiquitous and globally growing (see, for example, Lu et al., 2009). The American market absorbs well over 60 percent of the world's production of illegal drugs. An estimated 30 million Americans are regular users of marijuana, and habitual marijuana use increased among U.S. adults over the past decade, particularly among young minorities and baby boomers. The prevalence of marijuana abuse or dependence climbed from 1.2 percent of adults in 1991–1992 to 1.5 percent in 2001–2002, or an estimated 3 million adults 18 and over. That represents an increase of 800,000 people, according to data from two nationally representative surveys that each queried more than 40,000 adults in 2004. Among all adults aged 45 to 64, the rate increased by 355 percent, to about 0.4 percent of that population (Tanner, 2004). There are about 5–10 million cocaine abusers, and estimates for heroin addicts range from 200,000 to 900,000, with about half of them in New York City alone (Abadinsky, 2010; Goode, 2008; Walker 1993:574). Studies by the National Institute on Drug Abuse indicate that one-third of all college students will use cocaine at least once before they graduate (Meyer, 1989:1, 30). There is substantial evidence that the best predictor of cocaine use is heavy early marijuana use (Grabowski, 1984:vii). Close to 80 percent of all Americans will try an illicit drug by their mid-20s. Although the use of narcotics has decreased slightly since the 1990s, drugs are now far more available at cheaper prices and in greater purity and variety.

The illegal drug industry is simple and profitable. Its simplicity makes it fairly easy to organize, and its profitability makes it hard to stop. At every level, its pricing is determined by the level of risk of enforcement: the risk of seizure and jail, and the uncertainty that arises because traders cannot rely on the laws to enforce the bargains. For example, very conservatively, a Pakistani farmer receives about $90 for a kilo of opium. The wholesale price in Pakistan is almost $3,000. The American wholesale price is $80,000 on the street, at 40 percent purity; the retail price is $290,000 a kilogram. As for cocaine, the leaf needed to produce a kilo costs between $400 and $600. By the time it leaves Colombia, the price has gone up to about $1,800. On the streets in the United States, after changing hands for a few times, the retail price of a kilo of cocaine come to about $110,000, and in Europe, substantially more. The vast gap between the cost of production and the price paid by the end users obviously plays a role in the failure of drug polices. The producers see a modest return; the real profit is embedded mainly in the distribution chain, which is very hard to control effectively (see, for example, Marez, 2004).

The sheer volume of available drugs and the dollar amounts involved in their trade in the United States are phenomenal: some 3,900 tons of imported marijuana at a retail price of $84 per ounce; more than 12 tons of heroin at a street value of $290,000 per kilogram; and 2,500 tons of cocaine at $110,000 a kilo, retail (*Economist*, 2001:7; Paoli et al., 2009). In view of these numbers, it is interesting to note that, in 1993, the various federal agencies participating in the Federal-Wide Drug Seizure System (FDSS) (FBI, DEA, U.S. Customs Service, and U.S. Coast Guard) seized 3,345 pounds of heroin, 238,053 pounds of cocaine, and 752,114 pounds of marijuana—leaving the borders rather porous (U.S. Department of Justice, 1995:12).

The American cocaine market alone is worth over $100 billion a year. By contrast, the 1995 budget, which has not significantly changed over the years, devoted $13.2 billion to antidrug programs (U.S. Department of Justice, 1995b:10). More than two-thirds of it is going to measures that have consistently proved to be ineffective—police training for South America, swarms of planes and boats, radar balloons and drug agents at the borders, more jails, and battalions of police officers (Treaster, 1992). Less than a third is earmarked for treatment, rehabilitation, education, prevention, and international aid. With more than two million Americans now behind bars and up to 80 percent of them involved with powerful drugs like cocaine and heroin, rehabilitation programs offer a potent weapon for decreasing addiction, crime, and the spiraling cost of incarceration. Yet only a fraction of inmates—about 2 percent—undergo serious rehabilitation. It has been shown that every $1 invested in drug treatment saved $7 in future costs of crime and incarceration (Treaster, 1995). This conclusion is reinforced by Michael Massing (1998b) in his aptly titled book, *The Fix*, in which he contends that the hard-core users of heroin and cocaine are disproportionately poor, unemployed, and members of minority groups. Although hard-core users are only one-fifth of total users, they consume three-fourths of the cocaine and heroin used in America and are responsible for most of the pathological behavior that elicits public and governmental responses. If we could provide appropriate treatment to anyone in this population who wanted it, Massing maintains, the whole drug problem would diminish, as would the crime and illness associated with it.

Legally, psychoactive drugs are classified into three basic categories—legal drugs (alcohol, caffeine, and nicotine); prescription drugs (amphetamines, barbiturates, and tranquilizers), which must be prescribed by a physician; and illegal drugs (marijuana, heroin, and hallucinogens), which may not be sold under any circumstances. Cocaine and morphine make up a subcategory. They have limited medical use and high potential for abuse. The categories are not based on the potential harm or addictive quality of the drugs. Under the federal Controlled Substance Act of 1970, marijuana and heroin are classed together, although heroin is physically addictive and marijuana is not.

In the United States as well as in other countries, marijuana has reached a kind of a low-profile status, and it is no longer a symbol of rebellion or creativity (see, for example, Sandberg and Pedersen, 2009). Its use on college campuses is down, and prices have leveled off. Unlike most other drugs, 60 percent of the marijuana consumed in the United States is produced domestically. Marijuana is the largest cash crop in the United States, more valuable than corn and wheat combined. Using conservative price estimates, domestic marijuana production had a value of $35.8 billion in 2006 (Gettman, 2006)—a noticeable increase from 1986 when it was already worth $18.6 billion (Glassman, 1986:12) along with concomitant increases in job opportunities for producers, distributors, criminal justice personnel, and so on. For example, an investment of $500,000 into plants and about 100 workers for four months including incidental costs, such as generators, PVC pipes, and so on, could result in a return of about $120 million once the processed product is sold on the open market (Millman, 2009).

Despite intensive eradication efforts, domestic marijuana production has increased tenfold over the last 25 years from 1,000 metric tons (2.2 million pounds) in 1981 to 10,000 metric tons (22 million pounds) in 2006 according to federal government estimates (Gettman, 2006). Marijuana is the top cash crop in 12 states, one of the top three cash crops in 30 states, and one of the top five cash crops in 39 states. The domestic marijuana crop is larger than cotton in Alabama; larger than grapes, vegetables, and hay combined in California; larger than peanuts in Georgia; and larger than tobacco in both South Carolina and North Carolina. The quality of U.S. grown marijuana is much higher than that grown in Mexico and other exporting countries with the exception of British Columbia, Canada. This is also reflected in the price; the Mexican variety, with a lower content of THC (the active narcotic in marijuana) brings in about $500 to $700 a pound while Washington State–grown marijuana can command up to $6,000 a pound (Millman, 2009).

According to the FBI's Uniform Crime Report (2010), close to 800,000 individuals were arrested on marijuana charges in 2009. This number far exceeds the total number of arrestees for all violent crimes combined, including murder, rape, robbery, and aggravated assault. Eighty-eight percent of those arrested were charged with possession only. Convicted marijuana offenders are denied federal financial student aid, welfare, and food stamps, and may be removed from public housing. In many cases, those convicted are automatically stripped of their driving privileges, even if the offense is not driving related. In several states, marijuana offenders may receive maximum sentences of life in prison. The cost to the taxpayer of enforcing marijuana prohibition is staggering—over $13 billion annually. The harsh nature of punishments for marijuana offenses is even more disturbing if one considers the racial bias of the War on Drugs. According to data collected by the National Household Survey on Drug Use & Health, on an annual basis, the overall difference between drug use by blacks and whites is quite narrow. However, a recent national study found that African-Americans are arrested for marijuana offenses at higher rates than whites in 90 percent of 700 U.S. counties investigated. In 64 percent of these counties, the African American arrest rate for marijuana violations was more than twice the arrest rate for whites. Questions of racial and ethnic bias affect the integrity of investigations, arrests, and prosecutorial discretion (see, for example, Rice and White, 2010).

Although there has been an increase in the arrest rates for the sale, transportation, and possession of illegal drugs, and more severe mandatory prison terms for conviction, criminal law has not been successful at effectively controlling illicit drug use in the United States (see, for example, Faupel et al., 2009). Some of the byproducts of the tremendous legal efforts to control drugs resulted in the formation of elaborate illegal organizations for the supply of illicit drugs. Many users turn to other criminal activities to support their habit. Drug laws have contributed to a situation in which politicians and police ignore drug traffic—usually because of payoffs. Because drug use is a victimless crime, the lack of complainant makes enforcement difficult. In enforcement, the police frequently use entrapment and illegal search and seizure tactics (Sheley, 1985:122). Furthermore, there is a potential for conflict and recrimination in the control of the flow of illegal drugs. The principal consumer countries are affluent and industrialized; the principal drug-producing countries are poor and basically agricultural (Paoli et al., 2009). Cocaine and heroin traffic in the western hemisphere is a particularly serious example of how this conflict of interests plays out (Martin and Romano, 1992:51–67). Consuming and producing countries vehemently accuse and blame each other and, depending on which side they are on, advocate either demand-side or supply-side solutions—controlling the demand of users in the United States for cocaine, as opposed to controlling the supply from South America. The concerns of the United States are fairly unambiguous. Cocaine imports have increased tenfold during the last decade, distribution patterns have become more sophisticated, and the abuse of cocaine and its derivative "crack" has become a serious problem (Rengert, 1998). The position of producing countries is also clear-cut. Elites there view antidrug campaigns with hostility because they impose significant new burdens and create formidable new challenges (Paoli et al., 2009; Rensselaer, 1989). There are powerful vested economic interests profiting from drugs, and in the past decade, Colombia alone has lost 23 judges, 63 journalists, four presidential candidates, and more than 3,000 soldiers and police officers in its attempt to moderate drug production (Samper, 1995).

In short, there is little prospect of effective control of drugs through the criminal law in the United States, or any other place (see, for example, Scherrer, 2010). Some even argue that the War on Drugs, at a cost of $16 billion annually, has corrupted the institutions of the nation, and no law enforcement agency has escaped the effects of the profit and racism that drive the drug trade and its criminalization (Baggins, 1998; Marez, 2004). The various punitive approaches—attacking drug production abroad, interdiction (seizing drugs in transit), and domestic law enforcement (arresting and incarcerating sellers and buyers)—have failed (Massing, 1998a, 1998b).

There are two controversial alternatives, however. The first is a consideration of drug addiction and drug use more as a medical than a legal problem with an emphasis on comprehensive treatment, as is done, to some extent, in Great Britain and the Scandinavian countries (De Kort and Korf, 1992).

The second is the legalization or decriminalization of drugs. As the influential *Economist* (2001) argues, drugs are dangerous, but so is the illegality that surrounds them. Because it is illegal, it cannot be regulated. Governments cannot insist on minimum quality standards for cocaine; or warn asthma sufferers to avoid Ecstasy; or demand that distributors take responsibility for the way their products are sold. With alcohol and tobacco, such restrictions are possible; with drugs, not. In legitimate commerce, the sale of drugs would be controlled, taxed, and supervised. Educational campaigns would proclaim their dangers. Through legalization, drugs would poison fewer customers, kill fewer dealers and bystanders, bribe fewer enforcement people, and raise more public revenue. Initially, there may be more users and more addicts. The recommendation of the *Economist* (2001:16) is simply "to set it free." The article contends that governments allow their citizens to engage in a variety of self-destructive things: to go bungee-jumping, to ride motorcycles and jet skies, to carry loaded guns (legal to carry loaded concealed weapons in many states), to drink alcohol, to play with explosives (fireworks), to have unsafe sex, to overeat, and to smoke cigarettes. Some of them are far more dangerous than taking drugs. It concludes that trade in drugs may be immoral or irresponsible, but it should no longer be illegal. The same theme is reverberated in Jacob Sullum's (2003) book, *Saying Yes: In Defense of Drug Use.* He highlights the injustice of punishing people for their politically incorrect choice of intoxicants and argues that politicized government agencies, antidrug activists, and a naïve national media have exaggerated the public's fear of the harmful effects of recreational drugs—a nice controversial position to debate (see, for example, Liska, 2008).

Finally, the tenfold growth of production over the last 25 years and its proliferation to every part of the country demonstrate that marijuana has become a pervasive and ineradicable part of the national economy. The failure of intensive eradication programs suggests that it is finally time to give serious consideration to marijuana's legalization in the United States.

Before moving to the next topic, there is a novel form of drug control that is worth noting for its unique cultural component. Because of the practically unchecked methamphetamine production in Myanmar close to the Thai border, it became the drug of choice in the hills of northern Thailand. Many farmers became drug smugglers and dealers (earning more in a day than they could in a month on rice fields), and drug use spread in the area fueling theft to pay for the little orange pills. One village seriously afflicted with the drug problem came up with an indigenous—and perhaps ingenious—way to combat the drug epidemic. The village elders threatened drug dealers and users with a terrifying fate for a Thai: If they died, no one would attend their funerals and no monk would say prayers for their souls. Thai Buddhists believe the soul will be consigned to hell if funeral rites are not performed properly. A well-attended funeral—a major affair with relatives and musicians—is a principal requirement for a proper cremation. When dealers and users in the village were told that they would be cut off from the community, the drug problem ceased to exist. The 53 known drug dealers in the village of 1,500 people gave up the trade, and the addicts were weaned from the habit (Tang, 2003).

Prostitution

If there is one area in the criminal law that arouses the most anxiety concerning public morals, it is sexual conduct (Scoular and Sanders, 2010). The range of sexual conduct covered by the law is so great and extensive that the law makes potential criminals of most teenagers and adults—especially with the increased availability and variety of cybersex (see, for example, Neumann, 2010). One of the justifications for such a complete control of sexual behavior is to protect the family system. A number of state laws control acts that would otherwise endanger the chastity of women before marriage, such as the variety of laws on rape (statutory and forcible) (Horvath and Brown, 2009), fornication, incest, and sexual deviance of juveniles. The criminal laws on adultery are also designed to protect the family by preventing sexual relations outside of marriage (Quinney, 1975:83–84). In addition, a complex set of federal and state laws controls the advertising, sale, distribution, and availability of contraceptives; the performance of abortion; voluntary sterilization; and artificial insemination (Weinberg, 1979). Because of the complexity and extensiveness of legal controls on sexual conduct and related matters, this section will be limited to a discussion of the legal controls of female prostitution. In the United States, estimates of women who make some or all of their living as prostitutes range from half a million (Clinard and Meier, 2010) to a million (Aday, 1990:108).

It is now recognized that laws throughout the world against prostitution discriminate against women (see, for example, Davis, 1993; Gangoli and Westmarland, 2006; Kempadoo and Doezema, 1998; Kuo, 2005; Matthews, 2008; Munro and Giusta, 2008; Scambler and Scambler, 1997). Many women's groups in America and abroad maintain that a woman should have the right to engage in sexual relations for pay if she so desires (Poel, 1995). However, law enforcement authorities do not yet share that position, and there is still a tendency to regard only the women as offenders and not their clients.

State laws vary on prostitution (Meier and Geis, 1997:27–65). In many states, solicitation is considered a misdemeanor punished by a fine or a jail sentence of up to one year. Frequent arrests, however, may result in a charge of felony. There are three broad categories of arrests for prostitutes: (1) for accosting and soliciting; (2) on a charge of "common prostitution," which can be subsumed under disorderly conduct or vagrancy; and (3) detention under health regulations (La Fave, 1965:457–463). Law enforcement of prostitution is sporadic, and much of the control is limited to containment. In addition to Nevada that permits prostitution with the exception of its three most populous counties, due to a legal loophole, prostitution is also legal in Rhode Island as long as it happens indoors (Aujla and Levitz, 2009).

There is a fair amount of discretion involved in the control of prostitutes. At times, there is practically no enforcement, and at other times, police conduct special campaigns directed at streetwalkers in certain neighborhoods. In general, most of the police control of prostitutes is aimed at the individual practitioners and streetwalkers (see, for example, Canter et al., 2009). The high-class call girls are relatively immune to legal control. So are those who use the Internet to make appointments and to screen clients. Interestingly, the online proliferation of prostitution is leading to a more white-collar john, who does not have to risk the stigma (and possibly arrest) of driving around, looking for a prostitute. In addition, many women (and men) advertise themselves as scantily dressed strippers, massage therapists, and escorts on the back pages of local weekly newspapers in most cities in the United States.

Laws against prostitution are attempts to control private moral behavior through punitive social control measures. The classic, influential, and ubiquitous Wolfenden Report expresses rather eloquently the rationale for the continued legal control of prostitution.

> If it were the law's intention to punish prostitution per se, on the grounds that it is immoral conduct, then it would be right that it should provide for the punishment of the man as well as the woman. But that is not the function of the law. It

should confine itself to those activities which offend against public order and decency or expose the ordinary citizen to what is offensive or injurious; and the simple fact that prostitutes do parade themselves more habitually and openly than their prospective customers, and do by their continual presence affront the sense of decency of the ordinary citizen. In so doing they create a nuisance which, in our view, the law is entitled to recognize and deal with. (1963:143–144)

The report also notes that prostitution has prevailed for many centuries, and it cannot be really controlled by criminal law. As long as there is a demand for the services of prostitutes and there remain women who choose this form of livelihood—even when there is no economic necessity for it—the Wolfenden Report (1963:132) concludes that "no amount of legislation directed towards its abolition will abolish it." Still, from time to time, community leaders and law enforcement agents would like to "clean up" some areas of the cities, and through these efforts, they persist in trying to suppress prostitution through the law (Lowman, 1992). There are also arguments that although most prostitution is voluntary, paternalistic prostitution laws in one form or another are morally justifiable (Marneffe, 2010).

One day, perhaps, community leaders and law enforcement agents will learn from history and will recognize that such efforts are futile in a free-enterprise society (see, for example, Phoenix, 2009; Wright, 2009). A growing number of critics argue that the criminal statutes improperly and unwisely extend the coverage of criminal law to harmless matters of private morality, such as commercial sex between consenting adults. Prostitution is legal (with some restrictions) in Canada. Similarly, in many European countries in 2010, prostitutes ply their trade legally, pay taxes, receive health and retirement benefits, and take regularly scheduled vacations. The Netherlands, where the sex industry is now a $1 billion business or 5 percent of the Dutch economy, just recently legalized brothels and the 30,000 or so sex workers now have a chance to get the basic labor rights, insurance policies, disability payments, education and retirement benefits, and paid vacations enjoyed by other citizens. Many prostitutes now are also setting themselves up as self-employed businesswomen with accountants, banks, and health insurance companies as clients (Daley, 2001). In Germany, the law required for years now that cities with populations of 500,000 or more designate 10 percent of their area as an "amusement" zone, with prostitution included among the amusements (*Wall Street Journal*, 1986:16) along with brothels that offer special deals (€60—check the current exchange rates for dollars . . .) for virgins with prostitutes trained in the delicate art of catering to customers who have never had sex (*Seattle Times*, 2006). Studies in New Zealand demonstrated how to regulate sex work without moral judgment and how to take the crime out of prostitution (Abel et al., 2010).

Influential critics (see, for example, Gangoli and Westmarland, 2006; Geis, 1979; Matthews, 2008) would revise these prohibitions to narrow the kinds of behavior they proscribe to acts that are clearly harmful to society. Prostitution is not considered one of them. The decriminalization of prostitution would, in essence, extend the practice of official tolerance already operative in many places (Adler and Adler, 1975:224). It would allow the police agencies, who already mostly disregard online and newspaper prostitution, to deal with more important matters, and it would probably help lower the number of sex crimes. Opponents of decriminalization argue for increased legal control of prostitution, because they believe it leads, for example, to other crimes, such as drug addiction, blackmail, assault, and even murder.

Gambling

Some 70 percent of the American public gamble (Lesieur, 1992:43), and certain forms of casino gambling are legal in many parts of the country (see, for example, Grinols, 2004; Lears, 2003; Wolfe and Owens, 2009). Nowadays, more than 90 percent of Americans live within 200 miles of a legal casino (O'Brien, 1998) where people legally bet some $640 billion a year and loose about $90 billion of that amount (Flynn, 2007:4). About one in four Americans visited offline casinos and around 12 million gambled online in 2005 and a quarter of so of male college students now play card games online at least once a month (*Economist*, 2006b:77). As the legal gambling business has spread across the country, a fast-spinning revolving door has also developed, creating a situation in which a state senator with no casino experience has, in an instant, become president of a major casino, a law-enforcement official from a state attorney general's office has gone on to become the chief executive of the nation's most profitable casino, and where top gambling officials from one state after another have resigned to pursue lucrative casino careers. Legalized gambling has become a growth industry and created a robust new market for politically connected executives, lobbyists, and consultants who "speak the language" of the regulators (Pierce and Miller, 2004; Pulley, 1998).

Legal and illegal gambling exist practically side-by-side, and participants often cross the line. In the victimless-crime literature, illegal gambling, just like drug use and prostitution, is considered a consensual transaction and a plaintiffless crime (see, for example, Cozic and Winters, 1995; Wolfe and Owens, 2009). The players are willing participants who generally do not notify the police that a crime has been committed. Enforcement activity therefore must be initiated by the police, who then act as the complainant on behalf of the community. By contrast, enforcement activity for other crimes, such as burglaries or muggings, usually occurs in response to citizen complaints.

Historically, the prohibition and regulation of gambling has largely been a function of the state. Federal involvement with gambling began in the late nineteenth century, when Congress put an end to the operation of corrupt lotteries by denying them mailing privileges and the ability to transact business across state lines. The next significant federal action dealing with gambling occurred in 1949, when Congress enacted legislation to eliminate the gambling ships that had been operating off the coast of California. Other actions dealt with the interstate transportation and transmission of wagering information and gambling paraphernalia. The Organized Crime Control Act of 1970 further extended jurisdiction over interstate gambling and made it a federal offense to operate certain illegal gambling businesses (Pierce and Miller, 2004). Congress also has affected gambling activities through the exercise of its taxing powers by levying excise and occupational taxes on gambling operations, and a stamp tax on gambling devices, and by subjecting gambling winnings to the federal income tax (Commission on the Review of the National Policy Toward Gambling, 1976:5).

Local police departments have the primary responsibility for gambling enforcement, although the role of state-level agencies is growing. The Commission on the

Review of the National Policy Toward Gambling (1976:44–46) identifies a number of control techniques used by law enforcement agencies. The commission notes that the most frequent source of gambling arrests is the direct observation of illegal gambling activity. Such arrests are primarily "nonserious," involving individual street players or low-level employees of gambling organizations. Arrests at higher levels—for example, large bookmakers or numbers offices—are rarely, if ever, made in this manner. They require investigation leading to a probable cause for search and arrest warrants. The use of informants in gambling control is widespread. Most police departments rely on this technique, as well as on undercover investigators who can often accumulate evidence against individuals and on operations by placing bets. In recent years, the use of electronic surveillance, authorized by Congress in 1968 under Title III of the Omnibus Crime Control and Safe Streets Act, became particularly widespread in the control of illegal gambling (see also Norris and Wilson, 2007). Electronic surveillance is best suited for the use of gambling investigation because of the dependence of gambling operations on telephones. One of the devices that is used is the pen register, which records phone numbers dialed from a particular telephone. By attaching a pen register to the telephone line of a gambling location, police can often identify additional locations and individuals involved in illegal gambling operations. There are also sophisticated surveillance technologies to monitor cell phone and other forms of cyberspace communications.

Of the tens of thousands of individuals arrested annually in the United States for gambling offenses, a relatively small proportion are convicted. Of those convicted, a very small percentage receive jail or prison sentences, or substantial fines. For example, during the six-year period from 1969 to 1974, there were 36,207 arrests for gambling in Chicago. Only 6 percent of those arrested were convicted. But there are exceptions to the generally low conviction rates for gambling. For example, approximately 70 percent of persons who appeared in Connecticut Circuit Court on gambling charges between 1970 and 1974 were convicted (Commission on the Review of the National Policy Toward Gambling, 1976:46–47).

Criminal law is ineffective in controlling and preventing people from engaging in illegal gambling. The parties involved in gambling do not complain about it, and a typical gambling transaction is probably more easily, rapidly, and privately consummated than is any other kind of illegal consensual transaction. It is much easier to place a bet with a bookie than to buy cocaine or have an encounter with a prostitute. Aside from the difficulties of detection, the criminal sanction for illegal gambling exerts little deterrent force. Generally, the penalties for those who are convicted tend to be light. Public opinion does not consider gambling as particularly wrongful, a sentiment both affected by and reflected in the lenience with which gambling offenders are treated (Packer, 1968:348). There seems to be an ambivalence in attitudes toward gambling. It is reflected in a resistance to proposals to reduce or eliminate reliance on criminal sanctions, accompanied by an equivalent resistance to any but the most sporadic attempts at enforcement.

Illegal gambling provides the largest source of revenue to organized crime (see, for example, Lyman and Potter, 2007; Wolfe and Owens, 2009). In fact, gambling laws are now justified as necessary to combat organized crime (Sheley, 1985:121). In most urban areas, bookmakers associated with crime syndicates specialize in bets on horse racing, professional football and basketball, boxing, hockey, and baseball. Increasingly, they are also involved in college football and basketball. Syndicates also run "numbers games," which involve placing a bet on the possible occurrence of certain numbers, such as the last three digits of the U.S. Treasury balance (Light, 1977). A complicated hierarchical organization is required to distribute the forms and to collect and pay off bets. Organized-crime syndicates employ "writers," "runners," or "sellers," terms to indicate the persons who accept numbers bets directly from bettors. Bets collected by them are given to a "pickup man," who forwards them to the next level in the hierarchy, the "bank." In larger operations, bets may be carried from the pickup man to another intermediary, the controller. Tickets with winning numbers are redeemed by cashiers or delivered by runners. In addition to bookmaking and numbers games, gambling syndicates also operate illegal casinos, "sponsor" backgammon tournaments, and provide opportunities for wagers to be made on a variety of activities—even the outcomes of political elections (Pierce and Miller, 2004).

Attempts to control illegal gambling consume a large amount of law enforcement time and resources. The problem is further compounded by online gambling, which is virtually impossible to control through legal means. On September 30, 2006, Congress rushed through a bill to stop banks and credit unions from processing payments to online gambling companies, adding to an already formidable legislative arsenal that outlaws most online gambling. But according to the critics of the bill, it is unlikely to produce the desired results. Gambling is tailor-made for cyberspace, and online gambling seems unstoppable; in view of evolving and creative technologies any prohibition can easily be circumvented (*Economist*, 2006b; Wall, 2009).

Ostensibly, control of gambling activities also includes fighting organized crime, maintaining a favorable public image of the police department, keeping undesirable activities or persons out of a city, and maintaining public order. The objective of controlling organized crime is reflected both in the intent of some gambling searches and in the view of the police that illegal gambling is related to organized crime. The objectives of preserving the department's public image and of maintaining public order are related, in that where open gambling, such as street cards and dice, is permitted to continue, citizens are likely to conclude that the police are either corrupt or derelict in their duty. In some instances, however, "meeting the quota" has become a principal stimulant for the control of illegal gambling by the police. In such instances, officers produce what may be called "symbolic" gambling arrests—that is, gambling arrests that meet the quota, thus fulfilling the department's stated policy of continuing enforcement activity.

An additional problem with gambling control is that most of the corruption of police and of the courts is associated with these offenses. Few police officers are willing to accept bribes from murderers, burglars, or other criminals whose acts are blatantly harmful and have identifiable victims. However, many police officers tend to feel that gambling is not particularly serious and that, in any case, it is impossible to eradicate. Hence, organized crime is often readily able to buy police protection for its activities. The Knapp Commission found corruption in the New York Police Department to be "at its most sophisticated among plainclothesmen assigned to enforce gambling laws" (Commission on the Review of the National Policy Toward Gambling, 1976:40). Participation in organized payoffs—a "pad"—netted individual New York plainclothes officers $300 to $1,500 a month. In return for protection, gambling establishments paid as much as $3,500 a month. Similarly, it was found that in Philadelphia, police throughout the city accept protection money from gamblers. It should be noted, however, that police corruption exists not only in gambling enforcement but in other areas as well (Punch, 2009). Investigations have also uncovered misconduct related to the enforcement of narcotics, prostitution, liquor establishments, construction-site regulations, and traffic (see, for example, Chambliss, 1978). These forms of police corruption are largely an urban problem and not limited to the United States (Klockars et al., 2004). In Canada, for example, corruption, abuse of authority, brutality, and fabricating evidence are fairly widespread, and police officers have been accused of receiving gambling kickbacks, stolen jewelry, and drugs; rigging evidence to put suspects behind bars in Toronto; dumping intoxicated Canadian Indians on isolated snowy roads to freeze to death in the prairies; and abusing drug addicts in Vancouver (Krauss, 2004).

One response to the difficulty and wastefulness in trying to enforce laws against gambling is to remove completely the criminal label. As the Knapp Commission recommended, "The criminal law against gambling should be repealed. To the extent that the legislature deems that some control over gambling is appropriate, such regulation should be by civil rather than criminal process. The police should in any event be relieved from any responsibility for the enforcement of gambling laws or regulations" (Wynn and Goldman, 1974:67). Although a number of similar suggestions have been made, the question of the decriminalization of gambling still remains a hotly debated and controversial issue. One of the concerns fueling this controversy is the estimate that some 1–2 percent of the adult population are probably pathological gamblers (people who chronically fail to resist impulses to gamble and for whom gambling interferes with other aspects of life) and an additional 2–3 percent are problem gamblers (Lesieur, 1992:49). Other estimates go even higher suggesting that 5 percent of the adult population, or some 10 million people, are compulsive gamblers.

A 2001 survey of 315 senior citizens (a relatively small sample size) who frequented riverboat casinos and bingo parlors to escape boredom suggested that they were particularly prone to develop gambling problems, and 11 percent showed signs of being pathological or compulsive gamblers (Young and Stern, 2001). The number of older adults who had placed a bet nearly doubled from 1975 to 1998, a period in which legalized gambling exploded. The rate of increase was much higher than for other age groups (Grinols, 2004). Elder adults remain a prime target for the industry. Casinos, in particular, court those over 65 and older with cheap buffets, free drinks, free transportation, money-back coupons, and other discounts.

For those under 21, estimates go as high as 15 percent with serious gambling problems. In the mordant words of one authority on gambling, "Compulsive gambling disorders may be for Generation X what cocaine and crack were for their parents' generation" (O'Brien, 1998). But the problem is not limited to the United States. According to a new study by the International Centre for Youth Gambling at McGill University, among Canadian youngsters aged 12 to 17, more than half are considered recreational gamblers, 10 to 15 per cent are at risk of developing a severe problem, and 4 to 6 percent are considered "pathological gamblers." The McGill study also found young adults aged 18 to 24 are two to four times more likely to develop a problem with gambling than the general adult population (Schmidt, 2003). With further liberalization and legalization of gambling, and there are strong arguments that gambling is bringing in jobs, capital development, and tax revenues (Flynn, 2007), activities thought to be associated with pathological and problem gambling (excessive borrowing, family problems, difficulties at work, psychiatric disorders, crime, and so on) would probably increase.

WHITE-COLLAR CRIME

Both at home and abroad, white-collar crimes are essentially crimes of privilege (Friedrichs, 2010; Green, 2006; Minkes and Minkes, 2009; Salinger, 2005; Shover and Wright, 2001; Zagaris, 2010), they of the suite rather than of the street. The term "white-collar crime" was coined by Edwin H. Sutherland (1949:9) and first used in an address to the American Sociological Association (ASS) in 1939. He criticized proponents of social disorganization and social pathology theories of crime and introduced class and power dimensions. "White-collar crime," he proposed, "may be defined approximately as a crime committed by a person of respectability and high status in the course of his occupation." He documented the existence of this form of crime with a study of the careers of 70 large, reputable corporations, which together had amassed 980 violations of the criminal law, or an average of 14 convictions apiece. Behind the offenses of false advertising, unfair labor practices, restraint of trade, price-fixing agreements, stock manipulation, copyright infringement, and outright swindles were perfectly respectable middle- and upper-middle-class executives (Croall, 1989; Reichman, 1989). Already a decade ago, check fraud alone represented a $10 billion loss for banks (Holland, 1995:96).

Gilbert Geis (1978:279; 1994) argues that "white-collar crimes constitute a more serious threat to the well-being and integrity of our society than more traditional kinds of crime," and workplace injuries, unnecessary surgeries, and illegal pollution consign far more people to the cemeteries than the offenses of traditional criminals. Moreover, as the President's Commission on Law Enforcement and Administration of Justice (1967b:104) concludes, "White-collar crime affects the whole moral climate of our society. Derelictions by corporations and their managers who usually occupy leadership positions in their communities, establish an example which tends to erode the moral base of the law." It raises questions about the equity of law and provides justification for other types of law violations.

The now classic textbook case of the $23 million "unauthorized loan" is illustrative of the question of equity of law dealing with white-collar crime. The defendants were charged with setting up a check-kiting operation: the art of repeatedly taking checks written on one account and quickly depositing them into another, and vice versa, staying a step ahead of the clearing system, and thus creating a false impression of the balances in the accounts. Once false balances have been created, a kiter can take out money against them, and that is just what perpetrators of this scheme did, leaving Marine Midland Bank holding the bag for a loss in excess of $23 million. The two already wealthy individuals found themselves indicted for the felony of grand larceny and the misdemeanor of scheming to defraud. And because larceny requires intent to deprive an owner of his or her property *permanently*, the defendants' repayment—as well as their ability to repay—played an important role in defense. Their attorneys argued that it was a *temporary* borrowing; they never intended to deprive the bank permanently of the funds. They insisted that they had no intention of keeping the money—so that what they were doing did not qualify as larceny. The jurors apparently agreed. The defendants were found innocent of the felony charge of grand larceny, which carries a possible seven-year prison sentence, because they claimed they intended to return the money *and* had the ability to pay. They were convicted only of a misdemeanor count of scheming to defraud, for which the maximum sentence is one year. The defendants unsuccessfully appealed the conviction (Cony and Penn, 1986).

The full extent of white-collar crime is difficult to assess. Many illegal corporate activities go undetected, and many wealthy individuals are able to evade taxes for years without being found out. One of the more recent examples is Robert Madoff who developed a sophisticated network of contacts across Jewish charities, synagogues, universities, and country clubs and managed to steal billions of dollars over a period of several years (LeBor, 2010).

White-collar crimes ("crimes in the suites" that are often dubbed crimes of middle classes [Green, 2006; Weisburd et al., 1991]) are generally considered somehow less serious than the crimes of the lower class ("crimes of the streets"), and there is often strong pressure on the police and the courts not to prosecute at all in these cases—to take account of the offenders' "standing in the community" and to settle the matter out of court. For example, a bank that finds its safe burglarized at night will immediately summon the police, but it may be more circumspect if it finds that one of its executives has embezzled a sum of money. To avoid unwelcome publicity, the bank may simply allow the offender to resign after making an arrangement for him or her to pay back whatever possible.

The concept of white-collar crime generally incorporates both occupational and corporate crimes (Coleman, 2006:5; Croall, 2010; Green, 2006; Salinger, 2005; Simpson and Gibbs, 2007). Some individuals commit crimes in connection with their occupations. For example, physicians may give out illegal prescriptions for narcotics, make fraudulent reports for Medicare payments, and give false testimony in accident cases. Lawyers may engage in some illegalities, such as securing false testimony from witnesses, misappropriating funds in receivership, and being involved in various forms of ambulance chasing to collect fraudulent damage claims arising from accidents. Corporate crimes are considered those illegal activities that are committed in the furtherance of business operations but that are not the central purpose of business. A convenient distinction between occupational and corporate crimes may be in the context of immediate and direct benefit to the perpetrator. In occupational crimes, generally the benefit is for the individual who commits a particular illegal activity—for example, the physician who receives money for giving out illegal prescriptions. In corporate crime, the benefit is usually for the organization (see, for example, Pearce and Tombs, 1998). For example, an executive bribes a public official to secure favors for his or her corporation. In this instance, the benefit would be for the corporation and not directly for the individual. The desire to increase profits is a crucial factor in a wide range of corporate crimes. The remainder of this section will focus on what is strictly called corporate crime. It is distinguished from ordinary crime in two respects—the nature of the violation and the fact that administrative and civil laws are more likely to be used as punishment than the criminal law.

In the United States, corporate crime did not exist until the nineteenth century (Croall, 2010; Salinger, 2005; Simpson and Gibbs, 2007). The reason for it is simply that there were no laws against dangerous or unethical corporate practices. Before the nineteenth century, corporations were free to sell unsafe products, to keep workers in unsafe conditions, to pollute the atmosphere, to engage in monopolistic practices, to overcharge customers, and to make outrageously false advertising claims for their products. By the end of the nineteenth century and the beginning of the twentieth century, increasingly laws were passed that attempted to regulate some of the more flagrant business practices that prevailed at the time. Examples are the Sherman Antitrust Act (1890) and the Pure Food and Drug Act (1906). Since that time, a vast array of laws has been passed to regulate the various facets of potentially harmful corporate activities.

The extensive nature of corporate crime is unquestioned today; it has been revealed by many government investigative committees and daily media coverage in one form or another (see, for example, Comer, 2003; Salinger, 2005; Simpson and Gibbs, 2007). In an influential study of the 582 largest publicly owned corporations in the United States, over 60 percent had at least one enforcement action completed against them in 1975 and 1976 (U.S. Department of Justice, 1979). The average number of actions initiated against these corporations for illegal activities (such as price fixing, foreign payoffs, illegal political contributions, and manufacture of unsafe foods and drugs) was 4.2.

In the 2010s, corporate crime is on the rise, and it is estimated that corporate crimes in the form of theft, accounting fraud, corruption, faulty goods, monopolistic practices, and similar law violations annually cost consumers between $174 billion and $231 billion (*Economist*, 2009:69; U.S. Department of Justice, 1979:16). The loss to taxpayers from reported and unreported violations of federal regulations by corporations is between $10 billion and $20 billion per year. About $1.2 billion goes unreported in corporate tax returns each year. Price fixing among corporations costs the consumer well over $65 billion a year (Simon, 2008). The loss alone from the electrical price-fixing conspiracy of the 1960s was nearly $2 billion, far greater than the total burglary losses during any given year. In 1979, nine major oil companies were sued by the U.S. Department of Justice for illegal overcharges of more than $1 billion. The companies were accused of charging too much for products derived from natural gas liquids and artificially increasing consumer costs. In contrast, the largest robbery in the United States thus far involved the June 26, 1990, heist of $11 million in cash from an armored car in Rochester, New York. Previously, the much-publicized Sentry Armored Car Company robbery of about $10.5 million in New York City in 1982 had been the largest robbery loss so far. (The losses are higher outside of the United States as exemplified by major robberies in recent years such the $44 million from a private cash sorting company in London in 2006; $70 million from Central Bank of Fortaleza, Brazil, in 2005; and the $50 million from Northwest Bank, Belfast, Ireland, in 2004.) But these cases are atypical; the typical robbery involves armed theft of about $250, burglary of about $350, larceny of about $125, and bank robbery around $2,000.

Undoubtedly, corporate crimes impose an enormous financial burden on society (see, for example, Croall, 2010; Sjögren and Skogh, 2004). In addition, it has been estimated that each year 200,000 to 500,000 workers are needlessly exposed to toxic agents such as radioactive materials and poisonous chemicals because of corporate failure to obey safety laws. Nearly half of all deaths among asbestos insulation workers are directly caused by exposure to that substance (Coleman, 2006). Many of the 2.5 million temporary and 250,000 permanent worker disabilities from industrial accidents each year are the result of managerial acts that represent culpable failure to adhere to established standards (Geis, 1978:279). Corporate crimes cause injuries to people on a larger scale than the so-called street crimes. Far more people are killed annually through corporate criminal activities than by the 20,000 or so individual criminal homicides; even if death is an indirect result, the person still died (U.S. Department of Justice, 1979:16).

Corporate crime is controlled by a variety of regulatory agencies. The control of corporate activities may be *prospective*, as in licensing, when control is exercised before deviant acts occur; *processual*, as in inspection where control is continuous; and *retrospective*, as when a lawsuit is brought for damages after deviance has occurred. These types of controls will be discussed further in the final section of this chapter. In addition, if a business concern defies the law, the government may institute, under civil law, an injunction to "cease and desist" from further violations. If further violations occur, contempt of court proceedings may be instituted. Fines and various forms of assessments are also used in attempts to control deleterious corporate activities, as, for example, in cases of levying fines on water and air polluters. At times, the government can also exercise control through its buying power by rewarding firms that comply and withdrawing from or not granting governmental contracts to those who do not (Nagel, 1975:341–352).

But, as Christopher D. Stone (1978:244–245) points out, "Whether we are threatening the corporation with private civil actions, criminal prosecutions, or the new hybrid 'civil penalties,' we aim to control the corporation through threats to its profits." Although corporations are subjected to federal sentencing guidelines (Podgor, 1994), which are rather controversial (Hemphill, 1993), corporate offenders are rarely criminally prosecuted and even more rarely imprisoned. A large proportion of these offenders are handled through administrative and civil sanctions, and the penalty is monetary. In a sense, the penalty imposed for violating the law amounts to little more than a reasonable licensing fee for engaging in illegal activity. Essentially, it is worthwhile for a large corporation to violate the laws regulating business. Typically, the fines are microscopic. For example, until 1955, the maximum fine a judge could levy against a company for violating the Sherman Antitrust Act was $5,000. In 1955, it was increased to $50,000, and in 1976, it was further increased to $250,000. This is not much of a deterrent to a multimillion-dollar company.

Controlling corporations through the law becomes, as Stone (1978:250) puts it, a "misplaced faith on negative reinforcement." Although there are now sophisticated detection and record-keeping technologies, forensic accountants, and other legal specialists (Lindquist, 1995), the law constitutes only one of the threats that the corporation faces in dealing with the outside world. Often, paying a fine is considered part of doing business. For a businessperson, reducing the profits by a lawsuit does not involve the same loss of face as losses attributable to other causes, such as being sued by the antitrust division, although "a mess" is "understandable." It is not a question of improving such behavior but a realization by businesspeople that it could happen to anyone. In financial reports, losses through lawsuits are explained in footnotes as nonrecurring losses.

Although there were signs of increased enforcement by federal agencies in early 2000—the U.S. Department of Justice, for instance, created a special task force to tackle corporate fraud in 2002 (*Economist*, 2004)—and local authorities (see, for example, Benson and Cullen, 1998; Calavita and Pontell, 1994), the current legal controls on corporate crime are inefficient. For example, because of the Bush administration's massive restructuring of the FBI after the terrorism attacks of 9/11, thousands of white-collar criminals across the country are no longer being prosecuted in federal court—and, in many cases, not at all—leaving a trail of frustrated victims and potentially billions of dollars in fraud and theft losses. The White House and the U.S. Department of Justice have failed to replace at least 2,600 agents transferred to counterterrorism squads, leaving far fewer agents on the trail of white-collar and corporate criminals. The number of crimes that the bureau has traditionally fought, including sophisticated fraud and embezzlement schemes, plunged dramatically. Overall, the number of criminal cases investigated by the FBI nationally has steadily declined. In 2009, the bureau brought slightly more than 20,000 cases to federal prosecutors, compared with about 31,000 in 2000—a 34 percent drop. White-collar crime investigations by the bureau have plummeted even more in recent years. In 2009, the FBI sent prosecutors 3,500 cases—a fraction of the more than 10,000 cases assigned to agents in 2000 (Federal Bureau of Investigation, 2010). Already hit hard by the shift of agents to terrorism duties, FBI offices also suffer from lowered staffing levels, making this hidden cost of the war on terrorism even more pronounced (Shukovsky et al., 2007).

Further, the government's response to corporate violations cannot be compared to its response to ordinary crime. Generally, penalties imposed on corporations are quite lenient, particularly in view of the gravity of the offenses committed, as compared with the penalties imposed on ordinary offenders. Few members of corporate management ever go to prison, even if convicted; generally, they are placed on probation or requested to carry some kind of community service (Podgor, 1994). If they go to prison, it is almost always for a very short time period. For example, a study found that, of the 56 federally convicted executives, 62.5 percent received probation, 28.6 percent were incarcerated, and the rest had their sentences suspended. The average prison sentence for all those convicted for white-collar crimes averaged 2.8 days (U.S. Department of Justice, 1979). Gilbert Geis (1978, 1994) points out that it is, indeed, ironic that the penalties for corporate crime are the least severe, even though they are given to the very persons who might be the most affected by them, or who might "benefit" the most from them. In other words, if these offenders are potentially the most deterred, an increase in punishment and the intensity of enforcement might result in the greatest benefit to society. As it stands now, however, the penalty for corporate crime is far less than the harm caused, and unlike those who commit violent crimes, perpetrators of corporate crime are not subjected to the "three strikes and your are out" mandatory sentencing guidelines (see, for example, Spohn, 2009).

SOCIAL CONTROL OF DISSENT

A universal, omnipresent, and pervasive governmental activity is the control of dissent (see, for example, Lovell, 2009; Sarat, 2005). Political trials, surveillance, and suppression of information and free speech are rampant in most countries as described in a book with an appropriate title: *Why Societies Need Dissent* (Sunstein, 2003; see also Hier and Greenberg, 2010). Some examples are: In Islamic countries, fundamentalists regularly ban books. The most blatant case is that of the writer Salman Rushdie, who was being threatened with death because of his book, *The Satanic Verses.* Ayatollah Ruhollah Khomeini called it blasphemy against Islam and in 1989 offered a million-dollar reward for the writer's execution. The offer was raised to $2.8 million by hard-liners in late 1998, although the Iranian government officially rescinded the reward in an attempt to improve relations with the West (*St. Louis Post-Dispatch*, 1998). Rushdie is now out of hiding, and in late 2000s, he has started to make public appearances for book tours and talk shows but is still under the watchful eyes of security guards). In Islamic countries, the press is state controlled, and dissidents, at best, are jailed. In African and Asian countries, journalistic fealty to the ruling dictatorship is demanded (take Singapore, for example); and the abuse of psychiatry to intimidate and torture dissidents in the former Soviet Union was well documented and loudly deplored by the West. In Canada, from the 1950s to the late 1990s, state agents spied on, harassed, and interrogated gays and lesbians, employing various ideologies to construct their targets (people who deviated from the norm) as threats to society and enemies of the state. National security was used as an excuse for regulation of sexual behavior (Kinsman and Gentile, 2010).

In China, the democracy movement continues to be suppressed in the aftermath of the 1989 Tiananmen crackdown (Branegan, 1998; Christenson, 1999; Diamant et al., 2005; Fein, 1992), and the abuse of psychiatry as a form of social control for dissent once again appears to be increasing. For example, the government has forcibly imprisoned members of Falun Gong in psychiatric hospitals. Galun Gong, a popular movement that advocates channeling energy through deep breathing and exercises, has been the target of government crackdowns with abuses reminiscent of the Cultural Revolution decades earlier. Hundreds of Falun Gong members have been taken to psychiatric institutions and drugged, physically restrained, isolated, or given electric shocks (*New York Times*, 2001c). There is also a development of a network of new police psychiatric hospitals—called *Ankangs*, which means "peace and happiness"—built in recent years. Chinese law includes "political harm to society" as legally dangerous mentally ill behavior. Law enforcement agents are instructed to take into psychiatric custody "political maniacs," defined as people who make antigovernment speeches, write reactionary letters, or otherwise express opinions in public on important domestic and international affairs contrary to the official government position. There are 20 Ankangs, with plans to build many more.

The United States is no exception. Although it has a history of welcoming dissent in the abstract, it punishes it in the concrete (Lieberman, 1972). Law supports the government as the legitimate holder of power in society (see, for example, Cram, 2006). The government in turn is legitimately involved in the control of its citizens. The principal objectives of the government are to provide for the welfare of its citizens, to protect their lives and property, and to maintain order within society. To maintain order, the government is mandated to apprehend and punish criminals. In a democratic society, there are questions, however, about the legitimacy of a government that stifles dissent in the interest of preserving order or waging war. In principle, in a democratic society, tradition and values affirm that dissent is appropriate. At the same time, for social order to prevail, a society needs to ensure that existing power relationships are maintained over time. Furthermore, those in positions of power, who benefit from the existing power arrangement, use their influence to encourage the repression of challenges to the government. Consequently, governments generally opt for the control and repression of dissent.

One way of controlling dissent is through the various selection processes used to place individuals into desirable social positions (Oberschall, 1973:249–250). In most political systems, the leaders have ways of controlling the selection and mobility of people through patronage systems, the extension of the government bureaucracy, and co-optation in its many forms. Loyalty and conformity are generally the primary criteria for advancement. Another form of control in this context is the dismissal of individuals who do not comply with the stated expectations and voice "unpopular" opinions. In some instances, the leaders can directly control the supply and demand of certain services and skills. For example, "by exercising influence on budgets, examinations, student stipends, and university expansion, a government can within a couple of years reduce the total number of students in higher education for the purpose of quashing a troublesome student movement and floating population of unemployed graduates that it has brought into being and subsidized" (Oberschall, 1973:250).

Control can also be achieved through the manipulation of the structure of material benefits (Janowitz, 1976; Mandell, 1975). For example, Frances Fox Piven and Richard A. Cloward (1993) contend that welfare programs serve as a social-control mechanism in periods of mass unemployment by diffusing social unrest and thus reducing dissent. They argue that public assistance programs are used to regulate the political and economic activities of the poor. In periods of severe economic depression, the legitimacy of the political system is likely to be questioned by the poor. The possibility of upsetting the status quo of power and property relationships in society increases. Demands grow for changing the existing social and economic arrangements. Under this threat, public assistance programs are initiated or expanded by the government. They cite case after case from sixteenth-century Europe to mid-twentieth-century America, documenting their thesis that social welfare has, throughout the ages, been used as a mechanism of social control and a way by the government to diffuse social unrest through direct intervention. They note, however, that when economic conditions improve, the relief rolls are cut back in response to pressures from those who employ the poor so as to ensure an adequate supply of low-wage labor.

Another option for the government to use in the control of dissent is its coercive social-control apparatus to deal with crime, enforce the law, and keep social interaction peaceful and orderly. As compared with other mechanisms, "a coercive response to social disturbances is the cheapest and most immediately available means of control to the authorities" (Oberschall, 1973:252). The government is expected by the citizens, and is required by law, to protect life and property and to arrest the perpetrators of illegal activities. In addition to these coercive responses to dissent, the government has in its arsenal a variety of less overt, though equally effective, control mechanisms. For example, David Wise (1978:399–400) points out that the Central Intelligence Agency (CIA), although prohibited by law from doing so, has engaged in domestic operations to monitor and control the activities of Americans. For 20 years, the CIA opened 215,000 first-class letters, screened 28 million letters, and photographed the outside of 2.7 million letters. During the Nixon era, in Operation Chaos, the CIA followed antiwar activists, infiltrated various antiwar groups, undertook illegal break-ins and wiretaps, indexed 300,000 names in its "Hydra" computer, and compiled separate files on 7,200 Americans. A 2007 newspaper article headline "Spy chief wants to expand surveillance" (Shrader, 2007) illuminates more recent proclivities along the same lines (Goold and Neyland, 2009).

From 1955 to 1975, the FBI investigated 740,000 "subversive" targets—including the renowned sociologist Talcott Parsons of Harvard University's Social Relations Department (Diamond, 1992:37) and Senator John Kerry, the 2004 Democratic presidential nominee (Glionna, 2004). The FBI has also engaged in illegal break-ins, installed taps on telephones, falsified the credit ratings of some individuals on the subversive list, obtained their tax returns, staged arrests by local police on narcotic pretexts, made anonymous phone calls to friends or family members of some targets telling them of immoral or radical conduct, provided distorted information to civil rights and antiwar organizations in an attempt to create dissension and disruption within the group, and tried to disrupt marriages of suspected dissidents by sending anonymous letters to husbands, wives, or newspaper gossip columnists (*Newsweek*, 1979:45). As late as 1972, the FBI had close to 7,500 "ghetto informants" on its payroll and still maintains a network of 1,500 "domestic intelligence" informants whom it pays $7.4 million a year (Wise, 1978:400).

The Internal Revenue Service (IRS), with more than 106,000 employees in 1998 (Worsham, 1998:17), is the most feared and powerful of all federal agencies. As possibly the most powerful instrument of social control in the United States, the IRS decides on a wide range of matters that are far removed from the collection of taxes (Burnham, 1989, 1996). The power of the IRS is based on several factors. It is the largest federal law enforcement agency. It has a computerized national database unmatched by any other agency. To collect information it deems necessary, the IRS has the power to order—without warrant—banks, employers, and others to provide data about a taxpayer. (Other law enforcement agencies *must* obtain a warrant to get such information.) Not surprisingly, revenue agents also mine information posted on social-networking Web sites such as Facebook and MySpace dealing with relocation announcements, financial boasts, or professional profiles and are steady users of various search engines such as Google (Saunders, 2009).

The IRS also has the authority to impose civil penalties. If a taxpayer feels that the penalty is not justified, the penalty can be challenged. However, because of the special nature of civil tax law, the legal burden of proving one's innocence almost always rests on the taxpayer. This is in contrast to the criminal law, where the burden of proving a suspect's guilt rests with the government. The IRS can also make a "jeopardy assessment"—that is, without prior approval of a judge, the IRS can seize the assets of any taxpayer suspected of contemplating flight. All these powers are stated in the some 2,200 pages of the Internal Revenue Code of the United States. It is worth noting that the IRS regulations interpreting the law require an additional 7,600 pages.

The average American may never have any dealings with the FBI, the CIA, or similar organizations, but he or she comes in contact at least once a year with the IRS, on April 15. The tax system in the United States essentially rests on voluntary compliance. At the heart of the tax system is the citizens' trust and belief that the government will not use the vast powers of the IRS to punish citizens for their political views. That confidence was rudely shattered by the events of Watergate.

The congressional investigations that followed showed that one harassing tactic of the Nixon administration directed at its "enemies" was to subject them to frequent tax audits. The IRS, under pressure by the Nixon administration, established a secret section that eventually became known as the Special Services Staff (SSS). Operating under what was called "red seal" security, and situated in the basement of IRS headquarters in Washington, the SSS acted like a clandestine intelligence unit, in close liaison with the FBI, and compiled files on 8,585 persons and 2,873 organizations (Wise, 1978:326). The SSS was "given responsibility for investigating and collecting intelligence on 'ideological, militant, subversive, radical and similar type organizations' and individuals (and) . . . 'non-violent' groups and individuals, including draft-card burners, peace demonstrators and persons who 'organize and attend rock festivals which attract youth and narcotics'" (Wise, 1978:327). The IRS, like the FBI, became an instrument for social control, making its own judgments about what political views and cultural preferences were acceptable.

The Army Intelligence unit and the highly secret National Security Agency (NSA) have both been actively involved in the surveillance of dissenters. The NSA for years was reading and listening in on international communications. In the 1960s, for example, Western Union, Winston International, and ITT Corporation made available copies of international cables to the NSA in "Operation Shamrock." Later, when some of the communications companies switched to storing their cables on magnetic tape, NSA transported the tapes daily to its headquarters in Maryland for copying and then back to New York the same day. When these round trips became too burdensome, the CIA, in the guise of a television tape-processing company, provided the NSA with office space to copy the tapes in New York.

The government, through these various intelligence agencies, has, indeed, created a system of institutionalized social control of dissent. The government has shown a strong tendency to closely watch the activities of people who threaten it by collecting, concealing, suppressing, and manipulating information (Moynihan, 1998). Obviously, the government has to exert some control over its citizens, but in exerting control, care needs to be exercised to protect individuals' rights as guaranteed by the Constitution. There is a thin line between governmental control of dissent and the creation of a police state. Technology is also a new disturbance to the delicate balance between the privacy rights of citizens and the growing power of government to invade privacy (see, for example, Bloss, 2010; Cox, 2006; Goold and Neyland, 2009; Rule, 2009). And this is further exacerbated by the relentless information gathering on the market transforming shoppers into "glass consumers" (Lace, 2005). We are all "glass consumers." Organizations know so much about us that they can almost see through us. Governments and businesses collect and process our personal information on a massive scale. Everything we do, and everywhere we go, leaves a trail (Nissenbaum, 2009).

This control technology is ubiquitous in the modern state. To illustrate the potentials of just one aspect of that technology, there are millions of computers in use in the federal government providing electronic access to more than 35 billion records. There is even a monitoring technology that records keystrokes on a personal computer (Schwartz, 2001). Social security numbers have become national "identifiers," and the protections of the 1974 Privacy Act are eroded because the information in the database can be used with little notice or recourse. "Computer matches"—the cross-checking of records by one agency against another—are conducted routinely (Havemann, 1986). This is how the government is withholding the income tax refunds of student loan and other loan defaulters. Well over a decade ago, the technology was already available to create an electronic dossier on every citizen in the United States (Ramirez, 1992; *Time*, 1991). Flowing from the September 11, 2001, terrorist act, the U.S. Department of Homeland Security has been created along with demands on the attorney general for the establishment of a cross-agency, cross-platform electronic system that includes face recognition, electronic finger printing, retinal scan technology, hand geometry assayers, face recognition software, and smart cards with custom identification chips that were already almost fully implemented around mid 2010s (see, for example, Casey, 2009; Martin, 2011).

Horror stories already abound. For example, for almost 30 years, a state legislative committee spied on 20,000 Californians, documenting their personal habits, social lives, and political and professional relationships, and it has yet to release the 80 cartons of information gathered (Kennedy, 1998). From time to time, target groups are even required to pay a fee for being tracked. For example, the United States Immigration and Naturalization Services (INS) has started to instrument a $90 fee for international students during the summer of 2001 to help pay for the technology that will track them. It too will have a nationwide computer data base. The rationale is to try to minimize the risk of terrorism by keeping close surveillance on foreign students (see, for example, Hamm, 2007). Perhaps it is time to start thinking about some effective controls and checks to be devised and imposed upon the users of this technology so that they do not overstep the boundaries as happened in the Nixon era. If not, as many social commentators suggest, privacy may just become extinct (Kerr, 2004), civil rights may be sacrificed for security (Welsh and Farrington, 2009), and there will be additional breakdowns of traditional boundaries between public and private space resulting in substantial reduction of autonomy and privacy (Suk, 2009).

ADMINISTRATIVE LAW AND SOCIAL CONTROL

A broadly and popularly held misconception about the law is that it consists almost entirely of criminal law, with its apparatus of crime, police, prosecutors, judges, juries, sentences, and prisons. Another misconception is that all law can be divided into criminal law and civil law. But the resources of legal systems are far richer and more extensive than either of these views implies (Summers and Howard, 1972:198). This section is concerned with how distinctive legal ways can be used to control what Robert S. Summers and George G. Howard (1972:199) call "private primary activity." They use this concept to describe various pursuits, such as production and marketing of electricity and natural gas; provision and operation of rail, air, and other transport facilities; food processing and distribution; construction of buildings, bridges, and other public facilities; and radio and television broadcasting. But these activities are not confined to large-scale affairs such as electrical production and provision of air transport. The list can be expanded to include provision of medical services by physicians, ownership and operation of motor vehicles by ordinary citizens, construction of residences by local carpenters, and the sale and purchase of stocks and bonds by private individuals. Private primary activities not only are positively desirable in themselves, but also are essential for the functioning of modern societies. These activities generate legal needs that are met through administrative control mechanisms (see, for example, Beermann, 2006; Warren, 2010).

Today, all kinds of services are needed, such as those provided by physicians, transport facilities, and electric companies. But an incompetent physician might kill rather than cure a patient. An unqualified airline pilot might crash, killing everyone on board. A food processor might poison half a community. In addition to incompetence or carelessness, deliberate abuses are also possible. An individual may lose his or her entire savings through fraudulent stock operations. A utility company might abuse its monopoly position and charge exorbitant rates. An owner of a nuclear waste disposal facility may want to cut corners, thus exposing the public to harmful radiation.

Private primary activities, Summers and Howard (1972:199) note, can cause harm, avoidable harm. At the same time, such activities can have great potential for good. Airplanes can almost be made safe, and stock and consumer frauds by fly-by-night operators can be reduced. Legal control of these activities is then justified on two grounds—the prevention of harm and the promotion of good. For example, in the case of radio and television broadcasting, laws can be concerned with both the control of obscenity and the problem of balanced programming, such as covering public affairs in addition to entertainment and sports. Control is exerted on private primary activity through administrative laws, primarily in the context of licensing, inspection, and the threat of publicity.

Licensing

The power of administrative law goes beyond the setting of standards and the punishing of those who fail to comply. Horack notes, "The belief that law enforcement is better achieved by prevention than by prosecution has contributed to the emergence of administrative regulation as a primary means of government control" (quoted by Summers and Howard, 1972:202). Requiring and granting licenses to perform certain activities is a classic control device. Licensing is pervasive, and by one estimate, at least 5,000 different licenses have been granted to more than 5,000 occupations (Simon et al., 1992:542). With so many groups being licensed in one state or another, licensing as a form of social control affects a substantial portion of the labor force. Nowadays, a license may be required to engage in an occupation, to operate a business, to serve specific customers or areas, or to manufacture certain products (see, for example, Tashbook, 2004). Physicians and lawyers must obtain specific training and then demonstrate some competence before they can qualify for licenses to practice. Here, licensing is used to enforce basic qualifying standards. Airplane companies just cannot fly any route they wish, and broadcasters are not free to pick a frequency at will. Underlying all regulatory licensing is a denial of a right to engage in the contemplated activity except with a license.

The control of professions and certain activities through licensing is justified as protection for the public against inferior, fraudulent, or dangerous services and products. But, under this rubric, control has been extended to occupations that, at the most, only minimally affect public health and safety. In some states, licenses are required for cosmetologists, auctioneers, weather-control practitioners, taxidermists, junkyard operators, and weather-vane installers. To be a manicurist in the state of Washington, one must take 600 hours of training and pass both a written exam and a skill demonstration, and to cut hair, one needs 1,000 hours of training and two tests. Movie projectionists need a license in Massachusetts; college math teachers in Florida; and drywall installers along with paper-hangers, upholsterers, and fence erectors in California (*Forbes*, 2004). Hawaii licenses tattoo artists; and New Hampshire, lightning-rod salespeople. In Delaware, 86 occupations are licensed, including circus exhibitors, bowling-alley operators, and billiard-parlor owners. Until slightly over a couple of decades ago, it was a misdemeanor for someone without a license to repair a watch in North Carolina. The penalty was a six-month jail sentence, the same as for practicing medicine without a license (*U.S. News & World Report*, 1979:70). In 2007, Louisiana still required flower arrangers to pass a design exam, one with a failure rate of about 50 percent. Critics charge that this exam, judged by already-licensed florists with established businesses, is meant only to keep potential competitors out of the business and to protect their economic interests.

In addition to requiring a license to practice these occupations, control is exerted through the revocation or suspension of the license. For example, under administrative law, the state may withdraw the right to practice from a lawyer, a physician, or a beautician, and it may suspend a bar or restaurant owner from doing business a few days, a year, or even permanently. A study by Roger L. Goldman and Steven Puro (2001) on the police points out that a very common approach to addressing misconduct in police departments is the revocation of the offending officer's license or state certificate, which is obtained after the completion of a state-mandated training. They note that revocation of license is more effective than termination, which does not really prevent an officer to obtain employment in another department. This little-known way of handling police misconduct by the general public has been successfully adopted by 43 states.

Local, state, and federal administrative controls through licensing are widely used mechanisms of social control. Administrative laws generally specify the conditions under which a license is required, the requirements that must be met by applicants, the duties imposed upon the licensees, the agency authorized to issue such licenses, the procedures in revoking licenses and the grounds that constitute cause for revocation, and the penalties for violations.

Inspection

Administrative law grants broad investigatory and inspection powers to regulatory agencies (Reed, 2010). Periodic inspection is a way of monitoring ongoing activities under the jurisdiction of a particular agency. Such inspections determine whether cars and trains can move, planes can fly (see, for example, Wald, 1998), agricultural products can meet quality standards, newspapers can obtain second-class mailing privileges, and so forth. Similar procedures are used to prevent the distribution of unsafe foods and drugs, to prohibit the entry of diseased plants and animals into the country, or to suspend the license of a pilot pending a disciplinary hearing.

In a variety of industries and businesses, government inspectors operate on the premises. For example, when a U.S. Food and Drug Administration (FDA) inspector finds botulism in soup, the manufacturer will withdraw the product from grocers' and manufacturers' shelves and destroy all cans—because of the unstated but understood FDA threat to prosecute through the U.S. Department of Justice (Gellhorn and Levin, 1997).

Inspections constitute a primary tool of administrative supervision and control. For instance, the nation's banks are overseen by the Federal Reserve Board and the Federal Deposit Insurance Corporation through visits by their inspectors for examination of the bank's records. A housing official may inspect buildings to determine compliance with building codes. In some instances, inspection takes place occasionally, such as when ensuring compliance with building codes. In other instances, inspection is continuous, as in food inspection. Both forms of inspection, sporadic and continuous, also exert pressure for self-regulation and contribute to the maintenance of internal controls specified by the law. At times, these inspections may also lead to proposals for corrective legislation governing regulatory standards.

Threat of Publicity

In small communities where people tend to know each other, adversely publicizing wrongdoers can have a significant effect on changing their behavior. Such a system of social control normally would not work in an urban industrial society for individual deviance. Large companies selling widely known brand name products might, however, be greatly influenced by the threat of well-circulated publicity. For example, the publicity surrounding the secret internal documents of the Ford Motor Company on defective and recalled Pintos, which showed that needed structural fuel tank improvements at the cost of about $11 per car and which could have prevented 180 fiery deaths a year, resulted in a significant drop in market share for the company (Fisse and Braithwaite, 1993).

Perhaps the most potent tool in any administrator's hands is the power to publicize (Gellhorn and Levin, 1997). A publicity release detailing the character of a suspected offense and the offender involved can inflict immediate damage. For instance, just before Thanksgiving in 1959, the secretary of health, education, and welfare destroyed practically the entire cranberry market by announcing at a press conference that some cranberries were contaminated by a cancer-producing agent. The effectiveness and power of publicity as a control mechanism were again confirmed by the announcement that botulism in a can of soup had killed a man. The publicity led to the bankruptcy of Bon Vivant Soup Company (Gellhorn and Levin, 1997). It should be noted, however, that this power of control is not confined to public officials. For example, the demise of the Corvair is directly attributable to Ralph Nader's book, *Unsafe at Any Speed* (1965), and his subsequent efforts.

In many areas, publicity serves a highly useful, if not indispensable, control function. The 1970 federal air-pollution legislation, for example, provides for making known to the public the extent to which each automobile manufacturer is complying with the auto emission standards of the United States Environmental Protection Agency. Quite often, polluting companies agree to cease and desist orders of administrative agencies out of fear of the consequences of adverse publicity (Nagel, 1975:347). Furthermore, in the enforcement of legislation protecting consumers against the manufacture and sale of impure food and drugs, the ability of administrative agencies to inform the public that a product may contain harmful ingredients can play an important role in preventing consumption of the product under investigation until the accuracy of this suspicion can be determined.

In some cases, however, firms that have a monopoly on their products, such as local gas and electric companies, are not likely to be hurt by adverse publicity. Agencies are, at times, also reluctant to stigmatize firms, because adverse publicity is considered a form of informal adjudication, although it is often used and justified by the notion that people have a right to know.

SUMMARY

This chapter has considered law as a mechanism of formal social control. Law comes into play when other forms of social control are weak, ineffective, or unavailable. Individuals and groups are led to behave in acceptable ways through the processes of socialization and external pressures in the form of sanctions from others. Mechanisms of social control through external pressures may be formal and informal, and include both negative and positive sanctions. Informal social controls are exemplified in the functions of folkways and mores. Informal social controls tend to be effective when there is intense social interaction on an intimate face-to-face basis, normative consensus, and surveillance of the behavior of members of the community (see, for example, Norris and Wilson, 2007). Formal social controls are characteristic of more complex societies with a greater division of labor and different sets of mores, values, and ideologies. Formal social controls arise when informal controls are insufficient to maintain conformity to certain norms. Laws are one type of formal social control. Other types of formal social controls rely on both penalties and rewards, whereas control through the law is exercised primarily, but not exclusively, by the use of punishments to regulate behavior.

The social control of criminal and delinquent behavior represents the most highly structured formal system used by society to attempt to control deviant behavior (see, for example, Brudner, 2009). The concept *legalization* describes the process by which norms are moved from the social to the legal level. It also entails the incorporation of specific punishments for special kinds of criminal law violators. The goals of punishment are retribution or social retaliation, incapacitation, and both specific and general deterrence. Punishment is a deterrent in situations that involve low-commitment individuals who engage in instrumental crimes. The death penalty, as the most severe form of punishment, remains controversial, and there is no agreement on its deterrent effect.

Formal control of deviant behavior is not limited to criminal sanctions. The use of civil commitment as a mechanism of legal control is more widespread. In civil commitment, there are no procedural safeguards available for the defendant. Civil commitment operates through the process of defining deviant behavior as a mental disorder, and it includes the involuntary commitment of alcoholics, drug addicts, sex offenders, and troublesome teenagers. It allows mental health professionals, particularly psychiatrists, to exercise considerable judicial power by placing individuals in institutions without the guarantee of a trial.

The United States invests enormous resources in controlling victimless crimes. These are crimes *mala prohibita* and are differentiated from other crimes by the element of consensual transaction or exchange. Those who are involved in these crimes are willing participants, who, as a rule, do not complain to the police that a crime has been committed.

It was shown that the legal control of victimless crimes, such as drug addiction, prostitution, and gambling, tends to be generally expensive, and ineffective, and often leads to the corruption of law enforcement agents.

White-collar crimes constitute a greater threat to the welfare of society than more traditional kinds of crime. The notion of white-collar crime incorporates both occupational and corporate crimes. Some persons commit crimes in connection with their occupation; others do it while promoting the interest of a corporation for which they work. Corporate crime is a relatively recent phenomenon in the United States. The three broad types of legal control of corporate activities are prospective, processual, and retrospective. In general, laws dealing with corporate crime are ineffective, and the sanctions are insufficient to act as effective deterrents. Corporations tend to consider law violation and the resulting fine as part of their regular business expenses.

The social control of dissent is accomplished through the various selection processes, the manipulation of the structure of material benefits, and the use of coercive control mechanisms. In the past, the American government has relied heavily on the operations of various intelligence agencies to create a system of institutionalized social control of dissent.

Control through administrative law is exercised in the context of licensing, inspection, and the use of publicity as a threat. A license is an official permit to engage in certain types of activities. In addition to requiring a license to practice certain occupations or carry out certain activities, control can also be exercised through the revocation or suspension of the license in instances of noncompliance. Inspection allows a way of monitoring ongoing activities under the jurisdiction of a particular agency. It may be sporadic or continuous, and both forms exert pressure for self-regulation and contribute to the maintenance of internal controls specified by law. The threat of adverse publicity is considered a powerful administrative control mechanism. Because most large companies are sensitive to adverse publicity, administrative agencies can use the threat of such publicity to ensure compliance with the law. In the next chapter, the law as a method of conflict resolution will be considered.

SUGGESTED FURTHER READINGS

Phillip Bean, *Legalizing Drugs: Debates and Dilemmas*. Bristol, UK: Policy Press, 2010. The war on drugs continues along with new legislations and debates about them. This book provides a balanced account of this moral, legal, and political minefield.

Roger Cotterrell (ed.), *Emile Durkheim: Justice, Morality, and Politics*. Burlington, VT: Ashgate, 2010.

Jack P. Gibbs (ed.), *Social Control: Views from the Social Sciences*. Beverly Hills, CA.: Sage Publications, 1982. A compilation of classic papers from influential scholars in several fields regarding the notion of social control, psychological, political—in their disciplines. Several conceptual, theoretical, and empirical issues are identified and discussed.

Allan V. Horwitz, *The Social Control of Mental Illness*. Clinton Corners, NY: Percheron Press, 2002. *Creating Mental Illness*, Chicago, IL: University of Chicago Press, 2002. Both books deal, albeit from a slightly different perspective, with series of case studies on the social control of mental illness in the theoretical framework of Donald Black's *The Behavior of Law*.

REFERENCES

Abadinsky, Howard. 2010. *Drug Use and Abuse: A Comprehensive Introduction.* 7th ed. Belmont, CA: Cengage/Wadsworth.

Abel, Gillian, Lisa Fitzgerald, Catherine Healy, and Aline Taylor (eds.). 2010. *Taking the Crime out of Sex Work: New Zealand Sex Workers' Fight for Decriminalization.* Bristol, UK: Policy Press.

Aday, David P., Jr. 1990. *Social Control at the Margins: Toward a General Understanding of Deviance.* Belmont, CA: Wadsworth.

Adler, Freda, and Herbert M. Adler. 1975. *Sisters in Crime: The Rise of the New Female Criminal.* New York: McGraw-Hill.

Allyn, David. 2004. *I Can't Believe I just Did That: How Seemingly Small Embarrassments Can Wreak Havoc in Your Life—And What You Can Do to Put a Stop to Them.* New York: Jeremy P. Tarcher/Penguin.

Ang, Audra. 2006. "China Tightens Rules on Executions," *Seattle Times* (November 1): A9.

Appelbaum, Paul S. 1992. "Civil Commitment from a Systems Perspective," *Law and Human Behavior* 16 (1) (February): 61–74.

Arrigo, Bruce A. 2002. *Punishing the Mentally Ill: A Critical Analysis of Law and Psychiatry.* Albany, NY: State University of New York Press.

Aujla, Simmi, and Jennifer Levitz. 2009. "Rhode Island Tires of Loophole on Prostitution." *Wall Street Journal* (September 5–6): A5.

Baggins, David Sadofsky. 1998. *Drug Hate and the Corruption of American Justice.* Westport, CT: Praeger Publishers/Greenwood Publishing Group, Inc.

Bailey, William C., and Ruth D. Peterson. 1994. "Murder, Capital Punishment, and Deterrence: A Review of the Evidence and an Examination of Police Killings," *Journal of Social Issues,* 50 (2) (Summer): 53–75.

Beckett, Katherine, and Theodore Sasson. 2004. *The politics of Injustice: Crime and Punishment in America.* 2nd ed. Thousand Oaks, CA: Sage Publications.

Bedau, Hugo Adam, and Paul G. Cassell (eds.). 2004. *Debating the Death Penalty: Should America Have Capital Punishment?: The Experts on Both Sides Make Their Best Case.* New York: Oxford University Press.

Beermann, Jack M. 2006. *Administrative Law.* 2nd ed. New York: Aspen Publishers.

Belluck, Pam. 1998. "Forget Prisons: Americans Cry Out for the Pillory," *New York Times* (October 4).

Benjamin, Daniel K., and Roger Leroy Miller. 1992. *Undoing Drugs.* Washington, DC: Drug Policy Foundation.

Benson, Michael L., and Francis T. Cullen. 1998. *Combating Corporate Crime: Local Prosecutors at Work.* Boston, MA: Northeastern University Press.

Berlow, Alan. 2001. "The Broken Machinery of Death," *American Prospect* (July 30): 16–17.

Bloss, William P. 2010. *Under a Watchful Eye: Private Rights and Criminal Justice.* Santa Barbara, CA: Praeger.

Boggs, Sarah L. 1971. "Formal and Informal Crime Control: An Exploratory Study of Urban, Suburban, and Rural Orientations," *Sociological Quarterly,* 12 (1) (Summer): 319–327.

Bosworth, Mary. 2010. *Explaining U.S. Imprisonment.* Thousands Oaks, CA: Sage.

Boyd-Caine, Tessa. 2009. *Protecting the Public? Executive Discretion and the Release of Mentally Disordered Offenders.* Devon, UK: Willan Publishing.

Branegan, Jay. 1998. "China—Photo-Op Diplomacy," *Time* (July 6): 36–37.

Brooks, Thom (ed.). 2009. *The Rights to a Fair Trial.* Burlington, VT: Ashgate.

Brooks, Thom. 2010. *Punishment.* New York: Routledge.

Bruce, John M., and Clyde Wilcox (eds.). 1998. *The Changing Politics of Gun Control.* Blue Ridge Summit, PA: Rowman and Littlefield.

Brudner, Alan. 2009. *Punishment and Freedom.* New York: Oxford University Press.

Bull, Melissa. 2009. *Governing the Heroin Trade: From Treaties to Treatment.* Burlington, VT: Ashgate.

Burbick, Joan. 2006. *Gun Show Nation: Gun Culture and American Democracy.* New York: New Press/W. W. Norton.

Burnham, David. 1989. "The Abuse of Power: Misuse of the IRS" *New York Times Magazine* (September 3): 24–61. 1996. *Above the Law: Secret Deals, Political Fixes, and Other Misadventures of the U.S. Department of Justice.* New York: Scribner.

Butterfield, Fox. 2004. "Study Tracks Boom in Prisons and Notes Impact on Counties," *New York Times* (April 30): A1; A9.

Calavita, Kitty, and Henry N. Pontell. 1994. "The State of White-Collar Crime: Saving the Savings and Loans," *Law & Society Review*, 28 (2) (May): 297–324.

Canter, David, Maria Ioannou, and Donna Youngs (eds.). 2009. *Safer Sex in the City: The Experience and Management of Street Prostitution.* Burlington, VT: Ashgate.

Casey, Timothy. 2009. *The USA Patriot Act: The Decline of Legitimacy in the Age of Terrorism.* New York: Oxford University Press.

Chambliss, William J. 1975. "Types of Deviance and the Effectiveness of Legal Sanctions." Pp. 398–407 in William J. Chambliss (ed.), *Criminal Law in Action.* Santa Barbara, CA: Hamilton Publishing Company. 1978. *On the Take: From Petty Crooks to Presidents.* Bloomington, IN: Indiana University Press.

Christenson, Ron. 1999. *Political Trials: Gordian Knots in the Law.* 2nd ed. Somerset, NJ: Transaction Publishers.

Christianson, Scott. 2004. *Innocent: Inside Wrongful Conviction Cases.* New York: New York University Press. 2010. *The Last Gasp: The Rise and Fall of the American Gas Chamber.* Berkeley, CA: University of California Press.

Clark, Ramsey. 1971. *Crime in America.* New York: Pocket Books.

Clinard, Marshall B., and Daniel J. Abbott. 1973. *Crime in Developing Countries: A Comparative Perspective.* New York: John Wiley.

Clinard, Marshall B., and Robert F. Meier. 2010. *Sociology of Deviant Behavior.* 14th ed. Belmont, CA: Wadsworth/Thomson Learning.

Coleman, James W. 2006. *The Criminal Elite: Understanding White-Collar Crime.* 6th ed. New York: Worth Publishers.

Comer, Michael J. 2003. *Investigating Corporate Fraud.* Burlington, VT: Ashgate.

Commission on the Review of the National Policy toward Gambling. 1976. *Gambling in America.* Washington, DC: U.S. Government Printing Office.

Conrad, Peter. 1996. "The Medicalization of Deviance in American Culture," Pp. 69–77 in Earl Rubington and Martin S. Weinberg (eds.), *Deviance: The Interactionist Perspective.* 6th ed. Boston, MA: Allyn and Bacon.

Cony, Ed, and Stanley Penn. 1986. "Tale of a Kite," *Wall Street Journal* (August 11): 1, 10.

Cook, Philip J. 1989. "The Economics of Criminal Sanctions." Pp. 50–78 in Martin Lawrence Friedland (ed.), *Sanctions and Rewards in the Legal System: A Multidisciplinary Approach.* Toronto, Canada: University of Toronto Press.

Costanzo, Mark. 1997. *Just Revenge: Costs and Consequences of the Death Penalty.* New York: St. Martin's Press.

Cox, Noel. 2006. *Technology and Legal Systems.* Burlington, VA: Ashgate.

Cozic, Charles P., and Paul A. Winters (eds.). 1995. *Gambling.* San Diego, CA: Greenhaven Press.

Cram, Ian. 2006. *Contested Words: Legal Restrictions on Freedom of Speech in Liberal Democracies.* Burlington, VT: Ashgate.

Croall, Hazel. 1989. "Who Is the White-Collar Criminal?" *British Journal of Criminology*, 29 (2): 157–174. 2010. *Corporate Crime.* Three-volume set. Thousand Oaks, CA: Sage.

Cukier, Wendy, and Victor W. Sidel. 2006. *The Global Gun Epidemic.* Portsmouth, NH: Greenwood Publishing Group.

Culver, John H. 1992. "Capital Punishment, 1977–1990: Characteristics of the 143 Executed," *Sociology and Social Research*, 76 (2) (January): 59–61.

Currie, Elliott. 1998. *Crime and Punishment in America.* New York: Metropolitan Books/ Henry Holt and Company.

Cusac, Anne-Marie. 2009. *Cruel and Unusual: The Culture of Punishment in America*. New Haven, CT: Yale University Press.

Daley, Suzanne. 2001. "New Rights for Dutch Prostitutes, but No Gain," *New York Times* (August 12): 1.

Dallaire, Bernadette, Michael McCubbin, Paul Morin, and David Cohen. 2000. "Civil Commitment Due to Mental Illness and Dangerousness: The Union of Law and Psychiatry within a Treatment-Control System," *Sociology of Health and Illness*, 22 (5) (September):679–699.

Darnton, Nina. 1989. "Committed Youth," *Newsweek* (July 31): 66–72.

Davis, Nanette J. (ed.). 1993. *Prostitution: An International Handbook on Trends, Problems, and Policies*. Westport, CON: Greenwood Press.

De Kort, Marcel, and Dirk J. Korf. 1992. "The Development of Drug Control in the Netherlands: A Historical Perspective," *Crime, Law, and Social Change*, 17 (2) (March): 123–144.

Diamant, Neil J., Stanley B. Lubman, and Kevin J. O'Brien (eds.). 2005. *Engaging the Law in China: State, Society, and Possibilities for Justice*. Stanford, CA: Stanford University Press.

Diamond, Sigmund. 1992. *Compromised Campus: The Collaboration of Universities with the Intelligence Community, 1945–1955*. New York: Oxford University Press.

Diesfeld, Kate, and Ian Freckelton (eds.). 2003. *Involuntary Detention and Therapeutic Jurisprudence: International Perspectives on Civil Commitment*. Burlington, VT: Ashgate/ Dartmouth.

Duff, Peter. 1997. "Diversion from Prosecution into Psychiatric Care: Who Controls the Gates?" *British Journal of Criminology*, 37 (1) (Winter): 15–34.

Eckholm, Erik. 1995. "Studies Find Death Penalty Often Tied to Victim's Race," *New York Times* (February 24): A1, A11.

Economist. 1990. "The Politics of Death" (March 24): 25–26. 1995. "The Waiting Game" (April 1): 19–21. 2001. "High Time: A Survey of Illegal Drugs" (July 28): 1–16. 2004. "The Case against the Prosecution" (February 28): 57–58. 2006a. "Ingenious Punishments: Their Object All Sublime—A Vogue for Shaming Wrongdoers" (October 14): 31. 2006b. "Special Report: Online Gambling" (October 7): 13–14, 77–78. 2007a. "Private Jails: Locking in the Best Price" (January 27): 60–61. 2007b. "Capital Punishment: Here is Thy Sting. More and More Countries Have Doubts about the Death Penalty" (April 28): 69–70. 2009. "Corporate Crimes on the Rise. The Rot Spreads. A Survey Reveals that Desperate Times Have Led to Illegal Measures" (November 21): 69. 2010. "A Matter of Life and Death: Setbacks for Opponents of Capital Punishment, but They Are Making More Progress than Meets the Eye" (March 27): 50.

Ehrlich, Isaac. 1975. "The Deterrent Effect of Capital Punishment: A Question of Life or Death," *American Economic Review*, 65:397–417.

Erikson, Kai T. 1966. *Wayward Puritans: A Study in the Sociology of Deviance*. New York: John Wiley.

Faupel, Charles E., Alan M. Horowitz, and Greg S. Weaver. 2009. *The Sociology of American Drug Use*. 2nd ed. New York: Oxford University Press.

Federal Bureau of Investigation. 2010. *Uniform Crime Reports for the United States, 2009*. Washington, DC: U.S. Department of Justice.

Fein, Esther. 1992. "Working to Nourish Democracy Where Minds Are Being Starved," *New York Times* (August 16): E9.

Ferguson, Christopher J. (ed.). 2010. *Violent Crime: Clinical and Social Implications*. Thousand Oaks, CA: Sage.

Finch, Emily, and Stefan Fafinski. 2010. *Identity Theft*. Devon, UK: Willan Publishing.

Fisher, Joseph C. 1997. *Killer among Us: Public Reactions to Serial Murder*. Westport, CT: Praeger Trade/Greenwood Publishing Group, Inc.

Fisse, Brent, and John Braithwaite. 1993. "The Impact of Publicity on Corporate Offenders: The Ford Motor Company and the Pinto Papers." Pp. 627–640 in Delos H. Kelly (ed.), *Deviant Behavior: A Text-Reader in the*

Sociology of Deviance. New York: St. Martin's Press.

Flynn, Sean. 2007. "Is Gambling Good for America?" *Seattle Times* (May 20): 4–5.

Focus on Law Studies. 2003. "Gun Laws and Policies: A Dialogue," 18 (2) (Spring): 1–20.

Forbes. 1985. "Startling Statistics" (November 4): 28. 2004. "Protecting an Innocent Public From Untrained Flower Arrangers" (April 26): 36.

Forst, Martin L. 1978. *Civil Commitment and Social Control.* Lexington, MA: Heath.

Foucault, Michel. 1977. *Discipline and Punish: The Birth of the Prison.* Trans. Alan Sheridan. New York: Pantheon.

Friedland, Martin Lawrence (ed.). 1989. *Sanctions and Rewards in the Legal System: A Multidisciplinary Approach.* Toronto, Canada: University of Toronto Press.

Friedman, Lawrence N. 1998. *American Law: An Introduction.* 2nd ed. New York: W. W. Norton & Co., Inc.

Friedrichs, David O. 2010. *Trusted Criminals: White Collar Crime in Contemporary Society.* 4th ed. Belmont, CA: Cengage Wadsworth.

Friendly, Alfred, and Ronald L. Goldfarb. 1967. *Crime and Publicity: The Impact of News on the Administration of Justice.* New York: The Twentieth Century Fund.

Gangoli, Geetanjali, and Nicole Westmarland (eds.). 2006. *International Approaches to Prostitution: Law and Policy in Europe and Asia.* Bristol, UK: Policy Press.

Garland, David. 2001. *The Culture of Control: Crime and Social Order in Contemporary Society.* Chicago, IL: University of Chicago Press.

Garofalo, James, and Maureen McLeod. 1989. "The Structure and Operations of Neighborhood Watch Programs in the United States," *Crime & Delinquency,* 35 (3): 326–344.

Geis, Gilbert. 1978. "Deterring Corporate Crime." Pp. 278–296 in M. David Ermann and Richard J. Lundman (eds.), *Corporate and Governmental Deviance: Problems of Organizational Behavior in Contemporary Society.* New York: Oxford University Press. 1979. *Not the Law's Business: An Examination of Homosexuality, Abortion, Prostitution, Narcotics, and Gambling in the United States.*

New York: Schocken Books. 1994. "Corporate Crime: 'Three Strikes You're Out?'" *Multinational Monitor,* 15 (6) (June): 30–31.

Gellhorn, Ernest, and Ronald M. Levin. 1997. *Administrative Law and Process in a Nutshell.* 4th ed. St. Paul, MN: West Publishing Company.

Gettman, Jon. 2006. "Marijuana Production in the United States (2006)," Volume 2 (December), *The Bulletin of Cannabis Reform.*

Glaser, Daniel. 1971. "Criminology and Public Policy," *American Sociologist,* 6 (6) (June): 30–37.

Glassman, James K. 1986. "Going to Seed," *New Republic* (August 25): 11–13.

Glionna, John M. 2004. "FBI Tracked Kerry's Anti-War Activities," *Seattle Times* (March 23): A4.

Goldman, Roger L., and Steven Puro. 2001. "Revocation of Police Officer Certification: A Viable Remedy for Police Misconduct?" *Saint Louis University Law Journal,* 45 (2) (Spring): 541–580.

Goode, Erich. 2008. *Drugs in American Society.* 7th ed. San Francisco, CA: McGraw-Hill College.

Goold, Benjamin J., and Daniel Neyland (eds.). 2009. *New Directions in Surveillance and Privacy.* Devon, UK: Willan Publishing.

Grabowski, John (ed.). 1984. *Cocaine: Pharmacology, Effects, and Treatment of Abuse.* NIDA Research Monograph 50. National Institute on Drug Abuse. Washington, DC: U.S. Government Printing Office.

Green, Stuart P. 2006. *Lying, Cheating, and Stealing: A Moral Theory of White-Collar Crime.* New York: Oxford University Press.

Greenaway, William K., and Stephan L. Brickey (eds.). 1978. *Law and Social Control in Canada.* Scarborough, Ontario, Canada: Prentice Hall of Canada, Ltd.

Grinols, Earl L. 2004. *Gambling in America: Costs and Benefits.* Cambridge, UK: New York: Cambridge University Press.

Gross, Samuel R., and Robert Mauro. 1989. *Death and Discrimination: Racial Disparities in Capital Sentencing.* Boston, MA: Northeastern University Press.

Haines, Herb. 1992. "Flawed Executions, the Anti-Death Penalty Movement, and the Politics of Capital Punishment," *Social Problems,* 39 (2) (May): 125–138.

Hallinan, Joseph. 2001. *Going Up the River: Travels in a Prison Nation.* New York: Random House.

Hamm, Mark S. 2007. *Terrorism as Crime. From Oklahoma City to Al-Qaeda and Beyond.* New York: New York University Press.

Hanawalt, Barbara A. 1998. *'Of God and Ill Repute'—Gender and Social Control in Medieval England.* New York: Oxford University Press.

Harcourt, Bernard E. (ed.). 2003. *Guns, Crime, and Punishment in America.* New York: New York University Press.

Havemann, Judith. 1986. "Federal Computers Are Putting a Glitch Into Laws on Privacy," *St. Louis Post-Dispatch* (July 12): B1.

Hemphill, Thomas A. 1993. "Penalties for Polluters: Finding a Fair Formula," *Business and Society Review* (Fall): 29–32.

Henderson, Harry. 2005. *Gun Control.* Revised ed. New York: Facts on File.

Henderson, Stephen. 2006. "Justice Show Divergence on Lethal Injection," *Seattle Times* (April 27): A5.

Hickey, Eric (ed.). 2003. *Encyclopedia of Murder and Violent Crime.* Thousand Oaks, CA: Sage Publications.

Hier, Sean P., and Josh Greenberg (eds.). 2010. *Surveillance: Power, Problems, and Politics.* Vancouver, BC: UBC Press.

Hil, Richard, and Gordon Tait (eds.). 2004. *Hard Lessons: Reflections on Governance and Crime Control in Late Modernity.* Aldershot, Hants, UK/Burlington, VT: Ashgate/Dartmouth.

Hilsenrath, Jon, and Brent Kendall. 2009. "Bernanke Falls Victim to Identity Theft," *Wall Street Journal* (August 28): A3.

Hoffman, Jan. 1997. "Crime and Punishment: Shame Gains Popularity," *New York Times* (January 16): A1, A11.

Holland, Kelley. 1995. "Bank Fraud: The Old Fashioned Way," *Business Week* (September 4): 96.

Holmes, Ronald M., and Stephen T. Holmes. 2010. *Serial Murder.* 3rd ed. Thousand Oaks, CA: Sage.

Hoo, Stephanie. 2003. "In China, Aggrieved Turn to Ancient Crime. Rat Poison Becomes Lethal Weapon of Choice for Those with a Grudge," *Seattle Times* (November 16): A17.

Horvath, Miranda, and Jennifer Brown (eds.). 2009. *Rape: Challenging Contemporary Thinking.* Devon, UK; Willan Publishing.

Husak, Douglas. 2010. *Overcriminalization: The Limits of Criminal Law.* New York: Oxford University Press.

Ignatius, Adi. 1989. "China's Golden Girls Monitor Neighbors," *Wall Street Journal* (August 1): A10.

Inciardi, James A., and Karen McElrath (eds.). 2008. *The American Drug Scene: An Anthology.* 5th ed. New York. Oxford University Press.

Irving, John. 1992. "Pornography and the New Puritans," *New York Times Book Review* (March 29): 1, 24–27.

Janowitz, Morris. 1976. *Social Control of the Welfare State.* New York: Elsevier North-Holland.

Jelinek, Pauline. 2006. "Identity Theft Hit 3.6 Million U.S. Households and Cost $3.2 Billion, Government Study Says," *Seattle Times* (April 3): A22.

Johnson, David T., and Franklin E. Zimring. 2009. *The Next Frontier: National Development, Political Change, and the Death Penalty in Asia.* New York: Oxford University Press.

Kaplan, David A. 1995. "Anger and Ambivalence," *Newsweek* (August 7): 24–29.

Karp, David R. 1998. "The Judicial and Judicious Use of Shame Penalties," *Crime & Delinquency,* 44 (2) (April): 277–294.

Kelleher, Michael D., and C. L. Kelleher. 1998. *Murder Most Rare: The Female Serial Killer.* Westport, CT: Praeger Trade/Greenwood Publishing Group, Inc.

Kempadoo, Kamala, and J. Doezema. 1998. *Global Sex Workers: Rights, Resistance, and Redefinition.* New York: Routledge.

Kennedy, Shawn. 1998. "California Weighs Release of Spying Records," *New York Times* (April 5): 18Y.

Kerr, Ian. 2004. "Look Out: The Eyes Have It." *Globe and Mail* (January 12): A11.

Kinsman, Gary, and Patrizia Gentile. 2010. *The Canadian War on Queers. National Security as Sexual Regulation*. Vancouver, BC: UBC Press.

Klockars, Carl B., Sanja Kutnjak Ivkovic, and M. R. Haberfeld (eds.). 2004. *The Contours of Police Integrity*. Thousand Oaks, CA: Sage Publications.

Krauss, Clifford. 2004. "Canadian Police Image Taking Hit Thanks to Scandals," *Seattle Times* (January 25); A13.

Kuo, Lenore. 2005. *Prostitution Policy: Revolutionizing Practice through a Gendered Perspective*. New York: New York University Press.

La Fave, Wayne R. 1965. *Arrest: The Decision to Take a Suspect into Custody*. Boston, MA: Little, Brown and the American Bar Foundation.

Lace, Suzanne (ed.). 2005. *The Glass Consumer: Life in a Surveillance Society*. Bristol, UK: Policy Press.

Landsman, Stephen. 1973. "Massachusetts' Comprehensive Alcoholism Law—Its History and Future," *Massachusetts Law Quarterly*, 58 (3) (Fall): 273–290.

Lears, T. J. Jackson. 2003. *Something for Nothing: Luck in America*. New York: Viking.

LeBor, Adam. 2010. *The Believers: How America Fell for Bernard Madoff's $65 Billion Investment Scam*. London, UK: Weidenfeld & Nicolson.

Lesieur, Henry R. 1992. "Compulsive Gambling," *Society*, 29 (4) (May/June): 43–50.

Levine, Martin Lyon (ed.). 2009. *Mental Illness, Medicine and Law*. Burlington, VT: Ashgate.

Lewin, Tamar. 1995. "Who Decides Who Will Die? Even Within States, It Varies," *New York Times* (February 23): A1, A13. 2001. "Breast-Feeding: How Old is Too Old?" *New York Times* (February 18).

Lieberman, Jethro K. 1972. *How the Government Breaks the Law*. Baltimore, MD: Penguin.

Light, Ivan. 1977. "Numbers Gambling among Blacks: A Financial Institution," *American Sociological Review*, 42 (6) (December): 892–904.

Lindquist, Robert J. 1995. "Private Investigators with Accounting Acumen: Forensic Accountants Can Aid Attorneys in Recognizing and Ferreting Out White-Collar Crime," *National Law Journal*, 17 (23) (February 6): B13.

Liptak, Adam. 2001. "When is a Fake Too Real? It's Virtually Uncertain," *New York Times* (January 28).

Liska, Ken. 2008. *Drugs & the Human Body*. 8th ed. Upper Saddle River, NJ: Prentice Hall.

Loh, Wallace D. 1984. *Social Research in the Judicial Process: Cases, Readings, and Text*. New York: Russell Sage Foundation.

Lott, R. John. 2003. *The Bias Against Guns: Why Almost Everything You've Heard About Gun Control Is Wrong*. Washington, DC: Regnery Publishing, Inc. 2010. *More Guns, Less Crime: Understanding Crime and Gun Control Laws*. 3rd ed. Chicago, IL: University of Chicago Press.

Lott, R. John (ed.). 2006. *Straight Shooting: Guns, Economics, and Public Policy*. Bellevue, WA: Merril Press.

Lovell, Jarret S. 2009. *Crimes of Dissent: Civil Disobedience, Criminal Justice, and the Politics of Conscience*. New York: New York University Press.

Lowman, John. 1992. "Street Prostitution Control," *British Journal of Criminology*, 32 (1) (Winter): 1–17.

Lu, Hong, Terance Miethe, and Bin Ling. 2009. *China's Drug Practices and Policies: Regulating Controlled Substances in a Global Context*. Burlington, VT: Ashgate.

Lyman, Michael D., and Gary W. Potter. 2007. *Organized Crime*. 4th ed. Upper Saddle River, NJ: Pearson Prentice Hall.

Magnier, Mark, and Alan Zarembo. 2006. "China Admits Organs Come from Prisoners," *Seattle Times* (November 19): A24.

Maguire, Kathleen, and Ann L. Pastore (eds.). 2001. *Bureau of Justice Statistics. Sourcebook of Criminal Justice Statistics—2000*. Albany, NY: The Hindelang Criminal Justice

Research Center/U.S. Department of Justice, Office of Justice Programs, Bureau of Justice Statistics. NCJ-171147.

Malcolm, Andrew H. 1989. "Capital Punishment Is Popular, but So Are Its Alternatives," *New York Times (*September 10): E4.

Mandell, Betty Reid (ed.). 1975. *Welfare in America: Controlling the "Dangerous Classes."* Englewood Cliffs, NJ: Prentice Hall.

Marez, Curtis. 2004. *Drug Wars: The Political Economy of Narcotics.* Minneapolis, MN: University of Minnesota Press.

Marneffe, Peter de. 2010. *Liberalism and Prostitution.* New York: Oxford University Press.

Martin, Gus C. 2008. *Essential of Terrorism: Concepts and Controversies.* Thousand Oaks, CA: Sage Publications.

Martin, John M., and Anne T. Romano. 1992. *Multinational Crime: Terrorism, Espionage, Drug & Arms Trafficking.* Newbury Park, CA.: Sage Publications.

Massing, Michael. 1998a. "Winning the Drug War Isn't So Hard After All," *New York Times Magazine* (September 6): 48–50. 1998b. *The Fix.* New York: Simon & Schuster.

Matthews, Roger. 2008. *Prostitution, Politics and Policy.* New York: Routledge.

McBarnet, Doreen. 2004. *Crime, Compliance, and Control.* Burlington, VT: Ashgate/ Dartmouth.

McDonald, Ian. 2006. "Corrections Corp. Finds Success Stir," *Wall Street Journal* (September 25): C1, C7.

McDonald, Mark, 2010. "China Leads the World in Executions, Report Says," *New York Times* (March 30): A1, A14.

McLeod, Jane D., and Eric R. Wright (eds.). 2009. *The Sociology of Mental Illness: A Comprehensive Reader.* New York: Oxford University Press.

Meier, Robert F., and Gilbert Geis. 1997. *Victimless Crime? Prostitution, Drugs, Homosexuality, Abortion.* Los Angeles, CA: Roxbury Publishing Company.

Melzer, Scott. 2009. *Gun Crusaders: The NRA's Culture War.* New York: New York University Press.

Meyer, Thomas J. 1986. "1 in 3 College Students Tries Cocaine, Study Finds; Bennett Urges President to Crack Down on Drugs," *Chronicle of Higher Education* (July 16): 1, 30.

Miethe, Terance D., and Charles A. Moore. 1986. "Racial Differences in Criminal Processing: The Consequences of Model Selection on Conclusions about Differential Treatment," *Sociological Quarterly*, 27 (2): 217–237.

Millman, Joel. 2009. "Mexican Pot Gangs Infiltrate Indian Reservations in U.S." *Wall Street Journal* (November 5): A1, A16.

Minkes, John, and Leonard Minkes. 2009. *Corporate and White Collar Crime.* Thousand Oaks, CA: Sage.

Morgenthau, Robert M. 1995. "What Prosecutors Won't Tell You: Capital Punishment Is the Enemy of Law Enforcement," *New York Times* (February 7): A25.

Moynihan, Patrick Daniel. 1998. *Secrecy: The American Experience.* New Haven, CN: Yale University Press.

Munro, Vanessa E., and Marina della Giusta (eds.). 2008. *Demanding Sex: Critical Reflections on the Regulation of Prostitution.* Burlington, VT: Ashgate.

Nader, Ralph. 1965. *Unsafe at Any Speed.* New York: Grossman.

Nagel, Stuart S. 1975. *Improving the Legal Process.* Lexington, MA: Heath.

Natarajan, Mangai (ed.). 2010a. *Drugs of Abuse: The International Scene.* Volume 1. Burlington, VT: Ashgate. 2010b. *Drugs and Crime.* Volume 2. Burlington, VT: Ashgate.

Neumann, Caryn E. 2010. *Sexual Crime: A Reference Handbook.* Santa Barbara, CA: ABC-CLIO.

New York Times. 1995a. "Can New York Live with It?" (February 26): F2. 1995b. "Handgun Use Rose in 1993, Report Shows" (July 10): A6. 2001a. "U.S. Prison Population Rises but Slows in 2000" (August 26): A1. 2001b. "O'Connor Questions Death Penalty" (July 4): A1. 2001c. "Contortions of Psychiatry in China" (March 25).

Newsweek. 1979. "Another Dirty Trick by the FBI" (September 24): 45. 2007. "Special Report: The Anatomy of Violence" (April 30): 40–46.

Nissenbaum, Helen. 2009. *Privacy in Context: Technology, Policy, and the Integrity of Social Life.* Palo Alto, CA: Stanford University Press.

Norris, Clive, and Dean Wilson (eds.). 2007. *Surveillance, Crime, and Social Control.* Burlington, VT: Ashgate.

O'Brien, Timothy L. 1998. "Gambling: Married to the Action, for Better or Worse," *New York Times* (November 8).

O'Connell, Vanessa. 2010. "New Front on Gun Rights. Saying NRA Isn't an Aggressive Advocate, Splinter Groups Jump into the Fray," *Wall Street Journal* (April 19): A3.

O'Connell, Vanessa, and Julie Jargon. 2010. "Stores Land in Gun-Control Crossfire. 'Open-Carry' Proponents Target High-Profile Chains to Test Public Acceptance, Triggering Backlash." *Wall Street Journal* (March 4): B1, B12.

Oberschall, Anthony. 1973. *Social Conflict and Social Movements.* Englewood Cliffs, NJ: Prentice Hall.

Ogletree, Charles J., and Austin Sarat (eds.). 2006. *From Lynch Mobs to the Killing State: Race and Death Penalty in America.* New York: New York University Press.

Ortiz, Jon. 2006. "Study: Embezzlers Grab $660B Yearly. Nearly Half Occur at Businesses with Fewer than 100 Employees," *Bellingham Herald* (July 5): B6.

Packer, Herbert L. 1968. *The Limits of Criminal Sanction.* Stanford, CA: Stanford University Press.

Paoli, Letizia, Victoria A. Greenfield, and Peter Reuter. 2009. *The World Heroin Market: Can Supply Be Cut?* New York: Oxford University Press.

Patrick, Brian Anse. 2010. *Rise of the Anti-Media: Informing the American Concealed Carry Movement.* Lanham, MD: Lexington Books.

Pearce, Frank, and Steve Tombs. 1998. *Toxic Capitalism: Corporate Crime and the Chemical Industry.* Brookfield, VT: Ashgate.

Peay, Jill (ed.). 2005. *Seminal Issues in Mental Health Law.* Burlington, VT: Ashgate.

Peppers, Todd C., and Laura Trevvett Anderson. 2009. *Anatomy of an Execution: The Life and Death of Douglas Christopher Thomas.*

Hanover, NH: University Press of New England.

Phoenix, Jo (ed.). 2009. *Regulating Sex for Sale: Prostitution Reform in the UK.* Bristol, UK: Policy Press.

Pierce, Patrick A., and Donald E. Miller. 2004. *Gambling Politics: State Government and the Business of Betting.* Boulder, CO: Lynne Rienner Publishers.

Piven, Frances Fox, and Richard A. Cloward. 1993. *Regulating the Poor: The Functions of Public Welfare.* Updated ed. New York: Vintage Books.

Podgor, Ellen S. 1994. "Corporate and White Collar Crime: Simplifying the Ambiguous," *American Criminal Law Review*, 31 (3) (Spring): 391–401.

Poel, Sari Van Der. 1995. "Solidarity as Boomerang: The Fiasco of the Prostitutes' Rights Movement in the Netherlands," *Crime, Law & Social Change*, 23:41–65.

Porter, Carrie. 2009. "'Armadillo' Plays Well in Peoria But Is Panned by Drug Dealers. Cops Use Old Brink's Truck to Shame Suspects; Video Cameras Add to the Drama." *Wall Street Journal* (August 17): A1, A4.

President's Commission on Law Enforcement and Administration of Justice. 1967a. *The Challenge of Crime in a Free Society.* Washington, DC: U.S. Government Printing Office. 1967b. *Crime and Its Impact—An Assessment.* Washington, DC: U.S. Government Printing Office.

Pulley, Brett. 1998. "From Illegal Gambling's Regulators to Casinos' Men," *New York Times* (October 28): A1, A20.

Punch, Maurice. 2009. *Police Corruption. Exploring Police Deviance and Crime.* Devon, UK: Willan Publishing.

Quinney, Richard A. 1975. *Criminology: Analysis and Critique of Crime in America.* Boston, MA: Little, Brown.

Radelet, Michael L., and Glenn L. Pierce. 1985. "Race and Prosecutorial Discretion in Homicide Cases," *Law & Society Review*, 19 (4): 587–621.

Radelet, Michael L., Hugo Adam Bedau, and Constance E. Putnam. 1992. *In Spite of Innocence: Erroneous Convictions in Capital*

Cases. Boston, MA: Northeastern University Press.

Ramirez, Anthony. 1992. "The FBI's Latest Idea: Make Wiretapping Easier," *New York Times* (April 19): 2E.

Reed, O. Lee. 2010. *The Legal and Regulatory Environment of Business*. 15th ed. Boston, MA: McGraw-Hill/Irwin.

Reichman, Nancy. 1989. "Breaking Confidences: Organizational Influences on Insider Trading," *Sociological Quarterly*, 30 (2): 185–204.

Reinerman, Craig. 1996. "The Social Construction of Drug Scares," Pp. 77–89 in Earl Rubington and Martin S. Weinberg (eds.), *Deviance: The Interactionist Perspective*. 6th ed. Boston, MA: Allyn and Bacon.

Rengert, George F. 1998. *The Geography of Illegal Drugs*. Boulder, CO: Westview Press.

Rensselaer, W. Lee, III. 1989. *The White Labyrinth: Cocaine and Political Power*. New Brunswick, NJ: Transaction Publishers.

Rice, Stephen K., and Michael D. White (eds.). 2010. *Race, Ethnicity, and Policing: New and Essential Readings*. New York: New York University Press.

Rich, Robert M. 1978. *Crimes without Victims: Deviance and the Criminal Law*. Washington, DC: University Press of America, Inc.

Roth, Randolph. 2009. *American Homicide*. Cambridge, MA: Harvard University Press.

Rule, James B. 2009. *Privacy in Peril: How We Are Sacrificing a Fundamental Right in Exchange for Security and Convenience*. New York: Oxford University Press.

Rusche, Georg, and Otto Kurchheimer. 2003. *Punishment and Social Structure*. New Brunswick, NJ: Transaction Publications.

Salinger, Lawrence M. 2005. *The Encyclopedia of White Collar and Corporate Crime*. Thousand Oaks, CA: Sage.

Samper, Ernesto. 1995. "Colombia's War on Drugs," *Wall Street Journal* (June 30): A16.

Sandberg, Sveinung, and Willy Pedersen. 2009. *Street Capital: Black Cannabis Dealers in a White Welfare State*. Bristol, UK: Policy Press.

Sarat, Austin. 2001. *When the State Kills: Capital Punishment and the American Condition*. NJ: Princeton University Press. 2005. *Dissent*

in Dangerous Times. Ann Arbor, MI: University of Michigan Press.

Saunders, Laura. 2009. "Is 'Friending' in Your Future? Better Pay Your Taxes First," *Wall Street Journal* (August 27): A2.

Scambler, Graham, and Annette Scambler (eds.). 1997. *Rethinking Prostitution: Purchasing Sex in the 1990s*. New York: Routledge.

Scherrer, Amandine. 2010. *G8 against Transnational Organized Crime*. Burlington, VT: Ashgate.

Schmidt, Sara. 2003. "Half of Teens in Canada Gamble: Up to 15 Per cent at Risk of Addiction," *Vancouver Sun* (October 14): A1.

Schur, Edwin M. 1965. *Crimes without Victims, Deviant Behavior, and Public Policy*. Englewood Cliffs, NJ: Prentice Hall.

Schwartz, John. 2001. "U.S. Refuses to Disclose PC Tracking," *New York Times* (August 25): A1.

Scoular, Jane, and Teela Sanders (eds.). 2010. *Regulating Sex/Work: From Crime Control to Neo-liberalism*. New York: Wiley-Blackwell.

Seattle Times. 2006. "First-Timer Deals at Berlin Brothel" (May 6): A2.

Sellin, Thorsten. 1959. *The Death Penalty: Report for the Model Penal Code Project of the American Law Institute*. Philadelphia, PA: Executive Office of American Law Institute.

Sheley, Joseph F. 1985. *America's "Crime Problems": An Introduction to Criminology*. Belmont, CA: Wadsworth.

Shibutani, Tamotsu. 1961. *Society and Personality: An Interactionist Approach to Social Psychology*. Englewood Cliffs, NJ: Prentice Hall.

Shilling, Chris, and Philip A. Mellor. 1998. "Durkheim, Morality and Modernity: Collective Effervescence, *Homo Duplex* and the Sources of Moral Action," *British Journal of Sociology*, 49 (2) (June): 193–209.

Shover, Neal, and John Paul Wright (eds.). 2001. *Crimes of Privilege, Readings in White Collar Crime*. New York: Oxford University Press.

Shrader, Katherine. 2007. "Spy Chief Wants to Expand Surveillance: Critics Question Need for Changes" *Seattle Times* (April 11): A5.

Shukovsky, Paul, Tracy Johnson, and Daniel Lathrop. 2007. "The FBI's Terrorism

Trade-Off: Focus on National Security after 9/11 Means That the Agency Has Turned Its Back on Thousands of White-Collar Crimes," *Seattle Post-Intelligencer* (April 11): A1, A13.

Simon, David R. 2008. *Elite Deviance.* 8th ed. Boston, MA: Pearson/Allyn & Bacon.

Simon, Jonathan. 2009. *Governing Through Crime. How the War on Crime Transformed American Democracy and Created a Culture of Fear.* New York: Oxford University Press.

Simon, Leonore, Bruce Sales, and Lee Sechrest. 1992. "Licensure of Functions." Pp. 542–563 in Dorothy K. Kagehiro and William S. Laufer (eds.), *Handbook of Psychology and Law.* New York: Springer-Verlag.

Simpson, Sally, and Carole Gibbs (eds.). 2007. *Corporate Crime.* Burlington, VT: Ashgate.

Sjögren, Hans, and Göran Skogh (eds.). 2004. *New Perspectives on Economic Crime.* Northampton, MA: E. Elgar Publishers.

Smith, Dwayne M., and Margaret A. Zahn (eds.). 1998. *Homicide: A Sourcebook of Social Research.* Thousand Oaks, CA: Sage Publications.

Smith, Stephen, and Ronan Deazley (eds.). 2010. *The Legal, Medical and Cultural Regulation of the Body: Transformation and Transgression.* Burlington, VT: Ashgate.

Smolowe, Jill. 1992. "Must This Man Die?" *Time* (May 18): 41–44.

Spitzer, Robert J. 2008. *The Politics of Gun Control.* 4th ed. Washington: CQ Press.

Spohn, Cassia. 2009. *How Do Judges Decide? The Search for Fairness and Justice in Punishment.* 2nd ed. Thousand Oaks, CA: Sage.

St. Louis Post-Dispatch. 1985. "25 Innocent People Executed, ACLU Says," (November 14): 6B. 1998. "Group Still Wants Rushdie Murdered, Raises Reward" (October 13): A6. 2001. "McVeigh Execution Is Planned to the Smallest Detail," (April 8): A5.

Stein, Rob. 2010. "Group Warns Doctors on Aiding Executions: We Are Healers. Penalties to be Imposed for Participation," *Seattle Times* (May 2): A19.

Stevens, Dennis J. 1992. "Research Note: The Death Sentence Inmate Attitudes," *Crime & Delinquency,* 38 (2) (April): 272–279.

Stolzenberg, Lisa, and Stewart J. D'Alessio. 2000. "Gun Availability and Violent Crime: New Evidence from the National Incident-Based Reporting System," *Social Forces,* 78 (4) June: 1461–1482.

Stone, Christopher D. 1978. "Social Control of Corporate Behavior." Pp. 241–258 in M. David Ermann and Richard J. Lundman (eds.), *Corporate and Governmental Deviants: Problems of Organizational Behavior in Contemporary Society.* New York: Oxford University Press.

Suk, Jeannie. 2009. *At Home in the Law: How the Domestic Violence Revolution Transforming Privacy.* New Haven: CT: Yale University Press.

Sullivan, Eileen. 2009. "Police Support Citizen's Terrorism Watch. Program Opens in Los Angeles." *Bellingham Herald* (October 4): A1, A2.

Sullum, Jacob. 2003. *Saying Yes: In Defense of Drug Use.* New York: J.P. Tarcher/Putnam.

Summers, Robert S., and George G. Howard. 1972. *Law: Its Nature, Functions, and Limits.* 2nd ed. Englewood Cliffs, NJ: Prentice Hall.

Sunstein, Cass R. 2003. *Why Societies Need Dissent.* Cambridge, MA: Harvard University Press.

Sutherland, Edwin H. 1949. *White Collar Crime.* New York: Dryden Press.

Sutherland, Edwin H., and Donald C. Cressey. 1974. *Criminology.* 9th ed. Philadelphia, PA: Lippincott.

Szasz, Thomas. 2003. *Ceremonial Chemistry: The Ritual Persecution of Drugs, Addicts, and Pushers.* Rev. ed. New York: Syracuse University Press.

Tang, Alisa. 2003. "Drug Abuse? Just Say No Funeral. Threat of Ostracism Cleans Up Thailand Village," *Seattle Times* (October 27): A11.

Tanner, Lindsey. 2004. "Habitual Marijuana Use Rises among U.S. Adults," *Seattle Times* (May 5): A8.

Tappan, Paul W. 1960. *Crime, Justice, and Correction.* New York: McGraw-Hill.

Tashbook, Linda. 2004. *Survey on Licensing.* Buffalo, NY: W.S. Hein.

Terry, Don. 1998. "Survivors Make the Case against Death Row," *New York Times* (November 16): A12.

Time. 1991. "Nowhere to Hide," (November 11): 34–40.

Timiraos, Nick. 2007. "Shooting Highlights Gun Divisions," *Wall Street Journal* (April 21–22): A7.

Tittle, Charles R. 1969. "Crime Rates and Legal Sanctions," *Social Problems*, 16 (4) (Spring): 409–423.

Tonry, Michael. 2010. *Thinking about Punishment: Penal Policy across Space, Time, and Discipline*. Burlington, VT: Ashgate.

Treaster, Joseph B. 1992. "Echoes of Prohibition: 20 Years of War on Drugs, and No Victory Yet," *New York Times* (June 14): E7. 1995. "Drug Therapy: Powerful Tool Reaching Few Inside Prisons," *New York Times* (July 3): 1, 9.

Tuft, Carolyn. 1998. "In the Past 10 Years, 8 in Illinois Were Sentenced to Die, Later Found Innocent," *St. Louis Post-Dispatch* (April 12): A7.

Tunnell, Kenneth D. 2004. *Pissing on Demand: Workplace Drug Testing and the Rise of the Detox Industry*. New York: New York University Press.

Turk, Austin T. 1972. *Legal Sanctioning and Social Control*. Rockville, MD: National Institute of Mental Health.

Turow, Scott. 2004. *Ultimate Punishment: A Lawyer's Reflections on Dealing with the Death Penalty*. Waterville, ME: Thorndike Press.

Tyler, Patrick E. 1995. "Population Control in China Falls to Coercion and Evasion," *New York Times* (June 25): 1, 6.

Unger, Roberto Mangabeira. 1976. *Law in Modern Society: Toward a Criticism of Social Theory*. New York: Free Press.

U.S. Department of Justice. 1979. *Illegal Corporate Behavior*. National Institute of Law Enforcement and Criminal Justice. Law Enforcement Assistance Administration. Washington, DC: U.S. Government Printing Office (October). 1995 "Drugs and Crime Facts, 1994," Bureau of Justice Statistics (June). 2006. "Identity Theft, 2004" (April).

2007. "Prison and Jail Inmates at Midyear 2005" (May). 2009. "Prisoners in 2008." Bureau of Justice Statistics (December).

U.S. News & World Report. 1979. "Red-Tape: It's Bad at Grass Roots, Too" (September 24): 69–72. 1995. "South Africa Eliminates 'The Noose'" (June 19): 14.

Vaughan, Diane. 1998. "Rational Choice, Situated Action, and the Social Control of Organizations," *Law & Society Review*, 32 (1): 23–57.

Vold, George B., Thomas J. Bernard, Jeffrey B. Snipes. and Alex B. Gerould. 2009. *Theoretical Criminology*. 6th ed. New York: Oxford University Press.

Wald, Matthew L. 1998. "F.A.A. Asks, Can Airliners Get Too Old To Fly Safely," *New York Times* (October 2): A20.

Walker, Samuel. 1993. "Reform the Law: Decriminalization." Pp. 569–579 in Delos H. Kelly (ed.), *Deviant Behavior: A Text Reader in the Sociology of Deviance*. New York: St. Martin's Press.

Wall, David S. (ed.). 2009. *Crime and Deviance in Cyberspace*. Burlington, VT: Ashgate.

Wall Street Journal. 1986. "No Longer Amused, Frankfurt Decides to Relocate Its Red-Light District" (July 28): 16.

Warren, Kenneth F. 2010. *Administrative Law in the Political System*. 5th ed. Boulder, CO: Westview Press.

Weinberg, Roy D. 1979. *Family Planning and the Law*. 2nd ed. New York: Oceana Publications, Inc.

Weisburd, David, Stanton Wheeler, Elin Waring, and Nancy Bode. 1991. *Crimes of the Middle Classes: White Collar Offenders in the Federal Courts*. New Haven, CT: Yale University Press.

Welsh, Brandon C., and David P. Farrington. 2009. *Making Public Places Safer: Surveillance and Crime Prevention*. New York: Oxford University Press.

Williams, Mary (ed.). 2003. *Is the Death Penalty Fair?* San Diego, CA: Greenhaven Press.

Winerip, Michael. 1992. "Where Life Is a Beach and Topless Is Now Legal, Trail Blazers Are Timid," *New York Times* (August 2): 19.

Wise, David. 1978. *The American Police State: The Government against the People*. New York: Vintage Books.

Wolfe, Alan, and Erik C Owens (eds.). 2009. *Gambling: Mapping the American Moral Landscape*. Waco, TX: Baylor University Press.

Wolfenden Report. 1963. Report of the Committee on Homosexual Offenses and Prostitution. Briarcliff Manor, NY: Stein & Day.

Worsham, James. 1998. "Can the IRS Be Fixed?" *Nation's Business* (May): 16–23.

Worsnop, Richard L. 1995. "Death Penalty Debate: Will Support for Executions Continue to Grow?" *CQ Researcher*, 5 (9) (March 10): 195–212.

Wright, Richard G. (ed.). 2009. *Sex Offender Laws: Failed Policies, New Directions*. New York: Springer Publishing.

Wyatt, Kristen. 2003. "CDC: No Proof Gun Control Cuts Violence," *Seattle Times* (October 3): A8.

Wynn, Joan Ransohoff, and Clifford Goldman. 1974. "Gambling in New York City: The Case for Legalization." Pp. 66–75 in Lee Rainwater (ed.), *Social Problems and Public Policy: Deviance and Liberty*. Chicago, IL: Aldine Publishing Co.

Yorke, Jon (ed.). 2009. *Against the Death Penalty. International Initiatives and Implications*. Burlington, VT: Ashgate.

Young, Virginia, and Eric Stern. 2001. "Elderly Are Called Prone to Gambling Problems," *St. Louis Post-Dispatch* (August 6): 1, 7.

Zaibert, Leo. 2006. *Punishment and Retribution*. Burlington, VT: Ashgate.

Zagaris, Bruce. 2010. *International White Collar Crime*. Cambridge, UK: Cambridge University Press.

CHAPTER

6

Law and Dispute Resolution

A core function of law is the orderly resolution of disputes. The purpose of this chapter is to examine the questions of why, how, and under what circumstances laws are used in disagreements between individuals, between individuals and organizations, and between organizations.

A NOTE ON TERMINOLOGY

There are a number of different terms used in the sociological and legal literature to describe the role of law in controversies. Terms such as *conflict resolution* (see, for example, Aubert, 1963; Doak, 2004; Ford Foundation, 1978; Kriesberg, 1982, 2007), *conflict regulation* (see, for example, Wehr, 1979), *conflict management* (see, for example, Haynes et al., 2004; Lewicki et al., 1992; Lord et al., 1978; Thomas, 1992), *dispute processing* (see, for example, Chase, 2007; Felstiner, 1974, 1975; Palmer and Roberts, 1998; Thomas, 1992), *dispute settlement* (see, for example, Gulliver, 1969; Miceli, 1998; O'Connell, 2003), and *dispute resolution* (see, for example, Bradney and Cownie, 2000; Coltri, 2010; Goldberg et al., 2007; Kawashima, 1969; Leeson and Johnston, 1988; Susskind and Cruikshank, 1987; Ury et al., 1988) or simply *disputing* (Abel, 1995) are often used more or less interchangeably.

Some scholars, such as Richard L. Abel (1973), William L. F. Felstiner (1974, 1975), Carrie Menkel-Meadow (2003), Michael Palmer and Simon Roberts (1998), and Paul Wehr (1979), contend that disputes are processed in society rather than settled, and conflicts are managed or regulated rather than resolved. Third-party intervention, whether through legal or nonlegal means, represents for them only the settlement of the resolution of the public component of the dispute or conflict, rather than the alleviation of the underlying forces or tensions that have created that conflict. Richard L. Abel (1973:228) epitomizes this position and chides anthropologists and sociologists who "have tended to write as though 'settlement' must be the ultimate outcome of disputes, 'resolution' the inevitable fate of conflicts." Then he adds that "it has recently become almost commonplace to observe that the outcome of most conflicts and disputes are other conflicts and disputes, with at most a temporary respite between them" (Abel, 1973:28).

Other authors point out that the actual dispute is preceded by several stages. For example, Laura Nader and Harry F. Todd (1978:14–15) in an influential book, *The Disputing*

Process—Law in Ten Societies, contend that there are three distinct phases or stages in the disputing process: the grievance or preconflict stage, the conflict stage, and the dispute stage. The *grievance* or *preconflict* stage refers to situations that an individual or a group perceives to be unjust and considers grounds for resentment or complaint. The situation may be real or imaginary, depending on the aggrieved parties' perception. This condition may erupt into conflict or it may wane. If it is not resolved in the preconflict or grievance stage, it enters into the *conflict* stage, in which the aggrieved party confronts the offending party and communicates his or her resentment or feelings of injustice to the person or group. The conflict phase is dyadic; that is, it involves only two parties. If it is not de-escalated or resolved at this stage, it enters into the final, dispute stage when the conflict is made public. The dispute stage is characterized by the involvement of a third party in the disagreement. P. H. Gulliver (1969:14) suggests that "no dispute exists unless and until the right-claimant, or someone on his behalf, actively raises the initial disagreement from the level of dyadic argument into the public arena, with the express intention of doing something about the denied claim." Ideally, then, a grievance is monadic, involving one person or a group; a conflict is dyadic; and a dispute is triadic, because it involves the participation of a third party, who is called upon as an agent of settlement.

The legal approach to dispute resolution entails the transition from a dyad of the conflicting parties to the triad, "where an intermediary who stands outside the original conflict has been added to the dyad" (Aubert, 1963:26). The stages discussed by Nader and Todd are not always clear-cut or sequential. A person may file a lawsuit without ever confronting the offender or one party may quit or concede at any stage in the disagreement.

When disagreements formally enter the legal arena (that is, trial), from the perspective of the law, disputes are authoritatively settled rather than processed through the intervention of third parties (that is, judges), and conflicts are resolved rather than simply managed or regulated. The use of the terms *conflict resolution* and *dispute settlement* is thus, in this sense, justified. In this chapter, I shall use these concepts interchangeably, and at the same time, I will repeatedly emphasize, in different contexts, that the law resolves or settles only the legal components of conflicts and disputes, rather than ameliorating the underlying causes. In brief, the law deals with disagreements that have been translated into legal disputes or conflicts. A legal resolution of conflict does not necessarily lead to a reduction of tension or antagonism between the aggrieved parties as evidenced by many, for example, of the 3 million or so Americans who annually get divorced (see, for example, Sarat and Felstiner, 1995, for a major groundbreaking work on the topic).

METHODS OF DISPUTE RESOLUTION

Disputes are ubiquitous in every society at every level, and there is a wide variety of methods for their management (see, for example, Chase, 2007; Coltri, 2010; Fiss and Resnik, 2003; Lauderdale and Cruit, 1993; Plett and Meschievitz, 1991). Most societies use fairly similar methods; the differences among them consist in the preference given to one method over others. Cultural factors and the availability of institutions for settling disputes will usually determine such preferences. There are two principal forms of resolving legal disputes throughout the world. "*Either* the parties to a conflict determine the outcome themselves by negotiations, which does not preclude that a third party acting as a mediator might assist them in their negotiations. *Or*, the conflict is adjudicated, which means that a third, and ideally impartial, party decides which of the disputants has the superior claim" (Ehrmann, 1976:82). These forms are used (and are sometimes intertwined) for the settlement of civil, criminal, and administrative suits. For nonlegal disputes, there are a variety of other means for settlement.

Simon Roberts (1979:57–59), a noted anthropologist, points out that in some societies, direct interpersonal violence constitutes an approved method of dispute settlement. Such interpersonal violence may be a way of retaliation for violence already suffered or a reaction to some other form of perceived wrong. Occasionally, physical violence may be channeled into a restricted and conventionalized form, such as dueling. In Germany before World War II, for example, dueling was a popular form of dispute settlement among university students, members of the officer corps in the military, and the nobility in general. Duels took place under controlled conditions and according to specific rules. The participants wore protective clothing, and usually the first sign of bloodletting marked the end of the dispute. It was often a question of honor to challenge the insulting party to a duel, which was, by convention, compelled to accept it. In the event of an insult or injustice (on the ramification of insults, see Neu, 2009), all the offended party had to do was to slap the offender (unlike today when they sue for slander or libel). This act was a challenge to a duel, and the parties involved promptly settled on the time and place. Dueling scars on one's face represented symbols of courage and high status.

Another form of physical violence is feuding (Gulliver, 1979:1). It is a state of recurring hostilities between families or groups, instigated by a desire to avenge an offense (insult, injury, death, or deprivation of some sort) against a member of the group. The unique feature of a feud is that responsibility to avenge is carried by all members of the group. The killing of any member of the offender's group is viewed as appropriate revenge, because the group as a whole is considered responsible. Nicholas Gubser (1965) describes a feud that lasted for decades within a Nunamiut Eskimo community caused by a husband killing his wife's lover. When a man is killed, in Gubser's words,

> The closely related members of his kindred do not rest until complete revenge has been achieved. The immediate relatives of the deceased . . . recruit as much support from other relatives as they can. Their first action, if possible, is to kill the murderer, or maybe one of his closest kin. Then, of course, the members of the murderer's kindred are brought into the feud. These two kindreds may snipe at each other for years. (1965:151)

At times, the feud can turn into a full-scale battle when, in addition to the families, the communities are drawn into a dispute. This happened from time to time in the famous feud triggered by a romantic interlude between the Hatfields of Virginia and the McCoys of Kentucky. The feud broke out in 1882 and lasted for several years.

Disagreement, at times, is channeled into rituals (see, for example, Rosati, 2009; Stewart and Strathern, 2010). For example, the parties to the dispute may confront each other before the assembled community and voice their contentions through songs and dances improvised for the occasion. In the form of a song, the accuser states all the abuse he or she can think of; the accused then responds in kind. A number of such exchanges may follow until the contestants are exhausted, and a winner emerges through public acclaim for the greater poetic or vituperative skill.

In some societies, shaming is used as a form of public reprimand in the disapproval of disputing behavior. Ridicule directed at those guilty of antisocial conduct is also used to reduce conflict. At times, the singing of rude and deflating songs to, or about, a troublesome individual is also reported as a means of achieving a similar end. Ridicule, reproach, or public exposure may also take the form of a "public harangue," in which a person's wrongdoings are embarrassingly exposed by being shouted out to the community at large (Roberts, 1979:62).

In attempts to resolve disputes, parties may choose to resort to supernatural agencies. The notion that supernatural beings may intervene to punish wrongdoers is rather widespread. This notion is often accompanied by the belief that harm may be inflicted by witches or through the practice of sorcery. In some societies, witchcraft and sorcery are seen as a possible cause of death and of almost any form of illness or material misfortune. Jane Fishburne Collier (1973:113–120), for example, identifies a variety of witchcraft beliefs among the Zinacantecos in Mexico. They include witches who send sickness, ask that sickness be sent, perform specific actions (such as causing the victim to rot away), control weather, talk to saints, or cause sickness by an evil eye. Collier notes, "Witchcraft beliefs underlie all of the reasons given for actions during a hearing" (1973:122). Consequently, in such societies the procedures for identifying witches or sorcerers responsible for particular incidences or misfortunes assume great importance in the handling of conflict (Roberts, 1979:64).

Of course, not all disputes are handled by violence, rituals, shaming, ostracism, or resorting to supernatural agencies (Chase, 2007). Some of these methods can be "domesticated" (Cobb, 1997), and most societies have access to a number of alternative methods of dispute resolution. These alternatives differ in several ways, including whether participation is voluntary, presence or absence of a third party, criteria used for third-party intervention, type of outcome and how it may be enforced, and whether the procedures employed are formal or informal (Administrative Conference of the United States, 1987:12–13). Before considering them, let us look at two other popular ways of coping with disputes: "lumping it" and avoidance.

Lumping it refers simply to inaction, to not making a claim or a complaint. Galanter says, "This is done all the time by 'claimants' who lack information or access or who knowingly decide gain is too low, cost too high (including psychic cost of litigating where such activity is repugnant)" (1974:124–125). In "lumping it," the issue or the difficulty that gave rise to the disagreement is simply ignored and the relationship with the offending party continues. For example, a college professor may not want to press a particular claim (say, for a higher increment) against the administration and continues his or her relationship with the university. A somewhat different form of withdrawal from conflict situations that seems likely to result in dispute is described by Carol J. Greenhouse (1989:252–273) in her study of Baptists in a southern town. The findings indicate that Baptists in the community consider disputing a profoundly unchristian act because the Bible states clearly that Jesus is the judge of all people. The implication is that to partake in a dispute is to stand as judge over another person. This would be an indication of lack of faith and a preemption of Jesus's power (1989:256).

Avoidance refers to limiting the relationship with other disputants sufficiently so that the dispute no longer remains salient (Felstiner, 1974:70). Albert O. Hirschman (1970) calls this kind of behavior "exit," which entails withdrawing from a situation or terminating or curtailing a relationship. For example, a consumer may go to a different store rather than press grievances. In consumer-transaction disputes, for example, "the exit option is widely held to be uniquely powerful: by inflicting revenue losses on delinquent management" (Hirschman, 1970:21), it can be considered not only expedient in dispute settlement but also a way of imposing sanctions. Avoidance entails a limitation or a break in the relationship between disputants, whereas "lumping it" refers to the lack of resolution of a conflict, grievance, or dispute for the reason that one of the parties prefers to ignore the issue in dispute, generally basing the decision on feelings of relative powerlessness or on the social, economic, or psychological costs involved in seeking a solution. Avoidance is not always an alternative, especially in situations when the relationship must continue—for example, with certain companies that have monopolies, such as gas or electric companies, or with the Social Security Administration or the U.S. Department of Health & Human Services. An important aspect of avoidance is the reduction of social interaction or its termination. Lumping behavior entails the ignoring of the issue in dispute while continuing the relationship.

Primary Resolution Processes

The primary dispute-resolution mechanisms can be depicted on a continuum ranging from negotiation to adjudication. In negotiation, participation is voluntary and disputants arrange settlements for themselves. Next on the continuum is mediation, in which a third party facilitates a resolution and otherwise assists the parties in reaching a voluntary agreement (Bush and Folger, 2005). At the other end of the continuum is adjudication (both judicial and administrative), in which parties are compelled to participate, the case is decided by a judge, the parties are represented by counsel, the procedures are formal, and the outcomes are enforceable by law. Close to adjudication is arbitration, which is more informal and in which the decision may or may not be binding. Negotiation, mediation, and arbitration are the principal components of what is referred to "alternative dispute resolution" (ADR) in legal parlance (Barrett and Barrett, 2004; Palmer and Roberts, 1998; Partridge, 2009). The movement is spreading to other parts of the world and in France, for example, recourse to ADR carries with it a fashionable progressive American connotation, and ADR is regularly promoted by the French authorities and legal scholars alike as a means of relieving the burden of the courts, of rendering dispute resolutions faster, simpler, and cheaper, and of "de-dramatizing" disputes to render their resolutions more satisfactory to the parties (Gaillard, 2000).

Because dispute resolutions are bread and butter issues in the legal profession, not surprisingly there is now mounting evidence that law firms are becoming uneasy about the spreading use of alternative means because the money- and time-saving potential for disputants can be considerable by discouraging potential litigation (France, 1995). Let us now consider these processes and some of their variants in some detail.

Negotiations in disputes take place when disputants seek to resolve their disagreements without the help of neutral third parties. Negotiation is a two-party arrangement in which disputants try to persuade one another, establish a common ground for discussion, and feel their way by a process of give-and-take toward a settlement. It involves the use of debate and bargaining (Lewicki et al., 2011; Raiffa, 1997). A basic requirement for successful negotiation is the desire of both parties to settle a dispute without escalation and without resorting to neutral third parties. Aubert states, "The advantage of negotiated solutions is that they need not leave any marks on the normative order of society. Since the solution does not become a precedent for later solutions to similar conflicts, the adversaries need not fear the general consequences of the settlement" (1969:284). When interests are contradictory to the extent that gains and losses must cancel each other out, negotiations are inadequate in resolving the conflict, and in such situations, parties may bring the case to court for legal settlement. In industrialized countries, such as the United States, lumping behavior, avoidance, and negotiation are the most frequent responses to dispute situations (Best and Andreasen, 1976).

Mediation is a widely used dispute-resolution method that interposes a disinterested and noncoercive third party, the mediator, between the disputants (Bush and Folger, 2005; Haynes et al., 2004; McCorkle and Reese, 2005, 2010). Unlike litigation, where the judge imposes the ultimate decision, the mediator does not make the final decision. Rather, the terms of settlement are worked out solely by and between the disputants. It can be an effective way of resolving a variety of disputes if both parties are interested in a reasonable settlement of their disagreement and often produces a more equitable outcome than other methods (Fitzpatrick, 1994). Mediation begins with an agreement. It is nonadversarial, and the basic tenet is cooperation rather than competition. The role of the mediator in the dispute is that of a guide, a facilitator, and a catalyst.

A mediator may be chosen by the disputants or appointed by someone in authority. A mediator may be selected because the person has status, position, respect, power, money, or the alleged power to invoke sanctions in behalf of a deity or some other superhuman force. (There is some empirical evidence that lawyers playing the role of mediators are considered effective by clients in dispute resolutions [Croson and Mnookin, 1997].) A mediator may have none of these but simply be a designated agent of an organization set up to handle specific disputes. Bringing disputes to a mediator may be the choice of both parties or of one but not the other party to a conflict, or it may be the result of private norms or expectations of a group which "require" that disputes be settled as much as possible within the group.

Mediation essentially consists of influencing the parties to come to an agreement by appealing to their own interests. The mediator may use a variety of techniques to accomplish this objective.

> He may work on the parties' ideas of what serves them best . . . in such a way that he gets them to consider the common interests as more essential than they did previously, or their competing interests as less essential. He may also look for possibilities of resolution which the parties themselves have not discovered and try to convince them that both will be well served by his suggestion. The very fact that a suggestion is proposed by an impartial third party may also, in certain cases, be sufficient for the parties to accept it. (Eckhoff, 1978:36)

Ideally, both parties should have confidence in the mediator, be willing to cooperate, listen to his or her advice, and consider the mediator as impartial. A mediator may also use warnings, promises, or flattery, or in some instances sophisticated software such as SplitUp or Family Winner based on the principles of game theory, and these are used primarily in domestic disputes (*Economist*, 2006), in attempts to reconcile differences between the parties. Eckhoff points out:

> The conditions for mediation are best in cases where both parties are interested in having the conflict resolved. The stronger the common interest is, the greater reason they have for bringing the conflict before a third party, and the more motivated they will be for cooperating actively with him in finding a solution, and for adjusting their demands in such a way that a solution can be reached. (1978:36)

The use of mediators is widespread, and already two decades ago there were more than 300 neighborhood justice resolution centers in the United States (U.S. Department of Justice, 1986:2), and in late 2000 there were more than 650. The initial idea for such centers came from Richard Danzig (1973). Using the example of resolving intratribal disputes by conciliation in Liberia, he suggested the establishment of neighborhood community moots. Such moots involve community members with shared values who might be able to resolve more effectively than courts those disputes that affect the disputants and the neighborhood, such as family and housing disputes and minor criminal charges. Although there is a great variation among centers in the types of cases they handle, almost all tend to concentrate on disputes between persons with an ongoing relationship. Participation in mediation is voluntary. The majority of disputants are referred to the centers by judges, police, prosecutors, and court clerks. Mediators include lawyers, law students, undergraduates, and laypeople. Before acting as mediators, they receive training in mediation techniques. These neighborhood centers are listed in the ABA's Dispute Resolution Project Directory, which is updated annually (American Bar Association, 2007).

There are many advantages of such neighborhood justice centers (McGillis, 1982). These nonjudicial forums can increase access to justice because of their low cost (or no cost), convenient hours, and location. Mediation provides a better process than other forums for handling disputes because participants are able to explore the underlying problems contributing to the dispute without legal formalities, time limits, and lawyers acting as intermediaries in the discussion. The reliance on informal alternatives also frees the courts to attend to more serious cases (Wright and Galaway, 1989) and is being used with increasing frequency in victim–offender mediation for nonviolent offenses in attempts to work out a restitution program as an option to a prison sentence (Reske, 1995; Zernova, 2008).

Related to mediation is the *ombudsman* process, which combines mediatory and investigatory functions in dispute resolution. In the classic Scandinavian model, the ombudsman is a public official designated to hear citizen complaints and carry out independent fact-finding investigations to correct abuses of public administration. In a traditional sense, ombudsmen are independent agents of the legislature and they can criticize, publicize, and make recommendations, but they cannot reverse administrative actions (Rosenbloom and Kravchuck, 2009).

The system is widely used as an alternative to courts in other countries. In Denmark, for example, courts are very rarely used by the consumer (Blegvad, 1983:207). Instead, the ombudsman negotiates with the firms in disputes on behalf of clients. In the United States, Alaska, Hawaii, Iowa and Nebraska have used ombudsmen at the state level, and more and more corporations, hospitals, and universities are beginning to rely on the process to correct organizational abuses and resolve internal disputes. Some newspapers and radio stations, in the format of "action lines," also perform the role of ombudsman in disputes. A major criticism against the ombudsman process is that the person acting as mediator often represents the vested interest of a particular agency, which suggests bias in favor of his or her employer. For example, the hospital ombudsman may be partial to the hospital and biased against the client (Marshall, 1985:108).

Arbitration is another way of involving a third party in a dispute. Unlike mediation, in which a third party assists the disputants to reach their own solution, arbitration requires a final and binding decision to be made for the disputants by a third party. Disputants agree beforehand both to the intervention of a neutral third party and to the finality of his or her decision. Unlike in courts, the proceedings in arbitration can remain private and participants can opt for simplicity and informality. Arbitration and other nonjudicial methods tend to reduce the cost of dispute resolution (Fine, 1988) because of the lack of opportunity to appeal the arbitrator's decision and especially when attorneys are not hired. It is also faster than adjudication because participants can proceed as soon as they are ready rather than waiting for a trial date to be set.

Nowadays, almost all collective bargaining contracts contain a provision for final and binding arbitration. Arbitration clauses are showing up more often in business contracts and even in executive employment letters (*New York Times*, 1986a:1F). The conduct of commercial arbitrators (such as the American Arbitration Association, with offices in major cities) is governed by a code of ethics. Many private organizations, professional groups, and trade associations have their own formal arbitration machinery for the settlement of disputes among members. Similarly, labor-management disputes are often brought before arbiters, designated in advance, whose decisions are binding by mutual consent of the disputants and ultimately enforceable by private sanctions and by the courts. In general, willingness to submit disputes to private but formal arbitration is characteristic of parties who have a commitment to long-term relationships (Sarat, 1989).

Arbitration is increasingly considered as an alternative to judicial and administrative processes. Compulsory arbitration, especially for small claims, can free courts for more substantial disputes, and depending upon the issues involved, it may reduce the cost to litigants and be a more effective way of solving problems. For example, in Philadelphia, a case that is under $10,000 is automatically assigned by the court to arbitration. Three arbitrators are selected by the deputy court administrator from a panel of lawyers. They make their decisions on the pleadings supplemented by oral arguments by the attorneys for the parties. It is estimated that the average arbitrated case costs one-fifth less per day than it would in the Philadelphia court system. Similar systems of compulsory arbitration exist in England, Germany, the Scandinavian countries, and China where arbitration is used quite extensively (Tao, 2008).

Adjudication is a public and formal method of conflict resolution, which is best exemplified by courts (Fiss and Resnik, 2003). Courts have the authority to intervene in disputes whether or not the parties desire it and to render a decision and to enforce compliance with that decision. In adjudication, the emphasis is on the legal rights and duties of disputants, rather than on compromises or on the mutual satisfaction of the parties. Adjudication is also more oriented toward zero-sum decisions than the other mechanisms I have noted. Courts require disputants to narrow their definitions of issues in the identification of the nature of their problems. Felstiner states, "Adjudication as a consequence tends to focus on 'what facts' and 'which norms' rather than on any need for normative shifts" (1974:70). In other words, courts deal with issues and facts. Consequently, they can deal only with disagreements, grievances, or conflicts that have been transformed into legal disputes. For example, in a divorce case, the court may focus on one incident in what is a complex and often not very clear-cut series of problems. It results in a resolution of a legal dispute but not necessarily of the broader issues that have produced that conflict.

Although courts occasionally seek compromise and flexibility, generally the verdict of the court has an either/or character: The decision is based upon a single definite conception of what has actually taken place and upon a single interpretation of legal norms. When a conflict culminates in litigation, one of the parties must be prepared for a total loss. Aubert says, "One aspect of legal decisions that is closely linked to their either/or character is the marked orientation toward the past" (1969:287). The structure of legal thinking is also oriented toward comparisons between actions and sanctions rather than toward utility and effectiveness. Because of this orientation, and because of the use of precedents, there is a fair amount of predictability in how similar cases will be settled by courts. Because the courts are dealing only with the legal issues, they do not take into consideration the possibility that the applicable legal facts and norms may have been influenced by different social conditions and that, in many instances, courts are treating only the symptoms rather than the underlying causes of a problem. With these limitations, the courts work "to clean up all the little social messes (and the occasional big ones) that recurrently arise between the members of the society from day to day" (Hoebel, 1954:280).

Hybrid Resolution Processes

In both the public and private sectors, the intervention of a third party—a person, a government agency, or other institutions—can often facilitate dispute resolution among conflicting parties (Ross and Conlon, 2000), and there are currently several "hybrid" dispute-resolution processes in use. The term "hybrid" is employed because these processes incorporate features of the primary processes discussed in the preceding section. The main ones include rent-a-judge, med-arb, and minitrial.

The _rent-a-judge_ process is basically a form of arbitration (Goldberg et al., 1985:280–309). In the process, the disputants, in an attempt to avoid the use of a regular court, select a retired judge to hear and decide a pending case as an arbitrator would. The same procedure is used as in court, and the decision of the judge is legally binding.

Unlike in arbitration, the "referee's" decision can be appealed for errors of law or on the ground that the judgment was against evidence, though such appeals are rare. In California, where this system of private judging is quite prevalent, former judges have decided on hundreds of cases. The system is considered both an alternative to adjudication and a sort of "rich-man's justice" that undermines public methods of dispute resolution and threatens constitutional values.

There are other hybrid processes of dispute resolution that have been used with considerable success (Goldberg et al., 2007). One is *med-arb*, in which the issues that were not solved by mediation are submitted to arbitration, with the same person serving first as mediator and then as arbitrator. Med-arb has been used often in contract negotiation disputes between public employers and their unionized employees. Another is the *minitrial*, which has been repeatedly utilized in a number of big intercorporate disputes. In this method, attorneys for each disputant are given a short time (not more than a day) in which to present the basic elements of their case to senior executives of both parties. After the presentation, the senior executives try to negotiate a settlement of the case, usually with the aid of a neutral advisor. If there is no settlement, the advisor gives the parties his opinion of the likely outcome if the dispute were litigated. This dose of reality at times helps to break the deadlock.

In this section, I have distinguished among a number of procedures used for settling disputes. Some are public, some private. Some are official, some unofficial. Some are formal, some informal. These procedures overlap, and each has its limitations and advantages. They are related in different ways to outcomes and consequences. A number of procedures may also be used for the settlement of a single dispute. Table 6-1 summarizes the salient features of the more widely used procedures.

Obviously, no one procedure is applicable to every kind of problem. A number of considerations appear relevant in the selection of a particular method. One is the relationship between the disputants; that is, is there an ongoing relationship between the disputants, such as business partners, or is the dispute the result of a single encounter, such as an automobile accident? When an ongoing relationship is involved, it is more productive for the parties to work out their difficulties through negotiation or mediation, if necessary. An advantage of mediation is that it encourages the restructuring of the underlying relationship so as to eliminate the source of conflict rather than dealing only with the manifestation of conflict (Bush and Folger, 2005). Another consideration is the nature of the dispute. If a precedent is required, such as in civil rights cases, litigation in the form of class action may be appropriate. The amount at stake in a dispute also plays a role in deciding on the type of dispute-resolution procedure. Small, simple cases might end up in small-claims courts, whereas more complex issues might require court-ordered arbitration, such as in contract negotiation disputes between public employers and unions. Speed and cost are other relevant factors. For example, arbitration may be speedier and less costly than a court trial. Finally, consideration must be given also to the power relationship between the parties. When one party in a dispute has much less bargaining strength than the other, as in the case of a pollution victim faced by a powerful corporation, an adjudicatory forum in which principle, not power, will determine the outcome may be desirable. In the remainder of this chapter, I shall consider why some disputants turn to legal mechanisms of

TABLE 6-1   Partial List of Characteristics of the Major Primary and Hybrid Dispute-Resolution Processes

Negotiation	Mediation	Arbitration	Adjudication	Rent-a-Judge	Minitrial
Voluntary	Voluntary	Voluntary, unless contractual or court-ordered	Nonvoluntary	Voluntary	Voluntary
Nonbinding	Nonbinding	Binding, usually no appeal	Binding, subject to appeal	Binding, but subject to appeal, and possibly, review by trial court	Nonbinding
No third-party facilitator	Party-selected facilitator	Party-selected third-party decision maker	Imposed third-party neutral decision maker	Party-selected third-party decision maker, usually a former judge or lawyer	Third-party neutral adviser
Informal and unstructured	Informal and unstructured	Procedurally less formal than adjudication	Highly procedural; formalized and structured by predetermined, rigid rules	Flexible as to timing, place, and procedures	Less formal than adjudication and arbitration
Presentation of proofs, usually indirect or nonexistent	Presentation of proofs less important than attitudes of each party	Opportunity for each party to present proofs supporting decision in its favor	Opportunity for each party to present proofs supporting decisions in its favor	Opportunity for each party to present proofs supporting decisions in its favor	Opportunity and responsibility for each party to present proofs supporting decisions in its favor
Mutually acceptable agreement	Mutually acceptable agreement sought	Compromise result possible	Win/lose outcome	Win/lose outcome (judgment of court)	Mutually acceptable agreement sought
Agreement usually included in contract or release sought	Agreement usually embodied in contract or release	Reason for result not usually required	Expectation of reasoned statement	Findings of fact and conclusion of law possible but not required	Agreement usually embodied in contract or release

(Continued)

TABLE 6-1 (Continued)

Negotiation	Mediation	Arbitration	Adjudication	Rent-a-Judge	Minitrial
Emphasis on disputants' relationship	Emphasis on disputants' relationship	Consistency and predictability balanced against concerns for disputants' relationship	Process emphasizes attaining substantive consistency and predictability results	Adherence to norms, laws, and precedent	Emphasis on sound, cost-effective, and fair resolution satisfactory to both parties
Highly private process	Private process	Private process unless judicial enforcement sought	Public process; lack of privacy of submissions	Private process, unless judicial enforcement sought	Highly private process

conflict resolution, under what circumstances they choose the law rather than some other procedures, and the limitations of the law in resolving conflicts.

DEMANDS FOR COURT SERVICES IN DISPUTE RESOLUTION

More and more Americans turn to the courts to tell them how to live their lives and there is an explosion in legalisms (Rosen, 2001). A topical *Newsweek* (2003) cover is "Lawsuit Hell" and the article on litigation is entitled "Civil Wars." Former Chief Justice Warren E. Burger aptly remarked that "our society is drowning in litigation" (quoted by Cross, 1992:647). Indeed, litigation is becoming a national pastime, and more and more people are telling their troubles to a judge (Haltom and McCann, 2004). The President's Council on Competitiveness (1991) lamented already close to two decades ago that in 1989 almost 18 million new civil cases were filed in state and federal courts—one for every 10 adults. Between 1960 and 1990, the number of lawsuits filed in federal district courts increased from about 90,000 to more than 250,000 and exceeded 276,000 by the end of 1993 and topped 300,000 at the end of the decade. In 2009, the number of filings reached almost 400,000 (Administrative Office of the U.S. Courts, 2010). During the same period, there were corresponding augmentations in the number of court employees, judges, and lawyers. By the onset of the twenty-first century, for example, there was already one lawyer for every 300 Americans. Because of questionable comparability of data, this is a rough comparison, but Japan has a lawyer–population ratio of about 1:10,000 (Stumpf and Culver, 1992:63). The ratio in Germany is approximately 1:2,500; in England 1:1,400; and in Sweden 1:5,200. These ratios demonstrate how the United States, which has about 5 percent of the world's population, accounts for roughly more than two-thirds of all the world's lawyers—well over a million in 2007 and growing.

The increase in district court cases, dramatic as it has been, is dwarfed by the growth of caseloads in appeals courts—from 3,765 in 1960 to 29,580 in 1983. This is an increase of 686 percent (Posner, 1996:65). By the end of 1993, the caseloads in appeals courts came close to 49,000; and over a decade and a half later, in 2009, almost 84,000 new appeals were filed (Administrative Office of the U.S. Courts, 2010:1). The same conditions prevail in state courts. For example, since 1960, the number of lawsuits has more than tripled in Massachusetts and doubled in Los Angeles County (Luten, 2009). Although New York City's population has not grown, its civil court caseload rose 50 percent from 1978 to 1984 (Lauter, 1986:46) and another 50 percent by 2006. This extraordinary rise in civil litigation coincidentally comes at a time when the courts are already inundated with criminal cases.

Two decades ago already, the cost of tort litigation was estimated to be between $280 billion and $300 billion annually (Epp, 1992:25), and these are rather conservative figures. By 2008, it exceeded $590 billion. In 2008, U.S. tort costs increased by 1.1 percent over 2007 figures according to the Towers Perrin 2009 Update on U.S. Tort Cost Trends (www.towerswatson.com). While overall economic growth was 3.3 percent, 2008 marks the fifth consecutive year of a decline in the ratio of tort costs to gross domestic product (GDP), as shown in Table 6-2. Forecasted growth for the coming years is expected to be around 3 percent. Over the past six decades, the increase in tort litigation costs was 2 percent higher than the increase in the GDP.

Tort litigation primarily involves claims or damages related to personal injury. About 47 percent of all torts involve lawsuits between individuals, 37 percent between individuals and business, and the rest between individuals and government agencies or hospitals (Haltom and McCann, 2004) A rather controversial study, carried out by a University of Texas finance professor, Stephen P. Magee (1989) and his associates, finds that predatory and frivolous lawsuits reduced the GDP to 10 percent below its potential during the 1980s—at a price tag of about $1 million per attorney. Legal fees, damage awards, and increased insurance premiums account for about $80 billion, representing a small fraction of the GNP. Most costs are indirect, such as time wasted in filing questionable suits; the loss

TABLE 6-2 U.S. Tort Costs Up Slightly in 2008; Long-Term Increases Anticipated		
Growth of U.S. Tort Costs and GDP		
Years	*Average Annual Increase in Tort Costs (%)*	*Average Annual Increase in GDP (%)*
1951–1960	11.6	6.0
1961–1970	9.8	7.0
1971–1980	11.9	10.4
1981–1990	11.8	7.6
1991–2000	3.2	5.4
2001	14.7	3.2
2002	13.4	3.4
2003	5.5	4.7
2004	6.0	6.6
2005	0.4	6.3
2006	–5.6	6.1
2007	2.1	4.8
2008	1.1	3.3
58 years (1951–2008)	8.9	6.9

of potential engineers, physicians, and scientists to the legal profession; and the withholding of certain products from the market to reduce the potential for liability action. The so-called tort tax is responsible for about 30 percent of the price of a stepladder and 95 percent of the cost of childhood vaccines. Influential reports by the Institute for Legal Studies (Epp, 1992; Galanter, 1992) attempt to refute these allegations and conclude that the case of economic growth versus the number of lawyers rests on frivolous claims. The controversy continues (Cross, 1992; Galanter, 1993; Haltom and McCann, 2004).

There are several explanations for the increase in civil litigation over time. Americans today tend to accept that being sued is the price of freedom, they seem more fascinated by litigation than people perhaps in any other society, and the legal system is more prone to frivolous lawsuits (a rather value-laden term) as a result. In a sense, it is a form of entertainment and a favorite indoor activity to see due process take its course on television as evidenced by the enormous onslaught and popularity of law-related programming (Rapping, 2004; Zobel, 1994). Some even argue that lawsuits are good for America (Bogus, 2001). For instance, product liability litigation has saved countless lives, brought critical information to light (along with labels that warn us about almost everything that could be potentially harmful), forced manufacturers to make products safer, and driven off the market unreasonably dangerous products when regulatory agencies or Congress lacked the political will to do so (Koenig and Rustad, 2004). From time to time, however, such litigations can get out of control. For example, toothbrushes seem like innocent little things. Inexpensive and simple to use, they make life a lot more pleasant for everybody. But in 1999, a couple of lawyers filed a class-action suit against several manufacturers arguing that toothbrushes are actually dangerous. When used improperly, the lawyers said, they can lead to discomfort, receding gums, and sensitive teeth—conditions that could, in extreme cases, cost a few thousand dollars to repair. If the plaintiffs' attorneys had been able to convince a jury that they were right, the defendants could have been hit with a judgment of $1 billion or more. The case was thrown out of court and dampened temporarily the proliferation of a new breed of dubious class-action suits (France, 2001:122). Another example would be drying laundry on clotheslines in front or back of one's home. There are some 3,000,000 private communities in the United States, and many forbid drying clothes outside (despite the obvious environmental benefits) because it is considered an eyesore, just like junk cars, and a marker of poverty that lowers poverty values and lawsuits are being used to clamp down on users of outdoors clotheslines (Urbina, 2009).

Some economists contend that litigation is related to the proportion of lawyers in the population and the relative expenditure on civil justice (Chinloy, 1989:8, 88–89, 90; Nelson, 2009; Olson, 2004). Basically, the more lawyers there are, the greater is the quantity of litigation. Lawyers are better informed about the legal system than the client, and as a result, there is an asymmetric exchange of information between them. Thus, an increase in the supply of lawyers can increase the demand for legal services and litigation. A comparable argument is applicable to medical care. Physicians are specialized and have more information on diagnosis and procedure than patients do. The same kind of asymmetric relationship exists as between lawyers and clients, and in both cases, there is an economic incentive (billable hours, fees, and so on) to suggest intervention. The increase in the number of lawyers also increases competition and reduces a variety of costs, such as the cost of retaining an attorney and lower contingency fees. The cost to the litigant decreases while the total cost of tort action goes up. The increase in the supply of lawyers results in more litigation, increasing the demand for lawyers. This spiral is fueled by incentives in the American legal system that encourage litigation, such as the lack of penalty to litigants. An effective way to moderate the quantity of litigation in this context would be to evoke the so-called English rule (Polinsky and Rubinfeld, 1998) (used in England and Japan, among other places), under which the defendant recovers costs against an unsuccessful plaintiff.

In addition to the hypothesis that the supply of lawyers accounts for the increase in court cases, it is possible that there has been an increase in the number of individuals who have, at one time or another, been involved in litigation. An expansion in the volume of litigation may result even from a small increase in the total number of litigants. Such an expansion may be attributed to changes in the social and political conditions that facilitate the translation of conflicts and disputes into lawsuits. Although litigation requires a substantial investment of time and money, in recent years a number of attempts have been made to reduce or redistribute such costs through, for example, the provision of free legal services. Because of the greater availability of inexpensive or free legal services to individuals who were formerly unable to afford to bring disputes to court, the amount of litigation also may have increased (Goldman and Sarat, 1978:41).

An additional explanation for the increase in the number of cases reaching the courts may be that although the number of litigants has not increased, the relatively few individuals or organizations (that is, repeat players) who typically use courts to settle disputes have in recent years simply found more occasion to do so. This resulted in a kind of assembly-line litigation aided by all-but-automated computerized litigation packets that are now available for products ranging from handguns to tires (France, 2001).

The increase in litigation is also related to the increase in the range and variety of legally actionable or resolvable problems.

> As the scope of law expands, as more legal rights and remedies are created, the amount of litigation increases as a result of the new opportunities for court action. As new rights are created, litigation may be necessary to clarify the way in which those rights will be defined and understood by the courts. Furthermore, the creation of new rights may direct the attention of organized interest groups to the judiciary. Interest groups may come to perceive litigation as a viable strategy for stimulating group mobilization to achieve the group's political goals. (Goldman and Sarat, 1978:41)

At the same time, it is also plausible that litigation is not viewed by the parties as an effort to settle a conflict; "instead it is a tactical engagement in a sustained war" (Barton, 1975:575). In such a situation, resolving the legal issue or the conflict becomes secondary to creating publicity for a cause or to obtaining a delay of decision through procedural grounds (see, for example, Skerry, 1998). An example of this is a situation in which general minority rights have priority over the resolution of a specific disagreement, such as alleged discrimination in hiring or promotion. It is also part of the so-called entitlement mentality evidenced by general demands rather than specific claims and epitomized by what one author refers to as the "rights talk" (Glendon, 1991). It is perhaps most pronounced in instances of prisoners' lawsuits where inmates claim that prisons have violated their rights to:

- an orthopedically correct wooden gymnasium floor.
- replacing worn-out running shoes (the judge in this Canadian case actually rules in favor of the plaintiff stating that there is an obligation to replace an inmate's shoes when they are inadequate from wear) (Schmitz, 2009).
- wear sunglasses.
- own Soap on a Rope.
- have Rolling Stone magazine delivered to isolation cells.
- practice martial arts.
- have two hot meals.
- low-cholesterol diet and prescription dandruff shampoo (filed by a death row inmate in California in addition to 15 other similar suits).
- silky women's lingerie, makeup and jewelry (by a 47-year-old male inmate).
- unlimited refills of Kool-Aid.
- larger pieces of cake because the ones served in the prison cafeteria are too small (Manning, 1995).
- In highly publicized 2004 case, a convicted murderer sued New York state for $650,000 for refusing to pay for sex-change operation. He wants the state to pay for hormonal therapy, breast implants, electrolysis, and genital reassignment surgery. He then wants to be transferred to a women's prison.
- In late 2010, a Google search on frivolous prisoners lawsuits came up with over 300,000 hits, a goldmine for many other examples.

Prisoners' lawsuits have been steadily increasing since the 1964 Supreme Court decision permitting prisoners to sue state correctional officials when conditions of confinement failed to meet constitutional standards. The Court had in mind complaints involving excessive force, inadequate medical treatment, and freedom of religious expression. Instead, the courts often ended up with a variety of frivolous suits, and now prisoners' lawsuits make up around 20 percent of all civil cases before the federal courts (Cox, 2009; *Newsweek*, 1995:6). This kind of court use has been dubbed as "recreational litigation," and fewer that 1 percent of such suits result in a verdict for the prisoner, and most are dismissed for causes that counsel would have foreseen. Note that constitutional right to an attorney does not apply to such civil cases (Dilworth, 1995). Finally, because of the huge price tag, some states have already passed laws that penalize inmates if a judge rules their lawsuits frivolous. The state can delay a parole hearing by two months or raid half of the inmate's prison bank account (Bell, 1995). But care must be exercised that frivolous lawsuits are not turned into a serious denial of rights.

Sheldon Goldman and Austin Sarat (1978:41–43) identify three generic factors that may explain litigation. The first they call *social development*. Variation in the frequency of litigation is a function of changes in the level of complexity, differentiation, and skill of the society in which courts operate. Social development and changes in the structure of society bring about increased reliance on courts to process disputes. In less-developed societies, as a result of stable and enduring contacts among individuals, disputes are easier to resolve informally. Consequently, courts play a less important role in disputes. In more complex societies, on the other hand, relationships are typically more transitory in nature, disputes often take place between strangers and under such circumstances, and informal dispute processing is impractical. Furthermore, in developed societies, there is no longer a single dominant ethos or a set of customs that results from heterogeneity, secularization, and the closer interaction among different subgroups with specific norms (Barton, 1975:574). For example, corporate executives and environmentalists offer radically different ethical norms for the same activities, such as potentially hazardous waste disposal.

The second generic factor that explains why disputes are translated into demands for court services is subjective cost/benefit calculations on the part of disputants. For some disputants, the decision to use courts is a relatively objective, well-thought-out decision, because they must calculate a "risk" factor and weigh what they may lose against the possible benefits of doing nothing or of using different methods of conflict resolution. For others, however, resorting to courts may be an act "that has value because of its cathartic effect, even though it may not produce tangible, material benefits" (Goldman and Sarat, 1978:42). In such a situation, vindictiveness, spite, or the desire for a "moral" victory outweighs the financial considerations. Moreover, the disputants' decision to use the court decreases the pressure upon them to resolve disputes by using nonlegal resources that they can mobilize. Informal and private settlements seem less likely where the parties have the option for legal recourse (Turk, 1978:224).

The third generic factor in litigation is the creation of more legally actionable rights and remedies by legislatures and courts. Goldman and Sarat state, "The greater the reach and scope of the legal system, the higher its litigation rate will be" (1978:42). To some extent, the expanded use of courts is attributable to the expansion of rights and remedies stemming from Supreme Court decisions. The growing scope of law increases litigation implicitly or explicitly by expanding the jurisdiction of the courts. The creation of new rights is likely to stimulate litigation designed to vindicate or protect those rights. For example, the "criminal rights explosion" of the 1960s followed the logic that the creation of new rights would stimulate subsequent litigations that, in turn, would create new rights that would require further litigation.

Thus, with the creation of new norms, courts actually (although unintentionally) promote disputing, because these new norms may lead to claims that otherwise would not have been asserted. For example, the 1973 Supreme Court decision in *Roe v. Wade* invalidating statutes prohibiting abortions led to a series of disputes concerning such issues as whether the federal government had to pay for abortion through its Medicaid program and whether hospitals receiving federal funds had to make facilities for abortions available. Moreover, in clarifying certain norms, courts may make other normative conflicts salient and thus more likely to be disputed. Thus, the abortion decision has also led to disputes over whether parents must consent to a minor's abortion and whether a husband can veto his wife's decision to terminate a pregnancy (Lempert, 1978:97–98). Even laws intended for other purposes can be used as dispute facilitators. For example, the racketeering law which was passed in 1970 as a weapon for fighting organized crime has been used against militant anti-abortion groups. A class-action suit filed by the National Organization for Women on behalf of some 900 abortion clinics claimed that anti-abortion leaders and their organizations, Operation Rescue National and the Pro-Life Action League, violated the Racketeer Influenced and Corrupt Organizations statute (RICO) by conducting a nationwide conspiracy to intimidate abortion providers and patients. A jury recently ruled in favor of the plaintiff and allows abortion clinics to seek additional damages for the costs of added security (*Economist*, 1998:32).

In addition, since the mid-1950s the courts have discovered a slate of new constitutional rights, protections, and entitlements for whole groups of people—for example, disenfranchised voters, women, Hispanics, homosexuals, weight-challenged people, prisoners, children, and mental patients. Each of these new rights in turn creates potentially conflict-laden situations conducive to further litigation. At the same time, questions are being raised by critics about the "rights industry" running amok and its impact on major institutions (Morgan, 1984).

Variations in Litigation Rates

There are two general ways of measuring judicial involvement in dispute settlement (Galanter, 1988; Kritzer, 1988; Lempert, 1978). It can be measured by the percentage of disputes that courts play some part in resolving, and by the percentage of the adult population who take disputes to courts. With both measures, there are some difficulties. As Richard Lempert (1978:99) points out, there are several ways in which courts contribute to dispute settlement:

1. Courts establish norms that influence or control the private settlement of disputes. For example, norms established in an appellate opinion resolving one dispute can lead other disputants to resolve their conflict without legal intervention.
2. Courts ratify private settlements and provide guarantees of compliance. For example, in divorce cases where the parties have already reached an agreement, courts ratify that agreement which carries with it the probability of sanctions should it be breached.
3. Courts can escalate the cost of disputing, thereby increasing the likelihood of private settlement.
4. Courts provide opportunities to disputants to learn about each other's cases, thus increasing the probability of private settlement by decreasing mutual uncertainty.
5. Court staff act as mediators to encourage consensual private settlement.
6. Courts resolve certain issues in the case, leading disputants to agree on others.
7. Courts authoritatively resolve disputes.

Thus, at times, it is difficult to determine the extent to which courts contribute to dispute settlement. The clearest case is when disputes are adjudicated and a settlement is imposed after a full trial. But many cases do not end up at trials. A settlement may be reached during a pretrial conference or through informal negotiations where the judge is a participant. Judges also exert informal pressure, even after litigation has commenced, and attorneys usually listen to the recommended solutions. Settlement is also encouraged by the mounting financial costs. Under the unique American rule that each side pays his or her own way (the "English rule," for example, as noted earlier, forces the loser to pay for fees and court costs for both sides), the plaintiff's lawyers who make big enough nuisances of themselves will usually get an out-of-court settlement. Defendants calculate that it is cheaper to settle than to try a case, even if there is a good likelihood that they will win. Thus, attempts to explore the dispute-settlement functions of courts over time must consider the different roles courts play and the influences they exert. Lempert notes, "Exploration is complicated by difficulties in measuring the various ways that courts contribute to dispute settlement, and these difficulties are compounded if the measures must allow comparisons over time" (1978:100).

Complications also arise in attempts to measure longitudinally the percentage of the adult population who use court services in disputes. The figures may be inaccurate to the extent that certain individuals or organizations are "repeat players" (Galanter, 1974). Moreover, many courts do not keep adequate records for long periods of time. Where records are kept, the record-keeping procedures vary. Historically, a number of minor courts, such as justice of the peace and magistrate courts, did not keep records. Over time, the court systems had changed through reorganization, and new courts were established and others were eliminated. There were also changes in the jurisdiction of many courts. Consequently, there are some questions about the validity and reliability of longitudinal studies that deal with rates of litigation over time. In view of these precautions, let us turn briefly to some studies that have challenged the idea that the dispute-processing function of the courts has increased in recent years as a result of social and economic changes.

In modern societies such as the United States, the use of courts as a forum for conflict resolution is on the increase as a result of societal developments toward increased complexity, heterogeneity, and the prevalence of impersonal and contractual relations. (Where else would a state—Missouri—sue an employee who objected to wearing a tie to work? After multiple trials and appeals, the employee lost—but for the record that was before the era of widespread informality in attire and manners at the work place.) There is even an argument suggesting that computers have made a major contribution to increases in litigation by making it feasible to engage in protracted, and occasionally frivolous, litigation (Gerson, 1994). Although data are available to support these contentions, some authors contend that social, economic, and technological developments do not necessarily lead to higher rates of litigation. For example, Lawrence M. Friedman (2005:338) argues that there is no evidence that nineteenth-century America witnessed proportionately less interpersonal litigation than mid-twentieth-century America, despite more cohesive kin and residential systems. Similarly, over time in Spain, the litigation rate "has remained remarkably constant and at a relatively low rate . . . the process of economic change does not seem to have affected the rate of litigation" (Jose Toharia, quoted by Grossman and Sarat, 1975:59).

A similar conclusion was reached by Vilhelm Aubert (1969) in his study of the Norwegian legal system. He notes that the demand for dispute resolution during the last 100 years has remained stable or has even decreased throughout a period characterized by vast social changes and great economic progress, whereas the demand for most other kinds of services has multiplied at a very rapid rate. Aubert concludes that "the pure legal model plays a modest part in actual instances of conflict resolution in Norway today" (1969:302). Similarly, Joel B. Grossman and Austin Sarat conclude that "industrialization is a useful predictor of levels of legal activity but not litigation rates; legal activity but not litigation rates appears to be greater in more industrialized areas" (1975:343). Their study was based on litigation rates in federal courts in the United States from 1902 to 1972.

In a study of the civil load of two trial courts in California between 1890 and 1970, Lawrence M. Friedman and Robert V. Percival sampled civil case files of the superior courts in two counties. They found that highly developed economic systems do not show growth in their litigation. On the contrary, rates tend to decline in the face of rapid economic growth in capitalist economies (Milhaupt and Pistor, 2010). Although they are careful about the generalizability of their data, they conclude that "the dispute settlement function in the courts is declining" (1976:296). They attempt to explain the decline in litigation by suggesting that uncertainty—a prime breeder of litigation—has declined in the law and that rules are more "settled" now than in 1890. The routine administrative function has replaced the dispute-settlement functions in these courts. It is plausible that the court itself—its style, its mode of operation—discourages its use for dispute settlement. In reanalyzing the data used by Friedman and Percival, Richard Lempert comes to the opposite conclusion: Although "the mix of judicial business has changed over the years" and there is "little reason to believe that courts today are functionally less important as dispute settlers than they were in 1890 . . . overall, I do not believe that we can conclude from the Friedman and Percival data that the dispute settlement function of courts . . . has diminished over time" (1976:133). Lempert further comments that the conclusion about the diminution in the dispute-settlement activity of trial courts is overstated because Friedman and Percival neglect the mediative activity of trial judges and court personnel (1978:131). This neglect is attributable, in part, to the difficulty, if not the impossibility, of measuring activities of courts over time.

In addition to these studies contending that social and economic developments, with their concomitant increases in the complexity and impersonality in social relations, do not lead to higher rates of litigation, there is also a substantial amount of differentiation in the use of courts in disputes among other nations. Americans are more likely to turn to the civil court system than are people in similar situations in other countries (Kritzer, 1991:407). Henry W. Ehrmann (1976:83–84) points out that litigiousness, the propensity to settle disputes through the judicial process, is a cultural factor of some importance. Studies that have attempted to compare such attitudes cross-culturally have used as a measure the index of civil cases initiated per unit of population. Some of the findings of cross-cultural studies counter widely held assumptions about the litigiousness of various nations. Indians do not exhibit a propensity for litigation and never resort to legal measures when alternative means to resolve a dispute are available, and in India, there is a decrease in court cases since the pre-independence period (Moog, 1993).

In citing a study by Brian Able-Smith and Robert Stevens suggesting that "in England 'the law' plays a less important role than in almost any other western country," Ehrmann (1976:84) provides figures to show an extraordinarily high litigation rate for Great Britain, "higher than that for Western Germany, whose population is frequently described as being addicted to solving conflicts by lawsuits." The litigation rate per 100,000 population in Great Britain was 3,605 in 1969, and 2,085 in the former West

Germany during the same year. Enormous differences also exist in the rate of litigation between Denmark and other Scandinavian countries. Resorting to the judiciary in disputes is about ten times higher in Denmark than in Norway, Sweden, or Finland. Ehrmann finds it difficult to explain the differences between these countries, especially in view of the fact that Norway has about three times as many attorneys per 100,000 population as Denmark.

It is also difficult to explain the relatively high litigation rates for Japan in relation to some Western European countries and in view of the contention that the courts are still not a highly valued site for conflict resolution. The litigation rate for Japan was 980 per 100,000 population in 1986—but still ten times lower than in California (Tanase, 1995:58). Comparable rates for Scandinavian countries for the same year were 683 for Sweden, 493 for Finland, and 307 for Norway. In an often-quoted article, "Dispute Resolution in Japan," Takeyoshi Kawashima (1969) discusses specific social attitudes toward disputes that are reflected in the judicial process. Traditionally, the Japanese prefer extrajudicial, informal means of settling a controversy. Often, an extension of apology can resolve a dispute. By contrast, in many countries, an apology has legal implications and is often admissible in legal proceedings. In this connection, it is interesting to note that to say sorry may not be so hard to utter in British Columbia, Canada, where in early 2010 the provincial government once again proposed legislation that would allow individuals and organizations to apologize without risking liability for damages or other penalties. There are also some preliminary findings suggesting that in the United States, apology seems to play a role in hospital litigations and patients are less likely to sue if they receive full disclosure and an apology, along with an offer of compensation (Landro, 2009).

Litigation in Japan presupposes and admits the existence of a dispute and leads to a decision that makes clear who is right and who is wrong in accordance with legal standards. This is contrary to the attitude in favor of a compromise that does not assign a moral fault to disputants. This attitude is related to the nature of social groups in Japan, which are hierarchical in the sense that differences in social status are reflected in degrees of deference and authority; the relations among individuals in social groups are intimate and diffuse. Legal intervention in disputes would upset the harmonious social relationships. As a result, Kawashima contends, the Japanese not only hesitate to resort to a lawsuit but also are quite ready to settle a dispute through informal means of dispute resolution, such as mediation and conciliation (see also Oda, 2009). The use of law is further discouraged by the lack of easy availability of lawyers and judges. Donald Black (1989:84) notes that the number of judges and lawyers per capita has declined in Japan since the 1920s. In fact, the total number of judges has not increased since 1890. Today, there is only one judge for every 60,000 persons, compared with one for every 22,000 a century ago. This is due to Japan's decision to place statutory limitations on the number of judges and prosecutors in its system (Westermann and Burfeind, 1991:162). The number of lawyers is much smaller in Japan than in the United States—some 12,000 as contrasted with a very conservative estimate of about 950,000 in the late 1990s. (It is worth noting that the population of Japan is less than half that of the United States.) A typical, uncomplicated civil case can take five or ten years to be heard (*Economist*, 1993:62).

Moreover, in Japan, the individual who asserts legal rights and insists on judicial intervention

> is thought to be "inflexible" and selfish. . . . Introduction of a lawyer into a business conference is thought to be an unfriendly act . . . equal to an explicit threat of litigation. . . . When acts such as drafting a contract or the bringing of a suit are unavoidable, the contract is made as short and flexible as possible, or the act of suit is viewed as deplorable, even by the plaintiff. . . . The law . . . goes directly contrary to the Japanese feeling that the relations (even business relations) should be based upon a warm subjective relationship which can solve every practical problem by mutual compromise and accommodation, regardless of formal rights and obligations. The most notable practical result of this attitude is a paucity of litigation in Japan. (Strick, 1977:209)

Undoubtedly, it is difficult to reconcile the differences between these arguments and the relatively high rate of litigation in Japan. It is possible that the attitudes toward the law as a means of conflict resolution are changing and that in urban areas there is a greater reliance on the judiciary to settle disputes. However, I have no recent data to support these contentions, and the puzzle has yet to be solved empirically in 2010.

Complete and reliable data are lacking also for the United States. However, the differences that exist between two neighboring states, Massachusetts and New Hampshire, are startling. In Massachusetts, the litigation rate for 1971 per 100,000 was 1,814, and in New Hampshire for the same year 345. The differences point to the likely fact that the socioeconomic characteristics of a state or the particularities of its historic court system will have an effect on people's inclination to take their disputes to the courts (Ehrmann, 1976:84). But why the difference in litigation rates between two neighboring New England states should be that enormous remains unexplained.

Even within a state, differences in litigation rates exist among cities of comparable size and characteristics. In a study of four Wisconsin cities, Herbert Jacob (1969:92) suggests that "political culture may be a significant explanatory device for accounting for the differences in litigation rates." A traditional political culture is characterized by a relatively low level of bureaucratization in government and a reluctance to invoke governmental processes. There is a greater reliance on private dispute-settling processes in a traditional culture than in a more modern one with a more highly bureaucratized government. In traditional political cultures, people make greater efforts to settle disputes between themselves as neighbors and friends, and they have greater opportunities to settle conflicts within the confines of established private relationships. In a modern political culture, personal relationships are more strained, individuals deal with each other more on a contractual basis, and they have, as a result, less confidence in using private dispute-settling procedures. At the same time, they are more willing "to invoke the public processes of government for solving their problems, be they a neighborhood-development program needing a city council decision or a creditor-debtor conflict which requires the services of a court" (Jacob, 1969:92). Jacob provides some evidence for his contention that the use of courts will be greater in more modern political cultures. In his study on debtors, he found that the process of taking a debtor to court to collect a loan occurs more frequently in modern political cultures. But, beyond that, available data do not permit one to make further generalizations concerning the impact of political culture on the "propensity to sue" (Kritzer, 1988) although it may play a role in encouraging excess consumption and subsequent inability to pay for the goods and services (see, for example, Ritzer, 2001, 2010).

As a final point, in the past few years the term *litigation explosion* has received considerable fresh publicity in the wake of the publication of Walter Olson's controversial book by the same title (1991). He contends that there is a "revolution" in civil litigation which he views as the "civil war in very, very slow motion." But is there really such an "explosion," or is it a myth? It depends on whom one asks. The estimated number of lawsuits filed each year varies from 18 to 30 million, but no one really knows the precise numbers (Jacob, 1995) at a cost to society of an estimated $200 billion a year (*Newsweek*, 2003:45). It is difficult to collect data from the antiquated record-keeping systems in courthouses around the country. Records are still filed in thousands of county seats and most kept on paper. With civil cases, each jurisdiction has its own system of cataloging the number of people suing and the kind of claim, making comparisons between courts difficult. Close to half of the states lump all civil claims together, making it difficult to tell how many are medical; malpractice, or product liability disputes. There is not enough incentive for local courts to spend money on anything but salaries and administration, and as a consequence there is a paucity of comparative statistical data. Federal court records are, fortunately for researchers, more sophisticated. With these caveats, let us return to the question of litigation explosion.

Richard A. Posner (1996) talks about the caseload "crisis" of federal courts. He notes that civil cases increased from 48,886 to 210,503, more than 330 percent, from 1960 to 1983 (1996:65). Appeals, as indicated earlier, increased 686 percent for the same time period. This trend continued well into the late 2000s as evidenced by comparable increase in civil filings in federal courts (Administrative Office of the U.S. Courts, 2010). Federal litigation has increased much faster than the population, and this is a significant fact (Haltom and McCann, 2004). But there are 50 state court systems in addition to federal courts where some 95 percent of cases are filed. State court cases number in the millions. Is there a litigation explosion in state courts similar to that in federal courts? A study of court filings in 25 states by the National Center for State Courts contends that the litigation explosion is a myth and that litigation rates actually declined between 1981 and 1984, the most recent year with available data (Lauter, 1986:46). The states that have shown an increase are the ones with large population growth, such as California, Florida, and Texas. A surprising finding was that even in small-claims courts, where simplified legal procedures are supposed to ease barriers to filing suits, filings have been decreasing. But despite the decline, there were some 13.6 million suits filed in state courts in 1984.

But filing a case does not necessarily mean that it is judicially resolved. Most cases do not reach the trial stage. This is particularly true in accident and personal injury matters. Insurance companies tend to settle most claims out of court. In California, for example, fewer than 1 percent of filed accident claims go to trial; the rest are settled along the way (Friedman, 1985:18).

Thus, what is important are not the numbers, but the types of cases filed. In recent years, whole new areas of litigation opened up, such as malpractice, product liability, and employment discrimination (see, for example, Luten, 2009). Social Security cases have burgeoned as the government has attempted to restrict benefits, and suits in which the government is seeking to collect money from individuals have grown 6,600 percent since 1975 (Lauter, 1986:46). Disputants in traditional cases such as contract disputes, consumer matters, landlord–tenant quarrels, and real estate are slowly discovering alternative mechanisms of dispute resolution. There is a change in the types of cases as courts respond to social and legal developments over the years. But there are still questions that researchers cannot answer with certainty: What kinds of cases come to court? Who wins? How often juries award damages, including punitive ones? And how much do plaintiffs get in cases settled before trial?

PREREQUISITES FOR THE USE OF COURTS IN DISPUTE RESOLUTION

Courts provide a forum for the settlement of a variety of private and public disputes. The courts are considered a neutral and impartial place for dispute processing. Other than criminal cases, legal disputes are processed in civil courts. Individuals and organizations who want to use the courts for dispute processing must meet certain legal requirements. At the minimum, plaintiffs must be able to demonstrate justiciability and standing (Jacob, 1969:17–19).

Justiciability means that the conflict is viable to trial and courts. The court must be mandated to provide a remedy. In the United States, most disputes are justiciable in one court or another, although the jurisdiction of particular courts varies. For example, federal courts are not permitted to grant divorces or adoptions or to probate wills. Various state courts exist for these and most other cases excluded from the federal judiciary. The potential litigant must turn the grievance into a legal dispute and must determine, with or without the aid of an attorney, whether the complaint is justiciable. Essentially, justiciability refers to real and substantial controversy that is appropriate for judicial determination, as differentiated from disputes or differences of a hypothetical or an abstract character. Furthermore, in some instances, the courts may not be authorized to intervene in certain types of disputes. For example, the Wagner Act forbade court intervention in most labor disputes.

Standing is a more severe limitation to litigation than justiciability. The theory behind standing is that individuals should be able to bring lawsuits only if their personal legal rights have been violated. For example, a taxpayer may not sue the government to prevent the expenditure of funds for an objectionable purpose because the ordinary taxpayer's stake in the expenditure is minimal. If one disapproves what the CIA or the Army Corps of Engineers are doing, one is supposed to take it up with Congress, not with the courts. Similarly, a mother-in-law cannot sue for a divorce: Such proceedings must be initiated by the husband or wife. It should be noted though that since the late 1960s, the doctrine of standing has been broadened by activist courts (see Judicial Lawmaking in Chapter 4) eager to solve the nation's problems (Frum, 1993). Various public-interest groups, as it will be discussed later, have used the court against private companies and government agencies.

Herbert Jacob (1969:18) points out that the limits to justiciability and standing are not social accidents. They are related to political compromises achieved over the distribution of powers and functions between various branches of the government and interest groups who had favorable access to one branch of government or another. The jurisdiction of courts in most cases is determined by legislation. The decision to present one kind of dispute or another in a court is a political one. For example, civil rights groups in the 1960s worked for the passage of laws that, among other things, gave federal courts broadened jurisdiction over disputes affecting civil rights, because they considered federal courts to be more favorably disposed to them than state courts or administrative agencies. The use of courts for collection purposes (in creditor–debtor disputes) or the settlement of complex public-policy disputes is also the product of legislative compromises brought about by interest-group pressures.

However, justiciability and standing are not the only limitations to the use of courts in disputes. There is also the old legal axiom *de minimus non curat lex*: The law will not concern itself with trifles. Trivial matters may not be litigated. For example, a court may refuse to hear a suit to recover a $10 overcharge even if the cause appears just (Lempert and Sanders, 1986:137). In addition, untold numbers of disputes arise over which the courts have clear jurisdiction and someone has standing to sue. But using the court is dependent on a number of considerations. These considerations are superimposed on the legal barriers to litigation.

Resorting to court services in disputes is voluntary for the plaintiffs; for defendants, participation in a legal dispute is involuntary. The plaintiffs approach the courts with different expectations and often through different circumstances from those of the defendants. Jacob notes, "Whereas the initiation of court action may promise relief to the plaintiff, it threatens deprivation for the defendant. Since the plaintiff initiates court action he can exert a certain degree of control over it, but the action often descends without warning upon defendants" (1969:19).

Economic resources for both plaintiffs and defendants are important in their decision to pursue a suit through trial and appeal. With the exception of magistrate courts and individuals who qualify for legal-aid services, plaintiffs are unlikely to use the courts unless they have sufficient funds to hire an attorney and bear the costs of litigation. The litigant must bear court fees for filing cases, for calling witnesses, and for compensating the jury. Disputants must also be able to afford the costs of delay, which occur when disputes are submitted to the courts. For example, automobile accident cases involving large sums of money do not reach the court dockets for several years in many large American cities. In the interim, the plaintiff has expenses. Often the cost of waiting must be calculated against the benefits of a quick settlement for only part of the claim. Obviously, for many people economic resources play an important role in the use of court services and may be decisive in out-of-court settlements.

Prior to initiating a lawsuit, individuals must recognize the relevance of court services to their problems. Jacob (1969:20) notes that the use of the judiciary varies with education, for better-educated individuals are more likely to differentiate between the courts and other agencies and be aware of their various services. Perception of the courts also varies with other factors, such as integration into a social group in which court usage has previously occurred or where it is relatively prevalent. Jacob says, "Thus it may be that certain ethnic groups of communities are more litigious than others. Members of such groups are more likely to perceive court action as relevant to their problems and consequently they become more frequent consumers of court services" (1969:20).

Socioeconomic status is also related to the use of the judiciary in disputes. Those who cannot afford a lawyer and the necessary court fees are less likely to litigate than those who have sufficient funds. Moreover, social status is related to the kind of court services that are used. In general, the poor are more likely to be defendants and recipients of court-ordered sanctions. Middle-class litigants are less likely to be subjected to court sanctions and more likely to benefit from the use of court services in their own behalf from the legitimization of their private agreements or from out-of-court negotiations.

A TYPOLOGY OF LITIGANTS

As noted in Chapter 3, the use of courts varies also by the types of litigants. Marc Galanter advances a typology of litigants by the frequency of the utilization of courts. Those who have only occasional recourse to the courts are called one-shotters, and those who are engaged in many similar litigations over time are designated as repeat players. Illustrations for the former include the wife in a divorce case and the auto injury claimant. The latter is exemplified by insurance or finance companies. Based on this typology, Galanter proposes a taxonomy of litigation by the configuration of parties. He comes up with four types of litigations—one-shotter versus one-shotter, repeat player versus one-shotter, one-shotter versus repeat player, and repeat player versus repeat player.

The largest number of cases involving disputes between one-shotters are divorces and insanity commitments. Disputes between one-shotters are "often between parties who have some intimate tie with one another, fighting over some unsharable good, often with overtones of 'spite' and 'irrationality' " (Galanter, 1974:108). The courts are used when an ongoing relationship ruptures and the law is invoked *ad hoc* instrumentally by the parties. When such disputes take place between neighbors or business partners, there may be a strong interest in vindication, and the court decisions are seldom appealed.

The second type of litigation, repeat players versus one-shotters, is exemplified by suits initiated by finance companies against debtors, landlords against tenants, and the Internal Revenue Service (IRS) against taxpayers. Except for personal injury cases, insanity hearings, and divorces, the great bulk of litigation is found in disputes between repeat players and one-shotters. Here, the law is used for routine processing of claims by parties for whom the making of such claims is a regular business activity. In many instances, courts authorize repeat players to borrow the government's power for their private purposes. Repeat players may use that power to achieve many objectives, such as to collect debts, oust tenants, or prohibit some harmful activity. In such a case, the plaintiff comes to court with a grievance. If the court considers the complaint a legitimate one, it issues a judgment or an injunction. The judgment authorizes the plaintiff to make use of the government's police power to effectuate it. Thus, a real estate agent may, for example, call on the sheriff to oust a tenant, to reclaim some property, to sell property belonging to a defendant, or to seize the defendant's wages or property. When the court issues an injunction on behalf of the plaintiff, it orders the defendant not to engage in the activity about which the plaintiff complained. If the defendant persists, he or she may be fined or imprisoned.

The third combination of litigants is one-shotters versus repeat players. Illustrations of this include tenant versus landlord, injury victim versus insurance company, student versus university, defamed versus publisher, client versus welfare agency, or sexual abuse victim by priest versus Catholic Church, which was the focus of extensive media attention during the mid-2000s (Lytton, 2008) and child abuse cases by priests continued to make headlines through 2010. Outside of the personal injury area, litigation in this combination is not routine. It usually represents the attempt of some one-shotters to invoke outside help to create leverage on an organization with which the individual has a dispute.

The fourth type of litigation is repeat players versus repeat players. Examples of this include litigation between union and management, purchaser and supplier, regulatory agency and firms of regulated industry, and church/state litigations focusing on value differences (who is right) rather than on interest conflicts (who gets what). With these types of litigation in the background, let us now turn to certain types of conflicts between individuals, between individuals and organizations, and between organizations where one of the disputants resorts to the judiciary in an attempt to resolve the conflict.

DISPUTES BETWEEN INDIVIDUALS

Even though most controversies between individuals never come to the attention of courts, the handling of interpersonal differences is a traditional function of courts. Most individual disputes involve one-shotters. For those individuals whose disagreements come before a court, the experience is likely to be the most intimate they will have had with the government, and the manner in which the dispute is handled is likely to have a marked effect on their attitudes toward the government. Judicial resolution of individual disputes also affects the distribution of values. Some people gain, others lose; some individuals are honored, others are stigmatized; and as with all types of disputes, a court decision seldom resolves the underlying conditions for the conflict.

Individual disputes include private litigation as opposed to organizations, criminal defendants, or state agencies. These disputes generally deal with the distribution of economic resources and a variety of noneconomic problems. Economic disputes include various claims associated with contests over wills, trusts, and estates, landlord–tenant controversies, and disputes over property, titles, and sales. The greatest distinction between economic and noneconomic individual disputes is that the former directly involve a conflict over the control of economic resources, whereas the latter, although often involving money, do not necessarily stem from economic conflicts. Noneconomic conflicts include allegations of slander and libel, custody cases, divorce proceedings, insanity commitments, and malpractice suits.

Courts often make an effort to encourage disputants to settle their differences by agreement, because this is a less costly way to reestablish an equilibrium, which any conflict is likely to disturb. Settlements may even be encouraged after the disputants have brought their complaint to a court. Such efforts may be initiated by the judge in pretrial hearings or in open court. The success of such efforts depends to a great extent on the skills of the judge and on the nature of the disputes. When the parties are unable or unwilling to resolve their disputes by agreement, and when they have decided against letting matters rest, formal adjudication must take over and will normally end in a decision that claims to be binding on the parties (Ehrmann, 1976:83).

In the adjudication of individual disputes, one party wins and the other loses. Robert B. Seidman (1978:213–214) points out that in situations in which parties want to, or must, cooperate after the dispute, both must leave the settlement procedures without too great a sense of grievance. If, however, there are opportunities for avoidance (that is, parties need not live or work together), then the disputants may continue their antagonism. Compromises tend to resolve the disputes in the sense that they reduce any continuing antagonism. Win-or-lose situations, however, will not ameliorate antagonism.

Therefore, disputants who wish to maintain an ongoing relationship will generally engage in compromise settlements. Businesspeople do not sue customers whose trade they want to keep. Married couples who want to stay together do not sue each other; instead, they consult marriage counselors who look for compromises.

The structure of social relationships thus plays a role in the decision as to whether to take a dispute to court. When continuing relations are important to the individuals involved in the dispute, they are generally more predisposed to resolve their differences through nonlegal means. In a now-classic paper, Stewart Macaulay describes the avoidance of the law as a way of building and maintaining good business relations. Businesspeople prefer not to use contracts in their dealings with other businesspeople. Macaulay says, "Disputes are frequently settled without reference to the contract or potential or actual legal sanctions. There is a hesitancy to speak of legal rights or to threaten to sue in these negotiations" (1969:200). Similar sentiments prevail in other countries. For example, "For a Korean, it is not decent or 'nice' to insist on one's legal right. When a person hauls another person into court, he is in fact declaring war on him. . . . He has lined himself up on the side of the bureaucrats to use the power of the state to oppress his fellow man. Thus, a Korean cannot think of law as anything other than oppressive. . . . This reluctance to maintain one's legal right is particularly pronounced in the area of property" (Hahm, quoted by Friedman and Macaulay, 1977:1026).

How the either/or court decision would militate against continuing relations is further illustrated by Jane Fishburne Collier in her work on the Zinacanteco Indians of southern Mexico. She points out that Indians who wish to preserve a valued relationship will seek a settlement procedure that promotes reconciliation.

> Cases end when an appropriate settlement has been found. In Zinacanteco eyes, an ideal settlement involves reconciliation: both sides agree to forget their differences and drink together, or the guilty person begs pardon and is forgiven through acceptance of a bottle of rum. Settlements often involve agreements to pay money or repair damages, though such agreements are seen as a part of the reconciliation process. A case that ends without reconciliation and drinking is considered less than satisfactory. (Collier, 1973:38)

However, continuing relationships are but part of a broader issue of whether to litigate in individual disputes. Nader and Todd point out: "It is not enough to state that because litigants wish to continue their relation they will seek negotiated or mediated settlement with compromise outcomes" (1978:17). In some instances, ties within the family itself may give rise to disputes over inheritance among brothers or sisters, or arguments between males and females over the males' attempts to control the behavior of their unmarried sisters. At the same time, social relations may act not as an impetus to conflict but as a constraint on escalation. For example, Barbara B. Yngvesson (1978:59), in her pioneering study of a small Scandinavian fishing village, notes that "disputes are focused less on *acts than on* people. What was done is *less important than who did it.* An act considered normal when done by a kinsman or fellow community member may generate an entirely different response when done by an 'outsider.' "

Thus, it is no longer sufficient to generalize that a preference for continuing relations will turn disputants to some kind of compromise or reconciliation mechanism rather than to litigation. In a variety of instances, disputants resort to legal rather than nonlegal ways, with the full awareness of the risks involved in their attempts to settle their disputes.

Practically an unlimited variety of economic and noneconomic disputes takes place between individuals and end up before a judge for decision. Some recent highlights of our litigious society are provided to illustrate the types of law suits filed—without concern for outcomes: People argue over cows in the corn and pigs in the garden (Karsten, 1998). A Panama City, Florida, waitress is suing her employer, Hooters. After winning a contest (not specified in the suit) that offered a Toyota for a prize, she says, she was blindfolded and presented with . . . a toy Yoda. A young woman brushed her teeth for two weeks with Crest Baking Soda toothpaste. She claims it misaligned and scarred her teeth, and she is suing both the manufacturer and the store that sold it to her. A woman sued the Crunch fitness chain for what she says are injuries sustained during a pole-dancing class (*New York*, 2010:13). A New Jersey couple whose home caught fire after a Pop-Tart was left unattended in the toaster is suing Kellogg and Black & Decker for damages (*Time*, 2001:15). People sue their school officials for disciplining their children, local governments when they slip and fall on sidewalks, get stuck by lightning on city golf courses, and even when they get attacked by a goose in a park (*Newsweek*, 2003:43–51). Such types of lawsuits are not limited to the United States. For example, a high school student in Trenton, Italy, faced with the prospect of having to repeat junior year because she failed math, hired a lawyer who argued that she was suffering from "irreversible psychological pathology," or math phobia. A regional court ruled that the condition made it impossible for her to study or master math and compelled the school to promote her to senior year (Leo, 2003). There is even a spoof of one of America's favorite indoor pastime—litigation—in the form of a computer game "So Sue Me!" (sosuemegame.com), which became available (and popular) in cyberspace in late 2006 for $34.95. The game's tagline is, "Sue your friends. Take their stuff." With increased frequency, the game is being played both on the computer and in the courtroom.

[Strong] Affluent litigants may want possession of boats, silverware, or family dogs. Married couples want a divorce, and unmarried ones argue over property rights. A client may sue his or her attorney for legal malpractice, and attorneys' malpractice insurance rates have been going up both directly and indirectly. Higher deductibles and exclusions for some kinds of exposure have contributed to indirect rises (Hazard, 1994). A patient may institute charges against a physician for medical malpractice. For example, a woman in New York sued her physician for an off-center belly button stemming from unsuccessful plastic surgery. (A jury awarded her $854,000 for damages incurred by having her belly button two inches off center.) In the context of medical malpractice, there are obvious litigation excesses; those who go to and collect are often not victims of negligence and that almost 60 percent of malpractice rewards go to lawyers (*New York Times*, 1995:14E). But physicians have decided to fight back for "litigious behavior" and an obscure Texas company run by doctors started a Web site, DoctorsKnowUs.com, that compiles and posts the names of plaintiffs, their lawyers, and expert witnesses in malpractice lawsuits in Texas and beyond, regardless of the merit of the claim (see, for example, Faust, 2010). They use the service to assess the risk of offering services to clients or potential clients. For fees listed as low as $4.95 a month for the first 250 searches and thereafter 2 cents a search, subscribers are invited to search the database "one person at a time or monitor any sized group of individuals for litigious conduct." They can also add names to the database "from official and unofficial public records." Those on the list of litigants in "predatory lawsuits" (patients, their attorneys, and expert witnesses) have a hard time finding a physician who would see them (Blumenthal, 2004). It should also be noted that total spending on medical malpractice, including legal-defense costs and claim payments in addition to premium, amounts to more than 1 percent of the total U.S. health care spending, well over 30 billion dollars out of a total of some 2.2 trillion in 2007 (Searcey and Goldstein, 2009).

But malpractice charges are not limited to physicians. A clergyman is charged with clerical malpractice and the plaintiff alleges that his advice to remain married to her husband caused her "severe trauma, insomnia, and a chronic lower-back problem" (*Saturday Review*, 1979:7). (As a result of this suit, an insurance company began to offer malpractice coverage for the clergy; for about $20 a year, $300,000 of protection will be provided. Today, several insurance companies offer such protection. In 1986, there were already some 2,000 cases involving the clergy, and more than $100 million has been awarded to those suing them [*New York Times*, 1986b:1F].) Since 1950, the total number of accusations against the Catholic clergy stands at more than 12,000 costing dioceses more than $1 billion (Zoll, 2006), and following priestly pedophilia scandals, several dioceses have filed for bankruptcy protection in the wake of thousands of sex abuse claims against priests. The child abuse problems are ubiquitous in other countries as well. For example, in Ireland one priest admitted abusing more than 100 children. Another said he had abused children every two weeks for over 25 years (*New York Times*, 2010). However, it should be noted that nowadays churches, just like any other organizations, who fire ministers for adultery or other sexual misconduct risk a countersuit for wrongful termination, defamation, or emotional distress (Rosen, 2001:49). Even judges are not immune today; nearly 3,300 nationwide have decided that they, too, need malpractice insurance. This lack of judicial immunity is the cause of approximately 300 insurance claims that have been filed already by judges annually between 1984 and 1988 (Hagerdon, 1989).

The American Tort Reform Association (ATRA) (2004) complains about "scapegoat litigation" (that is, Martha Stewart) in the wake of the rash of corporate bankruptcies (that is, Enron) and lawsuits involving mortgage and savings and loan companies in the late 1990s and mid-2000s. In the wake of the massive Toyota recall in early 2010, there is a resurgence of calls in the mass media for stronger product liability laws and a greater role for trial lawyers to safeguard public health and safety (Robinson and Calcagnie, 2010). They also contend that creditors and regulators are suing lawyers and investment bankers for alleged malpractice because they are the only solvent targets left. Such litigation, they claim but do not explain how, will result in higher prices and a reduction in the GDP by an average of $30 billion annually. A man from Maryland sued a marriage counselor, alleging emotional distress because the counselor had an affair with his wife. He put a $10 million price tag on the suit for alienation of affection (Stumpf and Culver, 1992:1). A man from Colorado filed claims against his parents for the sum of $350,000, charging that they gave him inhumane and inadequate care as a child, making it impossible for him to fit into society as an adult. A black man in Omaha, Nebraska, sued the makers of a Compton's Encyclopedia CD-ROM for $40 million, claiming that he and his children suffered emotional distress when, during a search, he mistakenly typed in the word nigger—instead of Niger—and the program called up several references (*Time*, 1995). A former St. Louis University law student bit the left buttock of the president of the student bar association of another law school in a bar. After graduation, she sued him for damages and a jury awarded her $2,500 in actual and $25,000 in punitive damages (Poor, 1990). A man from Florida filed suit against a nightclub, claiming he suffered whiplash when a topless dancer knocked him out with her breasts. To compensate for pain and suffering, mental anguish and loss of capacity for enjoyment of life, among other things, he is seeking more than $15,000 in damages (*Vancouver Sun*, 1998). To continue this litany of illustrations with another Florida case, a 15-year-old girl in West Palm Beach sued her prom date for standing her up. She sought compensation of $49.53 for the shoes, flowers, and hairdo that went to waste when her date failed to appear (Page, 1989). A final example: An administrative-law judge in Washington, D.C., sued a dry cleaner for $65 million for losing his pants. After two years of escalating legal costs and repeated offers to settle by now almost bankrupt dry cleaner, the judge is still advocating for his suit over the pants (Takruri, 2007). Such cases may strike many people as frivolous, amusing, and at times blatantly abusive and absurd. They may be, but at the same time they are illustrative of the spectrum of individual disputes that end up in court.

Data on patterns of outcomes in individual disputes are scarce. In adjudication, courts are supposed to decide disputes by reference to the facts of who did what to whom, and by identifying, interpreting, and applying appropriate legal norms. Sheldon Goldman and Austin Sarat (1978:514) suggest that this requires that judges remain neutral with regard to both the issues of the case and its result. They use the notion of result impartiality in referring to the extent cases are decided independently of the personal attributes of the parties involved. Impartiality is displayed when both parties in a dispute are given the same opportunities and are shown the same considerations. It requires that the judge not be influenced by an interest in the outcome or by attitudes toward the disputants and the particular situations in which they are involved (see, for example, Soeharno, 2010).

To study the question of impartiality, it is necessary to examine a number of decisions involving similar situations to discover whether over time different kinds of disputants are equally likely to gain favorable results. For impartial results, the pattern of decision should be random and should not consistently favor one type of litigant over another. For example, if courts in custody cases at times rule for the mother and at other times for the father, it may be concluded that they show equal regard for both sexes. However, if they consistently favor mothers over fathers, regardless of the facts or the applicable law, then the results would not be impartial.

Goldman and Sarat point out, however, that the difficulty with this way of determining result impartiality is that it does not take into account other factors responsible for variation from the standard of randomness that go beyond the attitudes and values of the judges. A most obvious factor is that, even if courts are impartial in their procedures, they may still produce biased results if the laws that they apply favor one type of litigant. This is particularly true in custody cases, because most state divorce laws still favor the mother.

The outcome of court decisions may also be influenced by the type of attorney that disputants are able to retain. Availability of resources to disputants directly affects the quality of legal talent they can hire. Access to a skillful attorney increases the likelihood of a favorable court decision, because courts assume that in individual disputes both parties can marshal the resources and legal skills needed to present a case effectively.

To an extent, these considerations can be useful in predicting the outcomes of individual disputes. In some instances, however, both parties may be able to afford delays and the services of highly trained attorneys, and to have convincing legal arguments on their side. In such instances, the determination of the outcome of the case will have to wait until the judge hands down the verdict.

DISPUTES BETWEEN INDIVIDUALS AND ORGANIZATIONS

In this section, I will discuss disputes between individuals and organizations. The first part of the section will consider individuals as plaintiffs and organizations as defendants. The second part will deal with legal disputes initiated by organizations against individuals. I will use the term *organization* to cover a broad range of social groups that have been deliberately and consciously constructed to achieve certain specific goals—hospitals, credit agencies, universities, General Motors, regulatory agencies, the American Medical Association, public-interest law firms, and so forth.

Disputes between individuals and organizations may take place over a variety of issues, many of which may be included in four general categories: (1) disputes over property and money (economic disputes); (2) claims for damages and restitution; (3) issues of civil rights; and (4) disputes concerning organizational actions, procedures, and policy. These broad categories of disputes are, of course, not mutually exclusive.

Economic disputes are exemplified by the following types of actions: suits for unpaid rent; eviction; claims for unpaid loans and installment purchases; foreclosures and repossessions; and suits on contracts and insurance policies.

Claims for damages and restitution most frequently involve automobile accidents and lawsuits against insurance companies (see, for example, Zernova, 2008). However, other forms of injury—for example, airplane accidents, faulty appliances, and medical and academic malpractices—also give rise to claims. Damage suits may also be initiated to compensate for losses sustained from the failure to honor a contract or to perform a service properly. Slander and libel actions also fall within this category (Shuy, 2010). Although money may change hands as a result of these actions, the actions themselves seek compensation for alleged improper behavior and its consequences. It should be noted that economic disputes and claims for damages and restitution also occur in individual disputes as well as in disputes between individuals and organizations.

Civil rights disputes include claims of discrimination by race, sex, or national origin in matters of employment, hiring, promotion, retention, pay, housing, and admission policies.

Other issues that may lead to civil rights disputes include other discriminatory practices, such as the exclusion of handicapped people and setting arbitrary age or educational limits (see, for example, McCrudden, 2004).

The final category of disputes includes challenges to a variety of actions, procedures, and policies of organizations. Decisions of zoning boards or tax assessors may be challenged as a violation of statutes or administrative procedures. Plaintiffs may seek a reversal of particular decisions, or a voiding of statutes or injunctions prohibiting the continued application of particular policies. In organizations that distribute benefits, such as the program of Aid to Families with Dependent Children (AFDC), food stamps, aid to the disabled, and Medicaid, there are disputes about the appropriate form of benefits, conflicting and inconsistent eligibility rules on employment and training incentives, and disputes about how administrators should deal with beneficiaries. In business organizations, disputes over policies governing warranties, replacement of defective products, or unethical collection practices also come to courts.

Usually, organizations are plaintiffs in the first category of disputes and defendants in the other three. In general, as Marc Galanter (1975) concludes, organizations are more successful as both plaintiffs and defendants than are individuals. They enjoy greater success against individual antagonists than against other organizations. Individuals fare less well contending against organizations than against other individuals. For example, in 2000 the retail-store chain Wal-Mart was hit with 4,851 suits filed by individuals, and currently it has about 9,400 cases open. Dozens of lawyers now specialize in suing Wal-Mart; many share documents and other information via the Internet. The allegations range from falls on slippery floors and icy parking lots to claims of being injured in shoppers' stampedes triggered by bargain hunting to employment discrimination practices. In the vast majority of cases (no exact numbers are available), Wal-Mart wins by aggressively fighting cases even when it would be cheaper for the company to settle (*Bellingham Herald*, 2001). It is interesting to note that Wal-Mart is sued more often than any other American entity except the U.S. government, which was sued more than 7,500 times annually since 2000 (Slater, 2003).

Galanter's conclusion is supported by the Wal-Mart example and reinforced by Donald Black's (1976:92, 1989:41–46) contention that law and organization are inversely related: Law is greater toward less organization. Over one-half of the plaintiffs in civil cases in the United States are organizations, and two-thirds of the defendants are individuals. Organizations win more often than individuals. In small-claims courts, as well, more organizations sue individuals than the other way around. In these instances, the plaintiffs nearly always win. For example, David Caplovitz (1974:222) found that legal actions against debtors in his sample of 1,331 cases, drawn from four cities, resulted in creditor victories in all but 3 percent of the cases. Moreover, if an organization loses its case against an individual, it is more likely to appeal, and, if it does, it is more likely to win a reversal.

Black also points out that "although any group is more likely to bring a lawsuit against an individual than vice versa, then, the likelihood of a lawsuit by a group increases with its organization. On the other hand, the likelihood of a lawsuit by an individual against a group decreases with the organization of the group" (1976:93). In other words, a large organization such as the IRS is more likely to sue an individual than the reverse. Organization, as Black notes, provides an immunity from law and "an offense committed by an organization or its representatives is less serious than an offense by an individual on his own, and the more organized the organization, the less serious it is" (Black, 1976:94).

Although organizations have a greater chance of winning and a higher frequency of initiating lawsuits, it does not mean that individuals do not sue organizations (see, for example, Hellman, 2004). On the contrary, individuals are taking their disputes with organizations to courts at an unprecedented rate. Workers increasingly seek compensation in courts for health damages, allegedly suffered in hazardous working environments. There is a rapid growth of suits by consumers claiming harm from defective products or harm suffered while on company premises. But still, well-resourced defendants generally outlast and outmaneuver plaintiffs. Litigation does not provide an even battle ground, and David does not have a reasonable chance of defeating Goliath. The legal arena is more like the Roman Coliseum where the lions almost always win (McIntosh and Cates, 2010). For the remainder of this section, I shall consider disputes initiated by individuals and organizations separately. For the former, I shall illustrate the use of law as a method of dispute resolution in academe, and for the latter, I shall discuss the use of courts as collection agencies in the field of consumer credit.

Law as a Method of Dispute Resolution in Academe

At the beginning of the second decade of the twenty-first century, law remains a potent force in institutions of higher learning in the United States (Gerstein and Gerstein, 2007; Oppenheimer, 2006) and is becoming more pronounced at all other levels of education (see, for example, Bissonette, 2009; Essex, 2009). Along with producing lawyers, our nation's colleges are increasingly producing work for them (Gajda, 2010). More and more disputes that develop on campuses in America are resolved outside the groves of academia. Students, faculty members, academic administrators, and their institutions are becoming litigants in steadily growing numbers. Over the years, a substantial amount of literature emerged on legal guidelines in institutions of higher learning (see, for example, O'Reilly and Green, 1992), about the offenses committed in academe in the name of political correctness and multiculturalism (Kors and Silverglate, 1998), and law's pronounced presence on the campus reverberates on most activities (Kaplin and Lee, 2006:1). Some examples are provided: A college basketball player sues his institution for admission to a bachelor's degree program so he can maintain eligibility for intercollegiate sports. Another student sues her institution for $125,000 after an instructor gave her a *B+* grade, which she claimed should have been an *A–*. As an unintended consequence of growing legalism on campus, due to concerns with probable complications, adverse administrative reactions, lengthy justifications, a myriad of memos, grievance committees, and even with the possibility of litigation, many faculty members are reluctant to fail a student or to assign a *D* or even a *C+* (And it would be a professional suicide for an untenured assistant professor to assign a low grade or dare fail a student in a "chip on the shoulder" course.) Acknowledging intellectual diversity and divergent performance on the grade sheet is a pedagogical fact of life — although fewer and fewer professors do it because of the fear of consequences and giving in to administrative and student intimidation (Johnson, 2003). Also, there are very few big-dollar lawsuits on campus although people are beginning to look more and more at the university as just another institution with a lot of money — there are some 50 colleges and universities with endowments over $1 billion (Oppenheimer, 2006). In essence, the process is the punishment for some perceived wrong, that is, being dragged through months of hearings and cross-examination as if the defendants were criminals—just like in punitive or manipulative sexual harassment allegations.

Faculty members are similarly active. In one case, a tenured professor sought an injunction after the college reduced his laboratory space from 1,000 to 300 square feet. Others have sued (successfully) claiming that the Teachers Insurance and Annuity Association-College Retirement Equities Fund (TIAA-CREF) illegally discriminated on the basis of sex. Transgender professors launch law suits about job discrimination in firing (Sataline, 2007). Sexual harassment suits in all directions are also quite popular nowadays, and we are beginning to see complaints initiated by tenured male white professors against adjuncts and others on faculty and staff (see, for example, Mundson, 2004), and there are concerns being raised by male law professors about talking to a female law student (still less a female colleague) without a witness present along with an open office door (Hunter, 2006). There are also issues of excessive monitoring of faculty members for the topics they teach as a form of infringement on academic freedom and administrative reactions to faculty unionization (Nelson, 2010). These and other types of lawsuits on campus will be considered in the context of faculty–administration, student–faculty, and student–administration relations.

The *faculty–administration* relationship in postsecondary institutions is defined by an increasingly complex web of legal principles and authorities. The essence of this relationship is contract law, but "that core is encircled by expanding layers of labor relations law, employment discrimination law, and, in public institutions, constitutional law and public employment statutes and regulations" (Kaplin and Lee, 2006:159). The growth in the number and variety of laws and regulations governing faculty–administration relations provides a fertile ground for grievances and coincides with an increase in the number of lawsuits stemming from that relationship.

Many legal disputes center on the meaning and interpretation of the faculty–institution contract. Depending on the institution, a contract may vary from a basic notice of appointment to a complex collective bargaining agreement negotiated under federal or state labor laws. In some instances, the formal document does not encompass all the terms of the contract, and other terms are included through "incorporation by reference"—that is, by referring to other documents, such as the faculty handbook, or even to past custom and usage at an institution. In the context of contract interpretation, legal disputes arise most often in the context of contract termination and due notice for such termination.

A number of suits instituted by faculty members to redress their grievances against university administrations have focused on faculty-personnel decisions, such as appointment, retention, promotion, and tenure policies; pecuniary matters affecting women and minority groups; and sex discrimination. (Faculty members who sue their institutions over sex discrimination have had only a 1-in-5 chance of winning their cases [*Chronicle of Higher Education*, 1989:A14].) As a result of civil rights legislation, hiring procedures must follow clearly established affirmative action guidelines. Many traditional practices of departments and universities are being questioned, such as the use of "the old boy network" and other selection processes not in compliance with these guidelines. Similarly, termination procedures must also follow specific guidelines and deadlines, and in recent years faculty members have increasingly resorted to lawsuits on the grounds of procedural matters.

Other potentially conflict-laden situations in academe arise from *student–faculty* relations. Students are increasingly considering themselves buyers of education, treating education like other consumer items; concomitantly, there is a growing emphasis on the proper return for their educational dollars (see, for example, Johnson, 2003). Well over a generation ago, Ladd and Lipset already commented: "In fact, the students are the 'consumers,' the buyers, the patrons of a product sold by the faculty through a middle-man, the university system. In economic class terms, the relationship of student to teacher is that of buyer to seller, or of client to professional. In this context, the buyer or client seeks to get the most for his money at the lowest possible price" (1973:93).

Because students are purchasers of education, they expect "delivery" of a product. In this context, the question of academic malpractice becomes important. Although the legal definition of academic malpractice is yet to be codified, it is generally considered as improper, injurious, or negligent instruction, and/or action that has a "negative effect" on the student's academic standing, professional licensing, or employment (Vago, 1979:39). Although the concept of academic malpractice is rather amorphous, several patterns have emerged. A faculty member may be charged with malpractice by a student who perceives a particular course as "worthless," or by a student who contends that he or she did not obtain any "relevant" information or that for some reason it did not fit into the student's general educational outlook, requirement, or area of concentration. In such instances, individual professors are charged, and the object of the lawsuit is usually the recovery of tuition money, and occasionally an intent to seek punitive damages, because the legal doctrine of *respondeat superior* (that is, the sins of the employee are imputed to the employer) is usually invoked. Several cases have been also litigated in which students have claimed contract damages for an institution's failure to provide bargained-for services. In a most extraordinary case, for example, the defendant–student has alleged in a counterclaim that Columbia University

> had represented that it would teach the defendant wisdom, truth, character, enlightenment, understanding, justice, liberty, honesty, courage, beauty, and similar virtues and qualities; that it would develop the whole man, maturity, well-roundedness, objective thinking and the like; and that because it failed to do so it was guilty of misrepresentation, to the defendant's pecuniary damage. (Vago, 1979:41)

In this case, the trial court granted the university's motion for summary judgment, which was sustained on appeal.

Disputes resulting from a failure of a student to pass an internal examination may also culminate in attempts to involve the courts. In such a situation, a student may question the expertise and competency of professors to evaluate examinations, or a department may be accused of following improper procedures during examinations. Questions of expertise and competency usually arise in the area of alleged academic overspecialization. (That is, is someone qualified to evaluate an examination in social psychology when his or her professed specialty is the sociology of law?) Issues of improper procedures often arise in the context of due process involving the department's or the university's failure to list specific guidelines for examination procedures, or to live up to those guidelines, or to provide clearly written guidelines and appeal procedures. But when it comes to strictly academic decisions made by faculty members about a student's academic career, the right of judges to overturn such decisions is limited. According to a 1985 Supreme Court ruling, "When judges are asked to review the substance of a genuinely academic decision . . . they should show great respect for the faculty's professional judgment," and courts are not "suited to evaluate the substance of the multitude of academic decisions that are made daily by faculty members" (Palmer, 1985:33).

The student's failure to pass a professional examination is another ground for lawsuits. Here the charge is usually that a given department "failed" to properly prepare the student to successfully take an external examination, such as a bar examination, and thus provided a "defective product." In a well-publicized case, a court ruled against a graduate of the Southern University Law School, who claimed the university was responsible for his failure to pass—on three occasions—the state bar examination. The court held that it was against Louisiana law to sue a state agency and that the university is such an agency; the court also noted that a properly drafted contract suit may have stated a "remediable" course of action (Vago, 1979:41).

Student–administration relations provide a third area for potential conflict in academe. Increasingly, suspension and dismissal procedures, the rights of students to organize, alleged censorship activities over student publications, and sex discrimination are being challenged by students in courts.

Although institutions of higher learning have the right to dismiss, suspend, or otherwise sanction students for misconduct or academic deficiency, this right is determined by a body of procedural requirements that must be observed in such actions. Under the due process clause, students are entitled to a hearing and notice before disciplinary action is taken. In general, several court rulings indicate a judicial trend toward increased protection of student rights, in both public and private institutions, in suspension and dismissal cases (Gerstein and Gerstein, 2007; Kaplin and Lee, 2006:379–604).

First Amendment rights have been increasingly cited in student–administration disputes. Under the First Amendment, students have a legal right to organize and use appropriate campus facilities. In some instances, however, postsecondary institutions retain the authority to revoke or withhold recognition and to regulate the organizational use of campus facilities. When a mutually acceptable and satisfactory balance between the organization's rights and the institution's authority cannot be attained, the organizing students may turn to the courts to settle their dispute with the administration, as has been the case, for example, with various gay rights organizations.

The First Amendment principles also apply to student publications. The chief concern here is censorship and administrative control over publications. In one case, for example, financial support for the campus newspaper was terminated on the grounds that the paper printed prosegregation articles and that it urged the maintenance of an all-black university. The court of appeals held that the administration's action violated the student staff's First Amendment rights. Other currently controversial issues include questions of obscenity and libel in the context of student publications.

Lawsuits against university administrations on the basis of alleged sex discrimination, particularly in athletics, are also becoming more numerous, fueled by the cultural acceptance of women in sports, the impact of Title IX federal statute which prohibits discrimination in education and the still existing broad disparities in funding between men's and women's sports (Brake, 2010; Kaplin and Lee, 2006:564–569). These involve, for example, the use of university sports facilities and locker rooms; funding for women's athletic programs; segregated versus unitary (integrated) athletic teams; scheduling games and practice time; the provision of equipment and supplies; travel and per diem allowance; publicity; and the provision of coaches, housing, and dining facilities.

The growing frequency and diversity of lawsuits as a method of conflict resolution in academe has important implications for contemporary higher education. Postsecondary institutions are the parties that are most adversely affected by successful litigation. The economic and social costs of such litigations can be enormous. In addition to hiring more and more on-staff lawyers as prophylactics advising faculty and staff on how to ensure themselves against liability, the need for universities to develop and maintain effective mechanisms of internal conflict management is obvious. The following section will consider disputes initiated by organizations against individuals in the domain of consumer credit.

The Courts as Collection Agencies

Disputes between individuals and organizations, where organizations are the plaintiffs, are most often triggered by disagreements over property and money. Such disputes are most prevalent in the creditor–debtor relationship, where the creditor is usually an organization such as a collection, finance and loan company, car dealership, department store, or hospital. In such situations, there is a gross power disparity between the debtor and the organization, the debtor is relatively ignorant of the technical aspects of the product, and the stakes are small in dollars but large in their impact on the debtor (Goldberg et al., 2007). Further, there is a fair amount of obvious taxpayer subsidy in debt collection, especially in situations where collection agencies initiate law suits against debtors, because much of the court time and the caseload of judges or court commissioners, especially at the lower levels such as the district court in the state of Washington, were devoted to a significantly disproportionate number of routine assembly-line collection agency-initiated litigation. In fact, a cursory examination of the dockets would reveal the high number of cases, often in the hundreds if not higher, handled by a collection agency lawyer who does little else other than filing and processing collections. (It would be an eye-opener for students of consumer credit and behavior to go down to the court house and watch the attorneys in action for speed and volume representing [for a set fee] collection agencies.)

Kagan comments, "If the extension of credit is the lifeblood of a dynamic commercial society, the forcible collection of unpaid debts is its backbone" (1984:324). When a debtor defaults on his or her contractual obligation to make payments, the standard legal remedy is for the creditor to sue in civil court. The purpose is to establish the legality of the debt and its amount. Of course, creditors "hope to collect the debt by invoking the power of the court, but even if they do not collect, a judgment against the debtor is still of value for income tax purposes. Bad debts are worth 50 cents in deductions on every tax dollar" (Caplovitz, 1974:191).

If the creditor is successful in the suit, he or she obtains a judgment against the debtor. Once obtained, there are a variety of legal remedies available for collecting the judgment, including garnishment, liens, and the forced sale of the debtor's property. As I noted earlier, a garnishment is a court order directing someone who owes or possesses money due to the debtor (such as an employer) to pay all or some of that money to the court, which then turns it over to the creditor (Bryant, 2004; Vago, 1968, 1971). A lien establishes a creditor's claim on property (such as a house or a car). A forced sale, such as foreclosure, involves seizure and sale of the debtor's property at an auction. The proceeds are then turned over to the creditor to satisfy the judgment. But lenders will continue to hold the debtors responsible for the difference between what they were able to recover through forced sale of a property and the actual amount owned on it. For example, if a car is reposed, the lender will try to sell the car, and considering cars lose substantial amount as soon as they leave the dealership, the sale price will be substantially less than what the debtor paid—or even owe. With lenders having no motivation to seek the best price, the car is most likely to be sold in an auction to used car dealers, and the debtor will owe the remainder. So if one owes $10,000 and the lender sells the car for $3,000, the debtor will still owe $7,000 on the car that he no longer owns. If the lender cannot collect, the debt will likely be assigned to a collection agency with extra fees, charges, threats and hounding, and a likely scarred credit report for seven years.

Prior to going to court, a creditor may resort to a number of social pressures and sanctions of varying severity, ranging from impersonal routine "reminders" and dunning letters or telephone appeals to get the debtor "in" to make some kind of "arrangement" with him and to remind or threaten him or her to personal visits to the debtor's home in an attempt to elicit payments or at least promises (Hobbs, 2008). At times, creditors resort to unusual extrajudicial methods of collection. For example, a London firm is using a rather unconventional method of extracting money from debtors—smell: "Smelly Tramps, Ltd. is just what it sounds: a motley crew of ragged, foul-smelling tramps, who specialize in dunning particularly evasive debtors. The tramps are really otherwise respectable chaps, dressed in disgusting clothes and treated with a special stomach churning chemical" (*Economist*, 1979:104). Their technique is simply to sit around the victim's office or home until he or she signs a check. Not to be outdone, a debt-collecting firm in Bombay, India, is employing six eunuchs who threaten to remove their saris if the defaulters do not pay up. The eunuchs' arrival at a debtor's home or office usually ensures he pays his debt rather than be embarrassed in front of colleagues or neighbors (*Vancouver Sun*, 1999:E3). In Spain, debt collectors use shame to recoup money. Since the middle ages, public shaming has been used as a tool of coercion across Europe. One illustration of the famous El Cobrador del Frac (The Debt Collector in Top Hat and Tails) will suffice. The agency recently had a case of a couple who did not pay an $83,000 wedding bill. The collection agency obtained a guest list and started to phone the guest asking them if they had the lobster or chicken and then asking them where to send the bill. The embarrassed bride and groom promptly paid up (Harman, 2010). Finally, a high-tech version of a debt collection is the automobile starter-interrupt device which is becoming an increasingly popular way for lenders to ensure that they get paid. It is a cigarette pack size contraption mounted under the dashboard, which flashes green when a car payment is made on time. When a payment is late, the device will not let the car start (Yao, 2006).

Another unusual and ingenious dunning technique has been successfully used by Paragon Cable of New York on customers who were reluctant to pay their cable-television bill. Instead of cutting off service completely, Paragon filled each of its 77 channels with C-SPAN's programming. Collection of overdue balances has improved dramatically since the company started its constant bombardment by the public-affairs network specializing in live broadcasts of the proceedings of the U.S. Senate and the House of Representatives (*U.S. News & World Report*, 1995:14).

When such dunning efforts fail and creditors have exhausted nonlitigation alternatives, they are likely to sue. A characteristic of most civil suits for debt is that the plaintiff usually wins by default. Most defendants are not represented by counsel. In fact, many of them are not present when their cases are heard. Their absence is treated as an admission of the validity of the claim, and a default judgment is entered against them. Such judgments are rendered in over 90 percent of consumer cases (Caplovitz, 1974:220–221).

There are a number of reasons why defendants fail to respond to summons and appear in court. Some recognize the validity of the creditor's claim and see no point in attempting to contest it or cannot afford an attorney to do so (Hobbs, 2008; Kagan, 1984). Others may simply find it impossible to leave work (with consequent loss of pay), travel to court, and spend most of the day waiting for their cases to be called. The fact that most courts are open from 9 A.M. to 5 P.M., hours when most debtors are at work, further contributes to default judgments. At times, the wording of a summons is so complicated and obtuse that many debtors simply cannot grasp what is at stake, or that they must appear if they are to avoid a default judgment. Others simply do not know that they are being sued. Instead of properly serving the summons, process servers in some areas (because of the inability to locate debtors or the fear of going into certain neighborhoods) destroy it and claim it has been served. Although accurate statistics on the frequency of such "sewer service" do not exist, it is evidently commonplace in many cities (Caplovitz, 1974:193–195). These individuals learn about suits against them the hard way—when a garnishment or eviction notice is served.

A comparable situation but with much greater consequences existed in South Africa until late 1995. A creditor would go to court complaining that he had not been paid. A judge would then issue a judgment against the debtor and a request for payment. If the debtor did not pay within 10 days, the judge would hold the debtor in contempt of the court and send him or her to jail for up to three months. But many debtors, just like in the United States, were never even aware of the court proceedings. In some cases, debtors were illiterate and did not comprehend what was going on. Often, the first sign of trouble was when the police van showed up to take them to prison. The imprisonment of debtors has been very common, almost always involving the poor. In the late 1980s, for example, one-tenth of South Africa's prison population has been incarcerated because of debt. It should be noted, however, that by one criterion—payment of outstanding obligations—the system of imprisoning debtors was rather effective. Most people paid off their creditors within days. Studies showed that while the average contempt sentence was 31 days, the average debtor spent only 9 days in jail. Most of the time, the incarceration of the debtor set off a family-wide scramble to come up with the money (Daley, 1995). Draconian debt laws still exist in other parts of the world, such as Dubai for example, where the risk of doing jail time for debt is high especially among foreigners who make up about 90 percent of the population (Worth, 2009).

Although I have focused on suits for debts, there are a number of other important types of actions initiated by organizations against individuals. Real estate companies regularly initiate legal action in the form of evictions against unknown thousands of tenants. The IRS continuously files suits against individuals (and at times organizations) for back taxes or for tax evasion. Radio and television stations regularly use the courts to settle disputes with former announcers or disc jockeys who have decided to join competing stations, contrary to the desires of their former employers. In the final section, I shall consider disputes between organizations.

DISPUTES BETWEEN ORGANIZATIONS

There are two general types of organizational conflicts: (1) conflict between groups within the organization and (2) conflict between organizations. For example, interorganizational conflict within a university includes disputes between the faculty and administration over issues of collective bargaining, unionization, faculty freedom, and staff reduction based on alleged financial exigencies (Kaplin and Lee, 2006; Westin and Feliu, 1988). Interorganizational conflict is exemplified by disputes between the university and the community over matters of zoning, land use, and tax-exempt status, or between the university and the federal government concerning compliance with federal regulations, such as occupational safety, pollution, and civil rights. It can also cut across national boundaries such as the current controversies surrounding the climate crises and other aspects of the global environment (Axelrod et al., 2010).

Although the emphasis in this section is on interorganizational disputes, the generalizations that will be made are, of course, applicable to intraorganizational disputes. Such disputes may arise between private firms, between private firms and government, between government agencies, and between public-interest groups and private firms or government, or both. After a brief consideration of the various types of interorganizational disputes, I will examine in greater depth the activities of public-interest law firms in environmental disputes. At this point it should be noted that although most environmental offenses are processed by regulatory agencies and corrected by civil and administrative remedies, there is an increased "criminalization" of environmental wrongs (see, for example, Situ and Emmons, 2001) and the trend is likely to continue.

Disputes between organizations cover a wide spectrum of participants and controversies. Businesspeople may take their disagreements to court over contract interpretation, trademarks, or alleged patent infringements. The federal government is involved as a plaintiff in suits to acquire land needed for federal projects (highways, dams, parks, buildings) which the acquiring agency is unable to purchase through negotiation, in actions to force private companies to comply with contracts with federal agencies, and in suits brought under the antitrust statutes. Disputes between the government and private firms arise over matters of licensing and regulation, labor relations, Sunday closing laws, and governmental contracts. The government is often the defendant in cases involving zoning and land use, location of public housing projects, and tax reassessment.

In recent decades, complex public-policy disputes and regulatory disputes stemming from the government's regulation of the economic and social systems have become more pronounced. The regulation of economic activities has become pervasive, and it involves important decisions about the distribution of goods and services.

Social-policy disputes develop when the government pursues broad national objectives that may involve or impinge upon many interests and groups, such as racial equality and economic opportunity, environmental protection, income security, and public health and safety. Examples of agencies with such objectives are the Occupational Safety and Health Administration, the Equal Employment Opportunity Commission, and the Environmental Protection Agency. In fact, all large-scale social welfare programs—cash transfers, food stamps, housing, health, and education—generate similar complex public-policy disputes (Ford Foundation, 1978:3; see also Mink and Solinger, 2004).

Regulatory disputes frequently involve difficult technical questions, often involving regulation by litigation (Morriss et al., 2009), whereas social-policy disputes raise difficult political and value questions. In both types of disputes, information about important variables is often incomplete or inaccurate, effects of alternative choices are hard to ascertain, and often there are no easy answers to cost/benefit questions or to questions of trade-offs among various interests. The various regulatory agencies discussed in Chapter 3, in addition to major policy issues, also process large numbers of routine disputes. For example, the Civil Aeronautics Board (CAB), in addition to allocating airline routes (large complex disputes), in any given year will also handle thousands of passenger and shipper complaints, tariff applications, and referrals. The U.S. Securities and Exchange Commission (SEC), in addition to a number of formal hearings annually, also rules on thousands of registration statements.

In many instances, the formal quasi-adjudicative procedures used by regulatory agencies are ill-suited to resolving large and complex disputes. Delays in settling disputes are frequent, and the situation is further compounded by the fact that some agencies traditionally engaged in economic regulations are now being asked to consider environmental claims as well. The regulatory process, in a sense, encourages conflict, rather than acting to reconcile opposing interests. When agencies grant licenses, set rates, or determine the safety of drugs, they often allow the parties to the proceedings to have a full adversary hearing with impartial decision makers, formal records, and rights of cross-examination and appeal. This leads the parties to approach the agency as if they were in a lawsuit.

Public-Interest Law Firms in Environmental Disputes

Since the mid-1960s, the types of activities associated with Ralph Nader and his consumer organizations and Centers for Law in the Public Interest (Reske, 1994), with the Sierra Club and its environmental programs, and with a new institutional form embodied in law firms that characterize their activities as partly or wholly "public-interest" law and "cause lawyering" (Sarat and Scheingold, 1998) have proliferated. Law students founded the National Association for Public Interest Law (NAPIL) in 1986 to create more opportunities for students and lawyers interested in this area of the law. There are 131 NAPIL chapters, and 3/4 of ABA-accredited law schools have them (Vargas and Bushnell, 1995). NAPIL also offers the Fellowships for Equal Justice to encourage law students to go into public-interest law but law students cannot pursue public-interest law because of their large law school debt. The average law-school graduate owes between $50,000 and $80,000 in student loans and cannot make ends meet working in the government or public-interest sectors, where the median starting salary for lawyers is just over $40,000 (Mangan, 2007). As a result, many idealistic students are giving up on potentially rewarding government and nonprofit jobs, and low-income people are being denied access to justice, according to the nonprofit advocacy group. Undoubtedly, more law students would enter public-interest law if there were a comprehensive, nationally funded loan forgiveness program for students entering the public interest field where they make less than half of what their classmates earn in large firms (Hoye, 1995).

Public-interest law is the term frequently used to describe the activities of the foundation-supported law firms that represent environmentalists and consumers and like groups, as well as test-case litigation in civil rights and poverty controversies. It is generally oriented toward causes and interests of groups, classes, or organizations, rather than individuals (Handler, 1976:99). Although public-interest law firms engage in activities such as lobbying, reporting, public relations, and counseling, litigation is by far their most important activity. Education, employment discrimination, consumer problems, and environmental problems are the four areas that account for the largest proportion of their activities.

Educational controversies include school financing, legal rights of students and parents, bilingual education, special education, the political activity of teachers, and various forms of politically "incorrect" activities (Leatherman, 1994). Employment discrimination activities consist of class-action suits against private and public discriminators and the government agencies responsible for enforcing fair employment laws. A typical lawsuit seeks to establish affirmative action plans for minorities or women in hiring and promotion. Consumer matters include attacks on import restrictions to lower costs to the consumer and to improve quality, product safety, and guarantee and warranty practices.

After civil liberties, environmental defense generates the highest volume of cases for public-interest law firms (Aron, 1989:26). Private groups often use the courts to pursue better environmental quality (Naysnerski and Tietenberg, 1992). For example, a group of environmental lawyers have already started to explore novel legal strategies to adopt against global warning (Bodansky, 2010; Seelye, 2001; Stone, 2010) and similar attempts are under way in other countries (Anand, 2004). Public environmental enforcement can occur at the federal level through administrative proceedings, or through either civil or criminal judicial action. Several of the foundation-supported firms, such as the Natural Resources Defense Council and the Environmental Defense Fund, concentrate exclusively on this area, whereas other firms, such as the Center for Law and Social Policy, devote substantial resources to this type of work (Trubek, 1978:151). Public-interest lawyers have been active in a variety of environmental domains. They have challenged dams and other water resources projects, raised questions about nuclear power plants, attacked the pricing policies of electric utilities, stopped the use of dangerous pesticides, and sought to improve enforcement of such major environmental statutes as the National Environmental Policy Act, the Clear Air Act, and the Federal Water Pollution Control Act (see, for example, Weibust, 2010). Accounts of environmental policy disputes regularly fill the daily press (see, for example, Almeida and Stearns, 1998). Disputes include such questions as "Shall we expand or contract our programs for flood control and stream channelization? Should we relax or tighten the rules governing air pollution? Should we build a dam on a scenic stream, or allow nuclear energy plants to damage aquatic life in the natural bodies of water they use for cooling?" (Trubek, 1978:152).

Environmental disputes typically fall into two broad categories—enforcement and permitting cases. Enforcement disputes come about when a public-interest group raises questions about a party's compliance with certain state or federal law setting specific environmental standards, such as air or water quality. Permitting cases involve disputes over the planned construction of new facilities, such as a dam or an airport. Environmental disputes are also different from more traditional disputes in several ways: Irreversible ecological damages may be involved; at least one party to the dispute may claim to represent broader public interest—including the interests of inanimate objects, wildlife, and unborn generations; and the instrumentation of a court decision may pose special problems (what will happen to the community if the major employer is forced to close a factory responsible for water pollution) (Goldberg et al., 1985: 403–404).

The background of the actors in environmental disputes may also be different. Unlike those involved in many other disputes involving racial discrimination in schools, housing, or employment, environmentalists do not come from oppressed groups. In fact, they tend to draw most of their support from the white middle class. More often than not, their commitment is born of ideology rather than of pressing social or economic need. Consequently, environmental disputes seem to lack the immediacy of disputes in other areas. Often, they go on for years. Unlike in other disputes, delay favors the dissidents, and environmentalists prefer to postpone as long as possible decisions involving, for example, permits to construct new facilities.

Over the years, there has been a steady growth in the number of environmental disputes in the United States as well as in all other advanced industrialized countries (see, for example, Applegate, 2004; Heidenheimer et al., 1990:308–344). This phenomenon can be attributed to the significant increase in public awareness that our civilization causes substantial and possibly irreparable damage to the natural environment and to the growing significance of public action affecting the environment. Consequently, the recognition of the costs that society pays for environmental damage and the failure of companies to internalize environmental costs leads to a proliferation of regulatory laws designed to protect the natural environment. Many environmental controversies are about the extent to which the government should regulate private-sector decisions that are considered contributive factors in environmental degradation (Rabe, 1991). At the same time, the government itself is also a potential cause of environmental damages. Public programs of many types, from flood control to mineral leasing, have a potential for environmental damage.

Environmental disputes are further complicated by the establishment of a number of mission-oriented government agencies, such as the Army Corps of Engineers and the various highway departments. These agencies are set up to carry out programs: build dams, construct highways, or develop nuclear power. Such activities may cause environmental harm, but if an agency recognizes this harm, it will be forced to curtail its own activities and thus undermine, at least in part, the justification for its existence. At the same time, because these activities are perfectly lawful, they tend to magnify the advantages of those organized groups that favor development and to increase the obstacles facing environmental groups that set out to challenge agency decisions (Trubek, 1978:157). Much environmental advocacy occurs in complex policy disputes. In many such disputes, the resources available to environmental advocates may be insufficient to ensure that their concerns receive the degree of attention from decision makers that they would if the full extent of their demands were reflected in their representational resources.

SUMMARY

We seldom see to eye to eye and opening with the basic premise that disagreements are ubiquitous in social relationships, this chapter has reviewed and analyzed the role of law as a method of dispute resolution. It was demonstrated that there is no consensus in the sociological and legal literature on the terminology concerning the role of law in controversies. The concepts of conflict resolution and dispute settlement were used interchangeably to show how the law resolves the legal components of conflict and disputes. It was repeatedly emphasized that the law does not deal with the underlying causes of conflict and does not reduce tension or antagonism between the aggrieved parties.

Nonlegal methods of dispute resolution include violence, rituals, shaming and ostracism, supernatural agencies, "lumping it," avoidance, negotiation, mediation, and arbitration. In industrialized countries, such as the United States, lumping behavior, avoidance, and negotiation are the most frequent responses to dispute situations. Adjudication is a public and formal method of dispute resolution and is best exemplified by courts. Court decisions have an either/or character, and the adversary nature of court proceedings forces disputes into the mold of a two-party conflict.

As a result of social developments, the increased availability of legal mechanisms for conflict resolution, and the creation of legally actionable rights and remedies, there is a growing demand for court services in dispute resolution. Data indicate that litigation rates in the United States have increased substantially during the last two decades. There are some authors, however, who challenge the notion that the dispute-processing function of the courts has increased in recent years as a result of social and economic changes. There are obvious difficulties in measuring litigation rates over time, and similar problems exist in cross-cultural studies of litigation rates.

Courts provide a forum for the settlement of a variety of private and public disputes. To qualify for the use of court services, at the minimum plaintiffs must be able to demonstrate justiciability and standing. Those who have only occasional recourse to the courts are called one-shotters, and those who are engaged in much similar litigation over time are designated repeat players. There are four combinations of litigations: one-shotter versus one-shotter, repeat player versus one-shotter, one-shotter versus repeat player, and repeat player versus repeat player.

Most individual disputes involve one-shotters. Such disputes include private litigation as opposed to organizations, criminal defendants, or state agencies. Because litigation is costly and time-consuming, courts often make an effort to encourage disputants to settle their differences by agreement. A preference for continuing relations will not, in general, deter individuals from litigation. Those disputants who are better organized and have more expandable resources fare better in litigations.

Disputes between individuals and organizations may take place over economic issues, claims for damages and restitution, issues of civil rights, and issues concerning organizational actions, procedures, and policy. In general, more organizations are plaintiffs and more individuals are defendants, and organizations tend to be uniformly more successful than individuals.

For disputes initiated by individuals against organizations, law as a method of conflict resolution in academe was used as an illustration. Faculty and student-initiated lawsuits against the university were considered in the context of faculty–administration, student–faculty, and student–administration relations.

Disputes between individuals and organizations, where organizations are the plaintiffs, were analyzed in the context of creditor–debtor relationships. When nonlegal methods of collection fail, creditors are likely to enlist the courts in the collection process. Of the legal devices available for collecting the judgments, garnishment of wages is used most frequently. A characteristic of most civil suits for debts is that the plaintiff usually wins by default.

Disputes between organizations cover a wide spectrum of participants and controversies. In interorganizational disputes, the activities of public-interest law firms in environmental disputes were examined. In general, the party that is better organized with greater resources and greater capacity to generate data will have a higher probability of influencing the outcome of the dispute.

SUGGESTED FURTHER READINGS

Jerold A. Auerbach, *Justice without Law?* New York: Oxford University Press, 1983. An exceptional review of nonjudicial methods of dispute resolution in a historical context.

Barbara A. Curran. 1986. "American Lawyers in the 1980s: A Profession in Transition," *Law & Society Review,* 20 (1): 19–52.

Law & Society Review, 15 (3–4) 1980–1981. A special and now classic issue on dispute processing and civil litigation.

Miriam K. Mills (ed.), *Alternative Dispute Resolution in the Public Sector.* Chicago, IL: Nelson-Hall, 1991. A compilation of judicious symposium papers on conflict-resolution approaches in labor relations, environmental issues, rulemaking, and a number of related conflict situations.

Richard J. Lazarus. *The Making of Environmental Law.* Chicago, IL: University of Chicago Press, 2004.

REFERENCES

Abel, Richard L. 1973. "A Comparative Theory of Dispute Institutions in Society," *Law & Society Review,* 8 (2) (Winter): 217–347.

Abel, Richard L. (ed.). 1995. *The Law & Society Reader.* New York: New York University Press.

Administrative Conference of the United States. 1987. *Sourcebook: Federal Agency Use of Alternative Means of Dispute Resolution* (Office of the Chairman).

Administrative Office of the U.S. Courts. 2010. *Federal Judicial Workload Statistics.*

Washington, DC: The Administrative Office of the U.S. Courts.

Almeida, Paul, and Linda Brewster Stearns. 1998. "Political Opportunities and Local Grassroots Environmental Movements: The Case of Minamata," *Social Problems,* 45 (1) (February): 37–57.

American Bar Association. 2007. *Dispute Resolution Program Directory.* Washington, DC: American Bar Association.

American Tort Reform Association. 2004. "Scapegoat Litigation Will Drain U.S. Economy an Average of $30 Billion Annually," press release (April 6).

Anand, Ruchi. 2004. *International Environmental Justice: A North–South Dimension.* Burlington, VT: Ashgate.

Applegate, John S. (ed.). 2004. *Environmental Risk, Volumes I and II.* Burlington, VT: Ashgate.

Aron, Nan. 1989. *Liberty and Justice for All: Public Interest Law in the 1980s and Beyond.* Boulder, CO: Westview Press.

Aubert, Vilhelm. 1963. "Competition and Dissensus: Two Types of Conflict and Conflict Resolution," *Journal of Conflict Resolution,* 7 (1): 26–42. 1969. "Law as a Way of Resolving Conflicts: The Case of a Small Industrialized Society." Pp. 282–303 in Laura Nader (ed.), *Law in Culture and Society.* Chicago: Aldine.

Axelrod, Regina S., Stacy D. Vandeveer, and David Leonard Downie (eds.). 2010. *The Global Environment. Institutions, Law, and Policy.* 3rd ed. Washington, DC: CQ Press.

Barrett Jerome T., and Joseph P. Barrett. 2004. *A History of Alternative Dispute Resolution: From the Wisdom of Solomon to U.S. v. Microsoft and Beyond.* San Francisco, CA: Jossey-Bass.

Barton, John H. 1975. "Behind the Legal Explosion," *Stanford Law Review,* 27 (February): 567–584.

Bell, Kim. 1995. "Prisoners Can Now Lose More Than Their Lawsuits," *St. Louis Post-Dispatch* (July 6): 1, 9.

Bellingham Herald. 2001. "Lawsuits a Volume Business at Wal-Mart" (August 19): E1, E.3.

Best, Arthur, and A. Andreasen. 1976. *Talking Back to Business: Voiced and Unvoiced Consumer Complaints.* Washington, DC: Center for the Study of Responsive Law.

Bissonette, Aimee M. 2009. *Cyber Law.* Thousand Oaks, CA: Corwin.

Black, Donald. 1976. *The Behavior of Law.* New York: Academic Press. 1989. *Sociological Justice.* New York: Oxford University Press.

Blegvad, Britt-Mari. 1983. "Accessibility and Dispute Treatment: The Case of the Consumer in Denmark." Pp. 203–219 in Maureen Cain and Kalman Kulcsar (eds.), *Disputes and the Law.* Budapest: Akademiai Kiado.

Blumenthal, Ralph. 2004. "In Texas, Hire a Lawyer, Forget About a Doctor?" *New York Times* (March 5): A1, A9.

Bodansky, Daniel. 2010. *The Art and Craft of International Environmental Law.* Cambridge, MA: Harvard University Press.

Bogus, T. Carl. 2001. *Why Lawsuits Are Good for America: Disciplined Democracy, Big Business, and the Common Law.* New York: New York University Press.

Bradney, Anthony, and Fiona Cownie. 2000. *Living Without Law: Alternative Dispute Resolution in Practice.* Brookfield, VT: Ashgate.

Brake, Deborah L. 2010. *Getting in the Game. Title IX and the Women's Sports Revolution.* New York: New York University Press.

Bryant, Amorette Nelson. 2004. *Complete Guide to Federal and State Garnishment.* 3rd ed. New York,: Aspen Publishers.

Bush, Robert A. Baruch, and Joseph P. Folger. 2005. *The Promise of Mediation: The Transformative Model for Conflict Resolution.* Rev. ed. San Francisco, CA: Jossey-Bass.

Caplovitz, David. 1974. *Consumers in Trouble: A Study of Debtors in Default.* New York: Free Press.

Chase, Oscar G. 2007. *Law, Culture, and Ritual. Disputing Systems in Cross-Cultural Context.* New York: New York University Press.

Chinloy, Peter. 1989. *The Cost of Doing Business: Legal and Regulatory Issues in the United States and Abroad.* New York, NY: Praeger.

Chronicle of Higher Education. 1989. "'In' Box" (January 25): A14.

Cobb, Sara. 1997. "The Domestication of Violence in Mediation," *Law & Society Review,* 31 (3): 397–440.

Collier, Jane Fishburne. 1973. *Law and Social Change in Zinacantan.* Stanford, CA: Stanford University Press.

Coltri, Laurie S. 2010. *Alternative Dispute Resolution: A Conflict Diagnosis Approach.* 2nd ed. Boston, MA: Prentice Hall.

Cox, Stephen. 2009. *The Big House. Image and Reality of the American Prison.* New Haven, CT: Yale University Press.

Croson, Rachel, and Robert H. Mnookin. 1997. "Does Disputing Through Agents Enhance Cooperation? Experimental Evidence," *Journal of Legal Studies,* XXVI (June): 331–348.

Cross, Frank B. 1992. "The First Thing We Do, Let's Kill All the Economists: An Empirical Evaluation of the Effect of Lawyers on the United States Economy and Political System," *Texas Law Review,* 70 (3) (February): 645–683.

Daley, Suzanne. 1995. "Court Tells South Africa to Stop Imprisoning Debtors." *New York Times* (October 1): A4.

Danzig, Richard. 1973. "Toward the Creation of a Complementary, Decentralized System of Criminal Justice," *Stanford Law Review,* 26 (1): 1–54.

Dilworth, Donald C. 1995. "Prisoners' Lawsuits Burden Federal Civil Courts," *Trial,* 31 (5) (May): 98–100.

Doak, S. Robin. 2004. *Conflict Resolution.* Chicago, IL: Raintree.

Eckhoff, Torstein. 1978. "The Mediator: The Judge and the Administrator in Conflict-Resolution." Pp. 31–41 in Sheldon Goldman and Austin Sarat (eds.), *American Court Systems: Readings in Judicial Process and Behavior.* San Francisco: W. H. Freeman & Company Publishers.

Economist. 1979. "The Odour of Solvency," 273 (7101) (October 6): 104. 1993. "Paper Stockade: Lawyers in Japan," 328 (7823) (August 7): 60–62. 1998 "Abortion and Extortion," 347 (8065) (April 25): 32. 2006. "March of the Robolawyers. Software: A New Program Uses Game Theory to Produce Fairer Outcomes when Dividing Property of Divorcing Couples," 378 (8468) (March 17): 12–14.

Ehrmann, Henry W. 1976. *Comparative Legal Cultures.* Englewood Cliffs, NJ: Prentice-Hall.

Epp, Charles R. 1992. "'Honey, They Shrunk the Economy!' An Empirical Examination of the Claim that Lawyers Impair Economic Growth." Working Paper DPRP 11-2 (March). Madison: University of Wisconsin, Institute for Legal Studies.

Essex, Nathan L. 2009. *The 200 Most Frequently Asked Legal Questions for Educators.* Thousand Oak, CA: Corwin.

Faust, David (ed.). 2010. *Ziskin's Coping with Psychiatric and Psychological Testimony.* New York: Oxford University Press.

Felstiner, William L. F. 1974. "Influences of Social Organization on Dispute Processing," *Law & Society Review,* 9 (1) (Fall): 63–94. 1975. "Avoidance as Dispute Processing: An Elaboration," *Law & Society Review,* 9 (4) (Summer): 695–706.

Fine, Erika S. (ed.). 1988. *Containing Legal Costs: ADR Strategies for Corporations, Law Firms, and Government.* New York: Butterworth.

Fiss, Owen M., and Judith Resnik. 2003. *Adjudication and Its Alternatives: An Introduction to Procedure.* New York: Foundation Press, Thomson/West.

Fitzpatrick, Robert B. 1994. "Nonbinding Mediation of Employment Disputes," *Trial,* 30 (6) (June): 40–44.

Ford Foundation. 1978. *New Approaches to Conflict Resolution.* New York: Ford Foundation.

France, Mike. 1995. "More Businesses Ask: Can We Talk, Not Sue?" *The National Law Journal,* 17 (28) (March 13): B1. 2001. "The Litigation Machine," *Business Week* (January 29): 116–123.

Friedman, Lawrence M. 2005. *A History of American Law.* 3rd ed. New York: Simon & Schuster. 1985. *Total Justice.* New York: Russell Sage Foundation.

Friedman, Lawrence M., and Stewart Macaulay. 1977. *Law and the Behavioral Sciences.* 2nd ed. Indianapolis, IN: Bobbs-Merrill.

Friedman, Lawrence M., and Robert V. Percival. 1976. "A Tale of Two Courts: Litigation in Alameda and San Benito Counties," *Law & Society Review,* 10 (1 and 2): 267–302.

Frum, David. 1993. "Free to Sue," *Forbes,* 151 (11) (May 24): 90–91.

Gaillard, Emmanuel. 2000. "Alternative Dispute Resolution (ADR) A La Francaise," *The New York Law Journal* (June 1): 1–3.

Gajda, Amy. 2010. *The Trials of Academe: The New Era of Campus Litigation.* Cambridge, MA: Harvard University Press.

Galanter, Marc. 1974. "Why the 'Haves' Come out Ahead: Speculations on the Limits of Legal Change," *Law & Society Review,* 9 (1): 95–160. 1975. "Afterword: Explaining Litigation," *Law & Society Review,* 9 (2): 347–368. 1988. "Beyond the Litigation Panic." Pp. 18–30 in Walter Olson (ed.), *New Directions in Liability Law.* New York: The Academy of Political Science. 1992. "The Debased Debate on Civil Justice." Working Paper DPRP (May). Madison: University of Wisconsin, Institute for Legal Studies. 1993. "News From Nowhere: The Debased Debate on Civil Justice," *Denver University Law Review,* 71 (1): 77–113.

Gerson, Stuart M. 1994. "Computers Generate Litigation Explosion," *The National Law Journal,* 16 (31) (April 4): A17.

Gerstein, Ralph M., and Lois Gerstein. 2007. *Education Law: A Practical Guide for Attorneys, Teachers, Administrators, and Student Advocates.* 2nd ed. Tucson, AZ: Lawyers & Judges Publishing Co.

Goldberg, Stephen B., Eric D. Green, and Frank E. A. Sander. 1985. *Dispute Resolution.* Boston, MA: Little Brown & Co.

Goldberg, Stephen B., Frank E. A. Sander, and Nancy H. Rogers. 2007 *Dispute Resolution: Negotiation, Mediation, and Other Processes.* 5th ed. New York: Aspen Publishers.

Goldman, Sheldon, and Austin Sarat (eds.). 1978. *American Court Systems: Readings in Judicial Process and Behavior.* San Francisco, CA: W. H. Freeman & Company Publishers.

Greenhouse, Carol J. 1989. "Interpreting American Litigiousness." Pp. 252–273 in June Starr and Jane F. Collier (eds.), *History and Power in the Study of Law: New Directions in Legal Anthropology.* Ithaca, NY: Cornell University Press.

Grossman, Joel B., and Austin Sarat. 1975. "Litigation in Federal Courts: A Comparative Perspective," *Law & Society Review,* 9 (2): 321–346.

Gubser, Nicholas J. 1965. *The Nunamiut Eskimos: Hunters of Caribou.* New Haven, CT: Yale University Press.

Gulliver, P. H. 1969. "Introduction to Case Studies of Law in Non-Western Societies." Pp. 11–23 in Laura Nader (ed.), *Law in Culture and Society.* Chicago, IL: Aldine. 1979. *Disputes and Negotiations: A Cross-Cultural Perspective.* New York: Academic Press.

Hagerdon, Ann. 1989. "Judges, Immune No More, Seek Malpractice Insurance," *Wall Street Journal* (July 26): 1B.

Haltom, William, and Michael McCann. 2004. *Distorting the Law: Politics, Media, and the Litigation Crisis.* Chicago, IL: University of Chicago Press.

Handler, Joel F. 1976. "Public Interest Law: Problems and Prospects." Pp. 99–115 in Murray L. Schwartz (ed.), *Law and the American Future.* Englewood Cliffs, NJ: Prentice-Hall.

Harman, Danna. 2010. "Where Debt Collectors Use Shame as a Tactic. In Spain, a Practice Dating to Medieval Times Is Now a Way for Firms to Recoup Money," *The Christian Science Monitor* (February 14): 13.

Haynes, John Michael, Gretchen L. Haynes, and Larry Sun Fong. 2004. *Mediation: Positive Conflict Management* Albany, NY: State University of New York Press.

Hazard, Geoffrey C. 1994. "Liability Coverage May Become Impossible to Obtain Under Traditional Procedures," *The National Law Journal,* 16 (28) (March): A17.

Heidenheimer, Arnold J., Hugh Helco, and Carolyn Teich Adams. 1990. *Comparative Public Policy: The Politics of Social Choice in America, Europe and Japan.* New York: St. Martin's Press.

Hellman, Hal. 2004. *Great Feuds in Technology: Ten of the Liveliest Disputes Ever.* Hoboken, NJ: John Wiley & Sons.

Hirschman, Albert O. 1970. *Exit, Voice, and Loyalty: Responses to Decline in Firms, Organizations, and States.* Cambridge, MA: Harvard University Press.

Hobbs, Robert J. 2008. *Fair Debt Collection.* 6th ed. Boston, MA: National Consumer Law Center.

Hoebel, E. Adamson. 1954. *The Law of Primitive Man: A Study in Comparative Legal Dynamics.* Cambridge, MA: Harvard University Press.

Hoye, William P. 1995. "High Cost of Doing Good; More Law Grads Would Enter Public Service with Loan-Forgiveness Plan," *ABA Journal,* 81 (January): 96–97.

Hunter, Ian. 2006. "What Next? Anti-Harassment Training in the Crib?" *The Globe and Mail* (December 29): A15.

Jacob, Herbert. 1969. *Debtors in Court: The Consumption of Government Services.* Chicago, IL: Rand McNally.

Jacob, Margaret A. 1995. "Reliable Data About Lawsuits Are Very Scarce," *Wall Street Journal* (June 9): B1, B2.

Johnson, Valen E. 2003. *Grade Inflation: A Crisis in College Education.* New York, NY: Springer.

Kagan, Robert A. 1984. "The Routinization of Debt Collection: An Essay on Social Change and Conflict in Courts," *Law & Society Review,* 18 (3): 323–371.

Kaplin, William A., and Barbara E. Lee. 2006. *The Law of Higher Education.* 4th ed. San Francisco, CA: Jossey-Bass Publishers.

Karsten, Peter. 1998. "Cows in the Corn, Pigs in the Garden, and 'the Problem of Social Costs': 'High' and 'Low' Legal Cultures of the British Diaspora Lands in the 17th, 18th, and 19th Centuries," *Law & Society Review,* 32 (1): 63–92.

Kawashima, Takeyoshi. 1969. "Dispute Resolution in Japan." Pp. 182–193 in Vilhelm Aubert (ed.), *Sociology of Law.* Harmondsworth, UK: Penguin Books, Ltd.

Koenig, Thomas, and Michael Rustad. 2004. *In Defense of Tort Law.* New York: New York University Press.

Kors, Alan Charles, and Harvey A. Silverglate. 1998. *The Shadow University: The Betrayal of Liberty on America's Campuses.* New York: The Free Press.

Kriesberg, Louis. 1982. *Social Conflicts.* Englewood Cliffs, NJ: Prentice-Hall.

Kriesberg, Louis. 2007. *Constructive Conflicts: From Escalation to Resolution.* 3rd ed. Lanham, MD: Rowman & Littlefield Publishers, Inc.

Kritzer, Herbert M. 1988. "Political Culture and the 'Propensity to Sue,'" Working Papers Series 9. Institute For Legal Studies. University of Wisconsin 9 (1) (July): 1–50. 1991. "Propensity to Sue in England and the United States of America: Blaming and Claiming in Tort Cases," *Journal of Law and Society,* 18 (4) (Winter): 400–427.

Ladd, Everett C., Jr., and Seymour Martin Lipset. 1973. *Professors, Unions and American Higher Education.* Domestic Affairs Study 16. Washington, DC: American Enterprise Institute for Public Policy Research.

Landro, Laura. 2009. "Hospitals Own Up to Errors; Some Finding That Confronting Mistakes Reduces Litigation—and Future Mishaps." *Wall Street Journal* (August 25): D1, D2.

Lauderdale, Pat and Michael Cruit. 1993. *The Struggle for Control: A Study of Law, Disputes, and Deviance.* New York: State University of New York Press.

Lauter, David. 1986. "Report Says Litigation Explosion Is a 'Myth,'" *National Law Journal* (April 28): 46.

Leatherman, Courtney. 1994. "A Public-Interest Law Firm Aims to Defend the Politically Incorrect," *The Chronicle of Higher Education,* 41 (13) (November 23): A18–A20.

Leeson, Susan M., and Bryan M. Johnston. 1988. *Ending It: Dispute Resolution in America.* Cincinnati, OH: Anderson Publishing Company.

Lempert, Richard. 1978. "More Tales of Two Courts: Exploring Changes in the 'Dispute Settlement Function' of Trial Courts," *Law & Society Review,* 13 (1) (Fall): 91–138.

Lempert, Richard, and Joseph Sanders. 1986. *An Invitation to Law and Social Science.* New York: Longman.

Leo, John. 2003. "Hey, we're all victims here," *U.S. News & World Report* (December 8): 80.

Lewicki, Roy J., Bruce Barry, David M. Saunders. 2011. *Essentials of Negotiation.* 5th ed. Boston, MA: McGraw-Hill/Irwin.

Lewicki, Roy J., Stephen Weiss, and David Lewin. 1992. "Models of Conflict, Negotiation and Third Party Intervention: A Review and Synthesis," *Journal of Organizational Behavior,* 13 (3) (May): 209–252.

Lord, William, Leonard Adelman, Paul Wehr, et al. 1978. *Conflict Management in Federal Water Resource Planning.* Boulder, CO: Institute of Behavioral Science, University of Colorado.

Luten, Susan Burnett. 2009. *California Civil Litigation.* 5th ed. Clifton Park, NY: Delmar Cengage Learning.

Lytton, Timothy D. 2008. *Holding Bishops Accountable. How Lawsuits Helped the Catholic Church Confront Clergy Sexual Abuse.* Cambridge, MA: Harvard University Press.

Macaulay, Stewart. 1969. "Non-Contractual Relations in Business." Pp. 194–209 in Vilhelm Aubert (ed.), *Sociology of Law.* Harmondsworth, UK: Penguin Books, Ltd.

Magee, Stephen P., William A. Brock, and Leslie Young. 1989. *Black Hole Tariffs and Endogenous Policy Theory: Political Economy in General Equilibrium.* Cambridge, MA: Cambridge University Press.

Mangan, Katherine. 2007. "Debt Keeps Many Law Graduates From Taking Government Jobs," *The Chronicle of Higher Education* (January 18): 1.

Manning, Carl. 1995. "Legal Party's Over, Inmates Told: Attorney General Clamps Down on Frivolous Suits," *St. Louis Post-Dispatch* (September 6): 1B.

Marshall, Tony F. 1985. *Alternatives to Criminal Courts.* Hampshire, UK: Gower.

McCorkle, Suzanne, and Melanie J. Reese. 2005. *Mediation Theory and Practice.* Boston, MA: Allyn and Bacon.

McCorkle, Suzanne, and Melanie J. Reese. 2010. *Personal Conflict Management: Theory and Practice.* Boston, MA: Allyn and Bacon.

McCrudden, Christopher (ed.). 2004. *Anti-Discrimination Law.* Burlington, VT: Ashgate.

McGillis, Daniel. 1982. "Minor Dispute Processing: A Review of Recent Developments." In Roman Tomasic and Malcolm M. Feeley (eds.), *Neighborhood Justice: Assessment of an Emerging Idea.* New York: Longman.

McIntosh, Wayne V., and Cynthia L. Cates. 2010. *Multi-Party Litigation. The Strategic Context.* Vancouver, BC: UBC Press.

Menkel-Meadow, Carrie (ed.). 2003. *Dispute Processing and Conflict Resolution: Theory, Practice and Policy.* Burlington, VT: Ashgate.

Miceli, Thomas J. 1998. "Settlement Strategies," The *Journal of Legal Studies,* XXVII (2) (June): 473–482.

Milhaupt, Curtis J., and Katharina Pistor. 2010. *Law & Capitalism. What Corporate Crises Reveal about Legal Systems and Economic Development around the World.* Chicago, IL: University of Chicago Press.

Mink, Gwendolyn, and Rickie Solinger (eds.). 2004. *Welfare: A Documentary History of U.S. Policy and Politics.* New York: New York University Press.

Moog, Robert. 1993. "Indian Litigiousness and the Litigation Explosion," *Asian Survey,* 33 (12) (December): 1136–1151.

Morgan, Richard E. 1984. *Disabling America: The "Rights Industry" in Our Time.* New York: Basic Books.

Morriss, Andrew P., Bruce Yandle, and Andrew Dorchak. 2009. *Regulation by Litigation.* New Haven, CT: Yale University Press.

Mundson, Gilda. 2004. "Falsely Accused," *The Chronicle of Higher Education* (May 26): 1, 7.

Nader, Laura, and Harry F. Todd, Jr. (eds.). 1978. "Introduction." Pp. 1–40 in *The Disputing Process—Law in Ten Societies.* New York: Columbia University Press.

Naysnerski, Wendy, and Tom Tietenberg. 1992. "Private Enforcement of Federal Environmental Law," *Law Economics,* 68 (1) (February): 28–48.

Nelson, Cary. 2010. *No University Is an Island. Saving Academic Freedom.* New York: New York University Press.

Nelson, Todd D. (ed.). 2009. *Handbook of Prejudice, Stereotyping, and Discrimination.* New York: Psychology Press.

Neu, Jerome. 2009. *Sticks and Stones. The Philosophy of Insults.* New York Oxford University Press.

New York. 2010. "The Neighborhood News" (January 18–25): 13.

New York Times. 1986a. "Staying out of Court," August 31, 1F. 1986b. "Suing the Clergy" (September 2): 1F. 1995. "Wrong Direction on Malpractice" (July 16): 14E. 2010. "Pope to Meet Irish Bishops on Child Abuse Scandal" (October 14): A1.

Newsweek. 1995. "Slammer Suits" (August 7): 6. 2003. "Lawsuit Hell: How Fear of Litigation Is Paralyzing Our Professions" (December 15): 43–51.

O'Connell, Mary Ellen (ed.). 2003. *International Dispute Settlement.* Aldershot, Hants, UK; Burlington, VT: Ashgate/Dartmouth.

Oda, Hiroshi. 2009. *Japanese Law.* 3rd ed. New York: Oxford University Press.

Olson, Walter K. 1991. *The Litigation Explosion.* New York: Dutton.

Olson, Walter K. 2004. *The Rule of Lawyers: How the New Litigation Elite Threatens America's Rule of Law.* New York: St. Martin's Press.

Oppenheimer, Mark. 2006. "College Goes to Court," *Wall Street Journal* (July 14): W9.

O'Reilly, Robert C., and Edward T. Green. 1992. *School Law for the 1990s: A Handbook.* New York: Greenwood Press.

Page, Clarence. 1989. "Filing Suit Means Never Saying 'Sorry,'" *St. Louis Post-Dispatch* (August 19): 3B.

Palmer, Michael, and Simon Roberts. 1998. *Dispute Processes: ADR and the Primary Forms of Decision Making.* London: Butterworths.

Palmer, Stacy E. 1985. "Supreme Court Curbs Judges' Right to Overturn Academic Decisions." *Chronicle of Higher Education* (December 18): 1–33.

Partridge, Mark V. B. 2009. *Alternative Dispute Resolution. An Essential Competency for Lawyers.* New York: Oxford University Press.

Plett, Konstanze, and Catherine S. Meschievitz (eds.). 1991. *Beyond Disputing: Exploring Legal Culture in Five European Countries.* Baden-Baden, Germany: Nomos Verlagsgesellschaft.

Polinsky, Mitchell, and Daniel L. Rubinfeld, 1998. "Does the English Rule Discourage Low-Probability-of-Prevailing Plaintiffs?" *Journal of Legal Studies,* XXVII (January): 141–160.

Poor, Tim. 1990. "Lawyer Sues Lawyer For Buttock Bite," *St. Louis Post-Dispatch* (April 19): 6.

Posner, Richard A. 1996. *The Federal Courts: Challenge and Reform.* Cambridge, MA: Harvard University Press.

President's Council on Competitiveness. 1991. *Agenda for Civil Justice Reform in America: A Report from the President's Council on Competitiveness.* Washington, DC: The Council (August).

Rabe, Barry G. 1991. "Impediments to Environmental Dispute Resolution in the American Political Context." Pp. 143–163 in Miriam K. Mills (ed.), *Alternative Dispute Resolution in the Public Sector.* Chicago, IL: Nelson-Hall.

Raiffa, Howard. 1997. *Lectures on Negotiation Analysis.* Cambridge, MA: PON Books.

Rapping, Elayne. 2004. *Law and Justice as Seen on TV.* New York: New York University Press.

Reske, Henry J. 1994. "Ralph Nader's New Project: Law Centers to Help the Small Group Instead of the Little Guy," *ABA Journal,* 80 (May): 32–33.

Reske, Henry J. 1995. "Victim-Offender Mediation Catching On: Advocates Say Programs, Typically for Nonviolent Offenders, Benefit Both Parties," *ABA Journal,* 81 (February): 14–16.

Ritzer, George. 2001. *Explorations in the Sociology of Consumption: Fast Food, Credit Cards and Casinos.* Thousand Oaks, CA: Sage Publications. 2010. *Enchanting a Disenchanted World: Continuity and Change in the*

Cathedrals of Consumption. 3rd ed. Thousand Oaks, CA: Pine Forge Press.

Roberts, Simon. 1979. *Order and Dispute: An Introduction to Legal Anthropology.* New York: St. Martin's Press.

Robinson, Mark, and Kevin Calcagnie. 2010. "Why We Need Trial Lawyers." *Wall Street Journal* (February 24): A 17.

Rosati, Massimo. 2009. *Ritual and the Sacred. A Neo-Durkheimian Analysis of Politics, Religion and Self.* Burlington, VT: Ashgate.

Rosen, Jeffrey, 2001. "In Lieu of Manners," *New York Times Magazine* (February 4): 49–51.

Rosenbloom, David H., and Robert S. Kravchuck. 2009. *Public Administration: Understanding Management, Politics, and Law in the Public Sector.* 7th ed. Boston, MA: McGraw-Hill.

Ross, William H., and Donald E. Conlon. 2000. "Hybrid Forms of Third-Party Dispute Resolution: Theoretical Implications of Combining Mediation and Arbitration," *The Academy of Management Review,* 25 (2) (April): 416–427.

Sarat, Austin. 1989. "Alternatives to Formal Adjudication." Pp. 33–40 in Sheldon Goldman and Austin Sarat (eds.), *American Court Systems: Readings in Judicial Process and Behavior.* 2nd ed. New York: Longman.

Sarat, Austin, and William L. F. Felstiner. 1995. *Divorce Lawyers and Their Clients: Power and Meaning in the Legal Process.* New York: Oxford University Press.

Sarat, Austin, and Stuart Scheingold (eds.). 1998. *Cause Lawyering: Political Commitments and Professional Responsibilities.* New York: Oxford University Press.

Sataline, Suzanne. 2007. "Who's Wrong When Rights Collide? Transgender Professor Claims Job Discrimination in Firing; School Cites Religious Freedom," *Wall Street Journal* (March 6): B1, B12.

Saturday Review. 1979. "Getting Hot under the Collar" (June 9): 7.

Schmitz, Cristin. 2009. "Multiple Killer Wins Lawsuit over Old Running Shoes," *Vancouver Sun* (September 28): B2.

Searcey, Dionne, and Jacob Goldstein. 2009. "Health Care's Intangible Cost: Legal Liability. Malpractice Coverage Amounts to a Fraction of Medical Spending, but Tests Conducted for Fear of Lawsuits Are Tougher to Quantify," *Wall Street Journal* (September 3): A13.

Seelye, Katharine Q. 2001. "Global Warning May Bring New Variety of Class Action," *New York Times* (September 6): A1, A6.

Seidman, Robert B. 1978. *The State, Law and Development.* New York: St. Martin's Press.

Shuy, Roger W. 2010. *The Language of Defamation Cases.* New York: Oxford University Press.

Situ, Yingyi, and David Emmons. 2001. *Environmental Crime: The Criminal Justice System's Role in Protecting the Environment.* Thousand Oaks, CA: Sage Publications, Inc.

Skerry, Peter. 1998. "The Affirmative Action Paradox," *Society,* 35 (6) (September—October): 8–16.

Slater, Robert. 2003. *The Wal-Mart Decade: How a New Generation of Leaders Turned Sam Walton's Legacy into the World's #1 Company.* New York: Portfolio.

Soeharno, Jonathan. 2010. *The Integrity of the Judge.* Burlington, VT: Ashgate.

St. Louis Post-Dispatch. 2001. "Employee Who Objected to Wearing a Tie to Work Loses Battle Against State" (April 1): D9.

Stewart, Pamela J., and Andrew Strathern (eds.). 2010. *Ritual.* Burlington, VT: Ashgate.

Stone, Christopher D. 2010. *Should Trees Have Standing? Law, Morality and the Environment.* 3rd ed. New York: Oxford University Press.

Strick, Anne. 1977. *Injustice for All.* New York: Penguin Books.

Stumpf, Harry P., and John H. Culver. 1992. *The Politics of State Courts.* New York: Longman.

Susskind, Lawrence, and Jeffrey Cruikshank. 1987. *Breaking the Impasse: Consensual Approaches to Resolving Public Disputes.* New York: Basic Books.

Takruri, Lubna. 2007. "Taken to Cleaners? Missing Pants Evolve into $65M Lawsuit," *Seattle Times* (May 4): A2.

Tanase, Takao. 1995. "The Management of Disputes: Automobile Accident Compensation in Japan." Pp. 58–83 in Richard L. Abel (ed.). *The Law & Society Reader.* New York: New York University Press.

Tao, Jingzhou. 2008. *Arbitration Law and Practice in China.* 2nd ed. The Hague, New York: Kluwer Law International.

Thomas, Kenneth W. 1992. "Conflict and Conflict Management: Reflections and Update," *Journal of Organizational Behavior,* 13 (3) (May): 265–274.

Time. 1995. "Last Call at the Bar" (March 20): 14. 2001. "Crowded Courts" (August 13): 15.

Trubek, David M. 1978. "Environmental Defense, I.: Introduction to Interest Group Advocacy in Complex Disputes." Pp. 151–194 in Burton A. Weisbrod, Joel F. Handler, and Neil K. Komesar (eds.), *Public Interest Law: An Economic and Institutional Analysis.* Berkeley and Los Angeles: University of California Press.

Turk, Austin T. 1978. "Law as a Weapon in Social Conflict." Pp. 213–232 in Charles E. Reasons and Robert M. Rich (eds.), *The Sociology of Law: A Conflict Perspective.* Toronto: Butterworths.

Urbina, Ian. 2009. "New Laws Let It All Hang Out: Clothesline Bans Stir Rights Battles, Energy Saver Seen by Some as Eyesore," *Seattle Times* (October 11): A2.

Ury, William L., Jeanne M. Brett, and Stephen B. Goldberg. 1988. *Getting Disputes Resolved: Designing Systems to Cut the Costs of Conflict.* San Francisco, CA: Jossey-Bass.

U.S. Department of Justice. 1986. "Toward the Multi-Door Courthouse—Dispute Resolution Intake and Referral," National Institute of Justice Reports, SNI 198 (July): 2–7.

U.S. News & World Report. 1995. "Graveling the Deadbeats" (July 31): 14.

Vago, Steven. 1968. "Wage Garnishment: An Exercise in Futility under Present Law," *Journal of Consumer Affairs,* 2 (1) (Summer): 7–20. 1971. "The Legal Problems of Low Income Consumers—Some Methodological Considerations," *Journal of Legal Education,* 23 (1): 165–170. 1979. "Consumer Rights in Academe," *Social Policy,* 9 (5) (March–April): 39–43.

Vancouver Sun. 1998. "Man Sues Nightclub for Whiplash From Stripper" (July 3): A15.

Vancouver Sun. 1999. "Global Capitalism Update: A Eunuch Approach to Collecting Bad Debts" (May 29): E3.

Vargas, Hector, and George E. Bushnell, Jr. 1995. "Toiling in the Vineyards: Young Leaders in Public Service Work Give Meaning to 'Professionalism,'" *ABA Journal,* 81 (March): 6–7.

Wehr, Paul. 1979. *Conflict Regulation.* Boulder, CO: Westview Press.

Weibust, Inger. 2010. *Great Leviathans. The Case for a Federal Role in Environmental Policy.* Burlington. VT: Ashgate.

Westermann, Ted D., and James W. Burfeind. 1991. *Crime and Justice in Two Societies, Japan and the United States.* Pacific Grove, CA: Brooks/Cole.

Westin, Alan F., and Alfred G. Feliu. 1988. *Resolving Employment Disputes Without Litigation.* Washington, DC: The Bureau of National Affairs, Inc.

Worth, Robert F. 2009. "Investors Flee Dubai's Draconian Debt Laws. Miss a Payment? Go to Prison," *Wall Street Journal* (September 13): A19.

Wright, Martin, and Burt Galaway (eds.). 1989. *Mediation and Criminal Justice.* London: Sage Publications.

Yao, Deborah. 2006. "With New Device, Late Car Payment Like a Dead Battery. Draconian Tool?" *Seattle Times* (June 13): A2.

Yngvesson, Barbara B. 1978. "The Atlantic Fishermen." Pp. 59–85 in Laura Nader and Harry F. Todd, Jr. (eds.), *The Disputing Process—Law in Ten Societies.* New York: Columbia University Press.

Zernova, Margarita. 2008. *Restorative Justice. Ideals and Realities.* Burlington, VT: Ashgate.

Zobel, Hiller B. 1994. "In Love with Lawsuits," *American Heritage,* 45 (7) (November): 58–65.

Zoll, Rachel. 2006. "Clergy Abuse: More Claims, Costs Rising," *Seattle Times* (March 31): A7.

CHAPTER
7

Law and Social Change

For quite some time now, law and society theorists have been preoccupied with attempts to explain the relationship between legal and social change in the context of development of legal institutions (see, for example, Anleu, 2009; Cox, 2006; McLeod and Thompson, 2010; Raz, 2009; Vago, 2004). These theorists, some of whom were discussed in Chapter 2, viewed the law as both an independent and a dependent variable in society and emphasized the interdependence of the law with other social systems. In light of the theoretical concerns raised earlier in the book, this chapter will further examine the interplay between law and social change. The law will again be considered as both a dependent and an independent variable—that is, as both an effect and a cause of social change. The chapter will also analyze the advantages and the limitations of the law as an instrument of social change and will discuss a series of social, psychological, cultural, and economic factors that have an influence on the efficacy of law as an agent of change.

The initial step in understanding the relationship between law and social change is conceptual. What is social change? The term *change*, in everyday usage, is often employed loosely—as demonstrated in the recurrent rhetoric of the presidential and other political campaigns at various levels—to refer to something that exists that did not exist previously, or to the demise or absence of something that formerly existed. But not all change is social change. Many changes in life are small enough to be dismissed as trivial, although at times they may add up to something more substantial and consequential. In its most concrete sense, social change means that large numbers of people are engaging in group activities and relationships that are different from those in which they or their parents engaged in previously. Society is a complex network of patterns of relationships in which all the members participate in varying degrees. These relationships change and behavior changes at the same time. Individuals face new situations to which they must respond. These situations reflect factors such as new technologies, new ways of making a living, changes in place of residence, and innovations, new ideas, and new social values. Thus, social change means modifications in the way people work, rear a family, educate their children, govern themselves, and seek ultimate meaning in life. It also refers to a restructuring of the basic ways people in a society relate to each other with regard to government, economics, education, religion, family life, recreation, language, and other activities (Vago, 2004).

Social change is a product of a multitude of factors and, in many cases, the interrelationships among them. In addition to law and legal cultures (Gibson and Caldeira, 1996), there are many other mechanisms of change, such as technology, ideology, competition, conflict, political and economic factors, and structural strains (see, for example,

Cox, 2006; McMichael, 2008, 2010). All the mechanisms are interrelated in many ways. One should be very careful not to assign undue weight to any one of these "causes" in isolation. Admittedly, it is always tempting and convenient to single out one "prime mover," one factor, one cause, and one explanation and use it for a number of situations. This is also the case with legal change: It is extremely difficult, perhaps impossible, to set forth a cause-and-effect relationship in the creation of new laws, administrative rulings, or judicial decisions. Although there are exceptions, as will be alluded to in this chapter, one should be somewhat skeptical and cautious concerning one-factor causal explanations in general and in particular about such explanations for large-scale social changes.

RECIPROCITY BETWEEN LAW AND SOCIAL CHANGE

The subject of whether law can and should lead, or whether it should never do more than cautiously follow changes in society, has been and remains controversial. The conflicting approaches of the British social reformer Jeremy Bentham and the German legal scholar Friedrich Karl von Savigny have provided the contrasting classical paradigms for these long-standing propositions. At the beginning of industrialization and urbanization in Europe, Bentham expected legal reforms to respond quickly to new social needs and to restructure society. He freely gave advice to the leaders of the French Revolution, since he believed that countries at a similar stage of economic development needed similar remedies for their common problems. In fact, it was Bentham's philosophy, and that of his disciples, that turned the British parliament—and similar institutions in other countries—into active legislative instruments bringing about social reforms partly in response to and partly in stimulation of felt social needs. Writing at about the same period, Savigny condemned the sweeping legal reforms brought about by the French Revolution that were threatening to invade Western Europe. He believed that only fully developed popular customs could form the basis of legal change. Since customs grow out of the habits and beliefs of specific people, rather than expressing those of an abstract humanity, legal changes are codifications of customs, and they can only be national, never universal.

Well over two centuries afterward, the relationship between law and social change remains controversial. Still, "there exists two contrasting views on the relationship between legal precepts and public attitudes and behavior. According to the first view, law is determined by the sense of justice and the moral sentiments of the population, and legislation can achieve results only by staying relatively close to prevailing social norms. According to the second view, law, and especially legislation, is a vehicle through which a programmed social evolution can be brought about" (Aubert, 1969:69). At one extreme, then, is the view that law is a dependent variable, determined and shaped by current mores and opinions of society. According to this position, legal changes would be impossible unless preceded by social change; law reform could do nothing except codify custom. This is clearly not so, and ignores the fact that throughout history, legal institutions have been found to "have a definite role, rather poorly understood, as instruments that set off, monitor, or otherwise regulate the fact or pace of social change" (Friedman, 1969:29). The other extreme is exemplified by jurists in the former Soviet Union, such as P. P. Gureyev and P. I. Sedugin (1977), who saw the law as an instrument for social engineering. Accordingly, "during the period of the transition from capitalism to socialism, the Soviet state made extensive use of legislation to guide society, establish and develop social economic forms, abolish each and every form of exploitation, and regulate the measure of labour and the measure of the consumption of the products of social labour. It used legislation to create and improve the institutions of socialist democracy, to establish firm law and order, safeguard the social system and state security, and build socialism" (Gureyev and Sedugin, 1977:12).

In 2010 these views still represent the two extremes of a continuum representing the relationship between law and social change. The problem of the interplay between law and social change is obviously not a simple one. Essentially, the question is not, Does law change society? or Does social change alter law? Both contentions are likely to be correct. Instead, it is more appropriate to ask under what specific circumstances law can bring about social change, at what level, and to what extent. Similarly, the conditions under which social change alters law need to be specified.

In general, in a highly urbanized and industrialized society like the United States, law does play a large part in social change, and vice versa, at least much more so than is the case in traditional societies or in traditional sociological thinking (Nagel, 1970:10). There are several ways of illustrating this reciprocal relationship. For example, in the domain of intrafamily relations, urbanization, with its small apartments and crowded conditions, has lessened the desirability (and the feasibility) of three-generation families in a single household. This social change helped to establish social security laws that in turn helped generate changes in the labor force and in social institutions for the aged. Changes in landlord–tenant relations brought about changes in housing codes, resulting in changes in tenancy relations. As a result of technological change, the relation of personal-property owners to other individuals has become more impersonal and frequently more likely to lead to injury. As a result, there have been alterations in the legal definition of fault, which in turn has changed the American insurance system. Finally, in the context of employer–employee relations, much of American labor history before the 1930s pointed toward the enactment of precedents and statutes guaranteeing the right to unionize, and once the Wagner Act was passed, the percentage of the labor force in unions drastically increased, although it has since reached a plateau (Nagel, 1970:11) and started to decline in recent years.

Although there is an obvious and empirically demonstrable reciprocal relationship between law and social change, for analytical purposes I will briefly consider this relationship as unilateral. To this end, in the next section I will examine the conditions under which social change induces legal change; then, in the following section, I will discuss law as an instrument of social change.

SOCIAL CHANGES AS CAUSES OF LEGAL CHANGES

In a broad historical framework, social change has been slow enough to make custom the principal source of law. Law could respond to social change over decades or even centuries (see, for example, Edgeworth, 2003). Even during the early stages of the Industrial Revolution, changes induced by the invention of the steam engine or the advent of electricity were gradual enough to make legal responses valid for a generation. Friedmann notes, "But today the tempo of social change accelerated to a point where today's assumptions may not be valid even in a few years from now" (1972:513). In the often-quoted dramatic words of Alvin Toffler (1970:11), "Change sweeps through the highly industrialized countries with waves of ever accelerating speed and unprecedented impact." In a sense, people in modern society are caught in a maelstrom of social change, living through a series of contrary and interacting revolutions in demography, urbanization, bureaucratization, industrialization, science, transportation, agriculture, communication, biomedical research, education, and civil rights. Each of these revolutions has brought spectacular changes in a string of tumultuous consequences and transformed people's values, attitudes, behavior, and institutions.

These changes further transformed the social and economic order of society. Contemporary society is characterized by a great division of labor and specialization in function. In modern society,

> interpersonal relations have changed; social institutions, including the family, have become greatly modified; social control previously largely informal has become formalized; bureaucracy, that is, large-scale formal organizations, has proliferated both in the private and public sectors; and new risks to the individual have emerged including the risk of disrupted income flow through unemployment, of industrial accidents, and of consumer exploitation; and increased chronic illness and physical impairments have accompanied the extension of life. (Hauser, 1976:23–24)

The emergence of new risks to the individual as a result of the attenuation of the various family functions, including the protective function, has led to the creation of legal innovations to protect the individual in modern society. Illustrations of such innovations include provisions for worker's compensation, unemployment insurance, old-age pensions, Medicare, and various forms of categoric and general provisions for "welfare" (Hauser, 1976:24).

Many sociologists and legal scholars assert on the bases of a large amount of accumulated data that technology is one of the great moving forces for change in law (see, for example, Cox, 2006; Volti, 2010). Just consider how shifting forms of technological literacy (ranging from the invention of writing through the mass production of legal texts brought about by the printing press to the use of computers and the Internet) have shaped law, the practice of law today, and the training of lawyers (Tiersma, 2010). There is also consensus in the literature that technology generally changes exponentially while social, legal, and economic systems change incrementally (for example, the laws have not kept pace with the rapid changes brought about by the digital revolution [Downes, 2009; Plotkin, 2009]). Law is influenced by technology in at least three ways:

> The most obvious . . . is technology's contribution to the refinement of legal technique by providing instruments to be used in applying law (e.g., fingerprinting or the use of a lie detector). A second, no less significant, is technology's effect on the process of formulating and applying law as a result of the changes technology fosters in the social and intellectual climate in which the legal process is executed (e.g., televised hearings). Finally, technology affects the substance of law by presenting new problems and new conditions with which law must deal. (Stover, quoted by Miller, 1979:14)

Technology moves so quickly that we can barely keep up, and our legal system moves so slowly that it can't keep up with itself. By design, the law is built up over time by court decisions, statutes, and regulations (Silverglate, 2009). Illustrations of technological changes leading to legal changes abound. The advent of the automobile and air travel brought along new regulations. The automobile, for example, has been responsible for an immense amount of law: traffic rules, rules about drunken driving, rules about auto safety, drivers' license laws, rules about pollution control, registration, and so on. Just as technology has given a big boost to the retail industry, it has also transformed retail crime. Using sophisticated tactics such as bar-code forgeries and fraudulent gift cards, criminals are stealing large amounts and many of the high-tech thieves belong to organized crime rings resulting in the formation of organized retail crime task forces among other control measures (Zimmerman, 2006). Still another example, in late 2009, the Brazilian Senate approved a bill that would permit consensual divorces to be filed and resolved on the Internet. Couples could file for legal separations, decide on alimony, and resolve property issues via the Internet. As of this writing, the House has not acted on it. Finally, with the advent of the Internet, bullying has taken on new meaning as bullies take to the Web to intimidate, harass, embarrass, and offend others. Through social networking sites, e-mail, text messaging, and cell phones, bullies can engage in a variety of activities without ever having to face their victims and often without consequences. Bullying now takes place in cyberspace and cyber bullying has now crossed the line into the criminal (McQuade et al., 2010).

New devices in crime detection (fingerprinting, DNA use, and electronic snooping, among a host of others) resulted in changes in the law, such as the kinds of evidence admissible in court (see, for example, Carr, 2009). The computer makes possible our present systems of credit, merchandising, manufacturing, transportation, research, education, dissemination of information, government, and politics. The computer also plays a significant role in cybercrime, the unleashing of viruses, worms, and other rogue programs onto victims' computers to disrupt them or steal information (Balkin et al., 2007; Jewkes and Yar, 2009). The Federal Bureau of Investigation (FBI) now ranks cybercrime, which causes over $14 billion in damages to businesses annually, as its third priority behind terrorism and espionage (Bryan-Low, 2006). Credit and debit card companies are especially vulnerable as evidenced by, for example, the arrest of a person who stole 130 million credit card numbers (Gorman, 2009). While law-enforcement officials are getting better at catching criminals who engage in cybercrime, they still have difficulties securing stiff penalties (Bryan-Low, 2007).

The computer and easy access to cyberspace, especially the Internet, also have inspired legislation on both the federal and the state levels to safeguard privacy, to protect against abuse of credit information and computer crime (although not too efficiently, as evidenced by the phenomenal increase in, for instance, identity thefts [see, for example, Finch and Fafinski, 2009; Lee, 2001; May and Headley, 2004]), and to require an employer to tell a job applicant who is rejected the source and nature of any adverse report on his or her credit or past record or opinions that caused the rejection. It even contributed to the rise of Internet police states, such as China where cheerful cartoon icons Jingjing and Chacha watch over people's surfing habits and censor Web pages the government does not like (York, 2006).

The success of the 2004 Mars Rover and subsequent explorations renewed interest in space law which was initially modeled on maritime law. The once remote possibility of space tourism, for example, is now just around the corner but liability questions abound. The helium 3 isotope, abundant on the moon, could make a fortune for anyone who mines it. And space's zero gravity promises attractive manufacturing opportunities. There are now businesses that sell rights to name stars and there is an entrepreneur in Nevada who claims a loophole in international law allows him to assert ownership of the moon (Weir, 2004). New regulations and treatises dealing with various facets of space explorations and rights are grinded out daily (Lyall and Larsen, 2009) and, not surprisingly, space law is "in," and more and more law schools (see, for example, McGill, and the University of Mississippi) are offering courses and programs on the new legal frontier of outer space.

Change in law may be induced by a voluntary and gradual shift in community values and attitudes. People may come to think that poverty is bad and laws should be created to reduce it in some way. People may come to condemn the use of laws to further racially discriminatory practices in voting, housing, employment, education, and the like, and may support changes that forbid the use of laws for these purposes. People may come to think that businesspeople should not be free to put just any kind of foodstuff on the market without proper governmental inspection, or fly any plane without having to meet governmental safety standards, or show anything on television that they wish. So laws may be enacted as appropriate and regulatory bodies may be brought into being as necessary. And people may come to think that the practice of abortion is not evil, or that the practice of contraception is desirable, or that divorce and remarriage are not immoral (Glendon, 1989; Jacob, 1988). Hence, laws governing these practices may undergo repeal or revision.

Alterations in social conditions, technology, knowledge, values, and attitudes, then, may induce legal change. In such instances, the law is reactive and follows social change. It should be noted, however, that changes in law are one of many responses to social change. But the legal response in some respects is important, because it represents the authority of the state and its sanctioning power. A new law in response to a new social or technological problem may aggravate that problem—or alleviate and help to solve it. Often, the legal response to social change, which inevitably comes after a time lag, induces new social changes. For example, laws created in response to air and water pollution brought about by technological changes may result in unemployment in some areas, where polluting firms are unwilling or unable to install the required pollution-abatement controls. Unemployment, in turn, may result in relocation, may affect the crime rate in the community, or may bring about coercive pressures from the disaffected. These correlations and chain reactions can be extended practically indefinitely. Thus, law can be considered as both reactive and proactive in social change. In the next section, the proactive aspect of law as an initiator of social change will be considered.

LAW AS AN INSTRUMENT OF SOCIAL CHANGE

There are abundant historical and cross-cultural illustrations in which the enactment and instrumentation of laws have been used deliberately to induce broad social changes in society (see, for example, Fernandes and Varley, 1998; Jimenez, 2010). With the advent of

Roman jurists, the notion of law as an instrument of social change became clearly conceptualized. Nisbet says, "The conversion of Rome from republic to empire could not have been accomplished except by means of explicit legal decree buttressed by the doctrine of imperial sovereignty" (2000:184). Since Roman times, great ages of social change and mobility almost always involved great use of law and of litigation. There are several illustrations of the idea that law, far from being simply a reflection of social reality, is a powerful means of *accomplishing* reality—that is, of fashioning it or making it. It is generally acknowledged that, despite the ideas of Marx, Engels, and Lenin that law is an epiphenomenon of bourgeois class society doomed to vanish with the advent of the Revolution, the former Soviet Union succeeded in making enormous changes in society by the use of laws (Dror, 1968). In Spain, during the 1930s, law was used to reform agrarian labor and employment relations (Collier, 1989:201–222). More recently, the attempts by Nazi Germany and later on by Eastern European countries to make wholesale social changes through the use of laws—such as nationalization of industry, land reform and introduction of collective farms, provision of free education and health care, and elimination of social inequities—are illustrative of the effectiveness of law to induce change (Eorsi and Harmathy, 1971). In China, when the Communist party came to power in 1949, virtually all vices that are ubiquitous in Western countries—prostitution, gambling, pornography, drug trafficking, and usury—were eliminated by government decree along with business operations that were dependent on profits from such activities (Brady, 1981; Muhlhahn, 2009). China also managed to moderate through law its population growth and as a result devote more of its resources to economic development and modernization (Diamant et al., 2005; Tyler, 1995). They established an effective women's health system that discourages large families through patient education, contraceptive choice, and heavy taxes for couples who choose to have an additional child (Rosenthal, 1998). In late 2000, China's one-child policy became more flexible, and affluent couples now can buy a "license" or a "permit" to have additional children, although at a substantial cost.

Acknowledgment of the role of law as an instrument of social change is becoming more pronounced in contemporary society. Friedmann says, "The law—through legislative or administrative responses to new social conditions and ideas, as well as through judicial re-interpretations of constitutions, statutes or precedents—increasingly not only articulates but sets the course for major social changes" (1972:513). Thus, "attempted social change, through law, is a basic trait of the modern world" (Friedman, 1975:277). In the same vein, Yehezkel Dror (1968:673) contends that "the growing use of law as a device of organized social action directed toward achieving social change seems to be one of the characteristics of modern society." Many authors, such as Joel B. Grossman and Mary H. Grossman (1971:2), consider law as a desirable, necessary, and highly efficient means of inducing change, preferable to other instruments of change.

In present-day societies, the role of law in social change is of more than theoretical interest. In many areas of social life, such as education, race relations, housing, transportation, energy utilization, the protection of the environment, labor movement, immigration, crime prevention, and alleviation of poverty, the law and litigation are important instruments of change (Aron, 1989:85–114; Milkman et al., 2010; Prosterman et al., 2010; Reed, 1998; Visher and Weisburd, 1998). In the United States, the law has been used as the principal mechanism for improving the political and social position of blacks. Since the 1960s, the courts and Congress have dismantled a racial caste system embedded in the law and in practice for generations. The old order was swept away by legislation, including the Civil Rights Act of 1964 and the Voting Rights Act of 1965, as well as by the commitment of billions of dollars to social welfare programs. In a relatively short time, these policies have produced notable effects. For example, the immediate results of the Voting Rights Act of 1965 were dramatic, particularly in states that had successfully resisted earlier attempts to end voting discrimination. The percentage of potential black voters registered in Alabama increased from 23 to 52 between 1964 and 1967. By 1969, it had gone up to 61 percent. In Mississippi, the increase was most significant, from 7 percent in 1964 to 60 percent in 1967, and 67 percent by 1969. Between the 1964 and 1968 presidential elections, overall black registration in the South increased by nearly one million voters. About 75 percent of the increase came in the six states that were fully covered by the act—Alabama, Georgia, Louisiana, Mississippi, North Carolina, and South Carolina. This effectively doubled the number of registered blacks in those states (Logan and Winston, 1971:27). The 1965 law, through its impact on black registration and voting, also had profound consequences for black political power. In 1965, there were some 70 elected black officials in the South. By 1969, their number had risen to 400. In 1981, there were approximately 2,500 elected black officials in 11 southern states, including a black mayor in Atlanta (Scher and Button, 1984:45). It would be erroneous to assume, however, that similar changes took place in other domains. For instance, since 1964, the median family income of blacks has vacillated between 54 and 62 percent of the figure for whites.

Similarly, in the former Eastern-bloc countries, the law was a principal instrument in transforming society after World War II from a bourgeois to a socialist one. Legal enactments initiated and legitimized rearrangements in property and power relations, transformed basic social institutions such as education and health care, and opened up new avenues of social mobility for large segments of the population. Legislation guided the reorganization of agricultural production from private ownership to collective farms, the creation of new towns, and the development of a socialist mode of economic production, distribution, and consumption. These changes, in turn, affected values, beliefs, socialization patterns, and the structure of social relationships.

There are several ways of considering the role of law in social change. In an influential article "Law and Social Change," Dror (1968) distinguishes between the indirect and direct aspects of law in social change. Dror (1968:673) contends that "law plays an important indirect role in social change by shaping various social institutions, which in turn have a direct impact on society." He uses the illustration of the compulsory education system, which performed an important indirect role in regard to change. Mandatory school attendance upgraded the quality of the labor force, which, in turn, played a direct role in social change by contributing to an increased rate of industrialization and modernization. He emphasizes that law interacts in many cases directly with basic social institutions, constituting a direct relationship between law and social change. For example, laws prohibiting racial discrimination in education have a direct influence on social change by enabling previously excluded groups to attend schools of their choice. He warns, however, that "the distinction is not an absolute but a relative one: in some cases the emphasis is more on the direct and less on the indirect impact of social change, while in other cases the opposite is true" (Dror, 1968:674).

Dror argues that law exerts an indirect influence on social change in general by influencing the possibilities of change in various social institutions. For example, the existence of a patent law protecting the rights of inventors encourages inventions and furthers change in the technological institutions, which, in turn, may bring about other types of social change.

For all modern societies, every collection of statutes and delegated legislation is "full of illustrations of the direct use of law as a device for directed social change" (Dror, 1968:676). A good example of social change directly induced by law was the enactment of Prohibition in the United States to shape social behavior. (It was also one of the more conspicuous failures, showing that there are limits to the efficacy of law to bring about social change, as I will discuss later.) Other illustrations of comparable magnitude include the abolition of slavery in the United States and the passage of the 1964 Civil Rights Act (Horowitz and Karst, 1969).

Another way of considering the role of law in social change is in the context of Leon H. Mayhew's (1971:195) notion of the possibility of either redefining the normative order or creating new procedural opportunities within the legal apparatus. He designates the former as an "extension of formal rights," illustrated by the pronouncement of the Supreme Court that defendants accused of serious crimes have the right to legal representation. The latter is termed the "extension of formal facilities" and is exemplified by the establishment of a system of public defenders who provide the required legal representation. The extension of formal rights and formal facilities has definite implications for the criminal justice system in the form of greater protection of individual rights.

A rather different perspective on law in social change is presented by Lawrence M. Friedman. He describes two types of change through law: "planning" and "disruption." Planning "refers to architectural construction of new forms of social order and social interaction. Disruption refers to the blocking or amelioration of existing social forms and relations" (Friedman, 2005:25). Planning through law is an omnipresent feature of the modern world. Although it is most pronounced in socialist countries (for example, five-year plans of social and economic development), all nations are committed to planning to a greater or lesser extent. Both planning and disruption operate within the existing legal system and can bring about "positive" or "negative" social change, depending on one's perspective.

Although revolution is the most distinct and obvious form of disruption,

> milder forms are everywhere. Judicial review is frequently disruptive. American courts have smashed programs and institutions from the Missouri Compromise to the Alaska pipeline. Activist reformers have played a sensational role in American life in the last decade. Ralph Nader is the most well-known example. . . . He stimulates use of legal process as a lever of social change. Much of his work is technically disruptive; it focuses on litigation and injunctions, on stopping government dead in its tracks, when it fails to meet his ethical and policies standards. Legal disruption can . . . include lawsuits; particularly after *Brown v. Board of Education*, reformers have frequently gone to court to upset many old and established arrangements. (Friedman, 1975:277)

Social change through litigation has always been an important feature in the United States. Whether the change produced by such action is considered "destructive" or "constructive," the fact remains that law can be a highly effective device for producing social change. For example, when the California Supreme Court destroyed the legal basis for the system of financing schools in the state, Friedman (1973:27) succinctly observed: "Many a *coup d'Etat* in small countries have achieved less social change than this quiet *coup d'Etat* in the courts."

Friedman considers social change through litigation, an American phenomenon, and raises the question, Will this spread to other countries? His response is that creative disruption of the judicial type presupposes a number of conditions that rarely coincide and are apparently not present in other countries to the same degree. These conditions include an activist legal profession, financial resources, activist judges, a genuine social movement, and what he describes as "the strongest condition"—that is, in the United States, "elites—the power holders—must accept the results of disruptive litigation, like it or not" (Friedman, 1975:278). Clearly, no socialist or authoritarian country will tolerate anything like the American form of judicial review. Their legal structures are not designed to accommodate these patterns.

The Efficacy of Law as an Instrument of Social Change

As an instrument of social change, law entails two interrelated processes: the institutionalization and the internalization of patterns of behavior. Institutionalization of a pattern of behavior refers to the establishment of a norm with provisions for its enforcement (such as desegregation of public schools), and internalization of a pattern of behavior means the incorporation of the value or values implicit in a law (for example, integrated public schools are "good"). Evan (1965:287) notes, "Law . . . can affect behavior directly only through the process of institutionalization; if, however, the institutionalization process is successful, it, in turn, facilitates the internalization of attitudes or beliefs."

Often law is an effective mechanism in the promotion or reinforcement of social change. However, the extent to which law can provide an effective impetus for social change varies according to the conditions present in a particular situation. William M. Evan (1965:288–291) suggests that a law is likely to be successful to induce change if it meets the following seven conditions: (1) The law must emanate from an authoritative and prestigious source; (2) the law must introduce its rationale in terms that are understandable and compatible with existing values; (3) the advocates of the change should make reference to other communities or countries with which the population identifies and where the law is already in effect; (4) the enforcement of the law must be aimed at making the change in a relatively short time; (5) those enforcing the law must themselves be very much committed to the change intended by the law; (6) the instrumentation of the law should include positive as well as negative sanctions; and (7) the enforcement of the law should be reasonable, not only in the sanctions used but also in the protection of the rights of those who stand to lose by violation of the law.

The efficacy of law as a mechanism of social change is conditioned by a number of factors. One is the amount of information available about a given piece of legislation, decision, or ruling. When there is insufficient transmission of information about these matters, the law will not produce its intended effect. Ignorance of the law is not considered an excuse for disobedience, but ignorance obviously limits the law's effectiveness. In the same vein, law is limited to the extent that rules are not stated precisely, and not only because people are uncertain about what the rules mean. Vague rules permit multiple perceptions and interpretations. (What does the expression "all deliberate speed" mean?) Consequently, the language of the law should be free of ambiguity, and care should be exercised to prevent multiple interpretations and loopholes (Carter and Burke, 2005).

Legal regulations and the required behavior of people to whom the law is addressed must be clearly known, and the sanctions for noncompliance need to be precisely enunciated. The effectiveness of the law is directly related to the extent and nature of perception of officially and clearly stated and sanctioned rules. Perceptions of rules, in turn, vary with their sources. Rules are more likely to be accepted if they reflect a notion of fairness and justice that is prevalent in society and when their source is considered legitimate (Jacob, 1995). It should be noted, however, that the contrast between legitimacy and legality can, at times, remain confusing. As Carl J. Friedrich (1958:202) observes, "Law must not be seen as operating only in one dimension of the state, but in the many dimensions of the community if we are to comprehend legitimacy as an objective pattern. Legitimacy is related to right and justice; without a clarification of what is to be understood by the rightness and justice of law, legitimacy cannot be comprehended either. Hitler's rule was legal but it was not legitimate. It had a basis in law but not in right and justice."

The responsiveness of enforcement agencies to a law also has an impact on its effectiveness (see, for example, Kerley, 2005). Law enforcement agents not only communicate rules, but also show that the rules are taken seriously and that punishment for their violation is likely. But for a law to be enforceable, the behavior to be changed must be observable. For example, it is more difficult to enforce a law against homosexual behavior than a law against racial discrimination in public housing. Moreover, law enforcement agents need to be fully committed to enforcing a new law. One reason for the failure of Prohibition, for example, was the unwillingness of law enforcement agents to instrument the law. Selective enforcement of a law also hinders its effectiveness. The more high-status individuals are arrested and punished, the greater the likelihood that a particular law will achieve its intended objective (Zimring and Hawkins, 1975:337–338). Laws regularly and uniformly enforced across class and group lines tend to be perceived as more binding than they would have been if they were seldom and selectively enforced, because enforcement establishes behavioral norms, and in time, as E. Adamson Hoebel (1954:15) puts it, "The *norm* takes on the quality of the *normative*. What the most do, others should do."

As a strategy of social change, law has certain unique advantages and limitations as compared with other agents of change. Although these advantages and limitations go hand in hand and represent the opposite sides of the same coin, for analytical purposes I will examine them separately. The following discussion will focus on some of the more obvious reasons why law can facilitate change in society.

ADVANTAGES OF LAW IN CREATING SOCIAL CHANGE

As it has been previously emphasized, identifying the perimeters of change and attributing change to a particular causal variable or a set of variables should always be undertaken with prudence. In many instances, the state of the art of social-change endeavors is not methodologically sophisticated enough to distinguish clearly among causal, necessary, sufficient, and contributory conditions to produce desired effects in society. Social change is a complex, multifaceted phenomenon brought about by a host of social forces. At times, change is slow and uneven and can be brought about by different factors to differing degrees. Change in society may be initiated by a number of means. Of these, the most drastic is revolution, aimed at fundamental changes in the power relation of classes within society. Others include rebellion, riot, coup d'etat, various forms of violent protest movements, sit-ins, boycotts, strikes, demonstrations, social movements, education, mass media, technological innovations, ideology, and various forms of planned but nonlegal social-change efforts dealing with various behaviors and practices at different levels in society.

Compared with this incomplete list of change-inducing forces, the law has certain advantages. Change efforts through law tend to be more focused and specific. Change through law is a deliberate, rational, and conscious effort to alter a specific behavior or practice. The intentions of legal norms are clearly stated, with a concomitant outline of the means of instrumentation and enforcement and sanction provisions. Essentially, change through law aims at rectifying, improving, ameliorating, or controlling behaviors and practices in precisely defined social situations—as identified by the proponents of a particular change. The advantages of law as an instrument of social change are attributed to the fact that law in society is seen as legitimate, more or less rational, authoritative, institutionalized, generally not disruptive, and backed by mechanisms of enforcement and sanctions.

Legitimate Authority

A principal advantage of law as an instrument of social change is the general feeling in society that legal commands or prohibitions ought to be observed even by those critical of the law in question. To a great extent, this feeling of obligation depends on respect for legitimate authority (Andenaes, 1977:52) and the perception of power (Ewick and Silbey, 2003).

The archetypal treatment of legitimate authority is that of Max Weber (1947). Weber defines "imperative coordination" as the probability that specific commands from a given source would be obeyed by given groups of persons. Obedience to commands can rest on a variety of considerations, from simple habituation to a purely rational calculation of advantage. But there is always a minimum of voluntary submission based on an interest in obedience. In extreme cases, this interest in obedience can be seen in the tendency for people to commit illegal acts when so ordered by authority (and for others to excuse such acts as not subject to ordinary morality). Examples of this include the defense used at the Nuremberg trials, at the Watergate hearings, and at the court-martial of Lt. William Calley for the My Lai massacre during the Vietnam War (Kelman and Hamilton, 1989). Obedience to authority can be based on custom, affectual ties, or a purely material complex of interests—what Weber calls "ideal motives." These purely material interests result in a relatively unstable situation and must therefore be supplemented by other elements, both affectual and ideal. But even this complex of motives does not form a sufficiently reliable basis for a system of imperative cooperation, so that another important element must be added, the belief in legitimacy.

Following Max Weber, there are three types of legitimate authority—traditional, charismatic, and rational-legal. *Traditional* authority bases its claims to legitimacy on an established belief in the sanctity of traditions and the legitimacy of the status of those exercising authority. The obligation of obedience is not a matter of acceptance of the legality of an impersonal order but, rather, a matter of personal loyalty. The "rule of elders" is illustrative of traditional authority. *Charismatic* authority bases its claim to legitimacy on devotion to the specific and unusual sanctity, heroism, or exemplary character of an individual and the normative patterns that are revealed or ordained. The charismatic leader is obeyed by virtue of personal trust in his or her revelation, or in his or her exemplary qualities. Illustrations of individuals with charismatic authority include Moses, Christ, Mohammed, and Gandhi.

Rational-legal authority bases its claims to legitimacy on a belief in the legality of normative rules and in the right of those elevated to authority to issue commands under such rules. In such authority, obedience is owed to a legally established impersonal order. The individuals who exercise authority of office are shown obedience only by virtue of the formal legality of their commands, and only within the scope of authority of their office. Legal authority is not entirely conceptually distinct from traditional authority, although the distinction is nonetheless worth having. In modern society, "legality" suggests a component of rationality that traditional authority seems to lack (see also Berg and Meadwell, 2004; Lassman, 2006). Indeed, during the transition to modernity, especially in the sixteenth and seventeenth centuries, authority tends more and more to be rationalized in distinctively legalistic and voluntaristic terms. "Rational" people "voluntarily" make a "contract," which generates the impersonal legal order.

Theory and research show that legitimate authority can wield considerable influence over both actions and attitudes (see, for example, Tyler et al., 1988). It can be the result of both the coercive processes involved and the individual's internalized values regarding legitimate authority. There is a tendency on the part of individuals to assume that the law has the right to regulate behavior and justify conformity to the law. To an extent, obedience to the law stems from respect for the underlying process: "People obey the law, 'because it is the law.' This means they have general respect for procedures and for the system. They feel, for some reason, that they should obey, if Congress passes a law, if a judge makes a decision, if the city council passes an ordinance. If they were forced to explain why, they might refer to some concept of democracy, or the rule of law, or some other popular theory sustaining the political system" (Friedman, 1975:114).

Acceptance of legitimate authority can also minimize the possibility of cognitive dissonance (discrepancies between action and cognition) by interpreting or construing legally prohibited action as "wrong" or morally bad. The law, consequently, not only represents accepted modes of behavior but also enforces and reinforces those accepted modes of behavior (Vining, 1986). Further, it defines the "correct" way of behaving in our daily lives. This effect is ingrained and institutionalized and is present even without the sanctions that are part of the enforcement machinery. In fact, most people in most situations tend to comply with the law without consciously assessing the possibility of legal sanctions or punishment. The legal definitions of proper conduct become subsumed to a large extent in individual attitudes toward everyday life and become part of internalized values.

The Binding Force of Law

There are numerous reasons that law is binding (Honore, 1987). They range from an assertion that laws are ordained by nature to the belief that law results from the consensus of its subjects to be bound. The immediate and simplest answer is that law is binding because most people in society consider it to be so. The awareness and consciousness of law by most people serve as the foundation for its existence. People generally submit their behavior to its regulations, although they may have many different reasons for doing so. Some may believe that in obeying the law, they obey the higher authority of the law: God, nature, or the will of the people (Negley, 1965).

Others consider the content of the law to command obedience, which, in turn, is seen as a compelling obligation (Ladd, 1970). The law achieves its claim to obedience, and at least part of its morally obligatory force, from a recognition that it receives from those, or from most of those, to whom it is supposed to apply. In addition to agencies that encourage obedience through the application of law, other ingredients are normally present and essential. They include an inner desire of people to obey, reinforced by a belief that a particular law is fair and just because it is applied equally, a feeling of trust in the effectiveness and legitimacy of the government, and a sense of civic-mindedness. They also include self-interest and the knowledge that most people obey the law and recognize it as having a certain morally rightful claim upon their behavior, or at the very least, that they behave as though they felt that way. Essentially, people follow the law because they feel that, as one author (Tyler, 2006) succinctly puts it, it is the "right thing to do."

Even when laws go against accepted morality, they are often obeyed. The extermination of more than six million Jews in Nazi Germany, clearly the most extreme instance of abhorrent immoral acts, was carried out by thousands of people in the name of obedience to the law. Stanley Milgram (1975:xii) contends that the essence of obedience is that individuals come to see themselves as instruments for carrying out someone else's wishes, and they therefore no longer view themselves as responsible for their actions. In many instances, the acceptance of authority results in obedience. For example, Milgram, interested in the phenomena of obedience and authority, has shown that people from a wide range of backgrounds will do morally objectionable things to other people if they are told to do so by a clearly designated authority. Under the guise of conducting experiments on the "effects of punishment on memory," he found that about two-thirds of his laboratory subjects willingly behaved in a manner *they* believed was painful or harmful to others. Even though "victims" cried out in pain, feigned heart attacks, and literally begged for the experiment to be terminated, most subjects continued to obey authority and deliver what they believed to be high levels of electric shock (Milgram, 1975). The study, in addition to showing that under certain conditions many people will violate their own moral norms and inflict pain on other human beings (see, for example, the mid-2004 media coverage and reactions to the abuse and torture of Iraqi prisoners by U.S. military personnel in various detention facilities in Iraq [Whitelaw, 2004] and subsequent similar activities going well into the early 2010s), succinctly underlines the notion that most people willingly submit to authority and, by extension, the law.

An additional reason for the binding force of the law may be that people prefer order over disorder and predictability of behavior. Individuals are creatures of habit because the habitual way of life requires less personal effort than any other and caters well to a sense of security. Obedience to the law guarantees that way. It also pays to follow the law—it saves effort and risk, a motivation sufficient to produce obedience. Obedience to the law is also related to the socialization process. People in general are brought up to obey the law. The legal way of life becomes the habitual way of life. From an early age, a child increasingly gains insight into the meaning of parental expectation, orders, and regulations and becomes socialized. This process repeats itself in school and in the larger society. All such discourses increasingly provide—or should provide—for participation of the maturing person. The individual, so to speak, shapes these regulations and makes them his or her own. In the process, discipline is replaced by self-discipline.

Sanctions

Sanctions for disobedience to the law are surely among the primary reasons that laws have binding force (Evan, 1990:72-73). As Hoebel eloquently states, "The law has teeth, teeth that can bite if need be, although they need not necessarily be bared" (1954:26). Sanctions are related to legal efficacy and are provided to guarantee the observance and execution of legal mandates, to enforce behavior. The sanctions recognized and used by legal systems are usually of a diversified character. In primitive societies, they may take the form of cruel punishments or social ostracism. In developed legal systems, the administration of sanctions is, as a general rule, entrusted to the organs of political government. Among the means of coercive law enforcement are punishment by fine or imprisonment; the imposition of damage awards, which may be carried out by executions into the property of the judgment debtor; the ordering by a court of specific acts or forbearances at the threat of a penalty; and the impeachment and removal of a public officer for dereliction of duty. As Hans Kelsen (1967:35) notes, the sanctions characteristic of modern legal systems go beyond the exercise of merely psychological pressure, and authorize the performance of disadvantageous coercive acts, namely, "the forceable deprivation of life, freedom, economics and other values as a consequence of certain conditions."

Robert B. Seidman (1978:100) points out that "laws more or less consistent with the existing social order need not rely upon the threat of legal sanction to induce behavior." However, not all laws are consistent with the existing social order, and an advantage of the law as an agent of social change is that potential violation of the law is often deterred by actual or perceived risk and by the severity of sanctions attached to noncompliance. Even the threat of sanctions can deter people from disobedience. In this connection, it should be noted that disobedience can often lead to an improvement in legal regulation, thus reducing the need for sanctions (Penalver and Katyal, 2010). Perhaps sanctions also play a part by inducing a moralistic attitude toward compliance (Schwartz and Orleans, 1970).

The types of sanctions used obviously vary with the purposes and goals of a law or legal policy. An essential distinction is whether the main purpose of a law is to prevent individuals from doing things that others in society oppose as being harmful or immoral, or whether the purpose of the law is to create new types of relationships between groups or individuals—essentially the difference between proscriptive and positive policy (Grossman and Grossman, 1971:70). The distinction is not always perfect. Positive policy-making often involves negative sanctions as well as positive rewards, although proscriptive policy-making usually involves only negative sanctions (Friedland, 1989). Rewards, such as federal contracts or subsidies, are frequently part of regulatory statutes attempting to change established patterns of economic behavior and have been used widely as an incentive for compliance with desegregation laws. Those who violate such laws not only lose prospective rewards but also may be liable for fines or criminal penalties. Grossman and Grossman point out: "Laws or statutes which seek positive societal changes of major proportion must rely as much on education and persuasion as on negative sanctions. For the carrot and stick approach to be successful, the latter must be visible and occasionally used" (1971:70).

The circumstances are different where the changes sought through the law are the reduction or the elimination of deviant behaviors. In such instances, the law does not provide rewards or incentives to dissuade individuals from committing such acts—only the possibility, if not the certainty, of detection and punishment. In such instances, the emphasis is on deterrence, punishment, and vengeance, and the objective is the elimination or the reduction of a particular type of behavior considered harmful.

There are, of course, additional discernible advantages of the law in creating social change. For example, the law as an instrument of change can effectively be involved in the context of John Stuart Mill's notion of the law:

(i) to achieve common purposes which cannot be left to the forces of supply and demand—such as education; (ii) to protect the immature and helpless; (iii) to control the power of associations, managed not only by the persons directly interested but by delegated agencies; (iv) to protect individuals acting in concert in cases where such action cannot be effective without legal sanctions; (v) to achieve objects of importance to society, present and future, which are beyond the powers of individuals or voluntary associations or which, if within their powers, would not normally be undertaken by them. (Ginsberg, 1965:230)

The list of conceivable advantages of the law as an instrument of social change is indeed incomplete. What has been said so far is intended simply to demonstrate that the law has a peculiar and unparalleled position among agents of social change. At the same time, it has certain limitations. Knowledge and an awareness of the limitations will help us to understand more fully the role of the law in social change, and they need to be taken into account for the use of the law in change efforts.

LIMITATIONS OF LAW IN CREATING SOCIAL CHANGE

In a period when alienation from virtually all social institutions proceeds swiftly, when there is widespread demoralization brought on by uncontrollable economic conditions, and when people are suffering from a "crisis of confidence," it would seem a bit absurd to advance the idea that the law is an expression of the will of the people. For the great majority of individuals, the law originates externally to them and is imposed upon them in a manner that can be considered coercive. In reality, very few individuals actually participate in the formation of new laws and legislation. Consequently, one of the limitations of the law as an instrument of social change is the possibility of prevailing conflict of interest, which tends to determine which laws are promulgated and which alternatives are rejected.

Other limitations bearing on the efficacy of the law as an instrument of social change include the divergent views on the law as a tool of directed social change and the prevailing morality and values. In the following pages, I will consider these limitations separately, and then examine a number of conditions conducive to resistance to change from sociological, psychological, cultural, and economic perspectives.

Conflicting interests arise out of scarcity. Access to scarce resources and highly cherished objects is limited in every society. In the struggle to achieve them, some individuals and groups win; others lose. Several decades ago, Max Weber had already recognized, as did Karl Marx before him, that many laws are created to serve special economic interests. Individuals with the control of ownership of material goods are generally favored by laws since "economic interests are among the strongest factors influencing the creation of law" (Weber, 1968:334). Weber further recognized that other special interests, in addition to the economic ones, influence the formation of law. Weber (1968:333) says, "Law guarantees by no means only economic interest, but rather the most diverse interests ranging from the most elementary ones of protection of personal security to such purely ideal goods as personal honor or the honor of the divine powers. Above all, it guarantees political, ecclesiastical, familial and other positions of authority as well as positions of social preeminence of any kind."

There are two important insights contained in Weber's points. The first is that conflict of interest provides the framework in which laws are framed and change is brought about. Consequently, social stratification in a society will determine to a large extent the part laws will play in bringing about change based on the selectiveness and preferences exercised by those who promulgate those changes. The second point concerns the significance of the use of power to back up those changes. Studies of the legislative, judicial, and administrative processes in a society could lead very quickly to a discovery of not only who wields the power in society but also what interests are significant and influential in that group. Thus, the law as an instrument of a change can be viewed in the context of the organization of power and the processes by which interests are established in everyday social life; the resulting changes might very well be evaluated in those terms.

In a sense it is obvious, understandable, and even tautological that the powerful make and administer the laws in society. If anything gets done, it is because somebody had the power to do it. At the same time, those who are powerful and influential tend to use the law to protect their advantageous position in society, and for them "the law in effect structures the power (superordinate-subordinate) relationships in a society; it maintains the status quo and protects the various strata against each other" (Hertzler, 1961:421).

Many legislative enactments, administrative rulings, and judicial decisions reflect the power configurations in society. Some groups and associations are more powerful than others, and by virtue of being at the center of power, they are better able to reinforce their interests than those at the periphery. Even members of the legal profession are considered "professional go-betweens" for the principal political, corporate, and other interest groups, and hence serve to "unify the power elite" (Mills, 1957:289). Furthermore, as I noted in Chapter 3, many people are often apathetic about or unaware of an issue, but even when they are concerned, they are frequently unable to organize and thus successfully impose their preference on the legislature.

Curiously, however, those who are supposed to be coerced or oppressed by a system of laws imposed upon them by a ruling minority often seem unaware of their coercion or oppression. Indeed, they are frequently among the strongest partisans of the existing legal system. It may be argued that they have been "indoctrinated" by the ruling establishment, which uses its power to confuse them as to their true interests. But this requires that we distinguish between what people define as their interests and what their "true interests" are, a distinction that has given rise to a great deal of complex, subtle, and inconclusive polemics.

There are numerous instances of racial and ethnic minorities, workers, and farmers organizing to promote what they conceive to be their interests. Blacks have been instrumental in the passage of a variety of civil rights laws (Fleury-Steiner and Nielsen, 2006; Scheingold, 1989). More recently, Spanish Americans succeeded in introducing bilingual education into high schools in areas with a large proportion of Hispanics. Labor was instrumental in the enactment of a series of legislation dealing, for example, with occupational safety and health, flex-time work schedules, collective bargaining, and unemployment compensation. Similarly, farmers have succeeded in furthering their interests through legal measures dealing, for example, with migrant workers, farm subsidies, the importation of certain food items, such as citrus fruits, and favorable export provisions. Does this not mean that racial and ethnic minorities, workers, and farmers are also a part of the power structure? And if they are, does this not mean that the distribution of power in society is more widespread and complicated than is suggested by writers who speak of a simple division of society into "the powerful" and "the powerless"?

It is debatable whether the existence of conflicting interests could really be construed as pointing to a serious limitation of the law as an instrument of change. The points raised concerning the power of certain interest groups are valid, but the actual mechanics of change through the law would in any case preclude inclusion of large segments of the population. Large-scale participation of the citizenry in legal change, even in a democratic society, is seldom feasible. But lack of participation does not necessarily mean lack of representation. In the United States and most parts of Europe, people do have access (although of varying rates) to lawmakers and to the legal apparatus, and their aspirations for change through the law are often realized.

Law as a Policy Instrument

A different school of thought on the limits of the law as an instrument of social change is epitomized by Yehezkel Dror. He contends that "law by itself is only one component of a large set of policy instruments and usually cannot and is not used by itself. Therefore, focusing exclusive attention on law as a tool of directed social change is a case of tunnel vision, which lacks the minimum perspective necessary for making sense from the observed phenomena" (Dror, 1970:554). He suggests that it is necessary to redefine the subject of "law as a tool of directed social change" and to consider it as part of other social policy instruments, because the law is but one of many policy instruments that must be used in combination. In the context of social problems such as race relations, public safety, drug abuse, and pollution, "the necessity to use law as a policy instrument should be quite convincing" (Dror, 1970:555). This view certainly has merits. At times, change through the law can and should be construed as an ingredient of a larger policy. For example, the passage of the Economic Opportunity Act took place in the context of a broader policy that attempted to alleviate poverty in the United States.

However, the law is often used as an instrument of change outside of the context of a broad policy-making framework. This is typically the situation in reform-oriented litigation, where the object is to alter a particular institutionalized practice. For example, the 1973 Supreme Court decision to overrule state abortion statutes (Marshall, 1989:145) and its 1992 restrictions on abortion were not carried out within specific policy considerations, and yet they obviously had a tremendous impact on women seeking to terminate pregnancy legally. Although judicial decisions are generally not rendered a policy instrument, because of the adversary nature of litigation, legislative and administrative reforms dealing with larger social issues should take place in a broader social policy-making framework such as environmental and natural resource management activities (Dean, 2006; Hill, 2006; Jordan, 2007; Sterner, 2003). Such an approach would greatly enhance the efficacy of the law as an instrument of change. To this end, Dror advocates the establishment of interdisciplinary teams of lawyers, social scientists, and policy analysts to engage in relevant studies and prepare policy recommendations. More and more lately, this seemingly common sense advice is being translated into practical applications and policy preparatory and advisory teams becoming interdisciplinary.

Morality and Values

The sociological literature recognizes, as James P. Levine (1970:592) notes, that the ability of the law to produce social change is probabilistic, contingent, and sequential. If a law is enacted or a court decision is rendered, it is probable that certain changes will follow, but the degree of change is contingent on certain prevailing circumstances. The law is sequential to the degree that it must precede certain desired changes, but because a large number of factors influence change, the time lag is not obvious. Moreover, a number of factors other than the law may have an effect on change in a particular area, which means that the cause-and-effect relationship between the law and change is very difficult to identify. Some of these factors are related to the prevailing morality and values in society (see, for example, Sterba, 2004).

Patrick Devlin (1965) argues that a society owes its existence less to its institutions than to the shared morality that binds it together. Although his thesis is only partly true, morality and values affect the efficacy of the law in social change. Obviously, society could not exist without accepting certain basic values, principles, and standards. On certain issues, such as violence, truth, individual liberty, and human dignity, a shared morality is essential. This does not mean, however, that all the values in our shared morality are basic and essential, or that decline in one value spells decline in all the rest. Moreover, not all our values are essential. Rules about property, for example, are not: Some principles about property are essential, but no society needs to have those very property principles that are characteristics of, for example, the United States—the principle of private ownership. A society could own all property in common without ceasing to count as a society.

In general, when the law is used as an instrument of social change, it needs the support of society. Schur says, "A good illustration of the systematic ineffectiveness of unsupported law is provided by the utter failure of legislation designed to enforce private morality" (1968:132). Thus, an obvious limitation of the law in social change appears when it tries to deal with what may be called moral issues in society. Laws prohibiting adultery, for example, have existed for centuries, but adultery remains a favorite indoor sport in the United States and elsewhere. Similarly, laws dealing with homosexuality and prostitution have generally been ineffective and not because of lack of trying (Kempadoo and Doezema, 1998; Nussbaum, 2010). In France, there is even a special *Brigade des Incivilités,* or Bad Behavior Brigade. The 88 special agents of this task force in Paris are dressed in civilian clothes and drive around in unmarked cars, and their principal mandate is to carry out a war on public urination, be it on the street, in the Metro, or in parks, with fines up to $644.00 for *urine sauvage* (Ferreira, 2009).

Sexual abuse of minors is prohibited by both criminal law and canon law, but a 2004 nationwide survey compiled by the John Jay College of Criminal Justice on the extent and causes of sexual abuse by members of the Roman Catholic clergy has found that 4,450 priests, 4 percent of the clergy, including several Jesuit University faculty members and presidents (Tu, 2006), (significantly higher than that of the percentage of the general population with the same charges) have been accused of sexually abusing minors since 1950 with a total cost of cases to the church well over $533 million (Goodstein, 2004). The well-known failure of the prohibition of alcohol through constitutional amendment and legislation to produce a truly "dry" society, or to keep most people from drinking, is another example of the limitation of the law to bring about social change in public "morals." The early 2004 attempt by a group of congressmen who introduced a bill in the U.S. House of Representatives (HR3687) to outlaw the expression on television and radio of seven well-known words including the four-letter terms for defecation, urination, fornication, and the female genitals, as well as compound words that imply one resembles an anus, perform fellatio, or engages in maternal fornication, is still another example of trying to influence morality (Saunders, 2004). But the use of these short, vigorous, and very familiar terms in the English language that tend to emerge, inter alia, in traffic jams, White House tapes, and at exam times, is unlikely to be influenced by the proposed legislation.

A comparable situation exists with regard to the prohibition of several kinds of drugs, especially marijuana (Kleinman, 1989). Interestingly, the marijuana laws have been called the "new prohibition," to underline the similarity to alcohol prohibition and the futility of legal control of consumption of those substances (Kaplan, 1971). Clearly, "behavior that is perceived of as satisfying important drives is more difficult to extinguish than behavior that satisfies less compelling drives" (Zimring and Hawkins, 1975:332). In fact, some argue that marijuana at least should be a source of pleasure, not pain or shame: "We should be free to cultivate and sell and buy this 'euphoriant.' The only controls should be those imposed to protect from bogus or polluted merchandise. With the dreadful example of Prohibition before us, it seems nearly unthinkable that we should have done it again. When will we learn that in a democracy it is for the people to tell the government, not for the government to tell the people, what makes them happy?" (Goldman, quoted in *Behavior Today*, 1979:8).

The link between law and morality in the making and unmaking of law raises two questions: (1) What needs to be done in considering a change in the law when moral opinion is divided? Are there criteria other than individual likes and dislikes to which appeal can be made? (2) How can the line be drawn between that part of morality or immorality which needs legal enforcement and that which the law ought to leave alone (Ginsberg, 1965:232; see also Raz, 2009)? In response to these questions, Morris Ginsberg suggests that the law ought to deal only with what can be ascertained on reliable evidence and with acts that can be precisely defined, and primarily with overt or external observable acts; and the law must, as far as possible, respect privacy. He contends that these are "principles of demarcation arising from the limitations inherent in the machinery of the law" (Ginsberg, 1965:238).

Thus, laws are more likely to bring about changes in what may be called external behavior. However, changes in external behavior are after a while usually followed by changes in values, morals, and attitudes. As Morroe Berger (1952:172) emphasizes, "While it is true that the province of law is 'external' behavior, it is also true that in an urban, secular society an increasing number of relations fall within this province. Thus the range of behavior that can be called 'external' is enlarged. At the same time, law can influence 'external' acts which affect or constitute the conditions for the exercise of the private inclinations and tastes that are said to be beyond the realm of law." The fact that a change in attitude is only partial at first does not make it any the less of a change. This is contrary to the arguments advanced decades ago by William Graham Sumner (1906), which since have been echoed by many, that "stateways cannot change folkways."

Sumner contended that the law is limited to the regulation of individual behavior, and it cannot be used to alter attitudes, values, and morality. There are many examples both to support and to refute this contention (see, for example, Peach, 2002). There are several instances where the promulgation of laws did not result in widespread acceptance by the population. For example, the U.S. Constitution asserted the equality of persons before the law without much effect upon increased opportunities for blacks or upon the prejudicial attitudes of many whites for generations. Similarly, the Indian Constitution purportedly outlawed discrimination against untouchables, which has not significantly changed the values and attitudes of most Indians (Seidman, 1978; Waughray, 2010).

On the other side of the debate regarding the power of law to change attitudes, there are several studies suggesting that law can, indeed, alter values and attitudes. For example, studies on the effects of desegregation in situations such as "armed forces units, housing projects, and employment situations indicate that change required by law has lessened prejudice" (Greenberg, 1959:26). Essentially, the purpose of the law is to change behavior, and in some measure the laws requiring whites to change their behavior in dealing with blacks have changed attitudes (Harris, 1977:168). However, it should be noted that there is no simple way to describe white attitudes toward black people. Although there has been an enormous shift toward more favorable racial attitudes, resistance to change in race relations is still widespread. Some forms of change, such as acceptance of blacks in work situations, are accepted. Other, more private kinds of change (for example, interracial marriage) are still resisted in many parts of the country. The idea of racial superiority is no longer characteristic of white attitudes. This conventional sign of racial doctrine seems to have changed for the better. This is reflected, in part, in the relative disuse of derogatory and stereotyped language. Until fairly recently, derogatory words and expressions were commonly used to describe blacks—and one hardly thought it was wrong to do so. Although such language is still used today, its use has greatly diminished.

But the law can change morality and values only under some conditions and those conditions need to be specified. As Robert B. Seidman (1978:156) notes, "The literature contains little more than speculations," and there is a great lack of empirical studies. In general, the law will more readily change morality and values where it first changes behavior. Such a change is usually followed by a justification of the new activity. To a great extent, however, the efficacy of the law depends much upon its adaptation to morality and values if it is intended to induce change (Fuller, 1969:38–91).

There is still much to be learned about when and under what conditions the law can not "only *codify* existing customs, morals, or mores, but also . . . *modify* the behavior and values presently existing in a particular society" (Evan, 1965:286). In change efforts through the law, the prevalence and intensity of moral feelings and values need to be taken into account in both preserving and altering the status quo.

RESISTANCE TO CHANGE

In addition to the limitations of law as an instrument of social change discussed in the preceding section, the efficacy of the law (as well as other mechanisms of change) is further hindered by a variety of forces. In the modern world, situations of resistance to change are much more numerous than situations of acceptance. Members of a society can always find a justification in some more or less practical and rational terms for active resistance to change. Often change is resisted because it conflicts with traditional values and beliefs and prevailing customs (Banks, 1998) or a particular change may simply cost too much money, and sometimes people resist change because it interferes with their habits or makes them feel frightened or threatened. Although the law has certain advantages over other agents of change, for a greater appreciation of the role of law in change, it is helpful to identify some general conditions of resistance that have a bearing on the law. The awareness of these conditions is a major, but often overlooked or underutilized, prerequisite for a more efficient use of law as a method of social engineering.

The sociological literature recognizes a variety of tendencies to ward off change that directly or indirectly have an effect on law as an instrument of change. The intent of this section is to discuss briefly, rather than to analyze in depth, a series of forces that act as barriers to change. For the sake of clarity, I shall consider resistance to change through law in the context of social, psychological, cultural, and economic factors. The categories are only illustrative, and this distinction is made only for analytical purposes, for many of these factors operate in various combinations and intensities, depending on the magnitude and scope of a particular change effort. As may be expected, there is a substantial amount of overlap among these factors. They are not mutually exclusive; in fact, often they are interrelated and interdependent, and many of them, depending on the purpose or rational of the investigation, may be subsumed under different categories.

Social Factors

There are several factors that may be construed as potential barriers to change. They include vested interests, social class, ideological resistance, and organized opposition.

Vested Interests   Change may be resisted by individuals or groups who fear a loss of power, prestige, or wealth, should a new proposal gain acceptance. There are many different types of vested interests for which the status quo is profitable or preferable. Most British lawyers and judges insist on wearing the arcane court uniform of wigs and ceremonial robes that became fashionable and subsequently mandatory under King Charles II in the late seventeenth century (Schmidt, 1992) to lend an air of solemnity, impartiality, and anonymity and to serve as a "leveler" for younger and less-experienced attorneys, although there is a move initiated by the Lord Chancellor, head of the Britain's judiciary, to wear business attire every day and save the knee breeches, silk stockings, and buckled shoes for special occasions (Jordan and Sullivan, 2006; *St. Louis Post-Dispatch*, 1998) and to shed the expensive bench, bar, and full-bottom wigs with long curls reaching to the shoulders costing close to $5,000 in 2009. But the debates about wearing wigs still make headlines in British newspapers, and there are still traditionalists who are reluctant to give them up (Bryan-Low and Bravin, 2009). Students attending state universities have a vested interest in tax-supported higher education, college administrators in obtaining endowments, and faculty in getting research money, often regardless of the source (Stein, 2004). Divorce lawyers constitute a vested interest and for a long time have fought efforts to reform the divorce laws. Physicians opposing various forms of "socialized medicine" constitute a vested interest. Residents in a community often develop vested interests in their neighborhood. They often organize to resist zoning changes, interstate highways, the construction of correctional facilities, or the busing of their children. In fact, nearly everyone has some vested interests—from the rich with their tax-exempt bonds to the poor with their welfare checks.

The acceptance of almost any change through law will adversely affect the status of some individuals or groups in society, and to the degree that those whose status is threatened consciously recognize the danger, they will oppose the change. For example, Gregory Massell (1973) reports that Soviet efforts in the early 1920s in central Asia to induce Moslem women to assert their independence from male domination was perceived by men as threatening to traditional status interests. The men reacted by forming counterrevolutionary bands and murdering some of the women who obeyed the new laws.

Social Class   Rigid class and caste patterns in general tend to hinder the acceptance of change. In highly stratified societies, people are expected to obey and take orders from those in superior positions of authority or power. The prerogatives of the upper strata are jealously guarded, and attempts to infringe upon them by members of lower socio-economic groups are often resented and repulsed. For instance, under the traditional Indian and Pakistani rigid caste system, members of different castes could not draw water from the same well, go to the same schools, eat together, or otherwise mingle. In most cases, for the upper classes there is a tendency to cherish the old ways of doing things and to adhere to the status quo.

In the United States, those who identify themselves as working-class people tend to agree more readily that legal intervention is necessary to rectify deleterious social conditions, such as guaranteeing employment opportunities and providing adequate medical care (Beeghley, 2007). By contrast, middle- and upper-class people tend to oppose government intervention in these domains. For other government programs (such as aid to education), class-related differences tend to diminish.

Ideological Resistance   Resistance to change through law on ideological grounds is quite prevalent. A good example of this is the opposition of the Catholic Church to legislation and court decisions dealing with the removal of some of the restrictions on birth control and abortion. Specifically, in 1982, a French pharmaceutical company announced that it had developed a pill that would end pregnancy if taken within seven weeks of conception. Advocates of reproductive freedom hailed the news, because the pill, known as RU-486, meant that abortions could be induced soon after conception in a doctor's office, without surgery. By the early 1990s, RU-486 was available in France, Britain, and Sweden. But protests by antiabortionists were driving its European manufactures to quit making it, and opponents in the United States helped block its introduction here by threatening to boycott the products of any drug company that sold it. In the face of such intimidation and moral condemnation, virtually no American company was willing to supply it in commercial quantities. Since its approval for sale by the U.S. Food and Drug Administration in the fall of 2000, RU-486 has been distributed in the United States by a pharmaceutical company specializing in women's health that gets it from a producer in China (Tone, 2001, 2009).

Another illustration of ideological resistance (which goes hand in hand with vested interests) is that by the medical profession to anything suggesting socialized medicine, including the enactment of the Medicare Law of 1965 (Allen, 1971:278–279). In general, the basic intellectual and religious assumptions and interpretations concerning existing power, morality, welfare, and security tend to be rather consistent and adversely disposed to change (Vago, 2004:224).

Organized Opposition   Occasionally, widespread individual resistance to change may become mobilized into organized opposition, which can assume formal organizational structure (for example, the National Rifle Association opposing gun control or the National Association of Retired Persons protesting changes in Social Security benefits), or it may be channeled through a social movement (for instance, the recent pro-life activities) or political action committees or lobbyists. In modern societies, with the multiplicity of informal and formal organizations often in conflict with each other, a variety of new organizations have developed to combat specific threats to the status quo. For example, members of the John Birch Society decry a whole range of social changes from racial integration to the acceptance and legal protection of pornography. As with the John Birch Society, the reemergence of the Ku Klux Klan is based on public opposition to social change but focuses mainly on changing race relations. These and similar organizations have resisted change that was under way, and although most of them have fought a losing battle, their delaying effects have often been considerable. At times, however, when organized opposition to change through law is not forthcoming, the consequences can be disastrous. For instance, more than six million Jews were slaughtered in concentration camps during World War II in part because they did not organize resistance to the changes beginning in the early 1930s in Nazi Germany (Vago, 2004:259).

Psychological Factors

Goodwin Watson (1969:488) remarks that "all of the forces which contribute to stability in personality or in social systems can be perceived as resisting change." Any detailed discussion of these psychological forces is obviously beyond the scope of this book (see, for example, Matsumoto and Juang, 2008). For the present purpose, I shall consider only habit, motivation, ignorance, selective perception, and moral development.

Habit From a psychological perspective, habit is a barrier to change. Once a habit is established, its operation often becomes satisfying to the individual. People become accustomed to behaving or acting in a certain manner, and they feel comfortable with it. Once a particular form of behavior becomes routinized and habitual, it will resist change. Meyer F. Nimkoff (1957:62) suggests that the customs of a society are collective habits; in particular, where sentiment pervades custom, custom is slow to change when challenged by new ideas and practices. To cite but a single illustration, attempts to introduce the metric system have met with considerable resistance in the United States. We are accustomed to miles and feel uncomfortable with kilometers; we prefer a quart of something to a liter of something. When the law is used as an instrument of social change to alter established customs, it is more likely that the achievement of acceptable rates of compliance will require an active reorientation of the values and behaviors of a significant part of the target population (Zimring and Hawkins, 1975:331).

Motivation The acceptance of change through law is also conditioned by a variety of motivational forces (see, for example, Ginsberg and Fiene, 2004). Some motivations are culture-bound, in the sense that their presence or absence is characteristic of a particular culture. For instance, religious beliefs in some cultures offer motivations to certain kinds of change, whereas in other cultures these motivations center on the preservation of the status quo. Other kinds of motivations tend to be universal, or nearly universal, in that they cut across societies and cultures (Foster, 1973:152). Examples of these motivations include the desire for prestige or for economic gain and the wish to comply with friendship obligations. Changes that may threaten the desire for economic gain or the attraction of prestige and high status will in general be considered threatening and likely resisted.

Ignorance Ignorance is another psychological factor generally associated with resistance to change. At times, ignorance goes hand in hand with fear of the new. This is often true in the case of new foods. Not too long ago, many individuals assumed that citrus fruit brought an acid condition to the digestive tract. Once it was proved otherwise, resistance based on the acid matter faded. Ignorance can also be a factor in noncompliance with laws designed to reduce discriminatory practices. For example, employers often make observations about nonwhites as a group relative to whites and then on that basis hesitate to hire individual nonwhites (Beeghley, 2007). Ignorance is obviously an important factor in prejudice when a preexisting attitude is so strong and inflexible that it seriously distorts perception and judgment.

Selective Perception Law, by design and intent, tends to be universal. The perception of the intent of the law, however, is selective and varies with socioeconomic, cultural, and demographic variables. The unique pattern of people's needs, attitudes, habits, and values derived through socialization determines what they will selectively attend to, what they will selectively interpret, and what they will selectively act upon. People in general will be more receptive to new ideas if they are related to their interests, consistent with their attitudes, congruent with their beliefs, and supportive of their values (Baker, 2005). Differing perceptions of the purpose of a law may hinder change. For example, in India the law provides for widespread distribution of family-planning information and supplies. But the use of contraceptive devices has been rejected by many Indian villagers because they perceive the law's intent to stop birth completely. In the United States, the early attempts to fluoridate city water supplies met with perceptions that a "communist conspiracy" was behind these efforts, and as a result they were resisted in many communities.

The way a law is written, as I noted earlier, also affects perception. For example, in their early stages most civil rights laws have been ambiguous and weak. The *Brown* decision is a good illustration. Calling for desegregation "with all deliberate speed" is too vague, too indefinite to bring about meaningful change. "Ambiguity always lends itself to individualized perceptions" (Rodgers and Bullock, 1972:199), and the individuals will interpret and perceive the meaning of the law in a way they consider most advantageous in the context of social changes, economic trends, and integration into the larger community locally, nationally, and internationally (Engel and Engel, 2011).

Moral Development   To a great extent, obedience to the law stems from a sense of moral obligation, which is the product of socialization. Only relatively recently, however, has there been some awareness of moral codes that are not necessarily linked to conventional external standards of right and wrong behavior, but represent internally consistent principles by which people govern their lives.

Perhaps the most extensive work on moral development was carried out by Gibbs (2010) and Lawrence Kohlberg (1964, 1967). He defines six stages in moral development. The first stage is described as an "obedience and punishment" orientation. This stage involves a "deference to superior power or prestige" and an orientation toward avoiding trouble. The second stage, "instrumental relativism," is characterized by naive notions of reciprocity. With this orientation, people will attempt to satisfy their own needs by simple negotiation with others or by a primitive form of equalitarianism. He calls these two stages "premoral." The third stage, "personal concordance," is an orientation based on approval and pleasing others. It is characterized by conformity to perceived majority beliefs. Such people adhere to what they consider to be prevailing norms. Stage four is the "law and order" stage. People with such orientations are committed to "doing their duty," and being respectful to those in authority. Stages three and four combine to form a conventional moral orientation.

Stages five and six indicate the internalized-principle orientation. Kohlberg calls stage five the "social contract" stage; it involves a legalistic orientation. Commitments are viewed in contractual terms, and people at this stage will avoid efforts to break implicit or explicit agreements. The final and highest stage of moral development is "individual principles." This emphasizes conscience, mutual trust, and respect as the guiding principles of behavior.

If the development theory proposed by Kohlberg is correct, the law is more or less limited depending on the stage of moral development of members of a society. In this context, David J. Danelski (1974:14–15) suggests that both qualitative and quantitative considerations are important. We would need to know the modal stage of the moral development of elites, of "average" citizens, and of deprived groups. If most members of a society were at the first and second stages, institutional enforcement would be essential to maintain order and security. Law would be least limited in a society in which most people were at the third and fourth stages of development. Law at the last two stages is probably more limited than at stages three and four, "but it might be otherwise if it is perceived as democratically agreed upon and consistent with individual principles of conscience. If it is not, it is likely to be more limited" (Danelski, 1974:15). The limits of law, in other words, appear to be curvilinear with respect to moral development.

Cultural Factors

When long-established practices or behaviors are threatened, resistance to change is usually strong, often on the basis of traditional beliefs and values. The status quo is protected and change is resisted. For example, the Mormons, on the basis of traditional religious beliefs, opposed laws threatening their polygamous marriages. Similarly, in India, where malnutrition is a problem of considerable magnitude, millions of cows sacred to Hindus not only are exempt from being slaughtered for food but also are allowed to roam through villages and farm lands, often causing extensive damage to crops. Eating beef runs counter to long-held religious beliefs, and as a result it is unlikely that the raising of cattle for food will be acceptable in India. Other cultural factors also act often as obstacles to change. They include fatalism, ethnocentrism, notions of incompatibility, and superstition.

Fatalism   Mead states, "In many parts of the world we find cultures adhering to the belief that man has no causal effect upon his future or the future of the land; God, not man, can improve man's lot. . . . It is difficult to persuade such people to use fertilizers, or to save the best seed for planting, since man is responsible only for the performance, and the divine for the success of the act" (1953:201). Basically, fatalism entails a feeling of a lack of mastery over nature. People have no control over their lives and everything that happens to them is caused by God or evil spirits. Such a fatalistic outlook undoubtedly results in resistance to change, for change is seen as human-initiated rather than having a divine origin.

Ethnocentrism   Some groups in society consider themselves "superior," possessing the only "right" way of thinking about the world and of coping with the environment. Feelings of superiority about one's group are likely to make people unreceptive to the ideas and methods used in other groups. As a result, ethnocentrism often constitutes a bulwark against change. For example, such feelings of superiority by whites have hindered integration efforts in housing, employment, and education among many other areas in the context of race relations (Asante, 2003).

Incompatibility   Resistance to change is often due to the presence in the target group of material and systems that are, or considered to be, irreconcilable with the new proposal. When such incompatibility exists in a culture, change comes about with difficulty. An illustration is the marriage-age law enacted in Israel in an attempt to induce changes in the immigrant population through legal norms. The law sets 17 as the minimum age for marriage with the exception of pregnancy and imposes a criminal sanction on anyone who marries a girl below the age of 17 without permission of the district court. By setting the minimum age at 17, the law attempted to impose a rule of behavior that was incompatible with the customs and habits of some of the sections of the Jewish population of Israel that came from Arab and Oriental countries, where marriage was usually contracted at a lower age. The act had only limited effect, and communities that formerly permitted marriage of females at an early age continue to do so (Dror, 1968:678).

Superstition Superstition is defined as an uncritical acceptance of a belief that is not substantiated by facts (Ambrose, 1998). At times, superstitions act as barriers to change. For example, in one situation in Zimbabwe, nutrition-education efforts were hampered because many women would not eat eggs. According to widespread belief, eggs cause infertility, make babies bald, and cause women to be promiscuous. Similarly, in the Philippines, it is a widely accepted idea that squash and chicken eaten at the same time produce leprosy. In some places, women are not given milk during late pregnancy because of the belief that it produces a fetus too large for easy delivery, and in other places, a baby may not be given water for several months after birth because water's "cold" quality will upset the infant's heat equilibrium. In some parts of Ghana, children are not given meat or fish because it is believed that they cause intestinal worms (Foster, 1973:103–104). Obviously, where such superstitious beliefs prevail, change efforts through law or other agents will meet some resistance.

Economic Factors

Even in affluent societies, limited economic resources constitute a barrier to changes that might otherwise be readily adopted. For instance, in the United States, almost everyone would readily accept the desirability of more effective controls on pollution, cheaper and more convenient systems of public transportation, effective welfare programs, and adequate health care for all. The fact that changes in these areas come very slowly is a matter not only of priorities but also of cost. Cost and limited economic resources in a society do in effect provide a source of resistance to change.

It is a truism that, like everything else, change through law has its costs. In most instances, the instrumentation of legislation, administrative ruling, or court decision carries a price tag. For example, the economic impact of federal regulations on institutions of higher education has been significant. The various affirmative action programs (which are becoming more prominent in other countries as well [see, for example, McHarg and Nicolson, 2006]) carry sanctions providing for the cutoff of *all* federal funding in the United States to institutions that do not comply with antibias laws. Compliance, in turn, results in increased administrative costs for postsecondary institutions, which are resisted in many academic circles and have contributed to the demands for modification of a variety of laws affecting higher education.

In addition to the direct cost of a particular change effort, the way costs and benefits are distributed also affects resistance. For example, when costs and benefits are widely distributed (as in Social Security), there is minimal resistance to programs. The cost to each taxpayer is relatively small; the benefits are so widely distributed "that they are almost like collective goods; beneficiaries will enjoy the benefits, but only make small contributions to their retention or growth" (Handler, 1978:15). Resistance will be forthcoming in situations where benefits are distributed while costs are concentrated. For example, automakers still resist (although not too successfully) legal attempts to impose more sophisticated pollution-control measures on cars.

Although a particular change through the law may be desirable (such as an effective and comprehensive universal health insurance plan in the United States), limited economic resources often act as barriers to such change efforts. Of the four sources of resistance to change, the economic factors are perhaps the most decisive. Regardless of the desirability of a proposed change, its compatibility with the values and beliefs of the recipients, and many other considerations, it will be resisted if the economic sacrifice is too great. Simply stated, regardless of how much people in a society want something, if they cannot afford it, chances are they will not be able to get it. As George M. Foster (1973:78) suggests, "Cultural, social and psychological barriers and stimulants to change exist in an economic setting . . . (and) economic factors . . . seem to set the absolute limits to change."

SUMMARY

Social change occurs constantly—although at varying rates—in contemporary societies, and it affects the lives of individuals in different ways. Changes in society are a product of a multitude of factors and, in many cases, the interrelationships among them. In addition to law, there are a number of other mechanisms of social change. All these mechanisms are in many ways interrelated, and one should be careful not to assign undue weight to any one of these "causes" in isolation.

Law is both a dependent and an independent variable in social change. The relationship between law and change is still controversial. Some maintain that law is a reactor to social change; others argue that it increasingly is an initiator of change. These two views represent the extremes of a continuum dealing with the relationship between law and social change. In modern society, law does play a large part in social change and vice versa.

More and more, law is being considered an instrument of social change. Today the role of law in change is of more than theoretical interest. In many areas of social life, such as education, race relations, housing, transportation, energy utilization, and the protection of the environment, the law has been relied on as an important instrument of change. Law influences social change directly and indirectly. It redefines the normative order, extends formal rights, and is used for planning purposes.

As compared with other agents of change, the law has several distinct advantages. The advantages of law as an agent of change are attributed to the perception that the law in society is legitimate, more or less rational, authoritative, institutionalized, generally not disruptive, and backed by mechanisms of enforcement and sanctions.

At the same time, the law has certain limitations in creating social change. It is not always able to resolve conflicting interests, and generally the powerful in society fare better than the less privileged and the unorganized. Law alone cannot deal effectively with social problems such as drug addiction, overpopulation, and corruption in government. These problems still defy adequate solution. Each is not a single problem but a complex of problems: Each generates a host of countervailing considerations—moral, economic, and otherwise—that compound the complexities. Further limitations flow from the inherent clumsiness of the instrument of the rule of law. One cannot easily foresee and take into account the situations to which a rule might apply. How many advocates of rent control for the poor could have anticipated the extent to which it would contribute to the perpetuation of the ghetto? How many legislators could have foreseen that subsidies to help farmers would result in reducing the number of farmers? The law is further limited by the divergences in values and moral codes, the difficulty in enforcing some laws, the occasional lack of clarity of law, and the questionable diligence in enforcing certain laws.

In addition to these limits on the law in social change, a variety of social, psychological, cultural, and economic forces may provide direct or indirect resistance to change efforts. The social factors include vested interests, social class, moral sentiments, and organized opposition. Psychological resistance may be triggered by habit, motivation, ignorance, selective perception, and the complexities inherent in moral development. Cultural barriers to change include fatalism, ethnocentrism, notions of incompatibility, and superstition. But the economic factors are perhaps the most decisive. Cost and limited economic resources effectively set a limit to change.

SUGGESTED FURTHER READINGS

A. Allott, *The Limits of Law.* London: Butterworths, 1980. An oft-cited critical analysis of the role and limits of law in social change.

Vilhelm Aubert, "Law and Social Change in Nineteenth-Century Norway." Pp. 55–80 in June Starr and Jane F. Collier (eds.), *History and Power in the Study of Law: New Directions in Legal Anthropology.* Ithaca, NY: Cornell University Press, 1989. A discussion of a series of changes in Norway brought about by the law.

Lawrence M. Friedman, *American Law: An Introduction.* 2nd ed. New York: W. W. Norton & Company, Inc., 1998. See in particular the section on law and social change.

Lawrence M. Friedman, *American Law in the Twentieth Century.* New Haven, CT: Yale University Press, 2002. A stimulating overview of some of the major legal and social changes in the United States.

REFERENCES

Allen, Francis R. 1971. *Socio-Cultural Dynamics: An Introduction to Social Change.* New York: MacMillan.

Ambrose, David. 1998. *Superstition.* New York: Warner Books.

Andenaes, Johannes. 1977. "The Moral or Educative Influence of Criminal Law." Pp. 50–59 in June Louis Tapp and Felice J. Levine (eds.), *Law, Justice, and the Individual in Society: Psychological and Legal Issues.* New York: Holt, Rinehart & Winston.

Anleu, Sharyn I. Roach. 2009. *Law and Social Change.* 2nd ed. Thousand Oaks, CA: Sage Publications.

Aron, Nan. 1989. *Liberty and Justice for All: Public Interest Law in the 1980s and Beyond.* Boulder, CO: Westview Press.

Asante, Molefi Kete. 2003. *Afrocentricity, The Theory of Social Change.* Revised and expanded. Chicago, IL: African American Images.

Aubert, Vilhelm (ed.). 1969. *Sociology of Law.* Harmondsworth, UK: Penguin Books, Ltd.

Baker, Wayne. 2005. *America's Crisis of Values: Reality and Perception.* Princeton, NJ: Princeton University Press.

Balkin, Jack M, James Grimmelmann, Eddan Katz, Nimrod Kozlovski, Shlomit Wagman, and Tal Zarsky (eds.). 2007. *Cybercrime. Digital Cops in a Networked Environment.* New York: New York University Press.

Banks, Cindy. 1998. "Custom in the Courts," *British Journal of Criminology,* 38 (2) (Spring): 299–316.

Beeghley, Leonard. 2007. *The Structure of Social Stratification in the United States.* 5th ed. Boston, MA: Person/Allyn and Bacon.

Behavior Today. 1979. "New Roundup," 10 (26) (July 9): 8.

Berg, Axel van den, and Hudson Meadwell (eds.). 2004. *The Social Sciences and Rationality: Promise, Limits, and Problems.* New Brunswick, NJ: Transaction Publishers.

Berger, Morroe. 1952. *Equality by Statute.* New York: Columbia University Press.

Brady, James P. 1981. "A Season of Startling Alliance: Chinese Law and Justice in the New Order," *International Journal of the Sociology of Law,* 9: 41–67.

Bryan-Low, Cassell. 2006. "Criminal Network— To Catch Crooks in Cyberspace, FBI Goes Global. Zeroing In on the Zotob Worm," *Wall Street Journal* (November 21): A1, A11. 2007. "Bugs Abound in Prosecuting Hackers: Complex Issues and Soft Laws Pose Hurdles When Trying Cases; Sentences Might Stiffen." *Wall Street Journal* (January 17): A8.

Bryan-Low, Cassell, and Jess Bravin. 2009. "A U.K. Court Without Wigs. New Supreme Court Bench, Patterned on America's, Stirs Debate." *Wall Street Journal* (October 17–18): A1, A10.

Carr, Indira (ed.). 2009. *Computer Crime.* Burlington, VT: Ashgate.

Carter, Lief H., and Thomas F. Burke. 2005. *Reason in Law.* 7th ed. New York: Longman.

Collier, George. 1989. "The Impact of Second Republic Labor Reforms in Spain." Pp. 201–222 in June Starr and Jane F. Collier (eds.), *History and Power in the Study of Law: New Directions in Legal Anthropology.* Ithaca, NY: Cornell University Press.

Cox, Noel. 2006. *Technology and Legal Systems.* Burlington, VA: Ashgate.

Danelski, David J. 1974. "The Limits of Law." Pp. 8–27 in J. Roland Pennock and John W. Chapman (eds.), *The Limits of Law.* New York: Lieber-Atherton.

Dean, Hartley. 2006. *Social Policy.* Malden, MA: Blackwell Publishing.

Devlin, Patrick. 1965. *The Enforcement of Morals.* New York: Oxford University Press.

Diamant, Neil J., Stanley B. Lubman, and Kevin J. O'Brien (eds.). 2005. *Engaging the Law in China: State, Society, and Possibilities for Justice.* Stanford, CA: Stanford University Press.

Downes, Larry. 2009. *The Laws of Disruption: Harnessing the New Forces That Govern Life and Business in the Digital Age.* New York: Basic.

Dror, Yehezkel. 1968. "Law and Social Change." Pp. 663–680 in Rita James Simon (ed.), *The Sociology of Law.* San Francisco, CA: Chandler Publishing Company. 1970. "Law as a Tool of Directed Social Change," *American Behavioral Scientist* 13: 553–559.

Edgeworth, Brendan. 2003. *Law, Modernity, Postmodernity: Legal Change in the Contracting State.* Burlington, VT: Ashgate.

Engel, David M., and Jaruwan S. Engel. 2011. *Tort, Custom, and Karma. Globalization and Legal Consciousness in Thailand.* Stanford, CA: Stanford University Press.

Eorsi, Gyula, and Attila Harmathy. 1971. *Law and Economic Reform in Socialistic Countries.* Budapest: Akademiai Kiado.

Evan, William M. 1965. "Law as an Instrument of Social Change." Pp. 285–293 in Alvin W. Gouldner and S. M. Miller (eds.), *Applied Sociology: Opportunities and Problems.* New York: Free Press. 1990. *Social Structure and Law: Theoretical and Empirical Perspectives.* Newbury Park, CA: Sage Publications.

Ewick, Patricia, and Susan Silbey. 2003. "Narrating Social Structure: Stories of Resistance to Legal Authority," *The American Journal of Sociology,* 108 (6) (May): 1328–1375.

Fernandes, Edesio, and Ann Varley (eds.). 1998. *Illegal Cities: Law and Urban Change in Developing Countries.* New York: St. Martin's Press.

Ferreira, Susana. 2009. "In Paris, Behavior Brigade Battles to Make *Oui-Oui a Non-Non.* Even the *Sanisettes* Don't Stem the Flow; Mr. Rebete Is a Whiz at Catching Offenders." *Wall Street Journal* (September 1): A1, A14.

Finch, Emily, and Stefan Fafinski. 2009. *Identity Theft.* Devon, UK: Willan Publishing.

Fleury-Steiner, Benjamin, and Laura Beth Nielsen (eds). 2006. *The New Civil Rights Research: A Constitutive Approach.* Aldershot, Hants, UK; Burlington, VT: Ashgate.

Foster, George M. 1973. *Traditional Societies and Technological Change.* 2nd ed. New York: Harper & Row, Pub.

Friedland, M. L. (ed.). 1989. *Sanctions and Rewards in the Legal System: A Multidisciplinary Approach.* Toronto, Canada: University of Toronto Press.

Friedman, Lawrence M. 1969. "Legal Culture and Social Development," *Law & Society Review* 4 (1): 29–44. 1973. "General Theory of Law and Social Change." Pp. 17–33 in J. S. Ziegel (ed.), *Law and Social Change.* Toronto: Osgoode Hall Law School, York University. 1975. *The Legal System: A Social Science Perspective.* New York: Russell Sage Foundation. 2005. "Coming of Age: Law and Society Enters an Exclusive Club." *Annual Review of Law and Social Science* 1 (December): 1–16.

Friedmann, Wolfgang. 1972. *Law in a Changing Society.* 2nd ed. New York: Columbia University Press.

Friedrich, Carl J. 1958. *The Philosophy of Law in Historical Perspective.* Chicago, IL: University of Chicago Press.

Fuller, Lon L. 1969. *The Morality of Law.* Rev. ed. New Haven, CT: Yale University Press.

Gibbs, John C. 2010. *Moral Development and Reality: Beyond the Theories of Kohlberg and Hoffman.* 2nd ed. Thousand Oaks, CA: Sage.

Gibson, James L., and Gregory A. Caldeira. 1996. "The Legal Cultures of Europe," *Law & Society Review,* 30 (1) (February): 55–85.

Ginsberg, Margery B., with Pablo Fiene. 2004. *Motivation Matters: A Workbook for School Change.* San Francisco, CA: Jossey-Bass.

Ginsberg, Morris. 1965. *On Justice in Society.* Ithaca, NY: Cornell University Press.

Glendon, Mary Ann. 1989. *The Transformation of Family Law: State, Law, and Family in the United States and Western Europe.* Chicago, IL: University of Chicago Press.

Goodstein, Laurie. 2004. "Citing Survey, CNN Says 4,450 Priests Were Accused of Abuse," *New York Times* (February 17): A1, A17.

Gorman, Siobhan. (2009). "Arrest in Epic Cyber Swindle: A 28-Year-Old Allegedly Stole 130 Million Card Numbers; 'Get Rich or Die Tryin.'" *Wall Street Journal* (August 18): A1, A4.

Greenberg, Jack. 1959. *Race Relations and American Law.* New York: Columbia University Press.

Grossman, Joel B., and Mary H. Grossman (eds.). 1971. *Law and Change in Modern America.* Pacific Palisades, CA: Goodyear.

Gureyev, P. P., and P. I. Sedugin (eds.). 1977. *Legislation in the USSR.* Trans. Denis Ogden. Moscow: Progress Publishers.

Handler, Joel F. 1978. *Social Movements and the Legal System: A Theory of Law Reform and Social Change.* New York: Academic Press.

Harris, Patricia Roberts. 1977. "Freedom and the Native-Born Stranger." Pp. 160–174 in Norman A. Graebner (ed.), *Freedom in America: A 200-Year Perspective.* University Park, PA: The Pennsylvania University Press.

Hauser, Philip M. 1976. "Demographic Changes and the Legal System." Pp. 15–29 in Murray L. Schwartz (ed.), *Law and the American Future.* Englewood Cliffs, NJ: Prentice-Hall.

Hertzler, J. O. 1961. *American Social Institutions.* Boston, MA: Allyn & Bacon.

Hill, Michael. 2006. *Social Policy in the Modern World.* Malden, MA, Blackwell Publishing.

Hoebel, E. Adamson. 1954. *The Law of Primitive Man: A Study in Comparative Legal Dynamics.* Cambridge, MA: Harvard University Press.

Honore, Tony. 1987. *Making Law Bind: Essays Legal and Philosophical.* Oxford: Clarendon Press.

Horowitz, Harold W., and Kenneth L. Karst. 1969. *Law, Lawyers and Social Change.* Indianapolis, IN: Bobbs-Merrill.

Jacob, Herbert. 1988. *Silent Revolution: The Transformation of Divorce Law in the United States.* Chicago, IL: University of Chicago Press. 1995. *Law and Politics in the United States.* 2nd ed. Ft. Washington, PA: HarperCollins College Publishers.

Jewkes, Yvonne, and Majid Yar (eds.). 2009. *Handbook of Internet Crime.* Devon, UK: Willan Publishing.

Jimenez, Jillian. 2010. *Social Policy and Social Change. Toward the Creation of Social and Economic Justice.* Thousands Oak, CA: Sage.

Jordan, Bill. 2007. *Social Policy for the Twenty-First Century.* Malden, MA: Blackwell Publishing.

Jordan, Mary, and Kevin Sullivan. 2006. "Some Brit Lawyers Itchin' to Ditch Wigs," *Seattle Times* (April 5): A2.

Kaplan, John. 1971. *Marijuana: The New Prohibition.* New York: Pocket Books.

Kelman, Herbert C., and V. Lee Hamilton. 1989. *Crimes of Obedience: Toward A Social Psychology of Authority and Responsibility.* New Haven and London: Yale University Press.

Kelsen, Hans. 1967. *The Pure Theory of Law.* 2nd ed. Trans. M. Knight. Berkeley and Los Angeles: University of California Press.

Kempadoo, Kamala, and Jo Doezema. 1998. *Global Sex Workers: Rights, Resistance, and Redefinition.* New York: Routledge.

Kerley, Kent R. (ed.) 2005. *Policing and Program Evaluation.* Upper Saddle River, NJ: Prentice Hall.

Kleinman, Mark A. R. 1989. *Marijuana: Costs of Abuse, Costs of Control.* New York: Greenwood Press.

Kohlberg, Lawrence. 1964. "Development of Moral Character and Ideology." Pp. 383–431 in L. Hoffman and M. Hoffman (eds.), *Review of Child Development Research,* Vol. I. New York: Russell Sage. 1967. "Moral Education, Religious Education, and the Public Schools: A Developmental Approach." Pp. 164–183 in T. Sizer (ed.), *Religion and Public Education.* Boston, MA: Houghton Mifflin.

La Piere, Richard T. 1965. *Social Change.* New York: McGraw-Hill.

Ladd, John. 1970. "Legal and Moral Obligation." Pp. 3–45 in Roland Pennock and John W. Chapman (eds.), *Political and Legal Obligation.* New York: Lieber-Atherton, Inc.

Lassman, Peter (ed.). 2006. *Max Weber.* Burlington, VT: Ashgate.

Lee, Jennifer. 2001. "Fighting Back When Someone Steels Your Name." *New York Times* (April 8): B8.

Levine, James P. 1970. "Methodological Concerns in Studying Supreme Court Efficacy," *Law & Society Review* 4 (1) (May): 583–592.

Logan, Rayford W., and Michael Winston. 1971. *The Negro in the United States,* Vol. 2, *The Ordeal of Democracy.* Princeton, NJ: Van Nostrand Reinhold.

Lyall, Francis, and Paul B. Larson, (eds.). 2009. *Space Law.* Burlington, VT: Ashgate.

Marshall, Thomas R. 1989. *Public Opinion and the Supreme Court.* Boston, MA: Unwin Hyman.

Massell, Gregory. 1973. "Revolutionary Law in Soviet Central Asia." Pp. 226–261 in Donald Black and Maureen Mileski (eds.), *The Social Organization of Law.* New York: Seminar Press.

Matsumoto, David, and Linda Juang. 2008. *Culture and Psychology.* 4th ed. Belmont, CA: Wadsworth/Thomson.

May, David A., and James E. Headley. 2004. *Identity Theft.* New York: P. Lang.

Mayhew, Leon H. 1971. "Stability and Change in Legal Systems." Pp. 187–210 in Bernard Barber and Alex Inkeles (eds.), *Stability and Social Change.* Boston, MA: Little, Brown.

McHarg, Aileen, and Donald Nicolson (eds.). 2006. *Debating Affirmative Action.* Malden, MA: Blackwell Publishing.

McLeod, Julie, and Rachel Thompson. 2010. *Researching Social Change. Qualitative Approaches.* Thousand Oaks, CA: Sage.

McMichael, Philip. 2008. *Development and Social Change.* 4th ed. Thousand Oaks, CA: Pine Forge Press.

McMichael, Philip (ed.). 2010. *Contesting Development: Critical Struggles for Social Change.* New York: Routledge.

McQuade, Samuel C., James P. Colt, and Nancy B. B. Meyer. 2010. *Cyber Bullying.* Santa Barbara, CA: Praeger.

Mead, Margaret (ed.). 1953. *Cultural Patterns and Technical Change.* Paris: UNESCO.

Milgram, Stanley. 1975. *Obedience to Authority.* New York: Harper Colophon Books.

Milkman, Ruth, Joshua Bloom, and Victor Narro (eds.). 2010. *Working for Justice: The L.A. Model of Organizing and Advocacy.* Ithaca, NY: Cornell University Press.

Miller, Arthur Selwyn. 1979. *Social Change and Fundamental Law: America's Evolving Constitution.* Westport, CT: Greenwood Press.

Mills, C. Wright. 1957. *The Power Elite.* New York: Oxford University Press.

Muhlhahn, Klaus. 2009. *Criminal Justice in China. A History.* Cambridge, MA: Harvard University Press.

Nagel, Stuart S. (ed.). 1970. *Law and Social Change.* Beverly Hills, CA: Sage Publications.

Negley, Glenn. 1965. *Political Authority and Moral Judgement.* Durham, NC: Duke University Press.

Nimkoff, Meyer F. 1957. "Obstacles to Innovation." Pp. 56–71 in Francis R. Allen, Hornell Hart, Delbert C. Miller, William F. Ogburn, and Meyer F. Nimkoff, *Technology and Social Change.* New York: Appleton-Century-Crofts.

Nisbet, Robert. 2000. *Twilight of Authority.* Indianapolis, IN: Liberty Fund, with new introduction. Originally published in 1975, New York: Oxford University Press.

Nussbaum, Martha C. 2010. *From Disgust to Humanity. Sexual Orientation and Constitutional Law.* New York: Oxford University Press.

Peach, Lucinda J. 2002. *Legislating Morality: Pluralism and Religious Identity in Lawmaking.* New York: Oxford University Press.

Penalver, Eduardo Moises, and Sonia K. Katyal. 2010. *Property Outlaws.* New Haven, CT: Yale University Press.

Plotkin, Robert. 2009. *The Genie in the Machine. How Computer Automated Inventing Is Revolutionizing Law and Business.* Palo Alto, CA: Stanford University Press.

Prosterman, Roy L., Robert Mitchell, and Tim Hanstad. (eds.). 2010. *One Billion Rising. Law, Land and the Alleviation of Global Poverty.* Chicago, IL: University of Chicago Press.

Raz, Joseph. 2009. *The Authority of Law. Essays on Law and Morality.* 2nd ed. New York: Oxford University Press.

Reed, Douglas S. 1998. "Twenty-Five Years after *Rodriguez:* School Finance Litigation and the Impact of New Judicial Federalism," *Law & Society Review,* 32 (1): 175–220.

Rodgers, Harrell, R., Jr., and Charles S. Bullock III. 1972. *Law and Social Change: Civil Rights Laws and Their Consequences.* New York: McGraw-Hill.

Rosenthal, Elisabeth. 1998. "For One-Child Policy, China Rethinks Iron Hand," *New York Times* (November 1): Y1, Y16.

Saunders, Doug. 2004. "A Republican Congressman Launches a Bill to Outlaw Seven Vulgarities from U.S. Airwaves." *Globe and Mail* (January 13): A3.

Scheingold, Stuart. 1989. "Constitutional Rights and Social Change: Civil Rights in Perspective." Pp. 73–91 in Michael W. McCann and Gerald Houseman (eds.), *Judging the Constitution: Critical Essays on Judicial Lawmaking.* Glenview, IL: Scott, Foresman/Little, Brown.

Scher, R., and J. Button. 1984. "Voting Rights Act: Instrumentation and Impact." Pp. 20–54 in Charles Bullock and Charles Lamb (eds.), *Instrumentation of Civil Rights Policy.* Monterey, CA: Brooks/Cole.

Schmidt, William E. 1992. "British Courts to Doff Wig? Verdict Asked," *New York Times* (August 23): 4Y.

Schur, Edwin M. 1968. *Law and Society: A Sociological View.* New York: Random House.

Schwartz, Richard D., and Sonya Orleans. 1970. "On Legal Sanctions." Pp. 533–547 in Richard D. Schwartz and Jerome A. Skolnick (eds.), *Society and the Legal Order.* New York: Basic Books.

Seidman, Robert B. 1978. *The State, Law and Development.* New York: St. Martin's Press.

Silverglate, Harvey. 2009. *Three Felonies a Day: How the Fed Target the Innocent.* New York: Encounter Books.

St. Louis Post-Dispatch. 1998. "Britons Take off Jackets, Hang up Their Customs and Relax Dress Codes" (September 2): A2.

Stein, Donald G. (ed.). 2004. *Buying In or Selling Out?: The Commercialization of the American Research University.* New Brunswick, NJ: Rutgers University Press.

Sterba, James P. (ed.). 2004. *Morality in Practice.* 7th ed. Belmont, CA: Thomson/Wadsworth.

Sterner, Thomas. 2003. *Policy Instruments for Environmental and Natural Resource Management.* Washington, DC: Resources for the Future.

Sumner, William Graham. 1906. *Folkways.* Boston, MA: Ginn.

Tiersma, Peter M. 2010. *Parchment, Paper, Pixels. Law and the Technologies of Communication.* Chicago, IL: University of Chicago Press.

Toffler, Alvin. 1970. *Future Shock.* New York: Random House.

Tone, Andrea. 2001. *Devices and Desires, A History of Contraceptives in America.* New York: Hill & Wang.

Tone, Andrea. 2009. *Age of Anxiety: A History of America's Turbulent Affair with Tranquilizers.* New York: Basic Books.

Tu, Janet I. 2006. "Abuse Cases Put Focus on Jesuits," *Seattle Times* (October 16): B1, B3.

Tyler, Patrick E. 1995. "Population Control in China Falls to Coercion and Evasion," *New York Times* (June 25): 1, 6.

Tyler, Tom R. 2006. *Why People Obey the Law.* Princeton, NJ: Princeton University Press.

Tyler, Tom R., Jonathan D. Casper, and Bonnie Fisher. 1988. *Maintaining Allegiance toward Legal Authorities: The Role of Prior Attitudes and the Use of Fair Procedures.* ABF Working Paper #8813. Chicago, IL: American Bar Foundation.

Vago, Steven. 2004. *Social Change.* 5th ed. Upper Saddle River, NJ: Prentice-Hall.

Vining, Joseph. 1986. *The Authoritative and the Authoritarian.* Chicago, IL: University of Chicago Press.

Visher, Christy A., and David Weisburd. 1998. "Identification of What Works: Recent Trends in Crime Prevention Strategies," *Crime, Law & Social Change,* 28: 223–242.

Volti, Rudi. 2010. *Society and Technological Change.* 6th ed. New York: Worth Publishers.

Watson, Goodwin. 1969. "Resistance to Change." Pp. 488–498 in Warren G. Bennis, Kenneth D. Benne, and Robert Chin (eds.), *The Planning of Change.* 2nd ed. New York: Holt, Rinehart & Winston.

Waughray, Annapurna. 2010. "Caste Discrimination and Minority Rights: The Case of India's Dalits." *International Journal on Minority & Group Rights,* 17 (2): 327–353.

Weber, Max. 1947. *The Theory of Social Economic Organizations.* Ed. Talcott Parsons. Glencoe, IL: Free Press. 1968. *Economy and Society,* Vol. I. Ed. Roph Guenther and Claus Wittich. New York: Badminster Press.

Weir, William. 2004. "Laws that are really out of this world." *Seattle Times* (February 8): A14.

Whitelaw, Kevin. 2004. "Shocking and Awful: A Series of Horrific Images and a big American Black Eye," *U.S. News & World Report* (May 17): 26–36.

York, Geoffrey. 2006. "Internet Police State," *Globe and Mail* (January 28): F3.

Zimmerman, Ann. 2006. "Creative Crooks, As Shoplifters Use High-Tech Scams, Retail Losses Rise," *Wall Street Journal* (October 25): A1, A12.

Zimring, Franklin, and Gordon Hawkins. 1975. "The Legal Threat as an Instrument of Social Change." Pp. 329–339 in Ronald L. Akers and Richard Hawkins (eds.), *Law and Control in Society.* Englewood Cliffs, NJ: Prentice-Hall.

CHAPTER

8

The Legal Profession

An appraisal of the legal profession and its steadily growing role in society touches on fundamental issues in sociological and sociolegal theory—issues involving power, social control, stratification, socialization, and the social organization of law work. This chapter examines the character of the legal profession and the social forces shaping it. It begins with a historical background of law, with an emphasis on the professionalization of lawyers and the evolution of the legal profession in America. Next, the chapter focuses on the legal profession today: what lawyers do and where, their income, and how they compete for business. The emphasis is then placed on the accessibility of legal services to the poor and the not so poor, followed by a portrayal of law schools and the training and socialization of lawyers into the profession. The chapter concludes with some comments on bar admission, bar associations as interest groups, and professional discipline.

BACKGROUND

The diverse cultural, religious, and social history and the emergence of the legal profession and the legal professional have long fascinated scholars in history, law, and sociology (see, for example, Grillo et al., 2009; Pue and Sugarman, 1999; 2003). In primitive societies, as noted in Chapter 2, custom and law coincided. The laws of a primitive legal system are unwritten and comparatively undifferentiated. Such societies have courts and judges but no lawyers. The courts are temporary, and when a violation of a law has occurred, the defendant is not represented by a "lawyer." Each individual is his or her own "lawyer," and everyone more or less knows the law. Although some individuals may be wiser than others and more skilled in social affairs, this skill is not considered a *legal* skill.

The development of the legal profession has been intimately connected with the rise and development of legal systems. The origins of the legal profession can be traced back to Rome (Brundage, 2010; Friedman, 1977:21). Initially, Roman law allowed individuals to argue cases on behalf of others; however, those persons were trained not in law but in rhetoric. They were called orators and were not allowed to take fees. Later on, by Cicero's time, there were jurists as well—individuals who were knowledgeable about the law and to whom people went for legal opinions. They were called *juris prudentes*, but these men learned in the law did not yet constitute a profession. Only during the Imperial Period did lawyers begin to practice law for a living and schools of law emerge. By this time, the law had become exceedingly complex in Rome. The occupation of lawyers arose together with a sophisticated legal system, and the complexity of that system made the Roman lawyer indispensable.

C. Ray Jeffery (1962:314–315) points out that by the Middle Ages, the lawyer had three functions—agent, advocate, and jurisconsult. The word *attorney* originally meant an agent, a person who acts or appears on behalf of someone else. In this role of agent, the lawyer appeared in court to handle legal matters in place of his client. In ancient Athens and Rome, an agent was allowed to appear in the place of another person. In France, however, a person had to appear in court himself, and in England, he needed special permission from the king to be represented in court by an agent. In France, by 1356, there were 105 *legistes* (men of law) representing clients in court (Jacoby, 1973:14).

The distinction between an agent and an advocate appeared when the lawyer went to court with his client to assist the client in presenting his case. In addition to law, the advocate was trained in the art of oratory and persuasion. In England, the function of the agent was taken over by solicitors and attorneys; the advocate became the barrister (trial lawyer). The function of a lawyer as a jurisconsult was both as a legal advisor and as a writer and teacher. Although contemporary lawyers perform essentially the same functions, the modern legal profession is fundamentally different. Friedman (1977:21) notes, "It is organized. It is lucrative. It is closed except to those who have undergone training or apprenticeship. It holds a monopoly of courtroom work and the giving of 'legal' advice."

THE PROFESSIONALIZATION OF LAWYERS

Traditionally, law was considered one of the three archetypical "learned" professions—the Church and medicine are the other two (Kritzer, 1990:5). But what is a profession, and what does the process of professionalization entail? In the sociological literature, professionalization implies the transformation of some nonprofessional occupation into a vocation with the attributes of a profession, and the specification of these could be discussed in great detail (see, for example, Macdonald, 1995). Foote (1953:371–372) captures the essential ingredients: "As a modicum, the possession (1) of a specialized technique supported by a body of theory, (2) of a career supported by an association of colleagues, and (3) of a status supported by community recognition may be mentioned as constituting an occupation as a profession." Also usually included in the discussion of professions are the ideas of a client–practitioner relationship and a high degree of autonomy in the execution of one's work tasks. Harold L. Wilensky (1964:143) has studied those occupations that are now viewed as professions, such as law, medicine, and the Church, and notes that they have passed through the following general stages in their professionalization:

1. Became full-time occupations
2. **a.** Training schools established
   b. University affiliation of training schools
3. **a.** Local professional associations started
   b. National professional associations evolved
4. State licensing laws
5. Formal codes of ethics established

Magali Sarfatti Larson (1977) provides additional insights into professionalization as the process by which producers of special services seek to constitute and to *control* a market for their expertise. Because marketable expertise is an important element in the structure of inequality, professionalization also appears as a collective assertion of special social status and as a collective process of upward mobility. She considers professionalization as an attempt to translate one type of scarce resources—special knowledge and skills—into another—social and economic rewards. The attempt by professions to maintain scarcity implies a tendency toward monopoly: monopoly of expertise in the market and monopoly of status in a system of stratification. She contends, "Viewed in the larger perspective of the occupational and class structures, it would appear that the model of professional passes from a predominantly economic function—organizing the linkage between education and the marketplace—to a predominantly ideological one—justifying inequality of status and closure of access in the occupational order" (Larson, 1977:xviii). For Larson, the following elements in the professionalization process are inseparably related: differentiation and standardization of professional services; formalization of the conditions for entry; persuasion of the public that they need services that only professionals can provide; and state protection (in the form of licensing) of the professional market against those who lack formal qualifications and against competing occupations. She contends that educational institutions and professional associations play a central role in attaining each of these goals.

A critical element in the professionalization process is market control—the successful assertion of unchallenged authority over some area of knowledge and its professional instrumentation (Abel, 2003; Flores, 1988). Until the body of legal knowledge, including procedure, became too much for the ordinary person to handle, there was no need for a legal profession. Before the thirteenth century, it was possible for a litigant to appoint someone to do his or her technical pleading. This person was not a member of a separate profession, for apparently anyone could act in that capacity. The person who did the technical pleading eventually developed into, or was superseded by, the attorney who was appointed in court and had the power to bind his employer to a plea.

"The profession of advocate," writes Michael E. Tigar (2000:157), "in the sense of a regulated group of (law) practitioners with some formal training, emerged in the late 1200s." Both the English and the French sovereigns legislated with respect to the profession, limiting the practice of law to those who had been approved by judicial officers. The profession of full-time specialists in the law and in legal procedures appeared initially as officers of the king's court. The first professional lawyers were judges who trained their successors by apprenticeship. The apprentices took on functions in the courtroom and gradually came to monopolize pleading before the royal judges. In England, training moved out of the courtroom and into the Inns of Court, which were the residences of the judges and practicing attorneys. The attorneys, after several reorganizations of their own ranks, finally became a group known as *barristers*. Members of the Inns became organized and came to monopolize training in the law as well as control of official access to the government. Signs of the professionalization of lawyers began to appear.

In England, the complexity of court procedures required technical pleading with the aid of an attorney, and oral argument eventually required special skills. By the time of Henry III (1216–1272), judges had become professionals, and the courts started to create a body of substantive legal knowledge as well as technical procedures. The king needed individuals to represent his interests in the courts. In the early fourteenth century, he appointed sergeants of the king to take care of his legal business. When not engaged in the king's business, these fabled sergeants-at-law of the Common Pleas Court could serve individuals in the capacity of lawyers.

A crucial event in the beginning of the legal profession was an edict issued in 1292 by Edward I. During this period, legal business had increased enormously; yet, there were no schools of common law, and the universities considered law too vulgar a subject for scholarly investigation. The universities were, at that time, agencies of the church, and the civil law taught there was essentially codified Roman law, the instrument of bureaucratic centralization. Edward's order, which directed Common Pleas to choose certain "attorneys and learners" who alone would be allowed to follow the court and to take part in court business, created a monopoly of the legal profession.

The effect of placing the education of lawyers into the hands of the court cannot be overestimated. It resulted in the relative isolation of English lawyers from Continental, Roman, and ecclesiastical influences. Lawyer taught lawyer, and each learned from the processes of the courts, so that the law had to grow by drawing on its own resources and not by borrowing from others. But the court itself was no place for the training of these attorneys and learners. It did, however, provide aid in the form of an observation post, called the *crib*, in which students could sit and take notes, and from which occasionally they might ask questions during the course of a trial.

Training for lawyers was provided by the Inns of Court. A small self-selecting group of barristers gave informal training and monopolized practice before the government courts of London, as well as judgeships in those courts. Barristers evolved into court lawyers (that is, lawyers who acted as the mouthpiece of their clients in court proceedings). Originally they were called "story-tellers" (Latin *narrators*); they told their client's story in courts, and this is their essential function to this day. The barristers' monopoly of court activities helped create a second group within the legal profession, named the "solicitors" (or "fixers"), who advised clients, prepared cases for trial, and handled matters outside the courtroom (Simpson, 1988:148–156). This group arose to meet the needs of clients, because barristers were too involved as officers of the court to be very responsible to outsiders. The barristers outranked solicitors, both by virtue of their monopoly of access to the court and through their control of training. Originally, solicitors were drawn from the ranks of those who attended the Inns of Court, and later they came to be trained almost entirely by apprenticeships or through schools of their own. At first, in the Inns of Court, lawyers lived together during the terms of court, and for them, the Inns represented law school, a professional organization, and a tightly knit social club, all in one.

Initially, universities such as Oxford and Cambridge saw little reason to include training such as it was practiced in the Inns in their teaching programs. (Until fairly recently, law was not regarded highly as a university subject. The number of law professors was small, and their prestige was rather low, because "law school was treated as the appropriate home for rowing men of limited intellect" [Simpson, 1988:158].) Only subjects such as legal history, jurisprudence, and Roman and ecclesiastical law were considered part of a liberal education to be provided by the universities (Kearney, 1970). University education was sought by "gentlemen," whereas legal training at the Inns of Court became the cheapest and the easiest route of social mobility for those who aspired to become gentlemen. Many sons of prosperous yeomen and merchants chose legal apprenticeship in an attempt to adopt a lifestyle associated with a gentleman. The appointment in 1758 of Sir William Blackstone to the Vinerian chair of jurisprudence at Cambridge marked the first effort to make English law a university subject. Blackstone thought it would help both would-be lawyers and educated people generally to have a "system of legal education" (as he called it), which would be far broader than the practical legal training offered in the Inns of Court. Blackstone may thus be considered the founder of the modern English system of university education in law (Berman et al., 2004; see also Carrese, 2003).

By the end of the eighteenth century, law in England had become a full-fledged profession. Members of the profession considered law a full-time occupation, training schools were established, universities began to offer degrees in law, and a professional association evolved in the form of a lawyers' guild. The practice of law required licensing, and formal codes of ethics were established. Knowledge of law and skills of legal procedures became a marketable commodity, and lawyers had a monopoly on them. The practice of law in royal courts was limited to members of the lawyers' guild, which in turn enhanced their political power, their monopoly of expertise in the market, and their monopoly of status in a system of stratification (see, for example, Frank, 2010). Access to the profession became controlled, and social mobility for those admitted assured. By the end of the eighteenth century, the name "attorney" had been dropped in favor of the term "solicitor," with the formation of the Society of Gentlemen Practicers in the Courts of Law and Equity, which was their professional society until 1903, when the Law Society came into being. In the following section, I shall examine the rise of the legal profession in the United States.

THE EVOLUTION OF THE AMERICAN LEGAL PROFESSION

The American legal profession, like the American government (see, for example, Gitelson et al., 2008), has its roots in English government organization. Colonial America was a transplant of English institutions, but with an emphasis on even greater decentralization. The practice of law in the pre-Revolutionary period was virtually monopolized by the upper class of merchants and planters, who did their best to emulate the English pattern of closed legal castes. In the South, wealthy planters tended to send their sons to the Inns of Court in London for legal training. In the northern colonies, bar associations developed in most of the populous places after 1750, beginning originally as social clubs, but gradually coming to control admission to practice. The colonial legislatures delegated to the courts the power of admission to practice before them. In the late eighteenth century, the local bar associations, in particular in New York and Massachusetts, were in turn delegated responsibility for recommending lawyers for admittance, amounting to de facto control; their numbers constituted a powerful political elite (Hurst, 1950:249–311).

Before the Revolution, lawyers were unpopular. Both the Puritans and the planters feared a secularized legal profession. The Puritans felt that the Bible was all the "law" needed and wished to combine their religion with law (for other similar perspectives, see, for example, Turner and Kirsch, 2009). The planters opposed lawyers because of the threat they posed to their political power. Lawyers became even more unpopular during the American Revolution than they had been before (Friedman, 2005:265). Because many lawyers were closely associated with the upper class in background and in interests, it was among this group that the British sympathizers were most concentrated. As a result, a substantial proportion of lawyers immigrated to England during wartime persecutions of Tories. The prevailing custom of the bar to limit practice to a small group of elites also contributed to lawyers' unpopularity, as did their efforts to collect wealthy creditors' claims in the period following the Revolution.

After the Revolution, the legal profession became more egalitarian, the distinction between barristers and attorneys—in imitation of the English system—disappeared with democratization of the legal profession, standards of admission to the bar became loosened, and bar associations crumbled and disappeared as their powers waned. Between 1800 and 1870, the power of admission to the bar was granted by local courts. In its most extreme form, this meant that admission in one court conferred no right to practice before others, although it was more usual for the right to practice in one court to enable one to practice before any other court in the same state. Centralized admission (more in theory than practice) was prevalent only in a handful of states and territories.

Neither college education nor a law degree was absolutely required for admission to the bar. The bar examination itself was usually oral and administered in a casual fashion. Legal education throughout the nineteenth century was similarly informal. The principal method of education was apprenticeship in a lawyer's office, during which the student performed small services, served papers, and copied legal documents. In his spare time, he read what law, history, and general books were available. Students in the offices of leading lawyers were often charged fees for apprenticeship.

The first law schools grew out of specialized law offices offering apprentice programs. They used many of the same techniques as the offices. The earliest such school was founded in Litchfield, Connecticut, in 1784. It proved successful and grew rapidly in size. In time, it gained national reputation and attracted students from all over the country. It offered a 14-month course, but the school gave no diploma. At that time, law degrees were of little worth. The system was not one of formal certification. The egalitarian caste of political power in nineteenth-century America extended to legal practice as well. The school taught law by the lecture method. The lectures were never published; to publish would have meant to perish, because students would have no reason to pay tuition and attend classes.

Along with other noteworthy developments in American higher education (Freeland, 1992), university law schools started gradually to replace the Litchfield type as the principal alternative to office training, but legal training at the university level was still rare. A few university professorships of law were established as far back as 1779 at William & Mary, 1793 at Columbia, as well as at Harvard in 1816 and at Yale in 1824. But attendance was spotty, and the courses given were short and informal, covering the same materials as apprenticeship programs and allowing students to drop in and out as suited their own convenience. Legal standards for passing the course were minimal, and only a single final oral examination was required at some universities. Even at Harvard in the mid-nineteenth century, the standards were very low, and "there were absolutely no examinations to get in, or to proceed, or to get out. All that was required was the lapse of time, two years, and the payment of the fees" (Friedman, 1998:242).

After 1870, a number of interrelated changes took place that established stratification within the legal profession and brought university law schools to an important position. A nationally prominent group of lawyers developed, and the bar (or the lawyers' union, although never called by that name) fought vigorously to protect the boundaries of the calling (Friedman, 2005:550). Simultaneously, university professors of law began to make claims for the scientific status of law. The bar association movement started and spread at the same time that farmers and workers were also organizing. The new establishment of bar associations led to efforts to restrict admission to the bar. In 1878, the American Bar Association (ABA) was formed (Friedman, 2005:563). After 1878, boards of examiners normally controlled by the local bar associations replaced the state supreme courts as the examining authority. Statewide boards were established and financed themselves out of applicants' fees. The boards were almost invariably controlled by the state bar associations. Professional self-regulation had taken another important step forward (Stevens, 1971:458–459).

Starting in 1870, the teaching of law began with the use of the case method at Harvard University. Instead of using the older system of text reading and lectures, the instructor carried on a discussion of assigned cases designed to bring out their general principles. The proponent of the case method, Harvard Law Dean Christopher Columbus Langdell, believed that law was a general science and that its principles could be experimentally induced from the examination of case materials. He rejected the use of textbooks and instead used casebooks as teaching materials; these were collections of reports of actual cases, carefully selected and arranged to illustrate the meaning and development of principles of law. The teacher became a Socratic guide, leading the student to an understanding of concepts and principles hidden as essences among the cases. Langdell also made it more difficult for students to gain admission. If an applicant did not have a college degree, he had to pass an entrance examination. A student was required to show knowledge of Latin by translating from Virgil or Cicero; on occasion, a skill in French was acceptable as a substitute for Latin. Langdell likewise made it harder for a student to get out. The length of legal education was increased to two years in 1871, then to three years in 1876. The lax oral examinations for the law degree were replaced by a series of written exams with increasingly formal standards. By 1896, Harvard required a college degree as a prerequisite for admission to law school (Friedman, 2005:530–532). Before that, in fact, there were more lawyers than college graduates in America (Stevens, 2001:73).

But the method remained attractive and suited the needs of the legal profession. It enabled the size of classes to expand, with one professor to every 75 students (Stevens, 2001:63). It exalted the prestige of law and legal training and affirmed that legal science stood apart as an independent entity distinct from politics, legislation, and ordinary people. Langdell provided grounds for certain important claims of the legal profession. Law, he maintained, was a science that demanded rigorous formal training. There was justification, then, for the lawyers' monopoly of practice. The bar association movement coincided with Langdell's rise to power. The two supplemented and complemented each other and further strengthened the lawyers' monopoly of practice.

The increased emphasis on professionalization and monopoly of the practice of law brought about concerted efforts to improve the quality of legal education, to raise admission standards, and to intensify the power of bar associations. Attempts to improve legal education meant, in practice, the adoption of the standards of the leading law schools. The adoption of formal-education requirements for admission to bar exams further strengthened the schools, and by 1940, three years of law school study were required by 40 states. At the same time, efforts were made to incorporate the standards of the leading law schools into the bar exam prerequisites by calling for the requirement of two years of college as preparation before law studies in 1921, a requirement that was adopted by two-thirds of the states by 1940. By 1950, three years of college had become the norm, and by the 1960s, four years of college was required. A law student of today would find it hard to believe that until the 1950s, the number of lawyers who had not been in college exceeded the number of those who had been (Stevens, 2001:209). The Law School Admission Test (LSAT) was ready for general use in 1948. The ABA, in 1929, established law school accreditation standards, and the bar-admitting authorities encouraged the ABA's accreditation efforts. Today, graduation from one of the 195 ABA-approved law school satisfies the legal-education requirement for admission to the bar (after passing the bar exam) in all jurisdictions in the United States.

For much of its history, the profession was dominated by white males. Not a single woman was admitted to the bar before the 1870s, and very few blacks (Friedman, 1998, 2002, 2005). Women, particularly married women, were not considered suitable for the practice of law. They were seen as delicate creatures and, just like children and lunatics, lacked full legal rights. By allowing women to practice law, the traditional order of the family would be upset. In a notorious opinion of a justice of the U.S. Supreme Court in 1873, "the natural and proper timidity and delicacy which belongs to the female sex evidently unfits it for many of the occupations of civil life. . . . The paramount destiny and mission of women are to fulfill the noble and benign offices of wife and mother. This is the law of the creator" (Stevens, 2001:82). Not until 1878 did federal courts open the door to women attorneys. Law schools began to admit women in 1869, although in many places, the courses of instruction were "open to the male sex only." In 1872, Charlotte E. Ray became the first black woman to graduate from an American law school (Smith, 1998). As of 1880, there were 75 women lawyers and 1,010 by 1900 (Stevens, 2001:83). By 1984, of the 649,000 lawyers, more than 83,000 were women (Curran, 1986:20, 25) and in 2009, female applicants to law school was 48 percent (Farmer, 2010). As a result, the proportion of women should soon approximate one-third of the profession.

The profession explicitly discriminated against blacks (Abel, 1986). They were excluded from the ABA until the 1950s and from many law schools. As recently as 1965, blacks made up 11 percent of the population but less than 2 percent of lawyers and only 1.3 percent of law students, half of them in all-black law schools. Even in 1977, only 5 percent of the country's law students were black (Friedman, 1998, 2002). By the 1990–1991 academic year, this figure had risen slightly, to 5.6 percent. Although law schools claim that they recruit aggressively for minorities, in 1992, blacks still made up just 3.4 percent of lawyers (Pollock and Adler, 1992:4), and in 2008, their representation was still around 4 percent.

Law firms were about as discriminatory as law schools. Many excluded Jews, Catholics, blacks, and women. Through the 1950s, most firms were solidly WASP (white Anglo-Saxon Protestant). Legal politicians argued that the profession was a means by which Jews, immigrants, and basically non-WASPs "might undermine the American way of life" (Stevens, 2001:100–101). By the 1960s, discriminatory hiring practices had started to decrease, but they have not yet fully disappeared. There are still signs of tokenism for blacks and women, and Jews are excluded from high-prestige fields (Heinz and Laumann, 1994). Income disparities and subtler forms of gender bias in promotion to top positions still persist (Keeva, 1995; Petersen and Saporta, 2004). One large study shows that only 14 percent of the partners are women in the nation's top 250 law firms (Blohm, 2006).

A 2001 survey of the 12 highest-grossing law firms in the United States by the *New York Times* (Glater, 2001a) finds that minority lawyers accounted for about 5 percent of the new partners in recent years at the seven firms that supplied such data. Some lawyers contend that while law schools have aggressively recruited minority students and many law firms have done the same for minority graduates, firms have been more reluctant to promote minority associates to partnership. One reason lawyers fail to offer a partnership is that minority lawyers are less likely to have relationships with important clients or to land a significant amount of business for the firm. But some minority lawyers say that they are not given the same opportunities as white lawyers to work with important clients, often because they do not have mentors who ensure that they have access to the best work. Finally, minority lawyers also cite of what they perceive to be a lack of opportunity for advancement within firms, and as a result, they opt for career opportunities in business, consulting firms, government jobs, or corporate legal departments.

There are also complaints about alleged disparate treatment of male and female lawyers in court in demeanor and language (Curriden, 1995a). Minority female attorneys claim that they lack support by white women and minority men attorneys, face both race and sex discrimination, and have difficulties establishing networks (Quade, 1995). Sexual harassment continues to be a problem. In a survey of the Ninth U.S. Circuit Court (California and eight other western states), 60 percent of women lawyers alleged that they have been sexually harassed by men involved in the court system (Woo, 1992). There is evidence to suggest that women's integration into the legal profession remains marginal despite their growing proportions in the field; they are still underrepresented in law firm partnerships and move slower than men toward these positions. Further, women exit from the legal profession at a much higher rate than their male counterparts (Kay, 1997). Another, and rather recent, development is the "Graying of the Bar" (King, 2006). As more and more baby boomers (an estimated 78.2 million people who were born between 1946 and 1964) turn 60, there is a growing concern that incompetence due to declining skills, failure to keep pace, or dwindling mental acuity may soon rise in the legal profession. It is turning to be a sensitive issue in a profession that traditionally honors its elders for long careers and may be a ground for age-based discrimination suits.

There have also been noticeable changes in the practice of law. Before the Civil War, much of legal business concerned land and commerce, representing primarily speculative interests in the West. After the middle of the nineteenth century, the most lucrative business came to center on the big corporations, beginning first with the railroads. After the Civil War, the position of general counsel for the railroads was the most highly esteemed legal position, and, during the same period, lawyers became closely involved with the major banks and began to sit on boards of directors. By the turn of the century, corporate law firms were edging to the pinnacle of professional aspiration and power (Auerbach, 1976:22). Lawyers were instrumental in the growth of corporations, devising new forms of charters, assisting companies to organize national business, while taking maximum advantage of variable state laws concerning incorporation and taxation. At the turn of the century, the emergence and proliferation of firms specializing in corporation law provided those lawyers who possessed appropriate social, religious, and ethnic credentials with an opportunity to secure personal power and to shape the future of their profession. But only lawyers who possessed what Gerald S. Auerbach (1976:21) calls "considerable social capital" could inhabit the world of the corporate law firm.

Through corporate law firms, the large modern-style law firm came into existence. Before the middle of the nineteenth century, law practice was individual or carried on in two-man partnerships. After 1850, partnerships dealing with business interests began to specialize internally, with one person handling the court appearances and the other taking care of office details. At the same time, business clients started to solicit opinions from law firms on legal aspects of prospective policies, a practice that gradually led to the establishment of permanent relationships between law firms and corporations. The size of major law firms began to grow. The prominence of the "Wall Street law firm," allied with major corporations, originated in the late nineteenth century, growing along with the corporations whose economic dominance such law firms helped make possible. Notes Friedman (2005:553), "By and large, the leading lawyers of the big Wall Street firms were solid Republicans, conservative in outlook, standard Protestant in faith, old English in heritage." It should be noted, however, that such large firms were, and are today, an exception. Close to half of all lawyers in private practice continue to practice alone, usually in a particular ethnic community, and this has undoubtedly been the case throughout history (Carlin, 1962). Generally, individual practitioners of law use the legal profession more as an avenue of social mobility than do their counterparts in large firms.

In addition to changes in the structure and functions of the profession, there have been substantial changes in its numbers. In 1850, there were approximately 24,000 lawyers in the United States. In the next 50 years, after the Civil War and the transformation of the American economy, there were significant changes in supply and demand. The number of lawyers increased to approximately 60,000 by 1880, and to 115,000 by 1900 (Halliday, 1986:62).

THE PROFESSION TODAY

Since the 1960s, law has become the fastest-growing of all professions in the United States. The number of lawyers increased from 285,933 in 1960 to 355,242 in 1970 and reached 649,000 in 1984 when already one out of every 364 people was a lawyer (Curran, 1986:20). In 2006, there were 1,116,967 attorneys, and the ratio was further reduced to one lawyer per 268 people. (But only one attorney seems to be available for every 7,000 *poor* Americans, and the ratio is one to 14,000 in the Chicano community [Spangler, 1986:6].) By contrast, as noted in Chapter 6, the population-to-lawyer ratios are much higher in other countries. In the early 1980s, for example, there was one lawyer for 1,431 people in Belgium, one for 963 in Scotland, and one for 599 in Ontario, Canada (Lewis, 1986:82). China, with a population in excess of 1.2 billion, has about 30,000 lawyers (Galanter, 1992:13). Close to the end of the twentieth century there were over 950,000 lawyers in the United States (Gross, 1998:26); their number has well exceeded 1.1 million by the dawn of the twenty-first century and it was close to 1.2 million in 2009. Table 8-1. shows the national lawyer population by states in 2008 and 2009. In 2007, about 30 percent

TABLE 8-1 National Lawyer Population by State				
State		*2008 # Attys Resident & Active*	*2009 # Attys Resident & Active**	*Index*
Alabama	AL	13,231	13,443	102
Alaska	AK	2,383	2,362	99
American Samoa	AS	58	45	78
Arizona	AZ	12.7M	13,028	102
Arkansas	AR	5,700	5,700	100
California	CA	148,399	149,982	101
Colorado	CO	1,8894	19,340	102
Connecticut	CT	19,013	19,427	102
Delaware	DE	2,326	2,392	103
Dist. of Columbia	DC	46,689	48,456	104
Florida	FL	59,353	61,426	102
Georgia	GA	27,327	27,457	101
Guam	GU	270	243	90
Hawaii	HI	4,126	4,100	99
Idaho	ID	3,330	3,221	97
Illinois	IL	61,359	58,457	95
Indiana	IN	13,364	14,379	106
Iowa	IA	6,959	7,036	101
Kansas	KS	7,355	7,951	101
Kentucky	KY	11,376	12,088	102
Louisiana	LA	16,965	17,279	102
Maine	ME	3,394	3,647	101
Maryland	MD	20,396	21,354	103
Massachusetts	MA	42,301	43,198	102
Michigan	MI	32,131	32,321	101
Minnesota	MN	21,344	22,448	102
Mississippi	MS	6,723	6,748	100
Missouri	MO	22,602	23,362	103
Montana	MT	2,344	2,885	101
Nebraska	NE	5,117	5,315	102
Nevada	NV	6,105	6,395	105
New Hampshire	NH	3,309	3,397	103
New Jersey	NJ	39,384	40,060	102
New Mexico	NM	5,367	5,342	105
New York	NY	150,342	153,352	102

State		2008 # Attys Resident & Active	2009 # Attys Resident & Active*	Index
North Carolina	NC	18,966	19,637	104
North Dakota	ND	1,345	1,381	103
North Mariana Islands	MP	127	128	101
Ohio	OH	36,344	37,467	102
Oklahoma	OK	12,357	11,511	93
Oregon	OR	11,344	11,332	102
Pennsylvania	PA	46,065	46,376	100
Puerto Rico	PR	12,354	13,071	IOS
Rhode Island	Rl	4,055	4,044	100
South Carolina	SC	8,361	9,059	101
South Dakota	SD	1,761	1,794	102
Tennessee	TN	15,199	15,855	104
Texas	TX	73,305	75,087	102
Utah	UT	6,315	6,568	106
Vermont	VT	2,183	2,185	100
Virgin Islands	VI	750	700	93
Virginia	VA	21,183	21,682	102
Washington	WA	22,376	22,973	103
West Virginia	WV	4,618	4,672	101
Wisconsin	WI	14,348	14,906	103
Wyoming	WY	1,337	1,322	99
TOTAL		1,162,124	1,180386	102

of lawyers were women, 5 percent were African American, 3 percent were Hispanic, and 92 percent were white (*New York Times*, 2010).

The number of lawyers in any society is a function of the social role assigned to lawyers (Dare, 2009; Friedman, 1977:24, 2005; Halliday, 1986; Susskind, 2009). The role of lawyers in society is conditioned by a variety of factors, such as the degree of industrialization, bureaucratization, complexity of business transactions, expansion of legal entitlements, growth of regulation, crime rates, and attitudes toward and availability of nonlegal methods of conflict resolution (for additional details, see Rostain, 2008).

Attorneys have never been popular, and "lawyers, on the whole, have a terrible image" (Friedman, 1998, 2002). Plato spoke of their "small and unrighteous" souls, and Keats said, "I think we may class the lawyer in the natural history of monsters." Thomas More left lawyers out of his Utopia, and Shakespeare made his feelings known in that famous line from *Henry VI, Part II*: "The first thing we do, let's kill all the lawyers." Undoubtedly, the adversarial system is costly not only in money (a controversial economist

[Magee, 1992] argues that lawyers cause a $600 billion reduction in the American economy annually) but also in trust. Polls show that the public has limited confidence in the profession. For example, in a 1993 ABA poll, 63 percent of people queried said lawyers make too much, 59 percent called them greedy, and 40 percent said the phrase "honest and ethical" does not apply (Shulins, 1994). In a 1998 Gallup poll, 46 percent of the respondents rated them as "low" or "very low" in honesty and ethical standards—just slightly above car salesmen if it is any consolation (Gross, 1998:26); however, a March 2007 Gallup poll showed some improvement, and only 36 percent of the respondents rated lawyers as "low" or "very low." (Nurses toped Gallup's annual survey on the honesty and ethics of various professions, followed by other medical professionals like doctors, veterinarians, pharmacists, and dentists. Car salesmen, developers and real estate agents, HMO managers, insurance salesmen, and advertising practitioners are rated as the least honest and ethical in the 2007 poll.) The trend continues. In a 2009 Pew Research Center (2009) poll, while 84 percent of the public held scientists in high regard, only 23 percent ranked lawyers positively. For comparison, teachers were ranked 77 percent, medical doctors 69 percent, engineers 64 percent, and even journalist were higher at 38 percent.

Headlines in professional and popular publications and book titles are anything but flattering. Some examples over the years are "The Lawyer as Liar" (Uviller, 1994); "Why Lawyers Lie: The Truth Is Not the Highest Priority in a Criminal Trial" (Abrams, 1994); "The Law According to the Chequebook—The Duplicity of Lawyers" (Fotheringham, 1994); "Who Ya Gonna Call? 1-800-Sue Me" (*Newsweek*, 1995); and *Beyond All Reason: The Radical Assault on Truth in American Law* (Farber and Sherry, 1997). Their perceived greediness is reflected in titles such as "How to Rob a Bank" (Frum, 1994) or "A King's Ransom" (Lerman, 1995) referring to Rodney King's lawyer, submitting a $1 million bill to the city of Los Angeles for his defense-related activities. In *Why Lawyers Behave As They Do*, Paul G. Haskell (1998) actually claims that the public is justified in its low opinion of the legal profession and explains the professional rules that govern how lawyers behave and that allow—or require—conduct that laypersons may find unethical. Catherine Crier (2002), in *The Case against Lawyers: How Lawyers, Politicians, and Bureaucrats Have Turned the Law into an Instrument of Tyranny, and What We as Citizens Have to Do about It*, decries a system of laws so complex that even the enforcers—such as the Internal Revenue Service—cannot understand them and excoriates lawyers who profit from inefficiency, injustice, and abuse. A germane *Newsweek* (2003) cover "Lawsuit Hell: How Fear of Litigation Is Paralyzing Our Professions" nicely captures many of these sentiments about the legal profession. And Marc Galanter (2005), one of the leading figures in law and society studies, takes a mordant approach by using a collection of over 200 lawyer jokes to illustrate popular sentiments toward attorneys in his well-received book, *Lowering the Bar: Lawyer Jokes & Legal Culture*. Richard A. Zitrin et al. (2007) in *Legal Ethics in the Practice of Law* argue that the delivery of legal and adjudicative services should not be governed solely by market forces and human acquisitiveness. And to end this illustrative sample of sentiments is Wendy Murphy's (2007) self-explanatory title, *And Justice for Some: An Expose of the Lawyers and Judges You Hate—and the Dirty Tricks They Don't Want You to Know About*. It should not come as a surprise that many lawyers are unhappy with their careers and lives in law as nicely captured by Nancy Levit and Douglas O. Linder's (2010) sardonic *The Happy Lawyer*. The question, "Why lawyers are so unhappy" was also raised by Martin E. P. Seligman, former president of the American Psychological Association (http://www.lawyerswithdepression.com/lawyersunhappy. asp. April 20, 2010), who noted that in a recent poll 52 percent of the lawyers described themselves as dissatisfied. Certainly, in view of their earnings, the problem is not financial. In addition to being disenchanted, Seligman notes that lawyers are in remarkably poor mental health. They are at much greater risk than the general population for depression, about 3.6 percent higher than employed persons generally. They also suffer from alcoholism and illegal drug use at rates far higher than nonlawyers. The divorce rate among attorneys, especially among women, is also higher than in other professions. Lawyers are the best paid professionals and yet they are disproportionately unhappy and unhealthy. And they seem to be aware of this; many are retiring early or leaving the profession.

Similar attitudes prevail toward lawyers in other countries. For example, in the former Soviet Union (even though Lenin himself was trained as a lawyer and actually practiced for a short time), lawyers were considered (as they are still today; see, for example, Oleinik, 2003) one of the most unnecessary, parasitic, and exploitative groups, ranking in esteem with priests and capitalists (Cameron, 1978:50). In India, the profession "has lost the social and moral prestige," and lawyers "go all out for money with little qualms about the image and morality of the profession" (Gandhi, 1982:33). In England, lawyers always have had a bad press. They have been depicted as hypocrites; greedy social parasites; pettifoggers, who, in the pursuit of their clients' interests, obfuscate real issues and use distinctions devoid of ethical merit; and being basically contemptuous of truth and unsympathetic and brutal in their behavior.

Although lawyer-bashing is a venerable tradition, in fairness to lawyers, much of their negative image is exaggerated, and they are probably not much worse than members of other professions. Some of the charges are due to their ubiquitousness, their sheer number (compare the size of listings of the various professions in the Yellow Pages), and guilt by association. They often deal with people in trouble—criminals, politicians, business people, and those seeking a divorce. At times, they articulate strong partisan interests, and it is no surprise that they are the object of strong sentiments. Although lawyers play a useful role and are sometimes admired, they are rarely loved. Probably no other legitimate profession has been as subjected to extremes of homage and vilification as lawyers (Bonsignore et al., 1989:241).

There are four principal subgroups in the legal profession: lawyers in private practice, lawyers in government service, lawyers in private employment, and the judiciary. In the United States, about 74 percent of lawyers are in private practice, 12 percent work for the government, 12 percent are in salaried positions in private industry, and the rest are in the judiciary, educational institutions, legal-aid programs, private associations such as unions, and other special-interest organizations. It is interesting to note, by contrast, that in Germany slightly over one-fifth of the bar are in private practice, and another fifth are employed by the judiciary. Proportionately, three times as many lawyers work for the government and twice as many are in private employment in Germany as in the United States (Rueschemeyer, 1973:32). There is no recent evidence to suggest that these proportions have changed at any significant way after the unification to the two Germanys in the 1990s and its entrance into the European Common Market.

In career patterns, self-image, and sheer numbers, lawyers in private practice constitute the central group of the American legal profession from which other types of practice are branching out. These lawyers generally work as either individual practitioners or members of law firms. The next section will consider the private practice of law in the context of solo and firm practitioners.

WHERE THE LAWYERS ARE

Law is big business in the United States, and legal outlays including the cost of litigation now accounts for upwards of 2.8 percent of the gross domestic product (GDP) (Krauss, 2007), more than steel or electric power. Each year, thousands of young adults graduate from law school, pass the bar, and enter the profession. They engage in a variety of activities in diverse settings. Some go into private practice; others find jobs in government or private industry. A few even decide not to stay in law (O'Hara and Ribstein, 2009).

Private Practice

A majority of lawyers (roughly 74 percent) in the United States are in private practice. Contrary to the popular image that is reinforced by television (Rapping, 2004), only a small proportion of lawyers engage in litigation. In private practice, lawyers perform a number of significant roles. One is *counseling*. Attorneys spend about one-third of their time advising their clients about the proper course of action in anticipation of the reactions of courts, agencies, or third parties. Another is *negotiating*, both in criminal and in civil cases. Plea bargaining is an example of negotiation and is widely used in criminal cases (Palermo et al., 1998). Pretrial hearings and conferences in attempts to reach a settlement and thus avoid a costly trial are illustrative of the negotiating role of lawyers in civil cases. *Drafting*, the writing and revision of legal documents such as contracts, wills, deeds, and leases, is the "most legal" of a lawyer's role, although the availability of standardized forms for many kinds of legal problems often limits the lawyer to filling in the blanks. *Litigating* is a specialty, and relatively few lawyers engage in actual trial work. Much of the litigation in the United States is generally uncontested in cases such as debt, divorce, civil commitment, and criminal charges. Some lawyers also engage in *investigating*. In a criminal case, for example, the defense attorney may search for the facts and gather background information in support of the client's plea. Finally, lawyers take part in *researching*—searching, for example, for precedents, adapting legal doctrine to specific cases, and anticipating court or agency rulings in particular situations. Much of such research activity is carried out by lawyers in large firms and appellate specialists. Experienced lawyers working in their specialty (or those working for a small fee) usually do little research (Klein, 1984:74–76).

The two extremes in private practice are represented by solo practitioners and big law firms, often referred to as *Wall Street firms*. In between, there are partnerships and small law firms of relatively modest size. There is now a growing trend of female attorneys setting up their own firms (Graham, 1995). Solo practitioners are generalists; they operate in small offices and are "the jacks-of-all-trades of the legal profession" (Jacob, 1995). Many of these lawyers engage in marginal areas of law, such as collections, personal injury cases, rent cases, and evictions. They face competition from other professionals, such as accountants and real estate brokers, who are increasingly handling the tax and real estate work traditionally carried out by the solo practitioner. Jerome E. Carlin (1962:209), a highly influential and often-cited scholar of the legal profession, points out that the pressures to make a living may force individual practitioners to submit to pressures to violate legal ethics, and in a later study, he suggests that indeed this is the case (Carlin, 1966). Lawyers in solo practice often act, Carlin notes, as intermediaries between clients and other lawyers to receive referral fees. In such an instance, the individual practitioner may become a businessperson rather than a lawyer, thus defeating his or her original purpose of becoming a professional in the first place. As Carlin concludes:

> In considering the work of the individual lawyer in Chicago, one is drawn to the conclusion that he is rarely called upon to exercise a high level of professional skill. This arises in part from the generally low quality of his professional training, but even more from the character of the demands placed upon him by the kinds of work and clients he is likely to encounter. Most matters that reach the individual practitioner—the small residential closing, the simple uncontested divorce, drawing up a will or probating a small estate, routing filings for a small business, negotiating a personal injury claim, or collecting on a debt—do not require very much technical knowledge, and what technical problems there are are generally simplified by use of standardized forms and procedures. (1962:206–207)

Carlin notes that these lawyers attempt to justify their low status in the profession by emphasizing their independence and pointing out that they are general practitioners and thus knowledgeable about all facets of the law. This notion of autonomy, however, does not compensate for their feeling of insignificance in the overall legal structure and their frustration over not realizing their initial high ambitions, although they are professionals. Carlin (1962:206) also suggests that these individual practitioners, like their counterparts in general practice in medicine, are "most likely to be found at the margin of (their) profession, enjoying little freedom in choice of clients, type of work, or conditions of practice."

Jack Ladinsky (1963), in an often-referenced classic study of a sample of 207 Detroit-area lawyers of whom 100 were solo and 107 were medium- to large-firm practitioners, reinforced Carlin's findings on individual practitioners. Ladinsky (1963:49) also found that individual practitioners come from minority religious and ethnic backgrounds, have parents of entrepreneurial or small-business status, and receive qualitatively and quantitatively inferior education more often than the lawyers in the law firm practice he included in the study. Ladinsky suggests that social background (religious preference of mother and occupation of father) is the strongest determinant of whether a lawyer goes into firm or solo practice. The quality of the law school is an important intervening variable. Ladinsky (1963:53) notes, "Social background describes two major career contingencies: level of technical skill and access to clients." Socioeconomic considerations and ethnic and cultural factors force solo lawyers toward local night school or Catholic university law schools. Ladinsky further points out that after graduation, relatively poor training and discrimination in firm recruitment make it difficult to get a prestigious firm job, and so solo lawyers end up doing low-paying, low-status work — that is, injury suits, divorce, petty criminal cases, and debt collection. They often develop a clientele of people of similar class, ethnic, and religious background.

There are also differences between individual and firm practitioners in acceptance of and compliance with ethical norms. Jerome Carlin (1966) found that the individual practitioner was the most likely to violate ethical norms (for example, soliciting kick-backs or making or arranging police payoffs), with the nature of the client and the type of case being important contributing factors in the violations. Because solo practitioners often represent individuals, as contrasted with corporations that are represented by larger firms, the quality of the lawyers involved adversely affects the legal representation that many individuals receive. Because these lawyers are often from minority groups, minority clients are the ones who are adversely affected. Moreover, many of the larger, more prestigious, and more ethical firms will not accept the kinds of cases the individual practitioner confronts, and in fact refer those cases to him or her so that the organization of the bar is such that ethical violations and ineffective practice are almost built into certain situations.

In a survey of the Chicago bar's attitudes toward a specific problem in professional ethics (ambulance chasing), Kenneth F. Reichstein (1965) documents essentially the same relationship between professional status and notions of professional ethics found by Carlin in New York. Even though selecting personal injury cases is prohibited by the canons of ethics, an elaborate social structure (that is, legitimating values, specialist practitioners, techniques, and so on) exists around this type of practice. Reichstein found that high-status lawyers (high income, corporate practice, large firm, and the like) were almost unanimous in strongly disapproving of personal injury practice (and those lawyers engaged in it), on the grounds that "it brings disrepute on the profession." On the other hand, low-status lawyers (low income, solo practitioners, and lack of established clientele) were more likely to give qualified approval of personal injury practice. Low-status lawyers base their attitudes on the rationale that "it is necessary to make a living," or "it prevents poor people from being taken advantage of." Reichstein also notes that "deviance" in this case is in no small part a product of elite control of the rule-making and enforcement machinery of the organized bar, which will be discussed later in this chapter. More recent studies on professional ethics support and reinforce the earlier conclusions (see, for example, Carle, 2005; Gunning et al., 2009; Rhode and Luban, 2005).

Practicing in large law firms is very different from solo practice. Toward the end of the first decade of the 2000s, more than 75 law firms in the United States had over 200 lawyers each — Chicago-based Baker & McKenzie is the largest firm in the world, with over 3,750 — along with hundreds of people in the supporting staff, including paralegals, business-trained administrators, librarians, and technicians, generating close to $12 billion in annual revenues (*Lawyer's Almanac*, 2010). Many of these large firms are becoming national and multinational in scope by opening up offices in several cities in the United States and abroad. These firms shy away from less profitable business — individual legal problems such as wills and divorces — in favor of corporate clients often with a global presence (Peel, 2006). It should be noted that because of the economic setbacks and retrenchments of 2009 and 2010, many large law firms face unprecedented stress. Several have dissolved, gone bankrupt, or significantly downsized in recent years. According to

Larry Ribstein (2010) in a recent paper, "The Death of Big Law," the basic business model of the large U.S. law firm is failing and needs fundamental restructuring. He suggests that there are at least three prerequisites to establishing the viable large legal services firm of the future. First, the firm must own a core of durable, firm-specific property. Second, the firm must be able to secure nonlawyer financing in a variety of forms. Third, coherent legal structures must evolve that are suitable for large law firms. Big Law's ability to meet these conditions is contingent on significant changes in the regulation of law practice. The *Economist* (2010), while commenting on these business models, warns that as lawyers adapt to survive a tougher climate, they will need to ensure that any changes do not put their culture of professionalism at risk and that while aggressively pursuing profits, they do not end up looking like "greedy bastards."

Unlike solo practitioners, firms maintain long-term relationships with their clients, and many are on retainers by large corporations. Large firms offer a variety of specialized services, with departments specializing in a number of fields such as tax law, mergers, antitrust suits, and certain types of government regulations. These firms deal generally with repeat players and provide the best possible information and legal remedies to their clients along with creative and innovative solutions for the clients' problems (Jacob, 1995).

Large firms have a pronounced hierarchical organization structure (Hagan et al., 1988; Nelson, 1988). Young lawyers are hired as associates. Beginning associates are seen as having limited skills, despite their elite education, and are assigned the task of preparing briefs and engaging in legal research under the supervision of a partner or a senior associate. In seven or eight years, they either become junior partners or leave the firm. For a new associate who has a strong desire to move into a partnership position, the competition with cohorts is very strong. Nowadays, it is almost as difficult for an associate in a "good" firm to attain partnership as it is for an assistant professor in sociology to get tenure and promotion at a "good" university.

Associates are on a fixed salary, whereas partners' incomes are based on profits. In most firms, law partners earn profits largely on hourly billings of associates: the more associates per partner, the higher the profits. How profits are divided among partners is usually decided by a small committee that looks at such factors as work brought in, hours billed, and seniority. The traditional rule is that associates should produce billings of about three times that of their salaries—a third goes to the associate, a third to overhead, and a third to the firm's profit. To use an example with round figures, an associate who earns $50,000 and whose time is billed at $75 an hour would have to put in 2,000 billable hours a year, or 38.5 billable hours a week, 52 weeks a year. That may not sound like much, but 2,000 billable hours usually means 50 hours or more at the office a week. (On the average, lawyers work 46.5 hours a week [Reidinger, 1986:44].) At most firms, lawyers' time is billed in six-minute or fifteen-minute units, with each nonbusiness conversation, personal phone call, and vacation day cutting into billable hours. No wonder many associates are workaholics and spend evenings and weekends in their offices.

One of the most complete analyses of law firms is Erwin O. Smigel's (1964) *Wall Street Lawyer*. Although the Wall Street law firm is not typical of the majority of law firms in the United States because of its size and type of practice, the contrast between this type of law practice and that of the individual practitioner illustrates the immense diversity within the legal profession.

The law firms investigated by Smigel perform a variety of functions. They are spokespersons for much of big business in the United States. But they not only represent business; many members of the firms also serve as members of the boards of directors of corporations they represent. These law firms also act as recruiting centers for high-level government service. Members of the firm are appointed to important government positions and seek national political offices. Many of their members are also active in various capacities in national, state, and local governmental agencies. Wall Street lawyers also participate in civic and philanthropic activities, such as the Metropolitan Opera, various museums, and other cultural and charitable affairs.

The Wall Street law firms are large, ranging from 50 to several hundred lawyers on the staff. Over 70 percent of the lawyers attended Harvard, Yale, or Columbia Law School—the elite schools of the nation—and were top students. The Wall Street law firms actively recruit these top individuals, and would prefer all their lawyers to have these credentials. In addition, the firms also look for the "correct" family background, which is considered important in making contacts that will bring business in the future. As might be expected, Smigel found very few black or women attorneys in the Wall Street firms. Similarly, relatively few Catholic lawyers were found in the Wall Street firms because of what are considered to be lower-class origins, poorer education, and immigrant parents. As compared with individual practitioners, the Wall Street lawyers have a superior education, both quantitatively and qualitatively. It should be noted, however, that not every graduate of prestigious law schools desires the kind of law practiced by the Wall Street lawyers. Smigel notes that many students feel that the specialization in the large law office is so great that they would soon become limited in their abilities. Others feel that they would be lost in such a setting, and their mobility opportunities impaired. Some law school graduates look upon the Wall Street firm as a postgraduate training period, using it as a springboard for future positions in industry and government.

The observations of Carlin and Ladinsky on solo practitioners and Smigel on large law firms are supplemented by the conclusions of John P. Heinz and Edward O. Laumann's (1994) seminal study of the Chicago bar. They note that much of the "differentiation within the legal profession is secondary to one fundamental distinction—the distinction between lawyers who represent large organizations (corporations, labor unions, or government) and those who represent individuals. The two kinds of law practice are the two hemispheres of the profession." Most lawyers, they add, "reside exclusively in one hemisphere or the other and seldom, if ever, cross the equator" (Heinz and Laumann, 1994:319). The two sectors of the profession are separated by the social origins of lawyers, the schools where they were trained, the types of clients they serve, office environment, frequency and type of litigation, values, and different circles of acquaintance; the two sectors "rest their claims to professionalism on different sorts of social power" (Heinz and Laumann, 1994:384). Large cities, Heinz and Laumann conclude, have two legal professions—one that is recruited from more privileged social origins where lawyers serve wealthy and powerful corporate clients, and the other from less prestigious backgrounds where lawyers serve individuals and small businesses. Thus, "the hierarchy of lawyers suggests a corresponding stratification of law into two systems of justice, separate and unequal" (Heinz and Laumann, 1994:385).

Government

Roughly 12 percent of the members of the bar in the United States are now employees of the federal, state, county, and municipal governments, exclusive of the judiciary. Malcolm Spector (1972) presciently suggests that taking positions in government agencies may be a strategy used by young lawyers for upward professional mobility. He considers employment with the government a mobility route into a more prestigious practice for the young lawyer handicapped by mediocre education or stigmatized by sex, religion, or ethnic background. Spector maintains that by pursuing a short-term career in a government agency, the young lawyer not able to initially break into "big league" firms gains valuable trial experience, specialized knowledge of regulatory law, and government contacts that eventually might be parlayed into a move to Wall Street or to private industry. Many of those entering public service are recent law school graduates who find government salaries sufficiently attractive at this stage of their careers, and seek the training that such service may offer as a prelude to private practice. Limitations on top salaries discourage some from continuing with the government, although in recent years, public service has become more attractive as a career.

A majority of lawyers serve by appointment in legal departments of a variety of federal and state agencies and local entities. The various departments and regulatory agencies, such as the justice and treasury departments and the Interstate Commerce Commission, employ thousands of attorneys. Others work in the various legal departments in cities dealing with matters such as planning, zoning, eminent domain issues, and so on. Still others are engaged as either public defenders or prosecutors. (It should be noted that prosecutors are the most powerful actors in the legal system. Their decisions have major implications on how crime is defined, who is charged, and the punishment they receive [Frohmann, 2009], and from time to time, there are serious concerns about prosecutorial power abuse [Davis, 2009].) Federal prosecutors, the United States attorneys, and their assistants are appointed by the president and are subordinate to the attorney general of the United States and their employment can easily be terminated as evidenced by the controversial firing of eight United States attorneys by the attorney general in early 2007. State prosecutors, sometimes known as *district attorneys*, are commonly elected by each county and are not under the control of the state attorney general. As a rule, lawyers in government are directly engaged in legal work, because law training is infrequently sought as preparation for general government service. However, a small but important minority, which is considered an exception to this rule, consists of those who have been appointed to high executive positions and those who have been elected to political office.

Private Employment

About 12 percent of lawyers are in private employment. These lawyers (often referred to as *house counsels*) are salaried employees of private business concerns, usually industrial corporations, insurance companies, and banks. Large corporations such as General Electric, AT&T, State Farm, and Liberty Mutual have huge legal departments with over 500 lawyers (*Lawyer's Almanac*, 2010). It is interesting to note that such multinationals, along with other products and services, are increasingly outsourcing litigation support research and analysis to countries such as India as a cost-cutting measure (*Economist*, 2006:6).

The growth of corporations, the complexity of business, and the multitude of problems posed by government regulation make it desirable, if not imperative, for some firms to have lawyers and legal departments familiar with the particular problems and conditions of the firm. In view of the increased complexity of business transactions and the growth of federal regulations, the proportion of the profession engaged in this kind of activity can be expected to increase in coming years. In addition to legal work, lawyers often serve as officers of the company, and may serve on important policy-making committees, perhaps even on the board of directors. Although lawyers in legal departments are members of the bar and are entitled to appear in court, their lack of trial experience means that a firm will usually hire an outside lawyer for litigation and for court appearances. Lawyers in legal departments of business firms do not tend to move to other branches of legal work after a number of years. Many of these lawyers have been in private practice or in government service. There is some horizontal mobility between government work and private employment, but not to the same extent as between government and law firms (Jenkins, 1977).

Judiciary

A very small proportion of lawyers are federal, state, county, and municipal court judges. Except for some inferior courts, judges are generally required to be admitted to the bar to practice, but they do not practice while on the bench. There is so little uniformity that it is difficult to generalize further about judges, other than to point out three salient characteristics that relate to the ranks from which judges are drawn, to the method of their selection, and to their tenure.

Judges are drawn from the practicing bar and less frequently from government service or the teaching profession. In the United States, there is no career judiciary such as is found in many other countries, and there is no prescribed route for the young law graduate who aspires to be a judge—no apprenticeship that he or she must serve, no service that he or she must enter (Carp et al., 2010). (This is in contrast to some other countries, such as Japan and France, where there are special schools for training judges. In Scandinavian countries, judicial training is acquired during a practical internship period following law school. In the former Soviet Union, judges often lacked formal legal training and were appointed on the basis of loyalty and Communist Party affiliation [Glendon et al., 2008].) The outstanding young law graduates who act for a year or two as law clerks to distinguished judges of the federal and state courts have only the reward of the experience to take with them into practice, not the promise of a judicial career. Although it is not uncommon for a vacancy on a higher court to be filled by a judge from a lower court, even this cannot be said to be the rule. The legal profession is not entirely unaware of the advantages of a career judiciary, but it is generally thought that they are outweighed by the experience and independence that lawyers bring to the bench. Many of the outstanding judges of the country's highest courts have had no prior judicial experience. Criticism has centered instead on the prevalent method of the selection of judges. There is also an increased awareness of the need for continuing education and practical training programs for new judges because attorneys with less experience are seated on the bench (Carnahan, 1992).

As I discussed in Chapter 3, in over two-thirds of the states, judges are elected, usually by popular vote and occasionally by the legislature (see also Streb, 2009). Since 1937, the ABA has advocated a system (the Missouri Plan) under which the governor appoints judges from a list submitted by a special nominating board, and the judge then periodically stands unopposed for reelection by popular vote on the basis of his or her record. Such a system is now in effect in several states. In a small group of states, judges are appointed by the governor, subject to legislative confirmation. This is also the method of selection of federal judges, who are appointed by the president, subject to confirmation by the Senate. The selection of judges is not immune from political influence, pressure, and controversy (Shuman and Champagne, 1997). Nor is it reflective of the racial and ethnic composition of the population. To illustrate, in 1992, of the 356 judges sitting on the states' highest courts, only 4.2 percent were black, and there was only one Hispanic. Of the 837 judges on the federal bench, 5.2 percent were black (Pollock and Adler, 1992:4). In the ensuing decade and a half or so, the situation has not changed, and the progress of minorities on the bench has been very slow at all levels.

A third characteristic is that judges commonly serve for a term of years rather than for life. For courts of general jurisdiction, it is typically four to six years, and for appellate courts, six to eight years. In a few state courts and in the federal courts, the judges sit for life. Whether on the bench for a term of years or for life, a judge may be removed from office only for gross misconduct and only by formal procedures.

REVENUE STREAMS: LAWYERS AND MONEY

Some quarter of a century ago, a *Wall Street Journal* article (1986:23) already boasted that one out of every nine lawyers is a millionaire, and the rest have an average net worth of one-half million dollars. The fiscal position of lawyers since that time has undoubtedly improved (see, for example, Cotterman, 2004), and in 2006, it was not uncommon to hear about newly minted attorneys starting at $145,000 (plus bonus) and by 2009 $160,000 and bonus and partners averaging about $2.4 million a year at top law firms (Stracher, 2006). (To put it in a broader perspective, law work, as noted earlier, accounts for 2.8 percent of the GDP and the share of that going to plaintiff's lawyers alone is more than $50 billion [Krauss, 2007].) After physicians, who averaged $195,000 during 2009, lawyers as a group are the highest-paid professionals, with an average annual income of more than $150,000. To put these figures into some kind of perspective, a glance at average faculty salaries during the academic year of 2009–2010 at public universities shows that full professors earned around $89,000; associate professors $60,500 and assistant professors about $50,500—and as in other professions, the gender gap in salaries persisted. Female full professors earned just 88 percent of what male full professors earned in 2010. The gap narrowed between male and female faculty members at the associate- and assistant-professor ranks. (*Chronicle of Higher Education Almanac*, 2010), and during the same period, the median family income (four-person families) was just under $60,000 and the per capita personal income was slightly over $30,000. Not surprisingly, a poll showed that almost one-half of the lawyers chose law because its income potential appealed to them (but only 21 percent wanted "to see justice done" and 23 percent had a desire to improve society) (see, for example, Reidinger, 1986:44). There is an unusually large range of income among lawyers, and a high proportion of income goes to elites. In most law firms, there is an "eat-what-you-kill" system under which profits are shared among partners according to how much business each of them brings in (*Economist*, 2004). A study found that 5 percent of law firm partners earned 35 percent of all income, whereas the bottom 19 percent of individual practitioners earned only 5 percent (York and Hale, 1973:16); these proportions have been relatively stable over the past generation. There are several factors that account for the variation in lawyers' income. They include the type of practice (firm or solo); the type of clientele (corporations or individuals with "minor" problems); the reputation of the law school; achievement in law school; the age and length of practice; the degree of specialization; and the region and population of the place of practice (generally, the larger the community, the greater the average income). (Salaries are continuously changing; the most recent figures are available on the Internet at Web sites such as *www.career-journal.com, www.salary.com,* and *www.careerbuilder.com.* These and similar sources also come handy for salary negotiations.)

In 2009, the median starting salaries of law school graduates in private practice ranged from a low of $69,000 in Dallas/Ft. Worth to a high of over $160,000 in New York City, excluding bonuses and perks (*Official Guide to U.S. Law Schools*, 2010). The compensation of associates in law firms is to a great extent determined by the size of the firm as shown in Table 8-2. In general, the larger the firm, the greater the median income of associates. For example, the median base salaries of first-year associates range from

TABLE 8-2	Median Starting Salaries for First-Year Associates by Firm Size					
	Firm Size — Number of Lawyers					
	2–10	*11–25*	*26–50*	*51–100*	*101–250*	*251 or more*
1996	$35,000	$41,500	$52,000	$58,500	$60,000	$70,000
1997	40,000	52,000	50,000	60,000	65,000	71,500
1998	39,500	52,000	53,000	61,000	60,000	75,000
1999	— 51,000 —		57,500	67,000	70,000	85,000
2000	— 60,000 —		63,000	70,000	75,000	110,500
2001	— 60,000 —		70,500	75,900	90,000	110,200
2002	— 53,500 —		75,000	75,000	90,000	110,000
2003	— 59,000 —		71,000	80,000	85,000	107,000
2004	— 65,000 —		72,900	81,000	88,500	110,000
2005	— 67,500 —		80,000	83,000	86,000	110,000
2006	— 67,000 —		80,000	85,000	90,000	120,000
2007	— 68,000 —		81,000	90,000	105,000	130,000
2008	— 73,000 —		92,500	95,000	110,000	135,000
2009	— 70,000 —		92,500	104,000	110,000	145,000
% change 1996–2009	— 37% —		78%	78%	83%	107%

$70,000 in small firms to $145,000 in firms employing more than 500 attorneys. After eight years as associates (relatively rare because after six or seven years they are made partners or asked to leave just like faculty members without tenure), their median base compensation range from $105,000 to almost $197,000.

Some unusually high starting salaries in New York City and other large cities (see Table 8-3) from time to time get a great deal of publicity in the media. Some firms offer new associates fresh from law school $165,000 and anywhere from $25,000 to $35,000 in additional bonuses if they had spent a year or two clerking for a judge. Investment firms were luring away highly qualified law school graduates with starting salaries in excess of $160,000. But there were very few such openings and usually they are filled by top graduates of elite law schools. Still, such high initial salaries jolt the legal profession, especially the expanding megafirms that compete with each other for a relatively stable pool of top graduates. Shortly after such publicity, a ripple effect push up salaries at major firms across the country. This is good news for young associates who work in some cases up to eight or nine years in the hope of joining the full partners, who split a firm's profit. Table 8-4 provides an idea of compensation for nonlaw firm jobs, Table 8-5 gives the median salaries nine months after graduation by type of employer in 2009, and Table 8-6 shows the median base salary for associates by year and firm size.

Law students also earn a substantial income during the summer when they work at law firms as interns. Because most law firms compete for top students after meeting them on annual trips at law schools around the country for fresh brainpower to build their

TABLE 8-3   Median Starting Salaries for First-Year Associates in Firms of 251 or More Lawyers — Chicago, Los Angeles, New York, and Washington, DC

	Chicago	*Los Angeles*	*New York*	*Washington*
1996	NA	$75,000	$85,000	$72,500
1997	$73,000	80,000	87,000	74,000
1998	80,000	82,500	87,500	80,000
1999	90,000	92,000	96,000	91,000
2000	117,500	125,000	125,000	114,050
2001	125,000	125,000	125,000	125,000
2002	125,000	125,000	125,000	120,000
2003	125,000	125,000	125,000	120,000
2004	125,000	125,000	125,000	120,000
2005	125,000	125,000	125,000	125,000
2006	132,500	135,000	145,000	135,000
2007	145,000	145,000	160,000	145,000
2008	160,000	160,000	160,000	160,000
2009	160,000	160,000	160,000	160,000
% change 1996–2009	114%	113%	88%	120%

Table 8-4 Median Starting Salaries for Selected Nonlaw Firm Lawyer Jobs			
	Prosecutors	*Judicial Clerks*	*Legal Services*
1996	$33,000	$35,000	$30,000
2008	50,000	50,000	41,750
% change 1996–2006	51%	43%	39%

TABLE 8-5 Median Salaries, Nine Months after Graduation in 2009	
Employer	*Salary*
All graduates	$68,500
Private practice	108,500
Business	69,100
Government	50,000
Academic/judicial clerkships	48,000

permanent ranks, they pay candidates rather well, and some summer associates can earn the weekly equivalent of close to $125,000-a-year salary during their "12-week job interview"—in addition to a variety of other perks ranging from dining in top restaurants to using company retreats.

Even before a decade or so, individual partners in top law firms averaged around $435,000 and senior associates about $350,000 (Stevens, 1995a), and the figures are undoubtedly much higher today. (If law firms could incorporate and go public, a highly debated and controversial issue [see, for example, Belford, 2004], they could tap the stock market through public offerings and thus enhance further the financial benefits to the partners. At the same time, allowing law firms to trade publicly would raise issues, among other things, of client confidentiality and set obligations to shareholders above those to clients.)

On the whole, lawyers in private employment do not fare as well as their colleagues in private practice. Table 8-7 provides a glance of some median salaries for various attorney job titles in private employment in 2009. These figures do not include bonuses, perks, and so forth. For large corporations, it is not unusual for chief legal officers to have a total compensation package (salary, bonus, profit sharing, insurance, company car, and various perks) well in excess of $2 million, and in large- and medium-sized enterprises, the average compensation package is around $900,000 for chief legal officers (*Lawyer's Almanac*, 2010). Some details by industry are as follows: Attorneys employed by manufacturing/extractive firms make significantly more (with a median total compensation of $158,500) than those employed by nonmanufacturing organizations ($108,500). The highest median incomes are among those employed by business services ($191,031); by manufacturers of electrical and electronic products ($185,650), aerospace and aircraft products ($184,521), transportation equipment ($175,487), and machinery and heavy equipment ($172,312); and by health care organizations and communications services (both $170,000). The lowest median incomes are manufacturers of food/beverage/tobacco

TABLE 8-6 Median Base Salaries by Associate Year and Firm Size (as of April 1, 2009)

Associate Year	Firm Size—Number of Lawyers															
	2–25		26–50		51–100		101–250		251–500		501–1,000		1,001+		All Sizes	
	Median	# Reported	Median	# Reported	Median	# Reported	Median	# Reported	Median	# Reported	Median	# Reported	Median	# Reported	Median	# Reported
First	$70,000	27	$92,500	30	$104,000	53	$110,000	76	$125,000	121	$135,000	117	$160,000	126	$130,000	550
Second	71,000	26	92,000	34	101,500	48	112,000	73	128,950	112	140,000	103	160,000	95	130,000	491
Third	70,000	25	98,000	35	102,000	48	115,000	71	135,000	108	143,500	106	170,000	95	135,000	488
Fourth	77,175	26	101,750	30	105,500	48	116,250	66	140,000	109	148,000	109	185,000	95	141,000	483
Fifth	94,950	20	104,000	33	110,750	48	120,000	67	147,325	102	160,000	101	210,000	95	150,000	466
Sixth	99,600	20	109,250	30	120,500	46	125,000	71	150,000	103	162,075	106	230,000	94	155,000	470
Seventh	116,000	14	110,700	25	121,500	42	127,775	66	165,000	95	170,000	105	237,250	86	165,000	433
Eighth	111,625	24	126,500	22	123,950	36	133,000	55	165,000	105	180,000	107	258,050	82	171,275	431
Summer Associates ($/week)																
First year	800	11	1,325	22	1,575	24	1,800	45	2,350	70	2,600	72	3,075	93	2,500	337
Second year	1,000	22	1,550	29	1,800	45	1,900	79	2,400	91	2,700	101	3,075	112	2,400	479
Third year	950	6	1,700	10	1,400	13	1,800	11	3,075	27	3,075	23	3,075	79	3,075	169

TABLE 8-7 Median Salaries of Attorneys in Private Employment in 2009	
Deputy chief corporate legal officer	$210,000
Managing attorney	195,000
Attorney, high-level specialist	145,000
Chief divisional or subsidiary legal officer	139,000
Senior attorney	106,000
Intermediate attorney	99,000
Attorney	70,000
Specialty administrator	57,000
Legal administrator	53,000
Senior paralegal assistant	50,000
Paralegal assistant	36,000

products ($92,820), nonprofit organizations ($93,325), insurance companies ($100,998), and educational institutions ($102,000).

Regarding paralegal compensation in law firms, the average salary for legal assistant managers was $84,000 in 2009. Legal assistants/paralegals (paralegals without supervisory responsibility) earned an average of $48,000 in 2009, and legal assistant clerks took home around $32,000. Annual bonuses added between 6 percent and 9.5 percent to average salaries in 2009, increasing with level of responsibility and expertise.

In general, the compensation of judges is lower than that of attorneys in private practice or private employment. Judges, magistrate judges, and magistrates had median annual earnings of $94,070 in 2009. The middle 50 percent earned between $44,970 and $120,390. The top 10 percent earned more than $138,300, while the bottom 10 percent earned less than $24,250. Median annual earnings in the industries employing the largest numbers of judges, magistrate judges, and magistrates were $112,720 in state government and $54,750 in local government. Administrative law judges, adjudicators, and hearing officers earned a median of $64,540, and arbitrators, mediators, and conciliators earned a median of $47,320. In federal courts, the following salaries apply: the chief justice of the U.S. Supreme Court earned $198,600, and the associate justices earned $190,100. Federal court of appeals judges earned $179,500 a year in 2008 while district court judges had salaries of $169,300 as did judges in the Court of Federal Claims and the Court of International Trade. Federal judges with limited jurisdiction, such as magistrates and bankruptcy court judges, had salaries of $155,756 Annual salaries of associate justices of states' highest courts averaged $145,194 in 2008 and ranged from $106,186 to $218,237. Salaries of state intermediate appellate court judges averaged $141,263 and ranged from $105,050 to $204,599. Salaries of state judges of general jurisdiction trial courts averaged $130,533 and ranged from $99,234 to $178,789. Most salaried judges are provided health and life insurance, and contributions to retirement plans are made on their behalf (*Lawyer's Almanac*, 2010). Judicial salaries are perpetually in a state of flux, and there is continuous pressure at local, state, and federal levels for increased compensation. It should be noted that while judges' compensation and salary increments come from the general revenue (tax) in the United States, in England, there is a move under way that the full costs of court services in most cases should be met by the users. Essentially it means that litigants' fees will cover the judges' pay (*Economist*, 1994:59).

In private practice, there are several ways lawyers generate income. Some charge by the hour for services rendered. For top firms, the hourly rates billed by senior partners approximate $1,500–$2000, and many good firms average $650–$850 an hour in 2009. That is also the range of going rates for established trial attorneys, and there is predictable media frenzy when legal fees reach an unusual amount, such as $7,700 per hour that was charged by the lead law firm in the *Commonwealth of Massachusetts v.Same, Liggett & Myers Tobacco Co.*, case (Beam, 2004:96).

When hourly rates are charged, the client signs an hourly retainer agreement specifying the amount of the retainer fee and the hourly charges by the attorney for all work done. A legal assistant's time is charged at a lower rate. All time spent on a client's case is billed, including phone calls (incoming and outgoing—the timer on the phone works both ways), travel time, waiting time in court, preparation time, office conferences, negotiations, meetings, drafting, legal research, and so on, in units of one-tenth or one-sixth an hour minimum. In addition, the client is responsible for all costs related to the case, such as court costs, filing fees, long distance phone calls, facsimiles, copying, postage, process server fees, consultant fees, transcripts, expert witness fees, and in some instances basic office supplies such as paper, paper clips, and so on. Upon the exhaustion of the retainer fee, monthly billing kicks in. If the bills are not paid, usually within 30 days, the attorney may refuse to perform additional legal services, and if any suit commenced to collect an outstanding fee, the lawyer shall also recover reasonable attorney's fees.

In recent years, law firm billing practices have come under close scrutiny (see, for example, Koppel, 2006). In addition to the amount, there are legal and ethical questions concerning billing practices. Such practices include "using a heavy pen," which means rounding up to the next time unit in measuring fractions of hours worked on a client's case. There is also "late time," adding to the bill extra hours that lawyers did not work. Another questionable practice is the "smell test," a crude way lawyers can tell whether a padded bill will seem exorbitant to the client. Then there are fictitious narratives using such phrases as "review of key documents" and "analyze defense strategy" to describe work never performed. The central character of Jeremy Blachman's (2006:56) novel, *Anonymous Lawyer*, captures, in a lighter vain, some of these billing practices. In his sardonic words, "I bill the time I think about these sorts of things. I call it 'research.' The clients never question it. 'Research' is code for surfing the Internet, 'drafting' is code for eating in your office, 'misc. legal forms' is code for ordering gifts online, and 'preparing for meeting' is code for taking a crap. Everyone knows. It's no big deal."

Of course, there is not a clear-cut line between aggressive and creative billing practices and fraud. Ideally, legal billing should be as simple as paying for a housecall by a plumber. Both charge by the hour, and they expect to be reimbursed for expenses incurred. However, it is not as simple as it sounds. Because lawyers charge hundreds of dollars per hour and incur thousands in expenses, any imprecision can be costly to the client. Associates, for example, who are expected to bill from 1,800 to 2,400 hours (the latter means 6.57 hours of *actual* work 365 days a year) often introduce a modest multiplier in the charges (most lawyers have timers on their phones and rounding off phone calls, so a one-minute call costs the client a full-time unit of six or fifteen minutes on the bill, or charging a full hour of work that includes lunch and a visit to the bathroom) (Moses and Schmitt, 1992). Through a process of legal alchemy known as double billing, lawyers can make two into four (take two hours of research spent on client A's legal problem, which turns out to be the same as client B's problem). Though double billing is condemned by the ABA, lawyers are not bound by ABA rulings, and they are free to bill both clients for the same work. Associates are even told that any time spent thinking about a client's legal woes, even while eating or jogging, should be billed (Stracher, 2001). Some clients are concerned with billing practices, and in response, larger law firms started to use Web tools to ensure greater transparency of legal bills; from their computers lawyers enter and continually track the amount of attorney time and costs that have been incurred in a particular case as well as specific breakdowns of partner, associate, or paralegal charges. Clients of law firms using such Web tools can have real-time and comprehensive pictures of legal costs through secure Web sites as well as access to court filings, correspondence, and other matters involved (Koppel, 2010).

In a highly controversial book, *Lawyers, Money, and Success: The Consequences of Dollar Obsessions*, Macklin Fleming (1997) notes that lawyers claim that the last hour worked in a 20-hour day is as productive as the first, and the client should happily pay the same rate for both. He contends that the modern law firm is a Ponzi scheme, to maintain its profit base; the firm must hire two new associates every time it adds a partner. The retainers charged by the partners must cover both these rainmakers' fees and the salaries of the lawyers who actually do the work.

In the United States, legal expenses can be as devastating as medical expenses. To most Americans, legal fees for justice seem almost criminal—about $5,000 for misdemeanors, $4,000 to $12,000 for non-trial felonies, and $25,000 and above for felony trials. Even the simplest traffic violation starts with a $1,000 retainer. Similarly, the legal fees in estate and probate provide the opportunity for large profits from legal work. Few people understand why a lawyer who fills out mostly standard forms for two hours at the closing of a $600,000 house deserves 1 percent, or $6,000, for his or her effort (which is the same for a $100,000 house or for a $10,000,000 house—still 1 percent). In probate, legal fees are determined usually as a percentage of the worth of the transaction—in this case, the value of the estate. Typical charges are 7 percent for the first $7,000 of the estate, 5 percent for the next $4,000, 4 percent for the next $10,000, 3 percent for the next $60,000, and 2.5 percent for the remainder. Once again, the amount of the fee is not necessarily related to the amount of work expended by lawyers, especially in cases where the value of an estate exceeds several million dollars. Nowadays, it is not unusual to hear of lawyers receiving multimillion-dollar fees, especially in large class-action suits such as the one against the Manville Corporation, which was sued by those who were exposed to the asbestos it manufactured. Mergers provide another avenue for lucrative fees. In addition to fees, percentages, and hourly charges, some lawyers and law firms are on retainers. A wealthy individual or a corporation pays a certain sum a year to a lawyer or a firm for a predetermined amount of legal work, for example, a maximum of 80 hours of consultation.

Lawyers also take cases on a contingency-fee basis (Cotterman, 2004). This is an arrangement whereby a lawyer receives a percentage of any damages collected. This practice is limited to a great extent to the American legal system, and most countries emulate England, which refuses to allow lawyers to work for contingency fees. Such fees in the United States are used primarily in medical malpractice, personal injury, and some product liability and wrongful death cases. If the plaintiff loses, there is no payment required for legal services; if he or she wins, the lawyer takes his or her expenses off the top, then gets a percentage of the remainder—from 10 to 15 percent on big airline-crash suits to 35 percent on smaller suits. For example, when an individual is awarded $1,000,000 in damages, the lawyer may get from $100,000 to $350,000. The system has its merits. It allows individuals who could not otherwise afford it to retain the services of an attorney. It encourages lawyers to screen out weak cases because they share the risk of litigation—if they do not win, they do not collect.

At the same time, the contingency-fee arrangement provides a motivation to seek high damages. Lawyers make substantial investments by hiring investigators, expert witnesses, and consultants to augment their chances of winning. Often, they invest a considerable amount of their time in cases that can drag on literally for years. But the payoff can be substantial. It is not unusual to hear of a jury award of about $15 million in a personal injury case (*U.S. News & World Report*, 1986:35–36). Although the average verdict award in specific personal injury cases is relatively modest (knee injury, $189,184; vertebrate fracture, $259,061; and cervical strain, $42,157), million-dollar verdicts are quite common. By 1995, there were already 703 million-dollar verdicts as compared with 127 in 1980 and 7 in 1970, and in the early and mid-2000s, the verdicts in litigations against tobacco companies were in excess of several billion dollars (Beam, 2004; *Lawyer's Almanac*, 2010). The average personal injury verdict was almost $70,000, and the highest award was over $100 million. Multimillion awards are commonplace. By contrast, in many other countries, awards do not even approximate the dollar amount of many American judgments. Courts aim to award the amount of money that will put an individual back in as close a position as he or she would have been without the injury and it covers only actual treatment and treatment-related expenses such as transportation to a clinic. Not surprisingly, contingency-fee law made more overnight millionaires than just about any legal business one could name. An extensive survey of the richest lawyers in America found that the big fortunes were made predominantly in contingency-fee work, not the corporate law and transaction planning that have always represented the height of lucrative law practice (Olson, 1991a:45).

It should be noted that, in addition to actual damages, *punitive* damages further increase the dollar amount involved in litigation. Punitive damages are not intended to compensate plaintiffs but rather to punish defendants where their conduct has been outrageous, grossly negligent, and close to criminal. Punitives may be awarded in many types of tort litigation, including medical malpractice, product liability, and insurance bad faith. In most states, however, the law gives little guidance to judges and juries in determining whether punitive damages should be assessed and in what amount (see, for example, Hastie et. al., 1998) although it should be noted that in a nationwide study of nearly 9,000 cases, it was found that judges and juries each awarded punitive damages in about 4 percent of the cases won by plaintiffs and generally in about the same proportion in each case (Glaberson, 2001). Attorneys have little to lose by pressing a punitive-damages claim, and, if they win, it can be an immense windfall for the plaintiff. It is not unusual to have punitive damages sought in the tens of millions of dollars (*Business Week*, 1989). Although a fraction of civil cases end with punitive damages (*New York Times*, 1995a:B12), the threat of punitive damages has become an effective bargaining chip in settlement negotiations. In insurance cases, for instance, claim settlements average 10 percent higher when claimants seek punitive damages. In an attempt to moderate the size of excessive punitive damages, there is a nascent movement to split civil trials into two phases, one dealing with liability and the other with punitive damages. If the liability and punishment issues were tried separately, or bifurcated, the jury would hear evidence and render a verdict only on the defendant's liability, then return to hear evidence on punishment issues and render a second verdict, similar to the proceedings in criminal trials. Opponents of two-phase trials claim that they would be more time-consuming, further strapping already busy courts (Harlan and Geyelin, 1992).

Although the contingency-fee arrangement does influence the amount of effort lawyers devote to a given case (Kritzer, 2004; Kritzer et al., 1985), the high legal fees and high damage awards create a number of problems. Medical fees are increasing to cover the cost of malpractice insurance. Some obstetricians and surgeons are walking away from their practices rather than pay insurance premiums of $400,000 or more per year. States, cities, and school districts are faced with substantial increases in their liability insurance and have started to phase out high-risk services such as recreation programs. Corporations are passing on to the consumers the cost of higher insurance premiums for product liability. With certain products such as new chemical contraceptives or tranquilizers, the fear of product liability suits has also driven many companies out of research that was directed toward the development of new birth control technology (Tone, 2001; 2009).

The general public is also unhappy with the prevalence of liability suits. In a public-opinion survey on the topic, seven out of ten people polled agreed with the statement that a major effect of liability suits is to give lawyers "much more money than they deserve" (*Society*, 1992:3). Almost two-thirds in the sample agreed that people often initiate frivolous lawsuits because the potential awards are substantial and they have practically nothing to lose. Much less than half of the 1,970 people surveyed (40 percent) said that a significant outcome of liability suits is the fair compensation of victims. About half agreed that individuals and companies act more responsibly because of the threat of litigation. Participants were divided over whether the number of malpractice, personal injury, and product liability suits is reasonable. Slightly over a third called them "mostly justified," and almost an equal number considered them "mostly unjustified." About 70 percent would limit punitive awards and would have a cap for lost wages and pain and suffering. Lawyers disagree with the results of the poll and argue that there is a discrepancy between public perception and reality. They contend that product liability suits are filed in only a small fraction of cases where people are injured, and that headlines showing large punitive awards are misleading because often those awards are sharply reduced by judges; trial lawyers further argue that strong product liability laws are vital to public health and safety regardless how passionate public debate is on tort reform (Robinson and Calcagnie, 2010).

A number of states are now considering measures to limit both the size of damage awards and lawyers' fees (Krauss, 2007). Some states have already imposed caps on the size of medical malpractice awards to $250,000. A few states are also imposing controls on what a lawyer can charge. In general, the new laws allow the traditional fees for prosecuting minor lawsuits but reduce them sharply for certain big-money cases that are costly and complicated to bring. Lawyers, of course, do not like these limitations. They contend that the contingency fee is the victim's key to the courthouse. It allows the poor to obtain the same high-caliber legal services as the rich. Many of the cases require much expense and preparation. If the suit is lost, the lawyer gets nothing; therefore, the one-third contingency fee is most reasonable. But it does not seem that cutting contingency fees would reduce the number of malpractice and other damage suits filed. Because of the high level of competition for business, if top lawyers bow out, others will still handle these cases. In states without caps on verdict size, there will still be huge damage awards and logjams in the courts.

COMPETITION FOR BUSINESS

The days of exorbitant legal fees for the profession may be numbered (Jones, 2007). As a result of the confluence of the steadily growing size of the profession, cost of legal products and services, downsizing, improved technology for tracking legal work, and the economic turbulence and downturn in 2009 and 2010, many lawyers are likely to enjoy even less prestige, less interesting work, less security, and lower pay scales in the future than their predecessors. For example, more and more law firms are asking new hires to defer their employment start date, and some firms delay the start dates for new associates by a year or more (Mattioli, 2009).

For years now, law schools have been churning out more lawyers than the profession can afford. The job market for lawyers is so tight that some are willing to take jobs as paralegals, especially in such markets as Los Angeles, New York, and Washington, DC; some would-be attorneys take interim jobs such as waitressing, bartending, or are seeking pro bono fellowships (Mattioli, 2009). In 1993, only about 70 percent of law school graduates found law-related jobs within six months of graduation (Samborn, 1995), and the situation has not improved substantially in the ensuing years (*Official Guide to U.S. Law Schools*, 2010). (In Scandinavian countries, by contrast, the bar is declining in size, and there is also a decrease in the proportion of law students to other students in most European countries.) In the prescient and unflattering words of former U.S. Chief Justice Warren E. Burger, "We may well be on our way to a society overrun by hordes of lawyers, hungry as locusts . . ." (*Time*, 1978:56). Not surprisingly, there is growing competition among lawyers for the consumer's dollars.

Two Supreme Court decisions have contributed to competition among lawyers for business. In 1975, the Court ruled that lawyers, like others in business, should not be allowed to fix prices. Until then, it had been standard procedure for lawyers' associations to issue "minimum-fee schedules," lists of the lowest fees members should charge for handling divorces, wills, and so on. Another important case gave lawyers the right to advertise. Two Arizona lawyers placed an ad for their firm in a local newspaper that violated the model code of professional responsibility formulated in 1969 by the ABA and adopted in Arizona by the state's supreme court. The lawyers were censured for their ad. They appealed the case to the U.S. Supreme Court, which decided in 1977 that state laws and bar associations prohibiting lawyers' advertising were in conflict with the Constitution's guarantee of free speech.

Historically, bar associations have strongly opposed advertising by lawyers (Cebula, 1998; Olson, 1991a, 1991b). In the common-law tradition, a lawsuit was considered an evil, albeit a necessary one. Lawmakers and judges considered litigation wasteful, expensive, time-consuming, and an invasion of privacy (Solovo, 2009). It was considered acrimonious, increasing hostility and resentment among people who could otherwise find an opportunity to cooperate and to settle their pecuniary or personal differences. It hindered productive enterprise, and society discouraged litigation where it was not absolutely imperative. Lawyers were forbidden to "stir up" litigation. Any attempt to drum up business as ordinary tradesmen did was discouraged. Lawyers were expected to wait passively for clients and to temper any entrepreneurial urge to solicit them (Olson, 1991b:27).

The demise of opposition to advertising began with a simple idea. Lawsuits came to be considered an effective way to deter misconduct and to compensate wronged persons. There was also a need to increase the demand for legal services, in part because law schools kept turning out large numbers of newly minted attorneys. Many attorneys and law firms began to view law as business, which requires the use of business marketing strategies (Savell, 1994). Of course, lawsuits are not the only products of lawyers. Much of their work can be seen as preventive, nonadversarial, or defensive, such as tax planning, contract negotiation, adoption, or document drafting. But all these activities can lead to a cycle of new demands and suspicions, for much of lawyering work contains an element of adversariness and assertiveness. Thus, an uncontested divorce can turn into a contested one, and advertising can entice aggrieved parties to seek out a lawyer to help them "to drop the spouse but keep the house."

At the prodding of the Supreme Court, bar associations have developed and subsequently refined guidelines to allow lawyers to advertise. Typically, these guidelines allow lawyers to indicate their education, specialties, public offices, teaching positions held, and memberships in professional organizations. They may also indicate other clients represented with those clients' permission, tell what credit arrangements are acceptable, and indicate fees for initial consultations and other services.

The number of lawyers currently advertising has risen sharply in over the years. Effective advertising generates approximately $8 in revenue for each advertising dollar (Kennedy, 1994). Young, small-town, small-firm, or solo practitioners who earn less than $35,000 are the most likely to try it. Older, big-city lawyers still shy away from advertising; 30 percent of lawyers aged 24–34 have tried it, compared with 11 percent in the 55-and-older age bracket, and 14 percent in the 45–54 age group. Lawyers are more likely to advertise in cities with fewer than 50,000 residents and less likely in cities with 1 million or more. Large legal clinics advertise heavily, especially on television, with slogans such as "no frill will—$25." Large law firms are least likely to advertise (ABA Journal, 1986:44). But, by 1992, more than 900 law firms spent close to $83 million on television advertising alone. As one attorney (who hypes his practice regularly on television) sarcastically remarked, "Who wants to wait 30 years to become a household name?" (MacLachlan, 1989:1BP). Nowadays, late-night television airs a steady drumbeat of messages inviting the audience to "dump their hubbies, stiff their creditors, and take their bosses to the cleaners" (Olson, 1991b:31). There are even microspecialists such as those who concentrate on spring break offenses at popular student destinations such as South

Padre Island, Texas, who post fliers with slogans such as "Got drunk? Got caught? Call Mike. He won't tell your mama" (Warren, 2007). These days, there are even manuals and how-to-do books for lawyers on how to advertise on their own (see, for example, Randall, 2002). A divorce attorney in Chicago, who may have been inspired by one of these, put a large billboard in Chicago in May, 2007, getting all the attention it was hoping to attract. The ad showed the well-toned barely clothed torsos of a man and a woman with the caption: "Life is short. Get a divorce." The ad overnight became controversial and was removed by order of city officials but not before generating a fair amount of publicity—and business for the divorce attorney (*Newsweek*, 2007).

Of course, members of the legal profession have not unanimously welcomed the changes. There is concern that lawyer advertising has contributed to the low public image of attorneys (Podgers, 1995). The profession has traditionally considered unethical the more obvious forms of competition—advertising and soliciting clients. The underlying belief of traditionalists is that increased competition leads to a decreased quality of service. The implication is that high fees indicate high quality. In fact, the U.S. Supreme Court said that lawyers had wrongly overcharged clients for decades, under the rationale that the dignity of the profession required it (Green, 1975:55). Many people avoid going to lawyers because they do not have the necessary information about specialization and because they believe that lawyers charge too much. To reach a larger segment of the population, lawyers could advertise the types of cases they handle and lower their fees. However, most bar associations, although they are developing guidelines, still treat advertising as something that is just not done. Attempts to lower fees are usually met with the old arguments about ethics and the quality of service. As a result, with some exceptions, the fees are steadily increasing, and few lawyers allow themselves anything more than the traditional one-line listing in the yellow pages—name, address, and phone number.

After advertising, the next step in competition for business was solicitation. Until 1985, bar associations discouraged lawyers from drumming up litigation against a particular opponent, such as a church or a business. In 1985, the Supreme Court, in *Zauderer v. Office of Disciplinary Council*, ruled that soliciting injury claims from the use of the Dalkon Shield, an intrauterine device, through advertisement is permissible. It created a precedent for lawyers recruiting litigants against all kinds of institutions and businesses. Lawyers now have the right to send letters to solicit the business of individuals known to have legal problems. Even in-person solicitation is no longer a taboo. From airplane disasters to mine accidents, the scene is characterized by a "ravenlike descent" of tort lawyers anxious to contact the victims or their relatives (although it is interesting to note that traditional patterns of disparate recovery based on race and gender still persist and women and minorities are still undercompensated in tort law [Chamallas and Wriggins, 2010]). For example, competition for business among lawyers was so intense in the well-known 1989 Exxon Valdez oil spill in Bligh Reef in Alaska's Prince William Sound that it was referred to as "tanker chasing." A commentator vividly captures this scene: "Liability lawyers and prostitutes fresh from nearby Anchorage are said to prowl the dark, smoky bars in search of clients. Townspeople aren't as concerned about the prostitutes as they are about the lawyers" (Olson, 1991b:32). (The same scene is being repeated during the Spring 2010 BP oil spill in the Gulf of Mexico; the BP lawsuits will dwarf those followed by the Exxon Valdez spill, and trial lawyers are dreaming of one of the biggest paydays since they feasted on tobacco litigation). One of the consequences of this well-publicized incident was the creation of a code of conduct for accident scenes by the Association of Trial Lawyers of America. In 1995, in a decision that may open the door to new restrictions on advertising by lawyers, the U.S. Supreme Court upheld a Florida rule that bars letters to accident victims or their relatives within 30 days of the accident (Freivogel, 1995:7A).

Some large law firms are becoming more competitive by adopting modern cost-management techniques and strategic planning and by experimenting with fixed fees for routine jobs for large-scale buyers of legal services (Jones, 2007). Others are starting to experiment with public relations firms to handle new contacts. Virtually every major law firm in the country has a partner for whom cost management has become a primary preoccupation. Many firms are also increasing the number and size of specialized departments, and there is a growth of "specialty firms," such as the type that specializes in labor law work on the side of management (Heinz and Laumann, 1994). The business of law in large firms, in fact, is turning out to be much like business in any field. Some law firms even provide written service guarantees promising to resolve issues to the clients' satisfaction, even if it means a reduction in legal fees (*New York Times*, 1995b:A13).

Competition for law business is not limited to the United States. In India, for example, the legal profession is "extremely crowded" (Nagpaul, 1994:66), and there is excessive and unrestrained competition among lawyers for clients. India has the longest written constitution incorporating ideas of basic rights, equalities, and social justice. Citizens are becoming more aware of their legal rights, the number of statutes enacted annually are staggering, and the courts are increasingly used as a forum for dispute resolution. In this legal environment, the author of an excellent study on lawyers bitterly complains that the profession has turned into a commercial business "bereft of all ideals, principles . . . there are no sacrosanct ground rules" and "the ruling passion of the Bar is greed and maximisation of economic gains" (Gandhi, 1982:153, 155–156). Many lawyers rely on "touts" or brokers to get business, and "touting" is a widely used, albeit highly unprofessional, activity. A tout may be a government clerk, a typist in the courtroom, a policeman, a village headman, or anyone with some prestige and visibility in the community. A tout befriends a potential client and refers him to a lawyer. He gets a commission from the lawyer, the seller of legal services, to whom he brings business. A tout may get up to 50 percent of the fee the lawyer collects from the client but receives no commission from the client. A tout works for only one lawyer, and good touts are sought after by lawyers. Successful lawyers have several touts "procuring" for them, and about two-thirds of criminal and one-third of civil cases are obtained through touts (Gandhi, 1982:108). In another study, it was noted that young lawyers were acting as touts for older, well-established attorneys primarily because they were unable to obtain professional work on their own (Nagpaul, 1994:69).

In this highly competitive climate, the clients are often cheated by unscrupulous touts and lawyers, who know they are vulnerable and expendable. The clients are helpless because they are ignorant of the law and unfamiliar with the legal arena. In rural areas in particular, most litigants are either illiterate or have a low level of formal education. They do not know where to find adequate and reasonable legal services and welcome the advances of touts with the promise of professional help. Once entrapped, they are passed on "among the various actors of the drama as a nutritious morsel and each has his mouthful of bite." Clients have no recourse, or even a chance to protest, because lawyers do not give them receipts for services rendered. Lawyers view clients as exclusive trading commodities and nonrepeat business and extract whatever they can from them the first time. They are even reluctant to be seen with clients unless they have a formal business arrangement. The touts associated with lawyers are equally ruthless and exploitative and, like lawyers, do not develop continuing relationships with the clients. Even the most notorious "shysters," "ambulance chasers," and "ticket-fixers" hungry for legal business in the United States do not come close to their counterparts in India when it comes to violating ethical codes and professional standards.

LEGAL SERVICES FOR THE POOR AND THE NOT SO POOR

More than a third of the U.S. population have at least one legal problem in a year, but only one in ten consults an attorney (Blohm, 2004; Shdaimah, 2009; Waldman, 1986). A frequently cited survey carried out for the ABA's Consortium on Legal Services and the public found that, in general, low and moderate income families do not seek legal help for their problems. Although 41 percent of the poor and 52 percent of moderate income families encountered at least one legal problem in the 1990s, 71 percent of the poor and 61 percent of moderate income families did not turn to attorneys for help with their legal problem. The legal problems faced by these people were mainly consumer issues and personal finance (Hansen, 1994; Kritzer and Silbey, 2003). A main, and obvious, reason is that law and lawyers are expensive. Many people who need or want a lawyer have trouble paying the price. But as Friedman (1998) comments, "Justice is for sale; but in a just society it should not be totally for sale." Consequently, under a 1963 Supreme Court decision, people involved in a serious criminal case who tell the court that they are too poor to pay a lawyer must be represented, usually by public defenders on the state's payroll (who generally bear the stigma of ineptitude) (McIntyre, 1987) or by court-appointed attorneys. Such defendants are now involved in well over half of the felony cases in the country (U.S. Department of Justice, 1992:4). An editorial in *Harvard Law Review* (1994) calls for federal legislation to ensure that capital defendants receive legal assistance that meets the standards of effective assistance higher than those applied in other criminal cases. Well over a decade later, there is still a shortage of qualified lawyers in capital cases, which places inmates at risk of missing crucial filing deadlines, possibly preventing them from raising appeal issues. In addition, two out of three appealed death sentences are set aside because of errors by defense lawyers. Increasingly, private law firms cannot afford or balk at spending up to a 1,000 potentially billable hours (about six month's time) on a death penalty case, and often they lack competent attorneys for such pro bono work. This forces inmates to rely on incompetent and often-overworked court-appointed lawyers who miss filing deadlines, fail to investigate cases, or submit inadequate appeals (Hines, 2001).

At the same time, the practice of the court appointing attorneys for the defense is unpopular among lawyers. It is damaging to their pocketbook, for they receive only nominal compensation for their services, and it interferes with their regular activities. Even though the compensation is more than modest, ranging from $15 to $20 per hour in Missouri to $40 per hour for courtroom work and $25 an hour for work out of court in New

York City (Fritsch and Rohde, 2001:1), from time to time, states run out of money to pay court-appointed lawyers for defending indigents. In Missouri, when the state ran out of money to pay court-appointed lawyers and the legislature refused to appropriate any more, the Missouri Supreme Court upheld compulsory service without compensation rather than see the criminal justice system come to a halt. As a result, all lawyers in the state, including real estate and merger specialists, were faced with compulsory service in criminal courts. Obviously, many of these attorneys were not specialists in criminal proceedings, which had a bearing on the quality of legal help that defendants received.

The plight of the indigent criminal defendants is further complicated in many instances by the absence of some basic legal work that their more affluent counterparts would have. For example, most lawyers appointed to represent the poor do not hire private investigators to look for witnesses or evidence. Most do not get expert witnesses, like psychiatrists or pathologists, to help challenge the prosecution's case. Most do not take the time to go to the scene of crime, and some do not even make a jail or prison visit to discuss the case with their clients. In New York, for example, a defendant facing life in prison may get a lawyer who spends as little as 20 hours on the case—half a week's work—and is paid as little as $693. A study of 137 New York homicide cases completed by court-appointed lawyers in 2000 shows that in 42 of them—nearly one-third—the lawyers did less than a week preparation, raising questions about their effort and thoroughness. Only 12 spent at least 200 hours—five weeks or more—investigating and preparing their cases, a sign of "appropriate diligence," according to legal experts (Fritsch and Rohde, 2001:27). The median for all cases was 72 hours, not quite two weeks' work.

At times, in part to maintain public confidence in the legal system (Podgers, 1994; Rhode, 2004), lawyers provide legal services *pro bono publico* (for the public good) for indigents (Granfield and Mather, 2009). From time to time, various bar associations have recommended that all lawyers engage in such endeavors. But many cannot afford it, and others, particularly those who work for large firms, are discouraged from doing so. Many large firms are reluctant to take on pro bono criminal-law work, divorce, housing disputes, and consumer problems because such cases would be regarded as unseemly by their corporate clients. A principal reason for the reluctance of large firms to represent "the poor, downtrodden, friendless, and despised" or to engage in public-interest causes is that that sort of legal work "would give offense to their regular clientele" (Heinz and Laumann, 1994:371). As some research findings suggest, pro bono work is also related to the economy. For example, during the boom times of the late 1990s, many of the nation's biggest law firms were inundated with business. In 1999, the roughly 50,000 lawyers at the nation's 100 highest-grossing firms spent an average of just eight minutes a day on pro bono cases. Because of the sluggish economy during the early 2000s, lawyers have more time, and in some areas, pro bono activities more than doubled between 1999 and 2003 along with an increase in the number of lawyers doing such work (Saulny, 2003).

In civil cases, the poor can gain access to lawyers through public or private legal-aid programs. As part of the War on Poverty program in the 1960s, the Office of Economic Opportunity established neighborhood law offices to serve the indigents. In 1974, much of legal-aid work was assumed by the Legal Services Corporation (LSC), which distributed money to 323 legal service organizations with a total of 1,200 offices around the country in the mid-1990s. In general, an individual is eligible for free legal services if he or she has income less than $9,338 a year, and a family of four qualifies if its income is less than $18,938 (Pear, 1995:A9).

Because of the number of activist lawyers in the program who fought and antagonized city hall as a result of mandatory involvement of private attorneys in the delivery of legal services to the poor, the corporation soon became controversial. There were attempts by former president Reagan in the early 1980s to phase the program out, but Congress balked. The LSC was under attack again in between 1983 and 1987 when it began a campaign of harassment and intimidation of guarantee programs through adversarial monitoring and evaluation processes. As a result, there were renewed efforts in Congress to phase it out over the five years to save $1.6 billion. As a result of financial cutbacks, in several states including large ones such as New York, the quality of legal services continues to decline along with representation of indigent defendants and increasing case loads for fewer and fewer attorneys (*New York Times*, 1998). Critics contend the LSC often advances a left-wing agenda of its own through lobbying and litigation at the expense of the poor, and there are other agencies that provide legal aid to the needy (MacLachlan, 1995; Pear, 1995; Rhode, 2004; Shdaimah, 2009). An example of one such organization is the American Bar Foundation , which is made up interdisciplinary teams of attorneys, paralegals, social workers, health providers, and educators in different states to work on a number of issues affecting the poor such as affordable housing, homelessness, environmental protection, and community revitalization (Grange and Schwartz, 1995).

The work of legal services' attorneys is concentrated in five main areas—family, consumer, housing, landlord-tenant, and welfare. To qualify, applicants must have proof of indigence and have a case that falls within the mandate of legal services. Of the 1.7 million cases handled by legal service lawyers in 2007, 33 percent involved family matters like child support, spouse abuse, and divorce. Twenty-two percent involved housing, 16 percent welfare and other government benefits, and 11 percent consumer issues. The rest dealt with education, employment, individual rights, and health care matters. Legal-aid attorneys cannot file class-action suits against the federal government or any state or local government, and they cannot take any case on which they might recover attorneys' fees. Such fees are sometimes awarded in Social Security, civil rights, and domestic relations (that is, palimony) cases. Litigations that involve contingency fees are not accepted, because private attorneys would handle them even for poor clients. It should be noted though that poor people are often unable to obtain private lawyers because the likely fees tend to be small and speculative (Pear, 1995). The Legal Services Corporation (2006) in a comprehensive report, "Documenting the Justice Gap in America: The Current Unmet Civil Legal Needs of Low-Income Americans," concludes that at least 80 percent of the civil legal needs of low-income Americans are not being met. Roughly a million cases are rejected annually because the 143 legal-aid programs nationwide lack the resources to handle them. These one million cases do not include the many qualified people who do not ask legal-aid programs for help, because they do not know the program exists, they do not know that they qualify, or they assume that help is not available to them.

A novel version of legal assistance for the poor is "Street Law." The concept is very simple. Volunteer lawyers set up folding tables for three hours at a main intersection on Saturday afternoon and dispense legal advice to anyone who wants it on everything from family issues to debt problems to landlord–tenant disputes. The program lets anyone speak to an attorney, free, for a few minutes. It is designed for quick advice and the consultations last for 10–15 minutes. Sponsored by Legal Assistance by Whatcom (LAW) advocates (Bellingham, Washington), a nonprofit agency that offers legal assistance to low-income people, Street Law's goal is to help those who cannot afford to otherwise obtain legal help. The program started initially to help homeless people and street kids in the downtown area who would seldom end up in a law office. (For the Seattle scene, see Beckett and Herbert, 2009, on the banishment of the homeless and its consequences.) Since its inception in 1994, the program helped hundreds of people at least to find out whether they have a legal issue to fight and, if so, how to proceed. These Saturday sessions, which are advertised in the local papers, also benefit lawyers because they are exposed to issues outside their normal specialties and often subjected to the kinds of cases they have not heard about since law school. On a personal note, I saw the lawyers sitting at their green folding tables with people lining up for advice on a balmy Saturday afternoon in July 2010, in Bellingham, Washington, and found the sight not only unusual but also most impressive.

Some of those who lack both proof of indigence and the means (or the will) to hire a private attorney started to take matters in their own hands in the form of "pro se litigants" (pro se means "for oneself" in Latin.) It is a do-it-yourself approach, and the growing volume of cases involving self-representation is beginning to put pressure on the courts. For example, clerks have to answer basic questions a lawyer would not need to ask. Judges say pro se litigants constantly ask them for help, raising questions of impartiality. Legal-aid advocates fear pro se litigants may not receive the same shot at justice because they are naive to the system (*St. Louis Post-Dispatch*, 2001). For those who do not wish to act on their own behalf, there are two relatively low-cost ways of obtaining legal services—legal clinics and prepaid legal plans.

A legal clinic is simply a high-volume, high-efficiency law firm. Because the cost per case is low, the firm can afford to set lower fees. Legal clinics build case volume primarily through advertising and publicity. They achieve efficiency by using systematic procedures, by relying heavily on standard forms, and by delegating much of the routine work to paralegals (nonlawyers trained to handle routine aspects of legal work). They concentrate on legal problems that are fairly common, such as wills, personal bankruptcy, divorces, and traffic offenses (Muris and McChesney, 1979).

Some clinics have established chain operations with hundreds of offices in various states and advertise heavily on late-night television, in TV guides, and neighborhood newspapers. Two-thirds of the clients have problems that do not require formal legal action. They are mostly money claims—rent deposits, suits by collection companies, and the like. When a case does not warrant the services of a lawyer, the client is informed how to go to small-claims court or how to negotiate with bill collectors. Of the cases that go beyond the first meeting, about half are divorces, wills, name changes, and adoptions. The fees are usually set in advance and are based on a published schedule. For example, they charge a flat fee of $300 (plus court costs) for a simple uncontested divorce as contrasted with $600 at a conventional firm. The offices are often located in shopping centers or other heavy traffic areas with easy access and plenty of parking. Attorneys are available during the day and the evening and on Saturdays. Credit cards are accepted, as are installment payments (Sullivan, 1979:9).

A second way of providing low-cost legal services is through prepaid legal plans, which work very much like medical insurance (Cotterman, 2004; Waldman, 1986). There are currently two basic ways used to finance such a plan. The organizer can sign up a group of people—a labor union or a credit union—and charge so many dollars per person per year. The other way is to sign up individuals one by one. Obviously, individuals who sign up are those who think they will be likely to use the service. Because more legal services will be used, the cost per person will be higher compared with the group method.

There are two general ways of selecting lawyers in prepaid legal plans (Rhode, 2004). Either there is a designated lawyer or a group of lawyers from which a client may select, or a client may pick any lawyer he or she prefers. In the latter case, there are usually limits on how much of the fee will be covered by the plan. In recent years, unions have been the prime movers in organizing prepaid plans. For example, a plan set up by the United Auto Workers is probably the largest in the country. It covers over 150,000 Chrysler employees, retired workers, and their immediate families. Thus far, though, prepaid plans have not grown as fast as the proponents expected. Individuals in general consider the need for legal insurance less urgent than the need for medical insurance. Another impediment to widespread prepaid legal plans may be the legal clinic. If many more legal clinics are established, fees for routine services are likely to decline throughout the profession. As a result, there will be less of a need for protection against problems that may come up. In other countries, however, the idea of legal insurance seems more appealing. In Germany, prepaid legal plans are widely accepted, and about 40 percent of the households carry legal-expense insurance.

LAW SCHOOLS

As of January 2010, a total of 200 institutions are approved by the ABA: 199 confer the first degree in law (the Juris Doctor or J.D. degree); the other ABA-approved school is the U.S. Army's Judge Advocate General's Legal Center and School, which offers an officer's resident graduate course, a specialized program beyond the first degree in law. The following six of the 200 law schools are provisionally approved: Charleston School of Law, Charlotte School of Law, Drexel University – Earle Mack School of Law, Elon University – School of Law, Liberty University School of Law, and Phoenix School of Law.

Overall enrollment in these institutions increased from 49,552 in the academic year 1963–1964 to 152,033 in 2008–2009. There was a corresponding increase in the number of degrees awarded during the same time period—from 9,638 to 38,065—with the largest number of 43,920 students graduating in 2006 (American Bar Association, 1995:67; *Official Guide to U.S. Law Schools*, 2010). The total J.D. attrition for the academic year 2008–2009 was 6,869, and first-year students accounted for 4,909 of the total. Over the years, attrition rates have remained in proportion to enrollment. Table 8-8 provides an overview of law school enrollment and degrees awarded data from 1963 to 2009.

In addition, seven states have provisions for "reading law" programs allowing people to pursue an independent study of law under a lawyer's tutelage to obtain legal licenses. Most require up to four years of study under a member of the bar, along the line of the traditional apprenticeship programs, and some require a year in law school. Students are tested regularly, and they follow a preset curriculum. The ABA opposes these

TABLE 8-8	Enrollment and Degrees Awarded 1963–2008 Academic Years								
Academic Year	Number of Schools	First Year Enrollment	First Year Male Enrollment	First Year Female Enrollment	Total J.D. Enrollment	Total J.D. Male Enrollment	Total J.D. Female Enrollment	Total Law School Enrollments	J.O. or LLB Awarded
2008–2009	200	49,414	26,007	23,407	142,922	75,954	66,968	152,033	43,588
2007–2008	198	49,082	25,864	23,218	141,719	75,523	66,196	150,031	43,518
2006–2007	195	48,937	26,322	22,615	141,031	74,946	66,085	148,698	43,920
2005–2006	191	48,132	25,550	22,582	140,298	73,685	66,613	148,273	42,673
2004–2005	188	48,239	25,335	22,904	140,376	72,938	67,438	148,169	40,023
2003–2004	187	48,867	25,499	23,368	137,676	70,649	67,027	145,088	38,874
2002–2003	186	48,433	24,846	23,587	132,885	67,706	65,179	140,612	38,605
2001–2002	184	45,070	22,816	22,254	127,610	65,134	62,476	135,091	37,909
2000–2001	183	43,518	22,019	21,499	125,173	64,540	60,633	132,464	38,157
1999–2000	182	43,152	22,144	21,008	125,184	65,822	59,362	132,276	39,071
1998–1999	181	42,804	22,485	20,319	125,627	67,675	57,952	131,833	39,455
1997–1998	178 (2)	42,186	22,777	19,409	125,886	68,971	56,915	131,801	40,114
1996–1997	179	43,245	23,843	19,402	128,623	71,500	57,123	134,949	39,920
1995–1996	178	43,676	24,214	19,462	129,397	72,436	56,961	135,595	39,271
1994–1995	177 (3)	44,298	24,986	19,312	128,989	73,181	55,808	134,784	39,710
1993–1994	176	43,644	24,585	19,059	127,802	72,668	55,134	133,339	40,213
1992–1993	166	42,793	24,468	18,325	128,212	63,568	64,644	133,783	39,425
1991–1992	176	44,050	25,277	18,773	129,580	74,470	55,110	135,157	38,800

Year								
1990–1991	175	44,104	25,512	18,592	127,261	73,164	54,097	132,433	36,385
1989–1990	175	43,826	25,104	18,722	124,471	71,358	53,113	129,698	35,520
1988–1989	174	42,860	24,465	18,395	120,694	69,762	50,932	125,870	35,701
1987–1988	175	41,055	23,549	17,506	117,997	69,077	48,920	123,198	35,478
1986–1987	175 (4)	40,195	25,704	14,491	117,813	69,893	47,920	123,277	36,121
1985–1986	175 (4)	40,796	24,286	16,510	118,700	71,214	47,486	124,092	36,829
1984–1985	174	40,747	24,512	16,235	119,847	72,950	46,897	125,698	36,687
1983–1984	173	41,159	25,110	16,049	121,201	74,840	46,361	127,195	36,389
1982–1983	172	42,034	25,898	16,136	121,791	76,252	45,539	127,828	34,846
1981–1982	172	42,521	26,710	15,811	120,879	77,634	43,245	127,312	35,598
1980–1981	171	42,296	27,024	15,272	119,501	78,667	40,834	125,397	35,059
1979–1980	169	40,717	27,227	13,490	117,297	79,763	37,534	122,860	34,590
1978–1979	167	40,479	27,155	13,324	116,150	80,375	35,775	121,606	33,317
1977–1978	163	39,676	27,748	11,928	113,080	81,430	31,650	118,557	33,640
1976–1977	163	39,996	28,642	11,354	112,401	83,058	29,343	117,451	32,597
1975–1976	163	39,038	28,566	10,472	111,047	85,027	26,020	116,991	29,961

programs, and the lawyer graduates are restricted to practice in their own states (Curriden, 1995b).

For many years, the first degree in almost all law schools was the Bachelor of Law (LL.B.). A few gave their J.D. degree to all students, whereas others reserved the J.D. for students graduating with honors. In recent years, all schools have changed to granting the J.D. There is no difference in the nature of the course of study for the two degrees. The master's degree (LL.M.) usually involves a one-year program combining coursework and research beyond the J.D.; the Doctorate of Juridicial Sciences (S.J.D.) is a graduate academic research degree that involves substantial advanced academic publishable work; and the Master's in Comparative Law (M.C.L.) involves advanced work for foreign-educated lawyers. In addition, a number of law schools offer "joint degrees"; that is, a law school in conjunction with some other college or school offers a combined program leading to a joint degree, such as Juris Doctor/Master of Public Administration degree. Some of the other popular joint degree programs combine law and medicine, law and psychology, law and hospital and health administration, and law and Russian and Eastern European studies and international relations. Joint degrees give students career management flexibility, and the additional degree is expected (or hoped) to open law firm doors in a competitive legal-job market (Sangchompuphen, 1995). More and more law schools are also encouraging students to take advantage of study-abroad opportunities and internship programs in other countries, and to learn a foreign language (Gilgoff, 2004).

Over the years, there have been substantial changes in the composition and characteristics of law students. Women have been dramatically underrepresented in the past both in law schools and in the profession. As late as 1970, women made up only 2.8 percent of the population of lawyers in the United States. In the 1980s, women started entering the profession in unprecedented numbers, and by 1984, almost 13 percent of lawyers were women (Curran, 1986:25). In 1970, 8.5 percent of law school students were women; in 2007, over 47 percent were women and they are poised to outnumber men in law school. In 1995, Roberta Cooper Ramo, a lawyer who once could not find work because of her sex, became the ABA's first female president (*New York Times*, 1995c:A13).

Historically, minorities, like women, have been extremely underrepresented in the legal profession. In 1970, black lawyers made up slightly over 1 percent of all lawyers—3,845, of whom 600 were located in the South (Leonard, 1977:4–5). The various minority-recruitment programs instrumented by most law schools in the late 1960s have increased the enrollment of minority-group students substantially over earlier years. But these groups still do not have representations within the law school populations anywhere near the percentage of the total population. Between 1970 and 2007, the percentage of minority students enrolled in law schools increased from 3.3 percent to over 20.6 percent of the total J.D. enrollment and minorities comprised 21.6 percent of first-year enrollment. The number of minority-group law students remains low, and there are discouraging indications that this is the most likely group to drop in numbers as the total registration slackens or even declines. Further, the number of black and Mexican-American students applying to law school has been relatively constant, or growing slightly, for two decades. But from 2003 to 2008, 61 percent of black applicants and 46 percent of Mexican-American applicants were denied acceptance at all of the law schools to which they applied, compared with 34 percent of white applicants (Lewin, 2010). As they are shut out of the legal profession, blacks and Mexican-Americans must turn to other careers. As a result, they may face lost opportunity costs in the form of lower mean incomes as they enter into lower paid occupations.

For the first time, in 1989, law school students around the country demonstrated and successfully exerted pressure on their institutions to hire more women and minority-group members as professors (Leatherman, 1989:A32). These and similar efforts in subsequent years resulted in major changes in the composition of law school faculties, and now close to half of full-time law school faculty are women and minority-group members.

Lawyers in the United States, just like lawyers in other parts of the world (see, for example, Trubek and Cooper, 1999), established a monopoly on the instrumentalities of the law and the right to practice in the courts. Similarly, law schools have a monopoly on the training of lawyers. They are the gatekeepers for the legal profession. Entry into the profession is conditioned by socioeconomic status and academic standing. Robert Stevens (1973), in a sample of eight law schools studied in 1960, 1970, and 1972, reconfirms that law schools tend to draw students from more affluent families. Students in general come from better-educated and richer families than the general population, and there is increasing homogenization of the college background of law students. In 1960, Stevens found that law schools recruited primarily humanists; by 1970, however, they were recruiting social scientists, and the numbers majoring in social sciences had doubled to more than a majority (Stevens, 1973:574–575).

Law school application is cyclical. The number of applicants to law schools reached a high in 1990. Since 1990–1991, when a record of 99,300 applicants vied for 44,104 spots, there has been a steady decline of college graduates applying to the nation's accredited law schools. By 1996–1997, the number of applicants had dropped 27 percent, to about 72,300, the sharpest drop in recent memory, but the number of openings had declined only slightly, to 43,245 (Mangan, 1998a). For two academic years, 2003–2004 and 2004–2005, the number of applicants exceeded 100,000 but dropped back again to slightly over 95,000 in 2005–2006 and 2006–2007 and showed a light increase for 2009–2010. By contrast, applications to medical schools are up by 4 percent, and there is an even higher percentage in business schools. The recurrent reasons for the decline in the number of law school applicants include limited job prospects, low morale at law firms after layoffs, other lingering effects of the legal recession (Mangan, 1998a; Stevens, 1995b), and the continuing abasement of the prestige and economic status of the profession as evidenced, for example, by newspaper headlines that linger on such as "More Scorn and Less Money Dim Law's Lure" in the influential *New York Times* (Johnson, 1995).

But this situation may be changing in view of the emerging signs of economic and political uncertainties in 2009 and early 2010. Now, as the job market in general is becoming more precarious for college graduates, law schools might be drawing more attention again with a concomitant increase in the number of applications along with the number of people taking the LSAT and the preparatory classes for it. But the number of applicants is likely to remain, if current trends continue, well below the nearly 100,000 who sought entry to law schools at the depth of the 1991 recession (Glater, 2001b) and during the academic years of 2003–2005. According to the Law School Admission Council, students are once again showing interest in applying to ABA-approved law schools in growing numbers. The last increase of comparable applicants was encountered in 1991.

According to preliminary 2010–2011 figures, the number of students applying to one of many law schools for the fall 2010 term is on the increase.

Although still more people apply to law school than can be accepted, about 70 percent of all applicants are accepted in at least one school. Admission to law school is competitive. The higher the reputation of a law school, the greater is the competition among students for the number of places. There are annual rankings of law schools by a number of popular magazines on a variety of criteria (see, for example, *U.S. News & World Report*, 2010). The status of a law school is related, to an extent, to the placement of its graduates. Graduates of law schools attached to elite colleges and universities (for example, Harvard, Yale, Columbia, and Chicago) are more likely to be employed in firms, whereas graduates of Catholic or commercial law schools are more likely to be found in solo practice (Ladinsky, 1967:222–232). The elite Wall Street firms have been most educationally selective in this regard, choosing not only from Ivy League law schools but also from a group whose backgrounds include attendance at elite prep schools and colleges (Smigel, 1964:73–74). Moreover, many lawyers graduating from high-status law schools do not practice in the lower-status specialties of criminal, family, poverty, and debtor–creditor law (Zemans, 1977). Because many students are motivated by a desire for financial rewards (Stevens, 1973:577), competition for admission in high-status law schools is further heightened. As a result, only a small proportion of applicants are accepted in elite national law schools. For example, in 2009–2010 academic year, at the top three law schools ranked by *U.S. News & World Report* (2010), 6 percent were accepted at Yale, 12 percent at Harvard, and 8 percent at Stanford. The percentage of those admitted at less prestigious schools is much higher. For example, Regent University (Virginia) admitted 45 percent and Thomas M. Cooley Law School (Michigan) 69 percent. Some of the Catholic universities also had a relatively high acceptance rate; for example, St. Louis University admitted 40 percent of the applicants (McGrath, 2006:75–78; *U.S. News & World Report*, 2010). But in addition to the quality and reputation of the law school, other factors enter into a decision to apply to a particular school, such as the desire to practice in the school's state, job opportunities upon graduation, the school's orientation toward social sciences, availability and extent of financial aid, job opportunities for a spouse while in school, attraction to the community or area where the school is located, student faculty ratio (7.3 at Yale, 11.4 at Harvard, 23.3 at William Mitchell College of Law, and 16.4 at St. Louis University, just to mention a few numbers) and, not the least, tuition.

Law school education is rather expensive (McGrath, 2006:87–89). In 2010, tuition and fees ranged from $4,291 (North Carolina Central University) to $48,004 (Columbia University, New York). After adding food, housing, cost of books, and personal expenses, the cost of a three-year law school education can well exceed $175,000 at the higher end. For example, the annual tuition and fees at elite schools such as Harvard were $43,900, at Yale $43,340, and at Stanford $44,121 for the academic year 2009–2010 (just for comparison, the per capita income was around $33,000). The minimum budget required at these schools is about $70,000 a year for a single student. At the lower end, tuition and fees for in-state residents at Georgia State University is $6,484 and $6,519 at University of Wyoming. Law schools generally admit only those with a college degree, which itself restricts the profession to those who can afford seven years of education beyond high school. If one goes to a state university where the cost of an undergraduate degree is a very reasonable, $5,000 a year, the direct cost is $20,000 for residents. If the modest yearly "income" of $20,000 is added (the amount a student might have earned had he or she not gone to college), the total "cost" of college education is $100,000. Add to this the cost of law school and forgone earnings, which is another $100,000, and a law degree from a state university around the bottom of the tuition scale will cost at least $200,000. And this is a very conservative figure. For those who cannot afford such expenses, the alternative is to attend a less expensive college, then go to law school part-time at night. But this option will take longer and will provide a lower-quality legal education than full-time enrollment. Approximately, 94 percent of law students rely on educational loans as their main source of financial aid for law school. The typical law student graduates with more than $94,000 in debt not counting the loans that he or she may have taken out as undergraduate.

Admission to law school is determined to a great extent by the combined scores of grade point averages in college and LSAT scores. Although they do not like to publicize the fact, law schools are not above admitting students based on nonacademic criteria such as alumni or substantial family donations. This process is referred to as "institutional interest," and in part justified by suggesting that it helps poorer students by bringing in extra money from donations (Myers, 1994). The LSAT is a nationally administered, standardized test taken by all law school applicants. Most people take the test only once; only about 18 percent take it twice and about 4 percent more than twice. In 2010, the test alone cost $132, registration $65, plus another $37 for handscoring and $12 per report to a law school—or $15 if the report is ordered after registration. Virtually all law schools also require that applicants submit the law school data assembly service report, a summary of their college transcript that the Law School Admission Council/Law School Admission Services prepare. The LSAT test and the basic transcript service for 12 months cost $252. There is also an application fee at most law schools, which can be as high as $75, making multiple applications an expensive proposition because the average applicant applies to 4.7 law schools. Letters of recommendation in support of one's application are generally submitted separately to law schools.

The LSAT has been used in various forms since 1948. The current version was administered the first time in June 1991. In the academic year 2009–2010, over 148,000 persons took the test, but only about two-thirds of them actually applied to a law school. The LSAT is a one-half-day standardized test. It consists of five 35-minute sections of multiple-choice questions designed to measure the ability to read with understanding and insight, the ability to structure relationships and to make deductions from them, the ability to evaluate reading, the ability to apply reasoning to rules and facts, and the ability to think analytically. There is also a 30-minute writing sample that is sent directly to the applicant's law school. The score is reported on a scale of 120 to 180, with 180 as the highest possible score (*Official Guide to U.S. Law Schools*, 2010). For tests administered before 1991, the scores ranged from 10 to 48. Applicants are advised not to take LSAT for practice because all scores will be reported to every law school one applies for admission. The test repeatedly came under criticism, and questions have been raised concerning the extent to which the LSAT can predict success in law school. Performance criteria of success in law school have traditionally been, and continue to be, grades obtained in formal course work. More and more studies conclude that the LSAT, or a combination of LSAT and grade point average, does not predict law school grades for practical purposes of selection, placement, or advisement for candidates seeking entrance into law school (Leonard, 1977:204). Even though there are questions about the validity and reliability of the LSAT to predict success in law school, all law schools require it as part of the admission process. The LSAT, like any admission test, is not a perfect predictor of law school performance. The predictive power of an admission test is limited by many factors, such as the complexity of the skills the test is designed to measure and the unmeasurable factors that can affect students' performance, such as motivation, physical and mental health, or work and family responsibilities. Despite these factors, the LSAT compares favorably with admission tests used in other graduate and professional fields of study.

It should be noted, though, that law schools are not alone in their dependence on some form of admission (or exclusionary) device. Americans have come to expect testing. The fact that some definitive scientific answer about the best way or ways to measure human abilities and potentials is still remote will not stop the process.

Socialization into the Profession

The purpose of law school is to change people; to turn them into novice lawyers; and to instill "in them a nascent self-concept as a professional, a commitment to the value of the calling, and a claim to that elusive and esoteric style of reasoning called 'thinking like a lawyer'" (Bonsignore et al., 1989:271). Chambliss and Seidman (1971:97) sardonically but correctly note, "The American law school education is a classic example of an education in which the subject matter formally studied is ridiculously simple, but the process of socialization into the profession is very difficult." The study of law is a tedious although not a challenging undertaking. After the first year, the work load in law schools tends to be light. The popular conception of law students' life as a mixture of long hours, poring over casebooks, and endless discussions of the contents of those books is more myth than reality. For many students, law school is a part-time commitment, and by the fifth semester, they have the equivalent of a two-day work week and discuss their studies rarely if at all. Says Stevens (1973:653), "At least intellectually law school appears to be a part-time operation."

The key to an understanding of the socialization of law students is best found through an examination of their principal method of instruction, the case or Socratic method (see, for example, Gee, 2010; Sullivan et al., 2007). As I noted earlier, the case method was initiated by Langdell in 1870 at Harvard, and it has since become the dominant form of instruction in American law schools.

The case method of education "generally involves an intensive interrogation by the teacher of individual students concerning the facts and principles presumed to be operative" in a particular case. The method is intended to accomplish two objectives. The first is informational: instruction in the substantive rules of law. The second

> is to develop in the student a cognitive restructuring for the style analysis generally called "thinking like a lawyer." In that analysis, a student is trained to account for the factual 'details' as well as legal issues determined by the court to be at the core of the dispute which may allow an intelligent prediction of what another court would do with a similar set of facts. The technique is learner centered: students are closely questioned and their responses are often taken to direct the dialogue. (Bonsignore et al., 1989:275)

This method of learning the law through court decisions, appellate opinions, and attempts to justify those opinions predominates at virtually every law school in the country and has not changed since its introduction in 1870. Historically, as well as today, the first year of legal education is the most dramatic of the law school's three years. The curriculum of the first year has become as well established in the past century as the teaching method. Nearly all of the more than 48,000 people who begin their legal education every fall are required to take what are generally thought of as the basic subjects—contracts, torts, property law, criminal law, and civil procedure. And for all of them, the effects of that education are considered to be equally predictable and far-reaching. It is during the first year that law students learn to read a case, frame a legal argument, and distinguish between seemingly indistinguishable ideas; then they start absorbing the mysterious language of the law, full of words like "estoppel" and "replevin." It is during the first year that a law student learns "to think like a lawyer," to develop the habits and perspectives that will stay with him or her throughout a legal career (Turow, 1977:60).

The ratio of the number of students to the number of faculty in law schools is markedly higher than that in any other field of graduate training. A low student–faculty ratio plays an important part both in the marketing strategy of law schools and in their ranking (*U.S. News & World Report*, 2010). A 1-to-20 faculty-student ratio is rather common at the best law schools, compared with about 1-to-6 ratio in graduate schools (Loh, 1984:735). The ratio is predicated on the assumption that law students, unlike other graduate students, are handled in large classes and that law professors, unlike other academicians, "have no research work to be done" (Manning, 1968:4). Although the emphasis on research is on the increase among law professors, students, especially during the first year, are taught in large classes. One striking advantage of the case method noted by educational administrators is its adaptability to large classes; indeed, there is an argument to be made for the proposition that the impersonality of the large class is helpful to the student called upon to perform under attack for the first time in his or her life. As stated by a law professor at Yale, "I prefer a hundred, I will work for a hundred and put on a good show; I'll go to sleep with ten or twelve. After you've taught a subject to a class of a hundred for two or three years, you can anticipate the questions and their timing. When I started, I was told, 'Pick four or five points and keep coming back to them; find the bright students and play them like a piano!' It works" (Mayer, 1967:83–84). This method requires the student to do his or her own work and to prepare regularly for classes. When a professor has a gift for posing hypothetical questions, and invents cases to supplement the real ones, the method can be extremely stimulating, pointing out to a student that the rule, as he or she has stated it, would produce a different result under other circumstances. This method also focuses attention on subtleties and provides a good background for logical reasoning.

Although the processes of legal education continue to produce lawyers to fill the present institutional roles calling for them, through methods that have worked and proved themselves consistently over the last century, a feeling of malaise and discontent has been growing among students and faculty at many of the nation's law schools (see, for example, Tushnet, 2008). Many students deplore the Socratic method's inconclusiveness, its failure to encourage creativeness, and its lack of intellectual stimulation (Stevens, 1973:636–638). The class atmosphere is considered to be a hostile one, with the hostility directed from the icily distant law professor toward the student on the spot. Law professors often ignore the emotional level of communication. The impersonal nature of education and mistrustful relations between faculty and students culminate in an intense emotional climate in the classroom, which can pose a threat to the students' self-esteem, self-respect, and identity. Elevated levels of depression and anxiety are ubiquitous among law students (Carney, 1990). Many complain of a high level of stress, which will stay with them during their professional careers (*New York Times*, 1995d: B15).

These unintended results of the Socratic method of teaching are generally rationalized by explaining that the method is meant to acclimate the students to "real life," "legal reasoning" (see, for example, Bankowski and MacLean, 2007), or "thinking like a lawyer" (Schauer, 2009; Sullivan et al., 2007). But it is difficult to see the relationship between the psychic damage and those stated goals, "and one often gets the feeling that the recitation of 'thinking like a lawyer' has become more a talismanic justification for what is going on than an articulated educational program" (Packer and Ehrlich, 1972:30). In addition to the tendency of the Socratic method to provoke anxiety, hostility, and aggression in the classroom, the domination by the law professor as an authority figure suggests that another aspect of law school training is to enforce a respect for authoritative power (Bonsignore et al., 1989:277). Women seem to dislike the Socratic method more than men. Other studies also find that men outperform women in law schools as measured by higher grades (Mansnerus, 1995). There are also some arguments that although law schools may teach students how to "think like a lawyer," they do not really teach them how to be a lawyer (Stracher, 2007).

Further, a large majority of lawyers perceive critical gaps between what they are taught in law schools and the skills they need in the workplace, and appropriate technologies are not being used to help close this gap. This was the core conclusion of a new study by the Berkman Center for Internet & Society at Harvard University (Koo, 2007) in partnership with LexisNexis, which found that more than 75 percent of lawyers surveyed said they lacked critical practice skills after completing their law school education. Today's workplace demands skills that the traditional law school curriculum does not cover. For the most part, attorneys work in complex teams distributed across multiple offices; nearly 80 percent of lawyers surveyed belong to one or more work teams, with 19 percent participating in more than five teams. Yet only 12 percent of law students report working in groups on class projects. Also, legal educators seriously underutilize modern computer technologies and computer simulation and networking, even in those settings such as clinical legal education, that are the most practice oriented, and neither law schools nor most workplaces provide new attorneys with a structured transition between school and practice. Yet, the method has proved to be remarkably resilient, and despite all the criticism against it, there has been no serious competitor (Stevens, 2001: xiv).

Essentially, the objective of law school education is to indoctrinate students into the legal profession. Questions that challenge the basis of the system are seldom raised, and law students define the problems presented to them within the framework of the existing system. The socialization of law students tends to make them intellectually independent, but at the same time, it restrains them from looking for radical solutions, "for throughout their law school education they are taught to define problems in the way they have always been defined" (Chambliss and Seidman, 1971:99). During law school, students change their political orientation in a conservative direction (Erlanger and Klegon,

1978). It is not surprising that "legal education seems to socialize students toward an entrepreneurial value position in which the law is presumed to be primarily a conflict-resolving mechanism and the lawyer a facilitator of client interests. The experience seems to move students away from the social welfarist value in which the law is seen as a social change mechanism, and the lawyer a facilitator of group or societal interests" (Kay, 1978:347).

Political values are often fused with the learning of law, and "students are conditioned to react to questions and issues which they have no role in forming or stimulating. Such teaching *forms* have been crucial in perpetuating the status quo in teaching *content*. For decades, the law school curriculum reflected with remarkable fidelity the commercial demands of law firm practice" (Nader, 1969:21). Students anticipate and law professors reinforce the notion that successful lawyers tend to be conservative and use conservative solutions. A financially successful lawyer needs clients who are able to pay fees. Business-people and rich people in general pay larger fees than wage earners and poor people. Successful lawyers represent successful clients, and such a lawyer "if not already attuned to the value-sets of his client, tends to adopt them" (Chambliss and Seidman, 1971:99).

In response to the escalating criticism of the socialization process of law students (see, for example, Sullivan et al., 2007), there is a growing emphasis on interdisciplinary work in law schools, and on joint degrees such as law and sociology, law and psychiatry, law and business, and law and just about anything. There is also a call for exportation (Brand and Rist, 2009) and globalization of legal education (Mangan, 1998b) and a trend toward "clinical" programs, which is becoming a standard curricular feature at more and more law schools (Schrag and Meltsner, 1998). The idea is to remove law students from classroom situations and place them during their second and third years in real situations, such as criminal defense offices and poverty-related neighborhood legal-aid offices. For many law students, clinical education is considered to be more "relevant" to perceived social needs, and they believe that it should contribute to providing better legal services for the poor and other unrepresented groups in society. Clinical education lends itself to being a separate activity and is by nature removed from the law school. Because active participation is fundamental in clinical education, in addition to learning "how to think like a lawyer," students learn "how to work like lawyers." It injects a sense of realism and gives the students a feel for the human factors in dealing with clients, judges, juries, and regulators—something difficult to impart in the classroom (*U.S. News & World Report*, 1992). However, in view of the prevailing academic ethos that rewards faculty more for publishing than for teaching, some universities look with disdain on innovations that seek to provide courses that are snobbishly referred to as "vocational training." Clinical education is also expensive: It is more economical to deploy senior faculty (who earn well in excess of $300,000 at top schools) to teach 150 students in a large lecture hall than to advise and supervise a handful in a time-consuming clinical program. Not surprisingly, other than some attempts at clinical education, law schools oppose the traditional curriculum, such as the establishment of comprehensive programs (similar to medical internships) to provide students with a more practical grounding in courtroom skills and other aspects of law practice (Jacobson, 1979:10). Also, as Paula Wasley (2007) notes while referring to a 2006 Law School Survey of Student Engagement, faculty–student interaction has a greater impact on students' perceptions of their own success at law school than does the amount of time they spend studying or participating in cocurricular activities like moot courts and internships. The survey found that students who felt their professors to be available, helpful, and sympathetic were generally more positive about their experiences at law school than their classmates who did not see their professors that way. Finally, law schools nationwide are facing attacks in courts, and legislatures as legal clinics take on powerful interests that few other nonprofit organizations have the fiscal resources to challenge. Law clinics, as they take on cases against companies and government agencies, find themselves targeted for budget cuts by legislators when they sue public agencies. The argument is that there is no reason that tax money should be used by these students to act like regulators. On the other side of the argument, the law clinics represent individuals and groups that could not otherwise afford attorneys, and by definition, such work often puts clinics on the opposite side of the government or powerful interests such as developers or those engaged in environmental pollution (Urbina, 2010).

BAR ADMISSION

The legal profession has defined the perimeters of the practice of law and carefully excluded all who cannot utter the password of bar membership. Recall the lockstep of the profession as it now operates. The process begins after college, when the performance of the aspiring lawyer is carefully measured by more or less standard grading processes, as further refined by the LSAT. Nowadays, only the strongest, as measured by those two criteria, have been allowed to enter the portals of legal education. There the refining process continues with study and examinations designed to test the same qualities that were measured on the LSAT. Finally, at the end of law school—again a graded performance—there is, for those who wish to practice law, a bar examination, which reviews fitness to practice by testing for the same qualities as did the LSAT and the law school examinations.

In the United States, the possession of a law degree does not entitle one to practice law. Because a lawyer is technically a court official, he or she must, in addition to legal training, be admitted to practice by a court. Historically, there were no criteria for admission to the bar, and it depended a great deal on the charity or leniency of a local judge. In most instances, to be admitted by one court was sufficient to practice before any court in a state, for each judge respected his or her colleagues' actions in admission proceedings. As a result, the standards of the most lenient judge in a state became the minimum standard for admission (Hurst, 1950:276–285).

The lack of standards attracted the attention of the ABA and state bars. Their concern was twofold. Easy admission permitted the entry of unqualified and unscrupulous lawyers whose work blemished the reputation of all lawyers. Furthermore, easy entrance into the legal profession allowed more lawyers to compete for the available legal business and depressed the income of lawyers.

There were several efforts by the ABA and state bar associations to restrict entry into the legal profession. They obtained legislation to lengthen the required training before application for admission could be accepted. Most efforts to restrict entry into the bar, however, were focused on requiring applicants to pass a standardized bar examination. Bar examinations have had their desired impact in reducing admission to the legal profession and increasing the standards of the profession The bar exam is a test administered by state bar organizations, which law school graduates must pass before being licensed to practice law. In some states, there may be other requirements, such as having completed three years of legal education. Each state's bar exam is unique but almost all states use a two-day format incorporating the nationally administered Multistate Bar Exam (MBE), a six-hour, 200 multiple-choice question examination as a component of their test. State-specific law is often tested on a second day, usually in essay format. In most jurisdictions, the bar exam is offered twice a year, in February and in July. The school's bar passage rate is also part of the ranking and recruitment process, and many guides rank law schools also on the best first-time bar passages rates (see, for example, McGrath, 2006:103–106; *U.S. News & World Report*, 2010).

Today, "no person who is not a member of the bar of another American or Common-Law jurisdiction should be admitted to practice until he has successfully undergone a written examination accomplished under terms and conditions equivalent to those applicable to all other candidates for bar admission" (American Bar Association, 1959:585).

In order to obtain a license to practice law, almost all law school graduates must apply for bar admission through a state board of bar examiners. Most often, this board is an agency of the highest state court in the jurisdiction, but occasionally, the board is connected more closely to the state's bar association. The criteria for eligibility to take the bar examination or to otherwise qualify for bar admission are set by each state, not by the ABA or the Council of the Section of Legal Education and Admissions to the Bar.

Licensing involves a demonstration of worthiness in two distinct areas. The first is competence. For initial licensure, competence is ordinarily established by showing that the applicant holds an acceptable educational credential (with rare exception, a J.D. degree) from a law school that meets educational standards, and by achieving a passing score on the bar examination.

The most common testing configuration consists of a two-day bar examination, one day of which is devoted to the MBE, a standardized 200-item test covering six areas (constitutional law, contracts, criminal law, evidence, real property, and torts). The second day of testing typically comprises locally crafted essays from a broader range of subject matters; however, in a growing number of states, nationally developed tests, such as the Multistate Essay Examination and the Multistate Performance Test), are used to round out the test.

In addition, almost all jurisdictions require that the applicant present an acceptable score on the Multistate Professional Responsibility Examination, which is separately administered three times each year.

The second area of inquiry by bar examiners involves the character and fitness of applicants for a law license. In this regard, bar examiners seek background information concerning each applicant that is relevant to the appropriateness of granting a professional credential. Because law is a public profession, and because the degree of harm a lawyer, once licensed, can inflict is substantial, decisions about who should be admitted to practice law are made carefully by bar examining boards.

Boards of bar examiners in most jurisdictions expect to hear from prospective candidates during the final year of law school. Bar examinations are ordinarily offered at the end of February and July, with considerably more applicants taking the summer test because it falls after graduation from law school. Some boards offer or require law student registration at an earlier point in law school. This preliminary processing, where available, permits the board to review character and fitness issues in advance.

Over time, bar examinations have had some unanticipated consequences. Because bar examinations follow a content pattern substantially identical to that borrowed from the law school curriculum, the pattern of the local bar examination, in turn, strongly inhibits change in educational programs. The extent to which a school introduces innovative programs or markedly deviates in its curriculum from traditional programs places its graduates at a competitive disadvantage in taking a bar examination. Moreover, because law schools are accredited according to, among other criteria, the number of students who pass the bar exam, and are often rated by students according to this standard, legal education has become very much examination-oriented in many states. Subjects included in the examination are required of the students, and courses in those subjects are often molded according to the questions asked on the examinations.

More and more law school graduates, in preparation for the local bar examination, take cram courses and sit through six hours of daily lectures for 6 to 12 solid weeks, memorizing endless outlines and gimmicks of local examinationship—which will be erased from their minds within months after the examination date. And more and more of them take out "bar exam loans," averaging $5,000, to pass the fiscal bridge between commencement and the first paycheck, to pay for living expenses and for the $1,100 to $1,500 cost of bar review course (Anderson, 1995). There is also a registration fee, which can be several hundred dollars and varies from state to state. Whatever improvement is made in law schools greatly increases the necessity of this type of cramming, unless the bar examinations change, too. Apparently, there is a payoff for intense preparation; the percentage of 1994 law school graduates who passed the bar exam was the highest in the past 25 years (Myers, 1995). The percentage of those passing the bar the first time remains relatively high, and in 2006, about 70 percent passed. There is a fair amount of variation in the percentage of those who pass the bar exam by state, ranging from, for example, 60 percent in California to 90 percent in Utah. Those who do not pass the first time can try it again—and again depending on state bar admission guidelines. Not everyone who passes the bar exam will seek admission to the bar.

In addition to educational qualifications of would-be lawyers, bar associations restrict admission procedures to those who are morally fit to become lawyers. Applicants for admission to the bar must have "good moral character" (the same way university faculty are expected to have good moral turpitude). But the definition of this standard is weak. Basically, it means that no one who has a serious criminal record can be admitted to the practice of law. In some cases, it has led to the refusal of a board of examiners to admit someone who has held (or still holds) unpopular political views, and during the McCarthy era, the ABA urged that all those who would become lawyers should take a loyalty oath as a condition of practice (Green, 1976:5). Although the standards are vague, historically the U.S. Supreme Court often upheld the authority of state courts to refuse admission to individuals whom the state deemed unworthy to practice law. Admission is a privilege that a court may withhold. Through such actions, bar associations effectively control the entry of some individuals who could potentially damage the image of the legal profession or directly or indirectly jeopardize the economic interests of its members as it will be discussed in the following section. (American Bar Association, 2007).

BAR ASSOCIATIONS AS INTEREST GROUPS

In addition to restricting entry into the profession and seeking to control the activity of their members, bar associations are interest groups actively engaged in the promotion of activities that the bar considers vital to its interests.

Much of the bar's activity concerns the organization and personnel of the courts. Bar associations attempted repeatedly to devise and to promote court reorganization schemes. Much of this effort went into the elimination of nonprofessional elements from the judicial process. The bar has also been active in seeking to influence the selection of judges. On the state level, where judges are often elected on a partisan or nonpartisan ballot, the bar association has frequently lobbied for a change in selection procedures that would give the bar a greater voice. The bar also influences the selection of federal judges, and it is now a standard procedure for the attorney general of the United States to seek the ABA's opinion about political nominees when choosing a name for submission by the president to the Senate. The bar is also active in promoting legislation that will benefit lawyers and the administrators of justice. For example, the bar actively promoted legislation against the unauthorized practice of law (UPL), which includes software programs and manuals for creating wills, contracts, or simple divorce papers (*Time*, 1998), in an attempt to safeguard its monopoly of legal services. UPL statutes are billed as a way of protecting customers from charlatans. But their practical effect has been to protect lawyers from lower-priced competition. The dispensation of legal advice has been defined so broadly that in recent years people have been investigated for typing up legal forms and for inspecting the siding on houses to see if homeowners are eligible to join a class-action suit against a manufacturer.

In addition to taking a leading part in shaping laws (especially on criminal and regulatory matters), structuring the legal system, and making recommendations for judicial positions, the national and state bar associations have often turned to politics to promote their professional and economic interests. Such efforts have resulted in, among other things, state regulations that limit the number of lawyers and raise the income of those who do practice. Associations of trial lawyers have also sought to influence state and national legislations or regulations that are regarded as affecting their economic interests. For example, trial lawyers opposed no-fault automobile insurance, whereby people in an automobile accident can collect from their own insurance companies without having to hire a lawyer, go to court, and establish liability—whose proponents say that it would save drivers some $40 billion annually in lower premiums (Passell, 1998). Other attempts of the bar to enhance the economic status of its members include the promotion of continued benefits for self-employed lawyers, permission for lawyers to practice before federal agencies without having to obtain special admission or take a special admission examination, promotion of a bill to remove ceilings on attorneys' fees in federal departments and agencies, opposition to bankruptcy reform that would remove lawyers from the proceedings, and opposition to the extension of the role of title companies in home closings at the expense of lawyers (Green, 1976:7). But because of the rising concern over the cost and quality of legal representation in the United States, there have been arguments that formally trained attorneys are not the best advocates in many situations. For example, in a well-documented book, *Legal Advocacy: Lawyers and Nonlawyers at Work*,

Herbert M Kritzer (1998) describes lawyers and nonlawyer advocates at work in four different legal situations—unemployment compensation claim appeals, Social Security disability appeals, state tax appeals, and labor grievance arbitrations—and concludes that nonlawyers can be effective advocates and, in some legal settings, more effective than many lawyers.

Organized bar also opposes the spread of legal self-help materials and the growth of the self-help industry, which dispenses step-by-step guidance for solving common legal problems and translating legalese into plain English. But books on how to avoid paying for lawyers have sold well for centuries. The popular eighteenth century tome, *Every Man His Own Lawyer*, advertised itself as a "complete guide in all matters of law and business negotiations."

Not surprisingly, publishers of self-help legal books and software are reporting brisk sales (Benjamin, 2001). These popular legal resources are useful for simple matters such as simple will, no-fault divorces, landlord–tenant disputes, bankruptcies, and other bread and butter issues that previously used to be the exclusive domain of lawyers. They specialize in routine paperwork—the legal equivalent of the common cold. Their books mostly guide people through tasks that lawyers delegate to their secretaries and paralegals, like setting up basic wills. The fee of $150–$400 per hour that attorneys usually charge for those services is quite a bit above the average nonlawyer's hourly wage, and some people seek more economical alternatives. Even though many lawyers invoke the old maxim that a person who represents himself "has a fool for a client," Nolo Press, founded in 1971 by two legal-aid attorneys and is one the more successful publishers of legal self-help material (100 or so titles annually), sells hundreds of thousands of books such as *How to Do Your Own Divorce in California*. Similar titles are available for other states, and judging by the numbers, they are being used. For example, 12.3 percent of the divorce petitions filed in St. Louis County were by do-it-yourselfers in 2003. Nationally, between 10 percent and 15 percent of divorce petitions are filed without the use of lawyers (Lhotka, 2003). It should be noted, however, that Nolo and other similar publishers also flag areas that require professional legal assistance, and they coach their readers about how to ask informed questions when they consult an attorney.

There are also video clips that deal with legal topics and the ubiquitous Internet for those who are wired (try www.nolo.com to see an illustration of the variety of legal products available in cyberspace). It is interesting to note that defendants without lawyers succeed more frequently in civil court but tend to flounder in more complex criminal cases that involve forensic evidence. In such instances, a judge must rule out mental illness and assess whether the accused is making an informed decision to cast aside representation. Examples of some high-profile criminal defendants who have fought their own legal battles are serial killer Ted Bundy; Jack Kevorkian, whose suicide machine brought him notoriety; and James Traficant, former Ohio congressman convicted on racketeering charges in 2001. September 11 accused co-conspirator Zacarias Moussaoui also tried to represent himself until a federal judged ruled against it in late 2003 on the grounds that he was clogging the court with frivolous legal filings filled with insults and threats (McCaffrey, 2003).

Of course, the bar associations, like all professional associations (and unions), have, as one of their primary functions, the promotion of the social, political, and economic interests of their members. Ideally, at least, there is a fundamental difference between the legal profession and other professions. Fred Rodell of Yale is quoted as stating that "while law is supposed to be a device to serve society . . . it is pretty hard to find a group less concerned with serving society and more concerned with serving themselves than lawyers" (Green, 1976:19). Thus, it is not surprising that the most discernible common cause of bar associations is the needs of their lawyers and those clients whose interests they regularly attend. Bar associations, in the final analysis, have been rather successful in preserving lawyers' monopoly on legal practice and the profession's lucrative role in society.

PROFESSIONAL DISCIPLINE

One of the characteristics of a profession is a code of ethics. A profession involves, among other things, a sense of service and responsibility to the community, and the conduct required of a professional is delineated in a code of ethics for that profession. A lawyer's code of ethics deals with his or her relations with clients, other lawyers, the court, and the public (Carle, 2005; Hazard and Dondi, 2004; Kauffman, 2009; Rhode and Luban, 2005; Rhode and Hazard, 2007).

The legal profession has long been concerned with the ethical forms under which lawyers operate. In 1908, the ABA published its *Canons of Ethics*. In 1969, it was revised and called the *Model Code of Professional Responsibility*. The standards of professional conduct promulgated by the code were adopted by most states. The code covered a variety of important rules from representation of conflicting interests and preservation of clients' confidences to matters of professional etiquette. In 1977, the ABA decided that the code was insufficient in view of the changing nature of the profession and established a commission to come up with a new, more realistic, and more practical set of ethical rules.

In 1983, the ABA adopted the *Model Rules of Professional Conduct and Code of Judicial Conduct* (American Law Institute, 1989). It contains a series of guidelines and rules on matters such as fees, confidentiality of information, certain types of conflict of interest, safekeeping property, UPL, advertising, and reporting professional misconduct. Some of these are from time to time modified at the ABA's annual meetings—allowing lawyers to disclose confidences when doing so prevents "reasonably certain death or substantial body harm" or prohibiting a lawyer from having sex with a client unless a consensual sexual relationship predated the professional contact. In this context, it is interesting to note that the language is much stronger than the ethical guidelines for other professional associations such as university professors or accountants.

The 2007 edition of the *Model Rules of Professional Conduct* provides an up-to-date resource for information on lawyer ethics. The topics include:

- Client–lawyer relationship   Addressing issues of competence, diligence, communication, fees, confidentiality, conflict of interest, safekeeping property, declining representation, sale of a law practice;
- The lawyer as counselor   The lawyer's role as advisor and intermediary;
- The lawyer as advocate   On meritorious claims, expediting litigation, fairness and impartiality, trial publicity, the lawyer as witness, special responsibilities of a prosecutor;

- Transactions with persons other than clients   Dealing and communicating with third parties and unrepresented persons;
- Law firms and associations   Examining the right to practice; responsibilities toward partners, associates, and nonlawyer assistants; UPL; restrictions on right to practice;
- Public service   Pro bono service and other community activities;
- Information about legal services   Advertising and other communications with prospective clients;
- Maintaining the integrity of the profession   Disciplinary and misconduct matters, including information on political contributions to obtain legal engagements or appointments by judge.

A serious weakness of the codes and model rules is that they are not binding on lawyers and the adoption of them is not required by local groups. The ABA exerts no control over state bars in this process. Furthermore, enforcement is not obligatory. Although the ABA advocates uniform standards in disciplinary procedures, it is unable to instrument uniform adherence.

Disciplinary authorities are supposed to make sure that only honest and competent people are licensed to practice law. In some states, the disciplinary committee operates under the auspices of the state court system. In others, the bar organization runs the disciplinary agency and investigates complaints but any sanctions are imposed by the courts. Although the procedures vary from state to state, the boards investigate complaints about alleged violations of professional rules of conduct.

In general, disciplinary sanctions, such as reprimand, suspension, or disbarment, are imposed only for serious instances of misconduct, such as criminal acts, mishandling of client's property, and flagrant violation of certain rules of professional conduct, such as breach of confidentiality. Some of these sanctions are in addition to possible criminal proceedings, which are handled separately by law-enforcement authorities, and they may publicize the sanctions as a form of "risk prevention" (Davis, 1995). Of course, unhappy clients can always sue their lawyers, and an indirect form of punishment is the very high cost of attorneys' malpractice insurance (Hazard, 1994; Rhode and Hazard, 2007). Other rule violations rarely evoke formal disciplinary action, although there is informal discipline in the form of expressed disapproval, which carries its own practical penalties, such as questions about one's professional reputation. It is interesting to note that, unlike psychiatrists and psychologists who for some time now have been ethically proscribed from sleeping with patients—and college professors with students—the ABA only recently took an official position on lawyers engaging in sexual relations with clients. A *National Law Journal* article headline nicely captured an opposing viewpoint, stating: "Draconian Sex Rules Premature" (Barker and Rhodes, 1992), although some states began to consider "attorney sex guidelines" baring most lawyer–client sex (Dilworth, 1993). In 2001, the ABA adopted a ban against lawyer–client sex. Sex between a client and lawyer can pose significant dangers to both the client and the lawyer. The client is often the vulnerable person in the relationship and can even personally depend on the lawyer, especially in family law or domestic relations cases. The lawyer needs a certain amount of emotional distance to keep his client's interests in mind as well. In today's litigious climate, sex between clients and lawyers, lawyers and employees, or even between two lawyers can create considerable ethical, professional, and legal risks for those involved.

Generally, the highest ethical standards are found among attorneys who work for large firms (Carlin, 1966:47–48) and represent big-business clients in more traditional fields such as patents and admiralty. Those who represent individuals in cases that are characterized as "unsavory," such as personal injury plaintiffs' work, divorce, and criminal defense, tend to have lower ethical standards (Heinz and Laumann, 1994). These are usually lower-status solo practitioners who practice before state courts. As Herbert Jacob (1984:62) notes, the more contact such attorneys have with lower courts, the less likely they are to comply with legal ethics: "The culture of lower courts—waiting around, exchanging gossip, litigating petty criminal and civil cases" promotes unethical conduct.

Violations of legal ethics may be punished by a reprimand, a temporary suspension of the license to practice law, or the revocation of the license (see, for example, Rhode and Hazard, 2007). Jerome E. Carlin (1966:170) found that only about 2 percent of the lawyers who violated ethical norms were even processed by the bar's disciplinary machine, and only 0.2 percent were officially sanctioned. In 1972, bar associations disciplined 357 lawyers, roughly one-tenth of 1 percent of practicing lawyers at that time (Garbus and Seligman, 1976:48). In 1984, 59,862 complaints were received by the disciplinary boards in 48 states. That number represents about 8 percent of all practicing attorneys. During the same year, 1,408 lawyers received public sanctions (disbarment, suspension, and public reprimand), and 1,833 received private sanctions (reprimand and formal admonition) (Austern, 1986:17). Although the bar spent more than $30 million for lawyer discipline, the enforcement of the ethical standards it has promulgated for the guidance of its members leaves something to be desired when only 5.4 percent of those who had complaints against them were subjected to either public or private sanctions. In 1994, the ABA created a nationwide, online database of disbarred and censured lawyers, some 25,000 to start with, to keep track of lawyers who move from state to state. The service is available to disciplinary authorities but not to consumer groups, because in case of the slightest inaccuracy, it could harm a lawyer's reputation and lead to potential lawsuits. Discipline boards and state bar associations welcome the service. Because each state regulates its own lawyers, discipline is complicated as lawyers become increasingly mobile and register in more than one state. Lawyers who are disciplined in one state can move to another, take the bar examination, and start over without alerting authorities or potential clients of the infractions (Stevens, 1994).

How serious are lawyers about professional responsibility? In a 1985 poll conducted for the *ABA Journal*, Reskin (1985:41) finds that professional responsibility is important to most lawyers; most are familiar with ethical codes in effect in their jurisdiction. Lack of familiarity with the code of professional responsibility is highest (15 percent) among lawyers who are not in private practice—law professors and government, legal-aid, and corporate law department lawyers.

Ethics are emphasized and considered extremely important among partners, according to 66 percent of the respondents. The group that places the greatest accent on ethics consists of lawyers earning more than $75,000 from the practice of law (76 percent). Ethics are not discussed or emphasized especially among solo practitioners (22 percent) and lawyers not in private practice (27 percent). These findings are consistent with studies on lawyers' ethics (see, for example, Carlin; 1966, and Heinz and Laumann, 1994) that suggest that high-status lawyers in firms are more likely to adhere to the ethical norms of the profession than their lower-status counterparts in solo practice.

Lawyers have an obligation to report known or suspected ethical violations by other lawyers according to the ethics rules and standards of the governing bodies (Pitulla, 1995; Rhode and Hazard, 2007). But only 7 out of 10 lawyers say that they would report a lawyer outside of their firm who acted unethically, and 6 out of 10 would report a colleague in their own firm. Because 71 percent say they have occasionally encountered dishonest opposing counsel, it is obvious that lawyers should be doing much more reporting. But they are not. Most complaints against lawyers are filed by clients or initiated by the bar council. It is rare that lawyers or judges report lawyer or judicial misconduct. The reasons for not reporting vary from "no use" because nothing would happen and it is not their responsibility to not wanting to ruin someone's career. About 40 percent of the lawyers who do not report misconduct fear that too much time would be taken up testifying in a disciplinary proceeding, do not know where to report the misconduct, or are afraid of being subjected to a lawsuit. Although lawyers claim that ethical conduct is important and the majority are willing to report violation of professional norms, in reality, they are reluctant to do it—which raises serious concerns about the efficacy of the internal modes of control of the profession.

There are also external modes of control of the profession, primarily from the federal government. Both the Federal Trade Commission and the U.S. Department of Justice are concerned with the delivery of legal services in matters of monopolistic restrictions (curbing the provision of legal services to poor and moderate-income people) and practices constituting restraint of trade (such as real estate agents filling out legal forms in closing a deal, which is considered "unauthorized" practice of law). The U.S. Securities and Exchange Commission also has authority to discipline lawyers who practice before it and engage in fraudulent activities by temporarily suspending or disbarring them.

Finally, there is the delicate and difficult problem of monitoring judicial conduct, as well as the relationship between clients and lawyers, lawyers and employees, or even between two lawyers. These relationships can create considerable ethical, professional and legal risks for those involved (see, for example, Morrissey, 2004). How can judges be protected from unfair attacks so that they can maintain their judicial independence and have, at the same time, effective mechanisms for the retirement or removal of those who do not perform their duties properly? In some states, the only procedure for removal of judges before the end of their term is impeachment by a vote of legislators. In others, committees of judges are empowered to investigate judicial incompetence and compel the retirement of a judge found unable to carry out his or her duties (Flood, 1985:42).

The problem is further compounded by the failure of most lawyers to report judicial misconduct that they have witnessed (Reskin, 1985:41). So far, the most dramatic measure for rooting out judicial corruption has been Operation Greylord (Flood, 1985:42). The Federal Bureau of Investigation (FBI) for three-and-a-half years investigated the largest court system in the country, with over 300 judges—the Cook County system, which includes Chicago. The investigation uncovered a variety of corrupt practices by some judges, such as favorable rulings, case referrals, and lighter criminal sentences in return for bribes. Judges also gave permission to attorneys to solicit clients in the courthouse. The FBI relied on agents to represent attorneys and criminals to infiltrate the court, and in one instance, a judge was wired to record conversations between corrupt lawyers and judges. As a result of the FBI investigation, several judges, lawyers, and court officials have been indicted for corruption; four judges so far have been convicted, and one acquitted.

SUMMARY

In all societies, the legal profession has been intimately connected with the rise and development of legal systems. Primitive societies had courts and judges but no lawyers. In such societies, custom and law coincided. No special legal skills were required before a court. With the development of court procedures, a class of skilled advocates emerged. The origins of the legal profession can be traced back to Rome. Lawyers, in the sense of a regulated group of practitioners, emerged in the late 1200s. By that time, the body of legal knowledge, including procedure, had become too much for the ordinary person to handle alone. Technical pleadings required the aid of an attorney, and legal business increased tremendously. In the fourteenth and fifteenth centuries, a secular class of lawyers emerged in England, and the law administered by the royal courts became independent, in some important respects at least, from Roman and canon law. To a large extent, English lawyers received their training in the Inns of Court, at the hands of the legal profession itself, and not in the universities. Blackstone's appointment to the Vinerian Chair of Jurisprudence in 1758 marked the first effort to make English law a university subject.

apprenticeships

Initially, in the United States, legal education was modeled after the British system. Many of the early upper-class American lawyers obtained their training in the Inns of Court. In the late eighteenth and early nineteenth centuries, general courses in law were established in many American universities. However, these courses were in time superseded by the development of university law schools—a form of professional legal education that, strictly speaking, has no counterpart either in England or on the continent of Europe.

Lawyers have established a monopoly on legal business, and the profession of law has become the fastest-growing of all professions in the United States during the last two decades. Although members of the profession have never been popular, lawyers rank high in prestige in the United States. There are four principal subgroups in the legal profession: lawyers in private practice, in government service, in private employment, and in the judiciary. The American legal profession is highly stratified. Lawyers in private practice who are solo practitioners in general tend to have a lower status in the profession than their counterparts working in law firms. The relatively low status of solo practitioners is attributed to their socioeconomic background and to the quality of education they have received. Many solo practitioners use the legal profession as a form of social mobility. Employment with the government is often considered a mobility route into a more prestigious practice for young lawyers. The proportion of lawyers in private employment is on the increase, and they handle only the work of their corporate employer. Some larger corporations today have legal departments that compare in size and excellence with those of the largest law firms. In the United States, there is no career judiciary, and there is no prescribed route for the young law graduate to become a judge. Judges are elected or appointed.

There is substantial variation in income by types of lawyers. Those in law firms and in private employment generally earn more than their counterparts in solo practice or in the judiciary. Income is related to the type of practice, the type of clientele, the degree of specialization, the size of the firm, the quality of education and achievement in law school, the age and length of practice, and the size and location of the place of practice. In recent years, there has been a growing competition for legal business. Although the minimum fee schedules have been abolished (at least in principle) and lawyers are now able to advertise, the cost of legal services is still beyond the reach of many people.

Law and lawyers are expensive. In criminal cases, the poor are represented either by public defenders or by court-appointed attorneys. In civil cases, the poor can gain access to lawyers through public or private legal-aid programs. Others with less limited finances resort to legal clinics or prepaid legal plans as a way of obtaining legal representation.

Contemporary lawyers must submit to a long period of training before becoming eligible to practice. This, however, is a recent development in the United States. Throughout the nineteenth century, legal training was haphazard. Most lawyers received their training in the office of a practicing attorney. They worked for him as a clerk, and by doing so learned the trade themselves. University training of lawyers in the United States did not really begin until after 1870. Today there are 195 law schools approved by the ABA. Entry into a law school requires a college degree, and applicants must have a high grade point average in addition to a moderately high LSAT score. The number of law students tripled during the past two decades, and the number of women in law schools increased almost twentyfold. However, minority students still represent a smaller proportion in law schools than their percentage of the total population. Law school education still relies heavily on the case or Socratic method, which has remained virtually unchanged since its introduction. The method is meant to acclimate the students to "legal reasoning," or to "thinking like a lawyer," but lately it has been subjected to criticisms that, for example, it fails to encourage creativeness and that it lacks intellectual stimulation. It also provokes anxiety, hostility, and aggression in the classroom. Law schools seem to socialize students toward an entrepreneurial value position, and questions that challenge the basis of the legal system are seldom raised. During law school, students tend to change their political orientation in a conservative direction. In response to the growing criticism of the socialization process of law students, law schools in recent years began to emphasize interdisciplinary work and clinical programs. However, concerted efforts to reform curriculum are still opposed.

To maintain standards and to control entry into the bar, law school graduates are required to pass a standardized bar examination in the state where they wish to practice. Bar examinations have stifled changes in legal education. Many students are preoccupied with passing the bar, which forces law schools to mold courses according to the questions asked on the examinations. Bar associations further restrict admission procedures to those who are morally fit to become lawyers. Applicants for admission to the bar must have "good moral character." Bar associations also act as interest groups in promoting social, economic, and political activities that the bar considers vital to its interests. They often act like other interest groups in pressing for adoption of measures desired by their members.

In an attempt to improve the negative public image of lawyers, and to assist the courts in rendering justice, the legal profession adopted a code of ethics in 1908. Although violation of the code of legal ethics may be punished by reprimand, suspension from the bar, or disbarment, only a very small proportion of lawyers who violate the ethical standards are ever subjected to disciplinary action. Ethical codes seem to be more enforced when the profession, rather than the clients or society at large, is threatened.

SUGGESTED FURTHER READINGS

Richard L. Abel, *Lawyers in the Dock: Learning from Attorney Disciplinary Proceedings.* New York: Oxford University Press, 2008. A discussion of a series of disciplinary proceedings with their precipitative factors and consequences.

Richard L. Abel and Philip S. C. Lewis (eds.), *Lawyers in Society: An Overview.* Berkeley, CA: University of California Press, 1995. A compendium of influential cross-cultural articles on the profession and practice of law by leading international authorities.

Maureen Cain and Christine B. Harrington (eds.), *Lawyers in a Postmodern World: Translation and Transgression.* New York: New York University Press, 1994. A collection of articles exploring how lawyers create the forms of power they and others deploy.

Marc Galanter and Thomas Palay, *Tournament of Lawyers: The Transformation of the Big Law Firm.* Chicago, IL: University of Chicago Press, 1991. A provocative study of the growth patterns of large corporate law firms.

Robert Granfield, *Making Elite Lawyers: Visions of Law and Beyond.* New York: Routledge, 1992. A fascinating and timeless empirical work on the conservatizing effects of legal education at Harvard on a broad cross section of students.

Kermit L. Hall and Peter Karsten, *The Magic Mirror: Law in American History.* 2nd ed. New York: Oxford University Press, 2009. An insightful, concise, and chronologically complete history of law in America.

Richard D. Kahlenberg, *Broken Contract: A Memoir of Harvard Law School.* New York: Hill & Wang, 1992. A 1989 Harvard Law School graduate paints a troubling picture of his alma mater. An eye-opening book for law school-bound students.

Anthony T. Kronman, *The Lost Lawyer: Failing Ideals of the Legal Profession.* Cambridge, MA: The Belknap Press of Harvard University Press, 1993. See in particular the second part that examines the realities of lawyering in three institutional settings—law schools, law firms, and the court—from a Weberian perspective.

Anthony T. Kronman (ed.), *A History of the Yale Law School: The Tercentennial Lectures.* New Haven, CT: Yale University Press, 2004. A collection of captivating readings on the emergence of Yale Law School.

Deborah L. Rhode, *Beauty's Bias: The Injustice of Appearance in Life and Law.* New York: Oxford University Press, 2010. Even the blindfolded Themis is affected by appearances, and Rhode describes some of the ways of how it is done.

Austin Sarat and William L. F. Felstiner, *Divorce Lawyers and Their Clients: Power and Meaning in the Legal Process.* New York: Oxford University Press, 1995. An insightful analysis of the activities of divorce lawyers.

Austin Sarat and Stuart Scheingold (eds.), *Cause Lawyering and the State in a Global Era.* New York: Oxford University Press, 2001. A compendium of interesting articles on a variety of causes and their lawyers.

Mark Simenhoff, *My First Year as a Lawyer: Real-World Stories from America's Lawyers.* New York: Walker and Company, 1994. Eighteen lawyers share the stories of their first year of practice, discussing the challenges and rewards of the day-to-day of novice attorneys.

REFERENCES

ABA Journal. 1986. "Lawyer Advertising Is on the Rise," 72 (April): 44.

Abel, Richard L. 1986. "The Transformation of the American Legal Profession," *Law & Society Review*, 20 (1): 7–17. 2003. *English Lawyers between Market and State: The Politics of Professionalism.* Oxford, UK/New York: Oxford University Press.

Abrams, Floyd. 1994. "Why Lawyers Lie: The Truth Is Not the Highest Priority in a Criminal Trial," *New York Times Magazine* (October 9): 54.

American Bar Association. 1959. "Better Lawyers for Tomorrow: Code Standards for Bar Examiners," *American Bar Association Journal*, 45 (June): 583–589. 1995. *A Review of Legal Education in the United States, Fall, 1994.* Chicago, IL: American Bar Association, Section on Legal Education and Admission to the Bar. 2007. *Standards and Rules of Procedure for Approval of Law Schools.* American Bar Association, Section on Legal Education and Admissions to the Bar. Chicago, IL: American Bar Association

American Law Institute. 1989. *Professional Ethics and Responsibility.* Boston, MA: The American Law Institute.

Anderson, Lisa. 1995. "Bridging the Income Gap After Law School: Graduates Turn to Bar Exam Loans," *New York Times* (July 2): 14F.

Auerbach, Jerold S. 1976. *Unequal Justice: Lawyers and Social Change in Modern America.* New York: Oxford University Press.

Austern, David. 1986. "How Lawyers Police Themselves," *Trial*, 22 (4) (April): 17.

Bankowski, Zenon, and James MacLean (eds.) 2007. *The Universal and the Particular in Legal Reasoning.* Burlington, VT: Ashgate.

Barker, William T., and C. Harker Rhodes, Jr. 1992. "Draconian Sex Rules Premature," *National Law Journal*, 14 (43) (June 29): 17.

Beam, Alex. 2004. "Greed On Trial," *Atlantic* (June): 96–108.

Beckett, Katherine, and Steve Herbert. 2009. *Banished: The New Social Control in America.* New York: Oxford University Press.

Belford, Terrence. 2004. "Law Firms Grapple with Going Public," *Globe and Mail* (February 2): B12.

Benjamin, Matthew. 2001. "Legal Self-Help: Cheap Counsel for Simple Cases," *U.S. News & World Report* (February 12): 54–56.

Berman, Harold J., William R. Greiner, and Samir N. Saliba. 2004. *The Nature and Functions of Law.* 6th ed. New York: The Foundation Press.

Blachman, Jeremy. 2006. *Anonymous Lawyer.* New York: Henry Holt and Company.

Blohm, Craig E. 2004. *The Great Society: America Fights the War on Poverty.* San Diego, CA: Lucent Books.

Blohm, Lindsay. 2006. *Presumed Equal: What America's Top Women Lawyers Really Think about Their Firms.* Bloomington, IN: AuthorHouse.

Bonsignore, John J., Ethan Katsh, Peter d'Errico, Ronald M. Pipkin, Stephen Arons, and Janet Rifkin. 1989. *Before the Law: An Introduction to the Legal Process.* 4th ed. Boston, MA: Houghton Mifflin.

Brand, Ronald A., and D. Wes Rist (eds.). 2009. *The Export of Legal Education: Its Promise and Impact in Transition Countries.* Burlington, VT: Ashgate.

Brundage, James A. 2010. *The Medieval Origins of the Legal Profession: Canonists, Civilians, and Courts.* Chicago, IL: University Of Chicago Press.

Business Week. 1989. "Punitive Damages: How Much Is Too Much?" March: 54–56.

Cameron, George Dana, III. 1978. *The Soviet Lawyer and His System.* Ann Arbor, MI:

Division of Research, Graduate School of Business Administration, the University of Michigan.

Carle, Susan D. (ed.). 2005. *Lawyers' Ethics and the Pursuit of Social Justice: A Critical Reader*. New York: New York University Press.

Carlin, Jerome E. 1962. *Lawyers on Their Own*. New Brunswick, NJ: Rutgers University Press. 1966. *Lawyers' Ethics*. New York: Russell Sage Foundation.

Carnahan, Douglas G. 1992. "Judges Need a Trade School," *National Law Journal*, 14 (32) (April 13): 15.

Carney, Michael E. 1990. "Narcissistic Concerns in the Educational Experience of Law Students," *Journal of Psychiatry & Law*, 18 (1) (Spring–Summer): 9–34.

Carp, Robert A., Ronald Stidham, and Kenneth L. Manning. 2010. *Judicial Process in America*. 8th ed. Washington, DC: CQ Press.

Carrese, Paul O. 2003. *The Cloaking of Power: Montesquieu, Blackstone, and the Rise of Judicial Activism*. Chicago, IL: University of Chicago Press.

Cebula, Mark A. 1998. "Does Lawyer Advertising Adversely Influence the Image of Lawyers in the United States? An Alternative Perspective and New Empirical Evidence," *Journal of Legal Studies*, 27 (2) (June): 503–518.

Chamallas, Martha, and Jennifer B. Wriggins. 2010. *The Measure of Injury: Race, Gender, and Tort Law*. New York: New York University Press.

Chambliss, William J., and Robert B. Seidman. 1971. *Law, Order, and Power*. Reading, MA: Addison-Wesley.

Chronicle of Higher Education Almanac. 2010. "Average Pay of Full-Time Professors, Public Institutions."

Cotterman, James D. (ed.). 2004. *Compensation Plans for Law Firms*. 4th ed. Chicago, IL: American Bar Association, Law Practice Management Section.

Crier, Catherine. 2002. *The Case against Lawyers: How Lawyers, Politicians, and Bureaucrats Have Turned the Law into an Instrument of Tyranny, and What We as Citizens Have to Do about It*. New York: Broadway Books.

Curran, Barbara. 1986. "American Lawyers in the 1980s: A Profession in Transition," *Law & Society Review*, 20 (1): 19–52.

Curriden, Mark. 1995a. "Female Lawyers See Bias in Their Arrests: Cursing and Culottes Were Unacceptable to Authorities in Texas, Florida," *ABA Journal*, 81 (March): 28–29. 1995b. "Lawyers Who Skip Law School: Seven States Allow Read-law Programs Despite ABA's Opposition," *ABA Journal*, 81 (February); 28–30.

Dare, Tim. 2009. *The Counsel of Rogues? A Deference of the Standard Conception of the Lawyer's Role*. Burlington, VT: Ashgate.

Davis, Angela J. 2009. *Arbitrary Justice: The Power of the American Prosecutor*. New York: Oxford University Press.

Davis, Ann. 1995. "Title Insurers Eye N.J. Lawyers under Ethics Cloud: Newly Opened Disciplinary Process Lets Them Keep Tabs," *National Law Journal*, 17 (30) (March 27): A7.

Dilworth, Donald C. 1993. "New York Tightens Rules for Matrimonial Lawyers, May Extend Coverage to Others," *Trial*, 29 (10) (October): 13–16

Economist. 1994. "Paying the Judge: Legal Costs (Litigant's Fees Hiked to Pay Judges' Salaries in Great Britain)" (February 26): 59. 2004. "Trying to Get the Right Balance" (February 28): 65–67. 2006. "Now the Hard Part: A Survey of Business in India" (June 3): 1–18. 2010. "Professional Service Firms: Laid-off Lawyers, Cast-off Consultants" (January 23):64

Erlanger, Howard S., and Douglas A. Klegon. 1978. "Socialization Effects of Professional School: The Law School Experience and Student Orientations to Public Interest Concerns," *Law & Society Review*, 13 (1) Fall: 11–35.

Farber, Daniel A., and Suzanna Sherry. 1997. *Beyond All Reason: The Radical Assault on Truth in American Law*. New York: Oxford University Press.

Farmer, A. 2010. "Are Young Women Turning Their Backs on Law School?" *Perspectives*:

A Magazine for and about Women Lawyers, 18 (4) Spring: 4–7.

Fleming, Macklin. 1997. *Lawyers, Money, and Success: The Consequences of Dollar Obsessions*. Westport, CN: Quorum.

Flood, John. 1985. *The Legal Profession in the United States*. 3rd ed. Chicago, IL: American Bar Foundation.

Flores, Albert (ed.). 1988. *Professional Ideals*. Belmont, CA: Wadsworth.

Foote, Nelson N. 1953. "The Professionalization of Labor in Detroit," *American Journal of Sociology*, 58 (4) (January): 371–380.

Fotheringham, Allan. 1994. "The Law According to the Chequebook—The Duplicity of Lawyers," *Maclean's*, 107 (43) (October 24): 60–61.

Frank, Christopher. 2010. *Master and Servant Law: Chartists, Trade Unions, Radical Lawyers and the Magistracy in England, 1840–1865*. Burlington, VT: Ashgate.

Freeland, Richard M. 1992. *Academia's Golden Age*. New York: Oxford University Press.

Freivogel, William H. 1995. "Limits on Lawyers' Ads Upheld," *St. Louis Post-Dispatch* (June 22): 7A.

Friedman, Lawrence M. 1977. *Law and Society: An Introduction*. Englewood Cliffs, NJ: Prentice Hall. 1998. *American Law: An Introduction*. 2nd ed. New York: W. W. Norton & Company, Inc. 2002. *American Law in the Twentieth Century*, New Haven, CT: Yale University Press. 2005. *A History of American Law*. 3rd ed. New York: Simon & Schuster.

Fritsch, Jane, and David Rohde. 2001. "Legal Help Often Fails New York's Poor," *New York Times* (April 8): 1, 27.

Frohmann, Lisa (ed.). 2009. *Prosecutors and Prosecution*. Burlington, VT: Ashgate.

Frum, David. 1994. "How to Rob a Bank, Sturdevant & Sturdevant Law Firm Sues Banks," *Forbes*, 153 (5) (February 28): 62–63.

Galanter, Marc. 1992. "The Debased Debate on Civil Justice." Working Paper DPRP 10-10. Madison, WI: University of Wisconsin, Institute for Legal Studies. 2005. *Lowering the Bar: Lawyer Jokes and Legal Culture*, Madison, WI: University of Wisconsin Press.

Gandhi, J. S. 1982. *Lawyers and Touts: A Study in the Sociology of Legal Profession*. Delhi, India: Hindustan Publishing Corporation.

Garbus, Martin, and Joel Seligman. 1976. "Sanctions and Disbarment: They Sit in Judgement." Pp. 47–60 in Ralph Nader and Mark Green (eds.), *Verdicts on Lawyers*. New York: Thomas Y. Crowell.

Gee, James Paul. 2010. *An Introduction to Discourse Analysis: Theory and Method*. 3rd ed. Milton Park, Abingdon, NY: Routledge.

Gilgoff, Dan. 2004. "Law Schools Go International," *U.S. News & World Report* (April 12): 58–62.

Gitelson, Alan, Robert Dudley, and Melvin Dubnick. 2008. *American Government*. 8th ed. Boston, MA: Houghton Mifflin.

Glaberson, William, 2001. "A Study's Verdict: Jury Awards Are Not Out Of Control," *New York Times* (August 6): A1.

Glater, Jonathan D. 2001a. "Few Minorities Rising to Law Partner," *New York Times* (August 7): A1, A6. 2001b. "Law School Beckons as Economy Slows," *New York Times* (August 24): A1, A7.

Glendon, Mary Ann, Paolo G. Carozza, and Colin B. Picker. 2008. *Comparative Legal Tradition in a Nutshell*. 3rd ed. St. Paul, MI.: Thomson/West Publishing Company.

Graham, Deborah. 1995. "Law's New Entrepreneurs," *ABA Journal*, 81 (February): 54–60.

Granfield, Robert, and Lynn Mather (eds.). 2009. *Private Lawyers and the Public Interest: The Evolving Role of Pro Bono in the Legal Profession*. New York: Oxford University Press.

Grange, Lori, and David Schwartz. 1995. "Lawyers Answer Public Service Call," *Human Rights*, 22 (1) (Winter): 34–36.

Green, Mark J. 1975. "The High Cost of Lawyers," *New York Times Magazine* (August 10): 8–9, 53–56. 1976. "The ABA as Trade Association." Pp. 3–19 in Ralph Nader and Mark Green (eds.), *Verdicts on Lawyers*. New York: Thomas Y. Crowell.

Grillo, Ralph, Roger Ballard, Allesandro Ferrari, Andre Hoekema, Marcel Maussen, and Prakash Shah (eds.). 2009. *Legal Practice and Cultural Diversity*. Burlington, VT: Ashgate.

Gross, Edward. 1998. "Lawyers and Their Discontents," *Society*, 36 (1) (November/December): 26–31.

Gunning, Jennifer, Soren Holm, and Ian Kenway (eds.). 2009. *Ethics, Law, and Society.* Volume IV. Burlington, VT: Ashgate.

Hagan, John, Marie Huxter, and Patricia Parker. 1988. "Class Structure and Legal Practice: Inequality and Mobility among Toronto Lawyers," *Law & Society Review*, 22 (1): 9–55.

Halliday, Terence C. 1986. "Six Score Years and Ten: Demographic Transitions in the American Legal Profession, 1850–1980," *Law & Society Review*, 20 (1): 53–78.

Hansen, Mark. 1994. "A Shunned Justice System: Most Families Don't Turn to Lawyers or Judges to Solve Legal Problems, Survey Says," *ABA Journal*, 80 (April): 18–20.

Harlan, Christi, and Milo Geyelin. 1992. "Tennessee Backs Punitive Damage Change," *Wall Street Journal* (May 8): B5.

Harvard Law Review. 1994. "The Eighth Amendment and Ineffective Assistance of Counsel in Capital Trials," 107 (8) (June): 1923–1940.

Haskell, Paul G. 1998. *Why Lawyers Behave As They Do.* Boulder, CO: Westview Press.

Hastie, Reid, David Schkade, and John Payne. 1998. "A Study of Juror and Jury Judgments in Civil Cases: Deciding Liability for Punitive Damages." *Law and Human Behavior*, 22 (3) (June): 287–314.

Hazard, Geoffrey C. 1994. "Liability Coverage May Become Impossible to Obtain under Traditional Procedures," *National Law Journal*, 16 (28) (March): A17.

Hazard, Geoffrey C. Jr., and Angelo Dondi. 2004. *Legal Ethics: A Comparative Study*. Stanford, CA: Stanford University Press

Heinz, John P., and Edward O. Laumann. 1994. *Chicago Lawyers: The Social Structure of the Bar.* Revised ed. Evanston, IL: Northwestern University Press; Chicago, IL: American Bar Foundation.

Hines, Crystal Nix. 2001. "Lack of Lawyers Blocking Appeals in Capital Cases," *New York Times* (July 5): A1, A5.

Hurst, J. Willard. 1950. *The Growth of American Law.* Boston, MA: Little, Brown and Company.

Jacob, Herbert. 1984. *Justice in America: Courts, Lawyers, and the Judicial Process.* 4th ed. Boston, MA: Little, Brown and Company. 1995. *Law and Politics in the United States.* 2nd ed. Ft. Washington, PA: HarperCollins College Publishers.

Jacobson, Robert L. 1979. "Law Schools Are Cool to Chief Justice's Ideas on Reforming Curriculum," *Chronicle of Higher Education*, 17 (18) (January 15): 10.

Jacoby, Henry. 1973. *The Bureaucratization of the World.* Trans. Eveline L. Kanes. Berkeley and Los Angeles, CA: University of California Press.

Jeffery, C. Ray. 1962. "The Legal Profession." Pp. 313–356 in F. James Davis, Henry H. Foster, Jr., C. Ray Jeffery, and E. Eugene Davis, *Society and the Law: New Meanings for an Old Profession.* New York: Free Press.

Jenkins, John A. 1977. "The Revolving Door between Government and the Law Firms," *Washington Monthly*, 8 (11) (January): 36–44.

Johnson, Dirk. 1995. "More Scorn and Less Money Dim Law's Lure," *New York Times* (September 22): A1, A8.

Jones, Ashby. 2007. "More Law Firms Charge Fixed Fees for Routine Jobs," *Wall Street Journal* (May 2): B1.

Kauffman, Kent D. 2009. *Legal Ethics*. 2nd ed. Clifton Park, NY: Delmar Cengage Learning.

Kay, Fiona M. 1997. "Flight from Law: A Competing Risks Model of Departures from Law Firms," *Law & Society Review*, 31 (2): 301–333.

Kay, Susan Ann. 1978. "Socializing the Future Elite: The Nonimpact of a Law School," *Social Science Quarterly*, 59 (2) (September): 347–356.

Kearney, Hugh. 1970. Scholars and Gentlemen: Universities and Society in Pre-Industrial Britain. Ithaca, NY: Cornell University Press.

Keeva, Steven. 1995. "Standing Up for Women," *ABA Journal*, 81 (April): 118–119.

Kennedy, Daniel B. 1994. "The Payback: The Way to Gauge the Effectiveness of Advertising is by the Business it Brings In,"*ABA Journal*, 80 (June) 62–65.

King, Marsha. 2006. "'Graying of the Bar' Fueling Concern in Court" *Seattle Times* (April 9): B1, B5.

Klein, Mitchell S. G. 1984. *Law, Courts, and Policy*. Englewood Cliffs, NJ: Prentice Hall.

Koo, Gene, 2007. "New Skills, New Learning: Legal Education and the Promise of New Technology" (March 26). Available at SSRN: http://ssrn.com/abstract=976646.

Koppel, Nathan. 2006. "Lawyer's Charge Opens Window on Bill Padding," *Wall Street Journal* (August 30): B1, B2. 2010. "Using Web Tools to Control Legal Bills. Big Law Firms Turn to Technology to Provide Clients with Real-Time Expenses, Automate Tasks," *Wall Street Journal* (January 5): B6.

Krauss, Michael. 2007. "Tort-Eating Contest: Competition Could Reduce Liability Costs," *Wall Street Journal* (May 2): A20.

Kritzer, Herbert M. 1990. *The Justice Broker: Lawyers and Ordinary Litigation*. New York: Oxford University Press. 1998. *Legal Advocacy: Lawyers and Nonlawyers at Work*. Ann Arbor, MI: University of Michigan Press. 2004. *Risks, Reputations, and Rewards: Contingency Fee Legal Practice in the United States*. Stanford, CA: Stanford University Press.

Kritzer, Herbert M., William L. F. Felstiner, Austin Sarat, and David M. Trubek. 1985. "The Impact of Free Arrangement on Lawyer Effort," *Law & Society Review*, 19 (2): 251–278.

Kritzer, Herbert M., and Susan S. Silbey (eds.). 2003. *In Litigation: Do the Haves Still Come out Ahead?* Stanford, CA: Stanford Law and Politics.

Ladinsky, Jack. 1963. "Careers of Lawyers, Law Practice, and Legal Institutions," *American Sociological Review*, 28 (1) (February): 47–54. 1967. "Higher Education and Work Achievement among Lawyers," *Sociological Quarterly*, 8 (2): 222–232.

Larson, Magali Sarfatti. 1977. *The Rise of Professionalism: A Sociological Analysis.*

Berkeley and Los Angeles, CA: University of California Press.

Lawyer's Almanac, 2010. 2010. Englewood Cliffs, NJ: Aspen Law and Business, a division of Aspen Publishers, Inc.

Lhotka, William C. 2003. "Do-It-Yourself Divorces." *St. Louis Post-Dispatch* (November 3): A1, A10.

Leatherman, Courtney. 1989. "Law-School Students Protest Scarcity of Female and Minority Professors," *Chronicle of Higher Education* (April 19): A32–A33.

Legal Services Corporation. 2006. "Documenting the Justice Gap in America: The Current Unmet Civil Legal Needs of Low-Income Americans." Washington, DC: Legal Services Corporation.

Leonard, Walter J. 1977. *Black Lawyers*. Boston, MA: Senna and Shih.

Lerman, Steven. 1995. "A King's Ransom: Excerpts from Rodney King Attorney's Bill," *Harper's Magazine* (April): 20–23.

Levit, Nancy, and Douglas O. Linder. 2010. *The Happy Lawyer: Making a Good Life in the Law*. New York: Oxford University Press.

Lewin, Tamar. 2010. "Law School Admissions Lag among Minorities," *New York Times* (January 7): A1.

Lewis, P. S. C. 1986. "A Comparative Perspective on the Legal Profession in the 1980s," *Law & Society Review*, 20 (1): 79–91.

Loh, Wallace D. 1984. *Social Research in the Judicial Process: Cases, Readings, and Text.* New York: Russell Sage Foundation.

Macdonald, Keith M. 1995. *The Sociology of Professions.* Thousand Oaks, CA: Sage Publications, Inc.

Mangan, Katherine S. 1998a. "Students' Odds of Getting into Law School Improve, but Their Qualifications Drop," *Chronicle of Higher Education* (January 23): A41–42. 1998b. "Law Professors, Calling Their Institutions Complacent, Urge Curricular Changes," *Chronicle of Higher Education* (January 16): A14.

McCaffrey, Shannon. 2003. "Moussaoui Can't Represent Self. Court-Appointed Lawyers Will Take Over Case." *Seattle Times* (November 15): A5.

McIntyre, Lisa J. 1987. *The Public Defender: The Practice of Law in the Shadows of Repute.* Chicago, IL: University of Chicago Press.

MacLachlan, Claudia. 1989. "Admissible—Advertising by Lawyers Gets Respectable Here," *St. Louis Post-Dispatch* (March 20): 1BP, 20BP. 1995. "Legal Services Come Under attack—Again," *National Law Journal*, 17 (31) (April 3): A12.

Magee, Stephen P. 1992. "How Many Lawyers Ruin an Economy?" Letters to the editor, *Wall Street Journal* (September 24) A17.

Manning, Bayless. 1968. "Introduction: New Tasks for Lawyers." Pp. 1–11 in Geoffrey C. Hazard, Jr. (ed.), *Law in a Changing America.* Englewood Cliffs, NJ: Prentice Hall.

Mansnerus, Laura. 1995. "Men Found to Do Better in Law School than Women," *New York Times* (February 10): B13.

Mattioli, Dana. 2009. "New Task for Law-Firm Hires: Finding an Interim Job First," *Wall Street Journal* (October 6): A18.

Mayer, Martin. 1967. *The Lawyers.* New York: Harper & Row, Publishers.

McGrath, Anne. 2006. *U.S. News Ultimate Guide to Law Schools.* 2nd ed. Washington, DC: U.S. News.

Model Rules of Professional Conduct. 2007. Chicago, IL: American Bar Association. Center for Professional Responsibility.

Morrissey, Siobhan. 2004. "Revising the Rules: Update of Judicial Conduct Code Will Address the Changing Justice System," *ABA Journal*, 90 (62) (February): 6–9.

Moses, Jonathan, and Richard B. Schmitt. 1992. "Lawyer's Billing Practices are Scrutinized," *Wall Street Journal* (April 6): B7.

Muris, Timothy J., and Fred S. McChesney. 1979. "Advertising and the Price and Quality of Legal Services: The Case for Legal Clinics," *American Bar Foundation Research Journal*, 1 (Winter): 179–207.

Murphy, Wendy. 2007. *And Justice for Some: An Exposé of the Lawyers and Judges* Who Let Dangerous Criminals Go Free. New York: Penguin Books Inc.

Myers, Ken. 1994. "Sometimes It's Not What You Know . . . Law Deans Debate Admitting Students for the Wealth and Influence They Bring," *National Law Journal*, 17 (4) (September 26): A1. 1995. "Based on Results of Bar Exam, Class of 1994 Is One of Brightest," *National Law Journal*, 17 (19) (January 9): A17.

Nader, Ralph. 1969. "Law Schools and Law Firms," *New Republic* (October 11): 21–23.

Nagpaul, Hans. 1994. "The Legal Profession in Indian Society: A Case Study of Lawyers at a Local Level in North India," *International Journal of the Sociology of Law*, 22: 59–76.

Nelson, Robert L. 1988. *Partners with Power: The Social Transformation of the Large Law Firm.* Berkeley and Los Angeles, CA: University of California Press.

Newsweek. 1995. "Who Ya Gonna Call? 1-800-Sue Me" (March 20): 36–37. 2003. "Lawsuit Hell, How Fear of Litigation Is Paralyzing Our Professions" (December 15): 43–51. 2007. "Perspectives" (May 21): 25.

New York Times. 1995a. "Mere Fraction of Civil Cases End with Punitive Awards" (July 21): B12. 1995b. "Where Legal Help Comes Complete with Guarantee" (August 11): A13. 1995c. "Woman Heads Bar Association" (August 11): A13. 1995d. "Rising Concern about Stress in Lawyer's Lives" (March 10): B15. 1998. "The Crisis at Legal Aid" (September 1): A24. 2010. "Law School Admissions Lag among Minorities" (January 6): A22.

O'Hara, Erin A., and Larry E. Ribstein. 2009. *The Law Market.* New York: Oxford University Press.

Official Guide to U.S. Law Schools. 2010. New York: Times Books/Random House, Inc.

Oleinik, Anton N. 2003. *Organized Crime, Prison and Post-Soviet Societies.* Burlington, VT: Ashgate.

Olson, Walter K. 1991a. *The Litigation Explosion.* New York: Dutton. 1991b. "The Selling of the Law," *American Enterprise* (January–February): 27–35.

Packer, Herbert L., and Thomas Ehrlich. 1972. *New Directions in Legal Education.* New York: McGraw-Hill.

Palermo, George B., Maxine Aldridge White, Lew A. Wasserman, and William Hanrahan. 1998. "Plea Bargaining: Injustice for All?"

International Journal of Offender Therapy and Comparative Criminology, 42 (2) (June): 111–123.

Passell, Peter. 1998. "A Call for 'Auto Choice' and Lower Premiums," *New York Times* (August 30): BU1, BU19.

Pear, Robert. 1995. "As Welfare Overhaul Looms, Legal Aid for Poor Dwindles." *New York Times* (September 5): A1, A9.

Pew Research Center. 2009. "Public Praises Science; Scientists Fault Public, Media. Scientific Achievements Less Prominent than a Decade Ago" (July 9).

Pitulla, Joanne. 1995. "Firm Commitments: Lawyers Cannot Ignore Duty to Report Ethics Violations by Colleagues," *ABA Journal*, 81 (April): 108–109.

Peel, Michael. 2006. "Reach versus Risk: Why Big Law Firms Are Split on the Merits of Going Global," *Financial Times* (December 14): 13.

Petersen, Trond, and Ishak Saporta. 2004. "The Opportunity Structure for Discrimination," *American Journal of Sociology*, 109 (4) (January): 852–901.

Podgers, James. 1994. "Chasing the Ideal: As More Americans Find Themselves Priced Out Of the System, the Struggle Goes on to Fulfill the Promise of Equal Justice For All," *ABA Journal*, 80 (August): 56–61. 1995. "Sorting Out Image, Ads, Ethics," *ABA Journal*, 81 (March): 94–95.

Pollock, Ellen Joan, and Stephen J. Adler. 1992. "Justice for All? Legal System Struggles to Reflect Diversity, but Progress Is Slow," *Wall Street Journal* (May 8): 1, 4.

Pue, W. Wesley, and David Sugarman (eds.). 1999. *Lawyers Culture and the Cultural Significance of Lawyers: Historical Perspectives*. Brookfield, VT: Ashgate. 2003 *Lawyers and Vampires: Cultural Histories of Legal Professions*. Portland, OR: Hart Publications.

Quade, Vicki. 1995. "There is no Sisterhood: Non-white Women Lawyers Say They're Still at the Bottom of the Heap," *Human Rights*, 22 (1) (Winter): 8–13.

Randall, Kerry. 2002. *Effective Yellow Pages Advertising for Lawyers: The Complete Guide to Creating Winning Ads*. Chicago, IL: ABA Law Practice Management Section.

Rapping, Elayne. 2004. *Law and Justice as Seen on TV*. New York: New York University Press.

Reichstein, Kenneth J. 1965. "Ambulance Chasing: A Case Study of Deviation and Control within the Legal Profession," *Social Problems*, 13 (1) (Summer): 3–17.

Reidinger, Paul. 1986. "It's 46.5 Hours a Week in Law," *ABA Journal*, 72 (September 1): 44.

Reskin, Lauren Rubenstein. 1985. "Lawyers Are Serious about Professional Responsibility," *ABA Journal*, 71 (December): 41.

Rhode, Deborah L. 2004. *Access to Justice*. New York: Oxford University Press.

Rhode, Deborah L., and Geoffrey C. Hazard, Jr. 2007. *Professional Responsibility and Regulation*. 2nd ed. New York: Foundation Press; St. Paul, MN: Thomson/West.

Rhode, Deborah L., and David Luban (eds.). 2005. *Legal Ethics: Law Stories*. Eagan, MN: Foundation Press.

Ribstein, Larry E., 2010 "The Death of Big Law" (January 5). University of Illinois Law & Economics Research Paper No. LE09-025. Available at SSRN: http://ssrn.com/abstract=1467730.

Robinson, Mark, and Kevin Calcagnie, 2010. "Why We Need Trial Lawyers." *Wall Street Journal* (February 24): A 17.

Rostain, Tanina (ed.). 2008. *Lawyers and the Legal Profession*. Volume 1. *Sociolegal Studies on the Legal Profession: An Overview*. Volume 2. *Elite Practices, Personal Legal Services, and Political Causes*. Burlington, VT: Ashgate.

Rueschemeyer, Dietrich. 1985. *Lawyers and Their Society*. Cambridge, MA: Harvard University Press.

Samborn, Hope Viner. 1995. "Post-Law School Job May Be as Paralegal: Trend More Pronounced on East and West Coasts Where Work Tough to Find," *ABA Journal*, 81 (March): 14–16.

Sangchompuphen, Tommy, 1995. "More Law Students Seek Joint Degrees to Boost Job Chances," *Wall Street Journal* (August 7): B8.

Saulny, Susan. 2003. "Voluntarism among Lawyers Surges, Encouraged by a Slumping

Economy. A Decade-Long Decline in Pro Bono Work Is Reversed." *New York Times* (February 19): A27.

Savell, Lawrence. 1994. "I'm Bill Low. File with Me and Win, Win, Win!" *National Law Journal*, 17 (3) (September 19): A23.

Schauer, Frederick. 2009. *Thinking Like a Lawyer: A New Introduction to Legal Reasoning.* Cambridge, MA: Harvard University Press.

Schrag, Philip G., and Michael Meltsner. 1998. *Reflections on Clinical Legal Education.* Boston, MA: Northeastern University Press.

Shdaimah, Corey S. 2009. *Negotiating Justice. Progressive Lawyering, Low-Income Clients, and the Quest for Social Change.* New York: New York University Press.

Shulins, Nancy. 1994. "Survey Says . . . Let's Bash All the Lawyers," *St. Louis Post-Dispatch* (April 30): 1D, 3D.

Shuman, Daniel W., and Anthony Champagne. 1997. "Removing the People from the Legal Process: The Rhetoric and Research on Judicial Selection and Juries," *Psychology, Public Policy, and Law*, 3 (2/3) (June/September): 242–258.

Simpson, A. W. B. 1988. *Invitation to Law.* Oxford, UK: Basil Blackwell.

Smigel, Erwin O. 1964. *Wall Street Lawyer.* New York: Free Press.

Smith, Clay J., Jr. (ed.). 1998. *Rebels in Law: Voices in History of Black Women Lawyers.* Ann Arbor, MI: University of Michigan Press.

Society. 1992. "Liability Suits," 29 (5) (July–August): 3.

Solovo, Daniel D. 2009. *Understanding Privacy.* Cambridge, MA: Harvard University Press.

Spangler, Eve. 1986. *Lawyers for Hire: Salaried Professionals at Work.* New Haven, CT: Yale University Press.

Spector, Malcolm. 1972. "The Rise and Fall of a Mobility Route," *Social Problems*, 20 (2) (Fall): 173–185.

St. Louis Post-Dispatch. 2001. "Do-It-Yourselfers Are Becoming More Common in Court" (March 25): A3.

Stevens, Amy. 1994. "A List of Bad Lawyers To Go On Line," *Wall Street Journal* (August

26): B1. 1995a. "Fewer Partners, More Mergers Enriched Top Law Firms Last Year Survey Shows," *Wall Street Journal* (June 24): B1. 1995b. "Law Schools See Sharp Decline in Applicants," *Wall Street Journal* (February 19): B1, B16.

Stevens, Robert. 1971. "Two Cheers for 1870: The American Law School." Pp. 405–548 in Donald Fleming and Bernard Bailyn (eds.), *Law in American History.* Boston, MA: Little, Brown and Company. 1973. "Law Schools and Law Students," *Virginia Law Review*, 59 (4) (April): 51–707. 2001. *Law School: Legal Education in America from the 1850s to the 1980s.* Union, NJ: Lawbook Exchange.

Stracher, Cameron. 2001. "How to Bill 25 Hours in One Day," *New York Times Magazine* (April 8): 74. 2006. "Cut My Salary, Please!" Wall Street Journal (April 1): A7. 2007. "Meet the Clients," *Wall Street Journal* (January 26): W11.

Streb, Matthew J. (ed.). 2009. *Running for Judge: The Rising Political, Financial, and Legal Stakes of Judicial Elections.* New York: New York University Press.

Sullivan, Colleen. 1979. "The Upstart Lawyers Who Market the Law," *New York Times* (August 26): A1, 9.

Sullivan, William M., Anne Colby, Judith Welch Wegner, Lloyd Bond, and Lee S. Shulman. 2007. *Educating Lawyers: Preparation for the Profession of Law.* San Francisco, CA: Jossey-Bass.

Susskind, Richard. 2009. *The End of Lawyers? Rethinking the Nature of Legal Services.* New York: Oxford University Press.

Tigar, Michael E. 2000. *Law and the Rise of Capitalism.* New York: Monthly Review Press.

Time. 1978. "Those #*X!!! Lawyers" (April 10): 56–66. 1998. "A Legal Press in Texas: A State Court Targets Self-Help Publisher Nolo Press for Making it too Easy to Bypass Lawyers" (August 3): 29.

Tone, Andrea. 2001. *Devices & Desires: A History of Contraceptives in America.* New York: Hill & Wang. 2009. *The Age of Anxiety: A History of America's Turbulent Affair with Tranquilizers.* New York: Basic Books.

Trubek, Louise G., and Jeremy Cooper. 1999. *Educating for Justice around the World: Legal Education, Legal Practice and the Community.* Brookfield, VT: Ashgate.

Turner, Bertram, and Thomas Kirsch (eds.). 2009. *Permutations of Order: Religion and Law as Contested Sovereignties.* Burlington, VT: Ashgate.

Turow, Scott. 1977. "The Trouble with Law School," *Harvard Magazine,* 80 (1) (September–October): 60–64.

Tushnet, Mark. (ed.). 2008. *Legal Scholarship and Education.* Burlington, VT: Ashgate.

Urbina, Ian. 2010. "Law School Clinics Face Backlash," *New York Times* (April 3): A1, A9.

U.S. Department of Justice. 1992. "Prosecutors in State Courts, 1990," *Bureau of Justice Statistics Bulletin* (March).

U.S. News & World Report. 1986. "Sky-High Damage Suits" (January 27): 35–43. 1992. "Realism on the Docket" (March 23): 70–74. 2010. "Exclusive Rankings, Schools of Law" (April 9): 75–77.

Uviller, Richard H. 1994. "The Lawyer as Liar," *Criminal Justice Ethics,* 13 (2) (Summer–Fall): 2–7.

Waldman, Peter. 1986. "Pre-Paid Legal Plans Offer Consultations, Follow-Up Calls and Referrals at Low Cost," *Wall Street Journal* (February 11): 33.

Warren, Susan. 2007. "Spring Break Is a Legal Specialty for Ben Bollinger: Florida Lawyer Enjoys a Spike in His Business; Defendants in Flip-Flops," *Wall Street Journal* (March 17): A1, A10.

Wall Street Journal. 1986. "Parties, Polls and Pejoratives: Lawyers Meet" (August 13): 23. Wasley, Paula. 2007. "Law Student Survey," *Chronicle of Higher Education* (January 8): A1.

Wilensky, Harold L. 1964. "The Professionalization of Everyone?" *American Journal of Sociology,* 70 (2) (September): 137–158.

Woo, Junda. 1992. "Sexual Harassment Is Found in Study of Federal Courts in 9 Western States," *Wall Street Journal* (August 5): B3.

York, John C., and Rosemary D. Hale. 1973. "Too Many Lawyers? The Legal Service Industry: Its Structure and Outlook," *Journal of Legal Education,* 26 (1): 1–31.

Zemans, Frances K. 1977. *Law School and Law Practice: Credentials for Professional Status.* Chicago, IL: American Bar Foundation.

Zitrin, Richard A., Carol M. Langford, and Nina W. Tarr. 2007. *Legal Ethics in the Practice of Law.* Newark, NJ: LexisNexis Matthew Bender.

9

Researching Law in Society

Empirical studies provide the background for many of the generalizations and conclusions reached about law and society in the preceding chapters. The intention of this chapter is to show how sociologists carry out such studies by describing some of the ways they research law and the methods they use to arrive at their findings. This chapter also demonstrates the significance and applicability of sociological research to the formulation, instrumentation, and evaluation of social policy. The general comments on methodological tools for research on law are not proposed to replace the more detailed technical discussions found in books on the various methods of social research (see, for example, Alford, 1998; Babbie, 2010; Bernard, 2000; Chambliss and Schutt, 2010; Feldman, 2009; Gray, 2010; Halliday and Schmidt, 2009; McIntyre 2005; Morse and Field, 1995; Nock and Kingston, 1990; Schutt, 2009; Westmarland, 2010; Yates, 2004). They are intended merely to provide an exposure to the strategies used in the study of the interplay between law and society and to highlight the methodological concerns and complexities inherent in such endeavors.

METHODS OF INQUIRY

There are several methods that can be applied in researching law in society, and more than a single method is usually involved in such a study. However, there are four commonly used methods of data collection in sociology: All other approaches are variations and combinations of these four methods. The four methods that will be considered are the historical, observational, experimental, and survey methods.

Of course, actual research is much more complicated than these methods indicate. All research is essentially a process in which choices are made at many stages. There are several methods and they are combined in various ways in the actual research. Methodological decisions are made on such diverse matters as the kind of research design (Bynner and Stribley, 2010) to be used, the type of research population and sample, the sources of data collection, the techniques of gathering data, and the methods of analyzing the research findings. The differences among the four methods are more a matter of emphasis on a particular data-collection strategy to obtain observable data for a particular research purpose than a clear-cut "either/or" distinction. For example, in the observational method, although the emphasis is on the researcher's ability to observe and record social activities as they occur, the researcher may interview the participants—a technique associated with the survey and experimental methods. Similarly, in the experimental method, the subjects are usually under the observation of the researcher and his or her collaborators. The information gained in such observations also plays a crucial role in the final analysis and interpretation of the data. Furthermore, historical evidence is often used in observational, survey, and experimental studies.

At all stages of social science research, there is interplay between theory and method (Morse and Field, 1995; Schutt, 2009). In fact, it is often the theory chosen by the researcher that determines which methods will be used in the research. The selection of the method is to a great extent dependent on the type of information desired.

To study a sequence of events and explanations of the meanings of the events by the participants and other observers before, during, and after their occurrence, observation (especially participant observation) seems to be the best method of data collection. The researcher directly observes and participates in the study system with which he or she has established a meaningful and durable relationship, as did, for example, Jerome H. Skolnick (1994) in his study of police officers. Although the observer may or may not play an active role in the events, he or she observes them firsthand and can record the events and the participants' experiences as they unfold. No other data-collection method can provide such a detailed description of social events. Thus, observation is best suited for studies intended to understand a particular group and certain social processes within that group. When these events are not available for observation as they occurred in the past, the historical approach is the logical choice of method for collecting data.

If a researcher wishes to study norms, rules, and status in a particular group, intensive interviewing of "key" persons and informants in or outside the group is the best method of data collection. For example, in a well-known study, Jerome E. Carlin (1966) interviewed approximately 800 lawyers in New York City for his study of legal ethics and their enforcement. Those who set and enforce norms, rules, and status, because of their position in the group or relations with persons in the group, are the ones who are the most knowledgeable about the information the researcher wishes to obtain. Intensive interviews (especially with open-ended questioning) with these persons allow the researcher to probe for such information.

When an investigator wishes to determine the numbers, the proportions, the ratios, and other quantitative information about the subjects in his or her study, possessing certain characteristics, opinions, beliefs, and other categories of various variables, then the best method of data collection is the survey. The survey method relies on a representative sample of the population to which a standardized instrument can be administered.

As a final point, the experiment is the best method of data collection when the researcher wants to measure the effect of certain independent variables on some dependent variables. The experimental situation provides control over the responses and the variables, and gives the researcher the opportunity to manipulate the independent variables. In the following pages, I will examine and illustrate these methods in greater detail.

Historical Methods

Sociologists generally are accustomed to studying social phenomena at one time—the present. But social phenomena do not appear spontaneously and autonomously. Historical analysis can indicate the possibility that certain consequences can issue from events that are comparable to other events of the past: history as something more than a simple compilation of facts. It can generate an understanding of the processes of social change and document how a multitude of factors have served to shape the present. The study of history also has an existential function. It informs us who we are, and that we are links that connect the past with the present and the future (Inciardi et al, 1977:27–28).

Historical research carried out by sociologists is a critical investigation of events, developments, and experiences of the past; a careful weighing of evidence of the validity of sources of information on the past; and the interpretation of the evidence. Historical research is important and valuable in sociology because the origins of the discipline have to be understood if contemporary theories and research are to be understood. As a substitute for direct data from the participants, contents from documents and historical materials are used as a method of data collection. These documents and materials can range from census data; archives of various types; official files such as court records, records of property transactions, records of poor relief administration, and tax records; and business accounts to personal diaries, witness accounts, propaganda literature, and numerous other personal accounts and letters. The researcher uses these available data sources to carry out what is generally referred to as secondary analysis; that is, the data were not generated or collected for the specific purpose of the study formulated by the researcher. Of course, the usefulness of the historical method depends to a large extent on the accuracy and thoroughness of the documents and materials. With accurate and thorough data, the researcher may be able to gain insights, generate hypotheses, and even test hypotheses.

Official records and public documents have provided the data for sociological analyses attempting to establish long-term legal trends. For example, William J. Chambliss (1964), as I mentioned in Chapter 1, has shown how the vagrancy statutes changed in England according to emerging social interests. The first full-fledged vagrancy law, enacted in 1349, regulated the giving of alms to able-bodied, unemployed people. After the Black Death and the flight of workers from landowners, the law was reformulated to force laborers to accept employment at a low wage. By the sixteenth century, with an increased emphasis on commerce and industry, the vagrancy statutes were revived and strengthened. Eventually, vagrancy laws came to serve, as they do today, the purpose of controlling people and activities regarded as undesirable to the community. Similarly, Jerome Hall (1952) has shown, on the basis of historical records, how changing social conditions and emerging social interests brought about the formulation of trespass laws in fifteenth-century England.

The historical method is also used to test theories. For example, Mary P. Baumgartner (1978) was interested in the relationship between the social status of the defendant and the litigant and the verdicts and sanctions awarded them. She analyzed data based on 389 cases (148 civil and 241 criminal) heard in the colony of New Haven between 1639 and 1665. She found, not unexpectedly, that in both the civil and the criminal cases, individuals who enjoyed high status received favorable treatment by the court than their lower-status counterparts. Another example to test theories is Lawrence M. Friedman and Robert V. Percival's (1978) survey of the caseloads of two California trial courts at five points between 1890 and 1970. As described in Chapter 6, the authors hypothesized that, over time, trial courts have come to do less work in settling disputes and more work of a routine administrative nature. They concluded that the dispute-settlement function of the trial courts has declined noticeably over time, a conclusion that has since been repeatedly questioned. A third example is Susan W. Brenner's (1992:5–174) analysis, which traces the use of precedents from pre-Norman England to the present, demonstrates that their use has changed as new ways have been established for making them more available, and shows how they implicitly justify a legal system's reliance upon stare decisis.

In addition to relying on official documents, the historical method may also be based on narrations of personal experiences, generally known as the *life-histories* method. This technique requires that the researcher rely solely on a person's reporting of life experiences relevant to the research interest with minimal commentary. Often, life histories are part of ethnographic reports. In such instances, they are referred to as "memory cases" (Nader and Todd, 1978:7). This method is useful to learn about events such as conflict or dispute that occurred in the past, particularly when there are no written records available. Obviously, this method has certain pitfalls, for life histories tend to be tainted by selective recall: Subjects tend to remember events that have impressed them in some way and tend to forget others. Although the life-history method has been little used in recent years, it serves several functions. First, it provides insights into a world usually overlooked by the objective methods of data collection. Second, life histories can serve as the basis for making assumptions necessary for more systematic data collection. Third, life histories, because of their details, provide insights into new or different perspectives for research. When an area has been studied extensively and has grown "sterile," life histories may break new grounds for research studies. Finally, they offer an opportunity to view and study the dynamic process of social interactions and events not available with many other kinds of data.

A noteworthy difficulty of the historical method lies in the limited accuracy and thoroughness of the documents and materials involved. Because the data are "compiled" by others with no supervision or control by the researcher, the researcher is, in fact, at the mercy of those who record the information. The recorders use their own definitions of situations, define and select events as important for recording, and introduce subjective perceptions, interpretations, and insights into their recordings. For example, how do the recorders define a dispute? In many instances, a dispute enters officially into the court records when it is adjudicated, and a settlement is imposed after full trial. But as I noted in Chapter 6, not all disputes are adjudicated. Many are settled informally in pretrial conferences, or judges may intervene in other less formal ways as well. Therefore, a researcher must ascertain the reliability and validity of documents. They should be verified for internal consistency (consistency between each portion of the document and other portions) and external consistency (consistency with empirical evidence, other documents, or both). Although the historical method provides details and in certain cases presents a processual view of events, often unmatched by other methods of data collection, it is desirable (when possible, of course) to combine this method with other data-collection methods.

Observational Methods

Observational methods can be divided into two types: those utilizing either human observers (participant observers or judges) or mechanical observers (cameras, tape recorders, audio-video equipment, and the like) and those directly eliciting responses from subjects by questioning (questionnaires, schedules, and interview guides). Observational methods can be carried out both in laboratory or controlled situations and in field or natural settings.

Participant observation has a long history of use in anthropological research. Thus, there is justification if the term conjures up the image of a social scientist living with some preliterate tribe, perhaps for several years. Indeed, much of our knowledge of primitive law comes from anthropologists who lived in traditional societies, such as Bronislaw Malinowski and E. Adamson Hoebel. Of course, for anthropologists, the opportunity to observe ongoing legal phenomena (outside of an institutional setting such as a court) depends on a combination of circumstances and luck: It means that the anthropologists have to be in the right place at the right time. Anthropological (and sociological) field researchers generally proceed by way of a kind of methodological eclecticism, choosing the method that suits the purpose (see, for example, the widely known works of Margaret Mead) and present circumstances at any given time. In summary, "Hence, unobtrusive measurement, life history studies, documentary and historical analysis, statistical enumeration, in-depth interviewing, imaginative role-taking, and personal introspection are all important complements of direct observation in the field worker's repertoire" (Williamson et al., 1982:200).

Many of the observational techniques are used in laboratory or controlled situations. For example, comparatively little empirical research has been performed with actual juries because of the legal requirements of private deliberations. Consequently, mock trials in which jurors or juries respond to simulated case materials have become a primary research vehicle. The mock trial permits both manipulation of important variables and replication of cases (Davis et al., 1977:327). Many of the laboratory jury studies deal with the deliberation processes preceding the verdict and how the verdict is reached by juries of diverse composition deliberating under various conditions (Loh, 1984:460–461). One method of analyzing deliberations is to audiotape or videotape the deliberations and then analyze their content (Kessler, 1975:73).

Observational methods have been used by sociologists extensively in field settings that involve direct contact with subjects and take place in relatively natural social situations (McCall, 1978:1), and they are often part of what is called "action research," the way to integrate knowledge with action (Reason and Bradbury, 2008). For example, in attempts to find out and understand how law typically works on a day-to-day basis, sociologists have focused on various aspects of the criminal justice system. The study of the public defender's office by David Sudnow (1965); studies of the police by Richard V. Ericson (1989), Maurice Punch (1989), and Jerome H. Skolnick (1994) among others; Frank W. Miller's (1969) study of prosecution; Donald J. Newman's (1966) study of conviction; and Abraham S. Blumberg's (1979) work on the entire criminal justice system, all point to the day-to-day working of law. These studies have also noted the role of discretion in the application or nonapplication of the law in legally equivocal and unequivocal situations. At each step in the criminal justice system, from the citizen's decision to lodge a complaint or to define the situation as one in which it is necessary to summon the police, to the judge's decision as to what sentence a convicted person should receive, decisions are made that are not prescribed by statutory law (Westmarland, 2010).

There are both advantages and limitations to observational methods. The advantages include the opportunity to record information as the event unfolds or shortly thereafter. Thus, the validity of the recorded information can be high. Often observations are made and information is recorded independently of the observed person's abilities to record events. At times, when verbal or written communication between the researcher and the subjects is difficult—for example, in studying primitive tribes—observation is the only method by which the researcher can obtain information. Finally, the observer need not rely on the willingness of the observed persons to report events.

There are also several limitations of observational research. The method is obviously not applicable to the investigation of large social settings. The context investigated must be small enough to be dealt with exhaustively by one or a few researchers. In the case of field-work, there is a great likelihood that the researcher's selective perception and selective memory will bias the results of the study. There is also the problem of selectivity in data collection. In any social situation, there are literally thousands of possible pieces of data. No one researcher can account for every aspect of a situation. The researcher inevitably pulls out only a segment of the data that exist, and the question inevitably arises as to whether the selected data are really representative of the situation. Finally, there is no way to easily assess the reliability and validity of the interpretations made by the researcher. As long as data are collected and presented by one or a few researchers with their own distinctive talents, faults, and idiosyncrasies, suspicion will remain concerning the validity of their rendering of the phenomena studied. Researchers often respond to these criticisms by suggesting that the cost of imprecision is more than compensated for by the in-depth quality of the data produced.

Experimental Methods

The prevalent method for testing causal relations by social scientists, especially psychologists, is the experimental method. An experiment may be carried out in a laboratory or a field setting, and it ideally begins with two or more equivalent groups, with an experimental variable introduced into only the experimental group. The researcher measures the phenomenon under study before the introduction of the experimental variable and after, thus getting a measure of the change presumably caused by the variable.

There are two common ways of setting up experimental and control groups. One is the matched-pair technique. For each person in the experimental group, another person similar in all important variables (age, religion, education, occupation, or any other variable important to the research) is found and placed in the control group. Another technique is the random-assignment technique, in which statistically random assignments of persons to experimental and control groups are made—such as assigning the first person to the experimental group and the next to the control group, and so on.

Experiments in sociology face certain difficulties (see, for example, Orr, 1998; Schutt, 2009). An experiment involving thousands of people may be prohibitively expensive, and the cost factor is often the decisive issue whether or not to embark on a project. It may take years to complete a prospective study. Ethical and legal considerations prohibit the use of people in any experiments that may injure them. The scientific community reacts strongly in those infrequent instances where human subjects have been used in a hazardous or harmful manner (Mintz and Cohen, 1976). When people are unwilling to cooperate in an experiment, they cannot be forced to do so (although occasionally they are tricked into unconscious cooperation). Moreover, when individuals realize that they are experimental subjects, they begin to act differently and the experiment may be spoiled. Almost any kind of experimental or observational study upon people who know they are being studied will give some interesting findings, which may vanish soon after the study is terminated. Experiments with human subjects are most reliable when the subjects do not know the true object of the experiment. But the use of deception in social research poses the ethical question of distinguishing between harmless deception and intellectual dishonesty.

Moreover, the law in the United States does not allow experiments that involve elimination of a right that the due process clause guarantees, under all circumstances. For example, there would be legal and ethical questions involved in the use of experimental methods in the study of legal services, welfare payments, or incarcerations. There are exceptions, however, such as the Wisconsin welfare experiment (DeParle, 1998) or the often-cited and controversial New Jersey guaranteed income experiments, a rare example of government-sponsored policy experimentation. These experiments involve the systematic selection of experimental and control groups, the application of the policy under study to the experimental groups only, and a careful comparison of differences between the experimental and the control group after the application of the policy.

The New Jersey guaranteed income experiments were designed to resolve some serious questions about the impact of welfare payments on the incentives for poor people to work. Debates over welfare reform have generated certain questions that social science could presumably answer with careful, controlled experimentation. Would a guaranteed family income reduce the incentive to work? If payments were made to poor families with employable male heads, would the men drop out of the labor force? Would the level of the income guarantee, or the steepness of the reductions of payments with increases in earnings, make any difference in working behavior? Because current welfare programs do not provide a guaranteed minimum family income, or make payments to families with employable males, or provide graduate payments in relation to earnings, these questions could be answered only through experimentation.

To assess the impact of guaranteed incomes on families with able-bodied men, the Office of Economic Opportunity sponsored a three-year social experiment involving 1,350 families in New Jersey and Pennsylvania. The research was undertaken by the University of Wisconsin's Institute for Research on Poverty. To ascertain the effects of different levels of guaranteed income, four guarantee levels were established. Some families were chosen to receive 50 percent of the Social Security Administration's poverty-line income, some others 75 percent, some others 100 percent, and still others 125 percent. To ascertain the effects of graduated payments in relation to earnings, some families had their payments reduced by 30 percent of their outside earnings, others 50 percent, and still others 70 percent. Finally, a control sample was observed—families who received no payments at all in the experiment but were matched in every way with families who were receiving payments.

The experiment began in 1968, and a preliminary report issued by the Office of Economic Opportunity (1970) showed that there were no differences between the outside earnings of families who were receiving guaranteed incomes (experimental groups) and those who were not (control group). More important, the experiment raised a series of questions (Rossi and Lyall, 1976). Do researchers have the right to withhold public services from some individuals simply to provide a control for experimentation? In the medical area, where the giving or withholding of treatment may result in death or injury, the problem is obvious, and many attempts have been made to formulate a code of ethics. In the area of social experimentation, what can be said to control groups who are chosen to be similar to experimental groups but are denied benefits so that they may serve as a basis for comparison? (see, for example, Tomossy and Weisstub, 2003).

Setting aside the legal and moral issues, it will be politically difficult to provide services for some people and not for others. Moreover, as noted earlier, people behave differently when they know they are being watched. Students, for example, generally perform at a higher level when something—anything new and different—is introduced into the classroom routine. This "Hawthorne effect" may cause a new program or reform to appear more successful than the old, but it is the newness itself that produces improvement rather than the program or the reform. Another problem in such experimentation is that results obtained with small-scale experiments may differ substantially from what would occur if a large-scale nationwide program were adopted. In the New Jersey experiments, if only one family receives income-maintenance payments in a neighborhood, its members may continue to behave as the neighbors do. But if everyone in the nation is guaranteed a minimum income, community standards may change and affect the behavior of all recipient families (Kershaw, 1969).

On a smaller scale, experimental methods have been used quite often, for example, in the study of jury deliberation (Hans, 1992, 2006; Jonakait, 2003; Simon, 1975), the evaluation of objections in the courtroom (Koehler, 1992), allocation of scarce criminal resources (Nagel and Neef, 1977), the impact of increasing or decreasing police patrol on crime (Zimring, 1989), and the determination of the effectiveness of pretrial hearings. In the last case, a controlled experiment was done to find out whether pretrial hearings were time savers or time wasters. Sociologists developed a design calling for a random assignment of cases by court clerks to one of two procedures: obligatory pretrial hearing in one group of cases and optional pretrial in the control group, where it was held only if one or both of the litigants requested it. The conclusion was that the obligatory pretrial hearing did not save court time; in fact, it wasted it (Zeisel, 1967:84). Persuaded by the experiment, the state of New Jersey changed its rules and made pretrial hearings optional.

Many experiments, such as those dealing with juror and jury behavior (Diamond, 1997; Jonakait, 2003; Kramer and Kerr, 1989) or with violence, are conducted in a laboratory situation. The widely publicized National Commission on the Causes and Prevention of Violence (1969), for example, relied heavily, although not exclusively, on the results of laboratory experiments for its final report. In one group of experiments, young children who were shown acts of violence and then later observed at play committed more acts of violence in their play than children who did not witness acts of violence. In another group of experiments, college students were told that they were participating in a "learning experiment" in which they must apply mild electric shocks at whatever level of intensity they wished to other "learners" if the "learners" made a mistake. The "learning experiment" was interrupted and some students were shown a violent film while others were shown a nonviolent one. When the "learning experiment" was resumed, the students who saw the violent film used slightly stronger shocks on their "learners" than those who had watched the nonviolent film.

Laboratory experiments, as important as they may be in revealing insights into human behavior, achieve rigorous and controlled observation at the price of unreality. The subjects are isolated from the outside and from their normal environment. The laboratory experiment has been criticized for its unnaturalness and questioned as to its generalizability. By contrast, experimental methods that are used in nonlaboratory settings increase the generalizability of results and lend greater credence to the findings, but concomitantly increase the difficulty of controlling relevant variables.

Survey Methods

Survey research aims for a systematic and comprehensive collection of information about the attitudes, beliefs, and behavior of people. The most common means of data collection are face-to-face interviews, self-administered questionnaires (for example, mail questionnaires), and telephone interviews. Typically, the questionnaire or the interview schedule is set up so that the same questions are asked of each respondent in the same order with exactly the same wording and the validity of surveys is dependent on the design of the questions asked (see, for example, Fink, 2009; Fowler, 1995; Groves, 2009). A survey deals with a representative sample of a population. Probabilistic sampling is essential to survey studies. Survey studies tend to be larger than is typically the case in observational or experimental studies. Usually, data are collected at one time, although a survey approach can be used to study trends in opinion and behavior over time. Because of its ability to cover large areas and many respondents, the survey method has become the dominant method of data collection in sociology.

Survey methods, like other research methods, have their pitfalls. Probably foremost among them is the response rate or the nonresponse rate. One of the important reasons for conducting a survey is that a survey deals with a large representative sample from a population and thus permits inference from the sampled data to the population. Because of this, it is essential that the sample maintain its representativeness, which may be affected severely when a substantial number of the respondents fail to participate in the study. The return rate for mail questionnaires is generally low; a 60 percent or higher return rate is considered rather good (see, for example, Mangione, 1995). Of course, for the interview survey, the expected response rate is higher than that of the questionnaire survey. In both cases, in addition to the subject's refusal to participate, other factors affect the response rate. They include the inability of the subject to understand the question, the possibility that the subject may have moved or died, and the physical or mental incapacitation of the participants. Although questionnaire and interview studies have a margin of error, they are still useful. For example, public officials seldom take a position on a public issue without first reviewing public-opinion polls, and legislators often delay casting a vote on an important bill until they receive the latest survey of voter opinion from their districts.

An illustration of the use of survey methods can be seen in the efforts of the U.S. Department of Justice to gain a more accurate measure of the extent of crime in the United States. For years, both law enforcement agencies and sociologists have had to rely on official records compiled by such agencies as the Federal Bureau of Investigation (FBI) to measure the amount of crime. However, there have been concerns about the accuracy of these reports, and many sociologists have suggested that officially recorded crime statistics are a far better indicator of police activity than they are of criminal activity.

For the past several decades, the U.S. Department of Justice (2006) has conducted sophisticated victimization surveys for the nation and several major cities in an attempt to supplement official crime records and to overcome some of the problems of accuracy therein. In victimization surveys, subjects in a large sample of the population are systematically interviewed to determine how many crimes have been committed against them. In addition to determining the volume of crime, the surveys are also used in developing a variety of information on crime characteristics and the effects of crime on the victims—victim injury and medical care, economic losses, time lost from work, victim self-protection, and reporting of crime to the police. There are three advantages of victimization surveys that make surveys superior to self-report studies and the FBI's *Uniform Crime Reports*. First, people are more willing to discuss crimes committed against them than the ones they have committed. Second, victimization surveys by design seek out information about crimes rather than waiting for victims to report them as is the case with the *Uniform Crime Reports*. Third, victimization surveys rely on more representative samples than the other sources of crime data. There are also some disadvantages to these surveys. They are rather expensive—costing well over a minimum of $300 per interview depending on access to subjects, ease of locating them, and time considerations that are conditioned by the length of questionnaires (the longer they are, the more time it will take)—and because they deal primarily with major cities, information is lacking for the majority of suburban and rural areas in the United States.

At times, large-scale surveys are carried out at the behest of the Congress. For example, the Ninety-third Congress passed an amendment to an educational bill in 1974 requiring the secretary of health, education, and welfare to conduct a survey to determine the extent and seriousness of school crime. This extensive study included 4,014 school principals, 31,373 students, and 23,895 teachers in 642 junior and senior high schools throughout the country who received questionnaires from Washington (Toby, 1980). The study reconfirmed the general belief that schools are plagued with real crime and showed, unexpectedly, that the crime problem was worse in junior than in senior high schools. The findings prompted a series of hearings in Congress but surprisingly little in the way of systematic national effort to reduce school crime. In other instances, however, the results of such extensive surveys—such as the studies by James S. Coleman and his colleagues (1966) on the effects of a large number of variables on educational achievement, which will be discussed shortly—contribute significantly to policy decisions.

Survey methods have been widely used also in a variety of cross-cultural studies dealing with knowledge and opinion about law (Tomasic, 1985:116–126), evaluation of the effectiveness of the law, prestige of the law, and legal and moral attitudes (Podgorecki, 1974:83–124). Some of these studies reveal important and unexpected findings. For example, a European study asked people of Poland, the Netherlands, and Germany whether they thought people should obey the law. They found significant national variations; more Germans (66 percent) than Poles (45 percent) or Netherlanders (47 percent) answered yes to this general question (Friedman and Macaulay, 1977:216). Several surveys have also found that the public knowledge in a number of European countries concerning legal topics is considerably poorer than assumed by the legal authorities and by many scholars. But lack of knowledge about the law is not limited to European countries. For example, many respondents in an Oregon study did not know that Oregon law provided, at the time of the survey, minors with the right to treatment for venereal disease, birth control information, and medical treatment without parental knowledge (Friedman and Macaulay, 1977:607–608).

THE IMPACT OF SOCIOLOGY ON SOCIAL POLICY

In every scientific field, there is distinction between pure and applied science. *Pure* science is a search for knowledge, without primary concern for its practical use. *Applied* science is the search for ways of using scientific knowledge to solve practical problems. For example, a sociologist making a study of the social structure of a slum neighborhood is working as a pure scientist. If this is followed by a study of how to prevent crime in a slum neighborhood, the latter study is applied science. An example of this would be an investigation of the impact of neighborhood watch groups and patrols on crime and vandalism rates (see, for example, Levitz, 2009) or the effectiveness of the post–September 11, 2001, measures such as the proposed enlisting of postal, UPS, and FedEx carriers, gas and electric company workers, telephone and television cable repair persons, sanitation workers, and others with access to private homes to report suspicious behavior to the FBI in the fight against terrorism (Martin, 2010; Sullivan, 2009).

Fundamentally, however, sociology is both a pure and an applied science. For unless a science is constantly searching for more basic knowledge, its practical applications of knowledge are not likely to be very practical. This explains, in part, why a substantial amount of sociological work is still generated for academic purposes and executed with disciplinary concerns in mind. Much of sociological knowledge remains within the boundaries of the discipline. Often, the consumers of this knowledge are other sociologists and their students. But, simultaneously, with the continuing development of scientific knowledge, social scientists are also concerned with the generation and dissemination of knowledge and information with potential applied or policy-relevant implications in addition to merely theoretical perspectives and concepts (Anderson, 2003; Dean, 2006; Farahany, 2009; Gupta, 2010; Hill, 2006; Jordan, 2007; Lempert, 1991; Lister, 2010; Meenaghan et al., 2004; Milne et al., 2009; Nagel, 1993; Towers, 2011). Social science research has long been used to help resolve empirical issues that arise in litigation (Monahan and Walker, 1991, 2010), and sociological knowledge and methodology can be useful in the formulation and instrumentation of social policy and in the evaluation of current policies or proposed policy alternatives (Moynihan, 1989). Contemporary sociologists are attempting to contribute toward improving conditions of life in society in a number of ways, and providing policymakers with information needed to make informed decisions is a mandated activity in American sociology today (D'Antonio, 1992:4). Other fields, such as economics, are already playing a significant role in policy matters. There are attempts to reformulate legal concepts in the language and equations of the marketplace. Many good law schools in the country now employ at least one economist, and policy reforms in fields as diverse as antitrust law, environmental regulation, and criminal sentencing bear the distinctive imprint of economic analysis (see, for example, Posner, 2001, 2007).

Theoretical knowledge can and should be translated into practical applications and the purpose of this section is to demonstrate how social science knowledge and expertise can have an impact on social policy (Anderson, 2011). But what is "social policy"? Although there is no consensus in the sociological literature on the term (Cochran and Malone, 2010; Lavalette and Pratt, 2006; Morris, 1979:1–13), *social policy* generally refers to purposive legal measures that are adopted and pursued by representatives of government who are responsible for dealing with particular social conditions in society. The term *policymaking* refers to the process of identifying alternative courses of action that may be followed and choosing among them (Scott and Shore, 1979:XIV). Following Robert A. Scott and Arnold R. Shore (1979:13–33), the impact of sociology on social policy can be ascertained by looking at sociology's contributions to policy recommendations and sociology's contributions to enacted policy. The former deals with specific sociological research endeavors carried out on social problems that have been used for the development of specific policy recommendations for governmental programs to diminish and ameliorate those conditions, and the latter has had a direct impact on enacted policy.

Contributions of Sociology to Policy Recommendations

The proposition that law should be seen in a broad social context is now almost a truism. "Widespread acceptance of the view that law is at least in part concerned with policy making, coupled with realistic enthusiasm for empiricism has resulted in increasing use of social science materials in resolving many legal problems" (Monahan and Walker, quoted by Freeman and Roesch, 1992:571). Over the years, there have been many instances in which sociological knowledge, perspectives, concepts, theories, and methods have been useful in connection with the development of policy recommendations (see, for example, Dean, 2006; Hill, 2006; Jimenez, 2010; Jordan, 2007; Meenaghan et al., 2004; Mink and Solinger, 2004; Mullard and Spicker, 1998). Perhaps the best-known illustrations of this are the various uses made of sociology in presidential commissions. These commissions include the President's Commission on Law Enforcement and Administration of Justice, the U.S. National Commission on the Causes and Prevention of Violence, the President's Commission on Obscenity and Pornography, and the President's Commission on Population Growth and the American Future. Sociologists were active in these commissions, and disciplinary research and knowledge were incorporated in the recommendations.

Sociology played an important role in the President's Commission on Law Enforcement and Administration of Justice. Social science concepts, theories, and general perspectives were of great utility to the commission in forming final recommendations, and "existing social science theories and data were drawn upon to formulate broad general strategies in the prevention and control of crime" (Ohlin, 1975:108). Sociologists also provided sensitizing concepts and theories that oriented the search for solutions of the crime problem. For example, studies of the correctional system and the operation of law enforcement in the courts raised doubts about the effectiveness of existing criminal justice policies and of rehabilitation and treatment efforts. On the basis of sociological data, the commission accepted the view that alternative systems of social control should be used in place of the criminal justice system when possible, recommended the possibility of decriminalizing certain offenses against moral or public order, and called for a reconsideration of consensual crimes, or "crimes without victims" (Ohlin, 1975:109).

James F. Short points out that sociologists made similar contributions to the work of the National Commission on the Causes and Prevention of Violence. The specific recommendations provided by sociologists were incorporated in the commission's progress report and "marked the high point of social science input to the Commission" (Short, 1975:84). Specific recommendations included the "relativity of attributions of legitimacy or illegitimacy to violence"; that the nature of violence is essentially social as opposed to biological or psychological; that there is a connection between perceived legitimacy of the law and effective legal control of violence; and that the notions of responsibility for violence and of "relative deprivation" often lie in the unresponsiveness of social institutions (Short, 1975:85).

One of the final recommendations of the President's Commission on Obscenity and Pornography resulted directly from sociological and other social science research on the personal, psychological, and social consequences of exposure to explicit sexual materials. The commission recommended that federal, state, and local laws prohibiting the sale, exhibition, and distribution of sexual material to consenting adults be repealed (Scott and Shore, 1979:17).

This recommendation was based upon extensive sociological investigation that provided

> no evidence that exposure to or use of explicit sexual materials plays a significant role in the causation of social or individual harm such as crime, delinquency, sexual and nonsexual deviancy, or severe emotional disturbance—Empirical investigations thus support the opinion of a substantial majority of persons professionally engaged in the treatment of deviancy, delinquency and anti-social behavior, that exposure to sexually explicit material has no harmful causal role in these areas. (Report of the commission, quoted by Scott and Shore, 1979:17)

A similar conclusion was reached by Berl Kutchinsky (1973) in his ground-breaking study of the effects of liberalizing pornography in Denmark. In fact, he found that concurrent with the increasing availability of pornography, there was a significant decrease in the number of sex offenses registered by the police in Copenhagen. He adds, "The unexpected outcome of this analysis is that the high availability of hard-core pornography in Denmark was most probably the very direct cause of a considerable decrease in at least one type of serious sex offense, namely, child molestation" (Kutchinsky, 1973:179). In a later study, Kutchinsky found a similar decrease in child molestation in Germany, which he attributed to an increased availability of pornographic material (U.S. Department of Justice, 1986:974). By contrast, the controversial report of the Attorney General's Commission on Pornography (U.S. Department of Justice, 1986) negates many of the conclusions of earlier studies and that of the 1970 commission report partly because, in the words of the commission chairman, "If we relied exclusively on scientific data for every one of our findings, I'm afraid all our work would be inconclusive" (*Newsweek*, 1986:18). No doubt many of the "proofs" in support of the report's conclusions were less than compelling (Boyle, 2010).

Sociological research also had an appreciable impact on the substance of the final report of the President's Commission on Population Growth and the American Future.

The commission recognized that although population growth played a minor role in the short run (30 to 50 years) as compared with technological, economic, and government policy considerations, "in the longer run, population growth would become increasingly important. The message for population policy, therefore, was that resource and environmental considerations implied prudence rather than crisis; that there were no benefits to be realized from continued growth, but that population was an indirect and ineffectual policy level for environmental problems" (Westoff, 1975:54).

Demographic research contributed importantly to other commission deliberations and recommendations. For example, it was shown that if women averaged 2.0 rather than 2.1 births, zero population growth could be achieved near the same level while immigration remains at the current volume. Notes Westoff (1975:55), "Although not a world-shaking scientific discovery, this bit of demographic intelligence was extremely important in the debate over immigration policy and was influential in defeating a recommendation to reduce the volume."

But one of the most important applications of social science research to policy formation resulted from the National Fertility Studies of 1965 and 1970. It makes a considerable difference in the nature of population policy whether the stabilization of population can be achieved largely through the prevention of unwanted births or whether more radical social changes are necessary to change the number of children desired. These two studies estimated that the elimination of unwanted pregnancy would result in a population growth rate that would be below replacement level. The policy significance of this finding cannot be overestimated. By concentrating on the improvement and distribution of methods of fertility control, a solution to the problems of population growth can be reached within politically acceptable means.

Sociological research also discovered an appalling amount of ignorance among the general public about population (for example, 60 percent did not know or could not guess the size of the U.S. population within plus or minus 50 million [it was approximately 315 million in January 2010]), which provided a ground for recommendations about population education. A research finding that only 20 percent of sexually active unmarried teenage girls report using any contraception regularly dramatized the recommendation that such information and service be provided to minors (Westoff, 1975:55–56). There were other contributions as well. Studies showing a negative relationship between income and unwanted births served as a rationale for governmental subsidization of family planning for the poor. An opinion poll taken by the commission has shown that about half of the American people felt that abortion is a private matter and should be decided solely by individuals and their physicians, a finding that was subsequently used to support a policy recommendation for liberal abortion (Scott and Shore, 1979:19).

On the basis of the involvement of sociologists in presidential commissions, Scott and Shore conclude that sociology has made a contribution to recommendations for policy in three ways:

> The first is through the use of sociological concepts that are said to provide new or unique perspectives on social conditions—perspectives that are based upon more than common sense and that may in fact be inconsistent with basic notions upon which existing policies are based. . . . Second, prescriptions for policy are

sometimes suggested by the findings of sociological research undertaken primarily to advance scientific understanding of society. . . . The third is the use of sociological methods and techniques of research to obtain information about specific questions central to the deliberations of Commissions. (1979:20–21)

Of these three uses of sociology, the third is by far the most common (see, for example, Deutscher, 1999). However, it should be noted that there is no way of precisely determining the extent to which sociology can or does contribute to policy recommendations. In many instances, the methods of empirical research, not the knowledge and concepts of sociology, have been directly responsible for policy prescriptions. Obviously, conducting research is not a skill possessed exclusively by sociologists. Moreover, there is no way of distinguishing between the contributions of intelligent and insightful individuals who happen to be trained as sociologists and the contributions of sociological knowledge and perspective as such. Consequently, care needs to be exercised in crediting the discipline's knowledge in all cases in which sociology has had an impact on policy.

Despite these qualifications, it is fair to state that sociological knowledge can and at times does have an impact on developing recommendations for social policy. "For this reason," as Scott and Shore (1979:23) observe, "sociologists can legitimately claim that their discipline has been and is relevant to the development of policy recommendations." That claim has been validated over the years as evidenced by the demand on sociology and sociologists in policymaking circles.

Contributions of Sociology to Enacted Policy

Although there is a growing influence of social science in law, measuring the impact of social science research remains a fairly difficult endeavor (see, for example, Anderson, 2003; Kraft and Furlong, 2009; Meenaghan et al., 2004; Mink and Solinger, 2004). Impact studies rely predominantly on citations for an indication of whether policymakers have used such research (Roesch et al., 1991:2–3). Counts of social science publications and findings cited in legal decisions could possibly underrepresent the influence of research because policymakers are reluctant to cite them even when they have influenced their decisions. Because of their training in law, they have a preference for legal scholarship and precedent rather than for social science methodology and statistics. Consequently, the extent of impact in some instances remains controversial; in certain cases, sociology is considered to have had a direct impact on enacted policy. A most widely cited illustration of this is the social science contribution to the 1954 Supreme Court decision outlawing segregation in public schools. Other examples of impact on social policy are sociological studies that resulted in the reduction of delay in the courts, changes in testimony procedures, changes in the procedures to select judges, the provision for counsel to the indigent, various cross-cultural studies on sentencing with policy alternatives (Walker and Hough, 1988), and releasing indigent criminal defendants whose trial is pending without bail. The last study, for example, showed that a careful screening and notifying of defendants released without any bond produced a higher percentage of court appearances than did the traditional bail bond system (Nagel, 1969:31–32).

A number of other examples may be cited to support the view that sociology has had an impact on enacted policy. They include the involvement of sociologists in programs to combat juvenile delinquency (U.S. Department of Justice, 2007; Bernard and Kurly-chek, 2010), to lower recidivism rates through the use of teen courts where defendants already pleaded guilty and have chosen to come to teen courts to have the matter heard by peers who will assign a sentence ranging from letters of apology to community service (Bartley, 2006; see also Alexander, 2006), to reduce school dropout rates, and to prevent narcotics addiction (in particular, studies dealing with attempts to reduce youth crime and delinquency problems contributed to the legislation that became the Juvenile Delinquency and Youth Offenses Control Act of 1961 [Katz, 1978:137]). Sociological research on talent loss as a consequence of inadequate educational opportunities for minority groups and persons of low socioeconomic status led to the enactment of remedial measures, such as the establishment of new scholarships and loan resources and the creation of federal programs like Outward Bound, Talent Search, and VISTA. In each instance, sociologists have contributed research and conceptual skills toward the "formulation of programs and policies that were eventually enacted to ameliorate social conditions deemed harmful to society" (Scott and Shore, 1979:24).

In social-policy research, sociologists doing scientific work are often confronted with problems and issues that have an impact on many people whose lives may be substantially altered or changed. To illustrate, a study that had a significant impact on the lives of many people in the United States is the so-called Coleman Report. In 1964, the U.S. Department of Education was authorized by the Civil Rights Act to undertake a survey and to make a report to the president and Congress in two years concerning the lack of availability of equal educational opportunities for individuals by reason of race, color, religion, or national origin in public educational institutions at all levels in the United States. Subsequently, a social survey on a huge scale was carried out by a social science team led by James S. Coleman, Ernest Q. Campbell, and their associates (1966). The survey included 570,000 school pupils, 60,000 teachers, and 4,000 schools. The final report is a 737-page document.

Following this monumental study, efforts at the national and regional levels involving financial support and structural changes on a large scale have been made for the purpose of achieving a better mix of students in schools and continuity of research activities in this area. One far-reaching policy outcome of the study was the decision of the federal government to instrument busing for the purpose of achieving integrated schools. The issue of busing, as I noted in Chapter 3, remains a controversial policy and has generated many protests, counterprotests, and even violence. Although the researchers involved in the original study may not agree with all the policies that have been formulated and instrumented, the study's policy influence has been substantial.

The preceding illustrations show some of the contributions of sociology to enacted policy. However, a great deal of applied sociological research has no discernible policy implications of any kind. Many of the recommendations are pragmatically useless (that is, too expensive to instrument) or are considered politically unrealistic or implausible by policymakers. Furthermore, policy questions are fundamentally political and not sociological questions (Kraft and Furlong, 2009). Often, policies are formulated and *then* relevant research is sought to support, legitimize, and dramatize (or even propagandize) these policies. Thus, it would be erroneous to assume that research generally precedes and determines policy actions. Additionally, some sociologists feel that they should not be directly involved through research in the development and instrumentation of social policy, and this position is epitomized by Daniel P. Moynihan (1969:193), who contends that "the role of social sciences lies not in the formation of social policy but in the measurement of its results." In the next section, I shall consider evaluation research and impact studies.

EVALUATION RESEARCH AND IMPACT STUDIES

The evaluation of enacted policy is as old as policy itself. Policymakers always have made judgments regarding the benefits, costs, or effects of particular policies, programs, and projects (Fitzpatrick et al., 2009; Mathison, 2005; Nathan, 2000; Orr, 1998; Rossi et al., 2004; Taylor and Balloch, 2005). Many of these judgments have been impressionistic, often influenced by ideological, partisan self-interest, and valuational criteria. For example, a tax cut may be considered necessary and desirable because it enhances the electoral chances of the evaluator's political party, or unemployment compensation may be deemed "bad" because the evaluator "knows a lot of people" who improperly receive benefits. Undoubtedly, much conflict may result from this sort of evaluation because different evaluators, employing different value criteria, reach different conclusions concerning the merits of the same policy.

Another type of evaluation has centered on the operation of specific policies or programs, such as a juvenile correctional reform (McGarrell, 1988), boot camp (Zhang, 1998), various police programs (Kerley, 2005), specific crime prevention programs (Knutsson and Tilley, 2009), or a welfare program. Questions asked may include: Is the program honestly run? What are its financial costs? Who receives benefits (payments or services) and in what amounts? Is there any overlap or duplication with other programs? What is the level of community reintegration of participants? What is the degree of staff commitment? Were legal standards and procedures followed? This kind of evaluation may provide information about the honesty or efficiency in the conduct of a program, but like the impressionistic kind of evaluation, it will probably yield little if anything in the way of hard information on the societal effects of a program. A welfare program, for instance, may be carried out honestly and efficiently, and it may be politically and ideologically satisfying to a given evaluator. However, such an evaluation will tell very little about the impact of the program on the poor, or whether it is achieving its officially stated objectives.

Since the late 1960s, a third type of policy evaluation is receiving increasing attention among policymakers. It is the systematic objective evaluation of programs to measure their societal impact and the extent to which they are achieving stated objectives. In 1967 and 1968, Congress altered some of the central pieces of President Johnson's Great Society legislation so that mandatory evaluation would be included in all programs, such as the Economic Opportunity Act of 1964. The intention was to monitor the progress of programs and to terminate those that did not seem to yield the desired level of results. There were also political benefits to be obtained by emphasizing evaluation. Low-cost experiments on social problems and rigid evaluation requirements could be used to subvert attempts to solve social problems through (expensive) direct social change or action programs. The contrast between the evaluation components required for war on poverty programs and those required for such "welfare" programs as urban renewal, railroad subsidies, and agribusiness subsidies points this up dramatically. Notes Morehouse (1972:873), "None of the older, well-established, and 'safe' domestic programs have evaluation requirements.... Program evaluation requirements were an important by-product of a general policy of bringing controversial programs under control."

For many, evaluation research quickly became a proper use of sociology in policy-related work (Babbie, 2010; Knutsson and Tilley, 2009; Scott and Shore, 1979:43). Rapidly, this use of social research in policy analysis became widespread, and an entire field of specialization has developed about methods and procedures for conducting evaluation research. Technically speaking, however, there are no formal methodological differences between evaluation and nonevaluation research. They have in common the same techniques and the same basic steps that must be followed in the research process. The difference lies in the following: (1) Evaluation research uses deliberate planned intervention of some independent variable, (2) the programs it assesses assume some objective or goal as desirable, and (3) it attempts to determine the extent to which this desired goal has been reached. As Edward A. Suchman (1967:15) puts it, "evaluative research asks about the *kind* of change the program views as desirable, the *means* by which this change is to be brought about, and the *signs* according to which such change can be recognized." Thus, the greatest distinction between evaluation and nonevaluation research is one of objectives.

Carol Weiss (1998:6–8) proposes several additional criteria that distinguish evaluation research from other types of research:

1. Evaluation research is generally conducted for a client who intends to use the research as a basis for decision making.
2. The investigator deals with his or her client's questions as to whether the client's program is accomplishing what the client wishes it to accomplish.
3. The objective of evaluation research is to ascertain whether the program goals are being reached.
4. The investigator works in a situation where priority goes to the program as opposed to the evaluation.
5. There is always a possibility of conflicts between the researcher and the program staff because of the divergences of loyalties and objectives.
6. In evaluation research, there is an emphasis on results that are useful for policy decisions.

Social policy evaluation is essentially concerned with attempts to determine the impact of policy on real-life conditions. As a minimum, policy evaluation requires a specification of policy objectives (what we want to accomplish with a given policy), the means of realizing it (programs), and what has been accomplished toward the attainment of the objectives (impacts or outcomes). In measuring objectives, there is a need to determine that not only some change in real life conditions has occurred, such as a reduction in the unemployment rate, but also it was due to policy actions and not to other factors, such as private economic decisions.

Thomas R. Dye (2008) suggests that the impact of a policy has several dimensions, all of which must be taken into account in the course of evaluation. These include the impact on the social problem at which a policy is directed and on the people involved. Those whom the policy is intended to affect must be clearly defined—that is, the poor, the disadvantaged, schoolchildren, or unwed mothers. The intended effect of the policy must then be determined. If, for example, it is an antipoverty program, is its purpose to raise the income of the poor, to increase the opportunities for employment, or to change their attitudes and behavior? If some combination of such objectives is intended, the evaluation of impact becomes more complicated, because priorities must be assigned to the various intended effects.

At times, as Friedman and Macaulay (1977:501) note, it is difficult to determine the purpose of a law or a program of regulation. They suggest that the determination of intent is complicated because many individuals with diverse purposes participate in the policymaking. Will consideration be given to the intention or intentions of the persons who drafted the statute or the judge who wrote the opinion creating the rule? To that of the majority of the legislature or court who voted for it? To that of the lobbyists who worked for the bill? To that purpose openly discussed or to the purpose that is implicit but never mentioned? They add that sometimes one can only conclude that a law has multiple and perhaps even conflicting purposes, but this is not to say that one can never be sure of the purpose of a law. However, one must be aware of the complexities of determining "purpose."

It should also be noted that a law may have either intended or unintended consequences or even both. A guaranteed-income program, for example, may improve the income situation of the benefited groups, as intended. But what impact does it also have on their initiative to seek employment? Does it decrease this, as some have contended? Similarly, an agricultural price support program intended to improve farmers' incomes, may lead to overproduction of the supported commodities.

The difficulties of measurement of impact are most acute for those areas of conduct where the behavior in question is hard to quantify and where it is hard to tell what the behavior *would* have been without the intervention of the law. The laws against murder illustrate the difficulties here. There is a fairly good idea about the murder rate in most countries, but no information at all exists about the contribution that the *law* makes to this rate. In other words, there is no way of determining how high the murder rate would be if there were, for example, no capital punishment for murder.

Knowledge of a new law by members of the legal profession also plays a role in the study of impact. For example, the Magnuson-Moss Warranty Act of 1975 was heralded as a major piece of legislation intended to protect the consumers against defective products. Did the new law help consumers with specific complaints about faulty products? Not much, according to research findings. Two years after the passage of the new law, one study concluded that "most lawyers in Wisconsin knew next to nothing about the Magnuson-Moss Warranty Act" and "many had never heard of it" (Macauly, 1979:118). The fact that many lawyers know little about laws that are intended to protect consumers obviously impairs the effectiveness of such laws. As this example shows, another problem confronting impact research is the assessment of knowledge of a particular law by those who are involved in its interpretation and application.

The study of impact is further complicated by the fact that policies may have effects on groups or situations other than those at which they are directed. These are called spillover effects (Wade, 1972). These spillover effects may be positive or negative. An illustration of the negative effects is the testing of nuclear devices, which may provide data for the design of nuclear power plants but may also generate hazards for the population. An illustration of a positive spillover effect is that when tariffs are lowered at the request of American exporters to increase their sales abroad, consumers in the United States may benefit from lower prices caused by increased imports that lower tariffs stimulate. Obviously, in the evaluation of impact, attention must also be paid to the spillover effects.

A given legislation may also have impact on future as well as current conditions. Is a particular policy designed to improve an immediate short-term situation, or is it intended to have effects over a longer time period? For example, was the Head Start program supposed to improve the cognitive abilities of disadvantaged children in the short run, or was it to have an impact on their long-range development and earning capacity? The determination of long-term effects stemming from a policy is much more difficult than the assessment of short-term impacts. For example, it will be next to impossible to determine if the regulation of the price of natural gas at the wellhead, a policy that began in the 1950s, really contributed to the controversial energy shortage in the late 1970s, as some now contend. If so, this would be a long-term effect of a policy with a negative spillover effect.

A rather rich literature of evaluation of actual and proposed programs of law has developed, using criteria derived from economics as its standard. This literature takes certain economic goals as its basic values and assesses legal programs as good or bad depending upon whether they most efficiently or rationally achieve the economic goals or make use of theoretically correct economic means. Of course, it is fairly easy to calculate the dollar costs of a particular policy when it is stated as the actual number of dollars spent on a program, its share of total government expenditures, how efficiently the funds are allocated, and so on. Other economic costs are, however, difficult to measure. For example, it is difficult to discover the expenditures by the private sector for pollution-control devices that are necessitated by air pollution control policy. Moreover, economic standards are hardly applicable to the measurement of social costs of inconvenience, dislocation, and social disruption resulting, for instance, from an urban renewal project. At the same time, it is also difficult to measure the indirect benefits of particular policies for the community. For example, the Social Security program may contribute to social stability as well as the retirement incomes of recipients. The problem of measurement is again apparent.

In addition to the difficulties inherent in the measurement of indirect costs and benefits, other complexities arise because the effects of a particular law may be symbolic (intangible) as well as material (tangible). Intended symbolic effects capitalize on popular beliefs, attitudes, and aspirations for their effectiveness. For example, taken at face value, the graduated income tax is a symbol of equality and progressiveness in taxation and draws wide support on that basis (Reed and Swain, 1997:70–112). In reality, the impact of income tax on many people, particularly the affluent, is noticeably reduced by provisions such as those for tax shelters. The result is that effective tax rates for the rich are substantially lower than commonly believed. What is symbolically promised is quite different from what materially results. There are other laws that appear to promise more symbolically than their instrumentation actually yields in material benefits. They include antitrust activity, regulation of public utility rates, and various antipoverty efforts. These endeavors attempt to assure people that policymakers are concerned with their welfare, although the real tangible benefits are limited.

These are some of the difficulties that need to be taken into consideration in measuring the impact of a particular law. There are several possible research approaches that can be used for measuring impact. One approach is the study of a group of individuals from the target population after it has been exposed to a program that had been developed to cause change. This approach is referred to as the *one-shot* study. Another possible approach is to study a group of individuals both *before* and *after* exposure to a particular program. Still another possibility would be the use of some kind of *controlled* experiment. But as I noted earlier in this chapter, in measuring the impact of law, one serious problem is the absence of control groups. As a result, one is rarely able to say with confidence what behavior would have been had a law not been passed or had a different law been passed. Outside of a laboratory setting, it is difficult to apply an experimental treatment to a group that one has matched in all significant respects to another group that does not receive the treatment, so as to control for all possible sources of distortion or error. This difficulty is further accentuated by ethical problems that often arise from such research methods as the random assignment of persons to different legal remedies. One should be also aware of some of the murky statistics that seem to proliferate in the context of policy effectiveness in combating particular problems such as the drug trade, sex trafficking, or terrorist financing (Andreas and Greenhill, 2010; Limoncelli, 2010).

The final consideration of evaluation research involves the utilization of results. As James S. Coleman (1972:6) states, "The ultimate product is not a 'contribution to existing knowledge' in the literature, but a social policy modified by the research result." In many instances, however, those who mandate and request evaluation research fail to utilize the results of that research. These people may feel committed to particular ways of doing things despite evidence that a program is ineffective. This is particularly true in instances where programs were instigated by political pressures such as the various endeavors in model-city programs, war against poverty, corrections, and drug and alcohol rehabilitation. As public interest waned in the later stages of these programs, there was no real pressure to incorporate the results of evaluation studies into the ongoing activities (Vago, 2004:411–417). There are, of course, a number of other ways initiators of evaluation research can respond to the results. They include the manipulation of research outcomes for their own interests, rationalization of negative results, and, in some instances where the findings are negative, dismissal of results. A recent book titled *Evaluation: Seeking Truth or Power?* (Eliadis et al., 2010) succinctly captures these dilemmas.

It is apparent that sociological expertise can be made relevant to social policy. Of course, it is a question of choice whether one would want to pursue primarily disciplinary or a policy-oriented applied sociology, although the two are not mutually exclusive. Sociology undoubtedly has a good potential to play an active, creative, and practical role on the formulation, instrumentation, and evaluation of social policy (Rogers, 1988). At the same time, as sociological knowledge and methods become relevant to and influential on policy, they become part of politics by definition. In such a situation, the contributions of sociology can become a tool for immediate political ends and propaganda purposes by justifying and legitimizing a particular position. Ideally, the objective should be to insulate, but not isolate, sociological contributions from the immediate vagaries of day-to-day politics, and to strike some sort of balance between political and sociological considerations, permitting neither to dominate.

SUMMARY

This chapter examined measures that are useful for advancing our understanding of law in society and considered the impact of sociological research on law and the applicability of such research to social policy. Several methods can be applied in studying law in society, and more than a single method is usually involved in an investigation. The methods of sociological research are the historical, observational, experimental, and survey studies. Historical analysis relies on secondary sources collected for purposes other than the researcher's intentions. Thus, a notable difficulty of the historical method lies in the limited accuracy and thoroughness of the documents and materials involved. In addition to relying on official documents, the historical method may also be based on narrations of personal experiences, generally known as the life-histories method. Although there are difficulties with the use of historical methods, they provide an aid in understanding long-term developments and change processes involved in the study of law.

Observational methods utilize either human observers or mechanical devices and procedures to elicit responses directly from the subjects by questioning. Many of the observational techniques are used in laboratory situations as, for example, the studies on jury deliberations. Observational methods are also used by sociologists in field settings, which involve direct contact with subjects and take place in relatively natural social situations. Observational methods have been used extensively to study the various facets of the criminal justice system and the legal profession.

Experimental methods are used to test causal relationships, either in a laboratory or in a field setting. Experiments in sociology face certain difficulties such as ethical, legal, and financial considerations. Although there have been several large-scale experiments dealing with law and a large number of laboratory studies, questions of generalizability of results still plague the researchers. The use of experimental methods also raises questions about the legitimacy of "manipulating" human subjects.

Survey methods are widely used in sociological research, and they generally involve a reasonably representative cross section of the population under study. Survey studies tend to be larger than is typically the case in observational and experimental studies, and data may be collected at one point in time or over time. Policymakers tend to rely on the results of surveys more than other methods of sociological inquiry.

Sociology, like all sciences, may be either pure or applied. Pure sociology searches for new knowledge, whereas applied sociology tries to apply sociological knowledge to practical problems. Although this distinction is often used in the sociological literature, sociology is both a pure and an applied science. Sociological knowledge and expertise have demonstrable relevance to and influence on social policy in terms of the discipline's contributions to policy recommendations and to enacted policy. Sociological knowledge, methods, and concepts have been used in a number of presidential commissions as grounds for policy recommendations, and a number of sociological studies have had a direct impact on enacted policy, such as the Coleman study on school desegregation.

There is an increasing involvement of sociologists in evaluation research and impact studies. There are specific requirements for the evaluation of many federal programs and activities designed to induce change in some area. The object of evaluation research is to determine how successful a particular change effort is in achieving its goals. Impact studies are concerned with the intent of those who formulated a legal rule or policy, whether or not a legal rule was responsible for the change, knowledge of a law by its interpreters, and spillover effects. Evaluation research allows policymakers to determine the effectiveness of a program, whether it should be continued or phased out, and what in-course adjustments, if any, are needed to make it more effective. In some cases, however, when the results of the evaluation are negative, the client might attempt to dismiss or rationalize the findings.

SUGGESTED FURTHER READINGS

R. Luckham (ed.), *Law and Social Inquiry: Case Studies of Research.* Uppsala, Sweden: Scandinavian Institute of African Studies, 1981. An enlightening compilation of nine background articles discussing the problems of sociolegal research in different parts of the world.

Stuart S. Nagel (ed.), *Research in Law and Policy Studies.* Greenwich, CT: Jai Press, Inc. Vol. 2, 1988, Vol. 3, 1990. A collection of interdisciplinary and cross-cultural empirical studies on various facets of law and society.

Stuart S. Nagel with Lisa A. Bievenue, *Social Science, Law, and Public Policy.* Lanham, MD: University Press of America, Inc., 1992.

An excellent and influential analysis of the various social science measures applicable to law and public policy.

Rita J. Simon, *The Jury: Its Role in American Society.* Lexington, MA: Lexington Books, Heath, 1980. A review of much of the major research that has been done on the American jury between 1950 and 1979.

Thomas J. Sullivan, *Sociology: Concepts and Applications in a Diverse World.* 8th ed. Boston, MA: Pearson Education, 2009. A primer on the basics of sociological research and its applications to policy concerns.

REFERENCES

Alexander, Rudolph, Jr. 2006. "Restorative Justice: Misunderstood and Misapplied," *Journal of Policy Practice*, 5 (1): 67–81.

Alford, Robert R. 1998. *The Craft of Inquiry: Theories, Methods, Evidence.* New York: Oxford University Press.

Anderson, James E. 2011. *Public Policymaking.* 7th ed. Belmont, CA: Wadsworth.

Anderson, Lisa. 2003. *Pursuing Truth, Exercising Power: Social Science and Public Policy in the Twenty-first Century.* New York: Columbia University Press.

Andreas, Peter, and Kelly M. Greenhill (eds.). 2010. *Sex, Drugs, and Body Counts: The Politics of Numbers in Global Crime and Conflict.* Ithaca, NY: Cornell University Press.

Babbie, Earl. 2010. *The Practice of Social Research.* 12th ed. Belmont, CA: Wadsworth Cengage.

Bartley, Nancy. 2006. "Teen Courts Put Youngsters at the Mercy of Their Peers," *Seattle Times* (December 23): A1, A13.

Baumgartner, Mary P. 1978. "Law and Social Status in Colonial New Haven, 1639–1665."

Pp. 153–174 in Rita J. Simon (ed.), *Research in Law and Sociology*, Vol. 1. Greenwich, CT: Jai Press, Inc.

Bernard, H. Russel. 2000. *Social Research Methods: Qualitative and Quantitative Approaches.* Thousand Oaks, CA: Sage Publications.

Bernard, Thomas J., and Megan C. Kurlychek. 2010. *The Cycle of Juvenile Justice.* 2nd ed. New York: Oxford University Press.

Blumberg, Abraham S. 1979. *Criminal Justice* 2nd ed. New York: New Viewpoints.

Boyle, Karen (ed.). 2010. *Everyday Pornography.* New York: Routledge.

Brenner, Susan W. 1992. *Precedent Inflation.* New Brunswick, NJ: Transaction Publishers.

Bynner, John, and Keith M. Stribley (eds.). 2010. *Research Design: The Logic of Social Inquiry.* Piscataway, NJ: Transaction Publishers.

Carlin, Jerome E. 1966. *Lawyers' Ethics: A Survey of the New York City Bar.* New York: Russell Sage Foundation.

Chambliss, Daniel F., and Russel K. Schutt. 2010. *Making Sense of the Social World: Methods of Investigation.* Thousand Oaks, CA: Sage Publications.

Chambliss, William J. 1964. "A Sociological Analysis of the Law of Vagrancy," *Social Problems*, 12 (1) (Summer): 67–77.

Cochran, Charles L., and Eloise F. Malone. 2010. *Public Policy: Perspectives and Choices.* 4th ed. Boulder, CO: Lynne Rienner Publishers, Inc.

Coleman, James S. 1972. *Policy Research in Social Science.* Morristown, NJ: General Learning Press.

Coleman, James S., Ernest Q. Campbell, Carol J. Hobson, et al. 1966. *Equality of Educational Opportunity.* Washington, DC: U.S. Government Printing Office.

D'Antonio, William V. 1992. "Sociology's Lonely Crowd—Indeed!" *Footnotes* (May 3): 4.

Davis, James H., Robert M. Bray, and Robert W. Holt. 1977. "The Empirical Study of Decision Processes in Juries: A Critical Review." Pp. 326–361 in June Louin Tapp and Felice J. Levine (eds.), *Law, Justice, and the Individual in Society: Psychological and Legal Issues.* New York: Holt, Rinehart & Winston.

Dean, Hartley. 2006. *Social Policy.* Malden, MA: Blackwell Publishing.

DeParle, Jason. 1998. "Wisconsin Welfare Experiment: Easy to Say, Not So Easy to Do," *New York Times* (October 18): Y1, Y20.

Deutscher, Irwin. 1999. *Making a Difference: The Practice of Sociology.* Somerset, NJ: Transaction Publishers.

Diamond, Shari Seidman. 1997. "Illuminations and Shadows from Jury Simulations," *Law and Human Behavior*, 21 (5) (October): 561–573.

Dye, Thomas R. 2008. *Understanding Public Policy.* 12th ed. Upper Saddle River, NJ: Prentice Hall.

Eliadis, Pearl, Jan-Eric Furubo, and Steve Jacob (eds.). 2010. *Evaluation: Seeking Truth or Power? Comparative Policy Evaluation, Volume 17.* Piscataway, NJ: Transaction Publishers.

Ericson, Richard V. 1989. "Patrolling the Facts: Secrecy and Publicity in Policework," *British Journal of Sociology*, 40 (2): 205–226.

Farahany, Nita (ed.). 2009. *The Impact of Behavioral Sciences on Criminal Law.* New York: Oxford University Press.

Feldman, Robin. 2009. *The Role of Science in Law.* New York: Oxford University Press.

Fink, Arlene. 2009. *How to Conduct Surveys: A Step-by-Step Guide.* 4th ed. Thousand Oaks, CA: Sage Publications.

Fitzpatrick, Jody, Christina Christie, and Melvin M. Mark. 2009. *Evaluation in Action: Interviews with Expert Evaluators.* Thousand Oaks, CA: Sage Publications.

Fowler, Floyd J. Jr. 1995. *Improving Survey Questions: Design and Evaluation.* Thousand Oaks, CA: Sage Publications.

Freeman, Richard J., and Ronald Roesch. 1992. "Psycholegal Education: Training for Forum and Function." Pp. 567–576 in Dorothy K. Kagehiro and William S. Laufer (eds.), *Handbook of Psychology and Law.* New York: Springer-Verlag.

Friedman, Lawrence M., and Stewart Macaulay. 1977. *Law and the Behavioral Sciences.* 2nd ed. Indianapolis, IN: Bobbs-Merrill.

Friedman, Lawrence M., and Robert V. Percival. 1978. "A Tale of Two Courts: Litigation in Alameda and San Benito Counties." Pp. 69–79 in Sheldon Goldman and Austin Sarat (eds.), *American Court Systems: Readings in Judicial Process and Behavior.* San Francisco, CA: W. H. Freeman & Company Publishers.

Gray, David E. 2010. *Doing Research in the Real World.* Thousand Oaks, CA: Sage Publications.

Groves, Robert M. 2009. *Survey Methodology.* 2nd ed. Hoboken, NJ: John Wiley.

Gupta, Dipak K. 2010. *Analyzing Public Policy: Concepts, Tools, and Techniques.* 2nd ed. Washington, DC: CQ Press.

Hall, Jerome. 1952. *Theft, Law and Society.* 2nd ed. Indianapolis, IN: Bobbs-Merrill.

Halliday, Simon, and Patrick Schmidt. 2009. *Conducting Law and Society Research: Reflections on Methods and Practices.* Cambridge, UK: Cambridge University Press.

Hans, Valerie P. 1992. "Jury Decision Making." Pp. 56–76 in Dorothy J. Kagehiro and William S. Laufer (eds.), *Handbook of Psychology and Law.* New York: Springer-Verlag.

Hans, Valerie P. (ed.). 2006. *The Jury System: Contemporary Scholarship.* Burlington, VA: Ashgate.

Hill, Michael. 2006. *Social Policy in the Modern World.* Malden, MA, Blackwell Publishing.

Inciardi, James A., Alan A. Block, and Lyle A. Hallowell. 1977. *Historical Approaches to Crime: Research Strategies and Issues.* Beverly Hills, CA: Sage Publications.

Jimenez, Jillian. 2010. *Social Policy and Social Change: Toward the Creation of Social and Economic Justice.* Thousands Oak, CA: Sage Publications.

Jonakait, Randolph N. 2003. *The American Jury System.* New Haven, CT: Yale University Press.

Jordan, Bill, 2007. *Social Policy for the Twenty-First Century.* Malden, MA: Blackwell Publishing.

Katz, James Everett. 1978. *Presidential Politics and Science Policy.* New York: Praeger.

Kerley, Kent R. (ed.). 2005. *Policing and Program Evaluation.* Upper Saddle River, NJ: Prentice Hall.

Kershaw, David N. 1969. *The Negative Income Tax Experiment in New Jersey.* Princeton, NJ: Mathematica.

Kessler, Joan B. 1975. "The Social Psychology of Jury Deliberations." Pp. 69–93 in Rita James Simon (ed.), *The Jury System in America: A Critical Overview.* Beverly Hills, CA: Sage Publications.

Knutsson, Johannes, and Nick Tilley (eds.). 2009. *Evaluating Crime Reduction.* Devon, UK: Willan Publishing.

Koehler, Jonathan J. 1992. "Probabilities in the Courtroom: An Evaluation of the Objections and Policies." Pp. 167–184 in Dorothy J. Kagehiro and William S. Laufer (eds.), *Handbook of Psychology and Law.* New York: Springer-Verlag.

Kraft, Michael E., and Scott R. Furlong. 2009. *Public Policy: Politics, Analysis, and Alternatives.* 3rd ed. Washington, DC: CQ Press.

Kramer, Geoffrey P., and Norbert L. Kerr. 1989. "Laboratory Simulation and Bias in the Study of Juror Behavior: A Methodological Note," *Law and Human Behavior*, 13 (1): 89–99.

Kutchinsky, Berl. 1973. "The Effects of Easy Availability of Pornography on the Incidence of Sex Crimes: The Danish Experience," *Journal of Social Issues*, 29 (3): 163–181.

Lavalette, Michael, and Alan Pratt (eds.). 2006. *Social Policy: Theories, Concepts, and Issues.* 3rd. ed. Thousand Oaks, CA: Sage Publications.

Lempert, Richard. 1989. "Humility Is a Virtue: On the Publicization of Policy-Relevant Research," *Law & Society Review*, 23 (1): 145–161.

Levitz, Jennifer. 2009. "Volunteer 5-0: Civilian Patrols Grow as Recession Puts Citizens on Guard." *Wall Street Journal* (September 8): A1.

Limoncelli, Stephanie A. 2010. *The Politics of Trafficking: The First International Movement to Combat the Sexual Exploitation of Women.* Palo Alto, CA: Stanford University Press.

Lister, Ruth. 2010. *Understanding Theories and Concepts in Social Policy.* Bristol, UK: The Policy Press.

Loh, Wallace D. 1984. *Social Research in the Judicial Process: Cases, Readings, and Text.* New York: Russell Sage Foundation.

Macauly, Stewart. 1979. "Lawyers and Consumer Protection Laws," *Law & Society Review*, 14 (1): 115–171.

Mangione, Thomas W. 1995. *Mail Surveys.* Thousand Oaks, CA: Sage Publications.

Martin, Gus. 2010. *Understanding Terrorism: Challenges, Perspectives, and Issues.* Thousand Oaks, CA: Sage Publications.

Mathison, Sandra (ed.). 2005. *Encyclopedia of Evaluation.* Thousand Oaks, CA: Sage Publications.

McCall, George J. 1978. *Observing the Law: Field Methods in the Study of Crime and the Criminal Justice System.* New York: Free Press.

McGarrell, Edmund F. 1988. *Juvenile Correction Reform: Two Decades of Policy and Procedural Change.* Albany, NY: State University of New York Press.

McIntyre, Lisa J. 2005. *Need to Know: Social Science Research Methods.* Boston, MA: McGraw-Hill.

Meenaghan, Thomas M., Keith M. Kilty, and John G. McNutt. 2004. *Social Policy Analysis and Practice.* Chicago, IL: Lyceum Books.

Miller, Frank W. 1969. *Prosecution: The Decision to Charge a Suspect with a Crime.* Boston, MA: Little, Brown and Company.

Milne, Janet E., Julia LeMense, and Ross A. Virginia (eds.). 2009. *Mountain Resorts: Ecology and the Law.* Burlington, VT: Ashgate.

Mink, Gwendolyn, and Rickie Solinger (eds.). 2004. *Welfare: A Documentary History of U.S. Policy and Politics.* New York: New York University Press.

Mintz, Morton, and Jerry S. Cohen. 1976. "Human Guinea Pigs," *Progressive*, 40 (12) (December): 32–36.

Monahan, John, and Laurens Walker. 1991. "Judicial Use of Social Science Research," *Law and Human Behavior*, 15 (6) (December): 571–584.

Monahan, John, and Laurens Walker. 2010. *Social Science in Law: Cases and Materials.* 7th ed. New York: Thomson Reuters/ Foundation Press, Inc.

Morehouse, Thomas. 1972. "Program Evaluation: Social Research versus Public Policy," *Public Administration Review*, 32 (6) (November–December): 868–874.

Morris, Robert. 1979. *Social Policy of the American Welfare State: An Introduction to Policy Analysis.* New York: Harper & Row, Publishing.

Morse, Janice M., and Peggy Anne Field. 1995. *Qualitative Research Methods.* 2nd ed. Thousand Oaks, CA: Sage Publications.

Moynihan, Daniel P. 1969. *Maximum Feasible Misunderstanding.* New York: Free Press. 1989. "Toward a Post-Industrial Social Policy," *Public Interest*, 96 (Summer): 16–27.

Mullard, Maurice, and Paul Spicker. 1998. *Social Policy in a Changing Society.* New York: Routledge.

Nader, Laura, and Harry F. Todd, Jr. 1978. "Introduction: The Disputing Process." Pp. 1–40 in Laura Nader and Harry F. Todd, Jr. (eds.), *The Disputing Process: Law in Ten Societies.* New York: Columbia University Press.

Nagel, Stuart S. 1969. *The Legal Process from a Behavioral Perspective.* Homewood, IL: Dorsey. 1993. *Legal Scholarship, Microcomputers, and Super-Optimizing Decision-Making.* Westport, CT: Quorum Books.

Nagel, Stuart S., and Marian Neef. 1977. *The Legal Process: Modeling the System.* Beverly Hills, CA: Sage Publications.

Nathan, Richard P. 2000. *Social Science in Government: The Role of Policy Researchers.* Updated ed. Albany, NY: Rockefeller Institute Press.

National Commission on the Causes and Prevention of Violence. 1969. "To Establish Justice, To Insure Domestic Tranquility." Final Report. Washington, DC: U.S. Government Printing Office.

Newman, Donald J. 1966. *Conviction: The Determination of Guilt or Innocence without Trial.* Boston, MA: Little, Brown and Company.

Newsweek. 1986. "A Salvo in the Porn War," July 21, 18.

Nock, Steven L., and Paul W. Kingston. 1990. *The Sociology of Public Issues.* Belmont, CA: Wadsworth.

Ohlin, Lloyd E. 1975. "Report on the President's Commission on Law Enforcement and Administration of Justice." Pp. 93–115 in Mirra Komarovsky (ed.), *Sociology and Public*

Policy: The Case of Presidential Commissions. New York: Elsevier.

Orr, Larry L. 1998. *Social Experiments: Evaluating Public Programs with Experimental Methods.* Thousand Oaks, CA: Sage Publications.

Podgorecki, Adam. 1974. *Law and Society.* London, UK: Routledge & Kegan Paul.

Posner, Richard A. 2001. *Frontiers of Legal Theory.* Cambridge, MA: Harvard University Press. 2007. *Economic Analysis of Law.* 7th ed. New York: Aspen Publishers.

Punch, Maurice. 1989. "Researching Police Deviance: A Personal Encounter with the Limitations and Liabilities of Field-Work," *British Journal of Sociology,* 40 (2): 177–204.

Reason, Peter, and Hilary Bradbury (eds.). 2008. *The Sage Handbook of Action Research: Participative Inquiry and Practice.* 2nd ed. Thousand Oaks, CA: Sage Publications.

Reed, B. J., and John W. Swain. 1997. *Public Finance Administration.* 2nd ed. Thousand Oaks, CA: Sage Publications.

Roesch, Ronald, Stephen L. Golding, Valerie P. Hans, and N. Dickon Reppucci. 1991. "Social Science and the Courts: The Role of Amicus Curiae Briefs," *Law and Human Behavior,* 15 (1) (February): 1–11.

Rogers, James M. 1988. *The Impact of Policy Analysis.* Pittsburgh, PA: University of Pittsburgh Press.

Rossi, Peter H., Mark W. Lipsey, and Howard E. Freeman. 2004. *Evaluation: A Systematic Approach.* 7th ed. Thousand Oaks, CA: Sage Publications.

Rossi, Richard H., and Katherine Lyall. 1976. *Reforming Public Welfare: A Critique of the Negative Income Tax Experiment.* New York: Russell Sage Foundation.

Schutt, Russell K. 2009. *Investigating the Social World: The Process and Practice of Research.* 6th. ed. Thousand Oaks, CA: Pine Forge Press.

Scott, Robert A., and Arnold R. Shore. 1979. *Why Sociology Does Not Apply: A Study of the Use of Sociology in Public Policy.* New York: Elsevier.

Short, James F., Jr. 1975. "The National Commission on the Causes and Prevention of Violence: Reflections on the Contributions of Sociology and Sociologists." Pp. 61–91 in Mirra Komarovsky (ed.), *Sociology and Public Policy: The Case of Presidential Commissions.* New York: Elsevier.

Simon, Rita James (ed.). 1975. *The Jury System in America: A Critical Overview.* Beverly Hills, CA: Sage Publications.

Skolnick, Jerome H. 1994. Justice without Trial: Law Enforcement in Democratic Society. 3rd ed. New York: MacMillan.

Suchman, Edward A. 1967. *Evaluative Research: Principles and Practice in Public Service and Social Action Programs.* New York: Russell Sage.

Sudnow, David. 1975. "Normal Crimes: Sociological Features of the Penal Code in a Public Defender Office," *Social Problems,* 12 (3) (Winter): 255–276.

Sullivan, Eileen. 2009. "Police Support Citizen's Terrorism Watch: Program Opens in Los Angeles," *Bellingham Herald* (October 4): A1, A2.

Taylor, David, and Susan Balloch (eds.). 2005. *The Politics of Evaluation: Participation and Policy Implementation.* Bristol, UK: Policy Press.

Toby, Jackson. 1980. "Crime in American Public Schools," *Public Interest,* 58 (Winter): 18–42.

Tomasic, Roman. 1985. *The Sociology of Law.* London, UK: Sage Publications.

Tomossy, George F., and David N. Weisstub (eds.). 2003. *Human Experimentation and Research.* Burlington, VT: Ashgate.

Towers, Chris. 2011. *Experiencing Social Policy: An Introductory Guide.* Bristol, UK: The Policy Press.

U.S. Department of Justice. 1986. *Attorney General's Commission on Pornography.* Final Report. Vols. 1 and 2 (July). Washington, DC: U.S. Government Printing Office. 2006. *Criminal Victimization in the United States* (September). 2007. *Annual Report of NIJJDP, Fiscal Year 2006.* National Institute for Juvenile Justice and Delinquency Prevention. Office of Juvenile Justice and Delinquency

Prevention. Law Enforcement Assistance Administration (March). Washington, DC: U.S. Government Printing Office.

Office of Economic Opportunity. 1970. Preliminary Results of the New Jersey Graduated Work Incentive Experiment, February 18. Washington, DC: U.S. Government Printing Office.

Vago, Steven. 2004. *Social Change.* 5th ed. Upper Saddle River, NJ: Prentice Hall.

Wade, Larry L. 1972. *The Elements of Public Policy.* Columbus, OH: Merrill Company.

Walker, Nigel, and Mike Hough (eds.). 1988. *Public Attitudes to Sentencing: Surveys from Five Countries.* Aldershot, UK: Gower.

Weiss, Carol H. 1998. *Evaluation Research: Methods for Studying Programs and Policies.* 2nd ed. Upper Saddle River, NJ: Prentice Hall.

Westmarland, Louise. 2010. *Researching Crime and Justice.* Devon, UK: Willan Publishing.

Westoff, Charles F. 1975. "The Commission on Population Growth and the American Future: Its Origins, Operations, and Aftermath."

Pp. 43–49 in Mirra Komarovsky (ed.), *Sociology and Public Policy: The Case of Presidential Commissions.* New York: Elsevier.

Williamson, John B., David A. Karp, and John R. Dalphin. 1982. *The Research Craft: An Introduction to Social Science Methods.* 2nd ed. Boston, MA: Little, Brown and Company.

Yates, Simeon J. 2004. *Doing Social Science Research.* Thousand Oaks, CA: Sage Publications.

Zeisel, Hans. 1967. "The Law." Pp. 81–99 in Paul F. Lazarsfeld, William H. Sewell, and Harold Wilensky (eds.), *The Uses of Sociology.* New York: Basic Books.

Zhang, Sheldon. 1998. "In Search of Hopeful Glimpses: A Critique of Research Strategies in Current Boot Camp Evaluation," *Crime & Delinquency,* 44 (2) (April): 314–334.

Zimring, Franklin E. 1989. "Methods for Measuring General Deterrence: A Plea for the Field Experiment." Pp. 99–108 in Martin Lawrence Friedland (ed.), *Sanctions and Rewards in the Legal System: A Multidisciplinary Approach.* Toronto, Canada: University of Toronto Press.

INDEX

A

Abadinsky, Howard, 3, 38, 83, 217
ABA Journal, 376, 401
Abass, Ademola, 5
Abbott, Daniel J., 196
Abel, Daniel G., 128
Abel, Gillian, 223
Abel, Richard L., 4, 12, 255, 346, 351
Abraham, Henry J., 83, 166
Abrams, Floyd, 356
Abrams, Kathryn, 65
Abramson, Jeffrey, 108, 126, 127, 128
Abramson, Jill, 172
ABSCAM, 128
Academe, dispute resolution in, 288–292
Academic malpractice, 290
Adams, Bert N., 38
Adams, Carolyn Teich, 298
Adams, Thomas F., 137
Aday, David P., Jr., 222
Adelman, Leonard, 255
Adjudication, 83, 89, 145, 167, 263, 285
   by administrative agencies, 134–135, 165
Adler, Freda, 223
Adler, Herbert M., 223
Adler, Stephen J., 108, 112, 114, 351, 365
Administrative agencies, 129
   adjudication by, 134–135, 165
   investigation by, 133
   organization of, 130–132
   process in, 132–135
   rulemaking by, 133–134, 164–165
Administrative Conference of the United States, 258
Administrative law, 11, 43
   inspection, 239–240
   licensing, 238–239

and social control, 237–241
   threat of publicity, 240–241
Administrative Office of the US Courts, 267
Administrative Procedure Act, 134, 135
Agger, Ben, 63
Agyeman, Julian, 13
Ahmed, Ali, 16
Aid to Families with Dependent Children (AFDC), 287
Air Quality Act of 1967, 184
Akers, Ronald L., 8, 9
Al-Azmeh, Aziz, 16
Albonetti, Celesta A., 122
Alexander, Gregory S., 13
Alexander, Rudolph, Jr., 52, 430
Alexeev, Michael, 15
Alford, Robert R., 415
Alienation, 63
Alker, Hayward R., Jr., 113–114
Allen, Francis R., 332
Allen, Katherine R., 65
Allyn, David, 201
Almeida, Paul, 182, 297
Alpert, Geoffrey P., 135
Alschuler, Albert W., 118
Alternative dispute resolution (ADR), 259
Althaus, Scott L., 173
Ambrose, David, 336
American Association of Retired Persons (AARP), 128
American Association of University Professor (AAUP), 128, 184
American Bar Association (ABA), 261, 350, 383, 394, 397
   code of ethics, 399–403
   Consortium on Legal Services, 379
   and law schools, 383–390

American legal profession, 348–353, 403
American Medical Association, 184
American Sociological Association, 228
American Tort Reform Association (ATRA), 284
Amicus curiae, 171, 187
Anaconda, 120
Analogical reasoning, 16
Anand, Ruchi, 297
Andenaes, Johannes, 320
Anders, George, 113
Anders, Gerhard, 61
Anderson, James E., 426
Anderson, Lisa, 396, 425, 429
Anderson, Patrick R., 120
Andreas, Peter, 435
Andreasen, A., 260
Andrews, Lori B., 110, 113
Ang, Audra, 204
Ankangs, 233
Anleu, Sharyn I. Roach, 309
An-Na'im, Abudullahi, 16
Appelbaum, Paul S., 213
Appellate court, 88, 370
Applegate, John S., 298
Arbitration, 259, 262, 264
Armor, David J., 177
Army Intelligence Unit, 236
Arnold, Thurman, 61
Aron, Nan, 297, 315
Arons, Stephen, 357, 390, 392
Arrigo, Bruce A., 38, 213
Asher, Herbert, 124
Attorney, 89, 112, 122, 345, 356
Aubert, Vilhelm, 6–7, 18, 255, 256, 260, 263, 273, 310
Auerbach, Jerold S., 25, 352, 353
Aujla, Simmi, 222
Austern, David, 401
Authentication, 186